Cambodia's Economic Transformation

NORDIC INSTITUTE OF ASIAN STUDIES
NIAS Studies in Asian Topics

21 Identity in Asian Literature *Lisbeth Littrup (ed.)*
22 Mongolia in Transition *Ole Bruun and Ole Odgaard (eds)*
23 Asian Forms of the Nation *Stein Tønnesson and Hans Antlöv (eds)*
24 The Eternal Storyteller *Vibeke Børdahl (ed.)*
25 Japanese Influences and Presences in Asia *Marie Söderberg and Ian Reader (eds)*
26 Muslim Diversity *Leif Manger (ed.)*
27 Women and Households in Indonesia *Juliette Koning, Marleen Nolten, Janet Rodenburg and Ratna Saptari (eds)*
28 The House in Southeast Asia *Stephen Sparkes and Signe Howell (eds)*
29 Rethinking Development in East Asia *Pietro P. Masina (ed.)*
30 Coming of Age in South and Southeast Asia *Lenore Manderson and Pranee Liamputtong (eds)*
31 Imperial Japan and National Identities in Asia, 1895–1945 *Li Narangoa and Robert Cribb (eds)*
32 Contesting Visions of the Lao Past *Christopher Goscha and Søren Ivarsson (eds)*
33 Reaching for the Dream *Melanie Beresford and Tran Ngoc Angie (eds)*
34 Mongols from Country to City *Ole Bruun and Li Naragoa (eds)*
35 Four Masters of Chinese Storytelling *Vibeke Børdahl, Fei Li and Huang Ying (eds)*
36 The Power of Ideas *Claudia Derichs and Thomas Heberer (eds)*
37 Beyond the Green Myth *Peter Sercombe and Bernard Sellato (eds)*
38 Kinship and Food in South-East Asia *Monica Janowski and Fiona Kerlogue (eds)*
39 Exploring Ethnic Diversity in Burma *Mikael Gravers (ed.)*
40 Politics, Culture and Self: East Asian and North European Attitudes *Geir Helgesen and Søren Risbjerg Thomsen (eds)*
41 Beyond Chinatown *Mette Thunø (ed.)*
42 Breeds of Empire: The 'Invention' of the Horse in Southeast Asia and Southern Africa 1500–1950 *Greg Bankoff and Sandra Swart*
43 People of Virtue: Reconfiguring Religion, Power and Moral Order in Cambodia Today *Alexandra Kent and David Chandler (eds)*
44 Lifestyle and Entertainment in Yangzhou *Lucie Elivova and Vibeke Børdahl (eds)*
45 iChina: The Rise of the Individual in Modern Chinese Society *Mette Halskov Hansen and Rune Svarverud (eds.)*
46 The Interplay of the Oral and the Written in Chinese Popular Literature *Vibeke Børdahl and Margaret B. Wan (eds.)*
47 Saying the Unsayable: Monarchy and Democracy in Thailand *Søren Ivarsson and Lotte Isager (eds.)*
48 Plaited Arts from the Borneo Rainforest *Bernard Sellato ed.)*
49 Cambodia's Economic Transformation *Caroline Hughes and Kheang Un (eds.)*

Cambodia's Economic Transformation

Edited by Caroline Hughes and Kheang Un

Cambodia's Economic Transition
Edited by Caroline Hughes & Kheang Un

NIAS – Nordic Institute of Asian Studies
NIAS Studies in Asian Topics, no. 49

First published in 2011 by NIAS Press
Nordic Institute of Asian Studies
Leifsgade 33, DK-2300 Copenhagen S, Denmark
Email: books@nias.ku.dk
Online: http://www.niaspress.dk

© NIAS – Nordic Institute of Asian Studies 2011

While copyright in the volume as a whole is vested in the Nordic Institute of Asian Studies, copyright in the individual chapters belongs to their authors. No chapter may be reproduced in whole or in part without the express permission of the publisher.

Printed in Thailand
Typesetting and layout: Donald B. Wagner

British Library Cataloguing in Publication Data

Cambodia's economic transformation. -- (NIAS studies in Asian topics ; 49) 1. Cambodia--Economic conditions--21st century. 2. Cambodia--Economic policy. 3. Economic development--Social aspects--Cambodia. 4. Poor--Cambodia. 5. Distributive justice--Cambodia. 6. Cambodia--Politics and government--1979-
I. Series II. Hughes, Caroline, 1969- III. Un, Kheang.
338.9'596'0090511-dc22

ISBN: 978-87-7694-082-9 (hbk)
ISBN: 978-87-7694-083-6 (pbk)

Contents

Figures vi
Tables vi
Contributors vii
Acknowledgements x

1. Cambodia's Economic Transformation: Historical and Theoretical Frameworks
   Caroline Hughes and Kheang Un   1
2. The Rise of Provincial Business in Cambodia
   Andrew Robert Cock   27
3. China's Aid to Cambodia
   Michael Sullivan   50
4. Growth in the Rice and Garment Sectors
   Sophal Ear   70
5. The Privatization of Cambodia's Rubber Industry
   Margaret Slocomb   94
6. Cashews, Cash and Capitalism in Northeast Cambodia
   Jonathan Padwe   110
7. The Politics and Practice of Land Registration at the Grassroots
   Sokbunthoeun So   136
8. Neoliberal Strategies of Poverty Reduction in Cambodia: The Case of Microfinance
   David J. Norman   161
9. The Politics and Profits of "Labour Export"
   Annuska Derks   182
10. The Political Economy of "Good Governance" Reform
    Kheang Un and Caroline Hughes   199
11. Party Financing of Local Investment Projects: Elite and Mass Patronage
    David Craig and Pak Kimchoeun   219
12. Local Leaders and Big Business in Three Communes
    Caroline Hughes, Eng Netra, Thon Vimealea, Ou Sivhuoch and Ly Tem   245
13. Accountability and Local Politics in Natural Resource Management
    Kim Sedara and Joakim Öjendal   266
14. NGOs, People's Movements and Natural Resource Management
    Roger Henke   288
15. Imagined Parasites: Flows of Monies and Spirits
    Erik W. Davis   310

Bibliography 330
Index 357

Figures

1. The Jarai farming system at Tang Kadon — 121
2. Selected area, not showing recent land sale — 132
3. The same area, showing land sales transacted recently — 133
4. Location where landholdings were surveyed — 145
5. CPP Working Group Structure — 224

Tables

1. Agriculture in Cambodia 2000–2006 — 82
2. Situation of Rubber Cultivation at 31 December 1968 — 96
3. The Jarai Agricultural Calendar — 123
4. Land Sales in Tang Kadon by Year, Differentiated by Seller and Buyer — 129
5. Land Sales in Tang Kadon by Year — 130
6. Transfer of land holdings in Voar Sar, Pneay and Khtum Krang Communes, Kampong Speu Province — 144
7. How people conduct land transactions before and after receiving land titles in Voar Sar and Pneay Communes, Kampong Speu Province — 153
8. Reasons for not registering land transfers at cadastral authority — 154
9. Number of borrowers of Microfinance as of March 2010 — 175
10. Case 1: District Working Group Composition — 226
11. Case 1: CPP support to the district, 2003–2007 — 227
12. Case 1: CPP support to the commune, 2003–2007 — 228
13. Case 2: CPP support to the district, 2003–2007 — 231
14. Case 2: CPP and Other Support to one selected commune (in USD), 2003–2007 — 232
15. Case 3: Party and Donor Support to the district, 1998–2007 — 235

Contributors

Andrew Robert Cock was Post-Doctoral Fellow in the Centre of Southeast Asian Studies at Monash University in Australia from 2009–2011. He is currently based in Japan at Waseda University in Tokyo undertaking research into global commodity traders. Recent publications on Cambodia include "Anticipating an Oil Boom: the 'Resource Curse' Thesis in the Play of Cambodian Politics," *Pacific Affairs*, 83.3 (2010) and "External Actors and the Relative Autonomy of the Ruling Elite in post-UNTAC Cambodia," *Journal of Southeast Asian Studies*, 41.2 (2010).

David Craig is Senior Lecturer in the Department of Sociology at the University of Auckland in New Zealand. He is the author of *Development Beyond Neoliberalism? Governance, Poverty Reduction and Political Economy* (London: Routledge, 2006), written with Doug Porter, and *Familiar Medicine: Everyday Health Knowledge and Practice in Today's Vietnam* (Honolulu: University of Hawaii Press, 2002).

Erik W. Davis is Assistant Professor of Asian Religions at Macalester College in St. Paul, Minnesota, in the US. He is the author of "Between Forests and Families: Death, Desire, and Order in Cambodia" published in *People of Virtue: Reconfiguring Religion, Power, and Moral Order in Today's Cambodia*, edited by Alexandra Kent and David P. Chandler (Copenhagen: NIAS Press, 2008); and "Imaginary Conversations with Mothers about Death," published in *At the Edge of the Forest: Essays in Honor of David Chandler*, edited by Anne R. Hansen and Judy Ledgerwood (Ithaca: Cornell University Press, 2008).

Annuska Derks is a Swiss National Science Foundation Research Fellow, affiliated with the Institute for Social Anthropology of Bern University and the Center for Asian Studies at the Graduate Institute for International and Development Studies in Geneva in Switzerland. She is currently based in Vietnam, where she is a Visiting Lecturer at the Faculty of Sociology of the Vietnam National University, Hanoi. She is the author of *Khmer Women on the Move: Exploring Work and Life in Urban Cambodia* (Honolulu: University of Hawai'i Press, 2008) and editor of the Special Issue of the Asian Journal of Social Science on *Bonded Labour in Southeast Asia*, 38.6 (2010).

Sophal Ear is an Assistant Professor of National Security Affairs at the US Naval Postgraduate School in Monterey, California in the US. He is the author of the award-winning article "Does Aid Dependence Worsen Governance?"

International Public Management Journal, 10.3 (2007) and has contributed to the *Wall Street Journal* and the *New York Times*.

Eng Netra is a PhD candidate and Australian Leadership Award-holder at Monash University in Australia. She is the co-author of three working papers published by the Cambodian Development Resource Institute: *Accountability and Neo-Patrimonialism in Cambodia: a Critical Literature Review* (Phnom Penh: CDRI, 2007); *Accountability and Human Resource Management in Decentralised Cambodia* (Phnom Penh: CDRI, 2009); and *Leadership in Local Politics of Cambodia: A Study of Leaders in Three Communes of Three Provinces* (Phnom Penh: CDRI, 2009).

Roger Henke is the Managing Director of the Summit Hotel in Kathmandu in Nepal and formerly Programme Manager at the Interchurch Organization for Development Cooperation (ICCO) in Phnom Penh, Cambodia. Recent publications include "Mistakes and their Consequences: Why Impunity in Cambodia is Here to Stay" in Edwin Poppe and Maykel Verkuyten, (eds.) *Culture and Conflict: Liber Amicorum for Louk Hagendoorn* (Amsterdam: Aksant, 2007) and a Cambodia Context Analysis for the Dutch Trade Union Confederation CNV (2010).

Caroline Hughes is the Director of the Asia Research Centre at Murdoch University in Australia. She is the author of *The Political Economy of Cambodia's Transition* (London: Routledge, 2003) and *Dependent Communities: Aid and Politics in Cambodia and East Timor* (Ithaca: Cornell SEAP, 2009).

Kim Sedara is Senior Research Fellow at the Cambodia Development Resource Institute in Phnom Penh, Cambodia. He recently completed a PhD at the University of Gothenburg in Sweden entitled *Where Decentralization Meets Democracy: Civil Society, Local Government and Accountability in Cambodia* (Gothenburg: University of Gothenburg, 2007) and is the co-author of "*Korob, Kaud, Klach*: In Search of Agency in Rural Cambodia," *Journal of Southeast Asian Studies* 37.3 (2006).

Ly Tem is a Research Assistant at the Cambodia Development Resource Institute in Phnom Penh, Cambodia. She is the co-author of a CDRI working paper entitled *Leadership in Local Politics of Cambodia: A Study of Leaders in Three Communes of Three Provinces* (Phnom Penh: CDRI, 2009).

David Norman is a Visiting Lecturer in the Department of Political Science and International Studies at the University of Birmingham in the UK. He has recently completed a PhD entitled "Interrogating the Dynamics of Cosmopolitan

Democracy in Theory and Practice: The Case of Cambodia" (Birmingham: University of Birmingham, 2010). Fieldwork for this chapter was funded by the Economic and Social Research Council in the UK

Joakim Öjendal is Professor of Peace and Development Research at the School of Global Studies at the University of Gothenburg in Sweden. He has co-edited three volumes on Asian politics: *Beyond Democracy in Cambodia: Political Reconstruction in a Post-Conflict Society*, edited with Mona Lilja (Copenhagen: NIAS Press, 2009); *Deepening Democracy and Restructuring Governance: Responses to Globalization in Southeast Asia* edited with Francis Loh (Copenhagen: NIAS Press, 2005); and *Regionalization in a Globalizing World*, edited with Michael Schulz and Fredrik Söderbaum (London: Zed Press, 2001).

Ou Sivhuoch is a Research Associate at the Cambodia Development Resource Institute in Phnom Penh, Cambodia. He is the co-author of a CDRI working paper entitled *Leadership in Local Politics of Cambodia: A Study of Leaders in Three Communes of Three Provinces* (Phnom Penh: CDRI, 2009).

Jonathan Padwe is an Assistant Professor in the Department of Anthropology at the University of Hawaii in the US. He recently completed a PhD dissertation entitled *Garden Variety Histories: Notes on Farming at the End of the World* (New Haven: Yale University, 2010).

Pak Kimchoeun recently completed a PhD dissertation at the Australian National University entitled, *A Dominant Party in a Weak State: How the Ruling Party in Cambodia has Managed to Stay Dominant* (Canberra: ANU, 2011). He is co-author of two working papers published by the Cambodia Development Resource Institute: *Accountability and Neo-Patrimonialism in Cambodia: a Critical Literature Review* (Phnom Penh: CDRI, 2007); and *Accountability and Public Expenditure Management in Decentralised Cambodia* (Phnom Penh: CDRI, 2008).

Margaret Slocomb has retired, but continues to write history. She is the author of *The People's Republic of Kampuchea 1979–1989: the Revolution after Pol Pot* (Seattle: University of Washington Press, 2003), *Colons and Coolies: the Development of Cambodia's Rubber Plantations* (Bangkok: White Lotus Press, 2007) and most recently *An Economic History of Cambodia in the Twentieth Century* (Honolulu: University of Hawai'i Press, 2010).

Sokbunthoeun So is a Senior Research Fellow at the Cambodia Development Resource Institute in Phnom Penh, Cambodia. He is the author or co-author of several articles on Cambodian land governance, including "Land Rights in Cambodia: How Neopatrimonial Politics Restricts Land Policy Reform," *Pacific Affairs* 84.2 (2011); "Land Rights in Cambodia: An Unfinished Reform," *Asia Pacific Issues* 97 (2010); and "The Politics of Natural Resource Use in Cambodia," *Asian Affairs: An American Review* 36 (2009).

Michael Sullivan is the Director of the Center for Khmer Studies, Siem Reap, Cambodia. Research for his chapter in this volume was funded by a grant from the Research Committee of the Association of Southeast Asian Studies in the United Kingdom (ASEASUK).

Thon Vimealea is a Research Associate at the Cambodia Development Resource Institute in Phnom Penh, Cambodia. She is the co-author of a CDRI working paper entitled *Leadership in Local Politics of Cambodia: A Study of Leaders in Three Communes of Three Provinces* (Phnom Penh: CDRI, 2009).

Kheang Un is an Assistant Professor of Political Science at Northern Illinois University in the US, previously visiting fellow at the Royal Netherlands Institute for Southeast Asian and Caribbean Studies, the University of Louisville's Center for Asian Democracy and the Center for Khmer Studies, Cambodia. He is currently a Fulbright Fellow at the Royal University of Phnom Penh in Cambodia. He has published a number of book chapters and scholarly journal articles on contemporary Cambodian politics and political economy.

Acknowledgements

The editors would like to thank the UK Government's Department for International Development for funding the workshop that led to this publication, via its Phnom Penh office. We would particularly like to thank Mr Tom Wingfield for facilitating this support. We would also like to thank BUILD Cambodia who generously contributed additional funds for the workshop. Kheang Un would like to thank the Center for Asian Democracy, University of Louisville, where he was resident as a visiting research fellow during the process of producing this collection, for its generous financial and academic support. Thanks also to the anonymous reviewers and to Gerald Jackson of NIAS Press for their invaluable help in finalizing the manuscript. We would both like to thank our families – Judy Ledgerwood, Paul Un and Tony Un; and Richard Brown, Alice Brown, Hephzibah Brown and Mary Elizabeth Brown – for their support and encouragement.

Note on Transliteration

The transliteration of Khmer in this volume is based on an adaptation of the Franco-Khmer transcription system developed by Frank E. Huffman in 1983. Place-names are left in their common spellings (i.e. Phnom Penh, Kampong Cham, etc.). Common words from Pali are also left in their common spellings (Dharma, Karma), particularly in the chapter by Erik Davis. Words in the Jarai language in Chapter 6 are left as transliterated by the author of that chapter, Jonathan Padwe.

1

CAMBODIA'S ECONOMIC TRANSFORMATION: HISTORICAL AND THEORETICAL FRAMEWORKS

Caroline Hughes and Kheang Un

7 JANUARY 2009 WAS THE scene of a spectacular celebration in Cambodia's capital city of Phnom Penh. The day marked the thirtieth anniversary of the fall of the infamous Khmer Rouge regime, led by Pol Pot, which caused the deaths of up to 2 million Cambodians in a horrific experiment in collectivization between 1975 and 1979. On 7 January 1979, a group of former Khmer Rouge commanders, who had fled across the border a year earlier to Vietnam, returned to Phnom Penh backed by an invading force from the People's Army of Vietnam, to find a scene of utter devastation. With backing from the Vietnamese army and advisors, the former KR commanders established the People's Republic of Kampuchea (PRK).

The emergence of the PRK, whose political organ, the Kampuchean People's Revolutionary Party (KPRP), is the forerunner of today's ruling Cambodian People's Party (CPP), was heavily determined by Cold War factors. The ousted Khmer Rouge had come to power following the defeat of American power in Indochina in 1975, and had implemented a radical effort to re-engineer society by destroying virtually all pre-existing social institutions, evacuating cities, and enforcing rigid and draconian regimes of production and distribution. Although allied with Vietnam during the American War, the Khmer Rouge had subsequently shifted towards China, and used the vilification of the Vietnamese as the historic enemies of the Khmers as the key explanation for the disastrous failures of their economic and agricultural policies.

With the assistance of the Vietnamese army, the new PRK leaders were able successfully to oust the Khmer Rouge from Phnom Penh and install themselves as the new government. However, the PRK faced considerable problems: the economy was shattered, society in chaos, and institutions of state all but destroyed. Supported by the Soviet Bloc, it attempted to rebuild the Cambodian state, economy and society based upon an imposed – although relaxed, compared with the Pol Pot years – version of Vietnamese-style socialism. However, it faced famine in the aftermath of the Pol Pot experiments; a major insurgency from regrouped Khmer Rouge troops on the Thai border, supported by Thailand and China; and a total Western trade and aid embargo, imposed in response to a perceived threat of Vietnamese and Soviet expansion in South East Asia.

But by 2009, the leaders of the former PRK had a great deal to celebrate. They had not merely survived the initial decade of civil war and insurgency from 1979 to 1989. They had also survived the end of the Cold War, the collapse of their key donor, the Soviet Union, and the withdrawal of the Vietnamese army. These events precipitated a United Nations peacekeeping operation in Cambodia from 1992–1993, designed to end the ongoing war between the Phnom Penh regime, on the one hand, and Khmer Rouge insurgents, who were allied with small royalist and republican groups on the Thai Border, on the other. The United Nations Transitional Authority in Cambodia attempted unsuccessfully to disarm and demobilize the combatants; it also held an election intended to resolve the question of who would rule Cambodia. The former KPRP, renamed the Cambodian People's Party (CPP) narrowly lost these elections to the royalists. However, having bludgeoned their way into coalition government, the party regrouped and won a series of increasingly impressive landslide election victories at local and national level from 1998 to 2008.

The UN peace process also facilitated the return of Western donors to Cambodia, and these made efforts to promote a post-Cold War multi-party liberal democracy in Cambodia during the course of the 1990s, alongside a neo-liberal "good governance" regime of state-building. This represented a challenge which the Cambodian People's Party has met with élan. Although the Cambodian government consistently failed to conform to Western donor prescriptions for good governance, by 2006 the Cambodian economy was growing at one of the fastest rates in the world. As a consequence of their political control and economic success, the CPP's leaders had achieved considerable international and domestic legitimacy, and had amassed huge personal fortunes. The thirtieth anniversary celebration in Phnom Penh was very much a CPP affair: paid for and organized by the party, with the party leaders fêted and cheered, and with party colours waving. Vast crowds joined in a spectacular extravaganza that was televised and broadcast across the country. Yet, the fact that many of them joined the celebration under pressure or in return for favours raises important questions about the nature of the new, post-war Cambodia and of the CPP's success.[1]

---

[1] Kheang Un has learned that students were pressured to join the crowds in return for an automatic passing grade. Government ministries were given the order to make notes of those who failed to attend the ceremony.

This seems, then, an opportune moment to consider the position of the CPP and its last few years of power in Cambodia. Assessments of Cambodia's emergence from warfare with international assistance over the course of the 1990s have in the main been evaluated against models of either democratization or "good governance". For the CPP themselves, however, political stability and economic development have been the key goals, and it is their record in respect to these that was celebrated so ostentatiously on 7 January 2009.

Until relatively recently, such a celebration would have been difficult to envisage. The ten-year anniversary of the fall of the Khmer Rouge, in January 1989, saw the party in disarray as the Eastern Bloc was set to crumble at the end of the Cold War, and the Vietnamese army prepared a withdrawal, leaving their Cambodian partners in a precarious position, financially and militarily. Wholesale free market reforms were on the agenda, in recognition of the failure of Cambodia's second socialist experiment, and the necessity of submitting to the UN peace process was becoming clear. For the CPP, the road ahead must have appeared highly uncertain.

By the twentieth anniversary of Liberation Day, in 1999, things were looking much better: Pol Pot was dead, and the war had just finished with the capture of the last Khmer Rouge insurgent commander, Ta Mok. Cambodia was the recipient of large amounts of international aid, and a swathe of new factories, making garments for export, were in full production. Almost all Western donors and diplomats had accepted the CPP's dubious and highly contested victory in the 1998 election as cancelling out the illegitimacy of its 1997 attack on its partner in government, the royalist FUNCINPEC,[2] which had defeated the CPP in the 1993 UN-organized elections. Yet for the last six months of 1998, post-election demonstrations and horse-trading over coalition formation entailed that by 7 January 1999 the first post-war CPP-led government had only just been sworn in, and the CPP appeared to be toeing a Western donor-imposed reform line assiduously in pursuit of further international aid and recognition.

By 2009, the Party had pulled far ahead of its competitors at home. Cambodia's warm relations with China, the promise of oil revenues, and the country's recent attractiveness to foreign direct investment entails that what Western donors think matters far less than it did before. Peace is well established throughout the country; new systems of governance have been created at the national and subnational levels that better cement the party's relations with the electorate; and the economy has been transformed. At the same time, the plunge into global recession

---

[2] FUNCINPEC is formally the acronym of the *Front Uni National pour un Cambodge Indépendent, Neutre, Pacifique et Cooperatif*; however, this full name is never used in Cambodia, and the acronym FUNCINPEC is simply transliterated into Khmer characters to form an invented word in Cambodian texts.

is already reverberating inside Cambodia, and may mean that the 7 January 2009 spectacular represents the last real reason to celebrate for quite some time.

This volume sets out to understand the way that Cambodia has changed in the last decade of political stability and rapid economic growth. The purpose of this is twofold. First, as one of the first countries to undergo UN peacekeeping in the 1990s, and as a country that now appears relatively secure from a reversion to civil war, Cambodia represents a historical example of a country that has emerged from post-conflict status and is integrating successfully into the world's most economically dynamic region. Yet Cambodia's political and economic trajectory took the route it did to a great extent in spite, rather than because of, the policies advocated by international organizations and post-conflict reconstruction experts. An analysis of Cambodia's trajectory out of the "conflict trap" and into a period of high economic growth is important for the field of post-conflict studies, since Cambodia pursued a course in which resistance to Western governance prescriptions for the institutionalization of transparent process figured prominently, in favour of the preservation of a discretionary arena within a shadow state for political horse-trading amongst former adversaries. This has been effective in producing political stability and economic transformation; but raises the question of how we should evaluate the Cambodian post-war compact.

Second, Cambodia's recent experience casts new light on the context for economic development in the Asia-Pacific region. Pursuing capitalist developmentalism a generation after South Korea, Thailand and Singapore, and in the decade following the Asian Financial Crisis, Cambodia emerged into a globalizing world, in which the significance of China, of short-term capital flows, and of powerful forces of regional and global integration figured far more prominently than before. Has Cambodia's recent rapid economic growth been merely accidental, or the product of state policy? What has the decreased poverty but widening inequality engendered by growth meant for social and political institutions? How has Cambodia achieved its economic success, given its regularly poor governance ratings, and what does this mean for the "institutions matter" orthodoxy that has influenced Western development policy for the past fifteen years? What does the emergence of China and the transformation of states in the light of globalization mean for the prospects for industrialization for small primary commodity producers in Asia? This collection of essays on Cambodia's development throws light on these questions and in so doing contributes to the ongoing research agenda examining the impact, and contestation, of neo-liberal policy in the political economy of East and South East Asia.[3]

---

[3] See for example, Richard Robison and Kevin Hewison, "Introduction: East Asia and the Trials of Neoliberalism," *Journal of Development Studies* 41.2 (2005): 183–196; Pasuk Phongpaichit and Chris Baker, *Thai Capital After the 1997 Crisis*, (Bangkok: Silkworm, 2008); Richard Robison and Vedi Hadiz, *Reorganising Power in Indonesia: the Politics of Oligarchy in an Age of Markets*, (London: Routledge, 2004); Vedi Hadiz, *Empire and Neoliberalism in Asia*, (London: Routledge, 2006).

In this introductory chapter, we aim to achieve two things. First we set out the historical trajectory of Cambodia's recent development, from an impoverished, war-torn state plagued by the continuing shadow of instability to a rapidly growing economy increasingly tightly integrated into regional and global markets. Second, we discuss the theoretical frameworks explaining this trajectory, notably the contributions and limitations of the neo-liberal approach that characterizes the assessments of international financial institutions giving aid to Cambodia; and the institutionalist approaches that characterized an earlier generation of studies of developmental success in South East Asia. We conclude with an examination of critiques of these. In critiquing the neo-liberal and institutionalist approaches, we use the concept of economic transformation, drawn from the work of Karl Polanyi, to examine the profound social and political changes that have taken place in Cambodia as a result of economic growth, and to analyse the implications of the past decade for the prospects of the Cambodian poor.

Cambodia's Emergence from Conflict

Between the end of the insurgency in 1998 and the first commune elections in February 2002, Cambodia remained a post-conflict country, characterized by weakness of governance institutions; a lack of reconciliation among the formerly warring parties; and an economy based upon short term unregulated and unplanned exploitation of resources for survival or profit.[4] As such, it shared some of the common problems of post-conflict states. It maintained a bloated and entrepreneurial armed force that was difficult to control and appropriated considerable resources as a result.[5] In part because of the menace represented by the armed forces, and the CPP's close association with them, political processes were tainted by the threat of violence.[6]

At the same time, civilian institutions of state were weak. For much of the period they were characterized by an uneasy truce between the CPP

---

[4] These characteristics bear a close correlation to the four pillars of post-conflict reconstruction identified by Hamre and Sullivan (2002), namely, security, justice and reconciliation, administration and development [Hamre, John and Gordon Sullivan, "Toward Post-Conflict Reconstruction," *The Washington Quarterly*, 25.4 (2002): 85–96]. Here, however, we focus on the legacies of warfare in these four areas rather than upon an external policy agenda for reconstruction.

[5] Bryden, Alison, Timothy Donais and Hyder Hanggi, Shaping a Security Governance Agenda in Post-Conflict Peacebuilding, Genever Centre for the Democratic Control of Armed Forces Policy Paper no. 11 (Geneva: Centre for the Democratic Control of Armed Forces, 2005), online at http://www.dcaf.ch/_docs/pp11_bryden.pdf, accessed 7 September 2010.

[6] Bigombe, Betty, Paul Collier and Nicholas Sambanis, "Policies for Building Post-Conflict Peace," *Journal of African Economies* 9.3 (2000): 323–348.

and FUNCINPEC, both of whom stacked ministerial departments with their supporters in a manner that precluded efficient administration. This was compounded by technical ineptness in performing everyday tasks, such as providing well-functioning schools and hospitals, because of brain drain, the persecution of educated elites in the 1970s, and the war-time tendency to deprioritize these areas, and to starve them of funds. Rule of law was weak, permitting the institutionalization of corruption in civilian institutions that were mined for resources by the patrons of neo-patrimonial political networks.

Integration, administration and development activities were made more difficult by the poor state of infrastructure. Economic activity in Cambodia as in many post-conflict countries was characterized by short-termism, motivated either by the immediate problem of survival, or the desire to strip and export the country's most valuable assets as quickly as possible before someone else took them by force. Investment was slow to emerge because of uncertainties regarding stability.

However, over the same period, the CPP-led government acted to address some of these issues. Greater stability was sought through the active pursuit of loyalties within the armed forces, including newly defecting insurgent units, within the state and within local government. To a great extent, this intensified corruption, which became endemic in state institutions. A variety of rackets from aid- and revenue-skimming to fine-collection and bribe-taking operated to shore up personal networks of loyalty within the elite and associated with the major parties of government.

Wider legitimation was pursued by means of a campaign of mass patronage, designed to win rural votes. A school-building programme organized by Prime Minister Hun Sen, which brought a Hun Sen school to hundreds of communes across the country, was a leading example of this. This kind of patronage was paid for from a number of sources. To most rural Cambodians, the funds seem to flow personally from Hun Sen's largess. In fact some of it was paid for by international aid donors, while some was funded by business tycoons whose businesses depend on the state for licences and permits. These tycoons included Sok Kong of the Sokimex company, who lent millions of dollars to the CPP during various crises from the late 1980s to mid-1990s, and subsequently received lucrative government contracts to supply imported petroleum and uniforms to the armed forces, and to supply imported medicines to the Ministry of Health;[7] Teng Bunma of the Thai Bunrong company, who claimed to have bankrolled key battles in the continued war against the Khmer Rouge in the 1990s, and who made a fortune smuggling cigarettes from Cambodia into Vietnam;[8] and

---

[7] Stephen O'Connell and Yin Soeum, "All That Glitters Seems To Be... Sokimex," *Phnom Penh Post*, 28 April – 11 May 2000, online at www.phnompenhpost.com, accessed 3 February 2007.

[8] Elizabeth Pisani, "Cambodia's Top Investor Scoffs at Rumors About Shady Past," *Asia Times*, 12 March 1996, online at http://www.ternyata.org/journalism/features/teng_boonma_profile.html, accessed 21 October 2008.

Mong Retthy, an old school friend of Hun Sen's, whose construction company built many of the Hun Sen Schools, and whose private port was used as an exit point for illegal narcotics.[9]

A third significant source of funds for patronage was the proceeds of a rampant conflict trade in timber, which devastated Cambodia's pristine forest, and was conducted by means of secret deals between the military, provincial and national government and logging companies. Many of these deals ran directly contrary to a series of formal decrees and laws issued by the central government under direct pressure of sanctions from the international financial institutions.[10] The military continued through this period to be active in smuggling enterprises, and a formal private sector of tax-paying, lawfully operating private companies was slow to emerge, with the single exception of the garment manufacturing industry. The latter was itself frequently regarded during the late 1990s as a fly-by-night industry, attracted by Cambodia's favourable export quotas to the US and Europe, but ready to pack up and leave at the first sign of trouble.

A turning point can be identified between the end of 2001 and the end of 2004. By 2001, the security situation had improved dramatically in both the city and the countryside, and the coalition government, led by the CPP with an acquiescent FUNCINPEC as a junior partner was stable. A number of events translated this generally improved situation into a consolidation of power in the hands of the CPP and Hun Sen himself. For one thing, from 2001, the lucrative timber trade began to be consolidated in the hands of the Prime Minister and his cronies, strengthening both the party and Hun Sen's position within it. For another, the first local government election was held in February 2002, delivering a landslide victory to the CPP in communes across Cambodia, as opposition parties proved unable to compete with the CPP's impressive patronage-fuelled electoral machine.

This consolidation of power changed the electoral landscape. Whereas during the 1990s, the opposition had been marginalized in rural areas by threats and violence, from 2002 onwards they found themselves looking on largely as bystanders, while the CPP honed an increasingly elaborate system of mass patronage and mobilization. It also altered the balance of power within the CPP. Following the 2003 national elections, the opposition parties refused to enter a CPP-led coalition for a full twelve months, denying the CPP the two thirds majority it needed in parliament to form a government. The opposition parties' strategy was to reject, not the CPP as a whole, but Hun Sen as an individual, in the hope that an internal party coup could achieve what electoral politics,

---

[9] See Global Witness, *Cambodia's Family Trees*, May 2007, http://www.globalwitness.org/media_library_detail.php/546/en/cambodias_family_trees, accessed 10 October 2007, 10.

[10] See Global Witness, *Cambodia's Family Trees*.

so far, had not, and unseat Hun Sen in favour of a less threatening leader from Hun Sen's long time rival network, the Chea Sim/Sar Kheng *khsae*. However, Hun Sen survived this interregnum; indeed, he emerged from it stronger than before, having apparently consolidated control over the military, and prevailed over an internal challenge from his long-time CPP rival Chea Sim. Shortly after these events, King Norodom Sihanouk, who had served either as the country's King or as one of its major political leaders almost continuously since 1941, abdicated from power. From this point onwards, the terms of the elite pact underpinning peace in Cambodia were largely settled.

This consolidation of power in the hands of Hun Sen was viewed warily by international observers: it represented the deterioration of democracy into populist electoral authoritarianism, and Hun Sen's dependence on patronage funded through corruption was antithetical to the promotion of good governance models within the state. The former was perhaps less troubling to Western donors after 11 September 2001 than it had been before. The latter continued to be a point of contention. However, the consolidation of power within Cambodia has permitted Cambodia's political institutions to become significantly better developed and more predictable now than ten years ago. Furthermore, the lack of professional expertise widely noted in reports in the 1990s is now much less pressing, as a new generation of educated young professionals enters public service. The failure of Cambodian state institutions to conform to Western liberal models and the influence of neo-patrimonial networks organized via the Cambodian People's Party is now a matter of political choice, rather than of technical incapacity.

The broader context for development has changed too. Donors, the government and the ruling party have invested heavily in infrastructure, such as roads, schools, clinics, training centres, markets, bridges, irrigation schemes and temples, transforming the context within which economic activity is carried out. The rapid improvement in human development indicators and the decline in the rate of poverty may in part be attributable to investment in infrastructure, as a result of mass patronage by the CPP government and investment via initiatives of the Association of South East Asian Nations and the Asian Development Bank (ADB), intended to integrate mainland South East Asia through new transport networks. The ADB's strategy of building a transport network to support what it calls "connectivity" in the Greater Mekong Subregion has led to increased economic activity and thus new prosperity in areas such as Koh Kong, Poipet and Kirivong, Prey Veng and Cambodia's north-eastern region, which a decade ago were considered dangerous and remote.

Problems such as entrenched corruption, the dysfunctionality of the judicial system and the importance of patron-client networks within state institutions are certainly attributable in part to continuities from the war years, but they also reflect the response of the Cambodian government to the particular nature of their insertion into contemporary aid regimes and global and regional markets. As the discussion below indicates, patronage in Cambodia is by no means sclerotic: it has played a dynamic role in the context of economic transformation, and key individuals within the business sector have shifted their position radically as Cambodia moves away from dependence on illicit conflict trades in timber, gems and narcotics, towards more respectable industries such as mining, cash crops and service industries. As such, these patronage networks are not merely a legacy of the past, but are specifically reproduced by contemporary decision-making.

The shift in the nature of Cambodia's integration into global trading regimes constitutes the final aspect of the move away from post-conflict status. In the 1990s, 85 per cent of the population were engaged in subsistence agriculture, forestry and fisheries, with low rates of productivity. Aside from the nascent garment industry, there was little manufacturing activity in the country. The exploitation of timber represented the main extractive activity, and was conducted in a manner which emphasized short-term expedience over long-term strategy.

In 2001, the government passed a Forestry Law and a Land Law which, although not fully implemented, reflect a shift in the nature of economic activity. Interest in stripping the remaining hardwood timber assets is declining – most of these assets in any case are already gone. Rather, there is great interest in the acquisition of land, in particular for agro-industry or for the purposes of speculation. This hunger for land on the part of large investors – both Cambodian and foreign - has prompted a mass expropriation of land from Cambodian farmers and from the urban poor, often violently and with the assistance of the military and police. As such it represents a violation of rights and produces severe social problems. Analysts of Cambodia's economic prospects have distinguished between the acquisition of land for agro-industrial investment and the acquisition of land for speculation, regarding the former as potentially contributing to economic development over the long term, whereas the latter merely represents profiteering. However, both land uses reflect a certain level of confidence in Cambodian institutions, either formal or neo-patrimonial. These can be relied upon to support particular types of land title distribution over the long term. As such, the new regime of land acquisition and exploitation, although abusive, corrupt and anti-poor, represents a step away from the short-term asset-stripping rationale of the post-conflict economy.

Meanwhile, the private sector has grown exponentially, with fixed investment approvals increasing tenfold between 2000 and 2006, driven by investments in tourism, manufacturing and mining. Clearly, the Cambodian state remains "fragile" as this is conceptualised in recent OECD work, as a state which fails to provide many core services to its citizens because it is "unable or unwilling to do so".[11] The Cambodian state is authoritarian, corrupt and based heavily upon neo-patrimonial institutions, whose survival and expansion represent key interests driving, and limiting, public policy. However, the significance of the specific legacies of conflict has declined markedly over the past few years.

From Post-Conflict Reconstruction to Economic Transformation

Given that Cambodia has left behind its post-conflict status, how should we characterize the current period of continuing change? In this study, we coin the term "economic transformation" to describe the current context. This economic transformation represents a visible change in the level and nature of economic activities from the 1990s to the 2000s. Although a slowdown is expected as a result of the global financial crisis, and may limit or reverse some of the political implications of economic success, it will not erase the transformations wrought over the past five years.

Some statistics give an indication of the empirical dimensions of this transformation. The economy has grown at an average of almost ten per cent per year over the past five years. The value of exports has tripled, while the flow of foreign direct investment has increased 12-fold since 2004.[12] Poverty has fallen and human development indicators have improved. At the same time, according to the World Food and Agriculture Organization, Cambodia lost almost a third of its primary tropical forests between 2000 and 2005,[13] and severe inequality has emerged and is growing, especially in terms of landholdings.[14] A recent estimate by the Land Coalition put the proportion of landless people at 20 per cent of the rural population, and the proportion of land-poor people at 25 per cent[15]. This is a figure that is considered to be rising, in view of the rash

---

[11] See OECD, 2006, *DAC Guidelines and Reference Series Applying Strategic Environmental Assessment: Good Practice Guidance for Development Co-operation*, OECD, Paris, cited in OECD, *Glossary of Statistical Terms*, online at http://stats.oecd.org/glossary/detail.asp?ID=7235, accessed 23 December 2008.

[12] US Department of State, Bureau of East Asian and Pacific Affairs, "Background Note: Cambodia," June 2008, online at http://www.state.gov/r/pa/ei/bgn/2732.htm#econ, accessed 11 October 2008.

[13] Global Witness, "Latest Threats to Cambodia's Forests," http://www.globalwitness.org/pages/en/threats_to_forests.html, accessed 10 October 2008.

[14] World Bank, *Sharing Growth – Equity and Development in Cambodia* (Phnom Penh: World Bank, 2007).

[15] Land Coalition (2007), *Landlessness and Land Conflicts in Cambodia* (Phnom Penh: Star Kampuchea).

of forced evictions from disputed land that have taken place over the past three or four years.

To date, studies of Cambodia's economic trajectory have been largely confined to analyses by the international financial institutions (IFIs) that engage with Cambodia as "development partners," or by research institutes focused on the specifics of particular industries or indicators. There is broad agreement within these studies as to the nature of the economic transformation that has occurred, and its limitations. For example, there is widespread agreement that while economic growth in Cambodia has been high, it has been narrowly based. Over the period from 1996 to 2006, the economy as a whole grew by an average of 8.7 per cent per year. Disaggregated by sector, the picture looks less promising. Manufacturing grew by 18.1 per cent per year over this period: within the manufacturing sector, garment production grew by 34 per cent. Construction grew by 12 per cent. These industries are confined to a small geographical area: particularly the area around Phnom Penh and Tak Khmau, and the corridor along National Route 4 to the main port of Sihanoukville. However, the garment industry in particular has proved flexible and relatively durable in response to changes in the nature of the global trading regime of which it is a part. The industry survived the end of the Multi-Fibre Agreement which guaranteed Cambodian exporters privileged access to US markets, and brokered a new deal which claimed a niche for Cambodian garments on the basis of their "ethically produced" status. The extent to which the ethical claims made are real is debatable, but the strategy worked, up until 2008, in securing markets for Cambodian goods.

Services performed well, growing at an average of 8.5 per cent, a performance particularly boosted by the 12.5 per cent growth in the tourism sector which saw the number of tourists increase from 289,524 in 1998 to 2,015,128 in 2007.[16] Again, tourism is narrowly concentrated in the town of Siem Reap, gateway to the ancient Angkor temple complex, and a recent study has found that tourism has little effect on poverty reduction in Cambodia, since revenues do not reach the poor.[17] Across the rest of the country, although agriculture remains the main occupation of 55 per cent of the population, it grew only slowly over this period, at less than 5 per cent per year, and some of this growth was driven by the expansion of the sub-sector of industrial agriculture, which grew by 10 per cent per year[18] The subsistence agriculture sector upon which the

---

[16] Ministry of Tourism, Tourism Highlights: Visitor Arrivals, Average Length of Stay, Hotel Occupancy and Tourism Receipts 1993–2003. Online at http://www.mot.gov.kh/statistics/tourism_highlight.pdf, accessed 7 September 2010.
[17] CDRI, *Pro-poor Tourism in the Greater Mekong Sub-Region* (Phnom Penh: CDRI, 2007).
[18] Sok Hach, "Cambodia's Economy: from Donor Dependence to Self-Sustaining Growth?" powerpoint presentation delivered at the workshop on Capital Market Development in Cambodia, Phnom Penh, 30–31 May 2007.

rural population largely depends remained poor. Consequently, the numbers of people leaving the land altogether and making a living in manufacturing or service industries increased sharply. The percentage of the (expanding) labour force employed in industry and services increased from 4 to 12 per cent and 20 to 25 per cent respectively between 1994 and 2004.[19]

Explaining Cambodia's Economic Transformation: the Good Governance Perspective

How should we evaluate this pattern of growth? Documents produced by Cambodia's development partners have been strongly oriented towards a "good governance" reform agenda, which reflects the thinking emerging from the World Bank and International Monetary Fund since the mid-1990s. The good governance agenda comprised a new emphasis upon four key ways in which the quality of government institutions affected prospects for development: the quality of public sector management; accountability; the legal framework; and information and transparency.[20] In the World Bank's thinking, these factors were considered to be crucial ways in which the state laid the foundation for efficient, market-led development.

Critics of the World Bank's position on governance have charged that despite its acceptance of the contention that "institutions matter", the World Bank has been reluctant to cede these more than a technical role. A series of World Bank publications produced within Cambodia illustrate the point: they have made little attempt to analyse in detail the nature of the relationship between the state and the emerging private sector within Cambodia. Cambodia's performance in terms of both governance and economy have been analysed with respect to prescriptive models of how an ideal relationship between government and the free market "ought" to work. As such, evaluations have measured development in Cambodia against an abstract and ahistorical entity – laissez-faire capitalism and the state institutions regarded as best suited to upholding it – rather than asking the politically sensitive but analytically significant question of what happened, how and why in the Cambodian context.

In 2004, the World Bank issued a major analysis of Cambodian governance practice entitled *Cambodia at the Crossroads*. The report drew upon IMF analyses of Cambodia's economic performance, and it represented both

---

[19] SIDA, *Employment and Growth in Cambodia: an Integrated Economic Analysis* (Stockholm: SIDA, 2006).
[20] Moore, Mick, "Declining to Learn from the East? The World Bank on *Governance and Development*," *IDS Bulletin* 24.1 (1993): 39–50.

a response to the Cambodian government's recently articulated "Rectangular Strategy for Growth, Employment, Equity and Efficiency in Cambodia", and a briefing paper for the forthcoming Consultative Group meeting between the Cambodian government and its main donors.

The 2004 report set out three challenges facing Cambodia, based on the mainstream thinking then current within the World Bank. First, the World Bank contended, Cambodia faced an imminent serious deterioration in its trading position, due to increased competition in the garment manufacturing sector following the end of the Multi-Fibre Trading Agreement. The Bank argued that without the protection offered by import quotas to its main markets in the United States, the garment industry, and the Cambodian economy, would languish. Second, the report criticized poverty levels characterized as high and stagnant, and human development indicators which are portrayed as off-track with respect to Cambodia's Millennium Development Goals. Third, the report relates these problems to "governance failures", in particular high levels of corruption and poor mechanisms for accountability. Ultimately, the report attributes these issues to "limited institutional capacity, . . . lack of trust among the elite, and strong resistance to reforms from powerful vested interests". These, the report continues, represent

> . . . the dark clouds from Cambodia's tragic past that have cast a shadow over what could be a bright future and that prevent the relatively young and weak institutions of restraint from working effectively to ensure accountability and transparency.[21]

The report does not consider the particular economic and political rationalities that underlie the distributions of power and resources that they describe. Moreover, even though the term "governance" appears in this report and reappears in others as a significant issue, there has been little analysis of the regime that the Cambodian government has erected since the end of the war in 1998 for attracting, regulating and influencing economic development. Rather, poor governance is related, in this account, to low economic growth, through three mechanisms. First, failures of governance lead to poor quality or insufficient investments in public good provision needed to improve human capital. Second, failures of governance lead to inequality in landholdings and misuse of natural resources, all of which reduce economic growth. Third, and "above all," the Bank argues, "corruption, inefficiency and the inability to enforce contracts and property rights combine insidiously to impose a high cost on domestic and

---

[21] World Bank, *Cambodia at the Crossroads* (Phnom Penh: World Bank, 2004), para. 11.

foreign investors... As a result private investment is deterred and economic growth is lower than it should be."22

This analysis reflected current wisdom on Cambodia at the time; however, new data on past performance and continued success confounds the World Bank's predictions. The World Bank itself produced two major reports in 2006 and 2007 that considered Cambodia's performance in terms of poverty reduction and equitable growth.23 These reports offered a picture that was mixed, rather than entirely gloomy. In terms of poverty reduction, the World Bank's figures suggested that poverty had declined from an estimated 47 per cent in 1994 to 35 per cent in 2004. Meanwhile, new human development indicators that became available in 2006 suggested that the decline in the headcount of individuals living below the poverty line had been accompanied by better rates of school enrolment and much improved figures for infant mortality.

The second report, investigating the spread of benefits from economic growth between 1994 and 2004, found that the profits had been shared inequitably between rich and poor, with the consumption of the rich increasing by an average of 45 per cent, and that of the poor increasing by only 8 per cent. This contributed to a widening gap between rich and poor; however, the World Bank pointed out that even the poor had achieved some rise in standards of living, and claimed that the gap between rich and poor seemed to have been established in the 1990s, while the conflict was winding down. The report argued that the gap remained substantially unchanged from 1997 to 2004, in the period of post-conflict reconstruction; but more recent World Bank estimates suggest that this lull in the pace with which inequality was widening between 1997 to 2004 ended during the subsequent period of transformation. World Bank figures presented in 2009 suggest an increase in the gini coefficient for inequality in Cambodia from 0.39 to 0.43 between 2004 and 2007; this compared to 0.35 in 1993.24 However, growth remained strong over the period, suggesting that the predictions of the 2004 report – that observably poor governance would lead to a decline in economic fortune – were over-simplistic.

The analyses offered by these three reports conform to the standard approach of the IFIs in conceptualizing economic growth as the product of the natural functioning of the market, with governance, good or bad, coming into play as a secondary factor. While bad governance can deter private investors, depressing economic activity, good governance is conceptualized as essentially

---

22 World Bank, *Cambodia at the Crossroads* (Phnom Penh: World Bank, 2004), para. 26.
23 World Bank, *Cambodia – Halving Poverty by 2015?* (Phnom Penh: World Bank, 2006) and World Bank, *Sharing Growth – Equity and Development in Cambodia* (Phnom Penh: World Bank, 2007).
24 Stephane Guimbert, presentation to World Bank Country Office Retreat, 28 May 2009, Siem Reap.

hands-off, entailing dispassionate regulatory rather than skilled political action. The World Bank's rankings of Cambodia on its key governance indicators over the period from 1996 to 2007 are unequivocally bad. Although one indicator, political stability, has improved substantially since 1996, two other indicators, voice and accountability, and government effectiveness, have improved marginally, while the remaining indicators – regulatory quality, rule of law and control of corruption – show a worsening performance. Only in political stability and regulatory quality does Cambodian governance even make it into the second quartile of countries. In terms of corruption, Cambodia is ranked in the bottom ten per cent of countries worldwide.[25] Given this apparent disjuncture between measures of performance and measures of outcome, the good governance perspective would appear to have limited explanatory power with respect to Cambodia's impressive rates of economic growth.

The Developmental States Perspective

A powerful strand of the East Asian literature has long countered the World Bank's neoliberal conception of development as an impersonal process governed by objective laws, and locates East Asia's performance, rather, in institutions conceptualized as specific historical conjunctions of business and politics. "Developmental states" was a term coined by neo-Weberian institutionalists to denote the small number of states, concentrated in particular in East Asia from the 1950s to the 1990s, that exceeded the traditional role of keeping order, and the IFI-mandated role of "getting prices right" to intervene directly in the economy as a means to successfully create comparative advantage for new industries. Economic success is an important aspect of the distinctiveness of developmental states. They differ, for example, from "predatory states," which also intervene in the market but through what Evans terms "klepto-patrimonialism": namely, the marketization of the state apparatus and collusion between bureaucrats, politicians and businesses in the interests of the outright theft of state resources.[26]

---

[25] World Bank Governance indicators rank countries according to their performance on a range of six issues: voice and accountability, political stability, government effectiveness, regulatory quality, rule of law, and control of corruption. Cambodia falls well below the halfway mark in all of these indicators; it falls in the bottom quartile in voice and accountability, government effectiveness and rule of law, and in the bottom ten per cent in control of corruption. See World Bank, *Worldwide Governance Indicators*, online at http://info.worldbank.org/governance/wgi/sc_chart.asp, accessed 11 March 2009.

[26] Peter Evans, "Predatory, Developmental, and Other Apparatuses: a Comparative Political Economy Perspective on the Third World State," *Sociological Forum* 4.4 (1989): 570–571.

Between these two extremes the institutionalist literature describes other categories of states, sitting in differing relation to business and capital: one category applied in South East Asia, specifically to the post-colonial Philippines, is "booty capitalism", in which "a powerful business class extracts privilege from a largely incoherent bureaucracy."[27] A further category is that of "crony capitalist states", often applied to Indonesia and sometimes to Thailand in the boom years of the 1980s and most of the 1990s. These variations are considered to depend on the structural characteristics of states, their relations to their societies, and particular historical developments such as wars and colonial experiences. [28]

In its ideal manifestation, a developmental state not only presides over economic transformation in terms of capital accumulation, but also engineers its emergence. The success of developmental states in economic transformation has been attributed to two intertwined characteristics, autonomy and embeddedness. Autonomy allows the state to formulate economic policies which are independent from the interests of the dominant socio-economic class.[29] State autonomy requires a strong, effective and insulated bureaucracy which approximates Weberian rational models. With shared background and training, and superior social and economic status, these bureaucrats established internal norms and rules which constituted a specific type of bureaucratic corporate identity and coherence.[30]

State autonomy also requires bureaucratic insulation, meaning that bureaucrats are not linked to special socio-economic groups: those who are connected to state elites through family ties and economic interests.[31] In other words, the bureaucracy do not serve as a tool to facilitate the interests of a particular social or economic group. Rather they serve as guardians protecting prioritized policies and economic sectors from potentially colluding forces among the politico-economic elites.

Insulation does not entail isolation; for a state to be developmental, its elites, particularly its bureaucratic elites, need to be enmeshed in social networks and business elites in a form that Peter Evans terms "embedded autonomy."[32] Embedded autonomy, in the neo-Weberian framework, allows the state to effectively and efficiently acquire information, formulate policies and allocate resources in

---

[27] Paul Hutchcroft, *Booty Capitalism: The Politics of Banking in the Philippines* (Ithaca: Cornell University Press, 1998), 20.

[28] Peter Evans, *Embedded Autonomy: States and Industrial Transformation* (Princeton: Princeton University Press, 1995).

[29] Peter Evans, Dieter Rueschemeyer and Thida Skocpol, *Bringing the State Back In* (Cambridge University Press, 1985), 350.

[30] Evans, *Embedded Autonomy*, 48–49.

[31] Donald Crone, "State, Social Elites, and Government Capacity in Southeast Asia," World Politics, 40.2 (1998): 255.

[32] Evans, *Embedded Autonomy*.

order to attain a set of shared goals or a set of state initiated objectives.[33] When it is effective, it is because this embeddedness is precariously balanced, such that these elites and the bureaucracies they lead are not captured by any particular social group for rent-seeking purposes. In some instances, states (like Malaysia and Singapore) employ authoritarian paternalistic and corporatist structures to protect themselves from interference by social groups, affording the state the ability to formulate and implement economic policies.[34]

From this position, developmental states use policy instruments at their command – tariffs, subsidies, quotas and capital – to promote entrepreneurship within society.[35] They also carry out tasks which the private sector is unable to take on, such as strategic research and development on new technologies.[36] With autonomy and embeddedness, the state can also engage in sectoral intervention in the economy, as in the case of agricultural development and labour-intensive exports in the early stage of development in Taiwan[37] and in information technology in Korea, Brazil, India and Taiwan.[38] Furthermore, the state, plays a role as "a surrogate for a missing capital market", when it intervenes in economic transformations through the provision of needed funding to industrialists through government controlled financial and banking institutions.[39]

How useful is this approach for evaluating Cambodia's transformation? One problem with the developmental states approach is the difficulty in determining the conditions in which just the right mix of embeddedness and autonomy arises. A variant of the literature which focuses on the wrong mix has emerged: "crony capitalism" is a term coined to refer to states that have insufficient autonomy to frame and meet developmental goals. Bureaucrats in crony capitalist states are unable to insulate themselves from a business elite, which dictates policy and transforms technocrats into dependent clients.[40] Business elites are given protection from wider social forces, and monopoly rights over extraction of state resources and certain sectors of the economy, in exchange for "patronage resources for political elites".[41] This use of the state to broker

---

[33] Evans, *Embedded Autonomy,* 12
[34] Crone, "State, Social Elites," 259–262.
[35] Evans, *Embedded Autonomy,* 13.
[36] Evans, *Embedded Autonomy,* 14
[37] Alice Amsden, "The State and Taiwan's Economic Development," in Peter Evans, Dietrich Rueschemyer and Theda Skocpol (eds.), *Bringing the State Back In* (Cambridge University Press, 1985), 78–106.
[38] Evans, *Embedded Autonomy.*
[39] Evans, "Predatory, Developmental, and Other Apparatuses," 569–570.
[40] Crouch, "Indonesia's 'Strong' State," in Peter Dauvergne (ed.), *Weak and Strong States in Asia Pacific Societies,* (Canberra: Allen & Unwin, 1998), 100.
[41] Crone, "State, Social Elites," 262.

a narrow pact between business and political elites operates at the expense of broad developmental goals pursued over the long term. Rather than the state fostering the "right" kind of state – capital – labour relations to foster broad-based development, the state and capital collude in draining the economy of assets at the expense of either developmental goals or the poor. This tendency is certainly observable in contemporary Cambodia.

Institutionalists focus on the institutional characteristics of crony capitalist states, and the difference between these and the characteristics of developmental states: the significance of neo-patrimonialism rather than meritocratic principles within the bureaucracy; inadequate rates of pay producing corruption;[42] corrupt rent-seeking practices; and the dependence of officials on their patrons.[43] These institutional features foster the tendency of bureaucrats to facilitate state – business collusion rather than productive collaboration, and therefore offer a useful checklist of items to be targeted by governance reform.

However, this distinction is idealized, turning upon a concept of rationality that is used to distinguish between nepotism and meritocracy; patronage and sound management; personalism and even-handedness. In this, the model in the literature has certainly been abstracted from reality: Chalmers Johnson's classic study of Japan's Ministry of International Trade and Industry (MITI), for example, revealed two important aspects of "lines of succession" within the ministry and its departments. The first is the strong personal connections between bureaucrats and business executives which generated the trust and loyalty that oiled the wheels of the system. The second is the ways in which the strong ties between bureaucratic and business elites prompted MITI to discriminate in favour of particular industries and firms. These aspects – a key part of MITI's success in Johnson's view – are hard to square with the claims that developmental states are based upon rational – legal values of meritocracy, professionalism and fairness.

Peter Evans meets this criticism by asserting that, while all forms of state – business relations can be corrupt and patrimonial, the degree and impact is different between developmental states and crony capitalist states. Although rent-seeking to benefit incumbents and their friends exists in developmental states, the degree of such practices is low and does not impede economic development.[44] In developmental states, states and businesses form strategic partnerships wherein

---

[42] Ben Schneider and Sylvia Maxfield, "Business, the State, and Economic Performance," in Sylvia Maxfield and Ben Schneider eds., *Business and the State in Developing Countries* (Ithaca: Cornell University Press, 1997), 15.

[43] Crone, "State, Social Elites," 265.

[44] Evans, "Predatory, Developmental, and Other Apparatuses," 563.

state elites favour certain businesses; but only in cases where the business in question share the state's strategic goals and is deemed capable of helping the state to achieve them. Connections between state officials and businesses in crony capitalist states tend to be patronage based, resting on "purely personal connections, favors, promises, and privileges",[45] rather than well-formulated policies consistently applied across certain industrial sectors.

Furthermore, it is argued that in crony capitalist states, state elites' favour toward certain businesses is based primarily on narrow political interests – exchanging state resources and other rents for political support and perquisites. Business and industrial policies create opportunities for corruption around the issuing of licenses, contracts, subsidies and privatized projects;[46] in crony capitalist states these are sold to raise funds for political parties, election campaigns and buying off political opponents. In sum, crony capitalist states are riddled with corruption; and such states lack economic initiatives and effective responses to changes in global and domestic economies. Because these states lack embedded autonomy from social forces, any rational change in policy amounts to an assault on the foundations of power and wealth on which the mutually beneficial business – state elite alliance rests.[47]

There are three problems with this position. First, the focus on policy, rather than on the balance of power between a tight elite of officials and bureaucrats plays out behind the scenes, renders it difficult to distinguish crony capitalism from developmentalism in real life. As a result, in some of the literature, the designation of a particular set of policies as rational as opposed to self-serving is dependent upon how well they turn out to work, rather than upon criteria defined and applied a priori. The Asian Financial Crisis shifted many South East Asian states, in the analyses of some observers, from the first category to the second almost overnight.[48] We can observe many of the features of crony capitalism in contemporary Cambodia, particularly during the post-conflict years of the late 1990s. But now that the key players are cleaning up their acts, a shift to developmentalism may be occurring, based upon institutionalized relationships such as the Government – Private Sector Forum. Like the democratic transitions much sought after in the 1990s, this kind of transition will be difficult, analytically, to spot until it is complete.

---

[45] Hutchcroft, *Booty Capitalism*, 14.
[46] Edmund Gomez, "Introduction: Political Business in East Asia," in Edmund Gomez (ed.), *Political Business in East Asia* (London: Routledge, 2002), 2.
[47] Richard Robison, "Authoritarian States, Capital-Owning Classes and the Politics of Newly-Industrialising Countries: the Case of Indonesia," *World Politics* 41.1 (1988): 65 and 71.
[48] Kanishka Jayasuriya and Andrew Rosser, "Economic Orthodoxy and the East Asian Crisis," *Third World Quarterly* 22.3 (2001): 381-396.

Second, the focus on policy, in the neo-liberal literature, and capacity, in the institutionalist literature, diverts attention from the way that changing structures of capital and social class may be producing new social forces that both constrain the state and offer new opportunities for new modes of governance. For Cambodian reformers and external intervenors, the degree of state insulation from powerful business interests is a significant question; but so is the evolving nature of those interests themselves.[49] As Hadiz and Robison suggest with respect to Indonesia, the issue of reform in the context of powerful predatory elites is not so much the question of how policy can be devised to deal with them, as how coalitions can be mobilized to contest their power.[50]

Third, the shock of the Asian Financial Crisis and the effect of the neo-liberal reforms imposed in its aftermath upon former developmental states have themselves raised the question of whether the age of developmentalism is past. The politics of late development at the turn of the millennium entail that the forces propelling economic development are not found merely within the Cambodian state and economy. Rather, they can best be understood as emerging from the process of Cambodia's late integration into the mainstream of rapidly globalizing regional and international networks of production and trade. The regional and global order Cambodia faces is one in which the neoliberal project of integration and marketization is gathering pace.

Kanishka Jayasuriya argues that the developmental states credited with leading East Asian development from the 1960s to the 1980s were the product of a particular relation of forces with their roots in the US system of security alliances during the Cold War and the Bretton Woods system of financial regulation. These two overarching systems made possible the variety of national, state-led developmentalism that characterized economic policy in South Korea, Singapore and Thailand. Their demise, and the globalization of production and finance that followed, prompted the transformation of developmental states into "regulatory states", organized around the regulation of global capital flows, rather than the direction of national development.[51] Similarly, Iain Pirie conceptualizes the transformation of the South Korean state as a consequence of neoliberal reform thus:

> Neoliberalism essentially involves the creation of a "new" state which seeks to support the functioning of market disciplines and the commodification of ever greater areas of social and economic life.[52]

[49] Vedi Hadiz and Richard Robison, "Neo-liberal Reforms and Illiberal Consolidations: the Indonesian Paradox," *Journal of Development Studies* 41.2 (2005): 223.
[50] Ibid., 222.
[51] Kanishka Jayasuriya, "Beyond Institutional Fetishism: From the Developmental to the Regulatory State," *New Political Economy* 10.3 (2005): 383–384.
[52] Iain Pirie, "The New Korean State," *New Political Economy* 10.1 (2005): 27.

Pirie documents this in advance of the Asian Crisis in the case of South Korea, while pressures to liberalize financial markets in Thailand have also been regarded as the trigger for the devaluation of the baht and the Crisis itself. Viewed from this perspective, the developmental state of the 1960s is already redundant. The globalization of production and finance forced its demise, and created new kinds of states in East Asia which operated as agents for marketization, whose key task is less the formulation of national strategies for development and more the local enforcer of international strategies for facilitating global markets. This perspective opens up the relationship between business and capital for scrutiny, not only on a national but also on a regional and international scale. As such, it allows us to move beyond the good governance vs neo-patrimonialism that has characterized much of the debate over Cambodia's economic transformation, to consider the nature of the balance of power between different forces inside and outside the country. Such forces include western aid donors, promoting neo-liberal projects of good governance, conceptualized in terms of the regulation of a region-wide market, and foreign and domestic investors seeking profits and influence. They also include government and party officials organized into various institutionalized hierarchies and networks of personal loyalty. Last and, unfortunately, usually least, they include the political struggles of the long-suffering Cambodian poor.

The Politics of Markets and Integration

Cambodia's emergence from its post-socialist, post-conflict situation in the 1990s was organized through the twin projects of bureaucratic state-building and rapid economic integration. These were characterized by massive, internationally funded projects to produce and rebuild both physical and administrative infrastructure. The process of bureaucratization had two facets. The first was an internationally sponsored process of state capacity building, in which capacity was conceptualized as a technical process of regulation. The second was a locally produced and highly politicized process of stabilization, in which stability was conceptualized as the distribution of status and power through an elaborate hierarchy of positions designed both to maintain existing ties of loyalty and obligation from the war years, and to forge and accommodate new ones.

This process of bureaucratization occurred alongside a rapid process of marketization, particularly with respect to land and natural resources but also, more recently, with respect to money and labour. The initial establishment of land ownership rights at the end of the 1980s was swiftly followed by a wave of the enclosure of commonly held resources in the 1990s. This was followed again in the 2000s by the expropriation of both inhabited and frontier land for agro-industrial development in the 2000s. The concept of economic transformation offers a key to analyzing the nature of this process of marketization, and particularly its effect on the poor. Karl Polanyi's coinage of the term "the Great Transformation" in 1944 referred to the wave of contestation and change that swept England between the late eighteenth and late nineteenth centuries, as the idea of "the market" was transformed from a reference to local and incidental places for buying and selling goods to *the* key structuring principle around which relations between land, labour and money were organized on a national scale. For the first time, Polanyi argues, market exchange was elevated to an end in itself – the paramount goal of the community – rather than subordinated to broader social goals.[53]

This elevation of a particular set of economic relationships to the status of natural law was the intentional effect of efforts by the new liberal bourgeoisie to transform the nature and significance of private property holdings. In supporting this move in the England of the Industrial Revolution, the guardians of state and their economic advisors were not acting as the technocratic facilitators of development, but as the violent enforcers of a regime of expropriation for profit. This process of land enclosure is central to economic transformation, and the process has historically been violent and unequal wherein, as Polanyi describes, the desire of the poor for "habitation" is pitted against that of the bourgeoisie to profit from "improvement". Polanyi notes the level of conflict involved in this process. The economic logic of enclosures, he maintains, involves a "tragic necessity by which the poor man clings to his hovel doomed by the rich man's desire for a public improvement which profits him privately".[54] Enclosure forms the basis of the market economy, producing a bourgeois class with surplus capital for reinvestment in industrialization, along with a dispossessed pool of labour to exploit.

Although Polanyi coined the term to refer to developments in England, state organs subsequently performed the same task across Europe and the Americas, and, by the 1870s, in the form of colonial administrations, across the Global South, where a wave of enclosures occurred, in the interests of resource-hungry industries in the metropoles. Post-colonial East Asian states, across the spectrum from developmental to crony capitalist, share a history of forced expropriation and violent suppression of protest, achieved with the active assistance or tacit approval of the state, although this varies in shape and form. Such variations ranged from the quasi-governmental and policing role acquired by the semi-private South Manchuria Railway Company in China in the 1930s, from whose

---

[53] Karl Polanyi, *The Great Transformation: The Political and Economic Origins of our Time*, (Boston: Beacon).
[54] Polanyi, 36.

ranks emerged some of the architects of MITI's post-war economic policy; to the violence used by the *chaebol* in the 1970s and 1980s to suppress trade unions in South Korea; and to the monopolization by the *Tentara Nasional Indonesia* (in collusion with the Suharto family) of the sandalwood, coffee and marble industries in East Timor.

From Polanyi's perspective, the triumph of capital was achieved at the point where developmentalism, conceptualized as the dominance of the market and the forcible incorporation of natural resources into a regime of private property, could be portrayed as the natural precondition for human progress, regardless of the human misery it caused. In other words, it is the ability to divert attention away from the costs of growth, rather than the ability to actually minimize or eliminate them, in the name of the rationality of the market that represented the key to the triumph of the developmental state. However, the relationship of the state to capital is crucial in terms of what Polanyi described as "the counter-movement". These are political struggles by the poor aimed at reforming state institutions that have presided over the process of marketization into organs capable of providing welfare and protection from the ravages of profit-seeking capital.

State, Society and Market in Contemporary Cambodia

The central argument of this volume is that, in contemporary Cambodia, marketization is certainly occurring. However, the accompaniment of rapid growth by widening inequality, the continued concentration of industry, and a dependence on contingent factors such as export quotas suggests that this is not the unfolding of a rational developmental policy. The establishment of physical security across Cambodian territory, via strategies of bureaucratization, was the prerequisite for this drive towards commodification of the basis of subsistence; but bureaucratization itself was undertaken in a manner which rendered the capacities of the state increasingly dependent upon the Cambodian People's Party. The latter has evolved into a sprawling entity with interests, alliances and subsidiaries in every government agency and every village; within the trade union and NGO movements; in the private sector; even among the supposed opposition parties.

Arguably, this dependence upon the party, despite the efforts of foreign donors to promote the regulatory state as an autonomous (although embedded) entity, reflects the slender foundations of the regulatory state. Developmental states, backed by force and with powerful weapons of fiscal policy, had real resources to deploy as a means to reward and contain real political constituencies. The regulatory state, by contrast, has little discretionary power and control, confined to expanding the latitude of the commercial interests it is simultaneously supposed to police, in a manner which considerably undermines the realm within which political accommodations are possible.

In Cambodia, this situation has promoted the power of leading figures within the Cambodian People's Party, whose informal relations with regional and global business partners, and whose personal control of both vast slush funds and of instruments of lethal force,[55] forms the political cement that the regulatory state lacks. As Andrew Cock and Michael Sullivan illustrate in their contributions to this volume, the influence of external capital allied with party politics dominates the regulatory power of a weak bureaucracy, undercutting the hands-off orientation of the regulatory state, but simultaneously creating the foundations for a politics of resource distribution that can be used to accommodate contending political demands.

The way in which this operates, and the impact on the economy and on relations between rich and poor, differs between sectors and regions of the country, depending upon the influence of different groups of domestic and external investors, and upon the status of the global market. We demonstrate this through the detailed analyses by Sophal Ear, Margaret Slocomb and Jonathan Padwe of four important sectors in the Cambodian economy: rice, garments, rubber and cashews. Each of the authors investigates relationships between state actors and investors. Each shows how these relationships are determined less by development policies framed by autonomous state institutions than by historically determined levels of influence of local and central power-brokers in the party and state, in conjunction with the interests of regional or national capital.

Next, the volume turns to the neo-liberal reform agendas promoted by Western donors in line with good governance models. These, it is argued, have had highly variable effects in this context. So Sokbunthoeun, David Norman and Annuska Derks discuss efforts, sponsored by Western donors, to intervene to construct efficient markets for land, money and labour in Cambodia, through land registration, micro-credit and labour export schemes. In each case, they conclude that the impact of these schemes can be destructive of the communitarian basis of rural livelihoods, but, in its individualizing effects, is highly variable from one person to the next. In this they concur with Padwe and Slocomb's accounts of the impact of privatization and commercialization in the rubber and cashew industries. From the ethnic Jarai, investing in cashew crops in the north-east, to the rubber-tappers in the plantations of Kompong Cham, to the customers of the ACLEDA bank, to Cambodian fish-wives working in

---

[55] With respect to the latter, the rise and rise of Hun Sen's personal bodyguard, now estimated to number around 7,000 members, is one example. The use of assassins to contain social movements, as in the killing of union leader Chea Vichea in 2004, is another example.

Thailand, neo-liberal marketization is creating new opportunities for economic advancement and even success. At the same time, it is destroying older coping strategies, and reducing both the incentive and the basis for collective action. Thus in each case, the very poorest are left marginalized, and, arguably, with reduced prospects of finding assistance.

Chapters 10 to 12 move on to discuss the functioning of institutions of state and party in this context. With respect to bureaucratic systems of governance, as Un and Hughes discuss in Chapter 10, the reception of neoliberal reform prescriptions for a transparent and technocratic regulatory state has similarly been highly varied. The key determinant of this variation is the extent to which strategies for consolidating state – business alliances are confronted by reform. This kind of reform has been permitted in areas of state action that are associated with the provision of services, such as water and healthcare, at least where organized social forces have not mobilized in support of the status quo. However, in parts of government that are most closely concerned with the policing of the private property regime, the erection of this kind of regulatory framework has faced concerted resistance from interested coalitions of forces, and this resistance has been coordinated and facilitated by the structures of the ruling Cambodian People's Party.

The elevation of the Party over the state in Cambodia reflects the way in which the Party has taken on stabilizing of political relations, through the monopolizing of the sources of discretionary patronage, as a means to massage relations both with regional and global investors and with the poor. For the Party, surrendering control of natural resources and land to an internationally sanctioned, rights-based regime would represent surrendering its ability to manoeuvre politically. Thus, as Michael Sullivan describes in his account of Chinese investment in Cambodia, it is the Party, rather than the state, that has forged relations with the Chinese government; and it is the Party, as David Craig and Pak Kimchoeun show, that has taken on the role of promoting legitimacy through the provision of mass patronage to the poor. This elevation of the Party has been decried as anti-democratic, non-transparent, and antithetical to good governance. Yet, there is also a suspicion, voiced privately by donors in Phnom Penh, that the reserve, by the Party, of a discretionary sphere within which such political accommodations can be forged, has formed the basis of stability in Cambodia – the kind of stability that is precisely lacking in many other post-conflict countries, where neoliberal forms of regulatory state-building have been more assiduously pursued.

What does this deal mean for the position of the poor? The potential for the emergence of a counter-movement that can protect the poor from the consequences of transformation forms the theme of the rest of the volume. Craig and Pak regard the mass patronage of the Cambodian People's Party as potentially holding the seeds of more democratic consultation over the disposal of resources. However, patronage is a double-edged sword, since it facilitates co-optation and intense surveillance of collective action at the village level, and this is antithetical to the prospects for organizing coalitions of forces to contest the power of the state – business alliance. The promotion of bureaucratic decentralization of political power through the institution of commune level elections has frequently been regarded by Western donors as providing an opportunity to contest these relations, by offering two important political opportunities to the rural poor: the opportunity to participate in development planning, and the opportunity to gain representation for political demands. However, the co-optation of the process by the party, and the strength of the business sector vis-à-vis the poor stacks the deck firmly in the direction of rich allies of the party.

Hughes, Eng, Thon, Ou and Ly find little prospect for empowered participation in their analysis of local leadership and big business, which focuses on the functioning of local councils in three communes. They show how in a commune where big business has significant interests in land and natural resources, the local council is powerless to deal with them; in a rice-growing commune where big business is not so evident, the party steps in with donations to co-opt local support. Öjendal and Kim, by contrast, find the prospects more promising in their analysis of the engagement of non-state community-based associations with local government. Taking a more developmental institutionalist perspective, they argue that while these associations are as yet having little practical effect in redistributing power, their presence entails that over time a greater capacity for organization and contestation will emerge among the rural poor.

Henke takes up this theme in Chapter 14, offering a practitioners' perspective on the difficulties of providing support to community-based organizations in the context of a donor effort which tends to focus more upon the promotion of liberal political relations than upon solidarity. For Henke, the power and resources of external donors threaten to overwhelm fragile coalitions at local level, especially since the leadership of such coalitions have a powerful interest in hitching onto donor resource flows rather than focusing on the dangerous business of local mobilization. Finally, Erik Davis argues that rising rural inequality and contested rural – urban relations have generated considerable discontent in rural Cambodia, but that expression of this remains sporadic, elliptic and obscure. He documents this through an analysis of the way tensions are expressed between urban and rural communities celebrating the festival of the dead.

2

THE RISE OF PROVINCIAL BUSINESS IN CAMBODIA

Andrew Robert Cock

SINCE 1997, CAMBODIA'S PRIME MINISTER Hun Sen has elevated himself above political competitors to the point where he seems to hold unparalleled power. As he has done so, a group of business entities has risen to prominence. The growth of these entities has been partially a function of their positioning so as to benefit from grants of state property and various licences and concessions. Control over land in the form of plantation developments has been a key element of this trend. Such a trend raises questions concerning the implications for political power of the emergence of these business entities, or "oligarchs". Does Hun Sen control them, or have they come to be increasingly able to influence and perhaps to a significant extent control Hun Sen? Does the emergence of these business entities point to a reshaping of the Cambodian polity – a movement away from a bureaucratic polity towards an oligarchic state?

Analysis of the burgeoning relationship between state and business in Cambodia points to the significance of two potentially conflicting dynamics: pressure for the institutionalization of "good governance" by providers of foreign aid; and growing regional economic interdependence. These dynamics are analysed in what follows as a means of investigating their impact on the nature of state – business relations. The accelerated economic growth experienced in Cambodia since 2003 has accompanied a significant change in dominant economic structures, shifting the role of the state away from the bureaucratic politics that characterized the state-building process of the 1980s and 1990s, and towards an oligarchic system more reminiscent of the "booty capitalist" model described with respect to the Philippines.

In bureaucratic authoritarian political systems or, more precisely, "the patrimonial administrative state", the dominant social force is the bureaucratic elite. Countervailing social forces are, by contrast, weak. Because the major beneficiaries of rent extraction are the bureaucratic elite, based within the state apparatus, economic activity tends to be shaped and to a large extent dominated by elements located within the state. A paradigmatic example is often taken to be post-World War II Thailand.[1] Other sometimes cited cases include Mobutu's Zaire and Suharto's Indonesia.

This type of merging of economic and political power can be contrasted with "the patrimonial oligarchic state".[2] In this case, the dominant social force – an oligarchy – has an economic base that is in key ways independent of the state apparatus. Nonetheless, access to the state is a major avenue of capital accumulation. Both forms of patrimonial political system exhibit a weak separation between the official and private spheres, but in the patrimonial oligarchic state, extra-bureaucratic forces overshadow the bureaucracy. A key purpose of this chapter is to discern how Cambodia's political development seems to be manifesting itself in terms of a shift away from a patrimonial administrative and towards an oligarchic state.

In traditional polities, a ruler's power often depended on his capacity to win and retain the loyalty of key sections of the elite. Lacking sufficient coercive capacity to enforce acceptance of his rule, the ruler sought to win voluntary allegiance by satisfying the aspirations, particularly the material interests, of supporters through the distribution of fiefs and benefices in exchange for tribute and loyalty. The Weberian concept of "patrimonialism" thus conveyed the notion of political administration operating as a personal affair, with no clear distinction between the public and private domains, and the state apparatus as a matter of norm directed towards the personal whims and discretions of those holding power. The patrimonial state contrasts with the notion of the predictable, rule-governed behaviour of the archetypal legal – rational bureaucratic state.

Scholars continue to deploy the concept to capture the particular dynamics of some contemporary state structures. These are states that are formally modern in the sense of being structured as, and claiming to operate as, legal – rational bureaucratic entities, but where the public – private divide necessary for their operation as true bureaucracies is blurred. In this "neo-patrimonial" context, the lack of a clear public – private division results in the state apparatus being crippled by an incentive structure that promotes administration directed towards particularistic interests and personal benefits. Decision-making may be directed towards the interests of specific groups able to exercise influence over the state apparatus, or be aimed at maximizing the personal benefits of the office holder.

---

[1] The classic analysis of the bureaucratic polity is Fred Warren Riggs, *Thailand: the modernization of a bureaucratic polity* (Honolulu: East-West Center Press, 1966).
[2] Such a contrast is developed in Paul D. Hutchcroft, *Booty capitalism: the politics of banking in the Philippines* (Ithaca: Cornell University Press, 1998), 46–55.

Paul Hutchcroft suggests that the Philippines' developmental trajectory can be traced to the endurance of a group of landed families that have manifested a particular kind of predatory relationship with the Philippine state. The relationship, critically, was influenced by the nature of the support garnered from external economic forces. Hutchcroft notes:

> Throughout modern Philippine history, one finds far more oligarchy building than state building: the oligarchic families have had ample opportunities, historically, to consolidate their power with the support of external forces, while the state has remained woefully underdeveloped.[3]

Hutchcroft's argument is that the state apparatus is easy prey to a powerful social class that enjoys an independent economic base outside the state but depends on particularistic access to the political machinery as a major avenue to private accumulation. Hence, the political dynamic is characterized as a process of "oligarchy building" as distinct from "state building".

A clear distinction needs to be drawn between the patrimonial oligarchic and the patrimonial administrative state. Both systems exhibit a weak separation between the official and private spheres, but in the oligarchic state, extra-bureaucratic forces overshadow the bureaucracy. Hutchcroft notes of the Philippines that "[t]he principal direction of rent extraction is the reverse of that found in bureaucratic capitalism: a powerful oligarchic business class extracts privilege from a largely incoherent bureaucracy."[4] In the Cambodian case, conceptualizing a shift between these two types of political system requires identifying central drivers of change. Two are of key importance. One relates to how competition is manifested within elite groups, and the second relates to the influence of providers of foreign aid. In the case of relatively small polities such as Cambodia, highly interpenetrated by supra-national economic forces, and a recipient of substantial foreign aid, externally sponsored governance reforms and the nature of economic integration are central to the shift between patrimonial administrative and oligarchic polities.

In broad terms, the shift to an oligarchic political system entails a diminished economic role for the state and an increase in the political influence of business entities.[5] The bureaucratic elite's penetration and control over the economic sphere is mutated into a business elite's penetration into the state's

---

[3] Hutchcroft, *Booty capitalism: the politics of banking in the Philippines*, 11–12.
[4] Ibid., 234.
[5] For a discussion of the concept of oligarchy in the context of Southeast Asia, see Richard Robison and Vedi R. Hadiz, *Reorganising Power in Indonesia: the Politics of Oligarchy in an Age of Markets* (New York: Routledge, 2004).

processes of policy formulation and decision-making.⁶ A number of factors need to be considered regarding shifts. One is the capacity of the state and how changes in state capacity correspond to its role in relation to the strategies of rule deployed by political elites. A second is the increase in the size or economic power of coherent business entities that are conceptually separable from business networks controlled from within the bureaucratic elite. A third relates to the channels of communication, inducements and pressures utilized by business entities to influence Cambodia's political apex. A fourth is the relationship between business entities and societal groups and the circumstances that govern when and how state actors are involved in the mediation of these relations. These four factors are reviewed below in the context of two key land disputes that arose in Cambodia between 2004 and 2008, to illustrate the contradictory position of Cambodian capital at present. Large-scale business entities are substituting for the more ad hoc and contingent ways in which state actors and their clients sought to position themselves to benefit from favourable access to state property and various licenses and concessions. Thus the analysis illustrates the ways in which the bureaucratic polity of the 1980s, where political and economic power were merged in the hands of a ruling class, is being eclipsed by a regionally networked oligarchic elite.⁷ This elite maintains opportunistic alliances with state actors, but operates independently of them. The cases also reveal the incipient tension between foreign-advocated processes of political institutionalization and economic integration, in this context.

---

⁶ For a broader comparative discussion of this dynamic process, see Andrew MacIntyre, "Business and government in industrializing Asia," in *Business and government in industrializing Asia*, ed. Andrew MacIntyre (Ithaca: Cornell University Press, 1994). In comparing Northeast and Southeast Asia, MacIntyre notes (p. 12): "The Southeast Asian states have either not attempted to involve themselves in governing the behaviour of firms to a similar extent, or, if they have (as in Indonesia), intervention has generally been poorly coordinated and subject to extensive manipulation by business people with powerful patrons in government."

⁷ Intertwined with state structures and invariably key beneficiaries of the exploitation and manipulation of state assets, Cambodia's ruling class is composed of top level administrative, political, police, and military officials, close prime ministerial advisors, ministers (including secretaries and undersecretaries of state), departmental heads, provincial and municipal governors, and senior party officials. Their relatives are often encompassed within this group. For the ruling class, opportunities for appropriation are vast, and the material perquisites that flow from their status and connections are substantial. Most members of this group operate or create their own patronage networks and are part of others.

The Reshaping of Provincial Business: Insights from Two Land Disputes

Case 1: The O'Yadaw land dispute: bureaucratic power, foreign aid, and indigenous rights.

In August 2004 Keat Kolney, sister of the Minister of Economy and Finance (Keat Chhon) and wife of a Secretary of State in the Ministry of Land Management (Chhan Saphan), acquired 450 hectares of land held by villagers of the Jarai ethnicity in Ratanakiri's O'Yadaw district. The process by which she acquired the land and defended herself against the protestations of villagers and legal proceedings initiated by legal aid NGOs illustrates the patrimonial administrative tendencies of the Cambodian polity. The case is an example of how a person closely connected to the ruling elite (via her family's ties to the most senior levels of the Cambodian state) utilized her status to make the machinery of the state at a lower level work to her advantage so as to embark on a provincial business venture.

Keat Kolney acquired 450 hectares of land in Ratanakiri's O'Yadaw district, Pate commune, aiming to convert the area to a rubber plantation. Of the area's Jarai inhabitants, 101 families allegedly sold parcels of land for $180 per hectare.[8] Over the following year and a half, disputation concerning the probity of the transaction, including whether it constituted a sale of land, simmered at the provincial level.[9] Three issues have been central to the dynamics of the dispute in the period since 2004:

1. The legality of the sale: did villagers sell the land willingly or were they duped? And could the land be legally sold under the terms of the 2001 land law given that at least some of it was forested and possibly all of it was the immovable property of an indigenous group?
2. The deployment of the court system: first by legal aid NGOs to contest the legality and legitimacy of the transaction and later by Keat Kolney as an instrument to dissuade villagers and their lawyers from pursuing the matter.
3. The role of local government officials: in facilitating the transaction and in limiting the attempts by villager representatives and their civil society supporters to contest the deal.

Each of these issues will be considered in turn.

---

[8] Kuch Naren, "R'kiri land dispute villagers approached for deal," *The Cambodia Daily (Weekly Review)*, 12–16 March 2007; Prak Chan Thul, "Lawyer insists R'kiri land deal is valid," *The Cambodia Daily (Weekly Review)*, 2–6 April 2007.

[9] The dispute seems to have received scant attention at a national level prior to January 2007.

In January 2007, twelve Jarai villagers represented by the Community Legal Education Centre (CLEC) and Legal Aid of Cambodia (LAC) launched a complaint in the Ratanakiri Provincial Court. The complaint, made against Keat Kolney, a former village chief, commune officials and the district governor, alleged that the land was obtained illegally. According to the complainants, they had been hoodwinked into the sale of their land because officials had informed them that Prime Minister Hun Sen had requested fifty hectares of their land so it could be distributed to disabled soldiers. More broadly, villagers complained that the transaction (whose nature remained contested) had involved the faking of various documents and bribery.

Keat Kolney's counter-claim, made via her lawyer, was that she had legally purchased the land and that each villager had thumb-printed a document agreeing to sell his or her individually managed plot. Given this procedure, Kolney claimed, the transaction was made in accordance with Cambodia's 2001 land law. With much of the land cleared so as to establish a rubber plantation, villagers felt that they had lost their livelihood. Sev Kem, one of the villager complainants noted: "They took away all of our farmland. . . . [A village official] has threatened me but the rest of the village stands together. We want our land back."[10] A statement issued by the Cambodian Human Rights Action Committee echoed such villager concerns and provides an indication of the type of pressure state institutions were to be placed under as a result of the dispute. According to NGO Forum Deputy Director, Ngy San, "Ratanakkiri is in crisis now – land-grabbing is out of control and devastating indigenous lives – and Kong Yu is emblematic of the worst of these cases." And LAC Director Peung Yok Hiep suggested that there was "no clearer example in Cambodia today of the rich and powerful exploiting the poor and marginalized."[11]

A further issue of legality related to whether the land, some or perhaps much of which being forested, could legally change hands. In this regard, CLEC lawyers claimed that the 2001 land law prohibited all private sales of collectively owned indigenous land.[12] A central purpose of provisions in the land law related to indigenous peoples was to reduce the tendency of ethnic minority groups to lose control over land and associated resources as remote regions came to be under the influence of market based social relations. Civil society groups

---

[10] Cited in Erik Wasson and Yun Samean, "R'kiri villagers file complaints over land sale," *The Cambodia Daily (Weekly Review)*, 22–26 January 2007.
[11] Ibid.
[12] Ith Mathoura, for instance, stated: "The contract was based on lies and fraud and under the 2001 Land Law, no one can individually sell collective [indigenous] land." Ibid.

sought to make a robust case that "land alienation" was worsening in much of the province.[13] Ratanakiri Provincial Governor Muong Poy contested such claims. In reference to an NGO Forum report on "land alienation", he argued that there were "no rich and powerful people who encroach on people's lands. ... The ethnic communities don't know the Land Law. We have been educating them not to sell the land."[14] However, Pen Bonnar, Ratanakiri provincial coordinator for ADHOC, stated: "Our organization has clear information and proof that many governors in various districts are deeply involved in the sale of community farmland."[15] The claim that land was purchased illegally because it constituted communal property was to be a key issue that lawyers for the villagers attempted to pursue through the courts.[16]

These two issues – misrepresentation or fraud in the transaction, and the legality of the transaction itself given provisions in the 2001 Land Law relating to the immovable property of an indigenous community – were subsequently the subjects of a petition by the villagers' legal representatives to the Ratanakiri Provincial Court. The successful use of the courts to mediate the case would suggest success in the drive towards institutionalization of good governance implicit in the reform agenda of foreign aid donors. Indeed, the villagers' access to legal aid reflects this, since it was facilitated by an externally sponsored drive to build civil society and rule of law in Cambodia in the 1990s, a drive which resulted in the emergence of several legal aid non-governmental organizations with a strong human rights and pro-poor focus.

However, attempts by legal advocates to use the court system in support of their clients were blocked. An injunction was unsuccessfully sought by villager legal representatives in March 2007 to halt rubber planting on the contested land.[17] Local officials called to the court failed to attend on the first two occasions that they were summoned. When they did attend in late April 2007, questioning of their role in the case was limited. According to Ratanakiri court

---

[13] See NGO Forum on Cambodia, "Land alienation in indigenous minority communities - Ratanakiri Province, Cambodia," (Phnom Penh: August, 2006). See also, Yun Samean and Douglas Gillison, "R'kiri's indigenous people losing land, culture," *The Cambodia Daily (Weekly Review)*, 5–9 February 2007.

[14] Yun Samean and Gillison, "R'kiri's indigenous people losing land, culture." The Provincial Governor was referring to NGO Forum on Cambodia, "Land alienation in indigenous minority communities - Ratanakiri Province, Cambodia."

[15] Kuch Naren, "Ratanakkiri villagers accuse officials of grabbing land," *The Cambodia Daily (Weekly Review)*, 19–23 February 2007.

[16] As Ith Mathoura, a lawyer engaged by CLEC noted, "The [villagers] are ethnic Jarai people. They have no right to sell the land and no one else has the right to occupy their land." Prak Chan Thul, "Lawyer insists R'kiri land deal is valid."

[17] Kuch Naren, "R'kiri court denies request to halt rubber planting," *The Cambodia Daily (Weekly Review)*, 12–16 March 2007.

clerk Prak Soeun: "We just asked [the officials] whether they really signed or not. . . . They recognized that they had signed, with the agreement from the villagers."[18] Ny Chandy, a lawyer from LAC, observed that the judge was working rather slowly on the case. He noted, "[The judge] seems to delay the time to find justice for the victims."[19] In May, attempts were made by Keat Kolney to settle the matter out of court, a process with which Ratanakiri Provincial Court Judge An Samnang may have had some involvement.[20] Villagers rejected this offer and subsequently sought to petition senior government officials in Phnom Penh. In a sense, a decision by their NGO supporters was made to pursue the matter via contact with the political elites, not just via the court system.

In mid June 2007, villagers attempted to meet with Ministry of Land Management Secretary of State Chhan Saphan, Keat Kolney's husband.[21] Undertaken in the lead up to a government – donor meeting, this politicization provoked a more active set of responses from the Ratanakiri Provincial Court. Perhaps to save the government from further embarrassment, villagers were summoned by the Provincial Court to return to Ratanakiri to negotiate with Keat Kolney.[22] Keat Kolney subsequently sought to use the Provincial Court and the Cambodian Bar Association as tools against the plaintiffs and their lawyers, a practice noted by the Cambodia Office of the High Commissioner for Human Rights as increasingly prevalent in land disputes.[23]

Keat Kolney countered the villagers' lawsuit by filing a complaint with the Cambodian Bar Association charging that seven CLEC lawyers and three lawyers from LAC had incited Jarai villagers involved in the dispute and were "politically motivated".[24] She also claimed that the lawyers had been unduly influenced by foreign advisors, made inappropriate cash payments to villagers, given false information to the media, and inappropriately dragged powerful

---

[18] Prak Chan Thul, "3 officials questioned in R'kiri land-dispute case," *The Cambodia Daily (Weekly Review)*, 23–27 April 2007.

[19] Ibid.

[20] See Prak Chan Thul, "Settlement offered in Ratanakiri land dispute". Three proposals were put forward by Keat Kolney as the basis for a settlement: the return of 50 of the original 450 hectares; construction of a three-room school; payment of money.

[21] Prak Chan Thul and Erika Kinetz, "R'kiri villagers take land dispute door-to-door," *The Cambodia Daily (Weekly Review)*, 11–15 June 2007.

[22] Prak Chan Thul, "Jarai villagers abandon gov't doorstep tactics," *The Cambodia Daily (Weekly Review)*, 16[sic]–22 June 2007; Thul, "Villagers summoned by R'kiri court in Keat Kolney land case," *The Cambodia Daily (Weekly Review)*, 16[sic]–22 June 2007.

[23] Saing Soenthrith, "UN envoy and villagers discuss land complaints," *The Cambodia Daily (Weekly Review)*, 11–15 December 2006.

[24] Erika Kinetz and Yun Samean, "Bar questions aid lawyers' legal standing over land-dispute case," *The Cambodia Daily (Weekly Review)*, 23–29 June 2007; Prak Chan Thul and Erika Kinetz, "Keat Kolney files complaint against 10 lawyers," *The Cambodia Daily (Weekly Review)*, 23–29 June 2007.

government officials into a private land dispute.25 Timed to coincide with the conclusion of the government – donor meeting, Kolney filed a counter-complaint in the Ratanakiri Provincial Court against six of the twelve villager representatives.26 Huon Chundy, program manager with CLEC, stated that he was aware of the complaint, noting: "We think that filing this lawsuit is a strategy to scare the community and some lawyers into making an agreement."27

As Keat Kolney launched this counter-case, the court began questioning villagers from O'Yadaw district about the land transfer deal. Prak Soeun, clerk of the court stated: "All the villagers answered that they have really sold the land to Lok Chumteav [Keat Kolney]. . . . They said that they thumb-printed to accept $20,000 for 450 hectares of land. . . . Each family received $400."28 Sam Rainsy Party Chief of Pate commune, Sev Nhang, later claimed that the villagers had been paid money ahead of making statements to the court. He noted: "The villagers told me that the former village chief taught them what to say [in court]. . . . They were given food to eat, cars to ride back and forth to the court to talk about the land sale agreement and to recognize it."29

Local government officials played roles in facilitating the initial "sale", disorganizing villagers as they attempted to complain, facilitating their select participation in Keat Kolney's counterclaim, and preventing or limiting access to the affected locality by outside groups. This kind of involvement reveals the ability of persons closely connected to senior levels of the Cambodian state to use their status to make the machinery of the state work to their advantage. In other words, it is suggestive of the operations of the patrimonial administrative state. Keat Kolney mobilized her personal networks to ensure that state structures at a local level operated to secure the acquisition of 450 hectares of land. With the state operating as a patrimonial network, the bureaucracy cemented a member of the ruling elite's control over this particular parcel of land.

---

25 Kolney's letter to the Bar Association stated: "Their activities seem to be politically motivated by advice from foreigners which affects the reputation of the government leadership, my husband, and my brother, and also affects national development." See Prak Chan Thul and Kinetz, "Keat Kolney files complaint against 10 lawyers."

26 Prak Chan Thul, "Villagers say Keat Kolney did not grab land," *The Cambodia Daily (Weekly Review)*, 21–27 July 2007. During the donor-government meeting, the Canadian delegation delivered an address in which they criticized the government for failing to act on the question of indigenous people's land rights. Michael Brownell, Mainland Southeast Asia Director for the Canadian International Development Agency, told the conference: "Not a single indigenous group has been issued with title in the six years since the adoption of the land law." See Prak Chan Thul and Kinetz, "Keat Kolney files complaint against 10 lawyers."

27 Cited in Prak Chan Thul and Erika Kinetz, "Keat Kolney files complaint over land dispute," *The Cambodia Daily (Weekly Review)*, 23–29 June 2007.

28 Prak Chan Thul, "Villagers say Keat Kolney did not grab land."

29 Prak Chan Thul, "Ratanakkiri villagers paid in Keat Kolney case: SRP official," *The Cambodia Daily (Weekly Review)*, 30 July - 3 August 2007.

According to the January 2007 villager complaint, local officials had falsely informed the Jarai community that if they did not sell 50 hectares of their land, Hun Sen would take it for distribution to disabled soldiers.[30] After the villagers apparently agreed to sell this parcel, families in Kong Yu received donations of $400 each and a sarong from Keat Kolney. Reportedly, local officials did not tell them that this money (and sarong) was in exchange for their land.[31] O'Yadaw district governor Heng Bun Phann subsequently denied the villagers' allegations that he had tricked them out of their land. He stated that local officials had banned the minority villagers involved in the dispute from selling their property, but they had refused to listen.[32] Former Kong Yu village chief Phoy Svagn also denied the villagers' allegations against him, claiming: "We cannot undo the sale, it is wrong to do that to the buyer. ... It is like selling a buffalo – you cannot ask for it back."[33]

We have already noted the involvement of local officials in assisting select villagers to provide evidence to support Kolney's counterclaim. However the most critical role of local officials was in the dual process of disorganizing villager attempts to complain and impeding the access of their external supporters. An early instance was during a February 2007 visit by Hun Sen to Ratanakiri province. During a ground breaking ceremony in the provincial capital Banlung, a representative of the twelve plaintiffs was blocked by police and bodyguards from handing over a petition to Hun Sen.[34] The neutralizing of the political intent of this act was defended by Minister of Information Khieu Kanarith, who insisted that the dispute was unconnected to the government and was a matter for the court to decide. He claimed: "Many villagers filed a complaint but it doesn't mean that the complaint is right. NGOs incited them to file a complaint."[35]

The extent and rationale underpinning the connections between Keat Kolney and local officials are difficult to specify. O'Yadaw district officials seemed to have played a role in facilitating communications between Keat Kolney

---

[30] Wasson and Yun Samean, "R'kiri villagers file complaints over land sale."

[31] Ibid. In March 2007, Chhe Vibol, Keat Kolney's lawyer issued a statement claiming that villagers and local officials had all agreed to the land sale. He claimed that village elders, tribal chiefs, and commune and district officials had participated in the deal: "The ethnic people themselves agreed to sell, no one forced them." See Prak Chan Thul, "Lawyer insists R'kiri land deal is valid."

[32] He noted: "Now the rubber trees are planted so what can we do? They sold and now they want it back, it is very unjust." Wasson and Yun Samean, "R'kiri villagers file complaints over land sale."

[33] Ibid.

[34] Yun Samean, "R'kiri land dispute petition blocked, claim villagers," *The Cambodia Daily (Weekly Review)*, 5–9 February 2007.

[35] Ibid.

and villagers contesting her claim to have purchased the land. When reports emerged in March 2007 of an attempt to broker an out-of-court settlement it transpired that an O'Yadaw district official, Sev Rith, had provided his phone for Keat Kolney to talk to villagers. Commenting to reporters, he noted: "She just needs to know the progress of the court in dealing with the villagers' complaints."[36]

Much of the role of local officials, once the case was brought before the courts, and in a sense politicized by villager attempts to meet with Keat Kolney's husband (Secretary of State in the Ministry of Land Management), was to limit access by outsiders, prevent organization of villagers, and prevent protest within the province. For instance, in September 2007, police and soldiers blocked Voice of Democracy (VOD) radio from hosting a public forum on land rights in Kong Yu village.[37] Ratanakiri Provincial Governor Muong Poy stated that Voice of Democracy had contacted him but that he had referred the group to the Ministry of Interior in Phnom Penh because, he claimed, the radio program was only permitted to hold meetings in Phnom Penh.[38] He noted: "I do not reject their request but I ask them to follow the Interior Ministry's instructions. ... Their activity in our province is not good. They want to make problems in our province, and they want our minorities to argue with each other."[39] The following month the CPP offered gifts to the residents of Kong Yu consisting of 10kg bags of rice, packages of salt and t-shirts.[40] The donations were handed out by deputy district governor Than Kang in the presence of two employees of the Progressive Farmers Association, a company linked to Keat Kolney.[41] Deputy District Governor Than Kang admitted that two of Keat Kolney's employees had been present for the donation ceremony, but claimed that it was only to help out. He stated that the donations "belonged to the Cambodian People's Party" and that they were meant to assist the poor and widows.[42]

A few days later, police blocked the Cambodian Center for Human Rights (CCHR) from holding a public forum at Kong Yu village, O'Yadaw district. Police established a roadblock around 3 kilometres from Kong Yu to prevent

---

[36] Kuch Naren, "R'kiri land dispute villagers approached for deal."

[37] Erika Kinetz and Thet Sambath, "Police, soldiers block land forum in R'kiri," *The Cambodia Daily (Weekly Review)*, 10–15 September 2007.

[38] The radio program was created by an organization called the Cambodian Center for Independent Media.

[39] Cited in Kinetz and Thet Sambath, "Police, soldiers block land forum in R'kiri."

[40] Prak Chan Thul, "Fearing trickery, villagers reject CPP donations," *The Cambodia Daily (Weekly Review)*, 19–23 November 2007.

[41] Ibid. According to news reports, the donation ceremony was filmed and villagers apparently feared that after accepting the rice and t-shirts, they might be accused of receiving payment for the land.

[42] Ibid.

the CCHR staff from access, with the result that around 100 villagers trekked to the site of the roadblock. While Ou Virak of CCHR stated that his organization had written to commune, district and provincial authorities to notify them of the planned forum, Commune police chief Ma Vichit stated that CCHR had not obtained the proper permission.[43] Provincial Governor Muong Poy stated that he had received a letter from CCHR but that the gathering had been blocked for security reasons: "We were worried there would be incitement on the land issue."[44]

The same rationale was used to justify attempts to block a visit to O'Yadaw by UN Special Representative for Human Rights Yash Ghai. Nab Bun Heng, Ratanakiri's provincial cabinet chief, stated that he had not received any information about Ghai's visit but that large gatherings would be prohibited. He stated that provincial authorities would "stop them if those villagers and Ghai are going to organize a big public meeting without asking permission from our authorities because it will affect public order."[45] Ghai's visit to O'Yadaw involved a standoff with local officials and claims that he had not obtained permission from local authorities. Sok Na, Royal Cambodian Armed Forces (RCAF) chief for O'Yadaw noted: "We are here to protect villagers from any problems. Any NGO who wants to come must get a letter from me because this village is under my control."[46] Later in December, police used fire trucks to disperse a march organized by human rights NGO ADHOC in the provincial capital, Banlung. The purpose of the march was to highlight forest and land crimes and to support Hun Sen's calls for an end to illegal logging and land grabbing. Ratanakiri Provincial Prosecutor, Mey Sokhan, stated that all gatherings of more than four people in Cambodia required official authorization.[47]

Yash Ghai's visit highlighted the pressure that governmental officials were coming under in terms of the mechanism by which the family of a senior official was able to harness the machinery of the state to her advantage. Ghai noted that

---

[43] He claimed: "We, the authorities, did not get any letter from the human rights organization". See Thet Sambath, "Police block human rights forum in R'kiri," *The Cambodia Daily (Weekly Review)*, 26–30 November 2007.

[44] Ibid.

[45] Kuch Naren and Emily Lodish, "UN envoy to visit Ratanakkiri to examine land disputes," *The Cambodia Daily (Weekly Review)*, 2–7 December 2007. Hor Ang, deputy provincial police chief, stated that he too was unaware of Ghai's visit. He noted: "I cannot say exactly whether we will stop him or not because we are not clear about his trip and how harmful it will be if he goes down to Kong Yu village. . . . Whatever we are going to do will be for public security and to prevent disorder."

[46] Erika Kinetz and Prak Chan Thul, "UN human rights envoy Yash Ghai visits Ratanakkiri villagers," *The Cambodia Daily (Weekly Review)*, 2–7 December 2007.

[47] Prak Chan Thul, "R'kiri police turn hoses on land protesters," *The Cambodia Daily (Weekly Review)*, 17–21 December 2007.

the Kong Yu case exemplified Cambodia's deep-seated networks of patronage and the failure of the courts to offer the powerless adequate means of redress.[48] The significance of Ghai's interventions lies less in the content of his statements than in the fact that the dispute was attracting considerable attention as a test case for governance reform. Its resolution via the courts, if successful, would amount to evidence of the consummation of the governance reforms promoted by Western aid donors. CLEC lawyer, Ith Mathoura pointed to this in stating that she hoped international scrutiny on the Kong Yu case would help to keep the proceedings transparent: "This is a message to the court. They have to try the case fairly. There are a lot of eyes watching."[49]

The effect of this scrutiny, albeit highly imperfectly, was to slow down this particular manifestation of the "politically determined capitalism" of the contemporary Cambodian polity.[50] Impeding this particular type of circulation of capital, it arrested to some extent the transformative potential of these types of patrimonial networks in rural Cambodia. The agents of resistance (in this case a group of twelve Jarai villagers and their legal team) were relatively well funded and the institutions through which they were seeking recompense have come under considerable scrutiny. No matter whether this particular group is ultimately successful, there will be incremental transformations of the bureaucratic apparatus as an outcome of repeated contacts with the externally promoted governance agenda. These will likely work to limit the scope for state agents to be directly involved in appropriating economic resources. As such, these cases differ significantly from cases involving oligarchs empowered by agendas of regional integration. We can gain a sense of how this plays out when we turn to examine another land dispute involving a scheme to create a sugar plantation and processing factory in Koh Kong province.

Case 2: The Koh Kong Plantation Company in Sre Ambel: economic liberalization, regional integration and the growing power of the oligarchs

Before considering this contrasting case, we must first draw out key elements of the process through which Cambodia is being integrated into regional economic structures. Cambodia's economic growth since 2003 has been in substantial part

---

[48] Kinetz and Prak Chan Thul, "UN human rights envoy Yash Ghai visits Ratanakkiri villagers."
[49] Ibid. Provincial Court Judge An Samnang's response was that he must remain immune to all extra-judicial influence, both from inside and outside the country. He noted: "We don't think about who has money and power. . . . All people are equal in front of the law. The most important thing is who has enough evidence."
[50] Phrase is from the "Author's Introduction" in Max Weber, *The Protestant ethic and the spirit of capitalism*, trans. Talcott Parsons (London: Routledge, 1992). See also Hutchcroft, *Booty capitalism: the politics of banking in the Philippines*, 18.

contingent on the impact of globalization on the domestic economy. But this growth has been harnessed by, and has disproportionately benefited, a small segment of the population able to tap into the state.[51] For instance, in harnessing aspects of the externally promoted reform agenda related to land tenure institutions, well-positioned business entities have been able to take advantage of aspects of Cambodia's natural resource base and geographical position in relation to fast- growing regional economies.

Beneficiaries of integration into regional production networks in contemporary Cambodia include businesses with economies of scale; those producing agricultural commodities processed in neighbouring states; those requiring access to foreign capital and knowhow; and those selling into neighbouring markets or exporting to the developed world. Cross-border trade drives commercialization of production in these sectors, promoting larger-scale business entities that, if foreign, often operate with a local partner. That business partner, by virtue of its foreign backing, is then poised to exert oligarchic power. This process has been accelerated due to two initiatives aimed at promoting regional integration in mainland Southeast Asia: the Initiative for ASEAN Integration, and the various projects to develop the Mekong Basin.

When Cambodia, Laos, Myanmar and Vietnam became members of ASEAN in the late 1990s, there was concern that the substantial income differential between newer and older members would lead to a two-tier ASEAN. Such differentials were a potential impediment to the project of regional integration that had increasingly become ASEAN's *raison d'être*. A key response to this has been the Initiative for ASEAN Integration (IAI). Following the ASEAN Ministerial Meeting of July 2001 and the release of the Hanoi Declaration on Narrowing Developmental Gap for Closer ASEAN Integration, ASEAN ministers set up an IAI Unit in the ASEAN Secretariat. IAI projects entail mostly studies and training or so-called "soft infrastructure". This is predominantly financed by older members of ASEAN or with funds mobilized by ASEAN from international financial institutions and developed countries. Funding for hard infrastructure such as transport linkages and energy transmission networks has been supplied by external sources including bilateral and multilateral donors. Much of this financing dovetails with the support of foreign aid providers for the development of the Mekong Basin.

Since at least the 1950s, the Mekong has been subject to development plans aimed at tying the river basin's states more closely together, through elaboration

---

[51] On trends in land ownership, see Caroline Hughes, "Cambodia in 2007: development and dispossession," *Asian Survey* 48.1 (2008): 71. Hun Sen observed, in relation to the launch of a 2007 World Bank report on inequality: "The Royal Government of Cambodia still has some concerns due to the fact that while there has been a reduction in the poverty rate, the trend of socio-economic inequality seems to be increasing." Cited in "Poverty down, inequality up in Cambodia: World Bank," *Kyodo News*, 12 June 2007.

of transport and energy infrastructure. Recent initiatives to this end include the Mekong River Commission established in 1995 with key financial contributions from European states. The Asian Development Bank (ADB) has, in addition, a large programme for the creation of a Greater Mekong Subregion (GMS) that ties in Thailand and parts of Southern China. The ADB's program, backed primarily by Japan and complemented by Japanese bilateral assistance, includes loans for infrastructure projects such as hydroelectric dams in Laos, road construction in Cambodia and Laos, and highways linking key cities in the region. China, likewise, has become a key contributor to the development of infrastructure regionally and in Cambodia.[52] Its aid and investment links with Cambodia have grown rapidly over the past decade, with China committing to provide more than US$200 million at an October 2008 summit. Much of this aid was earmarked for road construction in northern provinces.[53]

Intra-East Asian trade volumes have indeed expanded dramatically since the 1980s, with East Asia-China trade an increasingly important component of this. Some of the new trade from Southeast Asia to China is in medium-tech manufacturing (such as semiconductors and other computer components) originating in the more developed ASEAN economies. However, as Ian Coxhead points out, "A large and rapidly growing share of the trade is in natural resource products, and this dominates trade from the poorer countries of the region (Indonesia, Vietnam, Laos, Cambodia, and Burma)."[54] China's expansion has raised demand for an array of agricultural and natural resource products across the world, and Southeast Asia's geographic proximity makes it a particularly attractive place to produce the agricultural commodities that China needs. Quantities of plantation crops such as oil palm, rubber, coffee, and sugar cane have as a consequence grown phenomenally.[55] Coxhead suggests, on the basis of Relative Comparative Advantage data, "that the less advanced SE Asian economies are becoming major suppliers of natural resource products to the Chinese market, and in return importing a wide range of manufactures from China."[56] To grasp the implications for the structure of business of this project

---

[52] Jane Perlez, "China competes with West in aid to its neighbours," *The New York Times*, 18 September 2006.

[53] Ek Madra, "China to give Cambodia $215 mln to build roads," *Reuters News*, 3 December 2008; Thai News Service, "China/Cambodia: Chinese arrive with millions in aid," *Thai News Service*, 5 December 2008.

[54] Ian Coxhead, "A new resource curse? Impacts of China's boom on comparative advantage and resource dependence in Southeast Asia," *World Development* 35. 7 (2007): 1103.

[55] Ian Coxhead, "Development and the environment in Asia: a survey of recent literature," *Asian-Pacific Economic Literature* 17, no. 1 (2003); Coxhead, "A new resource curse? Impacts of China's boom on comparative advantage and resource dependence in Southeast Asia," 1103.

[56] Coxhead, "A new resource curse? Impacts of China's boom on comparative advantage and resource dependence in Southeast Asia," 1110. Coxhead reminds us that such a trend would take Southeast Asia back to its neo-traditional role.

of integration, we will turn to consider a second land dispute that contrasts with the Keat Kolney case and points to emergent patterns of provincial business.

Heightened global demand for natural resources and agro-industrial commodities raises questions as to the ways in which national elites in Southeast Asia have harnessed this process, and the contestation they face in so doing. How will state structures and business entities shift over time as particular types of economic ties between key consumers of agro-industrial commodities and the least developed parts of Southeast Asia are consolidated? To begin to answer these questions, we turn to consider a land dispute that contrasts in key ways with the Keat Kolney case.

The dispute that arose over land in relation to the Koh Kong sugar plantation scheme is suggestive of the oligarchical tendencies in the Cambodian polity. It points to the conversion of large sections of Cambodia's rural landscape into plantation schemes that take advantage of Cambodia's integration into the world economy.[57] This process represents the flipside of the governance agenda of foreign aid donors: through the land concession process, the government itself has placed business entities closely connected to Cambodia's elite and with access to foreign capital at the forefront of these development schemes.[58] The process contrasts sharply with the patrimonial administrative tendencies exemplified in Keat Kolney's plantation venture.

Contestation over land in the Koh Kong plantation area began in mid 2006 and involves around 500 families from three villages in Sre Ambel district's Chi Khor Loeu commune. The villagers are in dispute with two companies in which Ly Yong Phat, a Cambodian Senator and advisor to Hun Sen on investment, is the principal Cambodian investor.[59] At issue is an envisaged 20,000 hectare sugar plantation to be created by Koh Kong Plantation Co. The sugar cane grown in this scheme is to feed a sugar-processing facility created by Koh Kong Sugar Industry Co Ltd.[60] This development project emerged following a February 2006 agreement between Thailand

---

[57] One press report on contract farming noted: "Three Cambodian landlords have offered to lease 2.5 million rai [400,000 ha] of farmland to Thai companies. They want Thailand to develop the fields and create jobs for 10,000 people living in the area." See "Firms Eye Cambodian Agriculture," *The Nation*, 13 March 2006.

[58] See Sopheng Cheang, "Cambodian senate to be joined by prominent tycoons," *Associated Press Newswires*, 13 February 2006.

[59] The *Bangkok Post* reported that "Mr Phat, an adviser to Prime Minister Hun Sen on investment projects in Koh Kong, was instrumental in helping the venture secure the concession." See Aranee Jaiimsin, "Commodities / Sugar Industry Expansion; KSL joins partners in Cambodia venture," *Bangkok Post*, 7 August 2006.

[60] Ibid. The article notes that the two companies are joint ventures in which a Thai company Khon Kaen Sugar Industry Plc, holds 50% stakes. A Taiwanese company, Ve Wong Corporation holds 30% and Ly Yong Phat 20%.

and Cambodia aimed at enhancing trade, tourism and flows of investment capital.[61]

Cambodia's Minister of Agriculture, Chan Sarun, granted the land concession on which the plantation was to be established in August 2006. According to an *Agence Kampuchea Presse* report, the 19,100 ha of "unused land will transform to a big sugar cane farm in Cambodia under a land concession agreement between a local private company and a Thai investor."[62] Granted for 90 years on highly favourable terms, the concession agreement specified a holiday from leasing fees for the first five years, after which the fee would gradually increase from $1 per hectare to a maximum of $4 per hectare.[63] Of these terms, a representative of the Thai investor Khon Kaen Sugar Industry Plc (KSL) noted: "The favourable concession eliminates our concerns about Cambodian politics, land occupation and land price, so what remains as our risk factor is the climate for the crop."[64] Other conditions for the investment included a corporate tax holiday during the first nine operating years of Koh Kong Plantation Co and Koh Kong Sugar Industry Co. This was one of numerous schemes by business entities from neighbouring states driven to look for opportunities in Cambodia due to the growing scarcity of land in their own countries. For instance, in early November 2006 the Phu Rieng Rubber Company of Binh Phuoc Province in Southern Vietnam reportedly had conducted a geographical survey and "started reclaiming wasteland" to plant 20,000 hectares of rubber in Kratie Province.[65]

Koh Kong Sugar Industry was created to manage a mill when commercial operations commenced in 2009, capable of producing 50,000 tonnes of sugar initially, and rising to one million tonnes a year in 2010 and 2.5 million tonnes from 2011.[66] To begin with, all of the cane would come from plantations operated directly by Koh Kong Plantation Co, but over the longer term, 70 per cent would come from contract farmers.[67] The envisaged primary market for the

---

[61] Nation (Thailand), "Cambodia beckons Thai firms to pump in more investment," *The Nation*, 23 November 2006. See also, Thai News Service, "Thailand: Thais and foreigners interested in investing in sugar industry," *Thai News Services*, 1 September 2006.

[62] AKP, "Cambodian signs land concession agreement for sugar cane production," *Agence Kampuchea Presse*, in English, 8 August 2006. BBC Monitoring Asia Pacific (BBCAPP0020060808e288001p5), 8 August 2006.

[63] Aranee Jaiimsin, "Commodities / Sugar Industry Expansion; KSL joins partners in Cambodia venture."

[64] Ibid.

[65] Asia Pulse, "Asia Agribusiness," 1 November 2006. The quote is from the news report. The report noted that this represented the first step of the Vietnam Rubber Corporation implementing a project to plant 180,000 hectares of rubber in three Cambodian provinces, including Mondulkiri and Kampong Thom.

[66] Aranee Jaiimsin, "Commodities / Sugar Industry Expansion; KSL joins partners in Cambodia venture."

[67] Ibid.

sugar and its by-products (including ethanol) shifted between 2006 and 2007, perhaps due to the growing demand for biofuels. A 2006 *Bangkok Post* report refers to Cambodia as the primary market.[68] However, an August 2007 report suggests that Khon Kaen Sugar (the Thai partner in the two Cambodian joint-venture companies) was embarking on investments in Laos and Cambodia in order to export to the European Union under the EBA (Everything But Arms) quota.[69]

Despite the Koh Kong Plantation Co's ambitions to grow sugar cane over a significant area (20,000 hectares) we know much less about the dynamics of community protest, the role of local government, and the perspective of external actors when compared to Keat Kolney's business venture. Within a couple of months of the Minister of Agriculture's approval of the land concession, villager protests had compelled human rights NGOs, local government officials and company representatives to broker a deal that was supposed to address community concerns. A meeting was held in Chi Khor village, organized by NGOs and broadcast on the Cambodian television station CTN.[70] At a meeting attended by 300 villagers, Koh Kong deputy governor Bin Sam Ol, Sour Sitha (deputy governor of Sre Ambel), Sin Kheam (chief of Chi Kor commune), and Heng San (representative of Ly Yong Phat), an agreement was signed allowing Koh Kong Sugar to continue to plant sugar cane around the villages but only on the portions of land owned by the state.[71]

Views on the promise of this accommodation were mixed, but its handling by civil society supporters contrasted in significant ways from that of the Keat Kolney case. The positioning of villagers vis-à-vis relevant laws and dominant notions of development was quite different. Not being classed as "indigenous", the resident population had limited rights under the land and forest laws, and a lower profile as a social grouping deemed worthy of external support other than for the broad purpose of promoting their development. In this regard, Yong Phat commented (after watching the proceedings on television): "As you see we solved problems. ... We want to help develop the area and create employment and income generation for local people."[72] Human rights organizations,

---

[68] Ibid.

[69] Thai News Service, "Thailand: Khon Kaen Sugar Industry to go ahead with investments in sugar mills in Laos and Cambodia," *Thai News Service,*, 20 August 2007. On European Union trade preferences, see Sheila Page and Adrian Hewitt, "The new European trade preferences: does 'Everything But Arms' (EBA) help the poor?," *Development Policy Review* 20.1 (2002).

[70] Erika Kinetz and Lor Chandara, "Koh Kong villagers may triumph in land dispute," *The Cambodia Daily (Weekly Review)*, 13–17 November 2006.

[71] The agreement was signed by the local officials, three villager representatives, and officials from CCHR, LICADHO, and CLEC. For details on the agreement, see Ibid.

[72] Ibid.

however, were aware of a major loophole in the agreement that had been reached with the company. Very few villagers had land titles to the areas where they lived. Kem Sokha, director of the Cambodian Center for Human Rights, had reportedly claimed that local officials and company representatives had agreed that even if they didn't have paper documents, villagers would be able to use witnesses to establish they had lived on the land and were its owners. However, Bin Sam Ol, Koh Kong deputy governor, claimed: "If one has enough documents of all kinds to prove they own the land, they can claim [ownership]. ... But they cannot point their finger at here and there [and say] that it's their land."[73]

In January 2007, human rights and legal aid NGOs (LICADHO, Cambodian Center for Human Rights, and CLEC) sent a letter to Ly Yong Phat.[74] The letter stated that the sugar plantation companies (Koh Kong Plantation Co & Koh Kong Sugar Industry Co) had "blatantly violated" the agreement by clearing paddy fields and plantations owned by villagers. According to the letter, "[v]illagers have been subjected to threats, harassment, and worse. Rather than decreasing poverty in the area, the company's activities have increased poverty and unrest in Sre Ambel."[75] Koh Kong Provincial Governor Yuth Phouthang stated that he planned to send a committee to meet with villagers to attempt to solve the dispute. But he claimed that NGOs had no right to ask for a halt in Ly Yong Phat's clearing operations, because no one would want to develop land in the province if they saw NGOs causing trouble. He claimed that villagers did not have land titles.[76] He captured a central element of the difference with Keat Kolney's dispute in O'Yadaw when he pointed out: "Ly Yong Phat didn't take their land, the government gave the investment to him."[77]

The paradox of this dispute, in comparison to the Keat Kolney case, is that although occurring over a much larger area (20,000 hectares compared to 450 hectares) and entailing substantially more overt violence, external concern was much more limited compared to the profile of the indigenous communities of Cambodia's northeast. Keat Kolney's land grab may have been viewed as a flagrant case of poor governance.[78] However, no connection seems to have been

[73] Ibid.
[74] Prak Chan Thul, "Sugar tycoon is taking village land: rights groups," *The Cambodia Daily (Weekly Review)*, 22–26 January 2007.
[75] Details of the letter are contained in Ibid. According to Kek Galabru of LICADHO, "police and military police have come in uniforms with guns" to scare villagers off their lands and threaten them with arrest.
[76] Ibid.
[77] Prak Chan Thul, "Koh Kong land protestors still waiting in capital," *The Cambodia Daily (Weekly Review)*, 12–16 March 2007.
[78] Recall the Legal Aid of Cambodia (LAC) director's claim in reference to Keat Kolney that there was "no clearer example in Cambodia today of the rich and powerful exploiting the poor and marginalized." Wasson and Yun Samean, "R'kiri villagers file complaints over land sale."

drawn in relation to Ly Yong Phat's plantation venture between the integrationist policies of external actors such as the European Union or proponents of biofuels, and how apparently benign intentions emanating from distant northern capitals fomented violent processes of agrarian change at this particular frontier of global capitalism.[79]

The paradox of the process of enclosure associated with the plantation scheme and its implications for Cambodia's development is the three-way linkage between external investors and external markets, the violence of the process by which common lands are enclosed, and the implications that this economic development strategy has for the evolution of the Cambodian polity.[80] The Thai partner in the scheme (50% owner of Koh Kong Plantation Co and Koh Kong Sugar Industry Co) had invested in sugar production in Laos and Cambodia to take advantage of quotas set for developing countries. As a company representative noted: "That's why we have to set up in Laos and Cambodia….We could not access the EU market without the quota as the tariff for sugar from other developing countries was set at more than 100 euros per tonne."[81] From the perspective of local villagers this strategy of agrarian change was felt rather differently. As one resident of Chouk village noted:

> During the Khmer Rouge time, they said "everything belongs to everyone", and they provided food for us to eat. … Now they take our land, without paying anything, and they are happy and we are crying.[82]

Those who suffered the least under the Khmer Rouge – long-standing rural dwellers – faced the full brunt of development initiatives working to concentrate much of Cambodia's rural landscape under the control of a small group

---

[79] For instance, in late January 2007, six cows and buffalo were shot after wandering onto the sugarcane plantation. Earlier, in 2006, guards working for the plantation company had opened fire on a crowd of villagers trying to stop the bulldozers, with several wounded in the legs. Following the shooting of the cattle and the filing of a complaint with the provincial court, Koh Kong governor Yuth Phouthang ordered the plantation company to repay villagers. For details, see Kay Kimsong, "Governor: Koh Kong villagers to be paid for cattle," *The Cambodia Daily (Weekly Review)*, 12–16 February 2007. AFP, "Land grabs leave thousands destitute in Cambodia's heartland," *Agence France Presse*, 14 May 2007. In an interview with AFP, Ly Yong Phat conceded that guards had acted too forcibly: "I do not know why they opened fire. … We told the company to avoid this kind of problem again."

[80] On the concept of the rationalities of enclosure, see Andrew Robert Cock, "The interaction between a ruling elite and an externally promoted policy reform agenda: the case of forestry under the second Kingdom of Cambodia 1993–2003" (Ph.D. Dissertation, La Trobe University, 2007).

[81] Apornrath Phoonphongphiphat and Wilanwan Pongpitak, "Thai Khon Kaen plans rising sugar exports," *Reuters News*, 22 March 2007.

[82] Amy Kazmin, "Villagers fight for the right to a few hectares of Cambodia's tilling fields," *Financial Times*, 10 April 2007.

of business entities.[83] While reform-promoting external actors might work to oppose the patrimonialism associated with Keat Kolney's plantation venture, Koh Kong Plantation Co accorded much more closely with their conceptions of Cambodia's appropriate path to development.

Oligarchy-Building in Cambodia

Key features of the oligarchs are their tendency to benefit from access to state property, licensing arrangements, concession grants and various other types of discretionary rights. They are the business entities that have acquired the capacity to tap into the discretionary privileges perpetually generated by the operation of the Cambodian state. These business entities may be heavily involved in one particular business area, but tend to be diversified, or to aim in that direction. Family networks and marriages that tie them to the state apparatus are important. The emergence of this group reflects the enduring patrimonial character of the state and the weakness of the state apparatus in relation to powerful social forces.

Arguably, Cambodia's economic integration has helped to unhinge the political elite from the state apparatus even as the reform agendas of external actors have worked to strengthen the state. A process of "oligarchy-building" has occurred as the political elite have come to be attached in new ways to these emergent business groupings.[84] Oligarchs, by definition, exert a preponderant influence over parts of the Cambodian economy. While it is difficult to measure this influence quantitatively, it may be apparent in their ability to convert this economic influence into enduring political power. The two ways in which this occurs is via their modes of access to the state and their relationship with key political leaders. This may over time lead to a symbiotic relationship between oligarchs and power holders and produce an oligarchic system.

This is distinct from the patrimonial administrative political system. Compared to the dominant social role played by the bureaucratic elite in such a system, there is in an oligarchic polity a reduced direct role of the state in economic

---

[83] According to the *Financial Times*, since 1992, 57 companies, many with close connections to the CPP, had been awarded "economic land concessions" covering almost one million hectares. Ibid.

[84] The term "oligarchy-building" is taken from Hutchcroft, *Booty capitalism: the politics of banking in the Philippines*, 26. Coxhead is perhaps hinting at this process in suggesting that for Southeast Asian countries such as Cambodia, which have low levels of industrialization, "recent trends in the global economy, coupled with existing domestic regulatory and institutional weaknesses, now pose both direct and indirect threats to future expansion." See Coxhead, "A new resource curse? Impacts of China's boom on comparative advantage and resource dependence in Southeast Asia," 1099.

activities and capital accumulation. Importantly, an oligarchic system may vary because in certain periods political leaders may be able to dampen the role of the oligarchs and during other periods the oligarchs may be able to anoint political successors. So what evidence can we point to that is suggestive of these trends in Cambodia?

Pathways to access the state apparatus are changing in Cambodia. Always a major avenue of private accumulation through the interaction between favoured elites, would-be favoured elites, and senior government officials, key accumulators can no longer be so readily identified as members of the ruling elite. They tend, instead, to dominate particular industries and exhibit variable independence from the state.

No business can prosper in the medium term in Cambodia without cultivating connections to the state. But to the extent that an oligarchy has emerged, it is due to an increasing separation from the state, evidenced by a reduced direct role of the state apparatus as the conduit for rents; an increased reliance of state officials on business entities; an increased autonomy of business from the bureaucracy and perhaps from the regulatory environment; and a concentration of economic power.[85]

There is evidence that Cambodia meets these conditions. The role of the state apparatus in capturing rents is diminishing as regional integration weakens the grip of state officials to control patterns of trade and consumption. As the grip of state agents on economic activity has declined, officials have come to depend more directly on business entities for their livelihoods. Patrimonial networks have not shrivelled. Rather, they have adapted with business entities fulfilling patronage roles previously dominated by the state. Our examination of the two land disputes has analysed more substantively how this has occurred in terms of rural land development schemes.

The reform agenda of foreign aid programmes has retarded the evolution of oligarchic features, but regional economic integration has clearly accelerated them, because it has provided the conditions in which a small group of business entities are coming to occupy a preponderant position in relation to the Cambodian economy. Businessmen have also taken advantage of elements of the reform agenda, such as land reform, at the same time as they have managed to gain access to credit, and tie into regional production processes that have bolstered their position relative to other economic actors. Economic power, and

---

[85] By economic power, I mean the ability of an entity to frame the market conditions faced by other actors. This includes input prices (such as for labour) and the price of various outputs. Under certain conditions, when production processes or particular inputs are monopolized, economic power can be considered to have been concentrated. For our purposes, a particular area of interest is agro-industry and the accumulation of land-holdings by a small number of business entities.

a changed relationship with the state, has led to a shift in the nature of links with the ruling elite. Political leaders are less able to manipulate the state in accordance with the patrimonial administrative patterns that the Keat Kolney case illustrated. Rather, to acquire access to economic resources, political leaders are becoming more closely tied with these oligarchic business entities.

The structure of the Cambodian polity is being remade by overwhelming forces associated with its integration into the East Asian economic system. While aid provided by international donors and the policy reform agendas promulgated by Western aid agencies are seeking to strengthen the Cambodian state's ability to mediate the process of integration, such attempts are subsumed by the more fundamental imperative of furthering integration. In other words, integration is trumping the ambitions embedded in the governance agenda, and an oligarchic system seems to be emerging. In considering this development, it is worth keeping in mind Hutchcroft's suggestion that the patrimonial oligarchic state presents particularly obstinate structural barriers to the demise of patrimonial features and the creation of a more rational legal state. Rather than moving towards such an order, oligarchical rule is in the ascendancy in contemporary Cambodia. Hun Sen, master-builder of the patrimonial administrative state, may at the zenith of his power find himself increasingly restrained by his ties to the small number of business entities that have rapidly come to own or control much of Cambodia's material and financial resources.

3

CHINA'S AID TO CAMBODIA

Michael Sullivan

FOR SEVERAL YEARS, CAMBODIA HAS received unprecedented levels of approved Foreign Direct Investment (FDI) from China, and Chinese bilateral aid to Cambodia, in the form of grants and loans, has also increased dramatically. For the first time in 2007 China joined Cambodia's other foreign donors in pledging aid at the regularly held government–donor forums. This surge of Chinese interest in Cambodia through investment and aid raises the question of the implications for the Cambodian government's stated commitment to democratic reform. Within Cambodia's NGO community, and for western donors, a key issue is the lack of transparency and accountability surrounding investments, grants and loans. There is a concern that Chinese investment, supported by China's foreign policy objectives in the region, may act as a disincentive for the Cambodian government to follow through on its commitment to democratic reform. Indeed, it may reinforce the power of Cambodia's political–economic elite, who preside over a notoriously unaccountable, opaque and inherently corrupt state system.

This chapter examines these issues by investigating the nature of the relationship between Chinese investment and aid and Cambodia's political–economic elite, and the impact of this on the Cambodian government's relations with donors pushing for reforms. Such an investigation is a challenge; the lack of transparency and accountability surrounding Chinese aid makes reliable data difficult to obtain. Nevertheless, it is possible to offer some useful speculations on these relationships. The hypothesis presented is that new opportunities for rent-seeking and personal enrichment are available to Cambodian state power-holders and their business associates through Chinese investment and aid, to the detriment of the prospects for democratic reform. Chinese influence will make the already difficult task of pushing recalcitrant elements within the state down the reform path all the more difficult. The donor–government effort since

1998 to re-construct a modern rational legal state system has so far fallen well short of expectations, in key areas (e.g. legal and judicial and anti-corruption) reform. It is argued here, that any investigation of Chinese investment and aid in Cambodian must consider how current state arrangements have evolved since the late 1980s, and in what ways they may further entrench the power of the country's political economic elite.

The Surge in Chinese Investment in Cambodia

Figures from the Cambodian Investment Board (CIB) for January to December 2007 show that the Cambodian government approved 32 Chinese investment projects, amounting to almost US$481 million in registered capital and over US$2.6 billion in fixed assets. The projects included garment factories, telecommunications, fiber optics, pharmaceuticals, gold mining, agro-industry and elastic bands. A year earlier, in April, after a two-day visit by the Chinese Premier Wen Jiabao, the Chinese and Cambodian governments signed agreements on technical and economic cooperation in the fields of health, transnational crime, information technology, and grants and soft loans said to be worth $600 million.[1] This surge in Chinese investment is part of a broader increase in foreign direct investment which, if it continues beyond the Global Financial Crisis, could reduce Cambodia's dependence on overseas aid. China is not Cambodia's only investor (IMF figures suggest that in 2007, Thai, Vietnamese and Malaysian FDI exceeded Chinese), but overall from 2004 to 2007 Chinese investments approvals in total outstripped all others.[2] The most notable of these investments have been in hydro-electric dams, particularly the controversial Kamchay project in Bokor National Park in Cambodia's southwest.[3] Also, and symbolically, these emergent and strengthening Sino-Cambodian ties are visibly expressed in the construction with Chinese finance of the new Council of Ministers building in Phnom Penh, where political and economic power in Cambodia will reside.

This strengthening of Sino-Cambodian relations is relatively recent and reflects the re-structuring of the Cambodian state in the late 1980s. Prior to this, China's interests in Cambodia were shaped in turn by Cambodia's Cold

---

[1] Figures taken from Council for Administrative Reform webpage, online at http://www.car.gov.kh/hunsen/chinese_PM_080406_en.asp, accessed 10 May 2009.
[2] IMF, *Cambodia: Statistical Appendix,* IMF Country Report 09/48, February 2009, Table 17. "Cambodia: Investment Approvals by Origin and Sector, 2002–07," 19, online at http://www.imf.org/external/country/KHM/index.htm, accessed 12 August 2009.
[3] See, for example, Suy Se, "Chinese-funded hydro-dams bring hope and fear to Cambodia," *Agence France Presse* (AFP), 29 June 2008, Phnom Penh.

War foreign policy under Sihanouk in the 1950s and 60s and then support for Cambodia's communists from the late 1960s until a new coalition government was formed after the United Nations-managed elections in 1993.[4] Not until 1996 is a shift in China's attitude to Cambodia discernible. This shift manifested itself through exchange visits between senior Cambodian and Chinese government officials, including the then Co-Prime Minister Hun Sen. These exchanges produced trade, investment, and technical and economic cooperation agreements, as well as the pledging of Chinese non-lethal military and other forms of aid, laying the foundations for future cooperation and mutual support.

From the point of view of domestic Cambodian politics, these visits were significant in that they were almost exclusively made by members of the Cambodian People's Party (CPP), led by Hun Sen. They took place at a time when relations between Cambodia's two Prime Ministers had deteriorated precipitously, culminating in Hun Sen's violent removal of his partner Prince Ranariddh, leader of the royalist FUNCINPEC party, by military force in July 1997. Immediately following these events, Hun Sen closed down the Taiwanese trade liaison office in Phnom Penh. China's apparent willingness to continue to develop close relations with the Cambodian government in the aftermath of the July fighting seemed to confirm earlier speculations that the authorities in Beijing "favoured" the CPP as the more viable and credible business partner – a view shared privately by some Western diplomats in Phnom Penh also.[5]

Despite international condemnation of Hun Sen's violent removal of Ranariddh, his action fundamentally altered Cambodia's political landscape, placing Hun Sen and the CPP in a predominant position to exercise considerable control over subsequent elections in 1998. Although elections were deeply flawed, international election monitoring groups endorsed the CPP's victory; with the destabilizing struggle between CPP and FUNCINPEC thus resolved, political stability and security were swiftly achieved. With Hun Sen as sole Prime Minister, and after the final dissolution of the Khmer Rouge in 1999, the path was clear for a new engagement between the Cambodian government and international donors, to begin tackling Cambodia's dire socio-economic problems.

However, the manner in which the Cambodian state was being transformed, combined with the fall-out from the political turmoil and violence of the mid 1990s, raised questions concerning the future trajectory of political and socio-economic development. Since the late 1980s the CPP leadership had presided over the development of loyal political and economic networks intended to

---

[4] For a full account of the events of this period see, David Chandler, *A History of Cambodia* (4th edn., Boulder: Westview Press, 2008).

[5] See for example, Sorpong Peou, *Intervention and Change in Cambodia: Towards Democracy?* (New York: Palgrave Macmillan, 2009), 381–396.

protect their position ahead of the return of insurgent groups laying alternative claims to state control, and of the would-be UN-managed elections. By the late 1990s these networks were crucial resources used to consolidate Hun Sen's power. They ensured political stability and security, but at the cost of the emergence of a weak and corrupt state system. Ironically, for western donors the dilemma appears to be that the forces responsible for political stability and security are the very same whose interests are threatened by the proposed reforms.

The 'West', China and Cambodia

The nature of the engagement between Western donors and the Cambodian government since the early 1990s has taken a series of different forms. In the build-up to the signing of the 1991 Paris Peace Accords, the award of desperately needed western aid for reconstruction and development was made conditional upon the holding of multi-party democratic elections. From 1991 to 1995, engagement took place within the International Committee for the Reconstruction of Cambodia forum (ICORC). In 1996 an alternative mechanism, the Consultative Group (CG) annual meeting, was introduced in an effort to improve the coordination of external aid and the monitoring of government performance against the goals set out in the first *National Programme to Rehabilitate and Develop Cambodia*. In 2007 the CG mechanism was restructured and renamed the Cambodian Development Cooperation Forum (CDCF). For the first time, the meeting was chaired by the Royal Cambodian Government rather than by one of Cambodia's development partners, and included representatives from China.

Since the first "National Programme" the Cambodian government, with significant donor technical assistance, has produced a bewildering number of development strategies and reform planning documents. In 2004 it introduced its flagship "Rectangular Strategy for Growth, Employment, Equity and Efficiency in Cambodia". This was followed by a new National Strategic Development Plan 2006–2010 (NSDP), intended to operationalize the Rectangular Strategy. At the heart of the strategy is a commitment, agreed with donors, to key good governance reforms such as anti-corruption and legal and judicial reform.[6]

Since 1993, the Cambodian government has failed to make good on these commitments. This has not stopped donors from pledging aid at the annual CG meetings, while seeking different levers to try to pressure the government

---

[6] Hun Sen, *The Rectangular Strategy for Growth, Employment, Equity and Efficiency in Cambodia,* Presented to the First Cabinet Meeting of the Third Legislature of the National Assembly, Phnom Penh, July 2004, online at http://www.cdc-crdb.gov.kh/cdc/aid_management/RGC_Rectangular_Strategy_2004.pdf, accessed 12 August 2008.

into more action on key reforms. In 2000, donors introduced "benchmarks" for this purpose; when these failed, in 2004, Joint Monitoring Indicators (JMI) and Joint Technical Working Groups (TWG) were introduced across 18 government sectors to report on the JMIs at monthly Government–Donor Coordination Committee meetings.[7] By 2008 key reforms had still not been enacted; yet donors pledged over one billion dollars worth of aid, a significant increase from previous years. Indeed, repeated donor demands for government "actions not words" followed by donor inaction when no progress on these reforms is made, but rather the regular pledging of aid, is becoming something of a cliché among commentators in Cambodia.[8]

It could be argued that by increasing the pressure to reform, or making aid conditional, Cambodia's traditional donors run the risk of pushing the government even closer to China. Furthermore, pushing too hard could potentially destabilize the political situation, and this would be unacceptable from the donor's point of view. The evident lack of effective pressure being exerted on the government to implement what could be politically destabilizing reforms begs the question, is there any real difference between traditional donor aid and Chinese aid and investment? The Cambodian experience thus provides a useful case for examining the impact of Chinese investment and aid, if any, on Western donor notions of democratic reform and good governance.

China and Cambodia

China's policy of "going out" into the world to seek and secure access to natural resources and markets to fuel and sustain its own growth has resulted in the Chinese government and Chinese firms enticing Cambodian state power-holders with grants and loans, generous aid packages, and a culturally more amenable way of doing business. Consequently, there is a growing interest among western analysts concerning the reach and implications of China's so-called projection of "soft power", in places like Cambodia, in Southeast Asia more generally, and beyond. Analysts in US foreign policy circles, for example, use the term soft power to describe China's capacity to affect the behaviour of state power-holders in Southeast Asia. China is seen as using a variety of diplomatic, foreign assistance, trade, and investment initiatives to further its foreign policy goals. It

---

[7] NGO Forum on Cambodia, "The PRSP and CSO's Participation in Cambodia," report prepared for the Roundtable Discussion on NGO/CSO Experiences in PRSP Monitoring & Advocacy, Phnom Penh, May 2006, 4–5, http://www.ngoforum.org.kh/Development/Docs/PRSP%20in%20Cambodia.pdf, accessed 12 August 2008.
[8] Douglas Gillison and Kay Kimsong, "A Decade of Donor Meetings, Donor Discontent May Not Lessen Donor Largesse," *The Cambodia Daily*, 3 March 2007, 12.

has also been described as a "charm offensive" that favours political and cultural influence contrasting with China's military support for communist insurgencies in the region in the 1970s and 1980s. This seemingly more accommodating foreign policy in the region promotes a more benign international image emphasizing the "mutual benefits" of political, economic and cultural ties with its regional neighbours. Moreover, China's state policy of "non-interference" into the affairs of other states makes Chinese aid and investment particularly attractive to the poorer authoritarian and semi-authoritarian states like Laos, Burma and Cambodia.[9]

The projection of China's "soft power" in this way comes at a time when there is a perception of a gradual decline in the influence of Western countries in the region, particularly the US. Some commentators point out that since 11 September 2001, US diplomacy and aid have emphasized counter-terrorism at the expense of its own previous soft power strategy. Since the dissolution of the Soviet system in 1991 the use by the US and her allies of "hard" military power in Southeast Asia has been replaced by a softer approach focusing on exporting and promoting Western values and norms. Items such as democracy and democratization via free and fair elections, free market economics, human rights, technology transfers, and Western education were viewed as having universal attraction and value. However, failed or stalled experiments with democracy through less than free and fair elections in the early to mid 1990s, the 1997 Asian financial crisis and its consequences for development in the region, followed by the handling of the Iraq war (especially human rights abuses at the Guantanamo Bay and Abu Ghraib prisons) have exposed the inconsistencies and contradictions of Western liberal democratic development models. A Chinese approach therefore that appears not to promote a particular set of political and cultural values and norms may appear more attractive to some Southeast Asian states like Cambodia.

This is not to say that political and cultural values are not part of the Chinese approach to diplomacy, aid and investment. The Cambodian government, for example, has consistently and publicly supported the People's Republic of China's (PRC) "one-China policy", fully recognizing China's claims over Taiwan. In terms of culture and cultural ties, the role played by Cambodia's ethnic Chinese community is also a significant factor in the strengthening of relations between the two countries. After years of civil conflict, resulting in the deaths of many Sino-Khmer and the suppression of their cultural heritage, China is now actively supporting the rejuvenation of Cambodia's Chinese community in Phnom Penh. This has been achieved in a variety of ways, through the re-establishment

---

[9] Thomas Lum, Wayne Morrison and Bruce Vaughan, *China's Soft Power in Southeast Asia*, Congress Research Service Report, Order Code RL 34310, 4 January 2008, 2–5.

of Chinese-language schools, support for Chinese-Cambodian social organizations, and facilitating business links between private Chinese companies and indigenous Sino-Khmer and other Cambodian business interests.

Phnom Penh has since the eighteenth and nineteenth centuries been home to a large group of well-assimilated ethnic Chinese, the majority of whom are Teochiu dialect speakers. originating from Guangdong province on mainland China, but who also include speakers of other Chinese dialects from Hokkien, Canton, Hainan, and the non-geographic Hakka. This community, with support from the Chinese state, has since the early 1990s been active in promoting Chinese-language education in Cambodia. Chinese-language schools closed down by previous Cambodian regimes have now been reopened and are increasing in number. According to Paul Marks the success of the re-establishment of Chinese-language schools is marked by the fact that one elementary school in Phnom Penh has 10,000 students, making it the largest overseas Chinese school in the world. Moreover, it is estimated that up to 30 per cent of students attending Chinese-language schools are ethnic Khmer.[10] There has also been a revival in what Marks refers to as Chinese social institutions or 'guilds' under the auspices of an umbrella organization known as the Cambodian Chinese General Assembly. The assembly, also with China's support, performs a supervisory role, acting as guide for the Cambodian Chinese community in social and community affairs.[11]

Chinese-language education institutions and local Cambodian and Chinese organizations encourage links between indigenous Sino-Khmer business interests and investment by Chinese firms. In particular, the Chinese Chamber of Commerce and the Hong Kong and Macau business association are active in this regard. The Chinese Chamber of Commerce maintains close links with the Chinese embassy in Phnom Penh, and plays a central role in hosting the increasingly frequent arrival of trade and investment delegations from China. A number of Cambodia's prominent business tycoons and senators are themselves Sino-Khmers and are members of these organizations, or have close links with Chinese companies operating in Cambodia.

The combination of China's regional foreign policy of accommodation and non-interference for mutual benefit, and the resurgence of the Cambodian-Chinese communities' role in the country's economic development, affords the current Cambodian regime a good deal of latitude vis-à-vis its traditional Western partners. With no apparent political and economic reform strings attached to Chinese investment and aid, it provides the current Cambodian government with a convenient alternative to prescriptive Western models of development. Moreover, a lack of transparency and accountability associated

---

[10] Paul Marks, "China's Strategy in Cambodia", *Parameters,* 30.3 (2000): 92.
[11] See n.10 above.

with infrastructural projects and investment deals makes it easier for well-connected Cambodian elites to conduct business with the Chinese government and Chinese companies. Thus, Western donor attempts at the reform of a regime that ultimately guarantees the necessary political stability and security for development is perceived as being even more problematic with the presence of Chinese investment and aid.

The questions remain: will China's growing influence affect the manner in which decisions within the Cambodian state are made, and if so to what extent? How will this in turn affect the interests and behaviour of other national and international actors engaged in determining Cambodia's future, and with what results? In attempting to answer these questions much depends upon understanding and explaining the political and socio-economic context within which Chinese engagement, in all its forms, with the Cambodian state has taken and is taking place. As alluded to earlier, the post-1998 election period of relative stability followed by Hun Sen's consolidation of personal power after the 2002 and 2003 polls were key events in shaping Cambodia's post-conflict political trajectory. Electoral success — achieved by a variety of strategies including violence, intimidation, coercion, the mobilization of fear, vote buying, and party control of electoral authorities — has paved the way for a lucrative convergence of politics and business controlled by dominant CPP elements within the Cambodian state. This is seen by some as a natural progression since the 1980s in the development of personal networks of patron–clientism established by leaders of the CPP that have evolved into what has been more recently conceptualized as a neo-patrimonial model of state formation.[12]

According to this model the state functions to serve the personal and private interests of a limited number of powerful interconnected political–economic elites who co-exist with but subvert the authority of formal institutions that should in theory operate solely in the national interest. This model, which extends beyond the state into every sphere of society, has been successfully developed in Cambodia since the late 1980s, eventually succeeding in securing a stable enough environment within which the interests of these political–economic elites could be met and furthered in the early 2000s.[13] It is a model that would appear to be at complete variance with the idea of good governance promoted by Cambodia's Western development partners, who emphasize the creation of a modern legal–rational state as being the most efficient and effective vehicle for growth

---

[12] See Evan Gottesman, *Cambodia After the Khmer Rouge: Inside the Politics of Nation Building* (London: Yale University Press, 2003).
[13] For a full discussion of neo-patrimonialism in Cambodia see Pak Kimchoeun, Horng Vuthy, Eng Netra, Ann Sovatha, Kim Sedara, Jenny Knowles and David Craig, *Accountability and Neo-patrimonialism: A Critical Literature Review*, Working Paper No 34 (Phnom Penh: CDRI, 2007), Chaps 4–5.

and development. Since the start of the massive influx of international aid during and after the 1992–1993 United Nations operation, these interests within the Cambodian state have to a large extent become dependent upon technical and financial assistance provided by multi-lateral and bilateral donors.

Consequently, a tacit compromise between the government and its international partners seems to have been struck. Piecemeal reforms in the banking, financial, trade and land sectors, accompanied by incremental and limited improvements in health and education have been exchanged for regular dispersements of aid, and international legitimacy. More fundamental reforms in key areas like the judiciary, and the introduction, implementation and enforcement of an anti-corruption law, which would potentially threaten entrenched interests within the neo-patrimonial state, and thus deemed to be potentially destabilizing, have not been enacted.

It is the very nature of the relationship between the Cambodian state and its traditional development partners that has produced what has been termed a "hybrid" form of governance allowing the neo-patrimonial networks to flourish alongside elements working for piecemeal reform. As will be discussed in more detail below, the introduction of Chinese investment and aid into this hybrid system only serves to strengthen the neo-patrimonial networks. Moreover, China's policy of non-interference in the political affairs of its neighbours makes China's "way of doing business" more attractive to some Cambodian state power holders vis-à-vis traditional donors, who rhetorically at least are pushing a reform agenda. The point was made by Hun Sen himself when, referring to the way Western aid is pledged, he was quoted as saying that when China gives, "It doesn't say do this or that. We can do whatever we want with the money."[14] While it is true that over the years Cambodia's Western donors have repeatedly and publicly pointed out the Royal Cambodian Government's (RGC) lack of action regarding judicial and other key reforms, insufficient pressure has been brought to bear by them to address the debilitating and worsening problem of corruption. Thus Hun Sen's speeches of this kind merely serve to remind western donors of the growing influence of China.[15]

Chinese Investment and Decision-Making

What is being suggested here is that, while there may be significant theoretical or rhetorical differences between Chinese and Western approaches to development,

---

[14] Mathew Coghlan, *China's Poverty Footprint in Cambodia* (Hong Kong: Oxfam, 2008), 30.
[15] World Bank, *Cambodia at the Crossroads, Strengthening Accountability to Reduce Poverty* (Phnom Penh: World Bank, 2004); see also, "Donors Pledge More Than $900 Million," *Cambodia Daily*, 5 December 2008, 12.

there may be very little difference in the outcomes of decisions made by the RGC in their dealings either with the Chinese or with other donors. In other words, China's "no questions asked" policy results in no progress on reform. Western donors' criticism of a lack of action for the reasons discussed above has also produced no significant results in key areas. However, there is increasing interest in and criticism of the manner in which the RGC makes decisions about Chinese investment projects and aid. Most of this interest and criticism is related to decisions taken about large infrastructural projects, agri-business and land concessions involving Chinese. A number of Chinese SOEs for example are involved in large controversial infrastructural projects, the most notable being the Kamchay and Stung Atay hydropower dam projects. Systematic research to understand the process by which the Cambodian government approved these projects has been mainly conducted by groups concerned about the potentially negative environmental and social impact these projects will have on local communities.

The findings of this research show that the decision-making processes to approve these projects, particularly the Kamchay dam, are less than transparent. The approval of the Kamchay project took place between high-level Cambodian and Chinese officials without consultation with local authorities and the public; the contract was authorized by Hun Sen and awarded by the Ministry of Industry, Mines and Energy (MIME) to China's largest hydropower company Sinohydro Corporation.[16] It was to be financed through the $600 million aid package given to the Cambodian government by the Chinese in April 2006. Of particular concern for the researchers, aside from the exclusion of key stakeholders from the approval process, was that the actual Chinese source of finance for the project was not disclosed at the time. It was subsequently revealed that the actual lender was one of two of China's largest state-supervised export–import banks, China Exim.

Almost all Chinese overseas aid is channelled through these so-called "policy banks" in the form of soft loans and grants, and since they are state-run entities, their aid decisions are intimately tied to the strategic interests and foreign policy objectives of the Chinese government. However, as the researchers note, Chinese concern for the environmental and social consequences of these projects is "notably weaker", than their Western counterparts whose own standards are "less than admirable". Furthermore, the grants and loans channeled through these state entities are not attached to conditions concerning good governance or reform.[17] Other studies offer some interesting insights into how the negotiating and decision making processes surrounding Chinese grants and loans are

---

[16] See the report by Carl Middleton and Sam Chanty, *Cambodia's Hydropower Development and China's Involvement* (Phnom Penh: International Rivers/The Rivers Coalition in Cambodia/NGO Forum on Cambodia, 2008).
[17] Ibid., 35.

made. According to Matthew Coghlan's study Chinese Overseas Development Aid (ODA) is a mixture of grants and loans weighted considerably in favour of loans. As with traditional donors all grants are free and loans concessional.[18] Invariably, rates of interest for loans range from nought to two per cent, and the amount of the grant that is considered free within a loan is forty per cent. As Coghlan notes,

> The process of negotiating Chinese grants and loans usually begins during an official visit, when Hun Sen starts negotiations by making specific requests for China to consider helping particular projects. The Chinese government then specifies how much assistance there is available for Cambodia, and together both sides negotiate specific projects. The next step is for the Chinese government to begin the tendering process for Chinese contractors, with the winning Chinese contractors then presenting their budget for the projects. If the budget is less than expected, the Chinese government reuses the balance, if the budget is more, then the Chinese will usually supplement the budget. The contractors who are successful then begin the process of implementing the projects, which are then jointly monitored by both the Chinese and the RGC.[19]

The process described by Coghlan reinforces the argument that a lack of transparency and accountability can potentially create new rent-seeking opportunities for powerfully connected political and economic elites within the Cambodian state.

Land Concessions and Agri-Business

A lack of consultation and transparency surrounding grants and loans is not restricted to large public infrastructure projects. Controversies surrounding the awarding of land concessions and licences to foreign business interests, especially Chinese, with links to politically connected Cambodian companies are nothing new. Problems and issues related to politics and Chinese Foreign Direct Investment in the Cambodian garment industry, the powerhouse of Cambodia's economic growth in recent years, for example, have been well documented.[20] More recently, the forced eviction from Cambodia of the NGO Global Witness for exposing direct links between members of Hun Sen's family,

---

[18] Matthew Coghlan, *China's Poverty Footprint*, 12.
[19] Ibid.
[20] Caroline Hughes, *The Political Economy of Cambodia's Transition, 1991–2001* (London: RoutledgeCurzon, 2003), Chapter 8.

foreign business interests and the illegal logging trade has become something of a *cause célèbre* among national and international civil society groups critical of the government's relationship with domestic and foreign business interests.[21]

The lack of accountability and transparency surrounding the awarding of large economic land concessions to foreign companies focuses attention on a number of issues related to law enforcement, rural livelihoods and poverty. These economic land concessions are supposed to be an integral part of the Cambodian government's framework strategy to tackle rural poverty set out in the National Strategic Development Plan 2006–2010. They are regulated by the 2001 Land Law, and the Sub-Decree on Economic Land Concessions signed by Hun Sen in 2005, and are defined as instruments for the granting of state private land for agricultural and industrial–agricultural exploitation. They may also be granted for the purpose of investment in agriculture, rural employment, diversification of livelihood opportunities, and the generation of state revenues, and are restricted in size to 10,000 hectares. An eight-member Technical Secretariat on Economic Land Concessions was appointed by Hun Sen in 2006 to oversee the granting of concessions. According to a report by the Cambodia Office of the High Commissioner for Human Rights, by 2007 "over 943,069 hectares of rural land has been handed over to private companies for the development of large agri-business ventures".[22] This amounts to 59 economic land concessions owned by Cambodia's politically connected business elite, and 25 owned by foreign interests, 12 of which are Chinese nationals.

A major concern is the negative impact these concessions are having on the human rights and livelihoods of rural communities dependent upon the land and its resources. The report concludes that rather than promoting rural development and the reduction of poverty, "economic land concessions have compromised the rights and livelihoods of rural communities in Cambodia".[23] The problem is a familiar one of poor enforcement and non-compliance with the requirements of the land law and the Sub-Decree on Economic Land Concessions. In the majority of cases, what this means is that local communities and concerned civil organizations have not been given the opportunity to participate in the decision-making process concerning the award of these concessions. Consequently, in many instances, local communities have found that their land has been encroached upon, and as the report goes on to note there has been a detrimental impact on their livelihoods, and on employment and labour conditions, adverse environmental

---

[21] See Global Witness, *Cambodia's Family Trees* (London: Global Witness, 2007).
[22] Special Representative of the Secretary-General for Human Rights in Cambodia, *Economic land concessions in Cambodia: A Human Rights Perspective*, (Phnom Penh: Cambodia Office of the High Commission for Human Rights, 2007), Executive Summary.
[23] Ibid., 20. See also Chapter 12 of this volume.

impacts, violence and intimidation, and no effective means for local communities to seek recourse to address these problems.[24]

A key question asked by the report is who exactly the beneficiaries of economic land concessions are. Increasingly, research and analysis are beginning to reveal the extent to which influential Cambodian political figures, especially members of the senate or wealthy individuals, known as *Oknha*, who make generous cash or in-kind contributions to the CPP party-state, are involved in economic land concessions. The word *Oknha* was originally used to indicate a position of high-rank within the Cambodian civil service. More recently, however, it has been influential businessmen and not necessarily civil servants who have been rewarded with the title. Like other prominent Cambodian businessmen some of these *Oknha* are Sino-Khmer and have personal and business connections with mainland Chinese. In the absence of accurate and reliable data it is estimated that these individuals either own or have shares in eleven of the concessions, with perhaps more having interests in others, thus enabling powerful individuals to use different companies to circumvent the 10,000 hectare limit contravening the Land Law.[25] Some prominent examples include Senator Ly Yong Phat, who it is believed has ownership interests in two companies, both of which were granted adjoining concessions to develop a sugarcane plantation. Taken together they add up to nearly 20,000 hectares. Other examples include An Yang Yin Chang, a Chinese national and director of three companies granted concessions in Stung Treng province totalling almost 25,000 hectares.[26] Another senator, Lau Meng Khin, a director of two companies including the well known Cambodian company Pheapimex has controlling interests in concessions totaling 415,025 hectares in Kampong Chhnang, Pursat and Mondulkiri provinces.[27]

---

[24] Ibid., 3–13. This estimate was given to me during an interview with staff working for an NGO in Phnom Penh who researches these issues but preferred to remain anonymous.

[25] Carl Middleton and Sam Chanty, "Cambodia's Hydropower," 44–59.

[26] Special Representative of the Secretary-General for Human Rights in Cambodia, *Economic land concessions in Cambodia: A Human Rights Perspective*, (Phnom Penh: Cambodia Office of the High Commission for Human Rights, 2007), Executive Summary. The three companies are: Phou Mady Investment Group, Grand Land Agricultural Development and CG World Group.

[27] Ibid. Lau Meng Khin is also the deputy chairman of the Phnom Penh Chamber of Commerce, and an economic advisor to the Prime Minister, Hun Sen. His wife Cheung Sopheap, also known as Yeay Phou, or Grandmother Yeay, is closely linked to the Shukaku Company which was granted a 99-year lease to develop the Boeng Kak Lake area in Phnom Penh. Over 4,000 resident families in the area faced eviction, and according to newspaper reports were subjected to harassment and intimidation in an effort to force them to leave with inadequate compensation. The Shukaku Company was originally believed to be from South Korea. After complaints were lodged to the South Korean embassy in Phnom Penh it was revealed that the company was not South Korean. The company is believed to be Chinese, from Yunnan Province. Author interview with NGO official December 2008. See also, "The South Korean Embassy Denies that the Shukaku Inc. Company Comes from Korea," *The Mirror*, Phnom Penh, 28 October 2008.

The negative social and environmental impact of these concessions reported by national and international NGOs also highlights the nature of the relationship between politically connected business elites, local and national authorities, and individuals and communities adversely affected. There have been numerous cases of communities attempting to take action and protest against the activities of the concessionaires. In many of these cases their concerns have largely been ignored by the concessionaires and the local and national authorities, and in some instances protests have been met with violence. The UN human rights office has documented many of these cases. In one such case, in May 2006 villagers in Sre Ambel district, Koh Kong province, staged a protest against the presence and activities of the Koh Kong Sugar Industry Company and the Koh Kong Plantation Company. During protests at the concession site armed security guards, believed to be military personnel, confronted the protesters, resulting in one being shot and four others injured. Despite taking their case to the National Assembly and the Prime Minister's Office in 2007, and receiving assurances that the dispute would be resolved, the concessionaires did not stop encroachment on their land.[28]

Collusion between powerful economic elites and local and national authorities including the military and police to protect mutual interests is nothing new in Cambodia, especially in rural areas. In the context of complaints against the activities of the concessionaires, for example, complainants and community activists have been accused by government officials and company representatives of being "opposition party members". This collusion also has a negative impact on the activities of civil society groups and NGOs, who have faced restrictions preventing them from mobilizing communities to protest and register complaints. In a notable instance in Mondulkiri province communities protesting against the Chinese Wuzhishan concession found that they needed permission from local authorities to leave the province in order to attend meetings organized by NGOs. In other instances, communities have been prevented from organizing meetings, and civil groups have been warned by local authorities "not to incite villagers".[29]

Chinese Investment and Development

A general lack of transparency and accountability associated with Chinese aid and investment, combined with negative social and environmental impacts, raise questions concerning the overall short and long term benefits to be accrued for

---

[28] Special Representative of the Secretary-General for Human Rights in Cambodia, *Economic land concessions in Cambodia: A Human Rights Perspective*, (Phnom Penh: Cambodia Office of the High Commission for Human Rights, 2007), Executive Summary, 17–19.
[29] Ibid.

the majority of Cambodians. These questions tend to focus on the motives and interests of both the Chinese and Cambodian governments. On the one side, and as one might expect when considering a regional power, China's motives and interests are viewed by some as not being altruistic. As the president of the Chinese Chamber of Commerce put it, whether they are state-owned or private, the number one priority of companies investing in Cambodia is to make profits, and to strengthen China's position regionally.

That said, it is important to note that China views the development of the Greater Mekong Sub-Region (GMS), of which Cambodia and the Chinese province of Yunnan form significant parts, as a major regional priority. Since 1992 the Asian Development Bank (ADB) has been working closely with Japan in providing assistance to GMS countries including China, and in implementing a GMS programme aimed at achieving regional integration underpinned by "sustainable development". The programme focuses on six areas: transport, energy and telecommunications; the environment; human resource development; tourism and trade; private sector investment; and agriculture. However, it has been pointed out that in order to be fully realized the ADB's idea of sustainable development requires among other things "democratic governance". According to this view structural reforms and good governance are thus essential prerequisites for successful regional integration. It may possibly be the case, therefore, that for countries like Cambodia, the ADB's regional integration programme, acts as a further disincentive to reform.[30]

Moreover, another potential negative aspect of Chinese involvement in Cambodia is the notion of a dependent economic core–periphery relationship. Cambodia may be running the risk of finding itself on the periphery of, and dependent upon, China's core economic activities within its own territory. Natural resource extraction by Chinese companies and the export of primary commodities to China followed by the importation of cheap Chinese manufactured goods for Cambodian markets could hamper the country's prospects for industrial development. In this way, China's motives and interests are seen by some as being not as "friendly" as its diplomacy would suggest. Investments in infrastructure like roads and bridges and land concessions for resource extraction have, cynically, more to do with what China can get from Cambodia rather than with what Cambodia can gets from China.[31] Seen from this perspective China's interests, as pointed out by Françoise Mengin, are

---

[30] Kao Kim Hourn and Sisowath Doung Chanto, "ASEAN-China Cooperation for Greater Mekong Sub-Region Development," in Saw Swee-Hock, Lijun Shen, and Chin Kin-Wah, (eds.), *ASEAN-China: Realities and Prospects* (Singapore: ISEAS Press, 2005), 316–328.
[31] Opposition parliamentarian, interview with the author, Phnom Penh, December 2008.

very much strategic in terms of access not just to Cambodia's, but also to the region's natural resources, especially oil and gas.[32]

The Kamchay hydropower dam building project in Cambodia's southwest provides a good illustration of the perceived divide between the benefits and costs of Chinese investments and aid. Cambodia's electricity infrastructure is very basic, and the costs of unreliable supplies among the world's highest, placing major impediments in the way of further foreign investment and socio-economic development. It is estimated that when completed the Kamchay dam could generate US$55 million in electricity sales, supplying relatively cheap power for the capital Phnom Penh and the southern provinces of Kampot, Kep, Takeo and Sihanoukville. However, before the Chinese company Sinohydro was awarded the contract to build the dam in 2006, previous support for a feasibility study by the Canadian International Development Agency (CIDA) was withdrawn because of "poor social and environment standards" and high cost. Moreover, the unusually lengthy 44 year Build Operate Transfer (BOT) contract signed between Sinohydro and MIME has been criticized as benefiting the Chinese more than the government. In spite of these and other concerns related to transparency and accountability issues referred to earlier, the Kamchay dam project could potentially be of great benefit to Cambodia.[33]

Thus, the Chinese regard their involvement as being no different from that of any other investors or aid donors.[34] In the process of earning profits and consolidating its position regionally China's involvement will, so this argument goes, ultimately benefit all Cambodians in the long term. China's funding of large infrastructural projects, like the construction of roads, highways and bridges, will according to some sources have immediate benefits, allowing greater access to markets and services, and creating business and employment opportunities. Indeed, Chinese funding of infrastructure is challenging Cambodia's traditional donors like the ADB and the Japanese International Cooperation Agency (JICA).[35] Although there may be some negative short-term consequences for traditional livelihoods, in the long term from this perspective these benefits have the potential for reducing rural poverty.[36]

Other potential benefits often pointed out by proponents of a positive perspective will be derived by continued Chinese investment in the garment sector. The expected collapse of the sector after the termination of the Multi

[32] Françoise Mengin, "La présence chinoise au Cambodge Contribution à une économie politique violente, rentière et inégalitaire," Les Études du CERI No 133 (2007): 10–12.
[33] Carl Middleton and Sam Chanty, "Cambodia's Hydropower," 44–59.
[34] President, Chinese Chamber of Commerce, interview with the author, Phnom Penh, December 2008.
[35] Matthew Coghlan, "China's Poverty Footprint," 15–19.
[36] Ibid., 33.

Fiber Arrangement (MFA) and the United States Cambodia Trade Agreement on Textile and Apparel (TATA) did not materialize. On the contrary, according to the Garment Manufacturers Association of Cambodia (GMAC) the number of garment factories in Cambodia has doubled in the last five years. The GMAC has 295 members, 39 of which originate in China. Many of these companies are owned and managed by ethnic Chinese from other Southeast Asian countries and Hong Kong. Also, many have close links with the Chinese Chamber of Commerce in Cambodia, and the China Hong Kong Macau Expatriate and Business Association of Cambodia, who provide these companies with help and support in establishing their businesses and with dispute management.

The contribution of these companies to Cambodia's economic transformation is well known. In terms of employment alone the sector has employed approximately 300–350,000 workers, predominately women whose income it is has been estimated supports up to one million Cambodians.[37] Based on a cursory examination of sectors like manufacturing and infrastructural development projects there can be little doubt that Chinese investments in Cambodia's garment industry, and aid for projects like roads and hydro-electric dams, have and will continue to have some benefit for some Cambodians, and under the right conditions over time will have an overall positive impact on the country's socio-economic development. That said, both the manufacturing and infrastructural sectors are subject to the vicissitudes of the global economy. In the current global economic circumstances it is not clear to what extent these sectors may be adversely affected, making any sustainable long term socio-economic gains highly uncertain. Recent figures released by the Cambodian Ministry for Commerce, for example, show that garment exports for the first few months of 2009 were down by half, with twelve factories having to close. More disturbingly, in terms of employment and those it supports, it was estimated by the head of the Cambodian Free Trade Union that as many as 40,000 garment worker jobs have been lost since last year.[38]

In the final analysis, therefore, for the full benefits of these investments and aid to be realized, much will depend upon the behaviour, decision-making and actions of the government in the context of its relationship with China. It is precisely because of the nature of this relationship to date that critics, especially opposition members of the National Assembly, present a more negative view of China's capacity to have a positive impact on Cambodian development. Some argue that rather than making a positive contribution Chinese investment and aid is actually eroding the democratic and human rights gains made in the last eighteen years. The inference is that despite the apparent reluctance by donors

---

[37] Ibid.
[38] "Cambodia Garments Export Halve," *Agence France Presse* (AFP), Phnom Penh, 21 March 2009.

to push the government too hard over key reforms, western influence since 1993 has nonetheless succeeded in helping democracy take root and kept the human rights situation in Cambodia in the national and international spotlights. By contrast China's domestic anti-democratic and dire human rights record is well known. It is more likely therefore, according to this argument, that because of the strengthening of relations between the two countries the current Cambodian government will be even more disinclined to follow through on its commitments to democratic reform so long as China remains as a viable alternative to Western aid and investment.

The overall lack of transparency and accountability surrounding Chinese investment and aid, together with the adverse social and environmental effects of Chinese-controlled concessions, are a good indication of an approach to development that benefits a small but powerful well-connected Cambodian politico-economic elite in the short term, and not the majority of Cambodians in the long term. Indeed, China's policy of non-interference in the political affairs of host countries, and its seemingly "no strings attached" approach, actually undermines the limited but significant progress that has been made in human rights and democracy over the past couple of decades. As far as state power-holders are concerned the Chinese approach to development assistance makes for a refreshing alternative to the good governance prescriptions and demands made by the government's Western development partners. In practical terms this gives the ruling party a good deal of space to manoeuvre between its traditional donors and the Chinese, lending greater legitimacy to its own post-conflict approach to development, underpinned by the neo-patrimonial networks.

As far as civil society groups, both national and international, are concerned, China's impact on Cambodia's development trajectory is at best mixed. Clearly, the manner in which China has funded infrastructural projects and the conduct of the concessionaires is a major concern for national civil society groups interested in a more equitable and just model of development. For some international Non-Governmental Organizations, like Oxfam Hong Kong, Chinese investment and aid can be enormously beneficial to Cambodia and Cambodians provided the government is prepared to engage in dialogue with civil society groups to discuss the ways in which mutual benefits can be assured.[39] Again, it will be the responsibility of the current Cambodian government to implement the right kinds of policies and reform if a more just and equitable approach to development is to be realized. In the short to medium term at least, all indicators seem to point to business as usual.

In many respects, the task of validating the hypothesis put forward at the beginning of this chapter with hard data was always going to be difficult. Not

---

[39] Oxfam Hong Kong Representative, interview with the author, Phnom Penh, December 2008.

surprisingly, the gathering of evidence to substantiate assertions that Chinese investment and aid create further opportunities for rent-seeking by, and the personal enrichment of, well-connected political economic elites within the state and their business associates is limited by the sensitive political and economic nature of the issues involved. Equally, attempts to establish the ways in which China's growing influence affects decision-making within the current Cambodian state structure with regard to reform is constrained by the overall lack of transparency, accountability and effective broad-based public scrutiny. How this in turn may affect the interests and behavior of other national non-state and international actors engaged in Cambodia's future aid and development is however more easily discerned. Likewise, an insightful analysis of the overall long-term impact of Chinese investment and aid for Cambodian development can be made.

The transformation of the Cambodian state beginning in the late 1980s up until the formation of a government in 2004, following the 2003 parliamentary elections, has produced a political and economic system dominated by the personal power of the current Prime Minister, backed by those within the CPP loyal to him. Furthermore, the inclusion of a powerful politico-economic elite strengthens the CPP's national and international legitimacy, earned through the holding of regular flawed elections, and a rhetorical commitment to reform. In turn, this ensures regular disbursements of donor aid that help maintain and reproduce the system. The predominance of this small group subverts the effective operation of the state, rendering it endemically corrupt and prone to rent-seeking, severely limiting its capacity to deliver high quality goods and services outside the system. In recent years it has benefited from high levels of economic growth that has combined with stability and security to boost foreign investor confidence. At the same time, however, this has shifted attention away from the growing inequities and disparities within the wider Cambodian society that may possibly become greater, if as is expected the Cambodian economy is adversely affected by the global economic downturn.

Nonetheless, the introduction of Chinese investment and aid into this system at this time is likely to be captured by well-connected economic and political elites, creating more rent seeking opportunities that will continue to undermine national and international efforts to reform. The growing influence of China, backed by its soft power and non-interference approach to relations with its neighbours provides a useful counterbalance to those critical of the Cambodian government's lack of action on substantive reform issues. The strengthening of bilateral relations between China and Cambodia under these conditions gives confidence to Cambodia's state power-holders that the current governance arrangements are in actuality the best that could possibly have been hoped for given Cambodia's recent turbulent past. Criticism of these arrangements and strident calls for reform by dissenting voices are deemed, by those whose interests within the state they threaten, to be destabilizing, resulting in repression by quasi-legal and violent means.

Insofar as Cambodia's traditional Western donors are concerned, some commentators view China's resurgent role in Cambodian affairs, as a no-political-strings attached alternative, as weakening demands for the democratic reform of the Cambodian state.[40] Given the limited Western donors' response to successive Cambodian governments persistent failure to introduce key reforms in the last decade, there is no reason to think that Chinese investment and aid will make a significant difference either way. It is unlikely therefore that the growing influence of China in Cambodia will fundamentally alter the ways in which decisions at the highest levels of the state are made regarding Chinese investment and aid, and reform. On the positive side, there is the feeling that Chinese investment in infrastructure, roads, bridges and hydro-electric dams will ultimately benefit Cambodia and Cambodians in the long term, opening up access to markets and creating employment. On the downside, opposition critics envisage a democratic backsliding and a deterioration in the human rights situation as Western donor influence diminishes and Chinese influence grows.[41]

There is little doubt that improved infrastructure, especially serviceable roads and cheaper and reliable electricity, will improve the quality of life in terms of access and supply. However, this still requires a huge amount of investment, Chinese or otherwise, and the overall positive impact on socio-economic development and poverty alleviation remains uncertain.[42] Likewise, it is difficult at this early juncture to substantiate assertions that Chinese investment and aid will result in some kind of democratic regression. Suffice it to say, it is unlikely to directly result in democratic progress in the near future. There is plenty of evidence to show that, regardless of China's presence, the democratic principles introduced in 1992–1993 under the United Nations operation have been seriously undermined by the current regime, and human rights abuses continue to occur despite regular critical assessments of the Cambodian government's performance by Western donors.[43] That said, the small amount of research that has been conducted so far does suggest that unless the current Cambodian government manages Chinese aid and investment in an equitable, accountable and transparent manner, any benefits accrued from it are more likely to be outweighed by its adverse affects.

---

[40] Devin T. Stewart, "Damning Public Opinion: The Risks of China's Diplomacy in Cambodia," *Carnegie Ethics Online*, 4 April 2008, online at 2008, http//www.cceia.org/resources/ethics_online/0020.html, accessed 12 August 2009.
[41] Ibid.
[42] Matthew Coghlan, "China's Poverty Footprint," 33.
[43] See for example, Stephen Heder, "Hun Sen's Consolidation, Death or Beginning of Reform?" in Daljit Singh ed. *Southeast Asian Affairs 2005* (Singapore: ISEAS, 2005), 113–130.

4

Growth in the Rice and Garment Sectors

Sophal Ear

CAMBODIA HAS GROWN RAPIDLY IN recent years despite lacklustre governance. This chapter aims to explain this phenomenon from a political economy perspective by examining the complex relationship between the state (and by extension the ruling Cambodian People's Party or CPP) and the market across two different sectors: garments and rice. One (garments) is a vibrant export sector; the other (rice) might be an emerging export for the future. This chapter seeks to answer two questions. What explains Cambodia's double-digit growth despite poor governance? Why do some sectors thrive while others fail under the same conditions?

In answering these questions, the chapter uses the concept of "good enough governance" as a basis for analysing the nature of state–business (and by extension CPP–business) relations in Cambodia. Grindle first explained "good enough governance" as:

> ... accepting a more nuanced understanding of the evolution of institutions and government capabilities; being explicit about trade-offs and priorities in a world in which all good things cannot be pursued at once; learning about what's working rather than focusing solely on governance gaps; taking the role of government in poverty alleviation seriously; and grounding action in the contextual realities of each country.[1]

Revisiting the concept three years later, she argued that good enough governance was "not sufficient for guiding practice".[2] Perhaps realizing the increasing

---

[1] Merilee Grindle, "Good Enough Governance: Poverty Reduction and Reform in Developing Countries," *Governance: An International Journal of Policy, Administration, and Institutions*, 17.4 (October 2004): 525.

[2] Merilee Grindle, "Good Enough Governance Revisited," *Development Policy Review*, 25.5 (2007): 554.

gap between the good governance agenda and reality on the ground, the World Bank published *Governance Under Real-World Conditions* in 2008 to highlight the fact that "difficulties arise when attempts are made to apply what are often excellent technical solutions under real-world conditions"[3] and that

> ... human beings, acting either alone or in groups small and large, are not as amenable as are pure numbers. And they cannot be put aside. In other words, in the real world, reforms will not succeed, and they will certainly not be sustained, without the correct alignment of citizens, stakeholders, and voice.[4]

Thus, it is within the context of good enough governance as practised under real-world conditions that two key explanatory factors pertinent to the different growth outcomes observed in the garment and rice sectors are analysed; namely, the nature of businesses operating in the sector and the way their relationship to the government is organized; and the nature of the constraints upon production, including technical or external constraints, emerging directly[5] and indirectly[6] from poor governance.

State/CPP–Business Relations: The Oknha Economic Context[7]

Since the end of the civil war, the current political regime in Cambodia has proved successful in providing peace and stability, conceptualized as public

---

[3] Sina Odugbemi and Thomas Jacobson, eds., Introduction to *Governance Reform: Citizens, Stakeholders, and Voice* (Washington, DC: The World Bank, 2008), 1.

[4] Ibid.

[5] For instance, informal payments to customs or other parts of government increase the cost of doing business inside Cambodia and when it comes to exports from Cambodia.

[6] For instance the high cost of electricity or high transport costs because of government-granted concessions in petrol import (Sokimex has the country's only oil jetty at Sihanoukville Autonomous Port), poor infrastructure due to corruption, etc., could be improved with better governance. See World Bank, *Sustaining Rapid Growth in a Challenging Environment: Cambodia Country Economic Memorandum*, Poverty Reduction and Economic Management Sector Unit, East Asia and Pacific Region (Washington, DC: The World Bank, 2009), available: http://www.worldbank.org/kh/growth and World Bank and IFC, *A Better Investment Climate to Sustain Growth in Cambodia Second Investment Climate Assessment*, Poverty Reduction and Economic Management Sector Unit, East Asia and Pacific Region (Washington, DC: The World Bank, 8 January 2009), Draft for Discussion, for more on this. The latter finds that corruption is still the number one issue facing businesses in Cambodia and that electricity is a growing concern because of its high cost and unreliability.

[7] This section is drawn from Pak Kimchoeun, "Oknha and Advisors in Cambodia" (unpublished brief, dated 11 June 2008) with permission. The Oknha portion is based on an article by Duong Sokha, « Le prix à payer pour entrer dans la caste des oknhas, » (Ka-Set.info, 14 April 2008). Available: http://ka-set.info.

order, and a veneer of democracy, evidenced by the periodic holding of elections. Despite this, the quality of governance has been perceived externally as poor. Cambodia's ranking in Transparency International's Corruption Perception Index, for example, has dropped from 130 out of 158 in 2005 – the first year it was ranked – to 151 out of 163 in 2006, to 162 out of 179 in 2007. Perceptions of corruption emerge in part from the functioning of intra-elite patronage systems, running both vertically and horizontally, across and within ministries. These patronage systems have prompted a continual expansion in the number of positions in government, from one election to the next – creating an entire Senate in 1999, and the largest cabinet in the world, comprising one Prime Minister, seven Deputy Prime Ministers, 15 Senior Ministers, 28 Ministers, 135 Secretaries of State and at least 146 Under-Secretaries of State, in 2003.

This dramatic increase in the number of formal positions in government belies the true nature of political power in Cambodia. Only a few individuals hold it: the rest divide the spoils and are content to subsist on a modicum of influence. Key ministries for governance and growth include the Ministry of Economy and Finance, the Ministry of Commerce, the Ministry of Interior, the Office of the Council of Ministers, and – though a special case because of the guns it holds – the Ministry of National Defence.

Alongside the concentration of personal power in the hands of this narrow group of formal office-holders, in recent years larger numbers of Cambodian businessmen have been establishing connections with the government. Known as *'khnorng'* [literally, 'back' in Khmer and indicating backing from powerful patrons], government officials see such connections as a mechanism for eliciting gifts from businessmen, both for personal enrichment and from which to make party contributions during election periods. The establishment of webs of personal *'khsae'* [literally, 'string' in Khmer and indicating a connection] across the divide between the state and the private sector has expanded specifically through a web of patronage which operates beyond the bureaucratic elite, and links the business sector with key individuals in the ruling Cambodian People's Party (CPP). The logic of such an expansion is simple: power and money find a way to meet one another. In contemporary Cambodia, increasingly elaborate systems of honours known as the 'Okhna' and 'Advisor' systems show the mechanisms by which money and power connect.

The title of 'Okhna' comes from Cambodia's peerage system and is bestowed by His Majesty the King. It is designated for individuals whose "Contributions [to national reconstruction] valued in excess of US$100,000".[8] The title of Oknha is the preserve of businessmen interested in formalizing their relationship with

---

[8] Geoffrey P. Oldham and Brett Delahunt, *Cambodian Decorations of Honor* (Auckland, N.Z.: Milymen Books, 2004), 59.

the State (and by extension the CPP). As of April 2008 there were officially 220 Oknhas, of whom less than ten were women.⁹ Unofficially, the number could be significantly larger as some Oknhas obtain their title by directly contacting the Prime Minister and without going through the Decorations Department of the Council of Ministers. Gold (US$10,000–100,000), Silver (US$5,000–10,000), Bronze medals (US$1,000–5,000), and Certificates (US$500–1,000) exist below the title of Oknha.

The appellation of '*Tiproeksa*'¹⁰ [Advisor] differs from that of 'Oknha'. 'Advisors' are associated with a particularly powerful office holder, but in a personal rather than an official capacity. The number of advisors attached to the Cambodian government is unknown, but it is believed that the Senate President, Chea Sim, has more than a hundred, while Prime Minister Hun Sen has more than a thousand. The right to call oneself an 'advisor' to one of these high ranking personages derives from two sources. One is through outright payment via contributions to one of the working groups of the CPP. The other is through one's long term affiliation and/or service to the party. The amount of the contribution varies depending upon one's *khsae*. Knowing the right person could cost as little as US$10,000 to obtain the title; other pathways might cost US$50,000. The degree of power the title of 'advisor' brings also varies. Of the hundred advisors working for the Senate President, only a dozen receive a salary and may not have paid much for their position. These are mainly people to whom the party (even from the 1980s) owes a debt of gratitude for achieving something deemed significant or who have done some political favours for the party, such as defecting from an opposition party. Even the dozen who are paid may not actually engage in any advising. The Senate President only has two 'real' advisors, persons from whom he really seeks advice on issues such as appointments of people to key positions.

Advisors get to be called '*Ayodom*' [Excellency], a title of honour that can be helpful for doing business in Cambodia, though it does not imply wealth per se as would Oknha. Some advisors will have NGOs on the side, as their 'business'. Some advisors are sought after as business partners because they can use their political influence to gain access to the corridors of power and build the credibility of their business or organization. Gaining access is an elaborate and highly ritualized hierarchy-mediating dance for external investors, and is the reason why advisors (and Oknhas) are highly sought after, since their employment in the service of foreign investors seeking influence becomes necessary. Like Oknhas, advisors might also make substantial gifts to the person to whom

---

[9] Duong Sokha, *Le prix à payer pour entrer dans la caste des oknhas*.
[10] Based on Pak, "Oknha and advisors in Cambodia," interviews with a high ranking government officer (6 June 2008).

they are attached, to improve their relationship with those in power. One way of doing this is by offering company shares to their patrons. Finally, the distinction between advisors and Oknhas often blurs because an Oknha can also be an advisor to top party leaders such as Neak Oknha Kith Meng, who is an advisor to the Prime Minister (he was an interlocutor in the freeing of imprisoned human rights and labour activists in January 2006).

The relationship between politics and business runs deep in Cambodia. Nine Oknhas are Members of Parliament and Senators (all CPP), but more importantly, most ministers and many Members of Parliament have financial interests. Indeed a joint venture with a politician who makes no financial investment represents a well-recognized method of parlaying influence into assets. The idea of a conflict of interest does not arise because the separation between public and private is not clear within Cambodian modes of governance. This in turn makes it difficult to enact an anti-corruption law (much less implement one). A minister who receives a monthly consulting payment from a firm he "supervises" has argued that he worked outside business hours. A minister's spouse owning a million dollars worth of shares in a conglomerate registered by her husband's Ministry raises only Opposition eyebrows. An incoming minister who owns a large business that he will supervise as minister argues that no conflict of interest exists if he hands the business over to his spouse. Often, inexplicable wealth is explained by exceptional business acumen (by the spouse).

The proliferation of Oknhas and advisors, and their ever tighter relationship with hierarchies of political power are significant for prospects for growth because they can play a significant role in the economic life of Cambodia, from land ownership to controlling access to the corridors of power. Oknhas are captains of industry, often manipulating their political connections for personal gain, while advisors can become the equivalent of lobbyists who are the ultimate insiders.

Oknhas and advisors are unlikely to invest in sectors that require technical knowledge which they do not have and cannot or are unwilling to obtain from outside Cambodia. Instead, they are more likely to invest in those sectors that enjoy the highest returns with relatively short time horizons because of country risk and capital constraints. This is reflected in the sectors under discussion here: the garment sector does not enjoy an Okhna presence because of its international character: less than five per cent of garment factories in Cambodia are domestically owned. Rice is overwhelmingly domestically-owned, and has some active Oknhas, one of whom heads a rice millers' association. However, for official export, rice requires international technical know-how for Sanitary and Phytosanitary (SPS) measures compliance, measures which are meant to ensure that imports do not undermine national health and safety for importing countries.

Constraints on Growth

Ostensibly, the Cambodian government has provided an environment that is not unfriendly to the private sector. Cambodia offers generous tax holidays in comparison to the investment regimes of other countries in the region, according to Hing.[11] These holidays take the form of a complete exemption from the 20 per cent corporate tax on profit. The exemption period begins from the first year in which the project becomes profitable (but before the offset of losses).[12] The duration of these holiday periods can be up to nine years.[13] There is also a precedent for extensions of tax holidays. In June 2006, the Council of Ministers extended the corporate tax holiday on garment factories registered before 14 March 2005 by two years.[14]

However, this apparently laissez-faire attitude is to some degree counteracted by two further factors: the informal costs of doing business in Cambodia and the costs imposed by indirect failures of governance, such as poor health services and infrastructure. Indirect failures of governance can in part be explained in terms of historical failures to collect tax, facilitated by the inflow of large amounts of foreign aid to Cambodia. Cambodia's formal tax revenues, in the period between 2002 and 2006 for which data is available, never exceeded 8.2 per cent of GDP. This is an abysmal figure by world standards and on a par with Niger, Tanzania and Togo.[15] During the same period, Thailand bottomed at 15 per cent, while Indonesia and the Philippines never went under 12 per cent. This is also reflected in an anaemic domestic revenue performance.

Cambodia offers investor-friendly tax holidays that substitute a formal system of taxation for an informal one in which contributions are made from Okhnas and advisors in lieu of formal taxes on businesses. Indeed, were the informal payments (inclusive of corruption) to be converted to formal payments, revenues as a percentage of GDP would be within international norms, and

---

[11] Hing Thoraxy, "Cambodia Country Report by Dr. Hing Thoraxy," Foreign Direct Investment: Opportunities and Challenges for Cambodia, Laos and Vietnam, Hanoi, 16–17 August 2002 (Phnom Penh: Cambodian Investment Board, Council for the Development of Cambodia, 2002), 5. Available: http://www.imf.org/external/pubs/ft/seminar/2002/fdi/eng/pdf/thoraxy.pdf.
[12] http://www.embassyofcambodia.org.nz/investment.htm.
[13] Erik Wasson and Kay Kimsong, "Tax Holiday Extended, Bond Market Approved," *The Cambodia Daily*, June 17–18 2006.
[14] Ibid.
[15] All revenue and tax figures come from International Monetary Fund staff country reports cited in World Bank and ADB, "Cambodia: Enhancing Service Delivery through Improved Resource Allocation and Institutional Reform. Integrated Fiduciary Assessment and Public Expenditure Review," Report No. 25611 KH (Washington, DC and Manila: World Bank and the Asian Development Bank, September 8, 2003), ix. Available: http://www-wds.worldbank.org/servlet/WDS_IBank_Servlet?pcont=details&eid=000090341_20030924104425.

Cambodia could lessen its aid dependency. Anecdotal evidence suggests that authorities have consistently prioritized contributions from Oknhas, Advisors and their aspirants[16] over facilitating the payment of taxes to the point of a niche industry being created for the payment of taxes which, for a garment factory, costs approximately $35 per payment.[17] Tax payments, which must be in local currency, are notoriously difficult to make as officials cannot be bothered to count the cash and require taxpayers to wait in line for a day.[18] This has led to businesses specializing in facilitating tax payments for a fee, such as a money-changer (17)[19] who processes hundreds of tax payments for businesses and trades $2–3 million per day from a rented storefront. She confided that her business only pays $100 in taxes per month.

Action by government in fostering a functioning tax collection system runs counter to interests in safeguarding informal revenue streams. Aid flows have facilitated this strategy by providing a back-up flow of cash, particularly into the service sector, in line with Feyzioglu et al.'s (1998)[20] findings which show a negative empirical link in cross-country comparisons between aid flows and tax revenues. The problem with this strategy is that it reduces domestic pressure for accountability.[21] Bribe taxes enable a regime of low tax revenue collection to become sustainable – indeed, they make it less likely that tax reform will occur since doing so would threaten vested interests and also remove an income stream that benefits not only the state but the party.[22]

A study of 800 private sector firms throughout the country by the World Bank[23] revealed that 76 per cent of the firms surveyed identify at least some

[16] As Craig and Pak discuss in Chapter 11, Prime Minister Hun Sen has told a story about a king with three officials looking for ways to collect revenues – and after two of them tried taxing people and failed dismally, the third just went around all the businessmen and asked each one for a gift and raised the money in no time.

[17] Garment Factory Owner (26).

[18] One leading NGO with exceedingly close ties to the government had to appeal directly to the Prime Minister when it too suffered difficulties paying its employees' payroll taxes. An official later came in person to the NGO to apologize and it has not since had difficulties making payments, but this is more the exception than the rule.

[19] This chapter is based upon research interviews with 58 key informants drawn from government and the private sector.

[20] T. Feyzioglu, S. Vinaya, and Z. Min, "A Panel Data Analysis of the Fungibility of Foreign Aid," *World Bank Economic Review*, 121, (1998): 29–58.

[21] Paul Collier and David Dollar, "Development effectiveness: what have we learnt?" *The Economic Journal*, 114.496, (2004): F263.

[22] See also Sok Hach, "The Political Economy of Development in Cambodia: How to Untie the Gordian Knot of Poverty?" *Political Economy of Development* (Phnom Penh: Economic Institute of Cambodia, October-December 2005): 3. Available: http://www.eicambodia.org/downloads/files/ER10_politicaldevelopment.pdf.

[23] World Bank, *Cambodia at the Crossroads: Strengthening Accountability to Reduce Poverty*, Report No. 30636-KH, East Asia and the Pacific Region (Washington, DC: World Bank, November 15, 2004). Available: http://siteresources.worldbank.org/INTCAMBODIA/Resources/1-report.pdf.

of the laws and regulations affecting them as "unpredictable". The report also found that 80 per cent of sampled firms acknowledged having to pay bribes, while 71 per cent of large firms had to make frequent unofficial payments. The report calculated the so-called "bribe tax" to be 5.2 per cent of total sales revenue, although the term was changed to "unofficial payments" throughout the main text before publication.[24] The same report proffered an estimate of $120 million in corruption. Calavan et al. (2004),[25] writing a descriptive report for the United States Agency for International Development, estimated between $300–500 million, which could be as much as 12.5 per cent. Given such gloomy realities, one must still wonder how Cambodia managed to grow at double-digit rates in recent years. The unpacking of this mystery through two sectors will help elucidate what works, what may or may not work, and what doesn't work.

Rice and Garments in the Cambodian Context.

Both rice and garments were identified in 2005 in *Cambodia and WTO: A Guide for Business* published by the Ministry of Commerce (MoC) and the Mekong Project Development Facility (MPDF) of the International Finance Corporation as being potential export sectors, although the report was careful to note that "The selection of an industry does not mean that it, more than one not selected, is likely to be successful at exporting."[26] These sectors provide a success story and an emerging story by way of comparison and contrast. The next section of this chapter examines the ways in which each sector has managed to establish itself in the challenging governance environment, and the outlook and implications for governance and growth.

The garment sector: a Cambodian success story?

Two sectors, garments and tourism accounting for around 14 per cent of GDP each, have clearly stood out in the past decade for their tremendous contribution

---

[24] The find and replace feature missed (perhaps intentionally) one instance on page 97, although even that instance has been typed over (though a search will still find the term bribe tax).
[25] M. Calavan, S. Briquets, and J. O'Brien, "Cambodia Corruption Assessment," Prepared for United States Agency for International Development (Phnom Penh: USAID Cambodia and Casals & Associates, May-June, submitted August 19, 2004).
[26] MoC and MPDF, "Cambodia and the WTO: A Guide for Business" (Phnom Penh: Ministry of Commerce and Mekong Private Sector Development Facility, March 2005), 3. Available: http://www.mpdf.org/images/en/content/E3/Wed-Apr-20-03-16-11-CST-2005.pdf.

to growth. According to the Economic Institute of Cambodia, the garment sector has added an estimated 2 per cent annually to GDP since 1995, although this is tapering off.[27] The garment sector emerged in response to US trade preferences. In 1998–1999, the Clinton administration developed the US–Cambodian Trade Agreement on Textiles and Apparel (1999–2004), which linked market access (increasing quota) to labour standards. Cambodia is the only country where a trade-labour arrangement was agreed to and implemented, securing it a quota for exports to the US.[28] In addition, the Cambodian garment industry benefited from diversification effects, i.e. garment buyers seeking to diversify their sources, and from regional effects, i.e. being located in a region which is strongly engaged in textiles and garments. [29]

US trade preferences were made conditional on improving labour standards. Cambodia became the first and so far only country in which International Labour Organization (ILO) monitoring of labour standards was made mandatory.[30] The ILO's *Better Factories Cambodia* programme was instituted to "improve working conditions in Cambodia's export garment factories" through "independent monitoring", "finding solutions", and making "suggestions to management, training, advice and information".[31] Monitoring is done twice a year against a 480-point checklist compiled from a variety of sources including the Cambodian Labour Law and a range of buyers' codes of conduct.

Apart from benefiting workers, the Cambodian system appealed to brands embracing ethical approaches to manufacturing and corporate social responsibility. In 2005, garment buyers played a key role in applying pressure on authorities for the release of five activists: a union leader, a radio host, two human rights activists, and a lawyer, all of whom had been imprisoned for exercising their freedom of expression. One of these freed human rights activists created the Human Rights Party not long after his release and won three National Assembly seats in the 2008 election. It baffled senior government officials to see

[27] EIC, *Export Diversification and Value Addition for Human Development: Addressing the Impact of the Agreement on Textile and Clothing Expiration on Cambodia* (Phnom Penh: Economic Institute of Cambodia, June 2007), 12.
[28] So unprecedented was this linkage that a Harvard Business School case study on the US-Cambodia agreement was produced, HBS, "Worker Rights and Global Trade: The US-Cambodia Bilateral Textile Trade Agreement," Case Study 9–703–034 (Cambridge, MA: Harvard Business School Press, Revised 4 November 2004).
[29] This section is drawn from the contribution of Verena Fritz to the World Bank mission's scoping note.
[30] The ILO monitoring system is currently being rolled out on a voluntary basis to several other countries – Vietnam, Jordan, and Lesotho.
[31] Better Factories Cambodia, "Twentieth Synthesis Report on Working Conditions in Cambodia's Garment Sector," (Phnom Penh: Kingdom Of Cambodia International Labour Organization Better Factories Cambodia, 30 April 2008), 1. Available: http://www.betterfactories.org/content/documents/1/20th%20Synthesis%20Report%20Final%20(EN).pdf.

freedom of expression linked to labour and garment buyers, but the perception of human rights abuses can impact business.[32]

To date, Cambodia captures only a relatively limited share of the value chain and enjoys little value addition. Cambodia is only involved at the "Cut, Make, and Trim" phase of the value chain. Almost all inputs for the sector are imported, and the country does not have a textiles industry. More than 95 per cent of garment factories are foreign owned, and a significant part of the profits are repatriated. Direct contributions to the government budget have been limited since the sector enjoys import tax exemptions as well as tax holidays. In June 2006, 180 out of 270 firms then operating (specifically those firms which had applied for licences before 14 March 2005) became eligible for an additional two years of tax holiday when the Council of Ministers acted to support the industry in light of increasing competition from Vietnam and China.[33]

Nonetheless, the benefits to Cambodia have been substantial in terms of direct and indirect job creation and in terms of boosting overall GDP. Garments account for up to 80 per cent of recorded exports, for 350,000 direct and about the same number of indirect jobs. According to *Better Factories Cambodia*,[34] almost three quarters of the garment workforce are employed in large factories of 1,000 or more workers. Of these factories, about 175 are affiliated with a particular brand (with Walmart, Gap, and H&M as major players).[35] The percentage of women workers in these factories is 92.2 per cent.[36] Workers were employed at a legally mandated minimum wage of US$55 a month plus a $6 bonus to offset inflation.

Currently, the sector is under pressure. A significant slowdown of garments exports to the US was recorded for Q4 2007 and Q1 2008, but overall 2008 ended with a 7 per cent increase to US$3.15 billion.[37] A combination of factors weigh on Cambodian competitiveness in garments: productivity is lower than in key competitor countries, while some costs are higher (mainly: informal payments/bribes, transportation, electricity, and costs related to labour disputes), and its key US market is expected to undergo a recession (70+ per cent of garment

[32] For more on this, see Sophal Ear, "Change and Continuity in Cambodian Human Rights and Freedom of Expression: Learning from Experience," Report for Pact Cambodia Final Draft Revised 26 May 2006. Available: http://csua.berkeley.edu/~sophal/pact/pact.pdf.
[33] AP, "Cambodia Gives Garment Cos. Tax Holiday," Associated Press, 16 June 2006.
[34] Better Factories Cambodia, Twentieth Synthesis Report on Working Conditions in Cambodia's Garment Sector, 3.
[35] Labour organization management (28).
[36] Better Factories Cambodia, Twentieth Synthesis Report on Working Conditions in Cambodia's Garment Sector, 5.
[37] Xinhua News Agency, "Cambodian Garment Exports up 7% in 2008," 18 February 2009, online at http://news.xinhuanet.com/english/2009-02/18/content_10838964.htm, accessed 14 September 2011.

exports are destined for the US). The high cost and the unreliability of electricity is an issue for factories using the national grid as well as for those using their own diesel generators.

Key constraints facing the sector fall into three groups. External constraints include a slowdown in international demand due to worldwide recession. Internal constraints include those that are directly governance related, such as the high cost of export and facilitation, due to demands from the economic police of the Ministry of Interior for charges related to trucking goods to the port of Sihanoukville; formal and informal charges demanded by customs officials; and charges demanded by CamControl, an arm of the Ministry of Commerce created to monitor the quality of exports and imports under World Trade Organization rules. It is unclear where bribes begin and formal payments end because so much is left to the discretion of individuals who have bid for their government post and form only a small part of an overall pyramid of payments. Other internal constraints include those that are indirectly governance related, such as high labour turnover (partly due to poor public health services);[38] high cost and unreliable electricity supply; and high transport costs. Also included in the category of indirectly governance related constraints is the high number of strikes regarded by many as a symptom of the international regulatory regime, and of the Cambodian government's sponsorship of a range of unions as a means to undermine the independent Free Trade Union Workers of the Kingdom of Cambodia.

The internal governance environment for the garment sector is characterized by sins of omission (benign neglect) rather than sins of commission (active obstruction of activities through crippling demands for informal payments). During 1999 to 2004 Cambodia enjoyed preferential access to US markets, and taking advantage of this had two pay-offs for the Cambodian government: "looking good" at the international level (and in particular in its relations with the US), and the fact that the quota regime offered considerable rents. The garment sector offers insights into Mushtaq Khan's theory of "how patron–client networks . . . have allowed some types of value-enhancing economic transformations and prevented other types".[39] Allowing the garment sector to emerge was therefore a "win–win" situation for the Cambodian government.

---

[38] Factory Owner (26) also pointed to demographics of the industry – young 20-something women who will want to marry sooner rather than later (much to the owner's chagrin). The growth of the garment industry itself has social implications which are profound and contested. Is working in a garment factory a golden opportunity or rapacious exploitation? Is the only thing worse than being exploited *not* being exploited? Unfortunately, such normative questions are beyond the scope of this chapter.

[39] Mushtaq Khan, "The state and economic development: what role, what risks?" An ODI Poverty and Public Policy Group Event (London: Overseas Development Institute, November 22, 2006), 18. Available: http://www.odi.org.uk/events/states_nov06/ODI%20State%20and%20Development.pdf.

Even so, how did the garment industry establish itself in the challenging business environment of Cambodia? While some of Cambodia's Okhnas certainly have interests in garments, not one can be named as owning a garment factory. Foreigners have not generally invested in Okhna relations, seeing little benefit from any insertion into a patronage-based peerage system that means little to them. One garment factory owner (27) complained "Oknhas have done nothing to help. They have no money, no knowledge." The head of the industry's trade group, the Garment Manufacturers Association of Cambodia (GMAC), is Van Sou Ieng, a Sino-Khmer who was born in Cambodia, graduated from a French university in 1976, and has had a career in banking and finance (1979–1983), stocks and securities (1980–1986), and textiles (since 1986).[40] Indeed, while he lists his nationality literally as "Cambodia",[41] he found himself hard pressed to speak or deliver a speech in Khmer in May 2005 at the launch of the Cambodian Economic Association at which he was a speaker. Such is the foreign character of the garment sector itself, a character that may have helped insulate the industry from capture.[42]

Furthermore, the prevalence of such "outsiders" in the garment business has also offered greater potential for social capital formation through horizontal associational links when compared to domestically-based sectors, and individual owners in the sector have lobbied collectively for their interests, via GMAC.[43] GMAC was successful in persuading the government to award it an official role in the export of garments. Because of this, garment factories wishing to export must be members of GMAC, awarding the association authority in its dealings with the government. Furthermore, playing this key role in exports awards GMAC a key role as agent for the industry in the collection or negotiation of rents.

GMAC emerged as a result of the foreign nature of the sector: key actors within it have fewer pre-existing ties to facilitate individual deals, rendering collective action more attractive. GMAC's own website describes the "symbiotic cooperation between the garment manufacturers and the Royal Government

---

[40] Van Sou Ieng, "Biography of Mr. Van Sou Ieng" e-mail from an informant November 9, 2008.

[41] http://www.gmac-cambodia.org/memberpop.asp?memberID=24.

[42] Both the Khmer diaspora in Western countries and Chinese expatriates play significant roles across different sectors. The garment industry has a very strong Chinese element; ethnic Cambodians will send their children to Chinese-language schools so that they can work in middle management at garment factories doing accounting for example. Moreover, there is a strong Chinese ethnic component to business in Cambodia, and more generally throughout Southeast Asia. Cambodians of Chinese ancestry include virtually the entire Phnom Penh Chamber of Commerce. For example, the modern rice mill operating in Cambodia is from a former Chinese-Cambodian businessman. Cham Prasidh is an ethnic Chinese Cambodian, as is the Minister of MAFF, Chan Sarun. Of course, while the manufacturers of garments are Asian, the "buyers" are Western.

[43] Garment Factory Owner (27).

Table 1. Agriculture in Cambodia 2000–2006

	2000	2001	2002	2003	2004	2005	2006
Agriculture, value added (per cent of GDP)	35.9	34.4	31.2	32.0	29.5	30.8	30.1
Agriculture, value added (annual per cent growth)	-0.4	3.6	-2.5	10.5	-0.9	15.7	5.5
Agricultural land (per cent of land area)	27.0	27.7	28.3	28.9	29.6	30.3	27.0
Employment in agriculture (per cent of total employment)	73.7	70.2	..	..	..	..	..
Rural population (per cent of total population)	83.1	82.5	82.0	81.4	80.9	80.3	79.7

Source: World Development Indicators Online. The World Bank, Washington, DC. Accessed 11 November 2008. Available for purchase: http://publications.worldbank.org/ecommerce/catalog/product?item_id=631625

of Cambodia (RGC) that has stood the test of time until today".[44] The sector is also relatively uniform: most players are of medium size and external and face an international environment that is demanding in terms of quality standards and competitiveness.

Consequently, the garment sector is an example of how Grindle's "good enough governance" can emerge in Cambodia. Particular features of the sector have allowed demands for improvements in governance that have at least had partial impact. Any such impact may have positive spill-over effects for other sectors. However, as the garment sector is struggling for survival, there is as yet little evidence that it has the potential to be a catalyst for other forms of light manufacturing.[45] The intense involvement of external stakeholders has been

---

[44] http://www.gmac-cambodia.org.

[45] In fact, the exports of shoes to major markets declined in value terms between the first trimester 2007 and the equivalent 2008 period by around 15 per cent according to MoC, "Estimated Cambodian Export Data Under GSP/MFN Scheme to the Main Markets," Ministry of Commerce, May 2008.

important in bringing about this success of employment-intensive ("shared") growth, from the US administration's design of trade preferences, to the role of the ILO, to the fact that most investors in the sector are foreign, to various donor projects to help improve the sector's productivity.

A special regime allowed the sector the space to develop its relative competitiveness. Now the sector faces new challenges in terms of rising costs and a declining market. Thus far, Cambodia's governance improvements have been largely incremental in nature. It is unclear whether a continued gradual approach to solving bigger and "lumpy" governance-related issues (power generation and labour relations) will succeed. Solving these issues will not only help the garment sector to survive and flourish, but remove significant barriers for other sectors, improving Cambodia's overall competitiveness. Given low government effectiveness and coherence to date, it is not clear whether this is feasible.

Rice: An emerging export sector?

In 2006, agriculture's value added as a percentage of GDP was 30.1 per cent, a decreasing share due to continued growth in garments and tourism. However, 80 per cent of Cambodians live in rural areas and depend on agriculture. There is a consensus that the development of agriculture and agro-processing are key for Cambodia's survival in the global economy[46] following the end of the preferential quotas for the export of garments to the United States and the European Union, which had made that industry Cambodia's largest foreign exchange earner. Table 1 summarizes the importance of agriculture in Cambodia since 2000. 2003 and 2005 were banner years for growth of value added in agriculture.

While the total cultivation acreage of rice has shrunk marginally, and agriculture itself has been shrinking in terms of value added to GDP (nearly 36 per cent in 2000), it still exceeds both tourism and garments combined. Rice as a share of

---

[46] See for example Martin Godfrey, "Youth Employment Policy in Developing and Transition Countries - Prevention as well as Cure," Social Protection Discussion Paper Series No. 0320, Social Protection Unit, Human Development Network, (Washington, DC: The World Bank, October 2003). Available: http://siteresources.worldbank.org/SOCIALPROTECTION/Resources/SP-Discussion-papers/Labour-Market-DP/0320.pdf; World Bank, *Cambodia at the Crossroads*; IMF, "Cambodia: 2004 Article IV Consultation," Country Report No. 04/328, (Washington DC: International Monetary Fund, October 22, 2004). Available: http://www.imf.org/external/pubs/ft/scr/2004/cr04328.pdf; RGC, "Address by Samdech Hun Sen on the "Rectangular Strategy" for Growth, Employment, Equity and Efficiency: First Cabinet Meeting of the Third Legislature of the National Assembly at the Office of the Council of Ministers," (Phnom Penh: Royal Government of Cambodia, July 16, 2004). Available: http://www.car.gov.kh/relatedtopic/rectangular%20strategy.htm; Bretton Sciaroni, "The State of the Private Sector," Remarks made at the Consultative Group Meeting, December 5–7, 2004. Available: http://www.cdc-crdb.gov.kh/cdc/7cg_meeting/7cg_document/the_state_private_sector.htm; NGO Forum, "NGO Statement to the 2002 Consultative Group Meeting on Cambodia," Phnom Penh, June 19–21, 2002. Available: http://www.ngoforum.org.kh/Development/Docs/ngo_2002/ngo_2002.htm.

GDP in agriculture is 22 per cent, but 78 per cent of rural households grow rice.[47] Rice is the most important staple for Cambodians and essential for food security reasons. The story of rice is in many ways the story of shifting from subsistence farming into agro-processing, an area of well-recognized value-addition that Cambodia has yet to tap effectively for a number of reasons, including but not limited to lack of credit, high electricity costs, corruption, and technology issues.

Growing rice is not a highly capital-intensive activity when irrigation is available (the use of diesel-powered pumps is otherwise needed), although milling rice requires energy, capital, know-how and transport. The sector was for many years domestically oriented, but has increasingly become export-driven because of world prices and surplus production in recent years. During the 1960s, Cambodia was one of the key rice-exporting nations in the world, exporting far more than Vietnam according to data from the United States Department of Agriculture, and falling third behind Thailand and the United States in terms of net exports of milled rice.[48] Today, Cambodia is a small official exporter, with Vietnam as its primary customer.

Indeed, the RGC announced that it would export 120,000 tons of rice to Guinea at a "friendship" price of $600 per ton.[49] While this is a major discount compared to international prices, it does not take into account that Cambodian rice is 35 per cent broken and is therefore considered low grade compared to long-grain Thai or Vietnamese rice, which is less than 5 per cent broken.[50] Regardless, intervening events saw the failure of the agreement for technical reasons: no agreed way of paying for the rice and Cambodia's refusal to send rice before payment was received. The same failure to consummate reportedly happened with a rice deal involving Senegal which was announced in April 2008.[51] Notably, a joint venture ballyhooed in 2009 between the publicly-owned Green Trade Corporation (GTC) and the Indonesian conglomerate Racharvali,

---

[47] Jehan Arulpagasam, Francesco Goletti, Tamar Manuelyan Atinc and Vera Songwe, "Trade in Sectors Important to the Poor: Rice in Cambodia and Vietnam and Cashmere in Mongolia," in Krumm, Kathie, and Homi Kharas, eds. *East Asia Integrates: A Trade Policy Agenda for Shared Growth* (Washington, DC: World Bank, 2004), 199. Available: http://lnweb18.worldbank.org/eap/eap.nsf/Attachments/Chapter+9/$File/chapter+9.pdf argue that in Cambodia and Vietnam, "Most of the poor earn a living by growing rice, and the rice culture permeates the farming traditions of the region." The title of their chapter underscores the importance of rice in promoting shared growth as Cambodia integrates into the world economy.

[48] http://www.irri.org/science/ricestat/data/may2008/WRS2008-Table12-USDA.pdf.

[49] AKP, "Guinea to Import Rice from Cambodia," Agence Kampuchea Presse, Phnom Penh, 3 July 2008.

[50] As a rice miller (36) put it: "For now we can still follow the old system and we can export to Africa. They don't demand much quality."

[51] Xinhua, "Cambodia grants sale of 6,000 tons broken rice to Senegal," www.chinaview.cn, April 23, 2008. Available: http://news.xinhuanet.com/english/2008-04/23/content_8036128.htm.

said to have the potential to pump $300–500 million dollars to set up rice-processing plants in Cambodia,[52] has since evaporated.

Both Kuwait's and Qatar's Prime Ministers visited Cambodia in 2008 and Prime Minister Hun Sen visited Kuwait in January 2009. Referring to both countries on 6 August 2008, Hun Sen said "Those countries have oil but no rice . . . I think the Gulf can become our rice market."[53] His announcement came one day after the Kuwaiti Prime Minister's visit in which both countries discussed swapping technical assistance for arable land for the cultivation of quality rice for Kuwait.[54] Cambodia is in talks with several Asian (including South Korea and the Philippines) and Middle Eastern (including Kuwait and Qatar) governments to receive as much as $3 billion in agricultural investment in return for millions of hectares in land concessions to be leased for between 70 and 90 years,[55] according to Suos Yara, under-secretary of state responsible for economic co-operation at the Council of Ministers. It is not impossible to imagine that Asian and Middle Eastern investors (sovereign or otherwise) could become the external drivers of good enough governance in Cambodia's agricultural development. During Hun Sen's visit to Kuwait in January 2009, Foreign Minister Hor Namhong reported that the Kuwaiti government signed a Memorandum of Understanding with Cambodia to construct a $350 million hydropower dam and irrigation system in Kompong Thom province. The dam will be built in Kompong Svay district on the Steng Sen River, will produce 40 Megawatts for the surrounding area, and provide irrigation for 130,000 hectares of rice land,[56] all of which could come into service for rice cultivation for Kuwait.[57]

Nine million Cambodians engage in rice production, making collective action difficult if not impossible. The structure of the milling industry is rather opaque. It is known that there are several big rice millers; there used to be many small ones, but recently most of the small millers have gone out of business and trade paddy rice to Vietnam for milling. Of the remaining 200–300 rice mills said to exist,[58] there is little evidence that their owners are themselves Oknhas, at least not at any higher rate than entrepreneurs of similar small and

---

[52] Ros Soketh and Paul Vireze, "Green Trade Plans Venture With Indonesian Firm," *The Cambodia Daily*, 15 August 2008, 29.

[53] As quoted in DPA, "Kuwaitis to return to Cambodia for rice talks – Summary," Deutsche-Presse-Agentur, 6 August 2008.

[54] DPA, Kuwaitis to return to Cambodia for rice talks – Summary.

[55] Raphael Minder, "Cambodia holds land deal talks," *The Financial Times*, 20 November 2008. Available: http://www.ft.com/cms/s/0/2506f3c6-b72e-11dd-8e01-0000779fd18c.html.

[56] Leopard Cambodia Fund, "In the News," Monthly Newsletter Issue 9, January 2009.

[57] Nick Paton Walsh, "Cambodia farm land sold to wealthy nations," Channel4 News, January 29, 2009. Available: http://www.channel4.com/news/articles/politics/international_politics/cambodia+farm+land+sold+to+wealthy+nations/2914582.

[58] Estimates vary, but this figure has been cited by Economic Researcher (20).

medium enterprises. As a Rice Miller (36) lamented "Oknha ... do not invest in any long term business, they only invest in business that give them profit tomorrow." Indeed, if immediate profitability is any indicator, only a handful of Oknhas are known to operate in the sector, one of whom, Neak Oknha Men Sarun (who is also a CPP Senator), owns a flour mill which is believed to also include a rice mill and would fit his role as a rice wholesaler who has historically sold to the Cambodian military.[59] One of the leading rice millers is an Oknha, while another heads the state-owned GTC. Aside from these, the structure of the industry is described as one of many "small potatoes" and "little guys"; "the ones who grow" are reported to be "foreigners or well-connected domestics".[60] Rice is estimated to enjoy an internal rate of return of around 20 per cent,[61] a respectable rate anywhere else, but in Cambodia land speculation had, until recently, been far more profitable. One informant reported that there is one big rice mill with both government and Oknha involvement, while another big mill exports aromatic rice (50,000 tons per annum).[62] One bank official interviewed did say that although currently there is not much lending for agro-processing, it is preparing to move into this direction and preparing to lend money for the development of a rice mill with a 50 per cent government guarantee.[63]

It has been reported that there exists a Mafia-like element in the rice sector. One NGO rice expert made inquiries about buying rice to export to another Association of Southeast Asian Nations (ASEAN) member some years ago, and allegedly received a threatening phone call telling him to stop his activities or he and his family would be in danger. The victim believes he knows the politically-connected mastermind behind the threats, as this individual's company exported to the same ASEAN country already and did not want competition. For his own safety, he stopped further inquiries about exports. The important point to note here is that, given the atomized structure of the industry, there are relatively few Oknhas in the rice sector. This means that both the large investment and operating capital needed to build a state-of-the-art rice mill and purchase paddy rice in significant quantities may have to come from outside Cambodia, and indeed indications are that French investors have stepped up with a $20 million rice mill in Udong, while the $350 million Kuwaiti deal is said to involve securing large quantities of rice exports as Cambodia's repayment terms to Kuwait.

As in the garment sector, constraints in the rice sector may be (1) external or purely technical; (2) directly governance related; or (3) indirectly governance

---

[59] http://www.mensarun.com.kh/Aboutmessage.htm.
[60] Economic Researcher (20).
[61] Economic Researcher (20).
[62] Agricultural Adviser (30).
[63] Banker (14).

related. In the first category, Cambodia's comparatively low yields compared to its neighbours are caused by: poor soils, low extension and research capacity, and low capacity to export due to inability to meet hygiene standards. Better governance could improve all these things. In the second category, a heavy burden of informal payments affects enterprises above a certain size, along with informal charges for exporting via Sihanoukville. In the third category fall problems such as the lack of irrigation, the high cost of factors of production due to poor infrastructure and the failure to erect systems to help farmers meet export standards. High energy costs represent an important constraint on rice milling, preventing Cambodian millers from competing with their counterparts in Vietnam or Thailand. Consequently, Cambodian farmers export raw paddy; this earns invaluable income for farmers, but robs Cambodia of the ability to add value to the raw commodity.

Like garments, economic rents must invariably be shared with the economic police during the transport of rice within Cambodia; customs officials control the borders so any official or unofficial export must also go through them; line ministries such as Agriculture, Forestry and Fisheries no doubt play another important role in rent-seeking. As of 26 May 2008 through at least 31 December 2008, when a two month ban was partially lifted on the export of rice, the Ministry of Commerce controlled all exports of rice in excess of 100 tons. A 1.6 million tons export quota was announced, and exports of more than 100 tons had to be approved by the MoC. Only two entities were granted permission to export in excess of 100 tons *without* a licence: the MoC's public enterprise, GTC, and its partner, the National Cambodian Rice Millers Association, headed, as it happens, by the director of GTC. Shortly thereafter, Angkor Kasekam Roongroeung (AKR), a private rice miller that has successfully exported to Europe, obtained a licence through its governmental channels, which include Ministry of Agriculture, Fisheries, and Forestry Minister Chan Sarun, who is also an owner of AKR.

Having learned from its experience with garments whereby the MoC became a "Governance Focal Monopoly" for the garment industry (fostering "dialogue and coordination among public and private elites in which confidence is inextricably created on a basis that is simultaneously interpersonal, process-based and institutionalized)",[64] the MoC is acting not just as a gatekeeper, but as seller of rice between Cambodia and the international system. As of this writing, it is unclear whether an export licence is still required as informants reported that

[64] Nicolas Miesel and Jacques Ould Aoudia, "Is 'Good Governance' a Good Development Strategy?" Working Paper 58, Agence Francaise de Developpement (Paris: AFD, January 2008), 38. Available: http://www.afd.fr/jahia/webdav/site/myjahiasite/users/admirecherche/public/DT/WP_58_GB_pour_mise_en_ligne.pdf.

a meeting with Deputy Prime Minister Keat Chhon, who is in charge of the overall economy, in early January resulted in a decision to remove rice export licensing requirements from the MoC.[65]

International rice prices increased significantly in 2007 and 2008. This very strong increase was a surprise and a problem as it led to speculation and hoarding as well as a ban on exports to India and Vietnam (since lifted). Expectations are that prices will remain relatively high, although lower than their peak in the spring of 2008. Ultimately, whether Cambodians grasp the day with rice exports will depend largely on the rice millers of the country being able to exploit opportunities. Realistically, the prospects are not particularly encouraging at this stage. Collective action in rice has thus far not produced the results that were evident in garments as early as 1996 when an informal group banded together to create what would become GMAC. Garments benefited from externally imposed institutions like Better Factories and the Arbitration Council that incentivized buyers' willingness to purchase from Cambodia, initially because of the Multi Fibre Arrangement (MFA),[66] and later because of membership of the World Trade Organization (WTO).[67] While the rice sector has millers' associations that are still fighting for legitimacy, it does not have a certifying entity that could facilitate exports. There is patchy awareness of Everything But Arms (EBA), an initiative of the European Union under which all imports to the EU from Least Developed Countries such as Cambodia are duty free and quota free, with the exception of armaments, until September 2009. EBA entered into force on 5 March 2001 and represents export opportunity for Cambodia. But awareness of this opportunity is insufficient to prompt the rice sector to make the leap from domestic to export-quality production.

Moreover, there is disagreement over how much rice is actually exported as there are no reliable figures currently in existence. Export practices are quite visible: large quantities of rice are shipped on barges to Vietnam and Thailand. Since 2000, the surplus has clearly increased. There is now also a major shift in

---

[65] Given the opacity of how Cambodian policy is made and implemented (see Sophal Ear, "The Political Economy of Pro-Poor Livestock Policy in Cambodia," Pro-Poor Policy Livestock Initiative Working Paper No. 26 (Rome: Food and Agriculture Organization of the United Nations, August 2005), 16. Available: http://www.fao.org/ag/againfo/projects/en/pplpi/docarc/wp26.pdf some informants dismissed the decision as irrelevant given the nature of ministerial fiefdoms. In other words, it remains to be seen how the decision of an unpublicized meeting would, in fact, be implemented.

[66] Also known as the Agreement on Textiles and Clothing (ATC), the MFA governed the world trade in textiles and garments from 1974 through 2004. It imposed quotas on the amount developing countries could export to developed countries and expired on 1 January 2005.

[67] The WTO is a global international organization that deals with the rules of trade between nations. Its stated goal is to help producers of goods and services, exporters and importers conduct their business.

focus underway among donor programs, from food security to a more market-focused approach.

Outlook and Implications for Governance and Growth

Minister of Commerce Cham Prasidh initiated a Trade Sector-Wide Approach Program (SWAP) to consolidate ongoing trade and trade-related reforms to contribute more significantly to job creation, investment promotion, supply capacity enhancement and thus economic growth. This Program, it is intended, will adopt an integrated approach to policy development, capacity building, institutional reform and implementation through improved governance and accountability.[68] Government is said to be taking serious measures to support this initiative. The SWAP also involves the Ministry of Industry Mines and Energy and the Ministry of Agriculture, Forestry and Fisheries. The SWAP as such provides a framework, under which the government will then develop various concrete projects with specific donors. A second SWAP is also being prepared on Agriculture and Water, involving 10 Development Partners. Donors and government are also seeking to link up trade and agriculture efforts. While MAFF does not really have incentives to engage in these activities, it is keen to increase its role on Sanitary and Phytosanitary measures,which would give it gatekeeper (read discretionary) power over rice exports.

Currently, the SPS regime is fragmented and competition around it between MAFF and MoC's CamControl is a repeat of what is known to have happened with livestock, where CamControl sought to take charge of SPS over the objections of MAFF.[69] While CamControl is the quality control arm of the MoC, launched for the purpose of WTO-compliance which the MoC championed and for which the MoC is the focal ministry, other line ministries like MAFF do not feel that the MoC has the right to venture into its technical "turf" since the MoC has no technical expertise. More control over the SPS regime invariably means more rent-seeking opportunities for MAFF at the expense of the MoC.

What is apparent is that Cambodia will need to find buyers in order to clear markets.[70] These could be in China, the Philippines, Africa and India. While

---

[68] Cham Prasidh has also led the Garment sector's evolution and is now involved in trying to introduce textile manufacturing. As a manager of a labour organization (28) reported, "If anyone can move things forward to the next level, it would be him."

[69] See Sophal Ear, The Political Economy of Pro-Poor Livestock Policy in Cambodia.

[70] Agricultural Advisor (30) and Rice Miller (46): "Yes, it is a good opportunity that Cambodian rice will be allowed to import into EU without tax. But in the meantime, we should be ready to be strong in seeking partners who can provide funds to purchase rice for export."

EBA makes Europe more attractive, it is less likely to be a key market given that demand for long-grain rice is not strong there. Cambodia's 2–2.5-million-ton rice surplus, if this is an accurate estimate, would place Cambodia among the top exporters in the world currently. Several rice informants agreed that the challenge is how to produce large quantities of milled rice of a consistent quality.[71]

Like garment buyers, rice buyers will play an important role in stimulating investment as well as signalling what level of certification buyers want, whether it be broken rice (which can be used to make rice flour), organic rice, paddy rice, husked rice, semi-milled rice, etc. This offers interesting parallels to garments. However, the rice sector does not have a certifying/audit mechanism like Better Factories, a dispute-resolution mechanism like the Arbitration Council set up to mediate labour relations in garment factories, or strong leadership via an association like GMAC.

Currently, Cambodian exporters who wish to meet SPS for the export of rice can hire the services of a testing labouratory such as Intertek Testing Services (Cambodia) Co Ltd. The difference between Intertek and Better Factories is simple: Better Factories was externally imposed and provides a kind of public good subsidized by donors. Moreover, membership in GMAC is required for export, and membership in GMAC requires compliance with Better Factories. Intertek is merely one of a handful of Inspection, Testing & Evaluation Services firms in Cambodia for which compliance with SPS by exporting Cambodian agricultural firms is not subsidized by any donors and is certainly not cost-free. SPS, while required for export, costs each individual firm in fees for testing and acquisition of technical know-how.

Conclusion[72]

Garments and rice are two sectors that could be promising in Cambodia. One is already vibrant (garments) and one might be emerging (rice). Comparing these two sectors has underscored the importance of good enough governance for growth and how governance can improve and support growth in some sectors and not others. This helps explain the paradox of double-digit growth with relatively poor governance.

The garment industry is an example of good enough governance, where the Government (in particular the Ministry of Commerce) and firms (coordinated

---

[71] Rice Buyer (47), Agriculture and Agricultural Advisor (30), and Rice Miller (49).
[72] I thank Stephane Guimbert for allowing me to draw from his work, World Bank, *Sustaining Rapid Growth*, for this section.

by GMAC) worked together to create an environment that generated growth. The strategic vision developed by the RGC, with the US Government, helped align expectations for investors. The link to export quotas and the supervision by the ILO helped establish the credibility of these higher expectations. The rents for Government from managing quotas (which ended in 2005 as the MFA was dismantled) increased incentives. Subsequently, the existence of a strong and capable business association, GMAC, helped sustain support to the industry and create a sense of security, given GMAC's capacity to get things done with the RGC. This is for instance evidenced in the capacity of this hand-in-hand relationship to reduce trade costs, at a time when these costs were still increasing for other industries.

The roles of international drivers, foreign investors, domestic collective action mechanisms, and high stakes seem to have been critical in these achievements. External pressure was instrumental in creating the opportunity for growth in the sector. The Government's response was probably driven by the high stakes, with a very labour-intensive sector (now employing circa 350,000 workers) and significant rents from the quotas. Coordination within Government (which is often challenging given its fragmented nature) was ensured through the dialogue monopolized by the Ministry of Commerce and GMAC. Foreign investors helped sustain the Government's focus on the sector. GMAC became a pathway to solve collective action problems and maintain the necessary close relationship with the Government.

While Okhnas are sometimes captains of industry and at other times Godfathers in a Mafia economy, in garments they never played so much as a cameo role. No doubt the land on which many a garment factory is located is probably owned by an Oknha, but the factory itself is not. In rice, there are a few Oknhas of some prominence, but clearly they are outnumbered by hundreds of rice millers who have neither the means nor the inclination to obtain the title of Oknha. These millers are interested in finding the working capital to buy paddy rice for processing and to invest in new milling equipment from Thailand or Vietnam.

Indeed, rice has been limited to small amounts of milled exports, despite much larger unofficial exports of paddy rice. The recent dramatic increase in rice prices might provide the incentives to develop a hand-in-hand relationship between a champion in Government and a domestic industry, possibly – based on lessons from the garment sector – with a role for third-party monitoring and foreign investors. If nothing else, the growing interest from foreign countries in the Middle East and Europe in Cambodia's rice sector bodes well for internationalizing the character and technical capacity of rice production in Cambodia.

Author's Note

Funding for a longer version of this chapter, which also examined the livestock sector, was provided by the World Bank–Netherlands Partnership Program. This chapter would not have been possible without the help of Vannarith Chheang. For the longer version, I thank Verena Fritz, Stephane Guimbert, Kai Kaiser and anonymous reviewer(s) from the UK Department for International Development for comments. I thank Verena Fritz, Pak Kimchoeun, Pete Pin, and Stephane Guimbert for allowing me draw from their considerable insights; Sopheary Ou and Jim Chhor for research assistance, and most of all, the more than 50 informants willing to speak to me during my visits to Cambodia on a wide-ranging, sometimes maddening set of topics. For help before, during and after my visits to Cambodia, I am grateful to Huot Chea and Peng Seng. The views expressed are mine alone and do not necessarily reflect the views of the World Bank, its Executive Directors, the Department of the Navy, the Department of Defense, or the US Government.

Appendix: List of Informants

Note: The titles below have been generalized to prevent identification of informants. For example, several informants were heads of trade associations, which would make their identities obvious. Also, government officials do not have their ministries listed for the same reason. The number in parenthesis following that informant's title descriptor throughout the text now appears to the left of the list below and is randomly assigned.

Informants

1. Cambodian Economist
2. Management of International Conglomerate
3. Donor Staff Member
4. Member of Parliament
5. Livestock Expert
6. Entrepreneur and former Secretary of State
7. Travel Agency Owner
8. Head of a Government Department
9. Ambassador
10. Research Advisor, Higher Education (Public)
11. Research Advisor, Higher Education (Public)
12. Civil Servant
13. Ministry of Health Advisor
14. Banker
15. Banker
16. Donor Representative
17. Money-Changer

18. Sihanoukville Port Official
19. Sihanoukville Entrepreneur
20. Economic Researcher(s)
21. Banker
22. Head of a Government Department
23. Management of a Domestic Conglomerate
24. Management of a Private University
25. Associate Dean at a Private University
26. Garment Factory Owner
27. Garment Factory Owner
28. Labour Organization Management
29. Labour Union Leader
30. Agricultural Advisor
31. Donor Representative
32. NGO Economic Program Officer
33. Embassy Official
34. Agricultural Advisor to Minister
35. Agricultural and Livestock Expert
36. Rice Miller
37. Hotel Assistant Sales Manager
38. NGO Livestock Representative
39. NGO Rice Expert
40. Head of a Government Department
41. Deputy Head of a Government Department
42. Assistant Head of a Government Department
43. Rice Mill Floor Manager
44. Livestock NGO Representative
45. Livestock NGO Representative
46. Rice Miller
47. Rice Buyer
48. Travel Agency Owner
49. Rice Miller
50. Ambassador
51. Head of a Government Department
52. Senior Advisor
53. Advisor
54. Newspaper Editor
55. Veterinarian and Livestock Advisor
56. Post-Conflict Reconstruction Expert
57. Forestry Expert
58. Entrepreneur and CPP Member

5

The Privatization of Cambodia's Rubber Industry

Margaret Slocomb

In global terms, Cambodia is a minor natural rubber producer, contributing less than one per cent of the total product traded annually on international markets. Domestically, however, the rubber industry has always been regarded as a major contributor to national economic development, particularly in relation to its role as a reliable earner of foreign exchange. Cambodians are rightly proud of the achievements of their rubber industry, reputed to have once had the finest quality product and the highest yields in the world. The soil and climate of the eastern highlands and plateaux are ideal for the cultivation of *hevea brasiliensis*. Before the First Indochina War intervened, the rubber estates of highly capitalized French companies covering almost 70,000 hectares in the provinces of Kompong Cham, Kompong Thom and Kratie produced around one- third of total rubber exports from Indochina. During the decades of protracted civil war and failed social revolution, the rubber industry survived but suffered particularly from lack of investment in capital stock and replanting. Since 1993, as part of the macro-economic reform process, Cambodia's rubber industry has undergone a major transformation. This process coincided with a sustained period of strong commodity price growth stemming from weakening competition from the petroleum-based synthetic rubber product and the ever-increasing demand for raw materials from the People's Republic of China. It was argued that the Cambodian rubber industry, for so long in decline, might again play an important role in the country's economic development.

This paper argues that a revitalized rubber industry can, if properly managed, make an important contribution to the national economy, not only in terms of trade and revenue-raising, but also in terms of employment and skilling for the fast-growing and increasingly landless rural population. It examines (a) the reform agenda that has been adopted with relation to the industry and the progress of that agenda to the end of 2007, and (b) the scale and nature of the external assistance that has driven the reforms. In particular, it attempts to analyse the response of key stakeholders in the industry to the pressures for change that are conditional on the provision of that assistance. Lastly, it considers the role the state might play *vis-à-vis* the rubber industry after the plantations have been privatized.

Rationale

Cambodia's rubber industry was developed along monopolistic lines and in accordance with the general principles of French colonization as they were applied in Indochina before the Second World War. It was founded almost exclusively on the large estate model, unlike the one adopted in the Dutch East Indies and Malaya, for example, where the indigenous smallholder had a stake in the industry equal to that of the plantations. The typical agricultural estate model is capital extensive and labour intensive; large initial capital outlays are recouped from profits that are dependent upon high labour productivity. Cambodia's seven state-owned rubber plantations, currently scheduled for privatization as part of the broader macro-economic reform process, were originally created by French joint stock companies on this typical estate model and as separate industrial enclaves. They jealously guarded their autonomy and discouraged pressure from the Protectorate administration for labour reforms while, at the same time, using their substantial political power to successfully lobby the Metropolitan government for protective subsidies that would buffer them against economic shocks, such as that of the Great Slump of the early 1930s.[1]

Independence in 1953 had little effect on the way the industry was structured. The plantations remained in the hands of the big French companies. A handful of large European trading companies, in collusion with numerous local businessmen, ethnic Chinese for the most part, controlled the country's import – export operations. In an effort to put a halt to the lucrative manipulation of the rules and regulations of foreign exchange operations by these business interests, the Royal government, in 1963, nationalized trade, along with banking and insurance, and thus assumed control of rubber exports. A mixed-economy enterprise, Sonexim (*la Société Nationale d'Exportation et d'Importation*), was created and given responsibility for the trade monopoly. Although the highly unpopular nationalisation policy was revoked in 1968 at the initiative of Sirik Matak, and formally ratified by a *kram* or decree one month before he instigated the *coup d'état* in 1970, the new Republican government retained its monopoly

---

[1] For details of the rubber industry in the French colonial period, refer to Margaret Slocomb, *Colons and Coolies: the development of Cambodia's rubber plantations*, (Bangkok: White Lotus, 2007).

Table 2. Situation of Rubber Cultivation at 31 December 1968

Province	Area (hectares)			Production (kilograms)
	in yield	not in yield	total planted	
Battambang	–	20	20	–
Kompong Cham	39,619	17,578	57,197	46,835,667
Kompong Thom	80	54	134	36,255
Kampot	–	178	178	–
Ratanakiri	–	3,932	3,932	–
Kratie	3,471	1,275	4,746	4,125,465
Sihanoukville	214	157	371	87,008
Preah Vihear	–	88	88	–
Total	**43,384**	**23,282**	**66,666**	**51,084,395**

Of this total:

State Plantations = 4,547 ha of which

Ratanakiri	3,323
Kompong Cham	1,136
Preah Vihear	88

Family Plantations = 11,144.80 ha of which

Battambang	20
Kompong Cham	10,127.43
Kompong Thom	14
Kampot	178
Ratanakiri	609.57
Kratie	195.80

The rest are held by large private companies.

Source: ANC, Box 469, Royaume du Cambodge, Direction de l'Agriculture, Division de Statistique Agricole, *Rapport Annuel: l'Agriculture Cambodgienne en 1968–69.*

rights over the exports of rubber, along with those of rice and derivatives, maize, and precious or semi-precious stones.[2] It did so despite the organized and persistent lobbying efforts of the local business elite who had backed the coup, as well as pressure from the Khmer Republic's major donor, the United States of America, which typically rewarded successive market liberalization measures adopted by the government with generous military aid packages.

The Cambodian rubber industry reached its peak in the mid-1960s. Throughout the highly productive years from 1957 to 1966 rubber consistently accounted for around one-third of Cambodia's total exports; in some years, the value of rubber exports surpassed even those of rice and derivatives, Cambodia's export staple, despite the fact that the international market for natural rubber had been seriously affected by competition from the synthetic rubber industry that evolved in the aftermath of the Second World War. The value of this industry to Cambodia's image of itself as a modern, industrializing, independent nation in this period cannot be overstated.

The last figures for the state of the industry and for agriculture generally before war and revolution intervened are for 1968–1969. It had been a year of severe drought, so rubber production had fallen by around five per cent compared with the previous year to 51,084 metric tons (MT) and all except five per cent of total production was exported. The report from the *Direction de l'Agriculture* noted that 66,666 hectares were planted with hevea trees, or 1,300 hectares more than the previous year. In April and May 1969, however, US – RVN military aircraft sprayed a large area of the rubber plantations in Kompong Cham province with the defoliant "Agent Orange" and the damage was expected to further affect production in the following year.[3] By then, of course, the Second Indochina War would engulf much of the Cambodian countryside; the bulletin of the Cambodian Chamber of Commerce later reported that the rubber plantations had effectively stopped all activity by April 1970.[4]

Table 2, contained in the above report, illustrates the situation of the rubber industry on 31 December 1968. It shows the overwhelming influence of the big, foreign-owned plantations in Kompong Cham province and their vast size in proportion to the rest of the industry. At the same time, it indicates that an indigenous industry had grown strongly since independence, quite spontaneously

---

[2] *Kram* No. 426/70 of 12 February 1970, modifying *Kram* No. 149-CE of 16 November 1963. These decrees are published in the *Bulletin de Chambre Mixte de Commerce et d'Agriculture de Cambodge*, 17 February 1970, copy held in the State Archives of Cambodia (ANC), Box 165.

[3] For details of damage caused by the US–RVN (United States–Republic of Vietnam) aircraft, see Andrew Wells-Dang, "Agent Orange in Cambodia: the 1969 defoliation in Kampong Cham," online at http://www.ffrd.org/AgentOrange/cam1969.htm.

[4] The *Bulletin* (see n.2 above) was renamed *Le Cambodge Economique* in May 1970. Details are in issue of 17 November 1970.

and close to the perimeters of the large plantations, with a combined total of state plantations[5] and family plantations accounting for 15,691.80 ha or almost one-quarter of the total area under rubber cultivation.

Despite the optimism that usually accompanied government statistics before 1970, however, Cambodia's rubber industry was already in urgent need of major structural overhaul. The French economist Rémy Prud'homme warned in 1967 that natural rubber producers would not survive the challenge from synthetic rubber unless they reduced their production costs. The excellence of the redlands and the quality of organization on the plantations would, he believed, guarantee very high yields and steady growth, but labour productivity was stagnating, and given that labour was the main cost element for the industry, this was cause for concern. He believed that the prospects were not good and that annual foreign exchange earnings from rubber would stabilize at the then current level of around USD20 million, being insufficient to meet Cambodia's increasing need for foreign exchange.[6]

The plantations owned by the large private companies[7] referred to in the report quoted above were eventually nationalized in June 1974 by the United Front Revolutionary government that renamed itself Democratic Kampuchea in April 1975.[8] The plantations survived the civil war and revolution; in fact, a refugee told Charles Twining who monitored the economy of Democratic Kampuchea that the Khmer Rouge had maintained the rubber plantations quite well and had even exported relatively large quantities of latex product to Singapore.[9] The post-1979 government of the People's Republic of Kampuchea, desperate for foreign exchange, quickly re-established the plantations as state-owned enterprises, and by 1988 it claimed that the industry was producing 30,000MT of rubber from an area of 40,000 hectares, with a combined labour force of 26,000 workers.[10]

---

[5] The state plantations of the Sangkum period were chiefly at Tapao in Kompong Cham, an established plantation that was donated to the Royal government by France, and at Labansiek in Ratanakiri. The Labansiek plantation is still worked by solidarity groups.

[6] Rémy Prud'homme, *L'Économie du Cambodge* (Paris: Presses Universitaires de France, 1969), 152. Please note that American currency is denoted USD and Cambodian currency, the riel, is denoted as KR.

[7] The five companies were *Compagnie [des Caoutchoucs] du Cambodge* (Chup complex), *Société des Plantations Réunies de Mimot* (Memot complex), *Compagnie des Caoutchoucs du Mékong* (Stung Trâng complex), *Société des Plantations de Kratie* (Snoul), and *Société des Caoutchoucs de Kompong Thom* (Chamcar Andong and Chamcar Leu). See *Photo Souvenirs Du Cambodge - Sangkum Reastr Niyum - Agriculture, 1955–1969*, 89–90.

[8] George Hildebrand and Gareth Porter, *Cambodia: Starvation & Revolution,* (New York: Monthly Review Press, 1976), 92.

[9] Charles H. Twining, "The Economy," in Karl D. Jackson, ed., *Cambodia 1975–1978: Rendezvous with Death,* (Princeton: Princeton University Press, 1989), 135.

[10] Quoting figures from the General Direction of Rubber Plantations, Grant Curtis, *A Country Profile*: a *report prepared for the Swedish International Development Authority*, August 1989, 75.

Therefore, when the macro-economic reform process began in 1993, the rubber industry was still viable, although it was operating at a much-reduced level of productivity because most of the trees were old, as were the processing factories and other capital stock. After allowing for labour and other costs, the state plantations' combined annual contribution to the treasury was regularly around only one million dollars. On the other hand, there were four justifiable and sound reasons for maintaining the industry. In quick summary, these reasons are as follows: thanks to practically ideal natural conditions for the production of high quality latex, Cambodia had a long-established reputation on international rubber markets; the existing infrastructure, while dilapidated and under-financed, still reflected a proven capability of returning much-needed revenue to the state in foreign trade earnings; Cambodian technicians had the knowledge, experience and expertise to support the industry; a skilled workforce already existed and there was a further labour pool that could be accessed in the vicinity of the plantations.

It is fair to say, then, that in the climate of high demand for natural rubber that preceded the global financial crisis in the last quarter of 2008, a revitalised Cambodian rubber industry could indeed be expected to satisfy some of the demands of creditors and donors to diversify and expand the export sector, one of the cornerstones of the liberal market reform process that the Cambodian economy is undergoing. According to World Bank analysis, "As a small country competing in a globally-integrated, dynamic, and fast growing region, Cambodia's private sector-led growth strategy must be anchored in trade."[11]

Progress of the Reform Agenda

In September 1994, almost exactly one year after the Royal Government of Cambodia declared a commitment to public sector reform, it issued a sub-decree "on the Creation of a National Permanent Commission for Coordinating Privatization and the Promotion of Rubber Plantations".[12] The high-level commission was charged with setting up guidelines for the process of privatization, negotiating and coordinating agreements with domestic and foreign partners, and for preparing documents pertaining to the privatization of the plantations. The first of seven state-owned rubber plantations, Chup, was eventually

---

[11] World Bank Group, "Cambodia: seizing the global opportunity: investment climate assessment and reform strategy," August 2004, in Oum Sothea and Sok Hach, *Cambodia Economic Watch*, Issue 1, 2nd edn., Economic Institute of Cambodia, October 2004, 95–112.

[12] Royal Government of Cambodia, *Anukret No. 52/ANK/BK*, 6 September 1994. Ministry of Commerce, online at http://www.moc.gov.kh/laws_regulation/part8_sustainable/ank52_94_rubber.htm.

privatized in 2006; three more, Chamcar Andong, Boeung Ket and Memot, were submitted for tender in May 2007. Thus, even allowing for the intervening periods of political instability which undoubtedly retarded the process, the divestment of the state's prime agricultural assets, with total capital stock valued in 2001 at approximately USD150 million (KR420 billion), has been inordinately slow.[13] More importantly, the process has been conducted if not in secrecy then certainly without sufficient regard for public scrutiny that might satisfy criteria for transparency. While debate raged throughout the 1990s over corruption and exploitative practices in other major export industries, namely logging and garment manufacturing, civil society, particularly the local media, paid almost no attention to the ambiguous proprietary status of the rubber plantations or the uncertain future of thousands of rubber workers, their families and other plantation employees.[14]

In the head count of public sector employees conducted in early 1995, it was estimated that around 21,000 people were employed on the state's rubber plantations. The major donors judged this to be a heavy burden on the government's payroll, given that the plantations themselves were said to be in poor condition. Consequently, the Asian Development Bank made "development of a divestment plan for state-owned rubber estates" one of the fourteen policy measures that had to be undertaken for provision of a "soft" loan worth USD30 million to fund the government's Agriculture Sector Programme, delivered in two tranches in December 1996 and September 2001.[15] In the proposal it submitted for the loan, the Ministry of Economy and Finance noted that as nearly two-thirds of the total staff of the Ministry of Agriculture, Forestry and Fishery (MAFF) were employed in the rubber sector, it recommended that some of the counterpart funds in the loan be used to provide compensation to 17,500 workers who would be dismissed, combined with long-term leases of land for those who chose to continue cultivating rubber on a smallholder basis.[16]

External assistance to the plan for the development of smallholdings was provided by the French government in the form of the Smallholder Rubber Plantation Project (1999–2012) that has operations throughout Kompong Cham province in proximity to the big plantations. The project helps the participating

---

[13] A World Bank review quoted by the ADB, "Program Performance Audit Report on the Agriculture Sector Program (loan 1445-CAM[SF]) in Cambodia," July 2003, online at http://www.adb.org/ Documents/PPARs/ CAM/PPARCAM_27154.pdf.

[14] This criticism is levelled particularly at the English-language press which has much more genuine autonomy than newspapers and other media that are produced locally.

[15] ADB, "Program Performance Audit Report on the Agriculture Sector Program (loan 1445-CAM[SF]) in Cambodia," July 2003. Delivery of the second tranche was tied to preparation of the divestment plan.

[16] Ibid. Appendix 2 (dated 17 May 1996) of the completion report for loan No. 1445-CAM (SF), online at http://www.adb.org/Documents/PCRS/CAM/ln286–01.pdf.

farmers, the vast majority of whom own between two and five hectares, to secure formal title to their land, and provides long-term credit on generous terms; it also guarantees that the smallholder receives high quality rubber clones and ongoing technical support. In addition, the French Development Bank (*la Caisse Française de Développement*) made an early grant of USD5 million to help with the rationalization of the industry, and a French research organization gave considerable assistance to the re-establishment of the Cambodian Rubber Research Institute (CRRI) after a hiatus of twenty-five years. A major outcome of the rationalization assistance is that Cambodia itself is finally able to certify the quality of the rubber it produces and to sell it directly on to the international market. Previously, all rubber was sold through Vietnam which processed Cambodia's rubber for export; this represented an annual loss of approximately USD8 million from the real value of rubber exports.[17] A national rubber association was admitted to the International Rubber Association, and the CRRI was formally recognized as a regional certification body. After 2008 Cambodian rubber was marketed under its own label. These rationalization measures, in conjunction with the country's liberal investment law, represent attractive incentives for both domestic and foreign investment in the industry.

In 1999, all the state-owned rubber plantations were incorporated. According to separate sub-decrees, the estates of Chup, Peam Cheang, Boeung Ket, Krek, Memot (all in Kompong Cham province), Snoul (in Kratie), and Chamcar Andong (Kompong Thom province) became rubber plantation companies, with stock and shares still totally owned by the government but managed by separate boards of directors with full autonomy in financial transactions and day-to-day affairs. Their total concession area was estimated to be about 63,000 hectares, of which 68 per cent or 43,000 hectares were planted, although not necessarily providing a yield, as the ten-year regeneration programme that commenced in 1995 meant that saplings had not yet reached maturity. The largest, best maintained and thus most valuable of these corporations was the Chup Rubber Company.

The *Compagnie des Caoutchoucs du Cambodge* had established this plantation complex on two lots, one of 18,000 hectares and the other of 4,966 hectares, according to a provisional concession awarded in February 1922.[18] By 1930, the total area was worked as four estates: Chup (4,136.65 ha), Thmar Pitt [Pich] (5,190.75 ha), Peam Cheang (4,966 ha), and Chrap (2,332.70 ha), each with its own director and managed independently from each other, according to

---

[17] Daniel Ten Kate and Kay Kimsong, "France to Help Certify Rubber," *The Cambodia Daily*, 29 April 2004.
[18] ANC, RSC File 1108, "Report on the material and spiritual situation of the Tonkinese émigrés employed on the plantations of the *Compagnie du Cambodge* and *du Syndicat de Mimot*." Confidential. *Inspection des Affaires Politiques et Administratives*, 28 April 1927.

instructions from company headquarters based in Saigon. The combined workforce, all imported from Tonkin or Annam, was then 4,192 and overwhelmingly (91 per cent) male.[19] The indentured workers, housed in barracks, laboured a ten-hour day, with four free days per month, and received a ration of 700 grams of rice per working day in addition to wages that, before the economic slump forced a reduction, was a standard 40 centimes per day (30 centimes for women). Close to the Mekong and in a relatively populated area, these were the best managed of all the colonial rubber estates. In 1967, the last year for which plantation figures are available before nationalization, the *Compagnie des Caoutchoucs du Cambodge* had planted 21,261.60 ha and, apart from forty-five French nationals, it employed a fully indigenous workforce of 7,739 that, together with their families, represented around 20,000 people living in some thirty villages on the complex of plantations.[20]

It is interesting to compare these figures with those recorded in two studies conducted in 2001 and 2005 on the exploitation of child labour in the rubber sector; the first, conducted by the Center for Advanced Study (CAS), focused specifically on Chup while the other was a more general study carried out under the auspices of the International Labour Organization's International Programme on Elimination of Child Labour (ILO/IPEC).[21] Both relied to a considerable extent on information supplied by the General Department of Rubber Plantations of the agriculture ministry. The CAS study, using also written information from the management and statistics from the plantation's administration, described the Chup plantation as divided into three bases: Chup (3,220.16 ha), Thmar Pich (2,676.1 ha) and Chrap (1,932.15 ha).[22] This equals a total of 7,828.41 ha which is vastly less than the 21,000 hectares that were planted in 1967, or the 16,000 hectares in 1930, even allowing for the 5,000 hectares that make up Peam Cheang which will be privatized separately, or for the official claim that only 68 per cent of the plantations' total area is planted. These statistics lend weight to the claim that is often made by Cambodians close to the industry that the Cambodian People's Party has retained Thmar Pich plantation, or almost half of its original area according to the figures above, for its own purposes. Sources

[19] ANC, RSC File 9995, "A quarterly report on work in Kompong Cham plantations." No. 431CT from le Contrôleur du Travail to M. le Résident of France, Kompong Cham, 9 October 1930.
[20] *Photos-Souvenirs...*, 89.
[21] CAS, *Child Work and Child Labour at the Chub Rubber Plantation in Cambodia*, Phnom Penh, September 2001, webpage, online at http://www.cascambodia.org/child_plantation.htm and Ministry of Labour and Vocational Training and ILO/IPEC, "Experiences and Lessons Learned on Child Labour Monitoring: Rubber, Salt and Fishing Sectors in Cambodia," Phnom Penh, June 2005, online at http:// www.ilo.int/public/english/region/asro/ bangkok/library/download/pub05–13.pdf.
[22] The report does not state whether these figures are for total areas or for planted areas only. I assume that they are for planted areas.

say that it too will eventually be prepared for privatization, but, under these circumstances, it is unlikely that the process will be either transparent or of any benefit to the national treasury.

Otherwise, the privatization of the Chup Rubber Plantation Company has proceeded in a manner intended to act as a model for the divestment of the other SOREs (state-owned rubber enterprises). The privatization of the rubber industry is being conducted strictly according to "the letter of the law", despite or rather due to the fact that those laws have been dictated by the all-powerful executive arm of government and passed with little critical scrutiny from a weak and divided opposition in the National Assembly. Even the appropriation of Thmar Pich plantation by the ruling party (assuming that this is the case as it cannot be demonstrated and sources cannot be named) might be covered by Article 18 of the 1995 sub-decree "on Procedure for Privatization of Public Enterprise" which grants special privilege to employees and personnel who purchase their own enterprise or some part of their own enterprise's tangible properties.[23] While the process has observed all legal niceties, certainly enough to satisfy the major donors, this, however, seems not to have affected the way that big business has always been conducted in Cambodia since the colonial era. In the words of Cambodian economists Oum Sothea and Sok Hach, "Reform in Cambodia is difficult in an atmosphere where the state is 'captured' and manipulated by a group of elite to shape institutions and to control information and media reports in an effort to protect their own benefits at the expense of the social interest."[24]

As a corporation, from 1999 to the end of 2006, the Chup Rubber Plantation Company was an autonomous public entity. Thus, while it could manage its own finances and was responsible for covering any losses it incurred, management was governed by a board of directors that was dominated by government representatives selected from the Ministries of Finance and Agriculture, and from the Council of Ministers. The chief executive officer of Chup Rubber Company was Oknha Mok Kim Hong, a wealthy businessman with close ties to the ruling party. In August 2000, the prime minister declared the development of family-scale rubber plantations to be government policy and ordered the MAFF to speed up development of plantations throughout the country. In accordance with this policy and under the direction of Oknha Mok Kim Hong, the company purchased and developed the stock to create the 6,200-hectare Tumring plantation in Sandan district of Kompong Thom province. Approximately two-thirds of the total area was allocated to the company for industrial

---

[23] Royal Government, ANK 38 ANK/April 19, 1995. Html version of file online at http://www.mlmupc.gov.kh/ mlm/docout.php?ID=387.
[24] Oum Sothea and Sok Hach, *Cambodia Economic Watch*, 1: 69.

planting and the remainder to villagers for family-scale rubber production. Despite the fact that a major reason for privatising the SOREs was their general debilitation and consequent failure to generate much revenue for the state, there was no public discussion of Chup's investment in Tumring or the source of funds invested, even though Chup was still, according to law, a publicly owned entity and the new rubber plantation of 4,359 hectares would require an initial capital investment of at least USD10 million.[25] Presumably, the Tumring Plantation was included in the portfolio of Chup's assets when the corporation was submitted for private tender. The technologically advanced latex processing plant at Chup was owned and run by the Mong Retthy Group, also closely associated with the ruling political party, so it would be interesting to know how it fared after the corporation was privatized. The experimental station of the CRRI with around 500 hectares of heveas is also located in the grounds of Chup.

In short, far more is known about Chup than about any of the other six plantation companies that are to be privatized, yet what is publicly known about the privatization of the Chup Rubber Company is so slight as to be almost meaningless. The French company SOFRECO was named as the "privatization consultant" in the Letter of Invitation posted in the Cambodian press at the end of May 2007 calling for tenders for the sale of Chamcar Andong, Boeung Ket and Memot plantations. This advertisement signalled that Chup, the forerunner, had completed the privatization process, but the economic mission of the French embassy in Cambodia, on its website posted in mid-November 2006 observed, "The process of privatization, however, does not seem to have started."[26]

The State's Role Post-privatization

In June 2007, Cambodia hosted the Third Asean Rubber Conference in Phnom Penh. With 400 participants, this was the largest meeting ever held of producers in the region, which accounts for almost all the world's natural rubber production. The mood was buoyant as rubber was then returning record prices on the international market; from USD500 a metric ton in 2001, the price in mid-2007 had risen to around USD2,000/MT (and a year later it would be more than

---

[25] The unit price for planting and incubation (6 years) of heveas was calculated as USD2,460/ha in the Marubeni proposal, to be discussed later. This would put the cost of the Tumring plantation at around USD10 million, not counting the cost of the latex processing plant and other infrastructure. See *Summary for Rubber Tree Afforestation in Mondul Kiri Province, Cambodia*, Marubeni Corporation, March 2004, online at http://www.gec.jp/gec/en/Activities/cdm/FS200317SE.pdf.

[26] Ambassade de France au Cambodge, Mission Economique, *Le caoutchouc au Cambodge*, 14 November 2006, online at http://www.afd.fr/jahia...fiche-caoutchouc.pdf.

USD3,000/MT, before plunging to new lows following the downturn in late 2008[27]). At the conference, the secretary of state in charge of rubber, Teng Lao, predicted that the area of hevea-culture in Cambodia would more than double by the year 2015 to 150,000 hectares, with commensurate production of 150,000 tonnes.[28]

Some foreign investors have already expressed an interest in developing rubber plantations in Cambodia. Recent past experience involving the abuse of the land concession system in relation to Cambodia's forestry industry, however, has made most ordinary Cambodians sceptical of the motives of large-scale land developers. So far, two concessions, each within the legal limit of 10,000 hectares, have been awarded in the northeast provinces of Ratanakiri and Mondolkiri.[29] Under an agreement between the governments of Cambodia and Vietnam, six companies under the umbrella of the Vietnam Rubber Group, including the prestigious Phu Rieng and Tan Binh rubber companies, have also been allocated over 22,000 hectares of land in eastern Cambodia for plantation development. The Vietnamese companies have complained of costly land reclamation, a lack of skilled workers, materials and machines, as well as "hindrances" from import procedures.[30] Opposition party leader, Sam Rainsy, while agreeing in principle with the privatization of the rubber industry warned that any deal struck with investors should also include guarantees that plantation workers would not be fired or evicted. "If they want to buy the plantation and fire the workers," he is quoted as saying, "then it is a sign that they just want land or to cut down the trees."[31]

The crucial issue of labour has been absent from the process of privatization. It is a glaring omission from the requirements of the divestment plan that the ADB outlined, or from representation on the boards of directors of the rubber companies in the corporation stage, and from the heady ambitions of

---

[27] The Economist Intelligence Unit expected a fall of 44 per cent in average prices for rubber in 2009, as a result of the downturn in the global automotive sector and the improved competitiveness of synthetic rubber. Webpage, online at http://www.eiuresources.com, accessed 9 February 2009.

[28] Kay Kimsong, "Experts at Asean Conference See Bright Future for Rubber Market," *The Cambodia Daily*, 16–17 June 2007.

[29] The Heng Brothers Co. will develop a plantation in Ratanakiri while the Marubeni Corporation intends to develop a rubber plantation as a carbon sink in Mondolkiri. See *Cambodia's Family Trees*, Global Witness report, June 2007, online at http://www.globalwitness.org or Peter Leuprecht, *Land Concessions for economic purposes in Cambodia: a human rights perspective*, COHCHR, November 2004.

[30] VietnamNet, "Rubber group to expand plantation in Cambodia," *Business in Brief* 10/1/2008, online at http://english.vietnamnet.vn/biz/2008/01/763511/.

[31] Prak Chan Thul and John Maloy, "Government Wants To Privatize Rubber Plantations," *The Cambodia Daily*, 23 May 2007.

government ministers to vastly expand the area cultivated with rubber trees.[32] Labour, and specifically labour productivity, however, is the single most important determinant of viability for the rubber industry and especially for one based on the large estate model. Forty years ago, Rémy Prud'homme warned that the almost perfect natural conditions for hevea cultivation in Cambodia and the quality of the plantations' organization were insufficient to sustain profits unless labour productivity improved. The chaos that resulted from war and revolution masked that persistent flaw in the industry. History suggests, however, that privatization will not prove to be a panacea for the stagnation that has afflicted the industry for the past thirty years, and investors will soon discover that cheap labour, in itself, is not a cost advantage if productivity levels remain low.

Working conditions for the tappers and their families employed on Cambodia's rubber plantations today are not fundamentally different from those under which the indentured Tonkinese laboured in the 1920s and 1930s. The ten-hour day, the work regimen, the dependency on the company for shelter and food rations, and even the tools of the trade are the same. From interviews CAS researchers had with workers at Chup in 2001, they estimated that average earnings for a worker, depending on the season, were between USD30–40 per month, plus 44 kilograms of rice (including the children's allowance) and that the average household income was USD55–72 per month. More than half the monthly income was spent on food and rice and most families had no financial reserves. There was almost no community life in the plantation villages and everything, including schooling for the children and health care, was organized by the company. The work tools were basic: a tapping knife, a billhook, ceramic bowls, buckets, a scraper, and a ladder. At Chamcar Andong plantation, this author saw tappers use lengths of string to guide the flow of latex and a carefully placed leaf to direct it into the bowl.

While the relationship between management and worker may at best be described as paternalistic, with outsiders it is intimidating and sometimes violent. Most villagers in the CAS study were convinced that the Chup Rubber Company would never allow organizations from outside to work in the area. The ILO/IPEC report concurred with this, noting, "Because of these difficult conditions and the semi-autonomous management, no development organizations have

---

[32] The letter signed by the Minister of Finance appended to the proposal for the Agriculture Sector Programme loan claimed, ". . . only about ten per cent of potentially productive rubber land is currently under cultivation so the scope for expansion of rubber . . . is substantial." In May 2008, the Prime Minister said, ". . . the size of [the] rubber planting area is insignificant compared to its total potential area, especially on red basalt soil areas which cover more than 300,000 hectares in Cambodia." *Cambodia New Vision*, webpage, online at http://www.cnv.org.kh/2008_releases/07may08_sandan_rubber_tumring_speech.htm.

ever worked in the rubber plantation ... Labour inspectors or other social services have never monitored the plantation work ...". According to the management, in 1998 Chup created the Independent Trade Union of Cambodian Labourers, representing all 4,666 staff and workers, led by seven representatives of both employer and employees; the workers who were interviewed by CAS researchers, however, said they were unaware of its existence.

Rubber workers who have heard rumours about the government's plans for the privatization of the plantations fear eviction. Early in 2002, military police dismantled and then removed more than one hundred houses in a village attached to Chamcar Andong plantation, leaving homeless those rubber workers who had lost their jobs once the plantation cut down and sold the trees they used to work.[33] Many families who tap and weed the plantations and live in the plantation villages have no land of their own. Some of them were already working on the plantations in the 1980s when land redistribution was conducted in their home villages so they did not receive an allocation, while others took refuge in the plantations during the conscription drive for the K5 defence campaign because rubber workers were exempt from military service and the rights to the land they had previously occupied lapsed. More recently, impoverished and landless farmers from neighbouring Prey Veng province have created villages on the outskirts of the plantations and earn a small income by scavenging rubber scraps that they sell to middlemen. If caught, they suffer terrible penalties and sometimes death.[34]

Under such primitive conditions, labour productivity on the plantations can only stagnate. Once the state has divested itself of direct responsibility for financing and managing these enterprises, however, it can play the more constructive role of guaranteeing Cambodia's competitive advantage in the industry by taking steps to improve productivity, along the lines of those already adopted in the country's textile and garment manufacturing sector. In relation to labour, these steps include regular inspection by trained officers under the auspices of the International Labour Organization, enforcement of the 1997 Labour Law, and respect for workers' rights under international labour law to organize and bargain collectively for safe and improved working conditions and pay. There are historical precedents to support arguments for state intervention in this aspect of plantation management. In particular, the implementation of Varenne's Labour Code in 1927 rationalized employment conditions through the agency of a labour inspectorate that equalized conditions of employment

---

[33] Phann Ana and Matt McKinney, "Jobless Rubber Workers Evicted From Homes," *The Cambodia Daily*, 22 March 2002.

[34] Porter Barron, "Teen Suspected of Stealing Resin Shot Dead," *The Cambodia Daily*, 2 December 2003 and Chhim Sopheak and Lasse Karner, "Young Man Killed While Trying To Steal Rubber," *The Cambodia Daily*, 21 September 2005.

throughout Indochina's rubber plantations, thereby stabilizing the industry and boosting productivity levels.³⁵

Unfortunately, labour relations on the Cambodian rubber plantations have changed very little since that period of reform more than eighty years ago. Workers who are not free to bargain collectively are, therefore, at a severe disadvantage to deal with the changes that privatization must entail. Moreover, the current economic landscape offers scant hope that the state will adopt a responsible role once the process is completed. The World Bank Group report of August 2004 highlighted the lack of key institutions, most notably the rule of law, and attempts by the government to fill the institutional vacuum through administrative measures that have largely not worked, and instead have created opportunities for corruption.³⁶ At the same time, the report proposed the challenge that Cambodia now faced an historic opportunity to change its growth path. The Royal Government of Cambodia has entered its second decade having held relatively stable elections, and in the broader context of a growing, stable and integrating East Asian region. This provides a good context to undertake a second generation of reform not focused on the establishment of a market economy, but on enabling broad-based growth. This, in turn, the report notes, must involve addressing the real costs and issues that reduce productivity and profitability for the private sector, as well as broadening the base of economic opportunity and jobs.

Conclusion

Cambodia's seven state-owned rubber plantations, despite their historical role in the modernization of the economy as a major earner of foreign exchange revenues, have always been secretive, potentially dangerous places. The original colonial proprietors, because of their vast wealth and commensurate influence in the *métropole*, exercised power over the Protectorate administration and won profitable advantages for their stockholders. Meanwhile, within those gated enclaves in the eastern provinces of the country, the indentured workers struggled against violent retribution and exploitation to access rights to minimal wages and conditions provided by the labour code. From the scant information that can be gleaned about the privatization process that commenced in 1993, it would seem that little has changed in the way the Cambodian rubber industry

---

35 ANC, *Arrêté*, signed by Alexandre Varenne, 25 October 1927, *Journal Officiél de l'Indochine Française*, 1927, 3033–3042.
36 World Bank Group, "Cambodia, Seizing the Global Opportunity: Investment Climate Assessment & Reform Strategy," August 2004, in *Cambodia Economic Watch*, 95–112 or online at http://siteresources.worldbank.org/INTCAMBODIA/Resources/Global-opportunity.pdf.

is managed. To date, only one of the seven plantations, Chup, has completed a process that has been inordinately slow, deliberately non-transparent and conflated with layerings of political influence and links to the wealthy business elite. There has been little or no organized opposition to the process, least of all from the plantation workers who were never consulted in the first place. The nexus of political power and big business remains very close, while the situation of labour is still one of impoverishment and oppression.

The economic outlook in Cambodia at present does not augur well for genuine private investment, and if the state does not intervene to improve labour relations in the privatized plantations, the availability of cheap labour, in itself, will not be sufficient to maintain Cambodia's cost advantages in the rubber industry.

6

Cashews, Cash and Capitalism in Northeast Cambodia

Jonathan Padwe

How have Cambodia's people experienced the economic transformation that is now taking place? This chapter investigates the specific implications of Cambodia's economic transformation for farming communities in the northeast highlands, in this case in Ratanakiri Province, and attempts to understand the transformation and its effects from the point of view of its inhabitants. In particular, I look at the case of Tang Kadon village – where some 270 people live in a cluster of longhouses perched just a few kilometres from Cambodia's border with Vietnam – and at one of the principal economic responses that highland farmers have given to the increasing integration of the highlands into the regional and global economy.[1] Faced with increasing land scarcity and the destabilization of longstanding tenure arrangements, farmers in Tang Kadon and elsewhere have intensified their agricultural system, taking advantage of the opportunity afforded by their increased access to roads and markets, and producing and selling cashew-nuts for the world market.

Recognizing the agency of farmers at Tang Kadon in adopting this strategy and linking their economic and social life to that of a global commodities market, I argue that the farmers at Tang Kadon have ushered in a series of changes with far-reaching *implications* for their society. In this chapter, I investigate several of those changes in detail. In particular, I explore the shift that farmers there have made from subsistence agriculture to market production, from an economy based on "multiple monies" to one in which modern money predominates, and from a common property regime to one based on the private ownership of land. These shifts represent striking reconfigurations of highland society which have occurred in a relatively short period of time, and which have

---

[1] Tang Kadon is a pseudonym for the village where I lived and conducted ethnographic field research from 2005 to 2007.

repercussions for individuals and institutions in the highlands well beyond the immediate economic transformation that they form a part of. To illustrate these repercussions, I look at changes to fallowing and land-management practices that have emerged in concert with the increasing privatization of landholding, and with the gradual displacement of reciprocal labour arrangements by paid wage labour. The availability of market goods, the increased availability of modern money, and new ways of displaying wealth and status have also contributed to the reconfiguration of village and household living arrangements: wealthier families have now left the traditional longhouses, and have used income generated by selling cashew to build "modern" single-family houses. At the same time, the changing nature of household income, especially where the sale of land and cashews is concerned, has had an impact on the inheritance system and on the position of women within the household.

In analyzing these reorderings, I seek to place the literature on agricultural intensification into conversation with the body of work in economic anthropology inaugurated by the economic historian Karl Polanyi. One of Polanyi's great insights was to demonstrate that society's adoption of the self-regulating market as both ideology and organizing societal principle is characterized by the "disembedding" of a series of productive relationships from their social context. Polanyi based his notion of disembedding on the understanding that social relations are created through the actions of people engaging in productive activity. The conversion of that activity to a series of economic transactions thus necessarily disrupts and reconfigures society.[2] I find value in the notion that the shift to market production of cashew at Tang Kadon has radically transformed a series of productive relationships governing land, labour and money.

However, this is only part of the story. Rather than see in these events a stark story of cash as the disintegrator of social bonds, it is important to bear in mind the re-embedding that occurs, as new social relationships form in response to new conditions. Furthermore, no great effort is necessary to recognize that previous forms of social relationships were similarly open to inequality and domination. The widespread use of bonded labour and the participation of highlanders in reciprocal slaving raids in highlands in the nineteenth and early twentieth centuries attest to this. Finally, rather than view the current transformation at Tang Kadon as a moment of cultural dissolution in the face of a totalizing modernization, it is important to recognize the place of the current encounter within the history of wrenching social changes that accompanied insurgency, war, the American bombing, and the radical project of the Khmer Rouge regime. The

---

[2] Karl Polanyi, *The Great Transformation: The Political and Economic Origins of Our Time* (Boston: Beacon Press, 1957 [1944]). Polanyi's work, including his notion of disembedding, has been met with numerous critiques. Later sections of this chapter engage these ideas explicitly.

changes that have occurred in Tang Kadon during this period are part of the larger political and economic transformation that has occurred in Cambodia as a whole. While many of the cultural and political forces that were put into motion by war and reconstruction remain important today, in Ratanakiri as in other parts of the country military and security concerns have largely ceded to market capitalism, economic integration, and "development" as dominant forces of social change. And although the region's inhabitants are surely glad for the end of armed conflict, no one here is under any misconception about who the beneficiaries of this transformation have been: the "peace dividend" has accrued almost fully to the political elite and their cronies.[3] Indeed, during the transition, the vast majority of the natural assets of this region have been transferred from the productive care of its inhabitants to the hands of the state and to those able to make claims on its power.

For this reason, the frontier in Ratanakiri is not the free-for-all that it sometimes appears to be. The ability of some to act with freedom comes at the expense of those who are largely powerless to act at all. In the midst of the rapid changes that have occurred here, officials from the Prime Minister on down have decried the "anarchic" plundering of the region's natural resources and the haphazard nature of land speculation. Those assertions notwithstanding, as the other papers in this collected volume seek to make clear, economic transitions generally – and markets in particular – do not occur in the absence of social regulation. Rather, the exercise of state power coupled with the actions of powerful individuals and firms has been critical to the production of the current transition.

From Post-war Transition to Economic Transformation in Northeast Cambodia

In Ratanakiri province, as in other parts of Cambodia where communities depend largely on forest resources for their livelihoods, two sequential extractive bonanzas have given expression to the transformation from a post-conflict mode of political and social organization to the present period dominated by the entrenchment of a particular set of capitalist economic and social relations. Thus the timber boom of the 1990s may be understood as a post-war power-grab funded through the rapid conversion of forest resources into cash and political

---

[3] A report that frames the transition from the post-war to the present period of transformation in this way is International Crisis Group, *Cambodia: The Elusive Peace Dividend* (Phnom Penh and Brussels: International Crisis Group, 2000), http://www.unhcr.org/refworld/docid/3ae6a6e74.html, accessed 11 March 2009.

capital. The current period, beginning around the turn of the century, is better understood as a land-grab undertaken in the name of economic improvement, one marked by the conversion of large areas of land – either inhabited or used extensively by communities – into the private property of well-placed individuals and well-connected national and international corporate firms and investors. In each case, the use of the institutions of the state, and the role of development partners and foreign investment interests, have been critical to the encouragement of the specific political – economic formations through which the business of extraction and dispossession has been accomplished.[4]

The shifts in the Cambodian political landscape that culminated in the signing of the Paris Peace Agreement in 1991 also set in motion the timber boom that swept through Cambodia's forests throughout the ensuing decade. As Philippe Le Billon and others have demonstrated, the rush on Cambodia's forests correlated not only with opportunities afforded by the end of hostilities in much of the country, but also represented efforts by competing factions to fund their attempts to gain and hold political power in an unstable political environment.[5] The effects on Cambodia's natural resources were notable. According to FAO figures, during a ten-year period beginning in 1990, forested land as a percentage of national territory had decreased by 8 per cent, a staggeringly high rate.[6]

By the end of the decade, the consolidation of power in the hands of the ruling party and its affiliated business interests had transformed the political and economic regime of the early 1990s. Even as the efforts of the donor community and internal reformers resulted in a moratorium on the operations of logging concessionaires, a significant shift was occurring in the modalities through which large-scale "asset stripping" of natural resources for private and political gain took place. Chief among these was the awarding of economic land concessions to private firms. These concessions are intended to be used for productive enterprises, including industrial agricultural plantations of acacia and eucalyptus, palm oil, cassava, sugar-cane, corn, rubber, teak and cashew.[7] Concessions for agricultural

---

[4] Caroline Hughes treats issues of political economy during the transition period in great detail. See Caroline Hughes, *The Political Economy of Cambodia's Transition, 1991–2001* (London and New York: RoutledgeCurzon, 2003).

[5] Philippe Le Billon, "The political ecology of transition in Cambodia 1989–1999: War, peace and forest exploitation," *Development and Change* 31 (2000), 801; Philippe Le Billon, "Logging in muddy waters: The politics of forest exploitation in Cambodia," *Critical Asian Studies* 34, 4 (2002): 563–586.

[6] Food and Agriculture Organisation, *Global Forest Resources Assessment 2005: Progress Towards Sustainable Forest Management* (Rome: Food and Agriculture Agency of the United Nations, 2005). All rates of change and percentages based on FAO figures derive from calculations using data from Global Tables 1 and 4 contained in the report and downloaded at http://www.fao.org/forestry/fra2005/en/, accessed 7 June 2009.

[7] NGO Forum, *Fast-wood Plantations, Economic Concessions and Local Livelihoods in Cambodia* (Phnom Penh: NGO Forum on Cambodia, 2006), 50–51.

and other purposes had been awarded under various laws throughout the 1990s, and in 2001 a new land law formalized the process, including a stipulation that concessions are not to exceed 10,000 hectares in size. In fact, many of the concessions granted to date do exceed that size (the Pheapimex concession in Pursat and Kampong Chhnang Provinces alone is over 300,000 hectares big), and in many cases the companies obtaining the 99-year leases on these lands have not paid any rent to the government for the use of the land. By 2003, the total amount of land granted in concessions was over 800,000 hectares, or 4 per cent of the country's land area.[8] It is thus not surprising that between 2000 and 2005 the rate of deforestation *increased*, and indeed accelerated dramatically. This five-year period saw another 10 per cent reduction in the amount of standing forest in Cambodia, with forested land as a percentage of total land area decreasing by 6.2 per cent, the third fastest rate worldwide.[9]

Economic Transformation as Seen from Tang Kadon Village: Cashews, Cash and Capitalism

It is within this political and economic context that the changes occurring in villages and towns throughout the highlands must be understood. Northeast Cambodia, which was nominally under Lao and Siamese control until the early twentieth century, has traditionally been a marginal buffer area separating Cambodia, Laos and Vietnam. The area was until recently sparsely populated, with the vast majority of inhabitants belonging to highland ethnic minority groups that spanned the national borders imposed by the French and modified over the course of a century of war and political manoeuvring. Highland people lived in small settlements and practised swidden agriculture, an extensive form of agriculture combined with forest management and heavy dependence on forest resources. Swidden farming relies on the cutting of new fields from forested land; these are used for several years, after which they are fallowed for long periods, reverting again to forest before being cleared again years later to begin the cycle anew.

The Vietnam Wars and the Khmer Rouge regime had a significant impact on highland villages in Cambodia, and brought highlanders into a great deal more contact with ethnic Khmers, especially in military and government. In this respect, the policies of the Lon Nol and some aspects of Khmer Rouge rule

---

[8] Special Representative for Human Rights in Cambodia, *Land Concessions for Economic Purposes in Cambodia: A Human Rights Perspective* (Phnom Penh: United Nations Cambodia Office of the High Commissioner for Human Rights, 2004). This figure represents a reduction from the high of over 900,000 hectares in 1999.

[9] FAO, *Global Forest Resources Assessment* 2005.

(notably emphases on modernization and relocation) echoed the "Khmerization" policies of Prince Sihanouk, who had encouraged the migration of lowland Khmers to the region in the 1960s.[10] Yet it was not until recently that significant numbers of ethnic Khmers from the lowlands began migrating to Ratanakiri and Mondulkiri provinces, where the great majority of Cambodia's highland minorities live. The economic transformation of the region has thus also seen a significant and rapid shift in its ethnic composition, too. While census data are too unreliable to serve as an indicator of the changes that are occurring in the highlands, the increasingly important presence of Khmer settlers is felt in even the most remote villages of the province.[11] Throughout Ratanakiri's district and commune centres small collections of Khmer-owned shops have increasingly transformed themselves into market centres dominated by recent arrivals to the province. Expanding government bureaucracies, a thriving NGO sector, and a host of entrepreneurial activities are dominated by ethnic Khmers, many of them first-generation migrants seeking opportunity on a rapidly changing frontier.

Deforestation, large-scale agricultural enterprises, improved road networks, and a rapidly increasing population have led to significant changes in land tenure and land use patterns, and have significantly transformed the economic and environmental conditions within which highlanders practise agriculture. These changes can be observed through remotely-sensed data, including aerial photographs and satellite images. Studies using historical aerial photography coupled with present-day imagery have documented the accelerating fragmentation of the landscape and the interruption of the former processes through which swidden fallows were allowed to return to forest.[12] Basing their observations on remotely-sensed data, Mund and Seyha suggest that "Over the last 10 years, major agricultural activities in [the] Cambodian upland[s] have changed from mainly swidden and shifting cultivation of smallholders to large-scale economic land concessions and the restitution of already existing plantations."[13]

[10] Ruth Bottomley, "Contested Forests: An Analysis of the Highlander Response to Logging, Ratanakiri Province, Nor theast Cambodia," *Critical Asian Studies*, 34.4 (2002), 590.

[11] Regarding the unreliability of population data for Ratanakiri, see Maria Backstrom, Jeremy Ironside, Gordon Paterson, Jonathan Padwe and Ian Baird, *Indigenous Traditional Legal Systems and Conflict Resolution in Ratanakiri and Mondulkiri Provinces, Cambodia* (Phnom Penh: United Nations Development Programme/Cambodian Ministry of Justice Legal and Judicial Reform Programme, 2006), 96.

[12] Jefferson Fox, "Understanding a dynamic landscape: Land use, land cover, and resource tenure in northeastern Cambodia," in Stephen Joseph Walsh and Kelley A. Crews-Meyer eds, *Linking People, Place, and Policy: A GIScience Approach*, eds. (Boston, Dordrecht and London: Springer, 2002), 113-130.

[13] Jan Peter Mund and Seyha Sok, "Mapping Land Cover Changes," paper presented at Tropentag 2007, (Witzenhausen, Germany: 9-11 October, 2007), online at http://www.tropentag.de/2007/proceedings/node355.html, accessed 8 June 2009.

Highland society is rapidly changing today, and many of these changes represent engagements with changing economic circumstances. While many accommodations have been imposed from without, highlanders have also sought to take advantage of new opportunities afforded by the expansion of market capitalism here. One of the principal strategies has been the adoption of cashew-nut into the agricultural production system. The adoption of smallholder cashew production appears to have occurred in almost every farming community in Ratanakiri during the past fifteen years, and this rapid transformation of the agricultural system has also led to significant social and cultural shifts in highland society. In the following sections I look specifically at cashew farming, and at some of the changes occasioned by entry into agricultural production for a world commodities market.

Cashew Production in Cambodia

Improvements to roads and transportation infrastructure, the increasing capabilities of government extension services and various other small-scale development activities, and the series of policy and economic initiatives that have increasingly linked northeast Cambodia to regional trading partners, especially Vietnam, occurred just as Vietnam was solidifying its position as one of the world's leading exporters and processors of cashew-nut for the world market.[14] In 1990, Vietnam had become the world's second largest exporter of cashew-nuts, producing 140,000 metric tons annually; by 2000 that amount had almost doubled, and by 2005 Vietnam had surpassed India to become the largest producer of cashew-nuts for the world market, producing 827,000 metric tons, a production valued at USD 5.4 billion.[15] Vietnam's entry into cashew production was similar to the country's experience with coffee production for the world market. Vietnam's "coffee boom" occurred throughout the early 1990s, in concert with the Đổi mới reforms through which Vietnam began experimenting with market capitalism. The Central Highlands of Vietnam were the site of the coffee boom, and many of the elements of the transformation taking place in Cambodia's highlands today were evident during this period just across

---

[14] Cashew is an increasingly important crop: world production of cashew has grown 6% annually since the early 1990s, compared with 2.2% for other food crops; see Andrew McNaughton, *The Cambodian Cashew Industry: Assessment of Opportunities and Constraints for Rural Employment and Export Revenue Generation* (Phnom Penh: McNaughton and Associates/GTZ Cambodia, 2005), 17.

[15] FAO, FAOSTAT Database (Rome: Food and Agriculture Organization of the United Nations, 2008), http://www.fao.org/es/ess/top/commodity.html?lang=en&item=217&year=2005, accessed 24 November 2008.

the border. There, forested lands under communal management were quickly transformed into small and large-scale plantations, a transformation made possible by development and policy initiatives, a series of rapid investments in entrepreneurial activity in the agricultural sector, and the massive migration of an ethnically differentiated labour force – in this case ethnic *Kinh* (Vietnam's national ethnic majority) from northern Vietnam seeking economic opportunities in Vietnam's sparsely inhabited Central Highlands. When world prices for coffee declined rapidly, in part due to the scale of Vietnam's production, Vietnamese investors and growers turned to cashew as an alternative crop well-suited to the region's climate and soils.

Because land for cashew production in Vietnam was scarcer and more expensive than in neighbouring Cambodia, Vietnamese cashew processors and exporters soon began seeking raw cashew-nuts from Cambodian sources. This was in keeping with Vietnam's pattern of trade with Cambodia, and was encouraged by Vietnamese trade policy and development assistance strategy. As trade between Vietnam and Cambodia has increased – it is close to USD 1.2 billion annually – Vietnam has consistently provided aid in support of road-building and other projects to increase Cambodia's ability to continue exporting raw materials and commodities for processing in Vietnam. Recent trade agreements will allow Cambodian goods to enter Vietnam tariff free, and will incentivize the agricultural sector in Cambodia through the construction of a processing factory on or near the border.[16] Cambodian leaders similarly encouraged market production of cashew in the northeast, a policy that was in keeping with a long-standing effort by Khmer, and previously French, administrations to encourage highlanders to "modernize" by producing for the market economy. In Ratanakiri, this encouragement took many forms. In speeches, successive provincial governors echoed national politicians in calling for cashew production as a key development strategy for the province; district and sub-district level officials echoed these calls. At the same time, the provincial agriculture department launched a campaign to encourage highland villages to grow cashew.[17] Medium-scale landowners, many of them new to the province, had already begun to grow cashew for export.[18]

[16] May Kunmakara, "Processing Plant Aims to Boost Trade with Vietnam," *Phnom Penh Post*, 12 November 2008, online at www.phnompenhpost.com, accessed 8 June 2009.
[17] See interview with Soy Sona, director of the Provincial Agriculture Department, in Cat Barton and Cheang Sokha, "Keeping Farm in Family Hands," *Phnom Penh Post* 22 February 2008, online at www.phnompenhpost.com, accessed 8 June 2009.
[18] According to the World Bank, cashew in Cambodia "has been popular since land was provided to influential people under economic concessions for agricultural activities," World Bank, *Cambodia Agrarian Structure Study* (Phnom Penh: The World Bank, 2005), online at http://go.worldbank.org/7TSE15UXI0, accessed 3 April 2009.

Perhaps the most important encouragement, though, was the returns that cashew farming offered. A study by the Economic Institute of Cambodia suggested that during the period of maximum yield (when trees are aged 10–15 years), production costs including inputs and labour average $103 per hectare; assuming a yield of 0.7 tons per hectare, sold at $600 per ton, the net income per hectare would be $317; alternatively, Kang and Chan suggest a gross revenue of about $300, resulting in a net income of $200 per hectare.[19] It is likely that much smallholder cashew farming in Ratanakiri does not live up to the scenarios presented in these analyses. Many planters I spoke with suggested that they had not had enough information when they started planting, and that they had planted their cashew trees too close to each other. They also complained of poor results on the marginal lands they have planted. Additionally, they struggle with wildly fluctuating prices. Because almost all of the cashew produced in Ratanakiri is processed in Vietnam, the purchase price for cashew is set by Vietnamese buyers and depends not only on world demand, but also on the flow of cashew from Vietnam and elsewhere through the Vietnamese processing centres.[20] Even with all of these considerations, cashew plantation has boomed in Ratanakiri since the late 1990s.

Tang Kadon – A Remote Village in a Remote Province

Cashew farming came later to Tang Kadon village than it did to many parts of Ratanakiri. In a province that is often described as remote, Tang Kadon and the other villages of Nhang commune lie far away from Ratanakiri's main roads and town centres. Tang Kadon village is a circular grouping of longhouses to the side of a small road; along the road, a couple of Khmer settlers have recently built houses and set up a small shop and rice mill. East and north of the village an uninterrupted expanse of farmland and forest extends to the Sesan River and the O Chatai stream, which form Cambodia's national boundary with Vietnam. The remoteness of the area has not spared the village from experiencing the signal events of Ratanakiri's recent past. This border area formed part of the Ho

---

[19] Economic Institute of Cambodia, *Cambodia's Export Diversification and Value Addition* (Phnom Penh: Economic Institute of Cambodia and UNDP Regional Centre, Colombo, 2006), 34; Kang Chandararot and Chan Sophal, *Cambodia's Annual Economic Review* (Phnom Penh: Cambodian Development Resource Institute, 2003), 47; World Bank, *Cambodia Agrarian Structure Study*, 192–198.

[20] Cambodia's only processing plant, which purchased only 150 tons per year, closed in 2008. A report by the EIC suggested that higher energy prices in Cambodia comprised the main barrier to investment in processing capacity there. See Tracey Shelton, "Cashew market crumbling," *Phnom Penh Post* 29 September 2008, online at www.phnompenhpost.com, accessed 3 May 2009.

Chi Minh trail, and was heavily bombed during the American War. For purposes of security and control, the Khmer Rouge forcibly relocated Tang Kadon and neighbouring villages to the floodplain of the Sesan River, and from 1973 to 1978 the village was part of an agricultural collective dedicated largely to growing "wet" rice in large, seasonally inundated fields. Agricultural production was centrally planned and many aspects of social life were undertaken communally. There were many deaths from sickness, hunger and killing during this period, and the years following the fall of the Khmer Rouge were marked by dislocation and instability. The village was moved several times during the 1980s, before returning to a place on the Sesan River near its traditional location. Finally in the early 1990s they moved back to the forests where villagers were once again cutting small swiddens and growing upland rice varieties.

The abundance of forest there, and its proximity to Vietnam and to navigable waterways made the area an inviting target for illegal logging. A massive logging operation took place here in the late 1990s; according to villagers, the logging crews were Vietnamese and the operation was undertaken by the Vietnamese military in coordination with Cambodian authorities. In 2006, authorities informed villagers that the forests they rely on for building materials, food and land for farming had been had been granted as an economic land concession and would be converted to a larger rubber plantation. The 10,000 hectare concession was awarded to the Heng Brothers Development company; no input was sought from the residents of the five villages which will be most affected by the project.[21] The news provoked a minor timber boom as entrepreneurs rushed to beat the concessionaire to the forest resources. Villagers worked largely as labourers, cutting luxury wood that would be sold illegally to Vietnam. The operation was organized by the chief of the Cambodian border police post, who ran crews of Vietnamese woodcutters as well, and who arranged for the transfer of the timber across the border to Vietnamese buyers. Finally, in mid-2008, villagers reported that as many as 30 tractors had been brought across the border from Vietnam to begin clearing the forest for the concession. The work crews were Vietnamese, although as the forest was opened up villagers from Tang Kadon and neighbouring villages were recruited

---

[21] The Heng Company was previously implicated in illegal logging in Botum Sakor national park and is best known for its role as a logging concessionaire operating in the "special coupe" awarded in 2006 to provide wood for the construction of a new National Assembly building. That it is Heng Brothers who have been awarded the concession to Tang Kadon's forest demonstrates how closely events in a forest-dependent village like Tang Kadon are linked to the evolving "crony capitalist" aspects of Cambodia's new economy. In their work on the "special coupe", Heng Brothers cooperated with the Ly Chhuong Construction Company, a company reportedly owned by the son-in-law of Cheam Yeap, the CPP Parliamentarian who is also the chairman of the National Assembly Construction Committee – the committee that awarded the "special coupe". See Global Witness, *Cambodia's Family Trees: Illegal Logging and the Stripping of Public Assets by Cambodia's Elite* (Phnom Penh: Global Witness, 2007), 15.

to plant rows of rubber seedlings in the area that was formerly the site of their forest and old swidden fields.

The cutting of the forest and the establishment of the large rubber plantation, if it goes ahead as planned, will have a decisive effect on the village economy, and will dramatically constrain the villagers' agricultural and resource-use opportunities. Yet the agricultural system was already in the process of a far-reaching transformation by the time the tractors arrived. One of the most important developments in that transformation was the recent introduction of smallholder cashew production into the mix of agricultural strategies used by farmers. Just as in the rest of Ratanakiri, small cashew plantations, between 1 and 10 hectares in size, seem to be everywhere you look in Andong Meas district, along roads and near villages. During the harvest season, piles of 80kg burlap bags full of cashews are stacked near river crossings and in front of local stores, where shop-owners purchase the raw cashew-nut from farmers and sell them in market towns for a small markup.

These changes to the landscape are the outward manifestations of a recent and profound shift that affects all aspects of highland life. In producing and selling cashews locally, the inhabitants of Tang Kadon and their neighbours have linked their economic life to a global commodities market about which they have little information, and over which they have little control.[22] In doing so, they have in a short time become dependent on the annual cash earnings that their involvement in that market has generated. Their increasing involvement in the market economy has in turn been accompanied by the rapid transformation of long-standing systems of common-property management of land and resources into a system of private property in land. And these changes have, finally, led to rapid cultural and social changes within Jarai society and between the Jarai and their newly arrived Khmer neighbours. In the following sections, I address these transformations in turn.

---

[22] The alienation of cashew growers from the final product of their labour is almost complete. Not only growers, but buyers and traders I spoke with, who had more formal education and, supposedly, more sophistication in the market, had little or no idea what processed, edible cashew-nuts looked like, or even that they were used as a food product after processing. This is a common attribute of global agricultural commodity chains. That alienation was central to Mintz's analysis of sugar production: for Mintz, the processes of exploitation that produce the disadvantageous position of agricultural labourers within the world economy also assure their ignorance of the final products to which their labour contributes. Sidney W. Mintz, *Sweetness and Power: The Place of Sugar in Modern History* (New York: Elisabeth Sifton Books, Penguin Books, 1985).

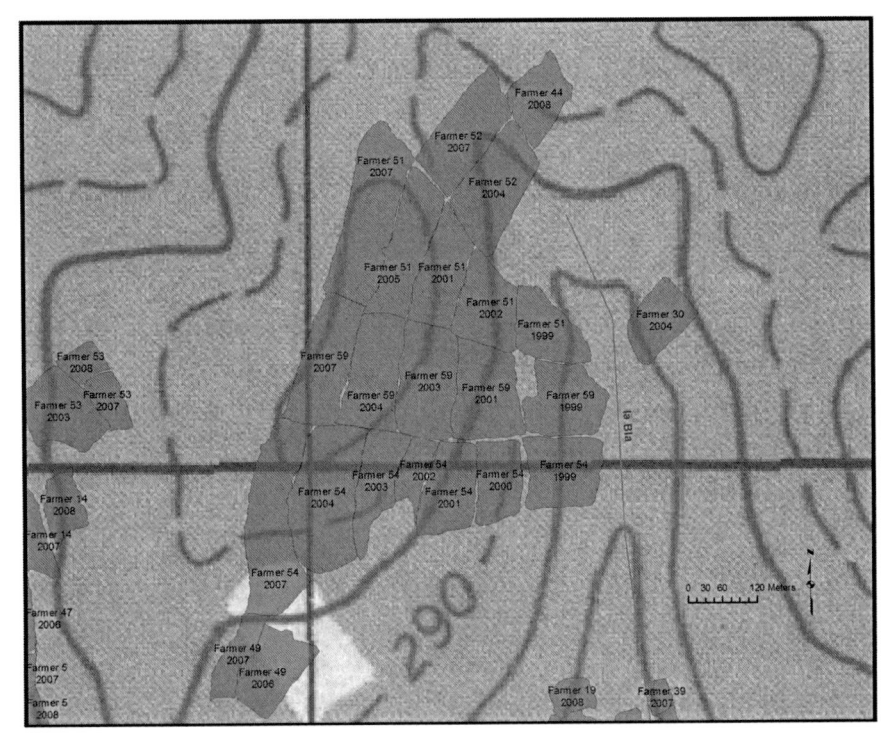

Figure 1. The Jarai farming system at Tang Kadon.

The Changing Swidden System

Tang Kadon is a village of approximately 270 inhabitants, which in 2008 was divided among 50 family units of varying sizes.[23] The basic outline of the traditional swidden system is easily grasped. Each family cuts a new field every year or two from an unused area of forest. Generally, a farmer will make the initial cutting in a new site close to a source of water (see Figure 1). During their first year there, the family will build a small house there, where they will spend most of the agricultural season. The following year, the farmer will cut another field, uphill from the initial location. During this second year, the farmer will continue to plant rice and other crops in the initial field. Whether a field is in its first year, or has been used previously, is one of several factors a farmer will take into consideration when choosing the crops and crop varieties to be used in a

---

[23] A 'family' in this sense represents the basic domestic unit of production in the village economy. Beyond their kinship ties, a family is a group of related individuals who work together and hold rights in common to an agricultural field or group of fields. Usually the family will include parents, their children who live with them, spouses of children who have not yet formed their own 'family,' and grandparents.

field. The yield of a swidden drops off precipitously after the first year of planting, as soil fertility drops and weeding becomes more arduous. It is this decline in yield that drives the system, necessitating the cutting of new forest. After a few years, when a field no longer provides an acceptable yield, it is fallowed, and will eventually grow back to forest. How frequently a family cuts new fields – and the size of the fields they cut – depends on many factors, including the location and purpose of the field, and the size and age of the family farming it. These latter factors are especially important, since they determine the supply of labour and the ability of the labourers to work. In general, though, newly-cut fields are slightly under one hectare in size, and families will cut perhaps three out of every four years.

This image shows a typical set of farm fields. The first fields were cut by three families who began working at this site together in 1999 (Farmers 51, 54 and 59). They cut fields near the Ia Bla stream in order to have water for family use, and cut new fields uphill in successive years. They were later joined by other families at this site. Prior to the introduction of small-holder cashew-nut production, the fields cut in 1999 would have been abandoned after they were no longer productive, followed by the next year's field, and so on.

Each year, then, the 50 families of Tang Kadon village cut between 20 and 40 hectares of forest. In the past, the impact on available forest resources of this annual cutting was offset by the constant reversion of old swiddens into forest land: for every new field cut, another was abandoned and allowed to revert to forest, so that at any given time a family would have only a few hectares of land under active cultivation. Furthermore, the village itself would move location from time to time, within the boundary of an area that could be considered the village's territory. Often these moves were initiated to overcome a spate of sicknesses or accidents, which villagers believe are caused by the malevolent activity of ghosts or spirits. Although some swidden fields were sited quite far from the village, many were in fact close, so the move provided an opportunity for thick forest to grow up in those areas as they were abandoned, and brought villagers into areas of forest that had not been cleared for a long time.

Incorporating cashew into this system, and into the diverse portfolio of crops that highlanders grow, was not an overly complicated process. Simply put, instead of fallowing their fields after three to four years of use, in today's system a farmer will begin to plant cashew on a given field in the second or third year of that field's existence. The cashew seedlings are planted at regular intervals throughout the field, and for the next few years it is still possible to intercrop rice and vegetables with the growing trees. After a year or two of intercropping, the farmer will cease planting new crops on the field. However, within four years of planting, cashews trees will begin to bear fruit. In the meantime, farmers would continue to cut a new field every year or so to grow sufficient amounts of rice and vegetables for household production. Cashew production undertaken in this way fits well with the annual agricultural calendar (see Table 3). Cashew seedlings are planted at the very beginning of the rainy season, just prior to planting rice and other vegetables. And the cashew harvest occurs during the rainy season, too; that is, it occurs well after the rice harvest is in, so farm labour is available for picking cashews. In fact, money from the sale of cashews arrives at an opportune time during the year: the period that stretches from the end of the dry season to the first rice harvest is traditionally a period of scarcity, and income generated by selling cashew allows families to buy rice during the shortfall.

The Jarai count months starting with the beginning of the agricultural cycle – that is, with the selection of a new field site; this accounts for the discrepancy between the 'Jarai Calendar' and the 'Gregorian Calendar.' This agricultural calendar is based on personal observation and interviews, on conversations with and unpublished reports by Jeremy Ironside.

The shift to cashew production represents an intensification of the agricultural system of a sort that is common in swidden systems throughout the world. The adoption of smallholder cashew is both a response to market opportunities as well as an intensification in the face of increasing land scarcity occasioned by encroachment,

Table 3. The Jarai Agricultural Calendar.

Jarai Calendar	12	1	2	3	4	5	6	7	8	9	10	11
Gregorian (Western) Calendar	1 (Jan)	2 (Feb)	3 (Mar)	4 (Apr)	5 (May)	6 (Jun)	7 (Jul)	8 (Aug)	9 (Sep)	10 (Oct)	11 (Nov)	12 (Dec)
Whole Farm – Conditions and Activities	Living in the Village, Funerals and Weddings		Slash, Cut, Burn, Clear Swidden Fields				Weeding					Living in the Village
Rice					Rice Shortage	Plant Upland Rice / Plant Lowland (Wet) Rice			Harvest Upland Rice (High Labour Demand) / Harvest Lowland Rice (High Labour Demand)			
Other Crops					Plant Maize, Beans / Plant Gourds, Tubers / Plant Sesame			Harvest Maize, Beans	Harvest Gourds, Tubers			Harvest Sesame
Cashew	Clear Grass, Weed Cashew			Plant Cashew	Cashew Harvest, Buyers in Village							

concessions and other forms of state-sanctioned enclosure.[24] Farmers in Tang Kadon began planting cashew in 1997 or 1998, and today all families plant cashew. In fact, cashew has become so much a part of the production system now that in the past several years there were only a few cases in which farmers fallowed old fields, and these decisions were largely made because of labour constraints. Thus the villagers of Tang Kadon have very rapidly made the significant and almost complete transformation from a long-fallow swidden agriculture system to a system of permanent cultivation. It is important to note that the shift to the new production system is not, of itself, necessarily permanent. The farmers' ability to rapidly alter their farming in response to changing constraints and opportunities not only disproves popularly held understandings of highland farming systems as archaic and non-dynamic, it also suggests that as conditions continue to change farmers are likely to change their strategies.

The move to permanent cultivation has significant implications for land availability and the distribution of farmland over the landscape. With permanent cultivation, the cutting of forest to make new agricultural fields is no longer offset by the reversion of fallow land to forest, as it would have been in the past. In the new system, each year, on average, a given family adds approximately one half hectare or so to the amount of land it maintains under cultivation. Were families to remain stable in size and age, we could assume that after a certain number of years they would no longer be able to provide the labour necessary to continue cutting and maintaining additional fields, although for a variety of reasons those limits have not been reached in Tang Kadon. Whereas a village cutting twenty to forty hectares of forest annually would formerly have had little net impact on the amount of available forestland, in today's system conversion of forest to agricultural land is cumulative, and, as might be expected, the amount of land under cultivation in Tang Kadon has indeed increased.[25]

---

[24] Intensification represents an increased investment of labour, capital or other improvements to a given area of land in order to increase productivity per land area, see Harold Brookfield, "Intensification and disintensification in Pacific agriculture: A theoretical approach," *Pacific Viewpoint* 13. 1 (1972): 78–96; Harold Brookfield, *Exploring Agrodiversity* (New York: Columbia University Press, 2001), 200–201. See also Ester Boserup, *The Conditions of Agricultural Growth: The Economics of Agrarian Change Under Population Pressure* (Chicago: Aldine, 1965); Christine Padoch, Emily Harwell and Adi Susanto, "Swidden, sawah, and in-between: Agricultural transformation in Borneo," *Human Ecology* 26. 1 (1998): 3–20; Michael R. Dove, "Theories of swidden agriculture, and the political economy of ignorance," *Agroforestry Systems* 1.2 (1983): 85–99; Bryant J Allen and Chris Ballard, "Beyond Intensification? Reconsidering Agricultural Transformations," *Asia Pacific Viewpoint* 42. 2&3 (2001): 157–162.

[25] At the end of the harvest in 2006, 2007 and 2008 I conducted surveys of all agricultural fields at Tang Kadon. With an assistant I walked the perimeter of each year's cutting of each family's set of agricultural fields, using a GPS machine (a handheld device running ArcPad software) to record the location and shape of fields, and using ArcGIS software to map and analyze the information collected from these surveys. The maps and analyses presented in this paper are based in part on this data.

In 1997, around the time that farmers began planting cashew, it is reasonable to assume that villagers were actively farming about 90 hectares of farmland. In 2007, farmers maintained about 227 hectares under cultivation (and cut a further 30 hectares in the 2008 agricultural season).[26]

Not only does the intensification of the swidden system signal an increase in demand on available agricultural land, it has also promoted the centralization and concentration of land under cultivation. As farmers have adopted cashew-nut production, over time both the amount and quality of available farmland close to the village has decreased.[27] Farmers suggest that the heavily-forested land to the east of the village presents the ideal landscape for cutting new fields. Yet even were that area not now claimed by the Heng Brothers concession, it is unlikely that anyone at Tang Kadon would actually go so far away to cut a new field. Formerly, distance from the village was not a major constraint on field location, since whole families lived in their fields for much of the year. Yet today it is necessary for farmers to locate farms in areas where they will have access to the roads and trails travelled by cashew-nut buyers – the more remote their farms, the lower prices they are likely to receive for the nuts. More importantly, because farmers need to harvest cashews at the same time that they are planting subsistence crops, they cannot simply leave their existing cashew fields untended during the rainy season. Farmers also report that theft of cashews is quite common when a family is known to spend long periods away from their fields.

Cashew production is also an important factor contributing to the decline in village mobility today. Villagers at Tang Kadon suggest that they are unlikely to move the village again. While moving the village provided a number of advantages for swidden farming, today village mobility is limited for many of the same reasons that constrain farmers from farming in remote locations. In both cases, capital improvements promote the tendency to remain in place. In farmers' fields, farmers invest labour in planting and maintaining cashew trees, and, knowing that they will have a long-term interest in these fields, they build sturdier field houses than they would have previously – indeed, many of the new houses that villagers are building with machine-sawn posts

---

[26] As I will discuss in the following section, a series of land sales undertaken by villagers, including the sale of many fields under cashew plantation, took place in 2007 and 2008, so that the amount of land managed by villagers in 2009 is in fact less than the 227 hectares that were under management in 2007.

[27] Less desired lands include those with poor soil, those on steep hills where erosion is harder to control, or those where the forest is not yet mature enough to produce a good burn. It is worth noting that the benefits to be reaped from cashew production incentivize farmers to put more land under cultivation. In this sense, the strategy is not only an intensification (the use of additional inputs per unit of land area) but also involves an extensive tendency to use more land for production.

and boards are located in their fields. This investment in *landesque capital*, in Blaikie and Brookfield's sense of the term, is mirrored by investments in village infrastructure, including the construction of 'modern' style houses, or the adoption of state- and NGO- sponsored development projects such as tube-wells and latrines.[28]

Global Commodities Markets and Markets for Land

Tang Kadon's entry into production of cashew-nut for the world market represents a significant shift in the nature of the village economy. Traditionally, that economy was based on subsistence agriculture: rice and most food was grown and consumed by villagers, although as Mathieu Guerín has shown, a system of exchange of surplus production between highlands and lowlands helped to regulate shortfalls in both areas.[29] Furthermore, "subsistence" should not be taken to indicate that the society was completely isolated. Rather, highlanders produced sesame and collected non-timber forest products including resins, honey and various animal products used in traditional medicine, which they traded with other highlanders, and with Lao and Vietnamese traders to obtain livestock, metal and ritual items including gongs and ceramic jars.[30] Trade was conducted almost exclusively through barter, and to date most of these traditional trade items continue to be obtained by barter, and are exchanged along traditional trade routes.[31]

While in recent years timber extraction, hydro-electric dams, rubber plantations and similar projects tied the highland economy to world markets in

---

[28] See Piers Blaikie and Harold Brookfield, *Land Degradation and Society* (London: Methuen, 1987), 9–10.

[29] Analyzing colonial-era records, Guerín found that years of unusually heavy rainfall favoured lowland rice production, but adversely affected highland production. Thus scarcities in the highlands occurred at the same time that lowland producers were likely to have surplus rice available to trade. Highland rice tended to do better during dry years, allowing highlanders to trade their surplus rice to lowlanders suffering shortfalls. Mathieu Guérin, "Essartage et riziculture humide, complémentarité des écosystèmes agraires à Stung Treng au début du XXème siècle," *Aséanie* 8 (2001): 35–55.

[30] Prior to French colonial rule, the slave trade was an additional and important element of trade between villages and between lowland and highland societies. Georges Condominas (ed.), *Formes Extrêmes de Dépendance: Contributions à l'étude de l'esclavage en Asie du Sud-Est* (Paris: Ecole des Hautes Études en Sciences Sociales, 1998). On traditional trading patterns see also Georges Condominas, "Aspects of economics among the Mnong Gar of Vietnam: Multiple money and the middleman," *Ethnology* 11. 3 (1972): 202–219.

[31] The very recent monetization of the highland economy may be inferred, for instance, from the fact that fines imposed through the traditional justice system continue to be reckoned in terms of livestock, although a system of equivalency now allows a fine levied in terms of buffalos to be paid with cash.

various ways, the adoption of smallholder cashew production has forcefully linked individual family welfare to prices determined by an international commodity market. Between 2002 and 2007, farmers in Tang Kadon reported obtaining prices of between 1400 and 4100 *riels* per kilo of cashew (between about USD 0.30 and 1.00). This high degree of variability is the product of the particular structuring of the cashew-nut market in Cambodia, where prices are determined by the needs of Vietnamese production facilities.[32] These fluctuations have become more important over time, as farmers have become more dependent on cash income for their livelihoods.

Increasingly, highland farmers depend on cash earned from the sale of cashew to purchase rice to supplement annual shortfalls. While there is no data available for the purpose of comparison, farmers report that total yields on their agricultural fields were higher in years past, an assertion that is supported by farmers own recognition that they presently grow rice and food crops on more marginal lands for longer periods than before. These reports suggest a sort of path-dependent outcome resulting from farmers' initial entry into the cashew market. As they have centralized their land-holdings close to the village and invested labour and capital in standing cashew plantations, yields from agricultural fields have likely declined. As a result, income from the sale of cashew-nut is an increasingly important element in the portfolio of production strategies employed by farmers to make ends meet. That is to say, as time goes on, farmers are producing less rice for their own consumption, and are instead purchasing rice with cash obtained from the sale of cashew-nut. The visible expression of this change can be found in the increasing percentage of the landscape that is occupied by smallholder cashew instead of secondary forest, especially if we recognize standing secondary forest to represent a long term investment in the building of soil fertility for future farming.

These changes are indicative of profound shifts in the nature of highland society, one of the most important of which is the transformation of the common property regime governing land use. It is a transformation that proceeds in part from the recent integration of the highlands into regional economic and national bureaucratic regimes. The actions of numerous agencies and governmental actors (such as government ministries with land-management mandates) and the enactment of a number of new legal instruments (such as the new Land Law) have sought to impose new bureaucratic and ideological norms regarding land ownership, undermining the legitimacy of long-standing arrangements governing land use and marginalizing the local institutions that enabled communities and families to resolve questions of land allocation.[33]

---

[32] Andrew McNaughton, *The Cambodian Cashew Industry*, 36.
[33] Backstrom, et al., *Indigenous Traditional Legal Systems*...

Nevertheless, two important economic factors have contributed to the shift from a system of common property rights in land to a system of private property rights. These are the increasing scarcity of land, on the one hand, and the increasing ability of land to produce income over time, on the other.[34] Land scarcity has been produced by government grants of land concessions, by the creation of large infrastructure projects, by the increasing amount of land occupied by recent Khmer settlers to the area, and by highlanders' decisions to rapidly expand their landholdings by keeping fields under permanent production instead of fallowing.[35] At the same time, land today remains useful to farmers for much longer than in the past. Whereas previously land lost its immediate economic value after two or three years of use, and was fallowed as soon as yields dropped off, today that same field under cashew cultivation will produce a stream of income for an indefinite period – perhaps as long as twenty years or more.

Land scarcity coupled with an increase in productivity over time has contributed to a shift in the way that land is valued and managed. Under the Jarai swidden system, land in a village's territory was controlled by the village, but individual parcels of land were not conceived of as the property of individual farmers. Rather land was used with the permission of spirits, or *yang*, who inhabited the landscape and required certain rules to be observed and rites be performed to ensure the harmonious relationship between the spirit and human world.[36] Property that could be transferred from individual to individual, or that could be passed down through the inheritance system, was limited to

---

[34] The literature on common property regimes and their erasures helps to draw attention to the role of power and political processes in structuring agricultural intensification; these are dimensions that are glossed over when the question is framed only with relation to human population or carrying capacity (as the "Boserup versus Malthus" approach to intensification often manages to accomplish). For an analysis that engages intensification and enclosure, and interrogates both through a theoretical reworking of Marx's notion of primitive accumulation, see Liza Grandia, *Unsettling: Land Dispossession and Enduring Inequity for the Q'eqchi' Maya in the Guatemalan and Belizean Frontier Colonization Process*, Ph.D. Dissertation, Department of Anthropology, University of California, Berkeley, 2006.

[35] Large infrastructure projects can make land unavailable and also displace inhabitants into neighbouring areas. The 720 megawatt Yali Falls Dam on the Sesan River in Vietnam has had significant downstream effects in Ratanakiri Province, Cambodia. In Nhang commune, several villages that formerly relied heavily on fishing in the Sesan have moved from locations along the river to upland areas where they now grow cashew and rely more heavily on agriculture than before. See 3S Rivers Protection Network, *Abandoned Villages along the Sesan River in Ratanakiri Province, Northeastern Cambodia* (Banlung, Cambodia: 3S Rivers Protection Network, 2007).

[36] Dournes suggests that for the Jarai, the relationship between the spirit world and the human world corresponds to and is complementary with the relationship between the world of humans and that of nature. Jacques Dournes, "Le milieu jörai: Éléments d'ethno-écologie d'une ethnie indochinoise," *Études Rurales* 53-54-55-56 (1974), online at http://etudesrurales.revues.org/document584.html, accessed 12 August 2009.

Table 4. Land Sales in Tang Kadon by Year, Differentiated by Seller and Buyer.

Year	Number of Land Sales	Sold By	Sold To	Hectares	Total Hectares owned by outsiders
2003	1	Village Chiefs	Khmer buyer	1.2	8.2
2004	3	Village Chiefs	Khmer buyers	2.6	10.8
2004	1	Individual	Khmer buyer	2	12.8
2005	3	Village Chiefs	Khmer buyers	2.3	15.1
2005	1	Individual	Khmer buyer	5.5	20.6
2006	1	Village Chiefs Tang Kadon and Neighbour	*Kromhun* of local authorities*	1000	1020.6
2006	7	Village Chiefs	Khmer buyers	8	1028.6
2006	1	Individual	Jarai buyer	1.5	1040.1
2006	2	Individuals	Khmer buyers	5.5	1045.6
2007	1	Village Chiefs	Khmer buyer	2.25	1047.85
2007	5	Individuals	Khmer buyers	17.5	1065.35
2008	1	Village Chiefs Tang Kadon and Neighbour	Khmer buyer	50	1115.35
2008	1	Village Chiefs	Khmer buyer	6	1121.35
2008	11	Individuals	Khmer buyers	30	1151.35

* A *kromhun* is a business enterprise, in this case a group of buyers composed of prominent authorities including some of the district governors.

livestock, harvested crops, ritual trade items like gongs and jars, personal effects, and items such as pots and pans, but did not include land. Rather, an individual's use of land was temporary. The clearing of a new field from the forest established a family's right to farm in the cleared area until the land ceased to be used for farming. Furthermore, the use of land was subject to a set of norms, and conflicts over land were resolved by meetings of the important men of the village.

In Tang Kadon village as elsewhere in Ratanakiri, this common property regime is gradually giving way to a system of private ownership of land. Now farmers have made informal claims to the land immediately in the path of their

Table 5. Land Sales in Tang Kadon by Year.

Year	Total Land Sales	Total Hectares Sold
2003	1	1.2
2004	4	4.6
2005	4	7.8
2006*	10	15
2007	6	20
2008	13	86

* Not including the 1000 hectare land sale made by Tang Kadon and a neighbouring village to a *kromhun* of local authorities.

annual cutting of new forest, and have held discussions about other areas where they will establish progressions of annually cut fields. Furthermore, those fields that are presently under their control are understood to be private property, although a number of the norms that govern the traditional common property regime continue to be respected.[37] Correspondingly, as money has become increasingly important in highland society, highlanders have begun to sell land, usually to outsiders. In Tang Kadon, in 2003 perhaps 5 to 10 hectares of land was being used by Khmer settlers, who had received the land through agreements made with the village chiefs. Since then, the number of land sales and the amount of land owned by outsiders or newcomers has increased dramatically (see Tables 2 and 3 and Figures 2 and 3).

Tang Kadon's Great Transformation

Cashew production at Tang Kadon and other villages in Ratanakiri only became possible as roads, communication networks, information and technology tied farmers there more closely to a global system of production, circulation and consumption of agricultural commodities. Many of the factors that made it possible for farmers to adopt this new agricultural strategy, particularly those

---

[37] For instance, farmers will not cut forest in a known burial site, they will not prevent other members of their village from using the paths that crisscross their property, and they continue to propitiate the *yang* inhabiting the areas where they farm. Baird, *Various Forms of Colonialism*, 124 - 37 describes spatial taboos including those governing land use among the Brao ethnic group.

that follow from the region's increasing connection to the circuits of global capitalism, are the same factors that have made agricultural intensification necessary. As I have sought to demonstrate in this chapter, the decision by farmers at Tang Kadon and neighbouring villages to grow cashew have contributed to sweeping changes in the highland agricultural system and in the system of land management and property rights. As Jarai highlanders at Tang Kadon have intensified their production system, their subsistence system has begun to rapidly incorporate elements of market capitalism. The production of one commodity – cashew-nuts – has contributed to and has been coincidental with the rapid commoditization of large sections of the highland economy. Not only items like motorcycles and radios, but also housing supplies and food are purchased through the market. Importantly, within a decade or two, throughout the highlands, land has become a commodity too, not only because the bureaucratic and economic orderings of the state have extended to a formerly remote hinterland, but also because highlanders themselves sought out the opportunities afforded by the market, and invested labour, capital and innovation into their landholdings. No sooner was land understood to embody economic value beyond its ability to produce subsistence for a few years, than it was traded and then sold to others, and the value obtained from those exchanges was used to purchase other goods and services.

Writing about the rise of the market economy as the predominant organizing principle of modern society, Karl Polanyi noted that "what we call land is an element of nature inextricably interwoven with man's institutions. To isolate it and form a market out of it was perhaps the weirdest of all undertakings of our ancestors."[38] For Polanyi, it was the commoditization of the factors of production – land, labour, and capital – that was a particularly troubling aspect of the market economy.[39] Because these productive forces were so completely ingrained within society, because they were social as well as economic forces, treating them as commodities required maintaining the fiction that they could be isolated from the systems within which they were embedded. The exchange

---

[38] Polanyi, *The Great Transformation*, 178.
[39] Polanyi's formulation of the fictitious commodity addresses land, labour and money, not capital *per se*, but as his emphasis is on the market economy's wresting of these items from their role as productive forces, it is money's role as capital that is at stake in his formulation. Bob Jessop has made the case that in an increasingly knowledge-driven global economy, knowledge should be considered a fictitious commodity as well. His insight corresponds nicely with Brookfield's assertion that land intensification is the product not only of farmers' investments of labour and capital, but also of their application of innovation to farming technique. Bob Jessop, "Knowledge as a Fictitious Commodity: Insights and Limits of a Polanyian Perspective," in Ayse Bugra and Kaan Agartan (eds). *Reading Karl Polanyi for the Twenty-First Century: Market Economy as a Political Project* (New York: Palgrave MacMillan, 2007); Brookfield, *Exploring Agrodiversity*, 201–202.

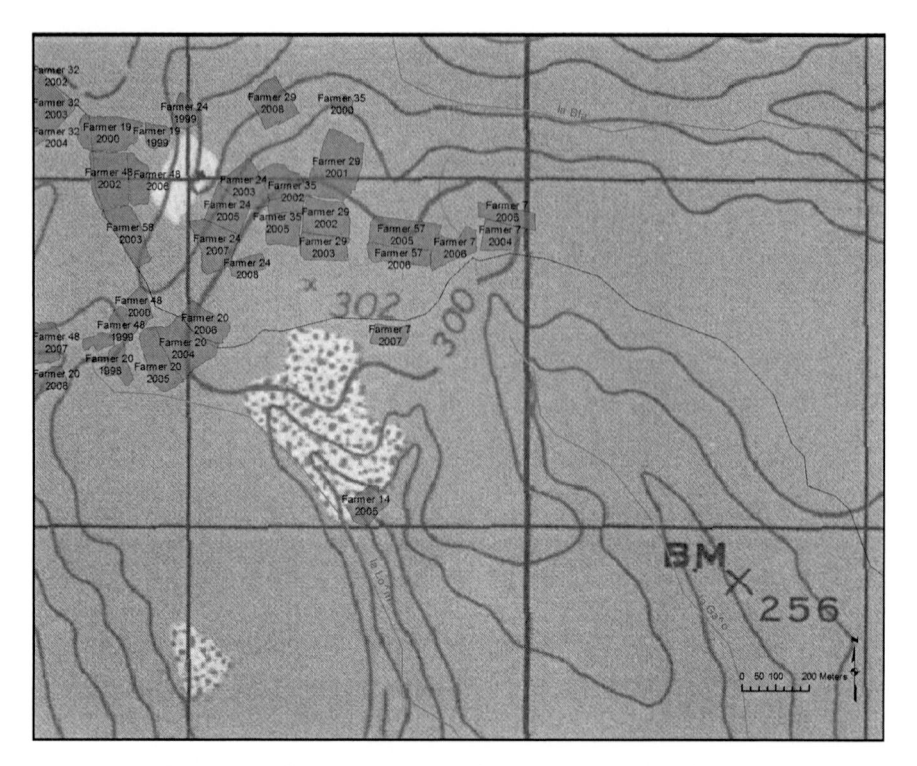

Figure 2. Selected area, not showing recent land sales.

of these forces as commodities thus necessitates the disruption of the societal bonds which they form a part of.

It is perhaps not surprising to find, then, that the transformation of Cambodia's highlands has involved not just the increased use of money and the adoption of private property in land, but also a rapid adoption of wage labour in place of the forms of labour exchange that were formerly common (and which continue to be relevant in various ways). Thus, to harvest rice or clear or weed fields, today wealthy Jarai farmers are hiring labourers to do the work, often labourers from other villages. This new system borrows some elements from the system of reciprocal labour sharing that continues to exist side by side with wage labour.[40] For instance, labourers are invited to partake of a jar of rice beer after the harvest is complete, even though they are often paid in cash and not with a share of the harvest. And of course, as more options for engaging in

---

[40] The Jarai system is not very dissimilar from that described by Matras-Troubetzkoy for the Brao. Jacqueline Matras-Troubetzkoy, "L'essartage chez les Brou du Cambodge: Organisation collective et autonomie familiale," *Études Rurales* 53–54–55–56 (1974), online at http://etudesrurales.revues.org/document579.html, accessed 19 August 2009.; Jacqueline Matras-Troubetzkoy, *Un Village en Foret: L'essartage chez les Brou du Cambodge* (Paris: Selaf, 1983).

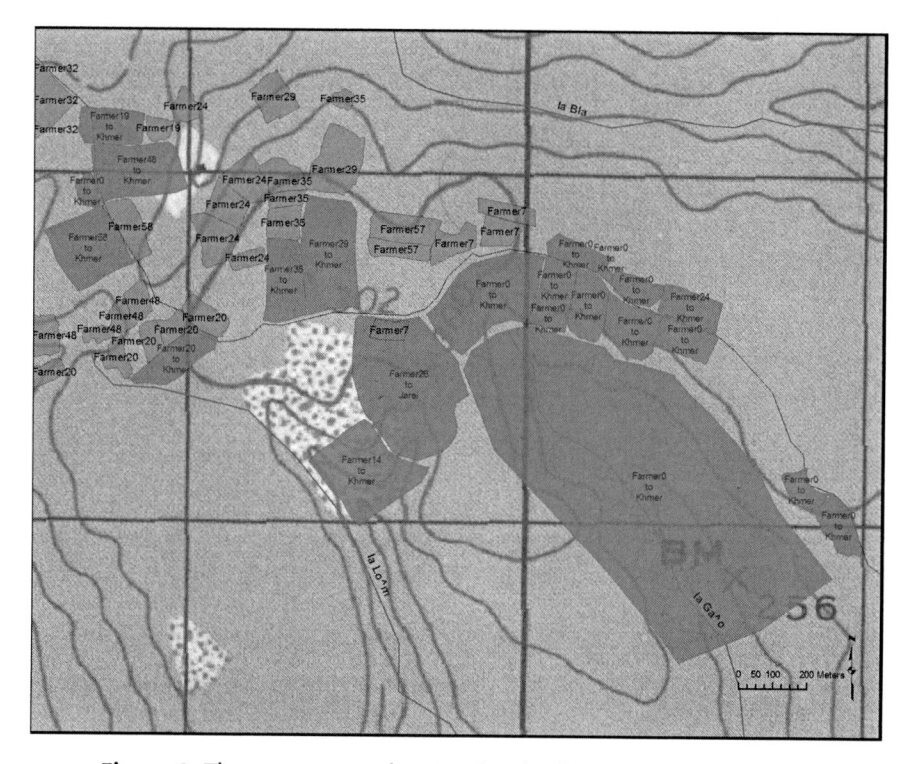

Figure 3. The same area, showing land sales transacted recently.

wage labour become available, those villagers who need to are engaging in *bwă kuli*, the Jarai term for the much-despised work as a coolie or manual labourer. Indeed, at Tang Kadon, several men, young and old, have become day-labourers for the Heng Brothers company, planting rubber seedlings on land that was formerly part of the village's forest.

In concluding this analysis of the ways in which highland farmers have adopted cashew production and in the process embraced some elements of market capitalism in the face of rapidly changing political and economic circumstances, it is worth briefly discussing just one of the social bonds that has been reconfigured by this transformation, that between men and women. It is said that a Jarai man enters a marriage with nothing but the clothes he is wearing, because heritable property passes down from women to their daughters. Men plan an active role in obtaining that property through trade, but thereafter it is held within the wife's matrilineal clan (called a *phung*). For the Jarai, residence is matrilocal – after marriage a new couple settles in the longhouse of the bride. This means that longhouses are composed of groups of sisters, their husbands and children, their grandmothers, and perhaps their female cousins and aunts, along with their immediate families. Children belong to their mother's *phung*, and marriage to a member of one's own *phung* is considered incestuous and is therefore prohibited. Furthermore, when a woman dies, her husband is expected to take one of her available, unmarried sisters as his wife. Otherwise, he must return the possessions the couple has acquired to the wife's family and additionally must pay a fine in order to sever the obligation. This system of sororate marriages is to a matrilineal clan system what the levirate is to patriliny – it keeps family wealth within the matriline, and keeps husbands attentive to the authority and status of the wife and her kin network.

The inheritance system and the cultural norms surrounding residence act as a brake on men's authority within the village and family. However, the recent embrace of private property in land has prompted a re-working of these arrangements. While money obtained from land sales may become the property of the family, and while wives are consulted when land is sold, the negotiating and contracting of land sales is undertaken by husbands (except where an unmarried woman is the head of the household). Furthermore, in many cases the money obtained from land sales is spent on the purchase of new houses, both on the farm and in the village. In the village, these are invariably 'modern' style houses – houses inhabited by a single family unit (that is, in a strictly economic sense, the family-as-unit-of-production which owned the sold land). Although the new house continues to be considered part of the longhouse from which it has broken off, in practice many of the norms governing the longhouse group are no longer observed. Thus the basic pattern of sociality within the longhouse is dramatically altered by the breakup into single-family units, suggesting that in the future the conceptual ordering which understands single-family houses as units within an imagined longhouse of a matrilineal clan may perhaps also lapse. Importantly, whereas longhouses formerly provided the visual evidence of group status within the village, today that status is displayed by the individual family house. The sale of land, linked, as it is, to the cashew boom and to the demographic and ethnic changes affecting the highlands, is thus intimately connected to the breakup of longhouses, and to the reconfiguration of status and social relations within the village.

All of the changes described here – the shift from common-property management to private ownership of land, the increasing use of wage labour, the increasing importance of modern money to the highland economy, and the changing roles of men and women in relation to property – are strongly linked to the current transformation of Cambodia's political economy that this volume seeks to understand. And all of these phenomena represent, to some degree, the sort of "disembedding" of the economy that Polanyi sought to describe. At issue for Polanyi was the importance of the market as a force for ordering social life. As he saw it, in market societies the forces of production and the social attachments they help to create become disembedded from the system of social relations within which they formerly inhered, and instead become subject to the market and to the processes of atomization and the effacement of social connection that markets are said to encourage.[41]

Yet while it seems evident that certain sorts of disembedding are occurring as part of Tang Kadon's transformation, it is necessary to take both the future and the past into consideration in applying any moral judgement on markets *per se* as they appear in this story. Longhouses, although they are often interpreted as embodying the collective spirit of communal living, can nonetheless house inequality: in Tang Kadon, the arrangement of longhouses in the village still recalls to some residents the former West to East hierarchical ordering of village space from elites to commoners to *ludn* (slaves and debt-bondsmen). And emerging relationships among Jarai cashew growers and the Khmer traders who now live among them represent a certain freedom to those who benefit from them, even as they are sometimes tinged with ethnic tension and resentment. It is within this emerging network of relationships that factors of production are now becoming re-embedded.

As the residents of Tang Kadon and their neighbours in the highlands find their society increasingly integrated into national and global markets, what is perhaps most striking is how complete a reversal this experience is from the last great cataclysm to affect social life there: the experience of collectivization under the Khmer Rouge, a period during which markets – and money – were reviled. Yet for all their ideological differences, these two crises share common traits. In both cases, an ideologically justified economic revolution has reached and reordered the most intimate aspects of social life, from labour-sharing arrangements on the farm to residence patterns in the household. And in both cases, there exists the potential that the rearrangements will dramatically transform peoples' lives. It remains to be seen what will result from the opportunities, as well as the constraints, presented by the present moment.

---

[41] Kathryn Ibata-Arens, Julian Dierkes, and Dirk Zorn, "Theoretical Introduction to the Special Issue on the Embedded Enterprise," *Enterprise and Society* 7. 1 (2006): 1–18; see also, David Graeber, "Debt, violence and impersonal markets: Polanyian meditations," in Chris Hann and Keith Hart (eds.), *Market and Society: The Great Transformation Today* (Cambridge: Cambridge University Press, 2009).

7

THE POLITICS AND PRACTICE OF LAND REGISTRATION AT THE GRASSROOTS

Sokbunthoeun So

IN THE CONTEXT OF BOTH post-conflict reconstruction and of economic transformation, the issue of secure access to land is always of critical concern. In Cambodia, the legacy of war and displacement has been exacerbated by poor land governance in the context of an emerging national market for land. The switch from collective ownership to private property at the end of the 1980s unleashed a flood of land disputes which has never really abated. Between 1992 and 1993, land ownership conflicts were the most common type of complaint filed to UNTAC's human rights office.[1] The rushed passage of a Land Law in 1992 intended to address the land issue exacerbated the problem, by allowing individuals to claim ownership on the basis of possession. This, according to a Cambodian government report, "set the stage for land grabbing and power abuses":

> As the Vietnamese withdrew from Cambodia, a massive land grab began, especially in Phnom Penh. Some officials began to act as though State property and vacant private property (or property that could be rendered vacant by the use of force) was theirs to occupy, "own" and therefore sell.... It has even been claimed that the 1992 law became a "get rich quick" manual for the upwardly mobile who knew how to satisfy the formal registration requirements: few rural families had managed to secure the necessary documentation to prove their land ownership rights.[2]

Press reports and protests over land disputes made the issue increasingly visible over the course of the 1990s, and a large and influential study by Oxfam in 1999,

---

[1] Judy Ledgerwood, "Rural Development in Cambodia: The View from the Village," in Frederick Z. Brown and David G. Timberman, (eds.) *Cambodia and The International Community* (New York: Asia Society, 1998), 132.
[2] Royal Government of Cambodia, *The Report of Land and Human Development in Cambodia* (Phnom Penh: RGC Supreme National Economic Council, 2007), 8.

which found rapid rates of land alienation due to indebtedness and expropriation, brought the scale of the problem to light.[3] In this context, a coalition of international donors put land policy reform onto the public policy agenda, and the result was the adoption of the 2001 Land Law, and the implementation of the Systematic Land Registration programme (SLR), which is the topic of this chapter.

Since the passage of the Land Law and the beginning of the SLR, the situation has continued to deteriorate. The scale of the problems is hard to capture precisely, since there is no central database recording land disputes. According to the Asian Legal Resource Centre, local NGOs registered around 150 cases of land grabbing between 2001 and 2003; this number rose to around 350 in 2004 and 2005, and then to 450 in 2006. The Centre suggested that in some of the worst affected provinces, such as Ratanakiri, home to indigenous communities, 30 per cent of lands may already have been lost to land-grabbers by 2006, and the rest remained under threat. A high-powered National Authority for Resolution of Land Disputes (NARLD), created in February 2006, received almost 2000 cases in 14 months.[4]

In 2007, the Cambodian Human Rights and Development Association (ADHOC) reported it had investigated 382 cases of land-grabbing, affecting 19,329 families, of whom about a quarter were in Phnom Penh.[5] According to ADHOC, 52 of these cases were related to large-scale development projects for public purposes, such as economic land concessions, while 191 cases comprised conflicts between farmers and civilian government officials or members of the armed forces.[6] Another local NGO, the Cambodian League for the Promotion and Defense of Human Rights (LICADHO) reported in 2007 that violence and intimidation were increasingly featuring in land disputes. LICADHO observed that "By far the greatest number of attacks against human rights defenders documented in 2007 concerned community activists targeted for their representation of fellow citizens in land disputes with powerful and business interests." LICADHO commented that verbal threats, including death threats, "are so commonplace that they go largely unreported" and added that the trend of threatening representatives of villagers with arrest, detention or "malicious legal charges" was "even more widespread

---

[3] Shaun Williams, *Where Has All the Land Gone?Land Rights and Access in Cambodia* (Phnom Penh: Oxfam GB, Cambodia Land Study Project, 1999).
[4] Asian Legal Resource Centre, "UN Human Rights Council/Cambodia: Landgrabbing, Corruption and the Rule of Law in Cambodia," *Human Rights Solidarity* 17.2 (2007): online at http://www.hrsolidarity.net/mainfile.php/2006vol16no02/, accessed 3 Feb 2009.
[5] Cambodian Human Rights and Development Association (ADHOC), *Human Rights Situation 2007* (Phnom Penh: ADHOC, 2008), 29.
[6] Ibid., 29–30.

than in previous years".[7] The Ministry of Planning, citing commune council records, reports that the total number of land disputes increased to 28,219 in 2005, compared to 26,353 in 2004, 25,442 in 2003 and 26,510 in 2002.[8] Figures reported in 2007 suggest rapid concentration of landholdings in Cambodia. In a five year period between 1999 and 2003/4, the top 20 per cent of the population had increased their share of landholdings from 59 per cent to 70 per cent, while the share of the poorest 40 per cent had declined from 8.4 per cent to 5.4 per cent.[9]

The SLR aimed to overcome the situation of tenure insecurity in Cambodia. It formalized and regulated undocumented land claims by registering all land and developing a centralized database of land ownership. Its ultimate goal was achieving cadastral sustainability, i.e. the maintenance of up-to-date information within the centralized database, which provides transparent ownership information crucial to the maintenance of tenure security. Yet, as the figures above suggest, SLR does not appear to have materially affected the rapid concentration of landholdings in Cambodia; nor does it appear to have reduced the violence and coercion that has accompanied this.

This chapter investigates the Systematic Land Registration Programme and draws three conclusions. First, the success of SLR rests on the acceptance and ability of individuals to meet their obligations *after* their land has been registered. All registered land owners are required by law to register subsequent land transfers at the cadastral authority, in order to ensure protection against a third party's claim. The Cambodian public have failed to follow the required procedures and register their land transfers at the cadastral authority, threatening the sustainability of the cadastral records and undermining the land registration effort. Second, the chapter explores the question of why the Cambodian poor appear to have resisted this major international effort on their behalf, and finds two reasons. The first reason is that SLR was inserted into a situation in which a prevailing system governing land transactions already existed. The second reason is that the institutions set up to support SLR were coopted and politicized, and thus they undermined the momentum for change arising from SLR, and failed to challenge the prevailing social conventions surrounding land

---

[7] Cambodian League for the Promotion and Defence of Human Rights (LICADHO), *Attacks and Threats Against Human Rights Defenders in Cambodia, 2007* (Phnom Penh: LICADHO, 2008), 15.

[8] Royal Government of Cambodia, *Cambodia Human Development Report 2007* (Phnom Penh: RGC Ministry of Planning, 2007), 56; the higher numbers reported are likely due to more comprehensive statistics, and the fact that NGOs tend to become involved only in conflicts that involve large numbers of families and which have human rights dimensions.

[9] Ibid., 48. It should be noted, however, that not all of this concentration is due to land grabbing: distress sales are also a major cause of land loss, and population growth since the mid-1980s has also produced a landless generation, now reaching adulthood.

claims. Because these social conventions only offer relatively weak security of tenure, the result has been continued uncertainty of land tenure. Finally, the chapter analyses land expropriation in the context of prevailing relations of power between rich and poor in the process of economic transformation and suggests that it is these relations of power which need to be reformed before a programme like SLR can achieve its objectives.

SLR and the Problem of Cadastral Sustainability: The Historical Emergence of the Quasi-Formal Land Transfer System

SLR may have succeeded in registering land parcels and issuing land titles initially, but it had difficulty achieving cadastral sustainability. Two factors contributed to this failure. First, historical turbulence together with a prolonged period of unregulated private land control created a "legal vacuum"[10] that gave rise to a "quasi-formal" property system of defining and transferring land ownership outside the state's control. This quasi-formal system is heavily identified with officials at local levels such as village and commune chiefs. Second, poor access to state services, either for land transfer registration or for seeking legal protection, greatly discourages people from using the system. Such poor access reinforces the preference for the existing "quasi-formal" system, threatens the sustainability of the cadastral records, and could eventually lead to the failure of SLR. In order to understand the current "quasi-formal" property arrangement, a brief discussion of the previous land holding practices is necessary.

The modern conception of private ownership did not exist in traditional Cambodian land holdings. Historian David Chandler writes, "The king, theoretically at least, was the lord of all the land in the kingdom, which meant that he could reward people with the rights to use it."[11] This kind of royal land grant was rare and was not the only way one could have land ownership. According to tenth-century inscriptions, ownership of land could also be secured through land transactions, which took place between two private individuals. Such transactions were sometimes patronized by the King and were made into a royal land grant at the request of the purchasers. There were also many records of land sales between private individuals in which the King played no role. The records contained agreements between buyers and sellers with names of land

---

[10] *Legal vacuum* was used by Jansen and Roquas to explain the emergence of the quasi-formal land holding practice as a result of the absence of any state regulations on land in Honduras. See Kees Jansen and Esther Roquas, "Modernizing Insecurity: The Land Titling Project in Honduras," *Development and Change* 29 (1998): 81–106.

[11] David Chandler, *A History of Cambodia* (Boulder: Westview Press, 1992), 16–17.

sellers, land boundary, and paid amount in forms of various goods such as gold, animals, and clothes.[12] Ownership through royal gifts or through purchases, however, seemed to have occurred among only those with power and wealth.

For the ordinary people, ownership of land could be claimed by clearing and settling on the land, a commonly known practice of "acquisition by the plough". In places where no one had worked before, people could plough and clear the land for subsistence farming as long as such action did not infringe on the rights of others.[13] In this mode of land holding practice, ownership rights to land could be secured through continuous cultivation on the land. Such rights were forfeited if the land was left fallow for three years.[14] The practice of clearing land for settlement and farming has not yet been fully given up in rural communities in contemporary Cambodia,[15] a practice that at times runs into conflict with modern legal claims to land.

Ownership based on land clearing and occupation was made possible by the high ratio of arable land to the total number of the population. Most Cambodian farmers worked on land that belonged to them.[16] Weak population pressure did not generate any need to regulate land ownership. "Local acceptance was proof of possession."[17] If the land was granted or purchased and was patronized by the king, the king served as the arbitrator if land conflicts occurred.[18] There were no cadastral records that maintained information on land ownership. The tax system was based on the amount of harvest rather than on land.[19]

The notion of private land ownership and modern land law was first introduced by the French colonial administration in 1884. The 17 June 1884 convention's article IX writes that "the land of the kingdom, up until today the exclusive property of the Crown, will no longer be inalienable. The French and the Cambodian authorities will proceed to establish private property in Cambodia."[20] Such introduction of alienable ownership law marked a major

---

[12] Merle C. Ricklefs, "Land and the Law in the Epigraphy of Tenth-Century Cambodia," *Journal of Asian Studies* 26 (May 1967): 412–414.

[13] Frank Van Acker, *Hitting a Stone with an Egg? Cambodia's Rural Economy and Land Tenure in Transition*, Discussion Paper No. 23 (Phnom Penh, Centre for Advanced Studies, 1999), 32–33.

[14] Serge Thion, *Watching Cambodia: Ten Paths to Enter the Cambodian Tangle* (Bangkok: White Lotus, 1993), 26; Chandler, *A History of Cambodia*, 17.

[15] Sovannarith So, Sophal Chan, and Sarthi Acharya, "An Assessment of Land Tenure in Rural Cambodia," *Cambodia Development Review* 5 (October-December 2001): 1.

[16] Charles Keyes, *Golden Peninsula: Culture and Adaptation in Mainland Southeast Asia* (New York: Macmillan Publishing Co. 1977), 144.

[17] Ibid., 26.

[18] Ricklefs, "Land and the Law in the Epigraphy of Tenth-Century Cambodia," 413.

[19] Thion, *Watching Cambodia*, 26.

[20] As quoted in Thion, *Watching Cambodia*, 29.

turning point in the land-holding practice ofn the country. The colonial law was fundamentally different from the traditional conception of land use. The king no longer enjoyed sole ownership of Cambodian land. Commoners could also have lawful possession and private ownership of land. The law also adopted a cadastral registration system, which provided owners with written legal evidence of land ownership.

Voan Lim, the Director in Charge of the Department of Cadastre,[21] explains that although private land ownership was introduced in 1884, there were only marginal changes to the traditional land tenure system until the adoption of the 1920 Civil Code. The Civil Code recognized two kinds of rights to land: ownership and possession rights. Possession rights could be attained through "fixed asset registration". which was announced by the government in 1925. It was conducted nationwide for a limited period of time through the commune office (*khum*), the lowest local administration, which was created in 1908 to facilitate various administrative issues at local level.[22]

The responsibilities of the commune chief (*mekhum*) included local governance (via a vital statistics officer), land certification (via a certifying officer), and land identification. These latter two responsibilities were crucial to the fixed asset land registration process. Individuals could register fixed assets at the commune office with help from the *mekhum*. The *mekhum* was charged with publicizing the fixed asset registration process, and filling in the fixed asset declaration form, with information provided by individual landowners. Once the fixed asset registration form was filed at the commune office, "The owner received a copy of the fixed asset declaration paper signed by the commune head and recognized as an occupying right document."[23] At the end of the fixed asset registration period, the fixed asset registration records were sent to the district cadastral office for recording into the land database.

This fixed asset registration process provided possession rights, as an initial step towards securing private land ownership rights. Individuals could receive formal ownership titles to land only after the fixed asset declaration was entered into the land database at the District Land Governance office. The entry of the fixed asset declaration into the land database required two further procedures. The first was technical measurement, which involved land mapping and required technical instruments to identify the shape, size, and photographic

---

[21] The Department of Cadastre was first created in 1896 to oversee procedure in land registration, which included the production and maintenance of a land database (land book) that recorded ownership and transfers of land. This land management body resembled the current one with its lowest unit of the department at the district level. See Voan Lim, "Land Regime In Cambodia," Unpublished Manuscript, 1997, 17.

[22] Voan Lim, "Land Regime In Cambodia," Unpublished Manuscript, 1997, 16.

[23] Ibid.

information of the land. The second was an administrative and legalization process that involved the legal identification of the owners.[24]

This new property system did not completely displace traditional land-holding practices, in which ownership was established by occupation on cleared forest land.[25] Article 723 of the 1920 Civil Code recognized the legitimate ownership rights of holders of newly cleared land if they had possessed the land peacefully for five consecutive years.[26] The cadastral authority did not issue ownership titles for all privately claimed land. Most of the land in the main rice-growing area was registered, but by 1975, 90 per cent had been registered only through fixed asset registration; only 10 per cent had been through the further processes necessary to establish full ownership rights.[27]

The fixed asset declaration was recognized as awarding legal possession rights to the land, whereas the ownership certificate was a formal private ownership right. These two forms of land control had different transfer procedures. Transfer of the possession rights was conducted at the commune office.[28] The transfer of the ownership rights required a written property transfer form and registration at the property registry or land governance office.[29] Consequently, the French and the post-independence governments, up to 1975, created two systems of formal land control that substantially differ in their transfer procedures. Since 90 per cent of the land was held only with fixed asset registration, the transfer with certification from the *mekhum* became a dominant mode of land transfer between 1925 and 1975.

Collectivization under Democratic Kampuchea (DK) from 1975 to 1979 eliminated all forms of private ownership including land. All records of ownership were destroyed.[30] The subsequent government, the People's Republic of Kampuchea (PRK, 1979 – 1989), continued the policy of collectivization; however, it was more moderate than under the DK period. By law between 1979 and

[24] Ibid., 16–17.
[25] Thion, *Watching Cambodia*, 41.
[26] Ray Russell, "Land Law in the Kingdom of Cambodia," *Property Management* 15.2 (1997): 103.
[27] Lim, "Land Regime In Cambodia," 17.
[28] This is based on three documents. Article 722 of the 1920 Civil Code stipulated that possession rights could be transferred with written documents on a certified form. A separate document by the director of the cadastre indicated that the *mekhum* served as a certifying officer. An anthropological study in a Khmer village by May Ebihara revealed that the Khum charged a fee of 20 riels for certifying the transfer. See Lim, *Land Regime in Cambodia*, 15; May Ebihara, *Svay, A Khmer Village in Cambodia* (Doctoral Dissertation, Columbia University, 1968), 518.
[29] Eng Sot, *Ka soeksa chbab kruap meatra knong kram rathpakveni* [Study of Law in Civil Code] (Phnom Penh: Ministry of Justice, 1967), 192.
[30] For more discussion on the political nature of the DK, see Kate Frieson, "The Political Nature of Democratic Kampuchea," *Pacific Affairs* 61.3 (1988): 405–427.

1989, all land belonged to the state. However, people were given a small plot for residential purposes. No land ownership documents were issued, and claims to own residential land were based on occupancy.[31]

Farmland was distributed among agricultural collectives known as *Krom Samaki* or solidarity groups. Each *Krom Samaki* comprised a small group of people between 10 and 15 families.[32] There were three categories of *Krom Samaki* differentiated by mode of management. The first was a "collective method of organization of the labour force by groups or teams" in which the farmland was collectively held and worked on by a small group of families and the produce was divided among the group members. The second category of *Krom Samaki* took the form of "mutual aid" in which the group's land was divided up for individual families to work on. Members of the solidarity group would then take turns to help each other in cultivating the land. The third category was basically individualized. The group's land was divided into individually held plots and was privately farmed.[33] Given the low productivity in the first two categories, the third category increasingly became the dominant form of land holding under the PRK. Economic reforms in 1989 marked the re-emergence of the legal recognition of private property in Cambodia.

What this history shows is that the practice of claiming and transferring land rights has not changed completely with the changes of political regimes, but has been reshaped under different legal regulations and the lax implementation of the regulations. Although Cambodia embarked on the process of cadastral development in 1925, it remained incomplete for the next fifty years. Ninety per cent of land between 1925 and 1975 was held only under possession rights, which could be legally transferred with certification from the commune chiefs. This practice of land transfer was apparently carried over and resumed in Cambodia immediately following the collapse of the Khmer Rouge regime, although not in its exact original format due to legal restrictions under the PRK. The PRK did not allow legal private ownership, but its poor implementation of collectivization gave rise to de facto private land rights, which lacked legal recognition but had tacit approval from the state. The third and least strongly collectivized category became the dominant form of landholding as the 1980s wore on, representing a considerable de facto privatization of land.[34] Within this context, the de facto private land holders in the 1980s developed a mutually

---

[31] Williams, *Where Has the Land Gone*, 9.

[32] This number is smaller in sparsely populated areas. See Ledgerwood, "Rural Development in Cambodia."

[33] Viviane Frings, *The Failure of Agricultural Collectivization in the People's Republic of Kampuchea 1979-1989* (Clayton, Australia: Center for Southeast Asian Studies, Monash University, 1993), 7, 16-18.

[34] Ibid., 36-37.

Table 6. Transfer of land holdings in Voar Sar, Pneay and Khtum Krang Communes, Kampong Speu Province.

Year	Cadastral Authority	Witnessed by local officials	Informal agreement between buyer and seller	Others	Total
1979	-	0	1	0	1
1980	-	1	0	0	1
1982	-	3	0	0	3
1984	-	3	2	0	5
1985	-	1	0	0	1
1987	-	0	1	0	1
1988	-	0	3	1	4
1989	0	3	0	0	3
1990	0	3	3	0	6
1991	0	1	1	0	2
1992	0	3	1	0	4
1993	0	5	2	0	7
1994	0	4	2	0	6
1995	0	2	0	0	2
1996	0	2	1	0	3
1997	0	8	0	0	8
1998	0	6	0	0	6
1999	0	4	1	0	5
2000	0	5	2	0	7
2001	0	3	1	0	4
2002	0	6	3	1	10
2003	0	8	2	0	10
2004	1	5	4	1	11
2005	0	10	1	0	11
2006	3	27	3	2	35
2007	0	13	5	0	18
Total	4	126	39	5	174

acceptable form of defining and transferring their "land ownership". Land plots were transferred either with a written agreement witnessed by local officials (village or commune chiefs) or informally with a mere verbal or written agreement between sellers and buyers.

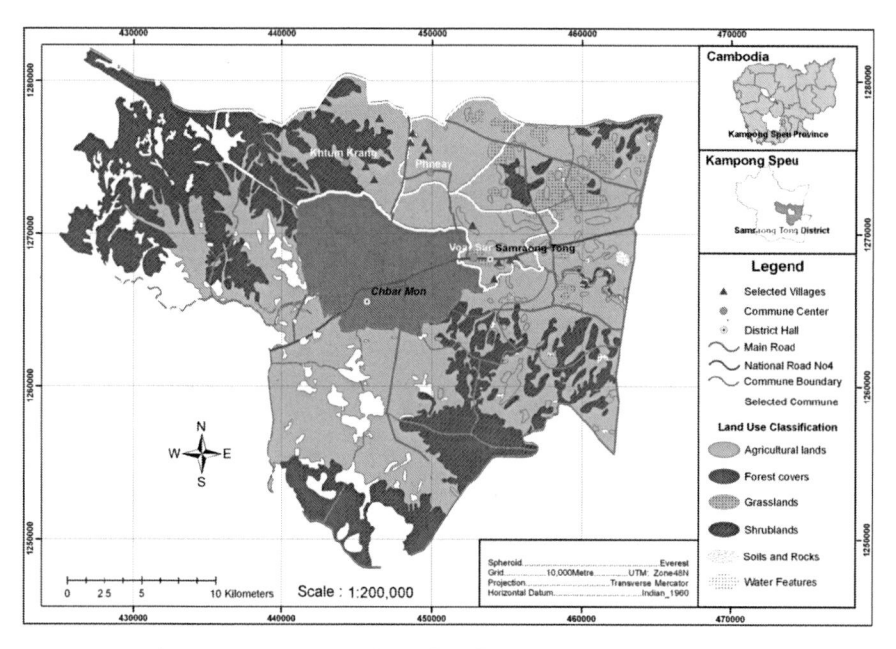

Figure 4. Location where landholdings were surveyed.
Source: BaseMap 2005 and JICA 2003.

The author's survey of 376 randomly selected respondents from three communes in Kampong Speu province carried out between August and October 2007 showed that 174 or 45 per cent of the respondents had been involved in land transactions since 1979. Sixteen of these transactions took place in the 1980s when they were formally illegal, eight with local officials as witnesses. The transfer of land holdings via a process of local authority witness began to re-emerge as early as 1980 and has been the major avenue for land transfer ever since (see Table 6). This pattern resembles the process of land transfer between 1925 and 1975.

Kompong Speu province was chosen as a site of research because it is one of the eleven provinces and cities[35] that were initially chosen for SLR. The province is 48 kilometres west of the capital city of Phnom Penh. It comprises eight administrative districts. At the time the survey was conducted, SLR was operating in Somrongtong district and had completed registration and issue of land titles in only two of the sixteen communes in the district. Both communes were included in the survey.

---

[35] The 11 provinces and cities initially included in SLR were: Takeo, Phnom Penh, Prey Veng, Kandal, Kompong Speu, Sihanouk Ville, Kompong Thom, Kompong Cham, Kompot, Siem Reap and Battambang.

The survey was conducted in ten villages of the two SLR communes, Pneay and Voar Sar, and in three villages of another neighbouring non-SLR commune, Khtum Krang. The standard of living of the people in the two SLR communes, Voar Sar and Pneay, differs substantially. The inclusion of both communes in the survey allows the examination of the variation in people's attitudes toward the formalized land holding within the sample. Voar Sar commune is in close proximity to an all-weather road, an urban area, and the district hall. Pneay is relatively rural and farther from an all-weather road. It is not much different from the non-SLR commune, Ktum Krang, which was included in the survey for comparative purposes. The standard of living in Voar Sar is relatively higher than in Pneay. Most residents in both communes rely on subsistence farming, although many farmers in Voar Sar have a second job. People generally call themselves farmers although some of them have a salaried job. Such characteristics are typical within rural Cambodia, where the majority of the population resides.

The reform of 1989 legalized the de facto private land right to allow individuals to legally own, possess, inherit, sell, and donate land parcels in their holdings. By law only registered land can be legally bought or sold. While the government provided land registration, it did not register all land plots, leaving a very large land area outside the state's regulation. Both human and technical resources for land registration were severely limited, leaving services available to only those who could pay a price. The 2004 *Cambodian Socioeconomic Survey* indicates that only 22.88 per cent of the people held land with an appropriate land title document fourteen years after the reform.[36] This figure left the majority of the people either holding land without documentation or only with documentation that lacks meaningful legal recognition (although with the apparent consent of the state). The failure of the state to register and regulate land ownership created a "legal vacuum", which was soon filled by the "quasi-formal" practice of land transfer, which began to emerge and evolve in the 1980s.

This practice is characterized by, in the words of Jansen and Roquas, a "combination of different elements from different normative spheres".[37] It features some elements of previous laws, some elements of the current land regulation, and some form of local adaptive practices, which emerge because of the state's

[36] This figure is widely contested by various people including researchers and Cambodian professionals working on the land issue in Cambodia. They believe that the percentage of people holding land titles is much smaller. One possible reason for such a high percentage is the confusion between land title and land title application receipts by people involved in the survey. People usually treat application receipts as if they were formal land titles, exchanging receipts instead of formal titles when buying and selling land. The people administering the survey may not have clarified the distinction between the two during data collection. See Thomas Markussen, *Land Titling in Cambodia — Findings From a Field Trip*, Mimeo, February 2006.

[37] Jansen and Roquas, "Modernizing Insecurity," 84–85.

failure to regulate private land ownership. For example, the transfer of land with certification or witnesses from the local authority was a legal practice between 1925 and 1975. It was illegal under the PRK since land was not allowed to be sold (although it did occur anyway). Following the economic reform of 1989, there was no legal provision that allowed the market transfer of unregistered land. The only relevant document was the Ministry of Agriculture 1992 declaration no. 296 that allowed usage of property transfer (sales, inheritance, or distribution) agreement forms. Despite the existence of such forms, most transactions were made through agreements witnessed by local officials.[38] By law, the transfer of all registered land is complete only when it is registered with the government's registry.[39] Since most land has not been registered and is held only with application receipts or without any sort of documentation, the mere transfer agreement witnessed by local officials seems to be a sufficient indication of property transfer.

This quasi-formal practice has increasingly been relied on by unregistered land holders, sometimes also by registered land holders,[40] as a means to transfer their land rights when they need to engage in land market transactions.[41] Immediately following the 1989 reform, many people filed applications for land titles and received receipts indicating that land title applications have been received at the cadastral authority, but they never received the appropriate documents. Yet, this application receipt is commonly treated as if it were a formal land title. It can be used as collateral to secure a loan from Micro Finance Institutions (MFI) at fairly low interest rates. At the same time, many people who did not apply for a land title continue to claim rights to land by occupation without any document. If a document is needed, for example for a microfinance loan application, undocumented land holders can ask the village and commune authorities to produce an "application for possessing and using land" for a small fee. The transfer of land rights, in this situation, be they inheritance or market transactions, are conducted through mutually acceptable procedures, which involve written agreements witnessed by local officials, at commune or village level, who are also

---

[38] In very rare cases, sales agreements are witnessed by higher level authorities, e.g. the District or Provincial Governor.

[39] Article 60, 1992 Land Law.

[40] There have also been many cases where registered land holders have bypassed the required registration of transfer in favour of a simple sales agreement witnessed by local officials. See Chan Sophal and Sarthi Acharya, *Land Transactions in Cambodia, An Analysis of Transfers and Transaction Records*, Working Paper 22 (Phnom Penh: Cambodia Development Resources Institute, 2002), 35.

[41] A similar situation is found in Honduras. See David Stanfield, Edgar Nesman, Mitchell Seligson, Alexander Coles, *The Honduras Land Titling and Registration Experience* (Madison, Wisconsin: Land Tenure Center, University of Wisconsin, 1990); Jansen and Roquas, "Modernizing Insecurity," 81–106; Rikke J. Broegaard, "Land Tenure Insecurity and Inequality in Nicaragua," *Development and Change* 36.5 (2005): 845–864.

expected to serve as witnesses when conflicts occur.[42] Those with some sorts of documentation, for example, a land title application receipt, hand over such documentation along with the written agreement during the transaction.

Local officials are heavily involved in the "quasi-formal" practice and also benefit substantially from such involvement. Their roles include not only witnessing land transactions but also an involvement in the enforcement of the agrarian contracts they have witnessed and the resolution of conflicts at local level, although their authority in this respect lacks a clear legal basis.[43] The Cambodia Agricultural Development Study Center (CEDAC) in its research on land transactions in Siem Reap, Kompong Thom, Sihanoukville and Ratanakiri suggests that agrarian contracts are not only land sales or purchases but also a "system for delegating use rights" or "derived rights", which include open-ended loans, fixed fee land rentals, share-cropping, pawning, and mortgaging. With the exception of mortgaging, which occurs only with a written agreement between farmers and MFI, all forms of agrarian contracts occur between farmers with either a verbal agreement or a written agreement witnessed by local officials. Verbal agreement has become less common. In the event of land conflicts, the people frequently avoid the state's formal authorities, e.g. the cadastral commission or the court, which have been legally assigned for resolving disputes. At the local level, they tend to keep conflicts local and seek mediation and resolution from local officials. Occasionally, they seek the help of politicians or "legal brokers".[44] This is especially the case when local officials collude with private interests, creating conflicts between private interests and the local people.

Limits to the "Quasi-Formal" System

This prevailing property system is reasonably operational, yet it is far from being efficient and not always peaceful. There are four important sources of land

---

[42] Sometimes, the people seek certification and witness from district chiefs or approach cadastral officials as witnesses in the transactions of their unregistered land. This kind of practice is still not within the government regulation since only registered land can be formally transferred and registered into the cadastral records. This practice is merely an attempt to seek witness from high level authority.

[43] For a detailed account of the role of local officials in conflict resolution at local level, see Fabienne Loco, *Between a Tiger and a Crocodile: Management of Local Conflicts in Cambodia, An Anthropological Approach to Traditional and New Practice* (Phnom Penh: UNESCO, September 2002).

[44] Sokha Pel, Pierre-Yves Le Meur, Vitou Sam, Lan Liang, Setha Pel, Leakhena Hay, and Sothy Im, *Land transaction in rural Cambodia: A synthesis of findings from research on appropriation and derived rights to land* (Centre d' Étude et développement agricole Cambodgien (CEDAC), August 2007), 226.

tenure insecurity in Cambodia, all of which come from the personalized nature of the Cambodian state that allows powerful individuals to manipulate the state and use the state's power to serve their own material and political interests.

The first source of tenure insecurity comes from the lack of uniformity in land-holding practices. Both undocumented land holders and holders with application receipts are vulnerable to counter-claims by other politically powerful and wealthy individuals, who have colluded with state agencies and issued themselves titles as counter-claims. While people who claim land based on occupation without any documentation may be more vulnerable to dispossession, the use of application receipts as proof of ownership is also deficient in form and is prone to conflict. This is because the receipt merely serves as an indication that land occupiers have filed a land claim at the cadastral department pending approval and title issuance. Multiple individuals could be holding application receipts to the same piece of land. In addition, the receipt, which is used as an indication of ownership, lacks the backing of the technical survey and cadastral mapping, with only rough estimates of boundaries, making boundary conflicts inevitable.[45] Moreover, these land title application receipt holders, even if they have settled or cultivated the land for a long time, are not protected by law. Such rights to land can be challenged when someone comes up with a formal ownership certificate.[46] Van Acker explains that various provisions in the Land Law and the Contract Decree no. 38 recognizes the first person who has registered the land in his or her name as "the legal owner".[47]

The second source of tenure insecurity comes from "forced transactions", in which land owners may be forced to sell land at a value well below the market price.[48] Powerful individuals, who obtain information about infrastructure development in a certain area from their contacts in the government, engage in large-scale purchases of land in the prospective development area for resale later at a much higher value. Such land purchases occur on land that has not yet been formally registered and are usually accompanied by the threat of seizure or violence. CEDAC shows two major forms of practices of land transactions, both of which are largely outside the state's regulation. The first is between local villagers and is based on mutually accountable localized social relationships among kinsmen, neighbours, and friends. The second is between local villagers and people from outside the community. It is based on an administrative

---

[45] In fact, 450,000 land titles had been issued by the cadastral department without appropriate mapping and measurement before 1995. See Van Acker, "Hitting a Stone with an Egg?", 38.
[46] Van Acker, "Hitting a Stone with an Egg?", 38.
[47] Ibid., 39.
[48] A similar situation is also found in Honduras. See Jansen and Roquas, "Modernizing Insecurity," 89–91.

and legal framework which is characterized by a "higher level of social ties and power relations".[49] This second form of land transactions involves the threat of seizure or violence, which forces individual land owners to sell their land at a price below the market value. In such a situation, many Cambodians prefer to sell their land and avoid trouble, especially when the other party appears to be overwhelmingly powerful.[50]

This kind of forced transaction often involves mediators or brokers between land buyers and owners of the land. Local officials are frequently found to have been involved in land brokerage, to have passed on threats and sometimes to have persuaded local people to sell their land.[51] The presence of threat in land transactions characterizes a crucial nature of tenure insecurity, which may not be remedied by simply documenting ownership without the effective support of institutions responsible for enforcing land rights.

The third source of tenure insecurity comes from the lack of a neutral and efficiently operating judicial system. Theoretically, the role of the court is to provide justice equally for the people, yet access to judicial services is hardly equitable and just. Many poor people fear that pursuing court cases will be costly and unpredictable. Seeking a legal solution requires payment for lawyers, court fees, travel and other expenses, and bribe payments for judges. In a case study on land expropriation involving poor people holding legal land titles, Elizabeth Kato provided an account of the their perception of the court as follows:

> "Go to the court against that rich businessman? I'd lose all my cows!" exclaimed one villager. "You don't have any cows," his neighbor pointed out. "Well . . . I'd lose everything, anyway." . . . The costs in terms of time and transportation would be more than they [villagers] could afford, and the outcome would still be very doubtful.[52]

Moreover, the court has also been used to threaten people into selling their land below the market value. For example,

> A villager in Siem Reap owned 1.5 ha of land and then sold it to the Kheng Sameth Company for the purpose of a golf course construction. Previously, she did not agree to sell this land as with this land she can grow sufficient rice to support her family. In 2003, the Kheng Sameth Company offered her $US 1 per m² and forced her to sell her land. But in 2004, the court requested

---

[49] Pel et al., *Land Transaction in Rural Cambodia*, 227.
[50] Luco, *Between a Tiger and a Crocodile*, 97.
[51] Pel et al., *Land Transaction in Rural Cambodia*, 28.
[52] Elizabeth Kato, "*We have the rights, they have the power,*" *A Case Study of Land Expropriation in Northwest Cambodia, Case Study #1*, (Phnom Penh, Oxfam GB, December 1998), 10.

her to solve this conflict, threatening that her land had no legal document. The court told her to sell with $US 0.5 per m² better than expropriation. She has agreed as her plot is located in the middle of the golf course and there is no road access. . . . another 8 families also faced the same situation of being forced to sell their land to the company.[53]

Consequently, disputes have not usually been resolved in court proceedings but rather are kept local for mediation by local officials and/or politicians or are organized into collective protest to appeal for help from top national level politicians.

The fourth source of insecurity is the threat of expropriation from the state following grants of large tracts of land in the form of economic land concessions to powerful politico-businessmen. The policy of awarding economic land concessions was adopted by the Cambodian government to increase government revenue through land rental, to promote private sector growth in agriculture and to alleviate rural poverty through employment generation. Recently economic land concessions have also taken the form of private housing development projects.

Economic land concessions are granted without either clear guidelines or prior public knowledge and create a situation of tenure insecurity for local people. The people who sell or are forced to sell their land in the peri-urban areas then either purchase or clear more land in the forested areas.[54] They claim land through settlement and utilization usually without any documentation, via the centuries' old practice to which rural Cambodian people still adhere. These practices lead them into conflicts with concessionaires who claim land through economic land concession rights usually granted via dubious processes by the government.

These tenure insecurity situations have been explained in term of "legal pluralism" in the existing literature. Legal pluralism is a "normative heterogeneity attendant upon the fact that social action always takes place in a context of multiple, overlapping semi-autonomous social field".[55] It denotes the coexistence of different normative orders, which at times run into conflict with one another. Individuals in different normative orders resort to different practices, which can be either legal or illegal, to claim the same piece of land.

Daniel Adler, Douglas Porter and Michael Woolcock maintain that the holding of land in the main residential and rice growing areas is relatively peaceful and secured despite the absence of formal land titles, and that conflicts over

---

53 Pel et al., *Land Transaction in Rural Cambodia*, 48.
54 Ibid., 28.
55 John Griffith, "What is Legal Pluralism?" *Journal of Legal Pluralism* 24.1 (1986), 38.

land are frequently found in forest lands, seasonal lakes and informal urban settlements, which are characterized by multiple competing norms. They identify three different normative orders, which conflict with one another and create a source of tenure insecurity for a vulnerable group of people who occupy land outside the main residential and cultivation areas. The first normative order is that of social norms, widely practised and perceived by the Cambodian rural dwellers. It is characterized by the deeply embedded traditional concept of ownership, the belief that ownership can be attained through the clearing and use of empty land without seeking appropriate documentation. The second normative order emerges from "neo-patrimonial administrative conventions", which are characterized by "a competing set of norms deriving from both previous regulatory regimes and practices that empower government officials at various levels to authorize transactions over lands within their administrative jurisdiction".[56] The final one is the "formal statute" or legal order which emerges out of the 2001 Land Law and the various other current regulations on land. The 2001 Land Law redefines people's rights to land by providing ownership rights to both residential and agricultural land through the issuance of legal documents. This law places a limitation on social norms. The clearing of "the state's public land" and the possession of such land following the adoption of the law becomes illegal. Yet, the law has not been effectively implemented to unify and harmonize all the competing norms. Instead it creates another layer of controls over the existing practices.[57]

What legal pluralism suggests is the coexistence of different competing norms, which are believed to be the sources of tenure insecurity. These different normative orders have been characterized by the differential use of rules among different groups of people, rules that at times clash with one another creating insecurity of land tenure. Sometimes, "Competing claims emerge even where none appear to be 'legal' in the narrow sense of the word."[58] In fact, while the problem of tenure insecurity in Cambodia characterizes the competing normative orders, tenure insecurity in Cambodia is more about asymmetric information and, even more crucially, unequal economic and political power between different parties to conflict. Powerful individuals are able to do more to serve their own interests.

[56] Daniel Adler, Douglas J. Porter and Michael Woolcock, "Legal Pluralism and Equity: Some Reflections on Land Reform in Cambodia," *Justice for the Poor* 2.2, April 2008, available at SSRN: http://ssrn.com/abstract=1133690. Studies by CDRI and CEDAC have arrived at similar conclusions about legal pluralism in the land sector, see Sovanarith So, Sophal Chan and Sarthi Acharya, "An Assessment of Land Tenure in Rural Cambodia," *Cambodia Development Review* 5 (October-December 2001): 3; and Pel et al., *Land Transaction in Rural Cambodia*, 226–227.
[57] Adler et al., "Legal Pluralism and Equity."
[58] Ibid.

Table 7. How people conduct land transactions before and after receiving land titles in Voar Sar and Pneay Communes, Kampong Speu Province

	After receiving land title		Before receiving land title		Total	
Cadastral Authority	4	9.3%	0	0%	4	3.1%
Witnessed by local officials	35	81.4%	64	74.4%	99	76.7%
Informal agreement between buyer and seller	3	7.0%	19	22.1%	22	17.1%
Others	1	2.3%	3	3.5%	4	3.1%
Total	43	100%	86	100%	129	100%

Given the deficiencies of the informal system, why do so many people still resort to it? The following sections discuss the limitations of SLR – limitations which preclude its emergence as a legitimate legal procedure to informal systems of land tenure.

Limits of the SLR System

Of all the respondents in the author's 2007 survey, 174 indicated that they have conducted land transactions of which 129 were conducted by people who resided in SLR communes. Of these 129, 86 and 43 conducted land transactions before and after receiving their land titles respectively, the imbalance in these figures reflecting the short time span between the distribution of land titles and the conduct of the survey.

According to Table 7, no substantial change in land transfer practice occurred after the distribution of land titles. About 90 per cent of people who transferred land after their land parcels had been registered, did not follow the required transfer procedure. Instead, most people either sought witnesses from local officials or reached verbal or written agreements among themselves in the process of conducting their land transactions.[59] Witness by local authority continued to be the prevailing form of land transfer practice. A wider set of

---

[59] The values of Chi squares for the different ways people conducted land transactions are statistically significant at .01 either before or after the people's receipt of land titles [Chi square =69.79 (2, 86) $p > .01$; Chi square = 73.37 (3, 43) $p > .01$].

Table 8. Reasons for not registering land transfers at cadastral authority.

Too costly		7	18.0%
Too complicated		9	23.0%
Everyone conducts land transaction at commune or village level		16	41.0%
Others	It's the buyer's task	3	18.0%
	Not necessary	1	
	The buyer wishes to transfer only at commune level	1	
	Trust	1	
	Don't know	1	
Total		39	100.0%

interviews with cadastral and local government officials confirmed that this pattern is not confined to the survey area, but is widespread in contemporary Cambodia.[60]

There were several reasons why people failed to register their land transfers. Of the 43 people who conducted land transactions following their receipts of land titles, 39 did not register their land transactions. These 39 people gave different reasons for their failure to register their land transfers (Table 8). For one group of people, the transfer of land witnessed by local officials represented simply an easily accessible avenue and an established practice (41 per cent). They chose their old way of doing things because everyone else did it that way and it remains acceptable among them even though it is illegitimate under the current Land Law. The decision of this group to register land transfer (or otherwise) was based upon the continued acceptability of customary practices among themselves, rather than being based upon the legal regulations. This response could be partly a result of lack of information. Given the fact that registering transfer qualifies the new owner for state protection against a third party claim, it should theoretically be in everyone's interests to register.

For another group, registering land transfers at the cadastral authority was either too complicated (23 per cent) or too costly (18 per cent). This group apparently had better access to information than the first group. They claimed either

---

[60] This study confirms the findings of the existing study. See, NGO Forum, *Land Titling and Poverty Reduction: A Study of Two Sangkat in Prey Nup District, Sihanoukville Municipality* (Phnom Penh: Analyzing Development Issues, NGOs Forum, November 2007).

to know someone (a friend or a relative) who had registered land transactions at the cadastral authority or to have tried inquiring about registering transfers by themselves. The complaints about the complicated and costly procedures are worth considering.

The legal procedure for transferring land ownership after land parcels had been registered required both parties to the land transaction to be physically present to thumbprint the sales agreement and to file a land transfer registration form at the District Cadastral Office, which is the lowest level of land governance authority, with reporting responsibility to the Ministry of Land Management, Urban Planning and Construction (MLMUPC).[61] This registration form also requires the approval of the district and provincial governors. District and provincial offices are usually situated at the urban centre. In some remote areas, travelling to these offices is a challenge due to cost and lack of means of transportation.

Moreover, there is a 4 per cent sales tax that needs to be paid at the provincial tax department. Only after the transfer agreement has been authenticated, the transfer registration form has been approved, and the cadastral transfer fee[62] and the tax have been paid, can the transfer of ownership be formally conducted.

Further complicating the issue is how the officials handle the transfer. The whole process of registering land transfers can take from 2 to 5 weeks (or even longer) with repeated follow-ups required to complete. Every time the transfer document crosses a desk, the payment of an informal fee is required. This process compares unfavourably with the quasi-formal process which requires just one day at the commune office, with no tax to pay.

By law, there is a 4 per cent sales tax based on the sales price plus a fixed cadastral service fee to conduct land transfer. The 2001 Land Law requires that sales agreements contain the sales price to a provide basis for the calculation of the 4 per cent tax liability. In addition, there is a 2 per cent tax on unused land as indicated in the Interim Land Policy paper.[63] There is currently no

---

[61] Article 65 of the 2001 Land Law indicates that "the transfer of ownership can be enforceable against third parties only if the contract of sale of immovable property is made in writing in the authentic form drawn up by the competent authority and registered with the Cadastral Registry Unit. The contract of sale itself is not a sufficient legal requirement for the transfer of the ownership of the subject matter." The competent authority in this context is the cadastral officials.

[62] This amount varies according to land types. It costs US$50 for residential land in Phnom Penh, Sihanoukville, Siem Reap, and Kandal, US$25 for residential land in rural area, US$30 for provincial town other than Phnom Penh, Sihanoukville, Siem Reap, and Kandal, and US$12.5 for agricultural land.

[63] Royal Government of Cambodia, *Strategy of Land Policy Framework: Interim Paper*, Phnom Penh, 6 September 2003.

clear valuation procedure or guideline to determine the market value of land systematically. While it is claimed that the Ministry of Economy and Finance's (MEF) tax department maintain information on land valuation for the purpose of taxation, this document is not made available to the public. Without a clear guideline for the estimation of tax, tax liability is unpredictable and amounts to whatever price the tax officials choose to set. [64] This situation makes it unpredictable and costly for individual land sellers and buyers to register land transactions. It is possible to ease the transactions by enlisting the help of a mediator, usually a cadastral official, to facilitate the complete transaction, including the payment of formal and informal fees as well as the negotiation of the tax payment with the tax officials. The cost can range between US$1,000 and US$2,000[65] in Phnom Penh and between US$350 and US$500 in rural areas depending on the land's size and value.[66]

To a certain extent, the tax payment for a land transaction does not necessarily inhibit people from registering their land transfers. It is the practice of rent extortion in the payment of tax, the charges of informal fees at every involved state office, and the long complex procedure that discourage people from using the cadastral registration system when conducting land transfers.

A 2002 study by CDRI indicated that the 4 per cent sales tax is never paid in full. This can be done with collusion from both cadastral and tax officials.[67] Corruption within the tax and cadastral offices presents problems for small land owners whose land value is low because informal fees are determined by the numbers of desks the transaction papers need to cross. In one example of a land transaction where the sale price was US$1,000, the cost of registering the transfer reached US$350.[68]

The high cost of registering a land transfer severely affects the sustainability of cadastral records since it limits access for many while also discouraging many others from meeting their legal land transfer obligation. The high and unpredictable cost of transfer registration greatly reduces the poor titled land holders' ability to comply with their legal land transfer obligation and affects the incentive of many others. In another example, a villager in Voa Sa wished

---

[64] G 3, Interview with author, 24 September 2007.
[65] A 2005 government's Land Valuation Study Report documented a higher informal fee in the amount of US$3000 in Phnom Penh. See Royal Government of Cambodia, *Land Valuation Study Report* (Phnom Penh: Ministry of Land Management Urban Planning and Construction, Land Mapping and Administration Project, 31 May 2005), 15.
[66] P 1, Interview with author, 24 October 2007.
[67] CDRI found differences in the leakage rate between provinces: in Kompong Cham and Battambang, only 20–30 per cent of the real price was recorded, while in Kandal and Sihanoukville it was 50–80 per cent. In Kompong Speu it was 40–60 per cent.
[68] G 12, Interview with author, 19 November 2007.

to give a fifth of his land plot – a patch measuring 2,000 square metres – to his eldest son as a wedding present. Since the land was registered in the father's name, a transfer procedure was necessary to legally transfer the portion in question to the son. The father visited the district cadastral office to inquire about the transfer, but he was asked to pay US$350 to have the land registered as two plots, one of which was to be registered under his son's name. He said he could not afford the cost; and given the small monetary value of his land, he would rather give his son US$350 if he had that money. He then visited the commune chief's office and requested a certification, which indicated his transfer of one fifth of his land to his son. He paid the commune chief R2,0000 or US$5.[69]

Furthermore, some interviewees who complained about the costly registration of land transfers believed that even if they invested a lot of resources to register their purchases, they would still need to pay more in bribes and fees in order to gain the protection of the state for their land in the event of a dispute. Given such poor access to state services, legal land title alone without political and economic power may not necessarily deter the threat of seizure from powerful people. As Daniel Bromley maintains "For dysfunctional governments to issue titles to slum dwellers or rural squatters is similar to governments issuing counterfeit currency. A mere title is no assurance at all that the issuing entity will act on the promissory note. In the absence of that assurance, a title can be a symbol of willful deceit."[70]

A relatively well-off villager interviewed in Pneay commune had bought many small titled plots of land without registering transfers at the district cadastral authority even though she was aware of the legal transfer procedure. Her perception was that she would not be protected by the state in the event of a conflict without paying bribes even when she had legally registered her purchases. She anticipated that the commune chiefs who witnessed her sales agreement would mediate or testify against any possible future conflicts should they occur.[71]

In sum, then, the key benefit from registering land transfers – tenure security protected by the state – is insufficiently certain to make it worth the cost, thanks to poor, but accurate, perceptions of the nature of the Cambodian court system. At the local level, most people tend to avoid legal proceedings at the court by keeping their disputes local and by requesting conflict resolution from the local authority, whose legal basis of intervention is unclear in the state's law.[72]

---

[69] V 1, Interview with author, 17 September 2007.
[70] Daniel W. Bromley, "Formalizing Property Relations in the Developing World: The Wrong Prescription for the Wrong Malady," *Land Use Policy* 26 (2008): 21.
[71] V 2, Interview with author, 4 September 2007.
[72] Pel et al., Land Transaction in Rural Cambodia, 226.

The high transaction cost and low benefits will not permit the institutionalization of a land holding practice based on the cadastral system.[73] As long as the cost continues to be high without substantial benefit, the established practice outside the state's regulation will continue to be an option among land owners despite its deficiency. Cambodia needs what Mancur Olson called a "structure of incentive"[74] to encourage a switch from current practice to a new form of centrally regulated cadastral registration system.

Land Tenure Institutions and Structures of Political Power

Land tenure insecurity prior to SLR was a multi-faceted issue caused by the actions of the predatory state, which favours the powerful at the expense of the poor. Much of the problem emerges from poor legal protection, widespread corruption, and poor land management systems; but these are all symptoms of underlying features of the Cambodian state. They cannot be resolved with a simple land registration process, unless important state services, such as the court, the police, and the land governance office, which is tasked with land registration and the maintenance of land ownership records, truly provide the backing for a legal order. Although an efficient cadastral registration system, introduced by donors, could potentially improve land management through the provision of transparent ownership information via the centralized land database, this kind of registration system is unlikely to take root in current conditions, where the average farmer is poor and weak, and where bureaucratic offices are underpinned by patrimonial structures supporting and defending practices of corruption.

The inability of SLR to develop an efficient cadastral registration system means that people will continue to use the "quasi-formal" system, reinforcing the plurality of norms governing land rights, and widening the divide between prevailing conceptions of land ownership on the part of the urban rich, and on the part of the rural poor. Although not all the urban rich people rely on the state-guaranteed land rights and register their land transactions, they increasingly do so in the light of the significant rise of urban land values. In rural areas, the poor are more likely to continue to use informal systems, due to their lack of financial resources and their familiarity with the informal systems.

---

[73] See, Douglass North, "Institutions," *Journal of Economic Perspectives* 5.1 (1991):102–104.
[74] Mancur Olson, "Big Bills Left on the Sidewalk: Why Some Nations are Rich, and Others Poor," *Journal of Economic Perspectives* 10.2 (1996): 6, 22–23.

Moreover, people who claim land without appropriate documentation will continue to be at risk of expropriation by the predatory state's action, in a context where land distribution has become a device through which political power is pursued and maintained. This is particularly the case in remote rural areas which have traditionally operated as a frontier available for settlement by the poor, but which are today the locus of large-scale development plans on the part of the government and big business. In fact, SLR has only been implemented in the relatively secure areas of well-established residential and agricultural land, leaving large areas vulnerable to competing claims.

In these unoccupied areas, the poor, reliant on traditional norms of land tenure, are at risk of running into conflicts with the state itself; in conflicts over "state land", possession rights do not award any kind of protection.[75] The conflicts are worsened when the state signs off such land in collusive deals of economic land concessions in favour of powerful private business interests.

One example of land conflict outside the SLR system affected more than 4,000 families living around Boeng Kak lake in Phnom Penh. This area, like other informal settlements in Phnom Penh, was excluded from land registration through the LMAP's SLR on the basis that ownership could not be granted on "state public land". In 2007 these families faced eviction following the government's lease of 133 hectares of the lake for the amount of US$ 79 million for a period of 99 years to a Cambodian construction company, Shukaku Inc.[76] The lake property is considered to be state public land, and therfore cannot be legally transferred or sold to private individuals; the government nevertheless awarded the land to a private company. The government went so far as to issue a sub-decree on 7 August 2008 re-titling the area as "state private land" to legitimize the leasing agreement.[77]

The *Phnom Penh Post* reported that the market value of the land around the Boeng Kak lake ranged between US$700 and US$1,000 per square meter, but the deal signed by the government with Shukaku netted the government only US$0.60 per square metre.[78] Ordinary people living on the lake faced eviction, and were forced to accept the paltry compensation of about US$8,000 for the

---

[75] Center for Advanced Study, "An Exploratory Study of Collective Grievances Over Land and Local Governance in Cambodia, (Phnom Penh: Center for Advanced Study and World Bank, 2007), 14.
[76] Allyster Hayman and Sam Rith, "Boeng Kak Lake Latest City Sell off," *The Phnom Penh Post*, 09 February 2007, online at www.phnompenhpost.com., accessed 12 August 2009.
[77] Sebastian Strangio and Chhay Channyda, "Who Owns the Lake? Debate Rages," *The Phnom Penh Post*, 03 October 2008, online at www.phnompenhpost.com, accessed 12 August 2009.
[78] Allyster Hayman and Sam Rith, "Lake Dwellers Among Thousands To Be Evicted," *The Phnom Penh Post*, 23 February 2007, online at www.phnompenhpost.com., accessed 12 August 2009.

takeover of their properties.[79] This case illustrates the use of state power to dispossess the poor for the benefit of powerful business individuals in collusion with government officials.

Faced with this state – business alliance, collective action has become one of the main instruments used to seek justice. Collective action has generated a certain degree of responsiveness from executive officials controlling the government. The executive officials are under pressure to respond to popular grievance, to ensure legitimacy and to avoid unrest. Prime Minister Hun Sen has warned of the negative consequences of increasing land grabbing and even declared a war against land grabbers with the approval of his party's Central Committee, although this war has yielded few successes.[80] As Hughes and Conway suggest, the ruling party needs to maintain its political legitimacy, "both democratic and patrimonial, in the eyes of a predominantly rural populace".[81]

Assistance from powerful individuals following collective action most of the time is limited and unsatisfactory; but it can prompt certain concessions from powerful parties to conflict. Such partial compromises result from the complex framework within which the incentives of the officials are shaped. The officials need to ensure (1) continuous electoral victories through the maintenance of their legitimacy as good patrons in the eyes of the Cambodian poor, (2) the achievement of the goal of developing the private sector, and (3) the continued presence of rent-seeking opportunities for self-enrichment and for the maintenance of their public posts.[82]

In the absence of a neutral and professional judicial system that provides equal protection to every person, people seek help from powerful individuals rather than seek formal legal protection. In this regard, tenure security is not so much about what kind of ownership paper one retains but who one is connected to and how much money or power one can use in support of one's claim. This was the problem of tenure insecurity in Cambodia prior to and after the introduction of SLR. Even if judicial reform can be achieved, the problem may not disappear entirely. However, the presence of an efficient court system that provides equal protection empowers the poor and the weak and could be expected to significantly alter the condition of tenure insecurity in Cambodia.

---

[79] One report indicates that the compensation was US$4,000. See IRIN, "Cambodia: Questions over legality of evictions in name of development," UN Office for the Coordination of Humanitarian Affairs, Phnom Penh, 18 August 2008.

[80] Samakum Thieng Tnoat, "Quarterly Summary of Land Conflicts in Cambodia," *Cambodia Eviction Monitor* 2 (July, 2007): 3–4.

[81] Caroline Hughes and Timothy Conway, *Understanding Pro-Poor Political Change: The Policy Process* (London: Overseas Development Institute, 2004), 33 as cited in Center for Advanced Study, "An Exploratory Study of Collective Grievances," 31.

[82] Center for Advanced Study, "An Exploratory Study of Collective Grievances," 31–32.

8

Neoliberal Strategies of Poverty Reduction in Cambodia: The Case of Microfinance

David J. Norman

This chapter traces the development of the microfinance sector in Cambodia, specifically looking at the way non-governmental organizations (NGOs) as traditional providers of microfinance have undergone a transformative process over the last decade into financial institutions as part of a changing commercial sector. These reforms are externally influenced through the global rise of microfinance "best practices", converging with international donor-driven "new public management" reforms of the NGO sector in Cambodia. The consequence is a commercially driven neoliberal strategy of poverty reduction, entailing a prioritizing of market expansion and self-sustainability at the heart of the emerging private-sector-oriented microfinance industry.

Microcredit/Microfinance: Some Conceptual Origins

Microcredit is a poverty reduction strategy that aims to provide small amounts of credit to the rural poor, not only for income generating activities but also for supplementing basic requirements such as food, health, housing and education.[1] In essence microcredit is about empowering the poor by giving them a chance to stand on their own two feet and create new business models, thereby instilling a sense of dignity and self-sufficiency without reliance upon welfare provision or other forms of economic dependency. In recent years there has not only been an expansion in outreach to the poor but also in the number of services microfinance institutions are able to offer. Originally restricted to

---

[1] Joy Deshmukh-Ranadive and Ranjani K. Murthy, "Introduction: Linking the Triad" in Neera Burra, Joy Deshmukh-Ranadive and Ranjani K. Murthy, *Micro-Credit, Poverty and Empowerment: Linking the Triad* (India: Sage Publications, 2005), 31.

small credit loans, microfinance today offers an array of financial products and services such as microinsurance, savings schemes, remittances and payments services.[2] The expansion of microfinance services and products is largely driven by the contemporary commercialization of the industry and its relationship with the competitive market.

Microfinance is increasingly seen as an important poverty reduction strategy. Many of the world's poorest are without sufficient access to credit: fulfilling this unmet credit demand will provide the poor with sufficient tools to acquire control and autonomy over their economic situation and break the vicious cycle of poverty. It is often cited in the literature that "the poor remain poor because they are powerless. Once empowered the poor are able to change their lives and overcome seemingly impossible odds."[3]

Microcredit began to emerge in the 1970s through experimental small-scale rural development projects tasked with opening up credit access for the poor. The founding of the Grameen Bank by Muhammad Yunus[4] in 1983 represented the start of a re-conceptualization of the poor as credit-worthy and capable of participating in economic markets. Yunus believed that some of the more extreme forms of poverty were breakable by bringing the poor into the financial market a radical position rejected at the time by the orthodox theories of economic development that saw the poor as outside of the financial system and thus excluded from its positive potential.[5]

The Global Mainstreaming of the Microfinance Sector

Microfinance remained firmly on the margins of international development throughout the 1980s as small-scale localized poverty projects. However in the mid 1990s the international donor community and key international organizations (the World Bank, United Nations, International Labour Organization etc.)

---

[2] See Brigit Helms, *Access for All: Building Inclusive Financial Systems* (Washington DC: World Bank, 2006), Joanna Ledgerwood, *Microfinance Handbook: An Institutional and Financial Perspective* (Washington DC: World Bank, 2002). In the literature this is what commonly differentiates microfinance from microcredit: the broadening of financial options rather than just focusing upon credit loans. It should be noted that the two terms are often used interchangeably throughout the literature; this chapter will, however, keep with the more common use of microfinance.

[3] CGAP, *Good Practice Guidelines for Funders of Microfinance: Microfinance Consensus Guidelines.* (Washington: CGAP, 2006) online at www.CGAP.org.

[4] Muhammad Yunus is often cited as the pioneer of microfinance and was awarded the Nobel Peace Prize in 2006 for his efforts at combating poverty through the use of microfinance projects.

[5] See Muhammad Yunus, "Grameen Bank, Microcredit and Millennium Goals," *Economic and Political Weekly* 39.36 (2006).

began to take an increasing interest in it, particularly in the wake of criticisms being received from inside and outside these organizations for the problematic implementation of Structural Adjustment Programmes.[6]

In response to this criticism a "Post-Washington consensus" approach was developed focusing upon "adjustment with a human face." The World Bank began to shift its emphasis to poverty reduction, and particularly to the development of national Poverty Reduction Strategy Papers as a focal point for directing reform in the economic systems of developing countries.[7] The shift to the "post-Washington consensus" entailed a re-focusing from the macro-political to the micro-political in order to tackle the recognised persistence of poverty and rising inequality within and among countries. Microfinance found itself elevated from the margins to the mainstream and an integral part of the new "global poverty reduction agenda".[8]

This agenda also entailed increased interest in the participation of civil society in development projects.[9] In this respect, microfinance was seen to contribute to a localized, non-state approach to micro-economic development. Global movements in microfinance found themselves in increasingly important partnership roles with global economic institutions like the World Bank, as the privileging of non-state approaches to poverty reduction gave microfinance global prominence.

1997 can be seen as a pivotal year in the increased mainstreaming of microfinance and its institutionalization in global development practices. The Consultative Group to Assist the Poor (CGAP) was established, comprising a global network of powerful donors (and partnering the World Bank) to assist in the global expansion and coordination of microfinance. In June 2004 microfinance received further recognition as a critical component in global poverty reduction when the G8 endorsed the "key principles of microfinance", which

---

[6] Structural Adjustment Programmes were part of the rise of the "Washington consensus"; large-scale public cut-backs and rapid privatization programmes (including a shift from state-led strategies to market-led strategies) representing the pinnacle of neoliberal economic development. See J. Williamson, "Democracy and the Washington Consensus," *World Development* 21.8 (1993).

[7] See Ben Fine, Costas Lapavitsas and Jonathan Pincus, *Development Policy in the Twenty First Century: Beyond the Post-Washington Consensus* (London: Routledge, 2003) and J. Stiglitz, "More Instruments and Broader Goals: Moving Toward the Post-Washington Consensus" (Helsinki: United Nations University/World Institute for Development Economics Research, 1998).

[8] Heloise Weber, "The Global Political Economy of Microfinance and Poverty Reduction: Locating local 'Livelihoods' in Political Analysis," in Jude Fernando (ed.), *Microfinance: Perils and Prospects* (London: Routledge, 2006), 44.

[9] A. Sarker, "New Public Management, Service Provision and Non-governmental Organizations in Bangladesh," *Public Organization Review* 5.3 (2005), G. Porter, "NGOs and Poverty Reduction in a Globalizing World: perspectives from Ghana," *Progress in Development Studies* 3.2 (2003).

have been translated into concrete operational guidance for the international donor community working with CGAP, and which established best practice methodologies for NGOs working in the field.[10]

The first "World Microcredit Summit Campaign" was also held in 1997 in Washington DC. The campaign summit was a global conference that brought together leading practitioners and policy-makers in the field.[11] At the summit, a universal document of intent and future aspirations was put forward and agreed upon by the participants. Core themes to be emphasized over the coming years were agreed upon including: reaching the poorest; empowering women; constructing self-sufficient finance systems; ensuring a positive impact on clients and families.[12] This increasing global recognition culminated in the United Nations World Summit's announcement of 2005 as the "Year of Microcredit" and recognising it as a critical tool in the effort to achieve the Millennium Development Goals (MDGs) on the grounds that, "Microfinance is one of the practical development strategies and approaches that should be implemented and supported to attain the bold ambition of reducing world poverty by half."[13]

The rise in prominence of the Microcredit Summit Campaign and the powerful role of CGAP demonstrate the links between global social movements advocating microfinance as a non-state solution to poverty reduction, and the elevating of microfinance by powerful economic institutions. This is part of a larger convergence between civil society and development occurring as part of the socially oriented "post-Washington consensus". This relationship, however, needs closer interrogation to uncover the unsurprising link between microfinance as a market-led poverty reduction strategy, and (contra post-Washington consensus rhetoric) the *continuation* and greater *intensification* of the neoliberal economic regime with its focus upon expansionary market rationality.[14]

Microfinance has been promoted and intertwined with mainstream neoliberal economics to construct an enabling environment to empower the poor in order for them to engage in self-help commercial and entrepreneurial

---

[10] CGAP, *Good Practice Guidelines for Funders of Microfinance: Microfinance Consensus Guidelines*.

[11] The 1997 conference brought over 2,900 people from 137 countries to participate. Since 1997 there have been global microcredit summits in 1998, 1999, 2002, 2006; throughout this period there have been successful regional microcredit summits, reflecting the growth and diversity of the sector (see www.microcreditsummit.org for a general overview).

[12] Joy Deshmukh-Ranadive and Ranjiani Murthy, 34.

[13] UNCDF, *Microfinance and the Millennium Development Goals: A reader's guide to the Millennium Project Reports and other UN documents* (Geneva: UNCDF, 2005), 5. online at www.yearofmicrocredit.org/docs/mdgdoc_MN.pdf accessed on February 2009.

[14] See Paul Cammack, "Neoliberalism, the World Bank, and the New Politics of Development," in Uma Kothari and Martin Minogue (eds.), *Development Theory and Practice: Critical Perspectives* (London: Palgrave, 2002) and Ben Fine, Costas Lapavitsas, Jonathan Pincus, 52–79.

activities regarded by neoliberals as the most appropriate path out of poverty. Muhammad Yunus himself notes that, "All it needs to get the poor people out of poverty [is] for us to create an enabling environment for them. Once the poor can unleash their energy and creativity, poverty will disappear very quickly."[15]

The Microcredit Summit Campaign claims "Microcredit allows families to work to end their own poverty - with dignity".[16] The concept of dignity (coupled with the rise out of poverty) is embedded within the business approach to poverty reduction: the aim is for anyone, no matter how poor they are, to have the opportunity to become an entrepreneur and thus a "somebody" imbued with dignity. In essence, in the rhetoric of microfinance, the market and its entrepreneurial (neoliberal) subject is privileged.[17]

The poverty reduction focus of microfinance, of expanding access to capital and combining this with an emphasis upon entrepreneurial empowerment, sits comfortably with the neoliberal rationality of individual self-help and the reduction of social welfare dependency to be replaced by an individual private sector emphasis. As Batliwala argues, "empowerment" was co-opted in the 1990s by conservative ideologies in their pursuit of dismantling welfare provisions. This is perceived as allowing power and control to be decentralized to "empowered" communities, who then look after themselves. The theme of 'empowerment' has been deprived of social content and wedded to the concept of the market and consumer choice as a method of access for those deemed powerless.[18]

From small-scale rural projects emanating from the Grameen Bank, microfinance has been incorporated into the larger international development architecture. There are still, however, numerous debates in the literature about whether microfinance is effective at poverty reduction and whether it can reach the poorest of the poor[19]. This is of less concern in this chapter, however; what is important is to understand how, in the case of Cambodia, microfinance

---

[15] Muhammad Yunus "Nobel Prize: ceremony speech," Nobel lecture presented at the Nobel Peace Prize ceremony on 10 Dec., 2006 in Oslo. Online at www.muhammadyunus.org/content/view/79/128/lang,en/ accessed February 2009.

[16] The Microcredit Summit Campaign "What is Microcredit," online at www.microcreditsummit.org accessed February 2009.

[17] Morgan Brigg, "Disciplining the developmental subject: Neoliberal power and Governance through Microcredit," in Jude Fernando (eds.), *Microfinance: Perils and Prospects* (London: Routledge, 2006), 77.

[18] S. Batliwala, "Taking the power out of empowerment – an experiential account," *Development in Practice* 17.4 (2007).

[19] See J. Copestake, "Inequality and the polarizing impact of microcredit: evidence from Zambia's copperbelt," *Journal of international development* 14.6 (2002), 743–755. Anne Marie Goetz and Rina Sen Gupta, "Who takes the credit? Gender, power, and control over loan use in rural credit programs in Bangladesh," *World Development*, 24.1 (1996). Nalia Kabeer, "Conflicts over Credit: Re-evaluating the empowerment potential of loans to women in rural Bangladesh," *World Development* 29.1 (2001).

has been introduced as an idealized form of poverty reduction and embedded within the dominant neoliberal development orthodoxy, and crucially to see what the repercussions are on socially-minded NGOs, when tracing the history of microfinance in Cambodia.

The Growth of Microfinance in Cambodia

Microfinance has in recent years become of increasing importance to the Royal Government of Cambodia as an integral tool to reaching its poverty reduction targets and stabilizing an inclusive credit market to the poor. The development of the second Socio-Economic Development Plan 2001–2005 and its subsequent inclusion in the National Poverty Reduction Strategy 2003–2005 highlighted microfinance as one of the government's priority poverty reduction actions. The National Poverty Reduction Strategy 2003–2005 adapted the second Socio-Economic Development Plan's targets to try and localize the Millennium Development Goals to Cambodian conditions, and in this way microfinance has been elevated as an example of NGOs, the private sector and international donors working together to decrease poverty in Cambodia. Since its elevation to being included in the National Strategic Development Plan 2006–2010 and the Financial Sector Development Plan 2001–2010, the industry has "evolved from a series of small, isolated projects into what is arguably the most sophisticated segment of the national financial services sector".[20] In 2006 a national summit on "Microfinance in Cambodia" was held, organized by the National Bank of Cambodia and the United Nations Development Programme. At the summit, the Prime Minister, Samdech Hun Sen, recognised the growing importance of microfinance to Cambodia, officially declaring 2006 as the "Year of Microfinance". Current World Bank president Robert Zoellick, visited Cambodia in August 2007 (his first to a developing country since becoming President in July) where he met local entrepreneurs and was given a brief overview of the microfinance industry in Cambodia, about which he remarked, "The success of the microfinance industry in Cambodia is remarkable given the challenging business environment and the difficulty of reaching rural and remote areas."[21] Despite these challenges the figures remain impressive; active borrowers with

---

[20] Vannak Chou, Simone di Castri, Sophea Hoy, Sovannsoksitha Pen, Engchhay Soung, *IDLO Microfinance Policy and Regulation Survey N1* (Rome: IDLO, 2008) online at http://www.idlo.int/Microfinance/Documents/Publications/1E.pdf.

[21] World Bank, "Local Bank Provides Hope to Thousands of Potential Micro-Entrepreneurs," August 2007 online at http://web.worldbank.org/WBSITE/EXTERNAL/COUNTRIES/EASTASIAPACIFICEXT/CAMBODIAEXTN/0,,contentMDK:21432545~menuPK:293861~pagePK:2865066~piPK:2865079~theSitePK:293856,00.html accessed February 2009.

access to rural credit and micro-business loans totalled over 464,122 clients in 2006, an increase of 27 per cent over the previous year.[22] The number of borrowers further increased to 624,000 clients at the end of 2007[23] and has grown to approximately 951,325 clients in the latest statistics released at the end of 2008,[24] demonstrating a vast level of expansion and greater levels of inclusion of rural households.[25] The high growth rate of the microfinance industry has been described as "a phenomenon that is relatively rare and could make Cambodia the envy of its neighbouring countries over the next few years".[26]

How has microfinance developed from small isolated projects to an impressive "sophisticated" industry that is continually expanding? What structural transformations have been undertaken, given Cambodia's economic and social fragility in recent decades? It is to these questions that the focus will now turn.

After 20 years of civil unrest had devastated the social and economic infrastructure of Cambodia (from 1970 to 1990), access to credit was virtually nonexistent outside of informal money-lending activities. In the 1990s Cambodia went through a transitional period with the introduction in rural villages of a cash-based economy. Subsequently, non-farming activities began to rise in importance in parallel with new marketing activities.[27] The underdeveloped urban banking system also underwent key changes to embrace the market and change from a monobanking system in 1989 to its first two-tier banking system, allowing the establishment of private commercial banks and constructing a centralized autonomous National Bank of Cambodia through the 1996 central banking law.[28]

By 2001 credit access for those outside the newly developing financial system (much of the rural poor) was still underdeveloped; the main suppliers of credit were from informal sources of NGOs practising microfinance. At this time it

---

[22] National Bank of Cambodia, *Annual Report 2006* (Phnom Penh: National Bank of Cambodia, 2006) online at www.nbc.org.kh.

[23] Vannak Chou, Simone di Castri, Sophea Hoy, Sovannsoksitha Pen, Engchhay Soung, 7.

[24] Cambodia Microfinance Association, "Information Exchange," 2008, online at www.CMA-Network.org/information.htm accessed on April 2009.

[25] Although these figures represent the expansion of the formalized sector since 2001, there are still numerous NGOs that have not transformed and work throughout various provinces which are difficult for statistical calculation.

[26] Sanjay Sinha, "Cambodia Microfinance Miracle," *Economics Today,* January 1–15th 2008

[27] Kim Sedara, "Agrarian Situation in Contemporary Cambodia: Overview of Case Studies in Cambodian Villages," *Cambodia Development Review* 6.2 (2002), 5. It is also worth noting that it was not until 1985 that market-orientated reforms were considered acceptable and heralded the rise of the private sector. See Asian Development Bank *Technical Assistance to the Royal Kingdom of Cambodia for Rural Credit and Savings Project* (Manila: Asian Development Bank, 1997) online at www.adb.org.

[28] Asian Development Bank *Cambodia: Financial sector Blueprint 2001–2010* (Phnom Penh: Asian Development Bank, 2001) online at www.adb.org.

was estimated that approximately 40 per cent of the population had no access to the formal banking sector, due to a weak financial architecture.[29] Compare this with statistics in 2009, suggesting that despite this "gap", demand for credit is rapidly being filled from outside of the formal banking system via microfinance. From a low 7–8 per cent coverage of the gap in 1997 to around 25 per cent today, the rise of microfinance has led one observer to note that at current rates of expansion, in the next five years approximately 95 per cent of the unmet credit demand will be filled.[30]

Microfinance, therefore, has been an important element in allowing greater access to credit for Cambodians outside of the formal banking system. Its earliest origins in the country can be traced to UNICEF in 1989 and the large ensemble of international non-governmental organizations (INGOs) and donors from 1990 onwards, arriving to offer aid and stabilize the country, whilst experimenting with small microcredit programmes.[31]

In order to regulate and coordinate this large influx of donor funded microfinance NGOs, the Royal Government of Cambodia established the Credit Committee for Rural Development (CCRD) in 1995. The CGRD was supported by the United Nations Development Programme to design a legal framework and establish the rules of the environment in which NGOs had found themselves operating in Cambodia. In order to modernize and tie the microfinance sector more closely to Cambodia's financial regulatory sector, the International Monetary Fund and the Asian Development Bank pressurized the CCRD in turn to place pressure upon the National Bank of Cambodia to take more responsibility and to implement more regulatory measures in the sector.[32] Following this pressure, in 1997 the "Supervision Office for Specialised Banks and Microfinance Institutions" was established in the Bank Supervision Department of the National Bank of Cambodia, highlighting the expansion and importance of microfinance to the development and financial sector.

This period of the 1990s can be seen as a period of the maturing of NGO activities in Cambodia, as microfinance projects became institutionalised through a sharing of objectives, principles and strategies in order to make development

---

[29] Ibid

[30] Sanjay Sinha, 11.

[31] The first to do so were the INGOs, Groupe de Recherche et d'Études Technologiques (GRET), Catholic Relief Services, and World Vision. They were joined by key international donors such as United Nations Children's Fund, International Labour Organization, United Nation Development Programme, Agence Française de Développement and the United States Agency for International Development (USAID). See Vannak Chou, Simone di Castri, Sophea Hoy, Sovannsoksitha Pen, Engchhay Soung, 2.

[32] Mark Flaming, Eric Duflos, Alexia Latortue, Nina Nayer, Jimmy Roth, *Country-Level Effectiveness and Accountability Review: Cambodia* (Washington DC: CGAP, 2005), 6.

coordination more effective.³³ NGOs were seen in this context as the key facilitators for the growth of microfinance. Their local knowledge and high mobility meant they were the ideal vehicle for supplying microcredit and various saving schemes to local poor communities. Their social objectives provided a platform in rural Cambodia for the pursuit of poverty reduction through expanding access to credit to the poor and offering various saving schemes, culminating in a multitude of coordinated projects.

Since the end of the 1990s, microfinance in Cambodia has undergone a period of rapid commercialization of the sector. This has involved a shift in NGO funding sources from donor to self-sustainability; significantly, it has also entailed a more professionalized and market-centred approach to poverty reduction. As they move from the margins to the centre of development assistance, Cambodian microfinance institutions are rapidly changing – they must now be seen to be businesslike and professional. At the heart of this transformation of the sector lies the intensification of neoliberal rationality in the construction of poverty reduction, like scaling up market expansion and the intensification of entrepreneurial identities. This entrepreneurial and business-orientated approach is not an isolated coincidence; it is part of a global managerial transformation of perceptions as to the way that organizations should be structured. This shifting attitude is part of the rise of New Public Management techniques that, emanating from western donors and development institutions, have permeated the organizational structures of NGOs in Cambodia. The chapter now interrogates what New Public Management techniques are, and how these principles create structural constraints on NGOs/microfinance institutions, forcing them either to adhere to market logic and contemporary "microfinance best practices", or risk being excluded from it.

New Public Management and the Shifting of a Paradigm

New Public Management is an important field of policy-making practice and scholarship that has rapidly risen in importance since the 1970s. The growth in interest in this field largely stems from the national economic crises of the 1970s and 1980s, which suggested a need for stricter control over public agencies, implemented in accordance with the neoliberal ideology of state bureaucratic reduction.³⁴ Despite many variations in what accurately constitutes the term, there is a consensus surrounding the core attributes of New Public Management

---

[33] Vannak Chou, Simone di Castri, Sophea Hoy, Sovannsoksitha Pen, Engchhay Soung, 2.
[34] Laurence Lynn, *Public Management: Old and New* (London: Routledge, 2006), 1.

which differentiate it from previous administrative methods. These attributes include a business-oriented approach to government, a preference for quality and performance management, deregulation, privatization, commercialization and marketization.[35] Competition forms an important tenet of New Public Management, deriving from the theoretical basis of public-choice theory, designed to motivate departments within organizations through internal competition and incentives.[36] The underlying management strategy parallels neoclassical economics (and rational choice theory), whereby public organizations are equated to a theory of the firm acting within market structures. Firms are formed and dissolved according to market opportunity, being led by external structures (for example shareholders require firms to act on market conditions in order to be efficient and have the highest performances).

New Public Management as an administrative practice became increasingly popular on a global scale; the World Bank recognized in 1991 that it needed to shift from a centralized administration to one that is more market-oriented.[37] The global spread of New Public Management as an overidingly neoliberal agenda brought the emphasis on managerialism and the private sector as a "best practice" ideology to be implemented throughout various public organizations.

Importantly, the globalizing trend of New Public Management as a transformative project has not only had an effect upon developing countries (especially when linked with the IMF's Structural Adjustment initiatives to privatize, deregulate and commercialize aspects of economic institutions) but has also had a significant transformative effect on how NGOs are managed. The reduction of state bureaucracies and demands for greater accountability have developed a general consensus among policy-makers that NGOs should step into important roles to relieve the government of bureaucratic overburden by forming networks with decentralized actors tasked with providing private sector services to the people.[38] New Public Management techniques have been implemented by donor-driven technical approaches to train and brief NGOs in order to help them carry out their roles in the support of various activities such as microfinance and poverty reduction in general. Within the NGO community there is an ongoing debate on how far NGOs should attempt to pursue strategies of New Public Management in order to raise levels of accountability and performance. Many have turned towards auditing as a standard method to remain accountable and, importantly, fundable.

---

[35] Ibid., 107.
[36] G. Gruening, "Origin and theoretical basis of new public management", *International Public Management Journal*, 4.1 (2001): 1–25.
[37] Laurence Lynn, *Public Management: Old and New*, 105.
[38] A. Sarker, 250.

New Public Management techniques have created a competitive environment that NGOs and microfinance institutions must now operate in, and international donors prioritize those actors who engage most effectively with the market, seeing them as more "professional", whilst penalizing those seen as inefficient and unprofessional.[39] CGAP's Country-Level Effectiveness and Accountability Review study emphasized that it is imperative that NGOs adapt to this new private sector development model. If there are reasons why an NGO cannot become an independent licensed institution then guidelines should be introduced for integrating the NGO into an existing microfinance institution in order for the microfinance sector to progress.[40] Also CGAP recommended that: "based on a competitive process, fund only registered NGOs that can become commercial, either by transforming into licensed microfinance institutions or by linking to sustainable microfinance institutions. Selection criteria could include the potential to become sustainable, including charging market interest rates; ability to reach scale quickly; commitment and capacity of management; and innovative delivery systems and product mix to reach unserved clients".[41]

It has started to seem natural that NGOs should follow the economization of the sector and internally adjust accordingly; if not, they risk becoming "inefficient" and failing to compete with contemporary development practices.

Microfinance in Cambodia: Towards Greater Commercialization

In Cambodia since the 1990s there has been a shifting in the structure of NGOs practising microfinance towards this neoliberal form of organizational management, and it has had a profound effect on the way that the industry as a whole has shifted towards a more commercial economic perspective of poverty reduction.

Following its establishment in 1995, the CCRD jointly wrote a review with the Asian Development Bank in 1996 which concludes that, although NGOs were the main supplier of rural credit, they were not expanding fast enough to reach the unmet demand for credit.[42] Following the publication of the report there existed a general consensus within the government and among western donors that NGOs would need assistance in order to engage more effectively

---

[39] In this respect NGOs and microfinance institutions become synonymous with inefficient/efficient, unprofessional/professional respectively.
[40] Mark Flaming, Eric Duflos, Alexia Latortue, Nina Nayer, Jimmy Roth, 6.
[41] Ibid., 17.
[42] Asian Development Bank *Technical Assistance to the Royal Kingdom of Cambodia for Rural Credit and Savings Project.*

with the unmet credit demand. Consequently, the conversion of microcredit NGOs into formal legal entities operating as Licensed Financial Institutions became a development goal.[43]

Under pressure from the Asian Development Bank and following various talks with leading donors, the National Bank of Cambodia decided to construct and implement a *Prakas* in 2000, requiring, under certain criteria, the transformation of NGOs practising microfinance into independent limited liability companies.[44] One of the greatest impacts has been that NGO microfinance programmes have been separated from their NGO parents to become microfinance institutions. In many cases entire NGO structures underwent a complete transformation in order to conform to the new 2000 regulations.[45]

Although the Royal Government of Cambodia effectively created the legal context for the creation of microfinance institutions, it is important to understand that the government faces strong pressure to avoid directly providing any financial service themselves to microfinance institutions, indeed under New Public Management principles they are expected only to develop policy frameworks that can enable a vibrant and competitive (private sector) market structure for microfinance to excel in.

Number eight of CGAP's influential key principles 2004 states that the job of the government is not to provide financial service to the poor directly but to construct a supporting policy environment.[46] It is a common (neoliberal) belief that governments usually have a negative effect and can often undermine the microfinance market. However, there is now a growing consensus that governments can be effective in working with donors and developing policy frameworks that can stimulate a vibrant and competitive microfinance structure rather than directly providing financial services themselves.[47] Governments have an important role to play in promoting private sector involvement when

---

[43] Asian Development Bank *Cambodia: Rural Credit and Savings Project* (Manila: Asian Development Bank, 2007) online at www.adb.org.

[44] This decision resulted in the creation of Prakas B7.00–06 on the licensing of micro-financing institutions, see National Bank of Cambodia, "Prakas relating to the implementation of law on Banking and Financial Institutions," 2000 online at www.nbc.org.kh/upload/english/prakas/Sup-Prakas2000.pdf, accessed November 2008.

[45] For a list of the criteria see Ibid. NGOs that meet the minimum requirements must be licensed and therefore this requires transformation. However those that do not (generally the smaller NGOs that do not have large credit portfolios) must still be registered, which for now does not require a shift in organizational structure.

[46] CGAP, *Good Practice Guidelines for Funders of Microfinance: Microfinance Consensus Guidelines*.

[47] CGAP, *Key Principles of Microfinance* (Washington DC: CGAP, 2004) online at www.cgap.org.

formulating poverty reduction strategies and elevating it to a leading role in development strategies.⁴⁸

The government-supported commercialization of NGOs is not a trend isolated to the Cambodian case and can be seen throughout the world where "Microfinance institutions are expected to follow on a linear path on which they transform themselves from informal evolving funds to NGOs, to licensed microfinance institutions."⁴⁹ Donors that had established and provided the funding for NGOs engaging with microfinance programs are now being replaced by "socially responsible investors and private finance institutions".⁵⁰· This involves new boards of shareholders and an entirely different funding structure from the original donor-dependency. One of the key areas of NGO-microfinance institution transformation therefore is the shifting in funding from top-down donor grants to bottom-up market-based private sector self-sufficiency.

In Cambodia there are currently 18 key organizations that are responsible for the delivery of microfinance services in Cambodia (see Table 9). They are seen as key for a number of reasons. Firstly, they make up a vast percentage of the entire microfinance sector.⁵¹ Secondly, they are the only members of the Cambodian Microfinance Association, an umbrella organization established to coordinate microfinance policy across Cambodia. Finally, they are made up of all the organizations that have applied and gained licenses at the National Bank of Cambodia and therefore all are commercial companies.⁵²

According to economic policy experts there are some common reasons why NGOs in general choose to convert into microfinance institutions. One of the primary reasons is to improve access to commercial funds. NGOs were previously dependent upon donor funding, but this becomes difficult to sustain financially whilst expanding an NGO's service outreach. Relatedly, limitations on service outreach are often combined with a limited range of financial services that can be offered by an NGO; for example most deal with credit only, and yet in order to mobilize savings effectively an NGO must transform into an microfinance

---

⁴⁸ Ibid.
⁴⁹ J. Conroy, "The challenges of Microfinance in Southeast Asia," in Nick Freeman (eds.) *Financing Southeast Asia's Economic Development*. (Singapore: Institute of Southeast Asian Studies, 2003), 141.
⁵⁰ Mark Flaming, Eric Duflos, Alexia Latortue, Nina Nayer, 6.
⁵¹ A report in 2004 suggested that ten of these institutions represented over 84% of all microfinance loans delivered, see Mark Pickens, Meas Thavy and Keo Kang, *Savings-Led and Self-Help Microfinance in Cambodia: Lessons Learned and Best Practices* (Phnom Penh: PACT, 2004).
⁵² Indeed in order to become a member of the Cambodian Microfinance Association network, NGOs must have gained a license or be in the process of gaining a license from the National Bank of Cambodia; thus they must also have transformed from an NGO to a microfinance institution.

institution in order to have the ability to attract a larger pool of clients.[53] With transformation, NGOs can access capital markets with ease, source capital more rapidly, and expand their loan portfolios at reasonable costs.[54]

These views are predicated upon the common assumption that it is of primary importance to create a professionalized, accountable and efficient microfinance industry, and that separating from donor funding requires closer conformity to market principles. Microfinance institutions in Cambodia have taken up this professionalized approach, and most have undergone internal structural changes in order to adapt to a more commercialized sector.

As an example, Hattha Kaksekar[55] underwent a transformation typical of the emerging pattern of NGO conversions to a microfinance institution in 2001. First they registered with the National Bank of Cambodia and, on completion of the transformation into a limited company with a three-year microfinance licence, took on a host of shareholders. The former NGO is now known as Hattha Kaksekar Ltd (HKL). HKL conducted a complete internal restructuring of the management and staff structure in order to become sustainable. Internal audit, credit, financial management information systems and human resource departments were newly formed in order to manage the company's expanded financial activities[56]. In 2004, HKL received its first rating by Micro-Credit Ratings International Ltd[57], and was congratulated for its financial transformation over the last three years to a sustainable company. 2004 also saw the company officially become self-sufficient in terms of operational status and yield a net profit increase of 195 per cent from the previous year.[58] In their 2006 annual report, HKL recognised that microfinance institutions are becoming more competitive and that there is still a sizeable market remaining; therefore they are focusing greater efforts, in line with other microfinance institutions, on market penetration and expansion.[59] HKL has therefore undergone a vast transformation to adapt to the changing microfinance sector. The early donor-based organization

---

[53] Gaamaa Hishigsuren, *Transformation of Microfinance operations from NGO to Regulated MFI* (USA: IDEAS, 2005).
[54] A. Campion and V. White, *NGO transformation* (Bethesda: Microenterprise Best Practices, 2001) online at www.microfinancegateway.org, 6.
[55] "Farmer's Hand," an NGO that was established in Cambodia with the help of Oxfam Quebec in 1996.
[56] Hattha Kaksekar Ltd "Annual Report 2003" online at www.HKL.com.kh.
[57] Micro-Credit Ratings International (M-CRIL) was established in 1998 to help facilitate the flow of commercial funds into microfinance. The aim of the organization is to provide a standardized tool to assess the financial worthiness of microfinance institutions to allow investors to understand the financial suitability of specific microfinance institutions, and be aware of their strengths and weaknesses for institutional capacity building.
[58] Hattha Kaksekar Ltd 'Annual Report 2004' online at www.HKL.com.kh 6.
[59] Hattha Kaksekar Ltd 'Annual Report 2006' online at www.HKL.com.kh 8.

Table 9. Number of borrowers of Microfinance as of March 2010.

ACLEDA	224,229
Angkor Mikroheranhvatho Kampuchea (AMK)	215,997
AMRET	212,919
Vision Fund Cambodia	96,013
Thaneakea Phum Cambodia (TPC)	92,872
Prasac	83,161
Credit	40,519
Hattha Kaksekar Ltd (HKL)	40,285
Sathapana	36,915
Seilanithih	12,617
Samic	11,529
Chamroeun (NGO)	8,982
Intean Poalroath Rongroerurng (IPR)	3,720
Maxima	2,493
Farmer Union Development Fund (FUDF)	2,325
Cambodian Business Integrated In Rural Development Agency (CBIRD)	2,003
Green Central Microfinance (GCMF)	991
Entean Akpevath Pracheachun (EAP)	195
Tong Fang Micro Finance (TFMF)	117
Farmer Finance	75
First Finance	54
YCP	48
Total	1,088,077

Source: Adapted from Cambodian Microfinance Association database available at www.cma-network.org. Practitioners in the microfinance industry claim that NGO-microfinance institutions bring a higher level of efficiency and financial performance than in their previous organizational NGO form. Microfinance institutions become more susceptible to the demands of the market once they become financially formalised; thus they must conform to the demands of customers in order to be competitive; their services and projects therefore become more efficient and attuned to the customer's needs. Banks and other formal financial institutions are reluctant to lend vast amounts of money to unregulated NGOs as these organizations struggle to leverage their equity base or offer a guarantee facility. A regulated microfinance institution however is subject to ongoing supervision and regulation; potential investors respond to increased security with increased investment. In Cambodia newly registered/licensed microfinance institutions are continuously regulated by the National Bank of Cambodia to ensure financial integrity.

has commercialized to become a self-sufficient (and expansion-oriented) economically viable microfinance organization.

ACLEDA[60] was initially established as the Association of Cambodian Local Economic Development Agencies, as a resettlement project of the International Labour Organization and the United Nations Development Programme, focusing on providing enterprise development training and supplying credit. After expanding to become a successful NGO, ACLEDA received strong support by donors such as the Kreditanstalt für Wiederaufbau, the United Nations Development Programme, the International Labour Organization and the United States Agency for International Development, who promoted the idea of a further transition from an NGO to a commercial institution and offered the NGO a wealth of technical and financial assistance.[61] According to ACLEDA's current managing director, In Channy, the organization took the decision to transform from an NGO to a public limited company and then a bank based upon some important factors. The first was to be able to expand their network to cover 14 of Cambodia's provinces. The second was that ACLEDA wanted to have the ability to operate at a profit to ensure sustainability (they had broken even financially in 1998). Access to funds is extremely difficult to obtain by NGOs in the contemporary development climate. To fill the unmet gap in demand for credit, NGOs like ACLEDA felt compelled to obtain greater access to commercial funds, thus there was a change in the structure of ownership and then the desired move towards licensing to become a public limited company capable of accessing funds from wholesale financial institutions and commercial banks.[62] Importantly, ACLEDA was forced to become a bank in order to comply with the 1999 law on banking which stipulates that the activities undertaken by ACLEDA are compatible with what the Royal Government of Cambodia calls a "specialised bank".[63] There was an inevitable cultural change when ACLEDA went through the motions of changing from an NGO to a microfinance institution – the organization took on a commercial attitude to better serve its clients. The management structure received an overhaul in order to deal with the complexities of expansion into commercial banking including strengthening the internal auditing function and bringing PriceWaterhouseCooper on board as external auditors. A new board of directors was established in order to bring

---

[60] Perhaps one of the most successful to undergo NGO-microfinance institution transformation, it is often viewed as the role model of Cambodian Microfinance.

[61] Mark Flaming, Eric Duflos, Alexia Latortue, Nina Nayer, 13.

[62] In Channy, "From NGO/Project to Micro-finance Institution: The Experience of ACLEDA Bank, Cambodia," from the FAO-APRACA Regional Workshop, Bangkok 2002 online at www.microfinancegateway.org, accessed on October 2008.

[63] Ibid., 5.

a broader range of skills and experience in the business sector.[64] ACLEDA therefore represents the trend in NGOs who felt that financial security could only be met by transforming the internal structure of the organization to a more professionalized, privatized shareholder approach in order to expand and become competitive in the market.

It is clear that many of the newly emerging microfinance institution structures are shifting priorities towards remaining competitive in the new market environment; thus they are shifting strategy to concentrate more on scaling up operations and increasing market share. As a senior member of a microfinance institution explained, throughout transformation there is still a consistent emphasis upon the poor and how best to serve poor clients; however, the private sector management style requires a priority shift towards expansion and competitiveness in order to meet unmet credit demand.[65] This shift in strategy is consistent with New Public Management principles and the new priorities of a competitive market: expansion as a way to include those who are excluded from the market. The priorities of the privatized microfinance institution equate with a neoliberal conception of poverty that views the ultimate priority of poverty reduction as ensuring everyone has access to credit. This shift has not always been easy for those involved in the sector, and indeed there are still questions raised over whether the current commercialized sector represents a form of "mission drift"[66] from the earlier conceptions of poverty reduction brought into Cambodia in the early 1990s.

Microfinance: Social and Commercial Tensions

An analysis by the Asian Development Bank of the sector's shifting commercial focus revealed that it wasn't as easy as first thought to merge the social NGO sector with a stronger private sector ethos as "Target NGOs were going through a corporate culture shock at being transformed into corporate entities."[67] This culture shock resulted in the Asian Development Bank's initial promise of a $20 million loan (to be channelled through the Rural Development Bank) being reduced to $5 million due to the underestimation of how many newly created

---

[64] Ibid., 5.

[65] Anonymous microfinance institution staff member, personal interview, Phnom Penh, 13 January 2009.

[66] According to Tanmay Chetan there is a major concern within the industry at the moment surrounding the potential repercussions of a market shift. See Tanmay Chetan "Are financial and social objectives mutually exclusive? The experience of AMK, Cambodia," *Small Enterprise Development* 18.1 (2007).

[67] Asian Development Bank, *Cambodia: Rural Credit and Savings Project*.

microfinance institutions would meet the criteria established in order to be able to qualify for the loan.[68] As the Asian Development Bank noted:

> The procedure for forming a company in itself was cumbersome as it involved shareholding decisions, the appointment of directors and officers, the formulation of memorandum and articles of association, etc. As this was a major transformation in corporate behaviour for financial institutions mostly operated by NGOs, the result was a great deal more time than envisaged was required for an LFI to qualify as a project participant.[69]

The transformation from an NGO to a microfinance institution has many implications that parallel the shifting perspective in contemporary microfinance policy directives, as Hishigsuren argues, "Balancing the composition of old-NGO and new-commercial staff and board members is difficult. It is not always clear how one can merge these values with poverty reduction."[70]

Clearly any cultural shift requires a break from the traditional approaches undertaken by the NGO. Campion and White believe that in order for the transition to be successful, microfinance institutions need to hire staff familiar with local markets and the business sector. The typical social service perspective associated with NGOs needs to be converted to a customer service orientation appropriate for a financial intermediary.[71]

Microcredit Ratings International Ltd found in its study on the impact of rating schemes for microfinance practice that many of its clients still suffer the usual weakness of newly converted microfinance institutions: namely, they lack the current business orientations which can severely limit sustainability. This, it is argued, is a product of microfinance institutions, emerging from NGOs and limiting market opportunities by not adequately "dispensing with a social agenda."[72]

Essentially the language from much of the international donor community suggests that market expansion (which is of the utmost importance for the

---

[68] The ADB loan expired in March 2006 and had successfully helped finance seven microfinance institutions: Hattha Kaksekar Ltd, Seilanithih Ltd, AMRET Ltd, Cambodia Entrepreneur Building Ltd, Thaneakea Phum Ltd, ACLEDA, Canadia Bank. These microfinance institutions (and two Banks) were the only microfinance institutions that had fulfilled the criteria established in order to receive loans via the RDB. See Asian Development Bank, *Cambodia: Rural Credit and Savings Project*.

[69] Ibid.

[70] G. Hishigsuren, "Evaluating Mission Drift in Microfinance: Lessons for Programs with Social Mission," *Evaluation Review* 31.3 (2006), 11.

[71] A. Campion and V. White, 10.

[72] Microcredit Ratings International Ltd, "The Impact of Rating... on Banking Practice and Resource Flows," 2002, 12. Online at http://www.sa-dhan.net/Adls/Microfinance/Rating/Impactofratingonmicrobanking.pdf accessed on November 2008.

neoliberal conception of creating an enabling environment for the poor to be given access to the market) and self-sustainability is being heavily hampered by the continuing social NGO structure that cannot "cope" with the competitive demands of the market. NGOs operating in microfinance often express concern and anxiety over the direction their organizations will take when converting into microfinance institutions, privileging market expansion. A member of a NGO currently going through the transformation process explained that his organization has always given a low priority to the expansion of market share and prefers to work on quality products with the small number of clients on its books. There is, however, a general fear that once they join the competitive market for funding (as opposed to being solely funded by their donor) there is always the chance that they will have to conform to other shareholder wishes of greater expansion in order to remain competitive and that this could represent an example of mission drift.[73] This can serve to highlight the differences between NGOs and microfinance institutions and the decisions they are faced with when left to the demands of the market. The process of attempting to merge these two cultures can prove to be a challenging task, yet it is undeniable that the commercial culture associated with neoliberalism is continually being promoted by shareholders and development agencies to the detriment of the social dimensions of poverty reduction.

Poverty reduction under a neoliberal commercial culture has clearly taken precedence over the development of alternative notions of the social aspects of poverty reduction. Microfinance draws the poor into the market and promotes microfinance as a method to pick up the social cost of neoliberal restructuring, thereby de-prioritizing the creation of alternative approaches such, as, for example, the organization of a state-provided welfare safety net.

Commercialized microfinance institutions have a tendency to focus on the "economically active poor", as opposed to the "poorest of the poor", the latter of whom are less interested in financial services and more in need of a subsidised provision of social services such as food, healthcare and education.[74] This is an important point; in Cambodia there is a problem developing surrounding "chronic indebtedness" in many rural communities. This is often caused by periodic droughts and floods and results in farmers having to borrow money in order to overcome food shortages.[75] Indeed Asian Development Bank country director Arjun Goswami surmised that in the wake of the global economic turbulence currently affecting Cambodia "the demand for MFI services will

---

[73] Anonymous NGO staff member, personal interview, Phnom Penh 11 January 2009.
[74] S. Ito, "Cambodian Microfinance: A Case of Successful Commercialization?" *Forum of International Development Studies* 37 (2008).
[75] K. Sedara, 5.

rise because of the impact of the slowdown on the poor - there will be a greater demand for their services and the poor will have to borrow more. The rural poor population may need to borrow for their very immediate necessities."[76] This rise in borrowing levels does not equate to entrepreneurial choice, but out of necessity in a country with no welfare state. Despite claims to the contrary from its advocates, neoliberal strategies do not imbue freedom of choice when faced with difficult economic climates, and increasing the amount of debt does nothing to help the coping strategies of the poorest in society.[77]

Conclusion

The microfinance industry in Cambodia has come a long way since the early 1990s. From small-scale, donor-funded NGO projects they have emerged as autonomous, self-sufficient, shareholder-based microfinance institutions.[78] This transformation can be traced to the recent pressure from international donors to instil neoliberal New Public Management principles into the NGO sector. Combined with the resulting new legislation in Cambodia, a competitive microfinance industry has been constructed where commercial organizations attempt to expand their outreach thanks to new, more efficient managerial structures. Poverty reduction is still at the heart of the microfinance industry but only in the dominant form of a commercial-based approach, characterized by the continual privileging of market expansion over other more social possibilities. A mission drift appears to have occurred, something that over the next decade will no doubt come increasingly to the fore of microfinance debates. The neoliberal vision of poverty alleviation promotes the expansion of the market to meet unmet credit demand, and when coupled with the self-sustainability of

---

[76] George Mcleod, "Microlenders weather the storm," *Phnom Penh Post*, 14 January 2009 online at www.phnompenhpost.com, accessed March 2009.

[77] Loans can become burdens on the poor; for example a study by Kleih et al. suggests that there are various limitations of microfinance schemes in Cambodia. One of these limitations is that they found examples of a number of people borrowing money from one NGO in order to refund a loan from another NGO that had previously helped them. See Ulrich Kleih, Sem Viryak and Un Kanika, "Guidelines to Improve Access to Microfinance by Poor Fishing, Processing and Trading Communities," *Cambodia Post-Harvest Fisheries Livelihoods project*, Final Draft, 2006, online at www.nri.org/projects/fishtrade/cphflp_microfinance_guidelines.pdf.

[78] It is frequently cited in the literature that CBOs and local NGOs are overly dependent upon international funding which hinders the development of a genuine grassroots democracy, for example see Caroline Hughes, *The Political Economy of Cambodia's Transition 1991–2001* (London: RoutledgeCurzon, 2003). The future of civil society's link with microfinance is an interesting one given that newly emerging microfinance institutions are becoming more self-sufficient and advocating only a technical role for donors rather than as the funding sources they once were.

microfinance institution, is seen as the fundamental method to contribute to the reduction of poverty in the country.

This view however is only effective if poverty reduction is viewed in such narrow economic terms as an enabling environment to be able to create the ability for the poor to become entrepreneurs and as a consequence increase levels of consumption. Early notions of empowerment that were brought in with donors in the 1990s were attached to nearly every project enacted, however these days it is becoming increasingly rare to hear the term empowerment employed in microfinance institution internal policy discussions and therefore in contemporary microfinance projects.[79] Empowerment has therefore become subsumed under the neoliberal rhetoric of market inclusion, emptying out its original critical and social origins. The neoliberal notion of empowerment has been criticised for not actively interrogating power relations within communities and the development of non-economistic notions of social capital. This diluted approach to empowerment fosters economic forms of inclusion through the market but fails to analyse the underlying structures of exclusion and dis-empowerment that can affect the social lives of the poor.[80] This links in with a concept of social empowerment different to the one promoted by advocates of neoliberal strategies: the ability of people to make decisions on matters that are important to themselves and not just about economic access to the market for material gain. This concept promotes the combating of social relations and structures of power that contribute to the dis-empowering of people in poverty.[81]

Undoubtedly microfinance in Cambodia has allowed access to credit and new sources of capital for those previously excluded from the formal financial system. Despite this, it has been elevated from a small alternative project focusing upon poverty reduction to become the win-win strategy destined to eradicate poverty through access to the market. This approach is problematic if poverty is viewed through a more social and welfare-orientated lens, and if questions are asked about the effects of chronic indebtedness and the continuing focus of a narrow, economic conception of development.

---

[79] Anonymous Microfinance institution staff member, personal interview, Phnom Penh 12 January 2009.
[80] C. Sardenberg, "Liberal vs. Liberating Empowerment: A Latin American Feminist Perspective on Conceptualising Women's Empowerment," *IDS bulletin* 39.6 (2008), 22.
[81] See S. Mosedale, "Policy Arena. Assessing Women's Empowerment: Towards a Conceptual Framework," *Journal of International Development* 17: (2005), and Srilatha Batliwala, "The Meaning of Women's Empowerment: New Concepts from Action," in Gita Sen, Adrienne Germain and Lincoln C. Chen (eds.), *Population Policies Reconsidered: Health, Empowerment and Rights* (Boston: Harvard University Press, 1994), 127–138.

9

THE POLITICS AND PROFITS OF "LABOUR EXPORT"

Annuska Derks

BESIDES GARMENTS, RUBBER AND RICE, Cambodia has during the past decade become increasingly interested in another "source for export", namely labour.[1] Following the examples of labour-exporting countries like the Philippines and Indonesia, the Cambodian government has started sending labourers abroad as a way to deal with the lack of employment opportunities at home and as a source of revenue for the country. The "export of labour" has now become part of an official policy to enhance professional skills and improve the living conditions of the people. Yet, considering the fact that Cambodian migrant workers tend to end up mostly as undocumented workers in low-paid, low-skilled, dirty and dangerous jobs, it is questionable whether they are in a situation that permits them to realize such lofty objectives. Media and NGO reports tend to highlight how Cambodian migrants abroad face deception, exploitation, rape, detention, enslavement and even death. As a result, the Cambodian migrant worker has become portrayed paradoxically both as development agent and as vulnerable victim. How do these contradictory representations of the migrant relate to one another? And, more importantly, how do they relate to the perspectives and experiences of the migrants themselves?

This chapter seeks to explore the conditions, practices and discourses regarding the "export" of Cambodian labour, and looks in particular at the implications for migrants working at the other side of the border.

---

[1] Formulation by Commerce Minister Cham Prasidh in Erika Kinetz, "Keeping Workers Safe," *Newsweek*, 11 April, 2008, online at http://www.newsweek.com/2008/04/11/keeping-workers-safe.html, accessed 18 June 2008.

Exporting Cambodian Labour

Cambodian labour is on the move. Although Cambodians have been migrating overseas for decades, government-orchestrated efforts to regulate and expand the flow of Cambodian labour overseas began only in 1995. More recently, the Cambodian government has made overseas employment part of its strategy for employment creation.[2] By stimulating demand for Cambodian labour overseas, the government hopes to be able to reduce un- and underemployment and at the same time to improve living conditions, enhance professional skills, and raise revenues for the state via remittances.

The Cambodian government is following here the example of other labour-sending countries. The most notable example is the Philippines, which in the 1970s began to encourage its citizens to migrate as a strategy to deal with unemployment at home and to increase foreign currency earnings. The Philippines has since become "the labour exporter par excellence".[3] About seven million Filipinos, almost nine percent of the population, can be found working in countries all over the world.[4] Due to the significance of their remittances for the economy as well as for the income of their families left behind, Overseas Filipino Workers are now also dubbed Overseas Filipino Investors.

This positive role assigned to migrants is interesting. Until not so long ago, migration was mainly regarded as a sign of development failure and of a state failing to deliver well-being and security to its citizens. It is now increasingly viewed as a solution to development.[5] This is largely related to the belief in the positive effects of migrant remittances and their contributions to raising incomes of poor households and injecting cash into disproportionately poor and rural communities.[6] According to what has also been dubbed the "new development mantra", remittances sent back by migrants abroad will not only help their families, but also their countries of origin. Migrants are accordingly assumed to become "the biggest provider of foreign aid".[7] And thus

---

[2] Royal Government of Cambodia, *National Strategic Development Plan 2006–2010* (Phnom Penh: Council of Ministers, 2006).

[3] Castles and Miller, *The Age of Migration. International Population Movements in the Modern World* (Hampshire and New York: Palgrave Macmillan, 2003).

[4] International Organization for Migration, *World Migration. Costs and Benefits of International Migration 2005* (Geneva: IOM, 2005), 239.

[5] Thomas Faist, "Migrants as Transnational Development Agents: An Inquiry into the Newest Round of the Migration-Development Nexus", *Population, Space and Place* 14 (2008): 22.

[6] Sarah Gammage, "Exporting People and Recruiting Remittances: A Development Strategy for El Salvador?", *Latin American Perspectives* 33.6 (2006).

[7] Devesh Kapur, "Remittances: The New Development Mantra?" Paper prepared for the G-24 Technical Group Meeting (Harvard University and Center for Global Development, 2003), 10.

international organizations, non-governmental organizations and state agencies alike have come to hail labour migration as a means of reducing poverty and as an important element within broader economic and social development strategies.

In line with this view, the Cambodian government now also promotes Cambodian labour as a "source for export". The use of the term "export" (*noam chenh*) in relation to labour is revealing. Labour is obviously seen as if it were just another type of commodity, one that can be purposefully dispatched abroad in order to provide opportunities for the poor and frustrated, and hence to reduce political instability – and increase state revenues. In Cambodia, as in many other parts of the world, migrants are thus treated as "a form of exportable commodified labour" by states that view their own citizens as one of their most valuable comparative advantages.[8]

As a result, a range of laws, bilateral arrangements and government bureaucracies have been developed to encourage and manage this flow of labour. The Cambodian government has started doing so much later than most neighbouring labour-sending countries. The sub-decree on the "export of Khmer labour overseas" dates from 1995 and describes in general terms the procedural measures for the sending of labour overseas under the direction of what was formerly called the Ministry of Social Welfare, Labour and Veteran Affairs (now the Ministry of Labour and Vocational Training). It stipulates the eligible candidates for working overseas (any Khmer worker above eighteen years registered at the Ministry of Labour), the requirements and obligations for companies wishing to recruit and send workers abroad, the terms and conditions of the employment contract, and the responsibilities regarding pre-departure training, monitoring and dispute settlement.

The sub-decree sets above all the legal guidelines for the role of the Ministry of Labour (the provider party) in authorizing and cooperating with private recruitment agencies (the receiver party). According to the procedures laid out in the sub-decree, private recruitment agencies should request the Ministry of Labour to provide candidate workers, i.e. those who have already been registered at the municipal or provincial Department of Labour. Recruitment agencies that are subsequently authorized to "export labour to work overseas" are required to deposit a surety fund of US $100,000 at the Ministry that may be used to compensate the workers in case the receiver party fails to implement any provisions of the work contract. More than a decade after sub-decree 57

---

[8] David Kyle and Christina A. Siracusa, "Seeing the State Like a Migrant: Why So Many Non-Criminals Break Immigration Laws", in Willem van Schendel and Itty Abraham, *Illicit Flows and Criminal Things. States Borders, and the Other Side of Globalization* (Bloomington: Indiana University Press, 2005), 156.

was brought into force, i.e. by the end of 2006, a total of forty-two recruitment companies were registered with the Ministry of Labour, out of which twelve had paid the required deposit and were thus officially licensed to operate.[9] In addition to these private recruitment agencies, the government also decided to set up a public agency for recruiting, training, sending and managing Cambodian migrant workers with the aim to provide migrant workers with a cheaper and safer labour migration channel.[10]

The increasing number of recruitment agencies indicates that sending Cambodian labour abroad has become a thriving business. Recruitment agencies act as intermediaries between workers and employers abroad. In order to find the workers for labour agents or employers in destination countries, they advertise job offers in the media. More importantly, however, is their reliance on brokers travelling in rural areas for face-to-face recruitment. Lee found that these brokers are often based in the villages themselves and that their intimate knowledge of the villages and their people allows them to easily identify candidate migrant workers.[11] The broker brings the candidate migrant workers to the recruitment company, which is usually based in or around Phnom Penh, and receives a commission for each recruited person.

Before being able to leave abroad, candidate migrant workers go through several administrative and training procedures. They are required to submit an application form and information form to the recruitment agent and to register at the Department of Employment and Manpower of the Ministry of Labour, after which they receive a migrant worker card. This card is necessary to obtain a passport from the Ministry of Interior.[12] The recruitment agency subsequently takes care of the passports and work permits, arranges the medical examination,

---

[9] Chen Chen Lee, *A Study into Exploitative Labour Brokerage Practices in Cambodia*, (COMMIT, 2007), 23. By September 2008 there were eighteen recruitment agencies licensed to operate for people wishing to work abroad according to a "Country Report for the Asia-Pacific High-level Meeting on International Migration and Development," presented by Thong Lim, Director of the Cambodian Immigration Department (22–23 September 2008).

[10] Additional decisions to promote cheap and safe migration were taken in a declaration (2006) on the need to provide Education on HIV/AIDS, Safe Migration and Labour Rights for Cambodian Migrants Abroad and a sub-decree on the provision of cheaper passports for migrants wishing to legally work abroad. See Sub-Decree 70 on the *Creation of the Manpower Training and Overseas Sending Board* (Royal Government of Cambodia, 2006); Maltoni, *Review of Labour Migration Dynamics in Cambodia* (Phnom Penh: International Organization for Migration, 2006), 18 and Hor Hab, "Passport Fees for Migrants to Drop," *Phnom Penh Post* (November 25, 2008). At the time of writing, the Ministry of Labour was in the process of formulating a new sub-decree aimed at improving the safety of workers and the monitoring of recruitment agencies (Will Baxter, "Govt to Launch Policy Protecting Migrant Labourers," *Phnom Penh Post* (June 14, 2010).

[11] Lee, *Exploitative Labour Brokerage Practices*, 35.

[12] Maltoni, *Labour Migration Dynamics in Cambodia*, 19.

provides pre-departure training, prepares the contracts (with the recruitment company and with the employer), and organizes the transport of the workers.[13] All in all, it may take several months before workers are eventually sent overseas. The costs of all these procedures, including food and accommodation during the pre-departure training – ranging between 350 and 480 US dollars for domestic workers going to Malaysia and between 900 to 1,100 US dollars for workers going to South Korea – are eventually borne by the migrant worker, generally by withholding the first four to six months of his or her salary.[14]

Up to the end of 2008, more than 25,000 Cambodians have been sent abroad within the framework of the government's labour export program.[15] The main destination countries are Malaysia, South Korea, and Thailand, with whom the government signed Memoranda of Understanding (2003 with Thailand; 2006 with Korea) or established official mutual labour cooperation (1997 with Malaysia, revised in 1999). The Cambodian government also signed agreements to send labour to Japan and Brunei, but the skills requirements of these destination countries are very high and can hardly be met within existing training programs. Cambodian labour is furthermore in demand in several other destinations countries with whom the government has not (yet) or only recently signed labour agreements, such as Hong Kong, Singapore and several Arab countries (Qatar, Kuwait, and Saudi Arabia).

The total number of Cambodian labour migrants abroad is, however, far higher than the figure of those who have left with licensed recruitment companies. There are also labour migrants who have become regularized after having entered the country of destination illegally. In 2008, 12,000 Cambodian migrants received work permits under the regular Thai registration policy, whereas more than 56,000 were documented through the nationality verification scheme in 2007 and 2008.[16] In addition, there are Cambodian migrant workers who remain undocumented in the countries of destination. There are no reliable statistics as to the number of undocumented Cambodian migrant workers abroad, but their number is estimated to be at least as high as the number of documented migrants.[17]

---

[13] After departure, the recruitment company officially remains responsible for monitoring the work situation and organizing the return of the workers after termination of the contract.

[14] Lee, *Exploitative Labour Brokerage Practices*, 25–26.

[15] More than 5,000 to South Korea, over 13,000 to Malaysia and more than 8,000 to Thailand, according to Seng Sakada, general director for employment at the Ministry of Labour, quoted in Chun Sakada, "Migrant Workers to Get Free Passports," *VOA Khmer*, 24 November 2008, online at http://www1.voanews.com/khmer-english/news/a-40-2008-11-24-voa2-90169237.html?refresh=1, accessed 3 April 2009; and in May Kunmakara, "Economic Downturn hitting Migrant Labour, Official Says," *Phnom Penh Post*, 29 December 2008.

[16] Data obtained from the Mekong Migration Network website at www.mekongmigration.org.

[17] Estimations of the number of undocumented Cambodian migrant workers in Thailand vary from 60,000 to 200,000; see Christopher Shay, "A Risky Path: Illegal Immigration Surges Despite Persistent Dangers," *Phnom Penh Post*, 06 February 2009.

This means that despite government objectives and regulations regarding the recruitment and placement of migrant workers abroad, informal networks remain the main source of support for those interested in working abroad, especially in neighbouring Thailand. Considering the relative ease with which these informal channels operate, and considering the considerable costs and time, as well as the bureaucratic hassle, of the formal migration scheme, it may not be surprising that most opt for illegal border crossing. Hence, while actively promoted by the government, labour migration takes place largely outside the gaze of the state.

Sending Abroad Victims or Development Agents?

When, as is the case for Cambodia, migrant-exporting schemes develop what Kyle and Siracusa call "a sort of grassroots development project without government authorization", sending states are generally less inclined to disrupt such schemes.[18] Their interest in finding an outlet for unemployed masses and in migrant remittances may after all be greater than the enforcement of a lawful "export" of their citizens.

Remittances are now often commended for having made possible a drastic improvement in the living conditions of millions of households in migrant-sending countries. They are considered to be typically destined for relatively poor families in rural areas that are most in need of capital and thus considered to be a more effective means of income distribution than large, bureaucratic development programmes or development aid.[19] It has often been pointed out that, on a global level, migrant remittances transferred to developing countries amount to substantially more than the sum of the annual Overseas Development Assistance (ODA) budget.[20] Besides being more elevated and effective than aid, remittances are also considered to be more resilient than capital flows or official aid and therefore resistant to economic downturns.[21] They are therefore viewed as an important source of finance for development, especially during this time of global financial crisis.[22]

---

[18] Kyle and Siracusa, "Seeing the State Like a Migrant," 157.

[19] Hein de Haas, "International Migration, Remittances and Development: Myths and Facts," *Third World Quarterly* 26:8 (2005), 1277.

[20] Faist, "Migrants as Transnational Development Agents," 21–22; Ninna Nyberg-Sorensen, Nicholas Van Hear and Poul Engberg-Pedersen, *The Migration-Development-Nexus: Evidence and Policy Options* (Geneva: IOM, 2002).

[21] Kapur, "Remittances: The New Development Mantra?"; Faist, "Migrants as Transnational Development Agents".

[22] World Bank, "Remittances May Buoy Developing Countries Caught in Financial Crisis", news report, 24 November 2008, webpage, online at http://web.worldbank.org/WBSITE/EXTERNAL/NEWS/0,,contentMDK:21996712~pagePK:64257043~piPK:437376~theSitePK:4607,00.html, accessed 3 April 2009.

Although remittances are unlikely to cure Cambodia of its aid dependency in the near future – ODA to Cambodia is still more than twice the officially recorded remittances – the increasing value of remittances indicates that it is going to be of growing importance as a source of revenue for the country. Migrant remittances have almost tripled within less than a decade. The World Bank estimated the total size of official remittances in 2007 at US$ 353 millions, or 4.2 per cent of the country's GDP.[23] This figure has, however, to be interpreted with some caution. One the one hand the actual size of remittances is arguably substantially higher since unrecorded flows through informal channels are not included. On the other hand the figure does not distinguish between remittances from Cambodian labour migrants and remittances from the Cambodian diaspora in countries like the United States and France, thus giving a distorted view of the amount of remittances sent back by Cambodia's labour migrants temporarily working abroad.

While it is difficult to estimate the actual remittances, it is even more difficult to assess the actual impact of migrant remittances on development at the local level. Several studies have pointed out that the causal link between migration, remittances and development is not as straightforward as it may appear at first sight. As Kapur has pointed out, contrary to the impression that remittances are a phenomenon affecting poor countries, the bulk of international remittances neither end up in the poorest countries (but in lower middle-income countries), nor in the poorest households.[24] Moreover, the positive effects of remittances suggested by macro-level analyses do not necessarily correspond with findings based on studies focusing on the local level. Some of the central issues to consider in this regard are related to the questions as to who migrates, whether migrants are in a position to remit, and how remittances are used.

Migration is commonly viewed as a result of poverty and a lack of local development options.[25] Migrants I talked to would give the standard answer to the question as to why they came to Thailand: "Because I am poor and I have no job". Yet, the general finding of most studies in migration is that "It is not the poorest who move but those with access to some resources, no matter how meagre these might appear".[26] Migration for work, especially cross-border, requires – besides able-bodied individuals, access to information and networks – a certain financial investment to cover the costs for transportation,

---

[23] World Bank, *Migration and Remittances Factbook 2008*, webpage, online at http://econ.worldbank.org/WBSITE/EXTERNAL/EXTDEC/EXTDECPROSPECTS/0,,contentMDK:21121930~menuPK:3145470~pagePK:64165401~piPK:64165026~theSitePK:476883,00.html, accessed 3 April 2009.

[24] Kapur, "Remittances: The New Development Mantra?" 7–8 and 16–17.

[25] Nyberg-Sorensen et al., "The Migration-Development Nexus".

[26] Ronald Skeldon, "Migration and Poverty", *Asia-Pacific Population Journal* 17.4 (2002), 71.

for recruitment, and for expenses along the way. The poorest of the poor do not have access to such resources.

This can clearly be observed in a village like Prey Tumpung, Prey Veng, which has during the past fifteen years specialized in labour migration. At the time of the latest village census in early 2008, the village chief counted among the little over 500 families 180 persons who were in Thailand and one person who had left for South Korea. They were especially young men who are part of a chain of migrants leaving their village temporarily in order to earn money as fishermen in Thailand. While rice farming remains the major source of income, villagers have halted the labour intensive and hardly profitable production of palm sugar with the arrival of remittances from migrants working abroad. These remittances have changed the outlook of the village, as they stimulated the construction of bigger, wooden houses and the purchase of cattle, motorbikes and mobile phones. The village chief joked that in his village even those looking after water buffaloes have mobile phones.

This development did, however, not spread evenly throughout the village. The poorest villagers still live in small, thatched houses and have no money to buy motorbikes, or to move in the first place.[27] Those aspiring to leave for Thailand need at least 100 dollars to pay for transport to the border, for food along the way, and for the services of a smuggler who helps migrants cross the "green border", organizes the transport to the place of destination in Thailand, and facilitates – ideally – the contact with a potential employer. Many migrants do not have this amount and rely on their families for access to credit from private moneylenders. This is even more pronounced for migration to other destinations. Since migration for work in South Korea has to go through legal channels, it requires a lot more money to cover the costs of the administrative procedures, of food and lodging during the training period, and of the ticket – which all together amounts to more than 1,000 dollars. Besides, in order to be accepted for work in Korea, one needs to have a certain level of education. It is therefore not surprising that the only person in the village who had the necessary money and education to leave for Korea belongs to a relatively rich family.

The higher investment may, however, also be expected to result in higher returns. Lucky migrant fishermen in Thailand may be able to receive a lump sum payment of 50,000 baht (almost 1,400 dollars) after one year of work, whereas migrant workers in a South Korean factory can earn up 1,000 dollars per month. This illustrates how "labour export" is in fact hierarchically ordered, with the poorest not able to move at all, the moderately well-off leaving along informal channels for Thailand, while the richest are able to work in destinations with

---

[27] Besides the money, the poorest families often lack the able-bodied household members who could move, such as in the case of families with small children or widowed women.

the highest returns. This means that the "export" of labour may, at least initially, reinforce income inequalities at the village level.

The benefits of remittances are most pronounced in the household of the migrant. Maltoni found in his survey on the impact of migration and remittances on communities in Prey Veng that remittances are invested in two main areas: satisfaction of basic needs (mainly food), and repayment of debt (related to health expenses and to the costs of migration). The prolonged absence of the main breadwinner leaves, according to Maltoni, the household relying heavily on the remittances from Thailand.[28] He therefore concludes that migration is a "short-term coping strategy to face unforeseen shocks". It is therefore questionable what the long-term effects of a reliance on migrant remittances will be. An unforeseen effect may be, as the village chief of Prey Tumpung observed, that the pupils in his village drop out early from school because they see others earn money abroad and want to follow them as soon as possible.

This is what happened to Nooy, one of the many migrants from Prey Tumpung. He was still at school when he visited a nearby village and met people who had worked in Thailand. They had to come back with amounts of money he knew he would never be able to accumulate by working in the rice field. He asked his mother to let him go to Thailand and earn money like the others, arguing that it would be a loss of money to continue studying. His mother took a loan of 300,000 riel (at the time about US $100) at a standard ten per cent interest rate to cover the costs of recruitment and transport. During his first time in Thailand, Nooy worked on a fishing boat in Trad. It took him almost half a year until he was able to send back enough money to repay the debt. He endured the hard conditions of work, including adapting to work at sea, extremely long working hours, and denigration by Thai supervisors for another year and a half, until it was time to *kit banhchi* ("stop the account book").[29] He received a lump sum payment of 50,000 baht (at the time almost US $2,000) which were invested back home in the upgrading of their family house and a TV set. Encouraged by this positive experience, he soon returned to Thailand to work for another two years on a fishing vessel. During his second stay in Thailand he managed to save a mere 20,000 baht, which he used to marry a woman from a nearby village. After marriage, Nooy returned to Thailand with the intention to earn money to support his wife. This time he was, however, not as fortunate. His employer claimed to have gone through a year of bad catches and low profits, letting Nooy return home empty-handed.

---

[28] Bruno Maltoni, *Impact of Remittances on Local Communities in Cambodia: The Case of Prey Veng*, Draft Report (Phnom Penh: World Bank, n.d.).

[29] The income of fishermen is not fixed, but based on a profit sharing that is calculated and paid in a lump sum after a fixed set of months (12, 24 or 30), when the boat owner closes the account books and calculates the profits from which the fishermen get a share.

Nooy's example fits well in the general pattern described in other studies that highlight how remittances are, in the first instance, besides repaying debts, often spend on upgrading housing, consumer articles and feasts. While such expenditures were long regarded as conspicuous consumption, there is now a more general consensus that houses, health and consumer items should not be simply dismissed as unproductive and non-developmental.[30] Expenditures on housing, health, transport and communication, as well as schooling of younger siblings, do after all contribute to improving sanitation and well-being, and broadening choices for migrants and their families. Besides, remittances are obviously also used on what are commonly considered to be more productive investments. In Prey Tumpung, migrant families have used the inflow of remittances to purchase fertilizers, land and draft animals, or to hire labour to till the land. Some return migrants have become private moneylenders providing money to aspirant migrants.

Yet, alongside these migrants who came back home well off are also those who fail to remit money. The hard conditions on boats, the extremely long working hours and a male-dominated environment contribute to a subculture in which young migrant men are easily tempted to use their earnings to pay for alcohol, sex and gambling during their short sojourns in the harbour. They, as Nooy called it, "forget their parents" (*phlech mae-ov*) and spend all their money on "going out" (*daoe leeng*). This leads some of them into a spiral of indebtedness from which they can only get out by means of continued labour.

Moreover, migration always involves certain risks. Villagers of Prey Tumpung can tell numerous stories of migrants who were cheated out of their wages by exploitative employers. The village chief himself lost his son-on-law who for unknown reasons fell from his boat at sea, and his body was never found. And he is not the only one. Villagers estimated that during the past fifteen years at least twenty men from their village had died in Thailand due to accidents and fights. The village chief therefore had an ambiguous attitude towards labour migration: on the one hand his village had experienced a high rate of development due to the sizeable out-migration to Thailand and the village chief did understand the desires of aspirant young migrants to follow suit; on the other hand he had seen too many accidents and difficulties related to working in Thailand and would rather see his villagers find work somewhere nearby or to go abroad through legal channels.

Abuse and violence have become a growing concern not only for the village chief of Prey Tumpung, but also for the Cambodian government as well as specialized international and non-governmental organizations. Media and

---

30 De Haas, "International Migration, Remittances and Development," 1274; see also Greame Hugo, *Migration and Development: A Perspective from Asia* (Geneva: IOM, 2003).

NGOs regularly report stories about "enslaved migrants", which typically start with the promises of a neighbour or *mekhyal* (here, broker) regarding high paying-jobs abroad and, after months of ordeal, end with a rescue operation or the support of an NGO. The focus of these stories was initially girls and young women in the sex business, but they currently also fell of women enclosed in foreign households and men trapped on fishing boats. These stories give us the impression that Cambodian labour has become a profitable commodity in the hands of unscrupulous traffickers and exploitative employers, leading migrant workers into situations in which they are no longer in active control of their own migration experiences and from which they eventually end up worse off.

This major focus on deceit and exploitation in relation to labour migration has even prompted Prime Minister Hun Sen to call on Cambodian workers in Thailand to return home in order not to be looked down on by (Thai) employers and not to have to work illegally.[31] This call was, however, probably more motivated by the Thai-Cambodian crisis in relation to the disputed Preah Vihear temple than the alleged improvements in the labour market and wage levels in Cambodia. For the majority of Cambodian migrants, Thailand is maybe not the most lucrative but definitely the most accessible country of destination.

Work and Life at the Other Side of the Border

The ambiguous attitude towards illegal migration, which is on the one hand tolerated because of its potential to bring in desired remittances and on the other hand condemned because of the risks of abuse, does not only hold true for states sending labourers abroad. Concerns regarding "national security" versus the quest for economic profit tend to be in the centre of the debate about illegal migration in the countries of destination. This is certainly the case with Thailand, which has seen a major inflow of migrant workers from its poorer neighbours since the 1980s. The booming economy in the 1980s and rising educational levels led Thai workers to look for more profitable jobs in services and high-tech industries, leaving menial and low-paid jobs in agriculture, construction, fisheries, manufacturing and domestic work to (mostly illegal) migrant workers. These migrant workers form on the one hand the backbone of the country's low-cost, labour-intensive industries, and on the other hand a constant worry to the country's national and health security. During the past two decades, the Thai government designed various policies in an attempt to control the large numbers of illegal migrants from Cambodia, Laos and

---

[31] Chean Sokha, "PM Wants Cambodian Workers in Thailand to Come Back Home," *Phnom Penh Post*, 2 October 2008.

especially Myanmar, thereby constantly navigating between pressure from the business lobby calling for lenient policies towards migrant workers in order to maintain their competitiveness in labour-intensive industries, and voices demanding stricter control of border checkpoints, increased penalties for both illegal migrants and employers, and improved monitoring of illegal migrants.[32]

In 2004, the Thai government started a comprehensive registration campaign with the objective to document all illegal migrants and their dependents by promising them an amnesty. The start was seen as a success: a total of 1.28 million migrants registered at the Ministry of Interior and received the permission to stay in Thailand either to work or seek employment or as dependants of migrants working in Thailand.[33] Migrants who had thus obtained work permits in Thailand were covered by most of the same labour regulations as Thai nationals and enrolled in a migrant health insurance scheme, making them less vulnerable to problems of illness and injury. The validity of the work permits was one year, with the possibility to renew them or to apply for new permits in the following years. Registration numbers have, however, decreased from year to year. In October 2005, 182,007 Cambodians had registered with the Ministry of Interior – representing 13% of all registered migrants in Thailand – out of which 75,804 had received work permits from the Ministry of Labour.[34] Only a third, or 24,754 Cambodians had renewed their work permits two years later in 2007.[35]

In Rayong, an industrial town on the eastern coast of Thailand, registration numbers dwindled from 18,714 in 2004 to 4,452 in 2007. This sharp decrease in registration numbers is, however, not so much illustrative of the actual number of Cambodian migrants in Rayong, but more of the difficulties related to the registration policy.[36] That actual numbers of Cambodian migrants in Rayong are higher than the official figures is clearly visible in Paknam, the harbour of Rayong city, also dubbed "Kambuja City". Cambodians are indeed all over the place: walking along the streets, buying daily necessities at the nearby small

---

[32] Yongyuth Chalamwong, "Government Policies on International Migration: Illegal Workers in Thailand", in Aris Ananta and Evi Nurvidya Arifin (eds.), *International Migration in Southeast Asia* (Singapore: ISEAS, 2004).

[33] Jerrold W. Huguet and Sureeporn Punpuing, *International Migration in Thailand* (Bangkok: IOM, 2005), 4.

[34] Maltoni, *Labour Migration Dynamics in Cambodia*, 24.

[35] After a halt in 2009, a new round of migrant registration and nationality verification took place in early 2010, along with the implementation of forceful measures to arrest and deport illegal migrant workers.

[36] The most often cited difficulties are: (1) limited registration period; (2) too expensive; (3) high turnover; (4) lack of actual protection/freedom of movement. The government under Prime Minister Abhisit Vejjajiva, in a response to economic downturn and increasing unemployment, has decided not to register new migrant workers and to crack down on illegal immigration.

shops, cooking food in front of small rooms in the alleys off the main road, and, above all, working on the fishing wharfs. The major presence of a Cambodian migrant community in this area is a relatively recent phenomenon. Initially it was young Cambodian men who came to work on the fishing boats, after Thais got access to jobs in the industrial and service sectors. In time the families of these migrants followed. Broadening opportunities for life and work made it possible for the wives and children of migrant men to settle in Rayong. Among them are also more and more young women: the daughters, sisters, cousins and neighbours who came along with migrant families in order to find jobs in seafood processing, local restaurants, factories or Thai households. Not surprisingly, attraction between young men and women has led to the creation of new families among young migrants, meaning Khmer style weddings in the harbour area and children born in local hospitals.

The case of Rayong is illustrative of the way in which labour migration may take on a dynamic of its own, unforeseen by government policies. Whereas the development of such a lively migrant community is often regarded as an undesirable result of chain migration outside the control of employers and authorities, the arrival of increasing numbers of migrants clearly serves the interests of those looking for a stable yet flexible workforce. Fishermen are considered to be a difficult-to-control and highly mobile group. The presence of wives and children may help to make workers more acquiescent and less mobile. Besides, fishing wharf owners have come to rely on cheap and flexible migrant labour not only for fishing, but also for the sorting and processing of fish, an activity that is now dominated by the wives, daughters and other relatives of Cambodian fishermen. By providing employment, police protection, housing – which migrants either have to rent or for which payment is deducted from wages – and the occasional food supplements (such as leftover fish), employers have thus accommodated migrant families in the harbour area.

Dha is one of tens of thousands of Cambodian migrants who have found a living in Rayong. Before she came to Thailand, Dha worked as a day labourer in the rice fields of better-off villagers earning 2,500 riel (25 baht) per day. Yet, after having seen several other villagers, including her younger brother, returning from Thailand with earnings she could only dream of, she decided she wanted to try her luck in Thailand. Her mother did not want her to go and refused to give her any financial support to pay the *mekhyal*, a fellow villager, who had helped to take her younger brother across the border. She therefore had to turn to a more supportive aunt to borrow 1,000 baht to cover her travel to the check point at Laem, pay for a *sambot*, a border pass that is valid for one day, and pay the person organizing her transport to Rayong, where she would stay with relatives while looking for work.

Dha found a job as one of the many fish selectors, sorting different species and sizes of fish that are brought on shore when fishing boats return after several weeks at sea. Depending on the amount of fish, she could earn around 200 baht per day – eight times the daily rate back home. Yet, as she soon was to find out, work was very irregular and living expenses were also a lot higher. Besides, she was severely constrained in her freedom of movement. Her border pass with which she had entered Thailand was obviously not valid any more – and at any rate not applicable for the Rayong region – meaning that she had to be constantly on the alert for police controls. She remembered:

> When I first came [to Rayong] the police came to arrest, but I managed to run away. The migration police came to arrest us all, oh, oh. I returned home only at midnight. They sat and waited at our homes. No, it was not easy when I first came to Thailand, not like now. I did not have a *ban* [registration card]. We locked the door everyday... The police came everyday, sometimes two or three times per day.

Dha was several times taken by surprise and caught by the police who threatened her with detention and deportation if she did not pay a fine of up to 2,000 baht – a large sum that had to be borrowed against high interest rates from fellow Cambodians.

Things became somewhat easier after she met and married a Cambodian fisherman who had lived and worked in Thailand for fifteen years. Due to his extensive experience as a fisherman on various boats and his fluency in the Thai language he had been able to move up to the position of *chiew* (supervisor) of the thirty-five fishermen on the boat of his current employer and hence to earn up to six times the amount of other fishermen on the boat. His employer facilitated Dha's registration card, deducting the costs of the registration procedure from her husband's lump sum payment after thirty months. Being documented meant that Dha was now permitted to work as a seafood processor at the wharf of her husband's employer, yet she was not able to change employer or sector. The registration card allowed her a greater freedom of movement within Rayong than undocumented or semi-documented migrants had.[37] Besides, due to her registration she also got access to the Thai health scheme, meaning that she could make use of the public health system for only thirty baht per consultation. Dha did so twice, namely for the birth of her two sons in Rayong hospital.

When I met her, Dha lived with her husband, who was often for extended periods of time out at sea. She was with her three and four year-old sons, and

---

[37] Some migrants pay 200 or 300 baht for a so-called *ban khae* or monthly card. This card is part of an unofficial agreement between employers and the local immigration police to protect the workers against arbitrary police raids.

a cousin, in a housing compound owned by relatives of their employer and inhabited exclusively by Cambodian migrants working in Rayong's fish industry. The houses were basically a row of rooms, each with a small bedroom and a bathroom inside. Dha's room was decorated with framed pictures of her parents, her husband's brother who had died at sea when he had tried to untangle a fishing net that had got stuck in the engine, a Buddha altar which Dha had rescued from the garbage, a TV-DVD set and a motorbike. Together with her mobile phone she possessed the most obvious tokens of their newly acquired wealth in Thailand.

After living for almost six years in Thailand, having created a new family on Thai soil, and staying in a community made up of fellow Cambodians, Dha seemed not to be rushed to return to live in Cambodia: "Here [in Thailand] we can earn money. Here we have electricity." Her way of life in Thailand comes, however, also with costs. Due to the expenses for housing, food, transport and the children, she has managed to save and thus remit a lot less than she would have misled. Indeed, the longer migrants stay abroad, the less money they tend to send back home (*skoal thai you leng sal luy*).

Still, Dha very well realized that her stay in Thailand is temporary. Her registration card has to be extended every year and with the fast changing political situation in Thailand one can never be sure whether current policies regarding migrant workers will be prolonged, or whether migration laws and enforcement strategies will become more stringent. Besides, her husband will not be able to continue working on the boat for ever: "He says he wants to go back to work in Cambodia when he has earned 100,000 [baht], because the work here is hard. He is old; he has already worked here for many years. . . It is exhausting."

She has, however, returned several times to Cambodia to visit her family. During her latest trip she brought back a younger cousin, who, like Dha when she first arrived, still has to get used to living in the small world that makes up her daily life and work in the margins of Thai society.

Making Sense of Migrant Careers

Dha's story vividly illustrates the realities of a grassroots migrant labour scheme outside the country's official "labour export" program. The constraints and choices that shape her migration experiences make it difficult to see her either as a development agent or as a victim. Cambodian migrant workers who, like Dha, cross borders in search for work move into a field marked by conflicting interests and unequal power relations involving sending and receiving states, recruiters, brokers, employers, and local authorities. Her trajectory from recruitment through informal village networks, crossing the border by means of an official border pass, becoming an undocumented migrant worker in the Thai fishing industry and becoming eventually so regularized as to facilitate the illegal entry and work of a cousin in Thailand, shows, however, how in the process apparent dichotomies between legal and illegal, documented and undocumented, have become blurred.[38]

Migration realities do here not necessarily correspond with the public perspective. Illegality is, as Hun Sen's remarks above indicate, commonly seen as being the main cause for the problems faced by migrant workers abroad. And since the perception is that, as Oum Mean, Under-Secretary of State of the Ministry of Labour, alleged, "legal workers are protected", the government promotes the sending of labour abroad through "proper channels", in other words through private recruitment companies working in alliance with the Ministry of Labour.[39] Yet, as Lee found, these recruitment companies are often more interested in profits than in organizing a safe and orderly migration, let alone monitoring the work situation at the place of destination.[40] She found numerous cases of malpractice and negligence by licensed recruitment companies, as well as several unlicensed and semi-legal companies sending Cambodian workers abroad, some to destination countries with which Cambodia has no mutual agreement on labour migration. The realities of the recruitment and placement of labour overseas thus make it difficult to neatly distinguish between "legal" and "illegal" practices in labour migration. Moreover, labour migration along the network of international employment agencies represents only a fraction of the estimated flow of labour abroad. Migrant workers draw on a myriad of legal, semi-legal and illegal schemes to cross borders and work abroad, often with the connivance of local authorities. At the place of destination documented, semi-documented and undocumented migrants conduct the same activities alongside one another on fishing boats and wharfs in order to get the work done that Thai citizens decline to do. Undocumented migrants, in other words, do not constitute a hermetically sealed community, but engage as neighbours, co-workers or consumers on a daily basis with other migrants as well as Thai citizens.[41]

It is important in this regard to be aware that when talking about the "illegality" of migrants, one is referring, as De Genova has stated, above all to a judicial status that entails a social relation to the state, above the receiving state.[42] It is a

---

[38] Cf Kyle and Siracusa, "Seeing the State Like a Migrant."

[39] Koun Leakhana, "Overseas Agencies Aid Migrant Workers," *Phnom Penh Post* (13 September 2008).

[40] Lee, *Exploitative Labour Brokerage Practices*, 34.

[41] Nicholas P. De Genova, "Migrant 'Illegality' and Deportability in Everyday Life", *Annual Review of Anthropology* (2002), 422.

[42] Ibid.

legal construct that is subject to change according to shifting economic and political situations, leading to either more permissive or more restrictive policies with regard to migrant labour and migrant labourers. As the case of Cambodian migrants in Rayong illustrates, "illegality" is – contrary to common belief – not necessarily correlated to the conditions of their work and is insignificant for many of the activities migrants engage in during their daily lives, but it does become an issue in certain contexts – namely those in which local authorities are involved. Yet, "legality" does not necessarily guarantee protection against police extortion and labour abuse.[43] It is therefore questionable whether "(il)legality" is the main "category" for migrant workers themselves.

Furthermore, as Dha's story shows, unauthorized labour migration is not in the hands of unscrupulous brokers conspiring with exploitative employers. Instead, labour migration is often organized within localized village and family networks, in which migrants themselves turn into brokers, recruiting and leading fellow villagers to work sites in Thailand. As an NGO-worker in Thailand remarked:

> When migrants leave their home for the first time, they need someone to take them from the village to Thailand; the second time they can go by themselves to the border and find an agent who can help them to cross the border; the third time they bring someone along with them.

This description definitely fits Dha's migration career. It places the role of the often negatively portrayed broker and trafficker – i.e. the one who helps the migrant to enter and work in a foreign country for profit – in a somewhat different light. Dha's story shows how family and village networks continue to play an important role in the place of destination by providing shelter, finding a job and facilitating the remittance of earnings.[44]

Dha's story exemplifies how the involvement of a growing number of people in organizing migratory movements has led to what has been called a "migration industry".[45] The increasing numbers of people moving across borders in search for work elsewhere has given rise to new possibilities to make money in these migratory movements. From recruitment agents, brokers, smugglers, transport agents, employers, house owners, shopkeepers, creditors and banks to police and migration officials, a range of people profit from the aspirations, needs, labour and earnings of migrants. In such a context, migration may easily lead to abuse, but it also entails a chance. And that is why so many are willing to take the risk.

---

[43] See also Eliane Pearson, *Underpaid, Overworked and Overlooked. The Realities of Young Migrant Workers in Thailand* (Bangkok: ILO, 2006).
[44] Ibid.
[45] Castles and Miller, *The Age of Migration*, 114.

10

THE POLITICAL ECONOMY OF "GOOD GOVERNANCE" REFORM

Kheang Un and Caroline Hughes

THE CHAPTERS SO FAR IN this volume have discussed relationships between business and governance, and the ways in which these play out in different sectors of the economy. In this chapter we focus on the state apparatus, and examine how the CPP-led government, since 1998, has steered a course between donor aspirations for good governance, party pressures to look after the interests of powerful insiders, and the need to deliver public goods and services. Consequently, we focus upon the politics of institutional reform within the Cambodian state apparatus, in four policy areas: health services and specifically the Health Ministry's response to the HIV/AIDS epidemic; the rehabilitation of the Phnom Penh water supply; judicial reform; and natural resource management.

Understanding the Cambodian response to donor-sponsored public administration reform requires contextualizing the state bureaucracy within the broader political economy of Cambodia's contemporary transformation. In the current economic transformation, the Cambodian state bureaucracy is facilitating the process of the enclosure of the commons and the concentration of productive resources in the hands of those with capital to invest, at the expense of the subsistence sector. This process of enclosure and concentration has been largely facilitated through the patronclient structure, and closely associated with strategies for the consolidation of political power through the forging of close ties with wealthy business people. Public administration reform has been subordinated to this process. The result has been the proliferation of corruption, cronyism and violence, at the expense of the rule of law, in those areas most closely associated with economic transformation. However, the state bureaucracy also has the task of mobilizing legitimacy for the regime and providing public goods for the purposes of development, and therefore in areas less closely related to the issues of enclosure and the concentration of productive resources, there is pressure on public servants to deliver better government. In areas such as service delivery and infrastructure provision, manager-leaders within the public service have the opportunity to seek effective ways of responding to the needs of the public.

A significant intervening factor in this context is the intrusion of Cambodia's Western aid donors, upon whom the state bureaucracy is financially dependent for its budgets, and who since 1998 have formalized a specific model of "good governance" which they seek to promote within the Cambodian bureaucracy. This good governance agenda has been made an explicit goal of government policy, both in RGC policy statements, such as the Rectangular Strategy and its Governance Action Plans, and in the Joint Monitoring Indicators established to enable the monitoring of bureaucratic reform by various government donor working groups. However, a 2007 study of government donor relations conducted by the Cambodian government suggested that Western donors are united in a suspicion of the Cambodian bureaucracy, and that as a result, aid tends to be channelled into discrete projects, ring-fenced off from mainstream government departments, relying on seconded staff earning extra salary supplements, and subject to tight reporting requirements.[1] For example, only 2 per cent of assistance to agriculture in 2007 was disbursed via broad ministry programmes rather than through discrete projects.[2] Other studies have commented on three issues: (1) the largesse awarded to donor project offices, at the expense of regular government departments; (2) the donors' unwillingness to use Cambodian government public financial management systems; and (3) the widespread use of foreign consultants. These forms of aid delivery reflect donor perceptions of the Cambodian state apparatus as corrupt and poorly functioning.

The government's response to this donor regime has been equivocal. While it has produced a raft of comprehensive reform plans which exactly match donor prescriptions, the implementation of these plans has been less impressive. Arguably, government support for reform peaked between 1999 and 2004, when the CPP was seeking international support, following two controversial elections, and when the country's economic transformation was still in its early stages. Subsequently, the government has appeared more cautious in its reform rhetoric. For example, its second Governance Action Plan, published in 2006, concludes with a warning:

> State Reform is a political venture made of a myriad of inter-dependent actions. It is more art than science. It is the art of the possible that is sustainable.

[1] Council for the Development of Cambodia, *The Cambodia Aid Effectiveness Report 2007* (Phnom Penh: CDC, 2007), online at http://www.cdc-crdb.gov.kh/cdc/aid_management/AER-Report-2007-FINAL.pdf, accessed 19 September 2007, 6.
[2] *Ibid.*, 24.

Reforming the State is a long arduous process that involves a complex range of activities that must mutually reinforce one another. It is not about doing a few things of drama with early results but of dubious cost benefits. This is particularly true in areas such as the fight against corruption, the legal and judicial reform and the administrative reform.[3]

The government's preoccupation with "sustainability" of reforms is connected to its repeated assertion of the need to safeguard gains in peace and stability. For the government, peace and stability is guaranteed by a highly personalist micro-managing of economic transformation and the dispersal of key resources via patronclient relations. Consequently, public administration reform in areas that are directly pertinent to this process has been extremely limited, as we will suggest in our analysis below of the failure of reforms in the judiciary and the natural resource management sectors.

In other policy areas, however, where the government regards effective service delivery and other provision of key public goods as important for the eliciting of legitimacy, there has been greater convergence between donor and government practices. Such convergence of practices is found for example in the cases of the Ministry of Health's response to HIV/AIDS, and in the rehabilitation and commercialization of the Phnom Penh water supply. Success in these two areas, we will argue, has been facilitated by the fragmentation of the Cambodian state, in a manner that not only permits but contains success in certain areas. This fragmentation has in part emerged through donor-prompted practices of agencification.

Agencification in service delivery derives from the New Public Management (NPM) reform movement that similarly fragmented state bureaucracies across the Western world in the 1980s and 1990s. The managerialist approaches to service delivery favoured by exponents of the New Public Management prompted the disaggregation of the state into a series of decentralized agencies intended to resemble firms rather than bureaucracies.[4] Within these agencies, appointed managers managed budgets and responded to consumers with a great degree of autonomy, and with reference to incentives designed to maximize efficiency. This model of organization was considered to elicit greater initiative and responsiveness from state officials, by freeing them from the red tape of hierarchical management structures, and allowing them "freedom to manage."

---

[3] Royal Government of Cambodia, *Governance Action Plan* (Phnom Penh: Council of Ministers, 2006), 69.

[4] Linda Kaboolian, "The New Public Management: Challenging the Boundaries of the Management vs. Administration Debate," *Public Administration Review*, 58.3 (1998): 190; Patrick Dunleavy and Christopher Hood, "From Old Public Administration to New Public Management," *Public Money and Management*, 14.3 (1994), 9–16.

Managerialism, and the New Public Management movement as a whole, has since fallen somewhat out of fashion in the West, largely because the fragmentation that it produces causes inefficiencies in governance. In Cambodia, however, this model lives on in donor-sponsored agencies, in the broader context of a relationship of deep distrust between donors and government, and of radically different interests in different wings of government, dependent, in large part, on the extent to which they are involved with the governance of resource ownership and exploitation, versus service delivery.

To some extent, managerialism contrasts with the logics of patron-clientism. Patron-clientism tends to value loyalty over efficiency, and prioritizes the maintenance of relationships over the achievement of performance targets. At the same time, the figure of the manager-leader galvanizing his employees to aspire to particular standards of service is not antithetical to patron-clientist models, given particular contexts. In particular agencies within the Cambodian state apparatus, arguably, these figures coincide; however, the extent to which this should be seen as a starting point for reform is questionable.

We conclude, after examining the two case studies, that in fact their "success" has not been achieved through combating neo-patrimonialism but by successfully forging an organizational culture in which both sets of values converge upon similar working practices. In other words, "reform" comprises the embedding of concepts associated with managerialism and new public management into a Cambodian context in a manner that pleases different power-holders, rather than transforming the Cambodian context itself. Second, we conclude that there are particular features of the issue areas studied which lent themselves to "success" in this regard, and marginality to the dynamics of economic transformation is one of these features.

Private Property Regime Management

The politics of the private property regime which has presided over a massive concentration of wealth and landholdings in Cambodia over the past twenty years can be illustrated by looking at two governance sectors that have been at the core of this regime: the judiciary and natural resource management. In these sectors, the government has resisted devolving power to either rules-based institutions or autonomous agencies, but has co-opted the latter into the heart of its patronage networks.

The judiciary is a key exemplar. The concept of judicial independence was incorporated into the Cambodian constitution following the 1993 UN-sponsored elections. The judiciary was constitutionally awarded the power of checks and balances, charged with review of legislative and executive acts, enforcement of constitutional provisions, and defense of civil, social and private property rights. However, the institutionalization of these powers has been contested between Cambodian elites and international donors.

Although judicial reform is a stated goal of the government, almost nothing has been achieved in this regard. Arguably, this failure stems from the significance of the judiciary for the property regime, and the resulting concern on the part of the government to maintain control over the judiciary. A number of factors have contributed to the successful co-optation of the judiciary. Low salaries are one factor. Until 2002 the average monthly salary for court officials was around US$14 a month, well below the minimum cost of living, virtually ensuring habitual corruption. As part of judicial reform, the salaries of judges and prosecutors have been substantially increased, but this occurred only once the danger of the judiciary flexing its new-found muscles in the context of the democratic aspirations surrounding the 1993 UNTAC election was long past.

In fact, judicial corruption in 2009 is not as widespread and uncontrolled as it was in the 1990s and early 2000s. It has become more co-opted, systematized and hierarchically controlled. A number of factors facilitated this. One is job insecurity. Laws to govern the tenure of judges and prosecutors, and thus award them independence from the executive, have been repeatedly stalled.[5] In the government's view, passing these laws means, as an official at the Ministry of Justice said, "setting a post to tie itself". At the same time, few institutional constraints have been imposed on judges' and prosecutors' activities. Corruption has become the norm.

The government has made cosmetic moves towards reform. For example, it created the Council on Legal and Judicial Reform, an institution placed under the direct control of the Council of Ministers, and co-led by senior ranking CPP members and close Hun Sen allies Dith Monty and Sok An. Such an august institution could, arguably, have empowered the judicial reform process. However, the glacial and apparently ineffective outcome of reform thus far reveals that the appointment of such high-ranking individuals portended the government's careful control of the process, rather than a determination to see judicial independence assured.

Other reform efforts have simply succumbed to the logic of corruption. A school created to professionalize the legal system became embroiled in patronage networks as *khsae* and bribes became the determinants of selection and placement processes.[6] Equally, continued financial control over the courts by

---

[5] World Bank, *Cambodia: Legal and Judicial Sector Assessment* (Phnom Penh: World Bank, 2003), 26.
[6] Caroline Huot and Sam Rith, "Hope of Justice Lies in School for Judges," *Phnom Penh Post*, 21 November–4 December 2003.

the Ministry of Justice empowers the ministry to intervene regularly in court cases. Meanwhile the miniscule size of the budget for the Ministry of Justice – projected to be US$5 million for 2007, of which the courts received a small fraction[7] – more or less determines the ineffective functioning of the judicial system.

Equally, the Supreme Council of Magistracy (SCM), constitutionally mandated to oversee and review the judiciary and to assist the King in ensuring the independence of the courts, has been dysfunctional since its establishment in 1998. According to articles 133 and 134 of the Constitution, the SCM is responsible for recommending all judicial appointments, and suspension of and disciplinary actions against judges and prosecutors, which are then executed by royal decrees.

Like other judicial institutions in the country, the SCM is regarded as politically dependent, subject to the CPP's influence, and functionally weak. Most of its current members, with the exception of the King and the prosecutor-general of the Supreme Court, are senior members of the CPP, some of whom also sit on the party's powerful Central Committee.[8] The institution has been accused of violating its own procedures: the SCM law provides for three seats to the council to be elected by the judges themselves. But according to the Office of the United Nations High Commission for Human Rights (UNHCHR), "no elections have ever been held for these three elected positions".[9]

The appointment and replacement of judges have also not followed constitutional procedures. Despite the constitutional stipulation that appointments of and disciplinary actions against judges and prosecutors must be decided by the SCM, past appointments appeared to contravene these principles. The SCM has not been effective in promoting effectiveness and independence within the judicial system but is itself imbedded in the overarching system of patronage. The SCM's lack of independence and transparency in turn has influence over a judge's decisions and behaviour. If a judge's decision deviates from the expected norm then he/she could be transferred to a remote province, a punishment that judges keep in mind when adjudicating sensitive cases. Despite the notoriously

---

[7] Royal Government of Cambodia Ministry of Economy and Finance, *The Medium-Term Expenditure Framework for Cambodia 2005–2007* (Phnom Penh: MEF, 2004) available online at http://www.mef.gov.kh/hnaron/mtef-2004/mtef7.htm, accessed on January 4, 2007.

[8] Lao Mong Hay (2003), "Institutions for the Rule of Law and Human Rights in Cambodia," online http://www.article2.org/mainfile.php/0501/223 accessed 20 May 2011.

[9] The United Nations High Commission for Human Rights, "Joint Public Statement: The United Nations Special Representatives of the Secretary General for Human Rights in Cambodia and the Special Rapporteur on the Independence of Judges and Lawyers Express Concern Over Judicial Independence in Cambodia in the Light of Recent Judicial Appointment," Geneva, 23 August 2007, available on line at Cambodia.ohchr.org/download.aspx?ep_id=334 accessed February 8, 2008.

corrupt and erratic nature of the court system, legal action by the SCM against corrupt practices and judicial misconducts is rare.

Persistent government unwillingness to implement meaningful reform in the judicial sphere represents the conflict between the rule-based governance demanded by the reform proponents and the personalist, hierarchical and discretionary elements of neo-patrimonialism. Lack of judicial strength and independence allows regular interference by the executive branch, and by powerful individuals associated with it, in court affairs. The degree and frequency of interference varies from one judge to another; but a general consensus among judges is that if there was intervention by high ranking government officials, judges and prosecutors needed to acquiesce.[10] The need to submit to such pressure derives from the judicial officials being linked in reciprocal relationships—whereby people return favours for what others did for them— or fear of being demoted or transferred to non-desirable post. "Influence of intervention from a higher authority depends on the individual judge," said one judge, but added, "Maintaining one's stance is difficult. For example, they used to help our interests. What can we do in such a case?"[11] Consequently, "It is unavoidable that court officials serve the interests of political parties and that the judicial system serves politics."[12]

Forest management is another case wherein efforts at creating a rational, legal-based administration have, over the past 25 years, consistently failed despite international pressure and an ongoing government rhetoric of reform. The sector is complicated as it involves many powerful actors. This complex web of networks renders the rationalization of the sector problematic. The fundamental problem is the desire to maintain a flexible and discretionary, rather than rule-based, control of natural resources. This desire was first conceived in the 1990s, as a means to tempt defections from insurgent armies and so produce national and political stability. Subsequently, it has been co-opted for the maintenance of power through patronage-based electoral exercises. In 1994 as a way to secure military allegiance, Cambodian leaders gave the military the right to control Cambodia's forests. The army, business people, forestry bureaucrats, politicians, and provincial authorities formed informal links through which the process of forest exploitation and the export of timber were facilitated to generate personal wealth and finance the civil war.[13]

---

[10] J 19, interview with author, 04 December 2002; J 15, interview with author, 14 November 2002.
[11] J 15, interview with author, 03 October 2002.
[12] J 3, interview with author, 02 October 2002.
[13] Phillipe Le Billon, "Logging in Muddy Waters: The Politics of Forest Exploitation in Cambodia," Critical Asian Studies, 34: 4 (2002): 570. The World Bank, *Cambodia: Enhancing Service Delivery Through Improved Resource Allocation and Institutional Reform* (Phnom Penh: World Bank, May 2003), 8.

With the achievement of internal peace following the demise of the Khmer Rouge guerrilla movement and power consolidation by the CPP and particularly Hun Sen following the 1997 *coup d'état*, the control of Cambodia's forests was transferred to the Ministry of Agriculture, Forestry and Fishery (MAFF). By the early 2000s the government had promulgated laws and introduced mechanisms to institute legal and rational governance of the forestry sector, such as the imposition of a total moratorium on logging and the establishment in 2002 of Forest Management Plans and Social Environmental Impact Assessments with specific action plans.[14] The action plans focus on the "decentralization, effectiveness, and accountability of forest management".[15] Furthermore, a new department—the Department of Forestry Administration (DFA)—was established with a mandate to promote the new management of the forest sector within the framework of deconcentration, focusing on critical elements of NPM such as merit-based staff recruitment, decentralized decision-making, responsiveness and accountability.

However, pressure from powerful interests and entrenched patronage permeated the sector, and the DFA was never as independent as it may have appeared. A relative of MAFF minister Chan Sarun was appointed as director of the DFA, and the broader staff selection process was "dictated by payment rather than competence;" by *khsae* rather than experience.[16] A critical component of the bureaucratic rationalization of forest management—decent salaries—was not instituted. While the salaries of forest officials are low and inadequate to support themselves, they are also required to pay kickbacks to their superiors.[17] With the military's role reduced to the transportation of timber, the relationships among business individuals, politicians, and forestry bureaucrats formed an iron triangle within which deals were made, often secretly, to profit through the award of forest lands to investors as land concessions or as special construction projects.

---

[14] Royal Government of Cambodia and Development Partners' Technical Working Group Forestry and Environment, "Forest Cover Change in Cambodia 2002–2006," paper prepared for Cambodia Development Cooperation Forum, 19–20 June 2007, 4

[15] Royal Government of Cambodia and Development Partners' Technical Working Group, *Forestry Outlook Cambodia 2008* (Phnom Penh: TWG on Forestry and Environment, 2008). Available online http://www.phnompenh.um.dk/NR/rdonlyres/3602743D-2288-4248-8FEB-2E1C57043785/0/ForestryOutlookCambodia2008.doc, accessed on March 30, 2009.

[16] Global Witness. *Cambodia's Family Trees.* Phnom Penh: Global Witness, 2007. Online at http://www.globalwitness.org/media_library_detail.php/546/en/cambodias_family_trees, accessed 10 October 2007, 60–61.

[17] Global Witness, 60–61; Royal Government of Cambodia Forestry Administration and Working Group on Natural Resource Management, *Forest Sector in Cambodia Part I: Policy Choices, Issues and Options*, Independent Forest Sector Review (Phnom Penh: Working Group on Natural Resource Management, April 2004), 102.

The new mechanisms have changed the patterns of the exploitation of forest land. On the one hand, the once widespread illegal logging by military units and provincial authorities has been stemmed. On the other, new practices of exploitation by what the international NGO Global Witness calls "kleptocratic elites" have been centralized.

External and internal accountability mechanisms have been consistently co-opted or undermined in the sector. For example, in 2001, the government passed a new Forestry Law and created a Forest Crimes Monitoring Unit (FCMU) to enforce it. The government then agreed to contract out oversight of the FCMU to an independent agency, and the environmental NGO Global Witness won the tender. However, when Global Witness exposed illegal and unsustainable exploitation of forests by high-ranking and well-connected business people, and the inability of an underfunded and politically co-opted FCMU to do anything about this, the government sacked the organization from the job and banned it from operating in Cambodia.[18] Subsequently, the exploitation of Cambodia's forests has been handled through the award of large areas of forest as economic land concessions under the Land Law, rather than as logging concession under the Forestry Law, avoiding the necessity of bothering the weak forestry regime at all.

The new framework for forest management is based on the Socio-Economic Development Plan and the National Poverty Reduction Strategy. However, the plan is rendered ineffective by political and business pressure and because the government has co-opted or undermined the institutions mandated to control concessionaires. Furthermore, the developmental potential of this regime is questionable. One independent review states: "One of the major assumptions underlying the system is unfounded, namely, that a concession system could deliver revenue to the state for national development."[19] While employment generated by the concession system is limited, weak enforcement of laws and a politicized legal system mean that the poor and ethnic minority communities tend to lose in most conflicts.[20] Furthermore, because the Forestry Administration lacks resources and finance to strengthen its staff, compounded by an absence of "external oversight or accountability mechanisms", rent seeking is widespread.[21] In one project, a logging company earned an estimate of US$13 million in a year and paid less than US$ 600,000 in taxes.[22] Similarly, the

---

[18] RGC FA and WGNRM, *Forest Sector*.

[19] Ibid., 61–63.

[20] Special Representative for Human Rights in Cambodia, "Economic Land Concessions for Economic Purposes in Cambodia: a Human Rights Perspective," (Phnom Penh: Cambodia Office of the High Commission for Human Rights, 2004), 8.

[21] RGC FA and WGNRM, *Forest Sector*, 83.

[22] Global Witness, 47.

Chinese government reportedly purchased US$ 16.2 million worth of Cambodian plywood between 2003 and 2005, but there were no records of exports and taxes at all.[23] Since 1989, Le Billon has estimated that Cambodia has exported 10 million cubic metres of timber, which is worth US$ 2.4 billion, of which only a small fraction (US$120 million) has made its way to the public treasury.[24] The government's concern to maintain tight control of the distribution of the profits of economic transformation, as a means to defend political power rather than to promote economic development, entails that institutions in this sector, as in the judicial sector, remain under-resourced, politicized, penetrated by patronage networks, and continually under attack from executive intervention.

Public Goods and Service Delivery

A rather different situation pertains in areas of governance where control over high rents and productive resources is not at issue, but where public goods or effective service delivery can serve the interests of legitimation. The water supply in Phnom Penh is one such area. Prior to its restructuring in 1996, despite abundant fresh water in and around Phnom Penh, the Phnom Penh Water Supply Authority (PPWSA) was unable to provide reliable, clean water to residents in Phnom Penh and its suburbs. While approximately 50% of Phnom Penh's population had access to running water, the service was unreliable and lasted on average only 12 hours a day.[25] As a result, people spent large amounts of time, energy and money on fetching and storing water. Furthermore, unclean water represented a threat to public health.

This situation was produced by two sets of factors: the legacy of conflict and the ongoing *modus operandi* of the rebuilding of the Cambodian state apparatus. Conflict had ensured that the water supply infrastructure had received inadequate maintenance and investment since the 1970s. The ongoing *modus operandi* of the state apparatus entailed that the PPWSA staff, like other public sector workers, were inadequately remunerated, leading to lack of discipline and incentive. Furthermore, the legal and institutional status of the PPWSA was complex. It was under the jurisdiction of the Ministry of Interior, which in turn placed it under the control of the Municipality

---

[23] Liam Cochrane, "Cambodia: can't see the forest for the thieves," *World Politics Review*, 6 June 2007, online at http://www.worldpoliticsreview.com/article.aspx?id=829, accessed 13 August 2009.

[24] Le Billon, 565.

[25] World Bank, *Implementation Completion Report on a Credit in the Amount of US$30 Million Equivalent to the Kingdom of Cambodia for an Urban Water Supply Project* (World Bank: Urban Development Sector Unit, East Asia and Pacific Region, January 2004), 2.

of Phnom Penh and its governor. Consequently, the PPWSA operated in a difficult technical, institutional, financial and administrative environment that rendered it an inefficient loss-maker. Unaccounted-for water lost to the system in 1993 was 80 per cent, one of the highest rates in Asia, and was projected to increase.[26]

Unlike other similar state agencies in Cambodia, the PPWSA has been able to transform itself into a financially stable, technologically advanced institution that is held up by its donors as a model of good governance reform. The World Bank's project evaluation in 2004 described the PPWSA's functioning as "best practice, certainly among developing countries".[27]

For the PPWSA, donors envisaged reform as focusing on two central questions. The first was changing a societal culture of free water usage to a market rationality of producer/consumer relations. The second was reorganizing the internal functioning of the agency in a manner which met donor demands with respect to financial and human resource management, and output efficiency measured in technical terms. This section offers an analysis of how the PPWSA was reconstructed over this period, so as to meet the contending needs of two key sets of power-holders. The first set includes international donors who invested large sums of money in the PPWSA, and who sought to promote market-oriented frameworks for service delivery and new public management principles for internal state organization. The second set comprised the government itself, and specifically the ruling CPP which was at the time engaged in using the state apparatus as a space within which relationships characterized by favour, protection, loyalty and reciprocity could be consolidated, and resources extracted to facilitate this.

The policy area of water in Phnom Penh, although subordinated to the state apparatus and consequently subsumed within the ambit of CPP ambitions to consolidate power, was not associated with significant vested political interests. Water supply was not a business in which powerful tycoons with links to the government held significant stakes. Before the project to upgrade the PPWSA began, the water industry was characterized by the provision of bottled and tanker water by a large number of small private enterprises. These enterprises provided a poor quality and expensive service, and the PPWSA's goal of replacing these with a better quality and cheaper service was not at odds with any particularly powerful interests within the government. Because high-level political interests were not at stake, the initial and general response of party leaders and political patrons in the Cambodian government to reforms within the PPWSA was indifferent rather than obstructive.

---

[26] *Ibid.*, 6.
[27] *Ibid.*, 6.

This facilitated a drive by donors, particularly the World Bank and the Asian Development Bank, to ring-fence the PPWSA from "political interference" through a formal grant of autonomous status. Both the World Bank and ADB made loans to the PPWSA conditional on autonomous status. One informant commented: "The government was not willing to give autonomy. But it is difficult to put donor money in if it doesn't function... Autonomy was on the donor agenda."

From the perspective of donors, the achievement of the grant of autonomy was crucial to success in creating the PPWSA as a rational oasis in a patrimonial desert. While autonomy prevented higher-level politicians and officials from interfering in PPWSA financing, staffing and planning, freedom to take responsibility for the workings of the agency permitted fast decision-making, accountability for those decisions, and transparency in financial and personnel management. Autonomy also placed the PPWSA in control of its own procurement procedures – an area where corruption is often a problem in Cambodian infrastructure development – and allowed it to manage its own finances, freeing the agency from pressure from high-level officials with vested interests in diverting revenues and expenditures into their own patronage structures. This helped the authority to manage relations with donors productively, and to maintain a healthy revenue stream that could be used to reward staff.

Additionally, institutional autonomy permitted internal restructuring of the institution in three important ways. First, the staffing structure was changed, with technical staff elevated to the board, and performance incentives attached to pay scales. The PPWSA launched the company employee pension scheme in Cambodia, and a rare merit-based hiring and promotions process, all of which are pioneering politics in Cambodia.

Second, measures of performance were subjected to new systems, based upon technical indicators, technological developments, and international benchmarks. For example, payment collection was strengthened by the introduction of sophisticated, centralised tracking systems that could compare the revenues coming in from payment-collectors with the amount of water being used in different parts of the supply network. Equally, internationally validated benchmarks for measuring water quality were introduced and quickly met, permitting the PPWSA to enjoy a variety of accolades internationally, including the award of the Ramon Magsaysay Prize for government service in 2006, and the ADB's crowning of PPWSA director Ek Sonn Chan as a "water champion". The applications of market-based management distinguish the agency from other parts of the state apparatus, where the raising of revenue for the party, and the consequent enjoyment of the Prime Minister's approbation, is a more common metric of success.

The third ingredient widely cited by donors for the PPWSA's success was the leadership of Ek Sonn Chan, who, under conditions of autonomy, was able to occupy the kind of managerial position touted as essential for effective, efficient and responsive service delivery. Ek Sonn Chan's management and leadership skills in this regard were the most widely cited factor in the success of the PPWSA, amongst donor informants interviewed. As such, the PPWSA in donor accounts appears to be a salutary example of managerial principles in practice, and an indication of what could be done with the Cambodian state, if only the Cambodian government would stop interfering with it.

However, a closer look at the ways in which ministry officials and Ek Sonn Chan himself have spoken about the evolution of the PPWSA suggests that there is an ambiguity in some of the key concepts in this story – namely, the nature of the PPWSA's "autonomy", the nature of the "reform" that has taken place within it, and the kind of "success" that has been achieved. This study suggests two qualifications to these concepts. First, "autonomy" does not represent a past decision but an ongoing negotiation, and in this respect the position of Ek Sonn Chan has been crucial, not merely as a manager, but as a high-ranking politician who is as adept at political manoeuvring within the Cambodian hierarchy as he is at experimenting with Western management models.

Second, "reform" does not represent a kind of modernizing transition, from traditional patrimonial attitudes to rational modern ones, but an embedding of particular practices and buzzwords within existing logics of appropriateness. As such, the "success" of the PPWSA does not represent the holy grail of the good governance agenda – the transferable template. Rather it represents an ongoing accommodation supported by distributions of power between individuals. These distributions of power are themselves determined by factors such as rank and status within the party and the state, and *khnang* and *khsae* (connections to powerful figures). Ek Sonn Chan's success emerges from his ability to use these to finesse the different perspectives of donors and government in a manner which permits the delivery of technical achievements and the protection and reward of subordinates.

Consequently, Ek Sonn Chan can as easily be regarded as a rather traditional type of leader in the context of Cambodian political culture. Historically, a powerful image in Cambodian politics has been that of the strong patron who is influential and ruthless, but who is at the same time clean, moral and selfless, and who works for the good of his clients. In a number of interviews conducted for this study, Ek Sonn Chan was described in these kinds of terms.

Ek Sonn Chan, interviewed for this project, acknowledged the need to finesse the potential contradictions between western management models and Cambodian expectations. For example, on the question of resisting pressure to hire the younger relatives of powerful or close acquaintances he commented:

> In Cambodia, reciprocity and empathy - *yok yual knea tov vinh tov mok* - is very important. It is very difficult to adopt western culture. We have to explain to those who wanted to have their relatives to work at PPWSA in a soft-friendly manner. We explain to them the technical requirements for working at PPWSA. So we use the principles of trial. Those who wanted to work have to work for free initially. If they are effective than we let them take a test. Sometimes, when they hear this they are scared.[28]

The achievement of Ek Sonn Chan, then, is perhaps to make quite radical changes within his organization while embedding these in practices that do not threaten existing logics of appropriateness implicit in models of official behaviour in Cambodian political culture.

At the same time, Ek Sonn Chan emphasizes two additional attributes of Khmer culture, seniority and credibility-influence (*teuk moat prai*), as underlying factors of his leadership success. Leadership capacity requires more than technical and scientific management as he commented:

> I am very concerned about the issue of institution-building. It is not a problem to find people with [technical] knowledge. But there are two pressing concerns: first, age and experience. I have lots of experience and I am old so I can mobilize people and I can scold my staff. Second [is] relationship with other institutions. I have many friends in other ministries and agencies. We cannot find people with these qualities yet.[29]

Here Ek Sonn Chan attributes the success of the institution of the PPWSA as a whole not to the "capacity building" emphasized uniformly by donors – "It is not a problem to find people with knowledge" – but explicitly to the maintainance of appropriate relationships that permit the exercise of power. Age and experience give Ek Sonn Chan the status to transform the expectations and practices of his staff internally; while the *khsae* that are conventionally used to award power in the context of the Cambodian state apparatus give him the ability to ward off interference from outside. It is the combination of these factors that allows him the luxury of experimentation with western management models which in Cambodian context are not self-legitimating.

Ek Sonn Chan's own status has also been important in persuading the PPWSA's customers to behave like customers. There was strong resistance, initially, among powerful individuals, towards accepting that water bills should be paid and that bill collectors had a right to demand payment. Success in reducing non-payment to almost zero came, at least initially, via a

---

[28] Ek Sonn Chan, interview with the authors, Phnom Penh, April 2006.
[29] Ek Sonn Chan, interview with the authors, Phnom Penh, April 2006.

very familiar trial of strength, and by the ability of Ek Sonn Chan to provide his workers with a very familiar type of *khnang*. Ek Sonn Chan commented, "Regarding state institutions, the success in collecting water fees is because I knew top leaders. We sometimes threatened them and sometimes we talked nice to them."[30]

Faced with the need to demonstrate an independent revenue stream to justify ongoing donor investment, Ek Sonn Chan was able to play a very familiar game to improve the PPWSA's finances. Ek Sonn Chan explained that he used his close *khsae* with senior figures in the military police to coerce certain recalcitrant senior military officers into paying their bills. As Ek Sonn Chan himself commented, replacing him as head of the PPWSA will be difficult primarily because of the need to mobilize high level support to protect the agency.

Furthermore, the agencification that facilitated the reform of the PPWSA could not necessarily be easily repeated in other sectors. A contrasting case in the field of infrastructure provision is that of Électricité du Cambodge (EdC), the major electricity supply company in Cambodia. EdC has a number of public private partnerships which are highly politicized. For example, the oil upon which its generation capacities are dependent is procured from a company called Sokimex, owned by Cambodian tycoon *Oknha* Sok Kong, a close ally of the government and Prime Minister Hun Sen. The presence of Sokimex in the sector significantly limits the prospects for EdC adopting market principles in its management style; as one donor informant commented: "The supplier of oil for electricity supply is Sokimex. If the bidding process was transparent it would be much easier. But Shell or other companies have no chance – only the local company has a chance. There is no player like that in the water industry."[31]

Our final case study is the Health Ministry's response to HIV/AIDS, which was effective in reducing the prevalence of HIV/AIDS and in providing care for people living with HIV/AIDS. The prevalence rate of HIV infection in Cambodia dropped from 3 per cent of adult population in 1997 to 2.5 per cent in 2000, 1.9 per cent in 2003,[32] and 0.8 per cent in 2007.[33] This success is commonly credited to the work of the National Council for HIV, AIDS,

---

[30] Ek Sonn Chan, interview with the authors, Phnom Penh, April 2006.
[31] Donor informant, name withheld for reasons of confidentiality, interview with the authors, Phnom Penh, April 2006.
[32] UNAIDS, "Addendum," dated 7 February 2005, to UNAIDS, *Country Profile: An Overview fo the HIV/AIDS/STI Situation and the National Response in Cambodia*, 5th Edition, (Phnom Penh: UNAIDS, December 2004).
[33] United Nations Childrens Fund (UNICEF) website, *Cambodia: Statistics*, webpage, online at http://www.unicef.org/infobycountry/cambodia_statistics.html, accessed 12 August 2009.

Dermatology and Sexually Transmitted Infections (NCHADS), established in 1998, and responsible for coordinating the response of the health sector to an emerging epidemic.[34] There has been much debate over the precise reasons for the decline in HIV prevalence in Cambodia, and over the degree of sustainability of this decline. However, two key policy responses are commonly cited as governance successes: the 100 per cent Condom Use Policy (CUP) and the roll-out of Anti-Retroviral Therapy to people living with HIV/AIDS through a programme called Continuum of Care for People Living with HIV/AIDS in Cambodia.[35]

The key programme associated with slowing the spread of HIV is the CUP, targeted at the commercial sex industry. The HIV epidemic in Cambodia was driven by commercial sex. Prevalence rates in the country were believed to be highest in the 1990s amongst sex workers and the police and the military, all of whom were monitored closely to chart the spread of the disease. The CUP was first implemented in trial areas in Cambodia in 1998, and expanded across the country in 2000. It involved local authorities, police, staff of government STI clinics, brothel owners and sex workers themselves, in ensuring the universal use of condoms during commercial sex. Under the policy, local authorities were required to produce maps of brothels operating in their areas, inform brothel owners of the CUP, ensure that adequate supplies of condoms were always available on the premises, register sex workers working within brothels, and ensure their regular attendance at government-run STI clinics. STI prevalence among sex workers was used as an indicator of brothel compliance with the CUP. Brothels that failed to comply were visited by government officials and could be threatened with closure.

The CUP ran alongside education programmes for police and military personnel, operated by NGOs in collaboration with the Ministries of National Defence and the Interior. Survey work, following the implementation of the policy, has produced evidence of behavioural changes among high-risk groups. Sex workers reported increasing condom use; military and police personnel

---

[34] The account of the National Response to HIV/AIDS is drawn from Caroline Hughes and Kheang Un, *Aid That Works, The Phnom Penh Water Supply Authority and the National Response to HIV/AIDS*, discussion paper (Phnom Penh: World Bank, 2006). It is based upon a series of interviews conducted by the authors in Cambodia in 2006 with Cambodian health officials, development partners and workers in Cambodian non-governmental organizations providing health services.

[35] Details of these programmes can be found in Royal Government of Cambodia Ministry of Health National Centre for HIV/AIDS, Dermatology and STD, National AIDS Authority and UNAIDS, *The Review of the 100% Condom Use Programme in Cambodia* (Phnom Penh: NCHADS/NAA/UNAIDS, 2003); and William Wells, *A Case Study of the Continuum of Care for People Living with HIV/AIDS in Cambodia: Linkages and Strengthening in the Public Health System* (Phnom Penh: NCHADS/World Health Organization, 2006).

report less frequent commercial sex; and awareness of HIV/AIDS appears to have increased among high-risk groups.[36]

The activism of NCHADS under its leader Mean Chivun has been regarded as key to this success. NCHADS has received huge amounts of aid money from international aid agencies: increasing from US$800,000 in 1994 to US$15million in 2002 and up to US$40million in 2006.[37] Partly, this increase is due to the probity with which NCHADS manages its money. Like the PPWSA, NCHADS has negotiated significant autonomy with respect to its budget from the wider Ministry of Health, and unlike most Cambodian state agencies, submits its books annually to international auditors. As with the PPWSA, the ability to wall off the agency from wider flows of money through the various networks operating within the bureaucracy has considerably increased the standing of the agency in the eyes of donors.[38]

The Director of NCHADS, Mean Chivun, was described by donors in similar terms to those used to describe Ek Sonn Chan – as someone who understood Western management practices, and applied them rigorously to his organization, and who was sufficiently high-ranking to be able to defend his organization from ministerial interference. Mean Chivun has been highly effective in gathering, collating and presenting data from a variety of institutions across the HIV/AIDS sector and across the country to provide a national-level picture of the health sector response, as a basis for the central management of annual workplans. Mean Chivun's hands-on management style, his ability to produce donor-friendly accounts and his willingness to submit them to auditing has been an important aspect of the strong relationship NCHADS has developed with international donors. Like the PPWSA, part of NCHADS's success is also due to performance-related salary supplements, which increase motivation to be part of the HIV/AIDS initiative. NCHADS has provided salary supplements for health centre staff working in HIV/AIDS-related areas at provincial, district, and commune levels. Thus NCHADS, like the PPWSA, is based upon a drive towards agencification under a manager who has been able to meet key donor demands in an effective manner.[39]

Like the policy area of water supply, HIV/AIDS is a policy area in which vested political interests associated with regime maintenance and resource distributions have not been an obstacle to effective action. On the contrary, a range of factors gave the central government a powerful stake in mounting an

---

36 Heng Sopheab, Knut Fylkesnes, Mean Chhivun, Nigel O'Farrell, "HIV Risk Behaviours in Cambodia and Effects of Mobility," *Journal of Acquired Immune Deficiency Syndrome* 41.1 (2006): 81–86.
37 Mean Chhivun, interview with the authors, Phnom Penh, April 2006.
38 Interviews with Cambodia's development partners, Phnom Penh, April 2006.
39 Ibid.

immediate response, and NCHADS's success in promoting 100 per cent condom use in commercial sex in part arises from the extent to which the agency was able to tap into some of Cambodia's most tightly-organized patronclient networks. The high rate of prevalence among urban police, for example, which was around 6 per cent in 1997,[40] could be regarded as a serious problem for core government interests. Similar prevalence rates were found in the armed forces. In the context of the political instability of the mid-1990s, control of the security forces was perhaps the most contested issue in Cambodian politics; for the Cambodian government, and particularly for the CPP which in 1997 had just consolidated control over the security sector, the prospect of an epidemic sweeping unpredictably through entire battalions may well have been a frightening one.

The significance of the sex industry in driving the epidemic also encouraged government openness on the issue, for two reasons. First, the proliferation of an openly functioning sex industry in Cambodia has routinely been attributed by the CPP to its arch-nemesis the United Nations Transitional Authority in Cambodia, which had been internationally and locally criticized for permitting its peacekeepers to patronize brothels. Second, it was arguably not difficult for local authorities and police to map brothels and establish relationships with their owners, since anecdotal evidence had long suggested that local government officials and security forces had in many places entered the commercial sex industry themselves, sometimes taking ownership shares in brothels, and frequently operating lucrative protection rackets around them.[41] The combination of relative ease in talking about the practices driving the epidemic, existing channels of communication between local government and the sex industry, and shocking statistics that led to dire predictions prompted a pragmatic response on the part of the government that was praised almost unanimously by our informants. In the 1990s, the epidemic threatened the government's core power base, and the government was able to use informal – even illegal – networks and connections to tackle this in a highly interventionist – even intrusive – manner.

The policy has not been entirely uncontroversial, however, and has been evaluated in two sharply different lights. In one light, the policy appears as an enlightened response, compared favourably with the tendency, in more conservative countries, to deny the existence of the commercial sex industry, or to

---

[40] Vonthanak Saphonn, *HIV Incidence Among Sentinel Surveillance Groups in Cambodia, 1999–2002*, power point presentation, Phnom Penh, 11 May 2004, online at http://www.nchads.org/Publication/dissemination/presentation%20in%20dissemination%20workshop%20english.pdf, accessed 12 August 2009.

[41] Nick Lenaghan, "Officials Implicated in Koh Kong Sex Trade," *Cambodia Daily*, 19–21 April 1996, 1; Lenaghan, "Pimps up for Hefty Sentences, but Reservations about New Law," *Phnom Penh Post* 8–21 March 1996, 13.

refuse to engage with it. This portrayal of the policy emphasizes the educational and treatment-oriented aspects of the programme, regarding these as empowering, and downplaying the compulsory nature of participation.

A different and more critical reading, however, sees the programme largely as one of brothel owners protecting their assets, rather than as sex workers protecting themselves. Critical reports cite interviews with sex workers, some of whom have been sold to brothel owners, who have described the humiliating and painful examinations they are forced to undergo without their consent, under the terms of the policy. Sex workers also described the poor treatment and judgemental attitudes they were subjected to in government clinics – attitudes which reinforced, rather than challenged, the sex workers' low expectations of what their government might be willing to do for them.[42]

Emphasis upon the compulsory nature of the programme transforms sex workers from active participants in their own self-protection into the disempowered and exploited victims of forced experimentation conducted with the interests of brothel owners and the government, rather than their own interests, at the forefront. However, this is certainly an ingredient of the policy's success. Given the realities of power distributions in the Cambodian shadow economy, it is perhaps unlikely that compliance could have been achieved in any other way. Success in reducing rates of infection among sex workers and their clients via the 100 per cent CUP was achieved via a combination of institutional autonomy and transparent management practices in the central organization, and the astute alignment of patrons and clients in the armed forces and the sex industry in pursuit of their own business interests via coercion.

The CUP is not the only success story in Cambodia's fight against HIV/AIDS. In the field of treatment NCHADS has developed a strong service-delivery structure allowing it to meet World Health Organization targets for the provision of Anti-Retroviral Therapies to people living with AIDS. However, to a great extent, NCHADS's efforts were facilitated by the activities of non-governmental organizations in the field. These NGOs were able to compensate for the inadequacies of the state healthcare infrastructure – providing education, advocating for patients, even paying for doctors to make housecalls. The ability of the centre to manage the funds transparently and to keep them strictly separate from the wider healthcare budget combined with the ability of grassroots organizations to fill in the cracks in state provision was decisive in this area. This again raises questions over models of reform which envisage the simple

---

[42] See for example, Network of Sex Work Projects, *The 100% Condom Use Policy: a Sex Workers Perspective*, webpage, 22 January 2003, online at http://www.nswp.org/safety/100percent.html, accessed 13 August 2009; David Lowe, *Perceptions of the Cambodian 100% Condom Use Program: Documenting the Experiences of Sex Workers* (Phnom Penh: USAID/POLICY Project, 2003).

movement of an agency along a scale from ineffective/irrational to effective/rational. Effective action, in this reading, requires the ability to frame problems in a manner that elicits cooperation and support from a range of actors with sharply varying sets of values.

Conclusion

Comparison of successes and failures in public administration reform suggests three conclusions. First, the government has consistently resisted any move which might lead to great institutional independence for agencies that are closely related to the property management regime that is supervising Cambodia's economic transformation. Furthermore, where successes in public administration reform have occurred, in areas related to the provision of public goods and services, a conception of change which sees irrational "Cambodian" practices being displaced by rational "Western" ones is misplaced. Leaders gain the discretion to experiment with Western management practices through the ability to negotiate autonomy –which is itself dependent upon the skilful playing of *khsae*. Moreover, within autonomous agencies, what is occurring is not a shift to Western modes of operation, but a blending of Western practices with a variety of different Cambodian norms and rationales. The outcome of this process will be highly differentiated across different sectors of the Cambodian state, but all its instantiations will be determined primarily by negotiated Cambodian logics, rather than by Western impositions. Finally, in areas, such as health, which are not fundamental to the maintenance and operation of neo-patrimonial networks, the government allows for the active participation of national and international civil society organizations providing effective, responsive and transparent management.

11

Party Financing of Local Investment Projects: Elite and Mass Patronage

David Craig and Pak Kimchoeun

The CPP party's dominance of Cambodian elections has been based on several factors, not least of which is the party's extraordinary ability to mobilize resources to build infrastructure at the local level. Facing opposition accusations of poor governance and corruption, the party has pitched itself as able to deliver post-conflict stability, and, even more prominently, roads, schools and irrigation in local communities. These infrastructure promises have played strongly to the party's rural base, which has consistently returned CPP politicians in almost every commune since elections began. As the party is well aware, this constituency is susceptible to promises of visible contributions delivered by powerful figures prepared to perform as patrons.

This performance has been impressive. During the 2008 campaign, the Prime Minister was featured daily on television reading out locally sourced lists of requests for construction projects; lists capped off by the triumphant, authoritative and impressive proclamation "Choun tam samnaumpo", which literally means "Granted according to your request". "Choun tam samnaumpo" has become a popular slogan used by other politicians announcing similar bequests elsewhere, and ultimately a catchphrase used in humour on radio and television, and even between children playing together.

The ability to deliver reflects the remarkable power of the CPP to use patronage and other means to organize, raise funds and motivate followers at all levels. Ministers, secretaries of state and senior staff of ministries campaign in provinces, districts and communes alongside provincial, district and commune officials and local business people, building the party's presence and contributing largesse. At the same time, they build their personal reputation and standing in the party. Most conspicuous here is *"doing construction"* (Khmer *sang sang*, erecting something tangible). Funds are provided for *sang sang* down through the party's subnational apparatus, as well as through parallel, politically identified entities (such as Hun Sen schools), or provided direct to (somewhat politicized) local pagodas and schools by individual patrons practising *saboraschun*, or charity.

The net result has been a plethora of projects, in fact contributed to by many, but publicly "giving face" to an elite party figure. In the last five months prior to the 2008 July elections, TV airwaves were replete with inauguration ceremonies of schools, roads, and irrigations, bearing the names of elite, party-identified patrons, but actually funded by an enormous range of contributors. Behind the face and ceremony, as this paper will show, was a good deal of substance. The amounts of money mobilized by the party, the commitment and accountability of those involved in delivery, and the integrity of the mechanisms used to move money and execute, compares well with that operating through formal channels, including the commune/*Sangkat* fund, which comprises the official state budget for development.

The formal commune/*Sangkat* fund system and the informal/party one are best considered together, both as modes of project-based local infrastructure support, and as complementary parts of a political strategy for winning votes that Nicholas van de Walle[1] calls mass clientelism, but we in this chapter call mass patronage[2]. Mass clientele/patronage arrangements, as we will elaborate later, are a combination of (1) harnessing patronage lines and political activists within the state executive system in order to (2) deliver largesse – and especially rural infrastructure – to a party's core constituencies, with the express aim of winning elections. Most importantly for this paper, it involves harnessing the accountabilities of a mass patronage system to deliver outputs, win elections, and possibly promote wider systemic change.

In Cambodia, this mass patronage strategy appears to have been successful as part of a wider consolidation of CPP dominance. Here, it seems, the kinds of project-based, infrastructure-oriented local development funding modalities supported through the national Decentralization and Deconcentration program might be thought to be all too compatible with the party's project of delivering such largesse to its rural base[3]. Donors, of course, have been at pains to emphasize the government's ownership of the formal Decentralization and Deconcentration process, and indeed most of the Commune/*Sangkat* funding

---

[1] Nicholas van de Walle, *The path from neo-patrimonialism: democracy and clientelism in Africa today*. Working Paper no. 3 (Ithaca: Cornell University Center for International Studies, 2007).

[2] See footnote 10.

[3] David Craig and Doug Porter, "Winning the Peace: Re-institutionalising conflict in Cambodia's politics and governance," paper presented at *Critical Approaches to Post-Conflict Policy: Post-Conflict Development or Development for Conflict?* University of Oxford, 25–26 June 2008.

(if not of the overall decentralization budget[4]) does come from a process largely interior to government. Certainly in the 2008 elections, the electorate were clearly being led to conclude that the CPP was responsible for orchestrating the bestowal of this largesse. And, to a significant extent, they were.

In this context, we explore van de Walle's suggestion that mass patronage can be seen as some kind of step along the way to something more democratic. There may be currently no sign of party funding scandals, or of eruptions in the press about corruption or influence-peddling as described in our opening quote. But things are certainly changing, and all the funding devices and modalities involved will shape future developments.

This chapter does two things: first it presents empirical material on party funding arrangements in Cambodian communes in three case study districts; and second it compares the accountability mechanisms inherent in party funding arrangements with the kinds of accountability offered by the institutions of state at local level. Since accountability represents one aspect of democratization, the analysis provides interesting lessons for both state and party.

Getting data on party financing was a learning-by-doing experience. While there is no overall budget for party activities, many provinces and districts – and especially district offices of the party – keep elaborate and formal records of spending in their areas. These practices are not nationally formalized in either party rules or national guidelines. However, each province is expected to know and be able to demonstrate project achievements. Most party officials consider this financing a generous act, a contribution that the party and its people make to help the community. Indeed party officials we talked to at several levels expressed a great deal of pride as they very happily showed us the lists of what are hailed as achievements.

For this paper we used records on party/elite support to the district and commune. District lists were typically provided by the party district headquarters, rather than the local government district office. However, the District Governor is usually also the district Party Chief. Lists are not kept at commune level, but interviews with commune chiefs were used to gain estimates of party support.

In cases one and two, we compare the estimated monetary value of support from the ruling party and its elites with the development component of the commune/*sangkhat* fund. However, the result of the comparison needs to be interpreted with care: generalizations cannot be made for the rest of Cambodia, and the separation between party, elite, state and even donors and NGOs is not always clear. Party elites influence state budget and donor support as well as

---

4 That said, of a total budget of over $80 million variously administered under National Council for Sub-National Democratic Development (NCDD) through decentralization and deconcentration arrangements, at least three quarters comes from international donors.

contributing their own funds: this was particularly evident in our second case study commune. The different kinds of networks converging on district and provincial working groups have important effects on the amount and nature of support received, and are highly varied. However, the cases show clearly the nature and dynamics of party state elite relationships in Cambodia: these are both systemic and national, and also highly place-, circumstance- and above all person-specific.

National, Central and Subnational Party Arrangements

District working groups and their *sang sang* and other activities are a national phenomenon. Each province is allocated to a central figure – someone with a historical or family connection to the area - who becomes head of the province working group. If this person is a minister, then it may be expected that many heads and members of district working groups will also come from that ministry, or from family and other members of the minister's networks. But central officials and other important centrally based actors are also drawn into working groups based on their own personal connections to places. Deputy Prime Minister Sok An, for example, takes charge of his home province of Takeo. Many Ministry of Interior officials assist Deputy Prime Minister and Minister for Interior Sar Kheng in Battambang.

Many ministry officials belong to their boss's working group, and support him or her in their role on the working group, travelling with the senior figure down to the district level, and acting as an executive entourage for their superior's political activities. Considerable contributions of time and money are required: even poorly paid central officials will contribute $20, $30, $50 a month to a fund held in the name of their District Working Group head. The head will also actively solicit money from central figures and networks, and supplement funds from their own (including family) resources. Those with positions, ministries or jobs that have "enough water" (i.e. are lucrative in one way or another) will be asked by a high-ranking party person to make a contribution, perhaps to their working group, or (sometimes via the central party) to a province where the head has less access to resources. Someone with control over issuing a permit or licence might ask those seeking the permit to make a contribution to their district, perhaps as large as a school building. Private figures also make large contributions, via whichever route or person they consider most appropriate to their own need to be seen to be contributing.

The fund-raising system thus appears to be very personalized. Ability to raise money means prestige, power and reputation: inability to raise money means spending more *time* and relying on others or on central party mechanisms to allocate money your way. Overall, this is a flexible and fungible funding mechanism.

Performance in this system is powerfully motivated. The level of voluntariness appears to be variable. It may be that with so many new actors crowding into the field, contributions are now demanded on a less coercive basis than previously. Certainly people at all levels are involved for a variety of reasons. Ambitious rising stars, everyday party members, or even people just wanting to hold onto high position, may feel no choice about contributing. Others actively and enthusiastically use this as a tactic for advancement and networking, and are usually rewarded. A few might seek exemption on the grounds that their positions require manifest political neutrality. Those entirely dependent on government for income sources have the most compelling incentives to participate. In any case, party contributions are closely watched, expected, acknowledged and calculated as a part of an overall assessment of a party member's (and especially a potential role or office candidate's) capability, loyalty, "internal solidarity" (willingness to fit into party arrangements), morality, influence, and potential for popular appeal.

Party Working Groups

Since the 1998 election, these activities have been arranged through the so-called "Working Group Helping the Local Level" (*krom kangea choh moulthan*), referred to here simply as the Working Group. The Working Group is drawn from but is not identical to the CPP formal organizational structure, which is composed of the Central Committee (and its Permanent Committee core) at the central level, and the provincial, district, commune, village and even group level at the sub-national level. From a personnel point of view, the state and party now overlaps almost perfectly at least at the sub-national level: usually the provincial governor, district governor and commune chief also serve the roles as the heads of provincial, district and commune party branches. This is a considerable change from the earlier post-UNTAC period, when governor and deputy positions among others were allocated along party lines.

The district is the most important level for Working Group organization. Here, people from all levels of the party come together to complement the party's tightly controlled local administrative network, which extends not just down to the village level, but to the sub-village '*krom*' comprising several households. The Working Group structure complements this network, providing a powerful mix of hierarchy and flexibility. The formal structure ensures and expands party networks to deliver votes, while the Working Group provides opportunities for

```
           Formal structure        Working group
                                     structure

              Central
                                   Chief Assignment      Fund-raisers

              Province                  Province


              District                  District

              Commune                   Commune          Implementers

              Village                   Village
```

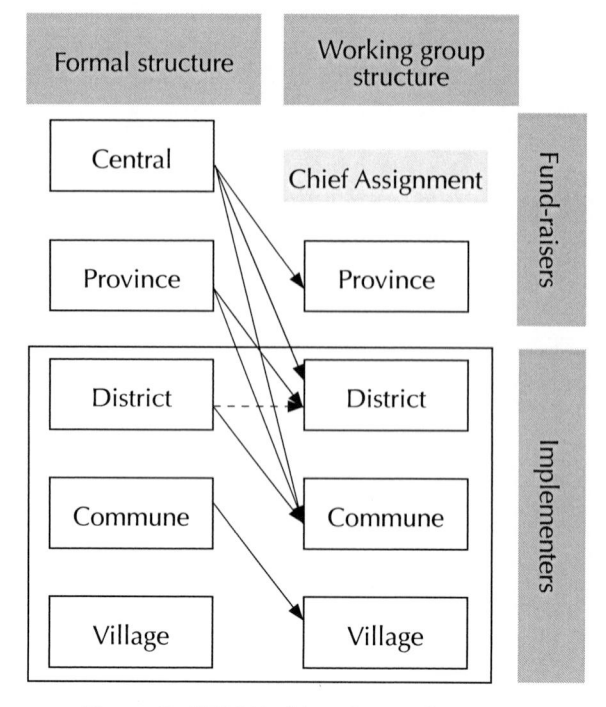

Figure 5. CPP Working Group Structure.

central and sub-national party officials to collaborate on project financing, to deliver legitimation.

Working Group officials take pride in their combined abilities: local understanding of local realities and the needs of the commune; the ability to mobilize resources from higher levels, via powerful central figures; and ultimately the capacity to deliver. Within the Working Group, people contact each other informally and this communication keeps the head of the Working Group regularly informed about what happens in the field.

Hierarchy and loyalty remain central characteristics of the system. Party activity clearly also happens in the context of a wider party and Khmer/Buddhist culture of gaining honour and respect by doing good. This cultural formation has several salient features. It involves a special connection to one's family homeland (*srok komnaoet*), and making a personal and public contribution there. This also involves "giving face" to powerful leaders and to the party (e.g. by contributing resources to fund a Hun Sen School, and staging elaborate ceremonies where they can receive public acknowledgement); "gaining face" by making big public contributions or by being effective in your electoral work, and influential and successful in relations with higher powers who might provide resources; "showing face" by regularly appearing at formal and informal meetings, demonstrating loyalty, assenting to consensus and registering some involvement; "saving face" by giving ceremonially prominent but undemanding, non-lucrative positions to older/senior cadres, even when these cannot make physical contributions.

Alongside this, well-recognized seniority, hierarchy, and respect for achievements and wartime service reinforces the overall authority and respect structure, and reinforces discipline and above all accountability. This means, for example, party activists can be rapidly mobilized for meetings. Horizontal accountability is achieved through competition to be seen to be achieving, and through consensus building. Younger members with smart ideas must never publicly be seen to contradict superiors, and must be very careful to prepare the ground before raising suggestions, often through a higher figure. Everyone, especially powerful central figures, but also low level activists, wants to be seen to succeed, to win, gain and give face. This produces caution about new and uncertain ventures, but it is balanced by a valorization of dynamism and capacity to deliver.

As at the national level, contributing to the local Working Group seems to be an occasion for both voluntarism and compulsion, and pride, trust, respect, even fear. Participating, however, currently means heavy personal commitments over a three year cycle, and ongoing commitment even in non-election years.

The District Working Group is the most active operational unit of the hierarchy; it is usually composed of about 100 people: 25–50 per cent from Phnom Penh; the rest from the provincial or district levels. Those from Phnom Penh are usually government officials, military or police, businessmen, and, rarely, parliamentarians. Under the District level are the commune, village and group levels, comprising local activists numbering about 1,000 per district. In all, this adds up to a very dense network. The head of the Working Group is very important for mobilizing resources. Very high-ranking government officials (minister and above) lead provincial working groups; a second tier (secretaries of state, department directors) lead district working groups; district governors might lead commune working groups, and commune chiefs are usually heads of village Working Groups.

A consistent labour division applies: heads and members of the central and provincial Working Groups raise funds, while district and commune groups identify, propose and sometimes execute projects. Money raised is partly from the head of the Working Group himself, and partly from his team and his networks with those outside the Working Groups. These "outsiders" can be anyone: local or international, government officials, businessmen, *saborochun* (benefactors) from abroad, etc. For instance, in some districts, local and central businessmen are said to be a source of contribution, while in one particular district, the head of the Working Group has been very successful in attracting international NGOs and donors to build various schools and roads in his area.

There are also cases where heads or members of Working Groups manage to allocate budget and staff of their line ministries or provincial departments to help in party projects.

Since the 2002 local elections, *communes* have been considered as a very important level of party hierarchy, particularly for legitimation with the people; but they are still considered subservient to the district party boss. For instance, we observed one party gathering, where around 30 CPP commune chiefs and councillors sat in a group in front of the district governor, while the district governor called them one by one by name to report on the status and number of activists recently inducted into the party in their communes. Three case studies illustrate the variation in arrangements and functioning of Working Groups.

Case 1: A well-off district with a resourceful district working group

Our first case is a fairly populous, well-off district in the north-west. It is close to the provincial centre, and has been experiencing rapid economic growth and urbanization. People there rely mainly on rice farming and trading. The CPP dominated the district in the 2008 election, taking about 60% of the votes cast.

The Provincial Working Group is chaired by and composed of some of the best resourced and highest ranked officials in the country. The District Working Group chair is a high ranking central official (based in Phnom Penh) who is also a businessman with a successful land speculation business both in Phnom Penh and various provinces. He is not a long-term veteran of the party, or of

Table 10. Case 1: District Working Group Composition.

Levels	Key players	Members
District	A central official who is also a rich businessman	87 members: 36 of whom are assigned from Phnom Penh; some are from ministries, some are businessmen.
Commune	A central official with a family connection to one of the deputy prime ministers	65 full members, only 5 of whom come from Phnom Penh. Out of these 5, one is a Deputy Prime Minister's relative, three are ministerial department directors, one from the Senate, and one is a police officer.

Table 11. Case 1: CPP support to the district, 2003–2007.

Type of spending	$	%
Schools	450,000	43
Road	35,000	3
Irrigation	255,000	24
Housing	52,000	5
Religion	173,000	16
Other infrastructure	85,000	8
Total	1,050,000	100
CSF (Development component)	487,000	

Sources: Except for CSF, the information above is based on District list on CPP Achievements

the official government bureaucracy. His reputation is of an opportunistic entrepreneur, who saw the commercial benefits associated with a government position. He is one of the new blood who have claimed an "advisor" (*tiproeksa*) position in exchange for his constant contributions to the party. As part of his party obligations, he takes care of his home district. Under him are other high ranking officials from Phnom Penh including a close relative of a deputy prime minister.

The district party branch of the CPP is located in the same compound as the District Office. In this case, the District Office has kept very good records of the Working Group's contributions since 2003, bound into a booklet entitled *A List of the CPP's achievements for 2003–2007*. The records provide a good summary of schools, roads, irrigations, and pagodas that have been built by the Working Groups, estimated by the district governor to be worth about $1,050,000. This is about 220 per cent of the $487,000 received over the same 2002–2008 period via the commune/sangkat fund. However, investment targets were differentiated: schools comprised 43% of the estimated total, while roads received only 3%. Irrigation is another big investment ($255,000 in value, or about 25% to total support) while religion (predominantly Buddhism) received also some contribution.

At commune level, by the commune chief's estimate, total CPP support amounted to more than twice the value of the commune/Sangkat fund. The district list includes only support that came directly through the working group. Commune interviews suggested that a further $200,000 had been given to six pagodas in the commune, not through the Working Group but through

Table 12. Case 1: CPP support to the commune, 2003–2007.

Sources	US$	Spending targets
CSF	59,500[a]	Infrastructure
Party/elite support estimate		
Through working group	160,000	Infrastructure
Individuals	200,000	Pagoda related
Direct hand-outs (over three elections)	42,000	Hand-outs to party members

[a] According to CSF database provided from PSDD, converted at exchange rate of 1USD=4,100.

individual *sobaraschon* donations from CPP elites. If each of the ten communes in the district received the same, total pagoda support could reach US$2 million over this period, an estimate borne out by the luxurious appearance of some pagodas in the area.

Another significant funding source that is not captured in the district's achievement list is the direct handouts made during the election campaign. In the case of the commune, an election year budget of $8,000 (32 million riels) was given to the Commune Working Group. Out of that, 85% is spent on cash and in-kind handouts for local people who are on the party list. In addition, members in the Working Group who are from Phnom Penh also provide about the same amount in hand-outs. For instance, in November 2006, when the CPP was preparing for February 2007 election, the hand-out was about $10,000 in the whole district, or about $1,000 for each commune. Based on this information, then, hand-outs for each commune during election periods is as estimated as follows:

Hand-outs from Commune Working Group: $8,000* 3 elections = $24,000
Handouts from members from Phnom Penh: $6,000*3 elections = $18,000,
Total: About $42,000 in hand-outs per commune

Assuming that each commune received more or less the same amount in hand-outs, the total for the ten communes would be $420,000 for the period from 2003–2007. If all the three figures are added together the total contribution for the period from 2003–2007 from the party and its elites must have been around $3.5 million dollars: seven times the state development budget.

The head of the Working Group is crucial in mobilizing resources. He is personally close to the district governor and district party officials. He provides a salary of about $40 per month to five CPP activists: three at the district (including the district governor), and three in the case of the commune (including the commune chief). Described as generous and accessible, he makes frequent visits, especially during election campaigns. Every time, he brings gifts and cash. District and commune people consider him resourceful, not only because he is a rich businessman, but also because he has good connections to the top, along with extensive networks (*ksae bandanh*). The commune chief said, "I discuss matters with him on the phone and when he agrees, he asks me to go to Phnom Penh, meet him at his home or office. He gives me $US5,000 at a time for arranging for contractors to build or repair roads". The Working Group also depends heavily on the popularity of the commune chief. The Working Group members make sure he feels he can access them personally, giving him their phone number, inviting him up to Phnom Penh for meetings and parties. He is addressed by central leader of the working group as *Pou* (Uncle), and he calls them *Lok* (Mister/Sir), to show respect. This is a part of a wider pattern in which central figures relate well to local ones around fund-raising and project identification, but do not necessarily entrust locals with implementation. The commune chief did not resent this – he said he did not want to be involved in money management since small scandals could cause him a lot of problems. He is however entrusted with cash for campaign spending.

Case 2: A poor district, with a not-so-resource-rich but influential working group head

The second case is a district located in relatively poor area, with around 60,000 voters registered for the 2008 election. Ninety per cent of the people there depend on rice farming, meaning that their main livelihood challenge has been drought and lack of irrigation. Fighting with the Khmer Rouge continued until 1998 in the district, limiting development prior to that year. The CPP has won increasingly convincingly in the district since 1993: in 2008, the party won more than half the popular vote. In the 2007 commune election, the CPP won in all communes, exceeding its 2002 performance, when it lost one commune. The opposition has been weak in the district, relying on an electoral promise that appeals almost exclusively to the poor that it will redistribute land to the people if it wins. The CPP, however, as in other provinces, relies on its ability to build and help the people through its elite groups, and on dividing and co-opting the opposition.

In contrast to the previous case, the head of the District Working Group here – who is also the head of the Provincial Working Group – is not known for his wealth and economic networks, but is respected for his very high position and influence in the party. A veteran himself, he is known to be a person of principle. He is respected among our informants for believing in party solidarity and the obligation to serve the people, rather than being driven by financial incentives. Because he is so influential and respectable, these personal values were observably espoused by party officials at district and commune levels.

Other members of the Working Groups include high ranking officials at central and provincial levels. Four out of seven members from the central level are assigned to the district because it is their *srok komnaoet*. Provincial-level members have been assigned to the district for their "potential" to help. They include a deputy governor and four line department directors from Agriculture, Land, Irrigation and Labour, who can use their formal influence to meet the most pressing needs of the district: agriculture and water. These high ranking officials (both central and provincial) usually bring some staff to work in the working group, altogether thereby adding about 20 people.

The records kept by the district office are not as complete as those in the first case: they list projects according to type and source, rather than according to value. They are, however, even more strikingly presented: the district governor showed us a single page table which on one side of the page detailed the numbers of official investments in the district, and on the other, in similar columns, listed the party's contributions. According to the CPP *provincial* development reports, the party regards irrigation as the main issue: various irrigation works have been constructed between 1998 and 2008, and about 85 per cent of the 91km of main canals constructed were provided in the name of the Prime Minister.

The name of the Prime Minister appears on almost every page of the provincial development reports, making it difficult to distinguish between support given by the state, the Prime Minister and the Working Group head. One part of one report, for example, reads as follows:

> Samdech Prime Minister together with the provincial working group and local people contribution have helped build 232 lines of sub-canals ... Samdech Prime Minister together with the Ministry of Irrigation, social funds and other NGOs have helped build 157 Watergates ... Samdech Prime Minister together with Ministry of Water Resources and Seila program has helped build 74 dams.

At district level, support from the party/elites focuses on two things: schools and irrigation related activities. Clearly here a full account of support mobilized through political means would need to consider all the projects influenced by the Provincial/ District Working Group head using his central party position to encourage line ministries into action in his district. As far as the full extent of this funding is concerned, however, we could not gain any clear or comparative sense of it.

The research team did however visit one commune in the district. Based on a list and estimations provided by commune officials, the biggest support

Table 13. Case 2: CPP support to the district, 2003–2007.

Type of spending	Units
Schools	75 rooms
Road	14 lines
Bridge	6 bridges
Pipe	75
Dams	3
Canal	5 lines
Pond	11
Pumping station	1
Wells	222
Rice	155 tons
CSF (Development component)	515,000

from party elites through the Working Groups was building 15 classrooms (costing around $US75, 000), presented as direct gifts from the Prime Minister. Rural roads also featured: about 9 km of earth road was built by the four prominent working group members, costing c. $70,000. The Working Group, with joint financing from the Cambodian Red Cross (highly politicized under the presidency of the Prime Minister's wife), has also helped dig 45 wells, each costing around $200. In sum, CPP support (including the well-digging support co-financed by the Red Cross) is estimated to be around 3 times of the development component of the Commune/Sangkat Fund for the commune, which is about $50,000 including the 2008 allocation[5].

Financing for religion was also very high. Here again, it is difficult to discern how much comes from the elites in the Working Group and how much is from local contribution. Among the five pagodas in the commune, four are financed by CPP Working Group elites, and the other by a royalist family. Three out of the four CPP-financed pagodas have been very well resourced. Since 2003, these three pagodas have received at least $400,000, partly given through elites formally identified with the Working Group. A key financier for one pagoda in this commune is a businessman who was born in the commune and now owns a construction company and garment factory in the provincial town; he claimed that he donated $50,000 for construction, along with other gifts, in memory of his mother.

[5] The CSF figure is based on the PSDD database.

Table 14. Case 2: CPP and Other Support to one selected commune (in USD), 2003–2007.

Projects	CPP	CSF	Donors
School	75,000	2,000	75,000
Roads[a]	70,000	40,000	25,000
Dams	None	3,000	12,000
Wells	9,000[b]	0	2,000

[a] This is based on the unit price given by the commune chief that 1,000m of the built roads might cost around $7,000 on average.

[b] Using estimation from the commune chief, one well might cost around $200 for 45 wells given from from the Cambodian Red Cross, led by the Prime Minister's Wife, Bun Rany.

Interestingly, there has been no party support for canal building in this commune: commune requests were refused by the Working Group because they were too expensive, but it may be relevant that other funding has been available. For example, there has been support from the World Food Program (WFP) in the form of "food for work" in the period from 2003 to 2008 to pay for local people to dig canals with a total length of 5,051 metres, with a value of around $12,000.

Some of the support given was in response to requests from the commune chief via the district governor, and some was given on the initiative of the Working Group members who regularly visit the area. The commune chief expressed satisfaction with the quality of the projects completed, but was concerned at the lack of ongoing maintenance. Commune officials reported feeling pressure to deliver votes in return for the party's investment and said that if votes do not increase, support could drop. The district's list of party/elite support, however, suggests that some communes have received much less than the case study commune: three of the 15 communes received nothing except food relief. The governor attributed this to the inactivity of Commune Working Group heads and members, and the ineffectiveness of commune chiefs in seeking support.

In these cases, variation in support seems unrelated to political performance, since the CPP did similarly well in all communes, but specific links to high ranking officials can be of significance. Most members of this District Working Group are not exceptionally rich; but the head is very influential in the party, and a number of development ministry officials are involved. "Formal" and party influence here created a new channel for seeking resources from state budgets to finance projects, in a kind of "pork barrel" approach. In 2006, an irrigation investment project was proposed to the working group. Because the project was too costly for the Working Group to pay for themselves, financial support was sought from a ministry. The head of the Working Group, through his party influence, secured this through informal channels first, ensuring that the formal request to the ministry was later accepted. The project was quickly implemented the following year. The request for the project would have been much less likely to succeed without this inside influence.

Two further interesting points arise from this case. First, recently created formal structures for decentralization – namely commune councils – complement the party system and improve the quality of local representation. In the 2002 election, the party "cleaned off" many unpopular commune chiefs, and for 2007 the party required that party candidates should be selected by party members, resulting in the voting off the party list of about one third of the first set of commune chiefs. One provincial party official claimed this as evidence of the party's awareness of the importance of genuine local democracy. Second, the party system has been used several times to provide matching funds for the commune/sangkat fund, allowing the implementation of larger projects. This suggests party funding complements, rather than competes with, other forms of support.

Case 3: A partly flooded district and a less pro-CPP commune

Our third and last case is a district located partly along the Mekong River, part of which is flooded almost every year. Within the district, the study looks at one commune which has received little support from the party, a commune where, perhaps not coincidentally, the CPP has performed less well.

With 52,000 voters, this district is located in a fairly prosperous province, relying on successfully combining rice farming, cash-cropping, and fishing. With so much water nearby, communes can use the commune/sangkat fund to dig small-scale canals, purchase or receive some small pumps from an elite charity, or rely on private companies charging fees for pumping the water. However, some areas have problems with floods, which destroy crops every year. Another challenge is the poor roads by which people travel to bring their produce to the nearby market. This is even more challenging for people living in communes that get flooded every year, in that roads are quickly washed out.

This is a district where the CPP was strongly challenged by the Royalist Party in both the 1993 and 1998 elections. Even now, the opposition party has been doing quite well in the area, despite the growing dominance of the CPP, especially since 2003.

Again, a great deal depends on the individuals involved. Here, the head of the Working Group holds a government ministerial position which gives him access to alternative financing, including international sources. His long tenure of this office means he has good networks with international donors and NGOs. He was born in the district and he has strong personal connections with it. Local people related a story of how spirits from one of the pagodas in the area saved his life during the war. His father is buried in the pagoda, and he regularly visits and prays there. There are also some other big names in the District Working Group: a senator, a high-ranking official from the Ministry of Health, a deputy chief of a national port, and an under-secretary of the Ministry of Rural Development.

Key informant interviews indicate that a wide range of people have made contributions. However, their names were rarely if at all listed in any public documents: often they made private contributions to development projects bearing the name of a prominent official, as a way of getting close to and expressing loyalty towards a patron, something that occurs nation-wide.

Very interestingly, the district records show that all the support from donors and NGOs has come to the district through the head of the Working Group. Recently, there has been more support from the South Korean government, which the head of the District Working Group has directed into the district. A Korean delegation was taken on a trip to the area and agreed to provide a dam worth $1 million. Discussions with local sources suggest that often local people do not know which projects are given by donors, and which by government.

In this case, the head of the Working Group is a religious man, with a strong belief in accruing merit. This is also evident from the list of contributions compiled at the CPP district party branch[6]. In all, there were 31 projects going into the district (2003–2007). One commune was the site of two very impressive (even luxurious) pagodas, construction of which must have cost tens of thousands of dollars. Here, the crucial factor appeared to be the religious conviction of the Working Group head and his close relation with the pagoda head.

Beyond the pagodas, simply adding up eight projects (2003- 2007) for which values were available, we arrived at a value of $78,000. Nonetheless, this amount too has been influenced by the pagoda: one commune chief in the area said he was compelled to compete or negotiate with pagoda committees to get them to agree to more Party Working Group support flowing to development and not just religious projects.

Communes in flooded areas of the district received less support, with interviews with one commune chief revealing very little support indeed. Virtually no support was reported from the period from 1993 to 2003, except for one secondary school built by Hun Sen, and two occasions of food relief also given by the Prime Minister during severe floods. It was only in 2007 that a project to

---

[6] It was noted that in the district, the district party branch and district office are allocated in the same compound, and the district governor is also the chief of the party branch at the level.

Table 15. Case 3: Party and Donor Support to the district, 1998–2007.

	From the party and its elites			Donors (influenced by Working Group head)
	Head of working group	Central party leadership including PM	Projects/ supports	
Schools				
2nd mandate	'A few rooms'	101 rooms	various cash contributions	46 rooms
3rd mandate	25 rooms	40 rooms	various cash contributions	49 rooms
Roads				
2nd mandate	3.1km	25km	various cash contributions	24.4 km
3rd mandate	32.0 km	None	2.8km	Few what?
Pagoda				
2nd mandate	—	No record	—	None
3rd mandate	31 projects	8 big projects	various cash contributions	None
Wells				
2nd mandate	30 wells	2 wells	various cash contributions	No record
3rd mandate	37 wells	None	various cash contributions	30 wells
Canals				
3rd mandate	4km	2.7 km	Various cash contributions	20.4 km

repair a 3.2 km flooded commune road was promised, provided the CPP won the 2008 election.

Two factors might explain this. First, since 1993 the commune strongly favoured FUNCINPEC and was home town to a high-ranking FUNCINPEC official who supported the pagodas there. Plus, there is no individual within the CPP elite who is originally from this commune. However, given the popularity of its commune chief candidate, the CPP just managed to win the last two commune elections. In preparing for the 2008 national election, then, the CPP was aiming to beat the Royalist party, and part of its strategy was to go to the commune and make promises. However, because the royalist activists are still good at mobilizing people, and because people here still feel bitterness from the war, and especially the period of the K5 campaign, the Royalists still managed to get about 50 votes more than the CPP. In fact, the commune is one of very few where FUNCINPEC still manage to win votes. As a result, the promised 3.2 km of local road was not given by the CPP.

The second factor has to do with local geographical variation: the fact that the commune is frequently flooded with significant damage to roads and some irrigation systems. As such, it is said, the Working Group finds the place not very good to "invest" in.

> The Working Group might have thought that people won't remember their help very long. Any roads built today will be washed away next year, and they have to build again. It is too expensive.

and repair his work. Finally, the district and commune chiefs, and the pagodas committees, despite their active roles in proposing projects, have had very limited roles when it comes to implementation. The head of the Working Group in this case has a nephew owning a construction company in provincial towns. Virtually all of the projects were contracted to his nephew, while the local authorities and pagodas just "waited to get whatever was built". The nephew was also asked to regularly come down to check, maintain and repair his work.

Interestingly too, what was being provided in this case was a focus beyond *sang sang*. In this case, "health funds" have been set up by the head of the Working Group, whereby he regularly provides financing to a fund managed by a close friend, who is also a rich businessman in the area.

Case Discussion

From the three cases, it seems that party/elite financing of local development projects can be very big – as big as seven times as in case 1 – or can be as small as 3 times in case 2. The party and its elites have not just used their own resources but also their political influence (over state budget allocation) and financial supports from donors and NGOs to help their "constituencies".

It is clear that the level of support can vary significantly both across districts and among communes within the same district. And, while we would need to investigate much more widely, it seems possible that areas that are less pro-CPP, and areas less well connected to central, wealthy and influential figures, are likely to receive less support. Therefore, although in general the support helps provide financing for development, it can result in a considerable horizontal imbalance. More importantly, party finance can be used as a very effective tool for political marginalization.

This support, in short, remains intensely personalized. This provides strengths and leaves weaknesses, not just in terms of horizontal inequalities. The strengths are in accountabilities, which in this system are powerful, based on culturally embedded modes of respect (*koruap*), trust (*tukchet*), fear (*klach*) and communication, and have low transaction costs. They are also an incentive and motivation: important people – at the centre and locally – will notice contributions of cash and effort.

It is grounded in virtue, emotion, and attachment to place. This is a contribution made to your birthplace, your public face, and your eternal destiny. Here, the connection to birthplace is clearly important for this generation of leaders, many of whom were themselves rice farmers. The support is also obviously powerfully politicized; it generates political accountabilities and incentives in ways which donor-oriented programs might not.

All this means the money contributed is what Khmers call "hot money": money with responsibilities attached, money you had better take care of. By contrast, some sectors of government budgets (especially recurrent operations and maintenance moneys) and a good deal of donor money can be considered "cool" or "cold" money: money that can be played around with relatively little consequence.

Some limitations are identified. First, it is likely that contributions have some alignment with electoral cycles, providing another element of irregularity. Second, like the commune/*sangkat* fund, the sum of money available for any particular project is small, ruling out needs that require relatively big investments. Third, investment has focused almost entirely on infrastructure and not service delivery, and on-going support for operations and maintenance is very rare. Where it does happen, it either relies on personalized accountabilities, or project-based maintenance not aligned with any regular maintenance schedule. Especially in the case of roads, this can be a recipe for disaster, as a laterite road not maintained over more than three years will often require a complete rebuild, meaning a huge investment loss. In general, the support has been focusing on having schools, but not on having motivated teachers to teach; on building rather than maintaining canals and pumping stations .

Overall, then, we think this system represents not so much a governing or infrastructure building system, as a political system which gives enormous scope to patronage. Given that, as seen below, patronage is where most resources are currently found, this is a terrific strength. But this also needs to be considered in terms of wider issues, including system capabilities, and the nature of political accountability.

Here, we might however say that the accountabilities involved in the party's system are of a specific, and perhaps limited nature. Their grounding in Khmer tradition is important and powerful. But it is also crucial, we think, to note that these are in the first instance patronage- based accountabilities deployed to largely political ends. They are, that is, the kinds of accountabilities you get from a patronage-based system that turns its attention to winning elections. As such, their potential for transforming wider administrative areas which to some extent need to operate along formal bureaucratic lines of accountability faces some constraints. Or, as we hope to show, it may be that leveraging these accountabilities into the wider system will be an important, but not straightforward, challenge for the government and its development partners.

There are also important implications in terms of multiparty and other/local democratic development. Clearly, these patronage-based supports represent an almost overwhelming electoral advantage for the CPP[7]. Certainly, the CPP are the only party in a position to afford a mass patronage system, or to make one work by combining political, executive and economic power. This situation is perhaps best captured in the CPP politicians' question as to why anyone should think the opposition Sam Rainsy party could look after poor Cambodians' interests: "They promise you a Mercedes, but they themselves ride a bicycle. How can they give you a Mercedes if they ride a bicycle?" While there is a certain plausibility to these claims in the current situation, we should also note that in fact this approach does not involve giving local people a Mercedes Benz. In fact, for all its elaboration and effort, mass patronage may be a reasonably inexpensive way of getting votes: perhaps less expensive than adequately funding teachers' salaries or good local health systems.

But again, this is not the end of the story. With political space now more consolidated and stable around these kinds of arrangements (and the party best able to deliver them), we might ask what further possibilities are emerging for ongoing development and change. In the discussion below, we consider what political accountabilities a unified system might bring, and how some of the accountabilities in the CPP party system might spill-over into the formal one.

Wider implications: Party Financing and Accountability

During a 2007 televised speech, Prime Minister Hun Sen told a revealing story. He was responding to criticisms of his government's tax and customs regimen, and its undermining by allegedly inaccurate customs declarations involving

---

[7] Though there is emerging evidence it doesn't always work. A forthcoming CDRI study shows voter preferences correlate with construction investments in quite surprising ways: contact Pak Kimchoeun for more details.

beer being imported from Thailand by a company reputedly connected with Deputy Prime Minister Sok An. A Chinese lord, he related, faced a revenue crisis which meant he would not be able to pay his imperial tribute. A leading court mandarin advisor proposed raising taxes on the peasantry, and another advised sending subjects to mine gold. Both were rejected as inefficient, unpopular and requiring unavailable time and manpower. But a third advisor asked for just twenty soldiers and a few days to solve the problem, and, in quick time, he duly returned with gold. It had been procured by simply taking the soldiers and going house by house around (other) high mandarins' residences.

In Cambodia, the "mandarins" are the elite neopatrons who personally and through lines of patronage control line ministries. Personalized control, bestowed on a personal basis by apex political figures, vests in them a lucrative, fungible and highly responsive revenue stream available for both political and strategic executive functions, and especially for elections. Most simply, this means Cambodia has a powerfully *neopatrimonial* state (that is, a formal bureaucracy occupied and governed by hierarchical patronage based on Khmer patrimonial modes)[8]. In this chapter, however, we want to elaborate this idea further, and open up discussion of what current arrangements might imply.

Following van de Walle[9], (neo)patronage arrangements of the kind familiar in Cambodia can be usefully contrasted with two ideal types. These two types are elite and mass clientelism, or, as we describe them, elite and mass patronage[10]. *Elite clientelism patronage* involves a powerful, relatively small and closely connected elite securing control over core ministries, assets, and private sector opportunities. A national elite in such circumstances might constitute just a few thousand people, often linked by military, central agency, investment and family ties. Elite patronage is a primary (post-) conflict mode of governing: it is basically oriented to securing one's family and supporters' physical and economic security in a time of threat, with little initial outlay on purchasing or legitimately acquiring resources. Here to be without an elite patron is to be in peril of death and hunger: and to be an elite patron is to orchestrate opportunities for clients in ways that will maintain their loyalty.

In other words, elite patronage reproduces itself from the top down by prebendalism: favour granted to a lower level to exploit a resource or a position

---

[8] Pak Kimchoeun, Horng Vuthy, Eng Netra, Ann Sovatha, Kim Sedara, Jenny Knowles and David Craig, *Accountability and Neo-patrimonialism: A Critical Literature Review*, Working Paper No 34, (Phnom Penh: CDRI, 2007).

[9] Van de Walle, *The Path from Neo-Patrimonialism*.

[10] Van de Walle calls them elite and mass clientelisms, perhaps because in many contexts, the clients' status, loyalty and actions are most important. But in Cambodia, we think it is the patronage that matters most: the ability of central political and neopatrimonial figures to personally and through their position command loyalty, pronounce the granting of requests, and win local elections.

to their own ends. Prebends thus get sanction (and often legal and other protection) from their boss or "back" (*khnang*) to go about doing (illegal) business. Protection here is both physical and legal, in impunity from legal prosecution, secured fairly cheaply by controlling or paying the courts. Prebendal/elite patronage builds what Cambodians refer to as a pipe (*tuy yo*) or line (*ksae*) for their patronage line: a base of clients ready and able to use their position to make money for themselves and (as a proportion) for their "back" or boss, while avoiding both formal and informal tax and rent. This doesn't require extensive liquid capital: resources, or lucrative gatekeeping roles in the security/ permit "checkpoint" economies can be allocated to close loyalists simply because the patron has come to control them, sometimes through violent or illegal means[11].

By contrast, mass patronage has important characteristics both additional to and divergent from the above. As suggested, the primary need of mass patronage systems is the winning of elections. This is done by two means: the allocation of jobs in the state mechanism according to party loyalty (so that employees become both voters and party activists at election time), and the allocation of resources accrued by the party by a number of means into mass patronage activities such as vote buying, provision of gifts and treats (in Cambodia, sarongs, bags of MSG, small cash donations), and the provision of local infrastructure projects by party, party-linked private charity, and the use of the government system in classic "pork-barrel" or populist politics ways to build local infrastructure, schools, clinics, and roads.

This kind of system, it will be clear, requires more up-front or liquid resources than a simple elite-focused system. The resources, however, need not be those of the formal revenue system: rather, they are more likely to be resources available from prebends, those beneficiaries of elite patronage, the mandarins of the Prime Minister's story. It is thus a system which emerges where resources are

---

[11] See Eng Netra, and David Craig, *Accountability and Human Resource Management in Decentralized Cambodia*, Working Paper no. 40 (Phnom Penh: Cambodia Development Resource Institute, 2009); Horng Vuthy and David Craig, *Accountability and Planning in Decentralized Cambodia*, Working Paper no. 39 (Phnom Penh: Cambodia Development Resource Institute, 2007); Caroline Hughes, *The Political Economy of Cambodia's Transition 1991–2001*(London: RoutledgeCurzon, 2003); Kim Sedara and Joakim Öjendal, *Where Decentralisation Meets Democracy: Civil Society, Local Government, and Accountability in Cambodia*, Working Paper no. 35 (Phnom Penh: CDRI, 2007); Judy Ledgerwood and John Vijghen, "Decision-Making in Rural Khmer Villages," in Ledgerwood (eds.), *Cambodia Emerges from the Past: Eight Essays* (DeKalb, Southeast Asia Publications, 2002); John Marston, *Cambodia 1991–94: Hierarchy, Neutrality and Etiquettes of Discourse,* PhD Thesis, University of Washington, 1994; Pak Kimchoeun and David Craig, *Accountability and Public Expenditure Management in Decentralised Cambodia*, Working Paper no. 38 (Phnom Penh: CDRI, 2008); Pak Kimchoeun, Horng Vuthy, Eng Netra, Ann Sovatha, Kim Sedara, Jenny Knowles and David Craig, *Accountability and Neo-patrimonialism: A Critical Literature Review*, Working Paper no 34 (Phnom Penh: CDRI, 2007).

available from a variety of sources, and can be tapped by either putting pressure on prebends to deliver proceeds from their lucrative positions in (rent-) rich ministries. For example, an official with the right to issue a licence for a financial institution or other business may ask the supplicant to build school rooms in some commune. In general, then, a mass patronage system relies less directly on illegal activities, and more on areas of discretion in and control of formal mechanisms of government and commerce. In this sense, it is more pervasively neopatrimonial than elite patronage systems. It extends its reach further down into the executive, into recruiting and other aspects of everyday human resource management[12]. And, for all its improved electoral responsiveness, it may be not particularly progressive in its ultimate outcomes. Mass patronage may well provide the elites with the legitimacy they need to hold onto massively privileged power and narrow demographic control both of the state and its assets, political organisation and its lines, and of the private sector. What seems clear, then, is that Cambodian politics combines aspects of elite with mass patronage in what are increasingly powerful and, from the point of view of the CPP, effective ways.

Looking Forward: Implications for Democracy and Accountability

The effusion of mass patronage in the 2008 elections was spectacular. Simply, party campaigns became venues for the display of new wealth and confidence among better off and elite sections of the community. The proceeds of Cambodia's remarkable economic growth, business development, land speculation, and neopatrimonial rents were channelled into *sang sang* and related campaign activities with extraordinary vigour. Contributions were made with an eye to securing support and patronage in the future, or perhaps to enabling an actor to become a public political figure himself. Perhaps this will change as deflationary effects spread to many of these sectors. But in general there was a confidence and even exuberance about what was now possible.

The party too was feeling that after a decade and a half of what they regarded as political instability, here was the possibility of something different. Party people in conversation would reiterate that the party knew the problems, and that now the new stability would give them a base for doing something about them, and legitimating both itself and Cambodian democracy. On the other hand, the results facilitated a consolidation of a dominant party order which might entail the closing of democratic space. But perhaps other spaces, perhaps not democratic in the same ways, are also opening up.

[12] Eng, et al., *Accountability and Human Resource Management*.

Whether this is true or not, there are implications for everyday issues including accountability in the public service. One important lesson from this for decentralization and de-concentration reforms concerns the ways accountability operates between the formal decentralized system and the Party Working Group System. Given some structural similarities between the two systems, it is worth asking whether aspects of the party system could be used in the state system, binding the party system more tightly to the formal arrangements of local government. Especially in delivery of local infrastructure, there has been what institutional theorists would call an *isomorphism* (similarity in form, partially because the two modalities arise from similar conditions[13]) between reform program activities and party activities. But in fact, the two systems work very differently in terms of political, institutional and personal accountabilities, the systems and incentives used to achieve them, and how and by whom those costs are borne. This so that each represents a kind of best practice, and that each might have lessons to teach the other. While we see isomorphism, we also see a clear separation or institutional *layering*[14] between the two systems, which seems equally crucial to understanding outcomes[15]. As we have noted, the political system includes many features of Khmer political and social life: hierarchy, respect, enforcement and fear, personalised patronage, opportunities and protection, respect for individual capabilities as an agent of the patron, competition to be trusted with resources, and so on. All these are the kinds of accountabilities that (only?) a Khmer, elite-mass patronage-based system has access to, and use for *sang sang* and winning elections.

For their part, the decentralization modalities rely on New Public Management modes of accountability[16], along with some related senses of effectiveness

---

[13] See Paul DiMaggio and Walter Powell, "The Iron Cage Revisited: Institutional Isomorphism and Collective Rationality in Organizational Fields," *American Sociological Review* 48.2 (1991): 147–160.

[14] Kathleen Thelen, "How Institutions Evolve: Insights from Comparative-Historical Analysis," in James Mahoney and Dietrich Rueschemeyer (eds.), *Comparative Historical Analysis in the Social Sciences* (Cambridge: Cambridge University Press, 2003), 208–240.

[15] As described by Thelen *ibid.*, 225 it typically involves attempts to reform a system, by bringing new devices or ways of doing business into it, but ends in "the partial renegotiation of some elements of a given set of institutions while leaving others in place". What happens is that vested interests within the old system are able to partially resist the reform by keeping their own systems functioning alongside the new one. Both survive alongside each other, doing similar things, though with separate revenue, budgets and lines of accountability. Layering also clearly happens when a certain group of actors simply wants to get a job done, and takes the most direct route to doing it, avoiding if at all possible entanglements with inefficient or rival systems alongside it.

[16] Jonathan Boston, *Public Management: the New Zealand Model* (Oxford: Oxford University Press, 1996); David Craig and Doug Porter, *Development beyond neo-liberalism: governance, poverty reduction and political economy* (London: Routledge 2006).

and efficiency. Typically, these modalities involve contracting based on narrowly defined outputs, clearly codified and allocated to individuals, followed up by audit and perhaps performance assessment. While they define and limit discretion, they may offer specific incentives for specific measured achievements. Perhaps most importantly, they stress accountability via surveillance or audit, directed to whether or not certain outputs have been generated. A common criticism of New Public Management is that it stifles professionalism and trust, through over-use of formal compliance measures that make people feel watched[17]. This in turn creates incentives to game the systems, and to find areas of autonomy not controlled by fine-grained surveillance. And, if performance incentives are not included or sustained, or if sanction is not actively imposed, these systems are highly prone to degeneration.

At the moment, the party's system seems to be as well resourced as the state system, and might be better grounded in Cambodian culture. This means the party system is, in present day Cambodia, better placed to generate aspiration, trust and crucial respect based on performance, as well as fear of the personal consequence of failure. It has, for example, a much stronger vertical accountability mode, in that powerful central officials and patrons keep a direct eye on local activities. All this bodes well for its institutionalization. Institutions are, by at least one founding definition[18], to be distinguished from mere organizations in that they effectively articulate higher, social, cultural and moral values, and thus enjoy a wide base of popular support.

In essence, then, we suggest that the party-led mass patronage system builds in trust, fear and respect and therefore more powerful kinds of accountability; it more successfully harnesses the limited electoral accountabilities in a dominant party system; it rewards participants and is demanding in terms of performance; it motivates the higher levels to listen to local voices; and it generates ceremonies that are enjoyed by many. Under such circumstances, those making decisions will perhaps prefer, like Prime Minister Hun Sen in commenting on the actions of the Chinese lord, to keep their money where they know they can control it in highly accountable ways. As one official we spoke to said, "If you were the one giving the money, what channel would you put it down? Would you put it down the state?"

What the decentralized state system needs, arguably more than anything else, is electoral accountability: electoral incentives to perform. It is crucial, then, to note that currently this electoral accountability does not seem to be being generated as much via the mainstream governmental system as it is via

---

[17] Christopher Hood, "The 'New Public Management' in the 1980s: Variations on a Theme," *Accounting, Organizations and Society*, 20. 2/3 (1995): 93–109.
[18] Philip Selznick, *TVA and the Grass Roots* (Berkeley: University of California Press, 1949).

the party patronage system. As long as the party is able to harness the kinds of accountabilities and effectiveness which emerge in a mass patronage context, it will retain control of a powerful electoral tool. It is a tool, however, which it may well be difficult to apply to the much more difficult business of enabling quality local services. Such services, it has been noted, involve local actors working with high levels of discretion around multiple, "intensive" transactions[19]. To be successful, they therefore require highly professional actors working with autonomy alongside high levels of formal and informal accountability.

There are also other areas where mass patronage is weak in guaranteeing outcomes, for similar reasons. Resource security for the poor in the contexts of enclosure and encroachment, and control of the police and judiciary are others. In these areas, the kinds of accountabilities provided strongly by patronage arrangements run almost exactly against the grain of what is required. It seems too that governance reform programs which operate in similar modes to mass patronage, delivering infrastructure through local project-focussed modalities, will also struggle to engage these same issues. Currently, what is clear is that the party has considerable the incentives to continue to rely on its control of the executive and its multiple sources of finance to deliver mass patronage. What more might be leveraged by its need for legitimacy, and rising popular demand, remains to be seen.

---

[19] Francis Fukuyama, *State Building: Governance and the World Order in the Twenty-First Century* (London: Profile Books, 2005); Michael Woolcock and Lant Pritchett, *Solutions when the Solution is the Problem: Arraying the disarray in Development*, Paper no. 10 (Washington DC: Center for Global Development, 2002).

12

LOCAL LEADERS AND BIG BUSINESS IN THREE COMMUNES

Caroline Hughes, Eng Netra, Thon Vimealea, Ou Sivhuoch and Ly Tem

THIS CHAPTER,[1] LIKE THE TWO subsequent chapters in this collection, shifts attention to questions of local politics in rural Cambodia and to the extent to which formal or informal arrangements at local level ameliorate or intensify the unsettling effect of transformation on Cambodia's poor. We proceed by investigating the extent to which villagers have been offered or have created avenues for resisting efforts to privatize, enclose or destroy natural resources on which livelihoods are based. We examine whether local governments, which have been elected since 2002, offer leadership to villagers in political struggles that might approximate a counter-movement to protect livelihoods and subsistence in the context of the transformation of forests, fisheries and land into commodities that are traded in national and international markets.

Understanding the role of local leaders in this process requires examining their function within the formal and informal institutions structuring the contestation between social forces in Cambodia. Consequently, this chapter begins with an outline of the forms of local government, the nature of local leaders' power and authority and the way that this has changed during the period of economic transformation. It then goes on to examine in detail the position of local leaders in three communes, which to preserve anonymity we

[1] The findings presented in this chapter are part of a larger research project on Local Leadership in Cambodia, conducted by the Democratic Governance and Public Sector Reform Team of the Cambodia Development Resource Institute (CDRI), with the assistance of Caroline Hughes, as part of CDRI's groundbreaking *Kechhnay* (Reform) Research Programme. Both CDRI and the *Kechhnay* Programme are funded by the UK Government's Department for International Development (DFID) and by the Swedish International Development Agency (SIDA), to whom grateful thanks are due. Further details of the project and the programme are available from the CDRI website at www.cdri.org.kh. This chapter reflects the views of the authors and not necessarily those of CDRI, DFID, or SIDA.

refer to here as Commune A, Commune B and Commune C. A is located in the north-eastern highlands, adjacent to an economic land concession in which large-scale logging is going on; B is a fishing community near the Tonle Sap Lake; and C is a commune in a traditional rice-growing district in the central plains. In each commune, the research team surveyed two villages to gather information as to the types of people villagers identified as leaders and the personal characteristics, networks and activities of these leaders. The resources upon which local leaders can draw in these different communes and the uses to which they put them, are the subject of this chapter.

Local Government in Cambodia

Cambodia's local authorities (*anhathua moulthan*) comprise the commune and village levels of government. The commune is a grouping of villages joined together for administrative purposes in an arrangement initiated by the French in the 1920s. The commune office represents the lowest level of the state's presence in rural Cambodia and is responsible for duties such as the registration of births, deaths and marriages and the keeping of electoral rolls. The village is a more organic entity and a source of local identity. Both communes and villages are led by a chief; while the commune chief is formally a state official, the village chief is not, prompting the hypothesis that the commune chief might be regarded as a government functionary, while the village chief is a representative of the people.

In fact, the relations between villages and communes have always been more fluid than this and recent decentralization reforms have altered the picture somewhat. In the sole study of village politics undertaken during the pre-war era, May Ebihara noted that the distinction between the village and the commune was unclear and that the division of responsibilities between them depended upon the personalities involved: an active commune chief might take on most of the tasks of local government if the village chief was a passive character and vice versa.[2]

Following the upheavals of the Democratic Kampuchea era, during which whole villages were relocated, boundaries redrawn and many old leaders replaced or killed, the incoming People's Republic of Kampuchea faced the task of reasserting local-level control in the early 1980s. They did so by a mixture of methods. In some villages, Khmer Rouge cadres were appointed; in others, previous or new leaders were selected. Elections were held in 1981 in some places, although alternative political parties and candidates were

---

[2] May Ebihara, *Svay, A Village in Cambodia*, unpub. PhD diss., Columbia University, 1969,

not allowed; in other places appointed chiefs were reconfirmed in their position.³

During the 1980s and 1990s, the role of the local authorities was security- and production-oriented. In the 1980s, the local authorities were responsible for two unpopular tasks: mobilizing young men for conscription and filling state compulsory rice purchase quotas.⁴ Since Cambodian villagers throughout the decade were reluctant to give up either their sons or their produce, successful prosecution of these tasks required a tough line. Local authorities were also responsible for policing, in a regime where a relatively high level of surveillance was maintained. Every commune maintained a militia which answered to the commune chief and had extensive powers of arrest; conscription and rice-procurement powers facilitated more subtle forms of coercion. Long-distance travel was not permitted without the written authorization of the commune chief; to be caught on the high road without the requisite papers was to risk being branded a Khmer Rouge insurgent.

In the 1990s, the situation changed: conscription and state rice-procurement drives ended, personal freedoms were much greater and the security situation gradually improved. But the structure of local leadership changed far less. In the three communes that are the subject of this chapter, 15 out of 29 local authority leaders had formed part of the local authorities since the early 1980s. The shake-up of national-level government presaged by the Paris Peace Agreements signed in 1991 had little effect on local authorities except to add electoral mobilization to their list of duties. In studies of the elections in 1993 and 1998, the local authorities were cited as significant sources of coercion, intimidation and human rights abuse.

Towards the end of the 1990s, things began to change again. The end of the war prompted the disbanding of local militias; at the same time, the extension of party patronage activities beyond the elite and towards the masses gave local authorities a new and more palatable task – ensuring the inclusion of villagers in the benefits of mass patronage, with exclusion reserved only for the most intransigent political dissidents. This marked a change from earlier practices in which the local authorities favoured a relatively small in-group of political loyalists and treated everyone else with a disdain that could easily turn violent. By the turn of the century, although local authorities were still blamed for intimidation around elections, tales of commune and village chiefs or policemen getting away with violent assaults, rapes and outrageous landgrabs had become

---

³ Margaret Slocomb, "Commune Elections in Cambodia: 1981 Foundations and 2002 Reformulations," *Modern Asian Studies*, 38 (2004): 456.
⁴ Sorpong Peou, *Intervention and Change in Cambodia: Towards Democracy?* (New York: St Martin's Press, 2000), 62.

far scarcer, as the Cambodian People's Party (CPP) began to attend more assiduously to its popular image and to rein in loose cannons at the local level.[5]

Billed as the first step in a grander campaign of decentralization and deconcentration of power, new commune elections set for 2002 presaged a qualitative shift in the nature of local governance. The new mandate for local governance is contained in the 2001 Law on the Administration and Management of the Commune/Sangkat and awards the communes the following functions: maintainance of security and public order; arrangement of necessary public services; encouragement of creation of contentment and well-being of citizens; promotion of social and economic development; protection and conservation of the environment and natural resources; promotion of mutual understanding and tolerance among citizens; and performance of "general affairs to meet the needs of citizens".[6] This expansive mandate focuses on developmental and administrative issues rather than security, in a shift which has transformed relations with constituents. Joakim Öjendal and Kim Sedara describe this as a transition from a relationship based primarily on fear to one based primarily on respect, a shift which they regard as a positive sign for the future emergence of grassroots democracy in Cambodia.[7]

This led to the first commune elections of 2002 which replaced the commune chiefs inherited from the 1980s with a newly elected, multi-party council, headed by a commune chief, representing the party with most seats, working alongside one or two deputies representing other parties with council seats and supported by a Ministry of Interior-appointed commune clerk. Subsequently, the commune councils appointed new village chiefs, deputy village chiefs and village gender focal people,[8] to replace the village chiefs appointed in the 1980s.

The centrepiece of commune governance is the production of the Commune Development Plan and the task of seeking funding for it. The discretionary budget available to communes are extremely limited. Councils can seek extra funding from district and provincial line ministries; from NGOs and donors; and from the party. As Craig and Pak described in the previous chapter, the latter funding source is by far the most lucrative. It has been facilitated by the establishment of district working groups reporting

---

[5] This characterization is taken from a comparison of data collected during programmes of interviews with directors of Cambodian human rights NGOs in 1996, 1999 and 2000. Comparison of data from the reports of the Special Representative for Human Rights in Cambodia confirms this picture. Interviews conducted by Caroline Hughes.

[6] Royal Government of Cambodia, Law on Administration and Management of Commune/Sangkat, 2001, Article 43.

[7] Joakim Öjendal and Kim Sedara, "*Korob, Kaud, Klach:* In Search of Agency in Rural Cambodia," *Journal of South East Asian Studies,* 31.3 (2006): 507–526.

[8] The village gender focal person is appointed in accordance with efforts to ensure women's representation on local committees.

to national level patrons, an arrangement which has also produced a closer relationship between local party officials, the national party and villagers on the ground.

In the context of both the decentralization of formal power and the reshaping of the party to better cement central–local ties of loyalty and patronage, local government has changed significantly in Cambodia over the past ten years. However, the shift to mass patronage raises the question as to the relationship between local government and big business, especially in those communes where economic transformation is taking place, through the appropriation of common resources and the conversion of smallholders into landless workers. Can local leaders intervene in this process and if so, what can they achieve for their constituents, given that they themselves are closely bound to a patronage machine which depends on the transformation for its functioning?

Local Leadership in Three Communes

Surveys of villagers in the three communes studied indicated that three types of leader were most commonly identified by villagers: local government officials (including commune chiefs, commune councillors, village chiefs and members of the village committee); spiritual leaders (including the abbot of the local *wat;* elders or *chas tum;* and lay preachers or *acha*); and influential business people in the area.[9] Of these groups, local government officials were the most readily identified and were regarded by the villagers surveyed as the most important. They were seen as having the most power and as being the first port of call for villagers who needed assistance or advice. Spiritual leaders and business people varied in their relevance to day to day life.

While the interactions between these sets of leaders varied in the two communes studied and is explored in the next section, four common themes emerged in surveys and interviews with villagers. First, it became clear that in all three communes there existed a local leadership group, based around the formal positions of commune and village chief, which had remained remarkably stable for at least twenty-five years. The members of these groups appeared to have close connections to one another: we observed them visiting one another and in the course of the research, they referred us to other members of the group. Most of these had held leadership positions since at least the early

---

[9] A fuller discussion of the survey methodology and a discussion of the range of Khmer terms that can be used to translate the word "leader" can be found in CDRI, *Local Leadership in Cambodia: a Study of Three Communes,* CDRI Working Paper series (Phnom Penh: CDRI, 2009), forthcoming.

1980s[10]; some had remained in the same position; others had moved up from militia to village committee, from deputy to chief, or from village to commune level; some had retired, but remained active and were frequently consulted by villagers and other leaders. These groups were composed of mostly male CPP members, aged between 45 and 60, with some older active retirees. The close bonds between members of these groups and their longstanding dominance in village affairs suggests that the upheavals transforming Cambodian politics at the national level had passed over these communes with barely any impact at all on the local secular leadership. Moreover, these groups were remarkably similar in composition across the three communes.

The data collected from villagers and from village leaders suggested that this group had expanded since 2002, under the influence of the decentralization programme. Although the demobilization of local militias had reduced the number of village positions available at the end of the 1990s, decentralization enlarged the leadership group again, by providing commune council positions in 2002 and deputy village chiefs and village gender focal point positions from 2006. This allowed more individuals to participate in the leadership group and also brought women into the group for the first time. Women entered the more junior positions,[11] despite the fact that the data we collected on educational backgrounds suggested they were on average better qualified than their male counterparts.

A second common finding that emerged from the survey of villagers was that, in discussing the local secular authorities, villagers had two different sets of terminology. Commonly, villagers used the legal term, *anhathua*, which translates as "authorities", to refer to village and commune leaders in a manner denoting correct and formal relations. However, they also used kinship terminology to refer to their leaders, in a strategic manner denoting different levels of respect and familiarity. The commonly used kinship terms of "*ming* (aunt)", "*pou* (uncle)" or "*ta* (grandfather)" were frequently used to refer to village chiefs who lived in close proximity to the villagers and were familiar to them. But the terms "*mae* (mother)" and "*ov* (father)" – or "*mae-ov*" for parents – were also used to denote local leaders who were not only familiar, but respected and venerated for their devotion to the care of their constituents.

---

[10] During research interviews with local leaders, the issue of whether they had been in leadership positions during the Khmer Rouge era, from 1975 to 1979, was found to be a sensitive one. Some interviewees were reluctant to give information on this period, and consequently a decision was taken amongst the research team to take 1979 as the starting point for the research.

[11] The exception to this is the Sam Rainsy Party commune chief in Commune A; however, she was regarded as an interloper rather than a member of the leadership group in this commune. Her position is discussed in more detail later in the chapter.

Use of "*mae*" and "*ov*" was reserved for referring to leaders who went beyond the formal requirements of their job and took on a relationship with villagers that was similar to that of parent to child. *Ov* also denotes a breadwinner, or head of the household. The shouldering of this kind of responsibility by a village or commune chief was referred to in terms of strong approval by villagers during surveys. A village or commune chief who also acted as an "*ov*" in taking care of the villagers, advising and guiding them on matters of personal conduct and morality, guarding their interests in the sphere of development and offering an example to the young, was a clearly articulated and apparently widespread ideal among the villagers surveyed.

It is significant, however, that among forty-six local leaders identified across the three communes, only one was actually regarded as reaching this ideal. This individual was a village chief from a settled rice-growing village in Commune C. This was a village in which there had been little inward migration and where there were few conflicts over land or natural resources. It was also a village which benefited from considerable assistance from an external patron, as the discussion below describes. As such, it might be considered a commune on the margins of transformation: a commune in which patterns of expectations were well-established and challenged relatively rarely. By contrast, in Communes A and B, in which economic transformation had taken a heavy toll, the terms "*mae-ov*" referring to idealized leaders acting *in loco parentis* were used to critique individuals whose behaviour fell far short of the ideal.

It is beyond the scope of this study to investigate the origins of this ideal, although it is tempting to speculate that it may be a legacy of the Sihanouk era of the 1950s and 1960s, when Prince Norodom Sihanouk ruled the country via his own "populist movement" the *Sangkum Reastr Niyum*. In his thousands of speeches made to peasants across the country in the pre-war era, Sihanouk referred to himself as the father of his people, using the formulation *Samdech Ov* (Lord Father). Sihanouk's personal interventionism, his active developmentalism and his assertion of moral authority based upon cosmological hierarchies described in patriarchal terms left a deep impression upon the terms of Cambodian political discourse, particularly because the horrors that followed his overthrow in 1970 have led to the pre-war era being viewed with a great deal of contemporary nostalgia. The use of the term "*ov*" arguably denotes aspirations for patriarchal leaders who can guide the village back to a future characterized by the comforts of reasserted tradition and increasing prosperity. The difficulty of actually achieving this reflect not merely the inherent unrealizability of goals based upon nostalgia, but also the particularly acute nature of this problem in a time of rapid transformation.

The third finding relevant to all three communes is the variability of the situation with respect to non-state community leaders, either as leaders of formal organizations or as leaders of spontaneous social movements emerging to combat particular issues. This is a surprising finding, since as Öjendal and Kim relate in the next chapter of this volume, non-state community-based organizations are becoming increasingly common in Cambodia. With respect to community level civil society, the three communes in this study each had quite different features, suggesting the need for caution in generalizing about the state of village-based civil associations in Cambodia.

In Commune C, the commune which had been the least overtly affected by economic transformation, we found a number of traditional self-help groups, including a funerals association, formed to assist with organizing funeral ceremonies; and some groups organized to help the most vulnerable members of the village. The leaders of these groups were drawn from the group of elders and from the village authorities.

Commune B, the fishery community, also contained some self-help organizations, for example a funeral association led by a village elder. There were also some savings associations, but these took a hybrid rather than strictly traditional form: although they operated along traditional lines, they were supported by external, professional NGOs. Interestingly, no villagers mentioned the leaders of these latter organizations as village leaders during the survey: we found out about them only when we interviewed a commune councillor who was responsible for them, suggesting that these associations operated more as an arm of local government than as independent non-state actors.

In Commune A, however, the community that was undergoing the most rapid change with deforestation and large flows of in-migration, we found no traditional self-help groups of these kinds. One villager interviewed commented, "In this commune, everyone just borrows money from ACLEDA." This reliance upon a commercial microcredit agency reflected not only the difficulty of organizing civil associations on traditional lines in situations where social ties are weak; it also reflected the fact that villagers were borrowing large sums of money to build houses with the timber they were cutting from the forest. Traditional saving associations could not supply this kind of capital, so villagers looked to banks instead.

From these three cases, it appeared that economic transformation was significantly changing if not destroying the kind of grassroots organizations that existed in Communes B and C respectively. Clearly much further research is needed to discover if this is a more general pattern in Cambodia; but if so, then it has significant implications for the question of leadership and for the question of the emergence of counter-movements of the poor.

Another kind of associational activity that has sparked interest in terms of movements of the poor is that of social movements, forming around the sort of resource conflicts that emerge from transformation. A recent World Bank study into such leaders called them by the Khmer term *mekhyal* ("masters of the wind")[12] – opinion leaders who step forward to lead in times of crisis, when villagers need to mobilize against the state.[13] They lead protests, boycotts and demands for assistance from higher-level politicians. In Commune B, such a mobilization had occurred recently over a land dispute; yet none of the villagers surveyed identified the leaders of this mobilization when asked to name leaders in the village, unless specifically prompted to name leaders of movements that emerged around land-grabbing.

There are a number of explanations for this. Some informants indicated that these leaders did not become more active on wider issues, but only when land-grabbing affected their own interests.[14] However, we also heard of one case, in Commune B, where a popular local farmer, who had successfully led the villagers to contest a land dispute against local authorities and had been active in water-user issues, was subsequently invited by the CPP to stand as their candidate in commune council elections. Villagers named this leader in the survey, but as a member of the local authorities rather than as a non-state leader. Subsequently, as a commune councillor, the same man was far less influential in new land-grabbing cases which pitted villagers against local authorities, suggesting that to some extent he had been co-opted into government rather than elected as a representative of grass-roots interests.

Similarly, in Commune A, we found a local leader who shared some of the same characteristics of independent influence. The leader in question was a widow who had a number of local business interests that had made her rich and influential. She acted as a money-lender in the village and many villagers relied upon her for this. She also owned some ceremonial items which she would rent out for families holding religious ceremonies. This lady achieved a growing reputation for having "salty spit (*teuk moat prai*)"[15] on the basis of these activities, although she had not been active in any social movements. Like the farmer in Commune B, this lady was invited to stand for the CPP in

---

[12] Centre for Advanced Study/World Bank Phnom Penh, *Justice for the Poor: an Exploratory Study of Collective Grievances over Land and Local Governance in Cambodia* (Phnom Penh: World Bank, 2006).

[13] This use of the term "*mekhyal*" is contested to some extent: *mekhyal* can also be translated as a "fixer" – someone who can get things done – and is used in a number of different spheres of life. Human traffickers are referred to as *mekhyal,* for example. A previous study of the *mekhyal* was conducted by William Collins.

[14] The survey was designed to interrogate a number of different Khmer terms for leadership. Alongside being asked to name local leaders, with a series of different Khmer terms used to translate "leader", villagers were also asked questions such as, "Who has influence in the village?"; "Who can get things done in this village?" and "Who can help you if you need assistance?" Consequently, we believe the findings to be robust and not simply a matter of terminology.

[15] A Khmer colloquialism: to have salty spit is to have influence and the ability to get things done.

commune elections and became a councillor. Whether this practice represented co-optation of locally influential individuals, as it appeared to in Commune B, or an attempt to recruit the best and brightest into local government is a question demanding further research.

The fourth finding across all three communes studied was the relatively narrower horizons of the poor and marginal. Respondents to the survey were selected from four different socio-economic groups: professionals and business owners; smallholders; poor and labouring families; and ethnic minorities. The results of the survey suggested a clear correlation between socio-economic status and willingness to reveal knowledge of the political sphere. Professionals and business owners were able to name the greatest variety of village leaders, expressed some knowledge of their activities and voiced criticisms of their achievements. The group of smallholders were also able to name a variety of leaders, at village and commune level, but appeared less willing or able to comment on the specifics of their performance. The very poor tended to name only their own village chief and appeared unfamiliar with the names of commune councillors; some were unable or unwilling to name any leaders at all. Members of the ethnic minority groups, which in these communes were all ethnic Chinese, informed us that they avoided contact with the local authorities as far as possible.

The villages in these three communes were dominated by a static, highly politicized and male leadership group inherited from the early 1980s. Any impression of an opening up of leadership in Cambodia's villages is not supported by this study, although the function of the commune level of government has changed dramatically and the co-optation of a wider leadership group may ultimately promote wider forms of representation. Despite a more developmental focus in commune mandates, the very poor appeared alienated from local leaders. Furthermore, in the two communes that had felt the pressures of economic transformation most sharply, those villagers who were prepared to share their opinions appeared disillusioned with local leaders. They expressed this disillusionment with reference to a form of leadership which perhaps has its origins in Sihanouk's ultimately unsuccessful style of rule in the 1960s, rather than in aspirations for the pluralization of the political sphere, or more specifically for democratic forms of representation.

Arguably, these findings can be explained with reference to the ways in which party patronage, state decentralization and economic transformation have interacted in the context of these communes, in a manner which promotes dependence and/or alienation rather than contestation. Consequently, this chapter now proceeds with an examination of the interaction between these different dynamics in each commune.

Commune A: Local Leadership on the Margins of an Economic Land Concession

Commune A is situated in north-eastern Cambodia, on the margins of an economic land concession. As such, it exists in the maelstrom of economic transformation. The journey to the commune took us along newly built highways connecting the area to the border with Vietnam; all along these roads, the view was clouded by the smoke of burning forests, with the most discernable feature of the landscape being a line of flame along the horizon. At first sight, the commune appears to be booming: there are newly constructed houses everywhere and enormous piles of freshly cut timber in every yard. Enquiry reveals this to be a last bonanza, precipitated by the award of the economic land concession. Everyone is rushing to cut as much timber as they can before the forest is gone forever. What will replace it in terms of livelihoods is a question no one can yet answer.

The local leadership group in this commune is typical of the findings across the three communes. Fifteen leaders were identified in the survey; of these, seven were current or former commune chiefs or councillors; four were village chiefs or deputy village chiefs; one was the village gender focal person; one was an *achar* or lay preacher; one was an elder and former village chief; and one was a locally-based *oknha* or businessman, a former official at the provincial department of transportation who went into business in 1990 as a contractor for a logging company and who had recently been awarded the 15,000 hectare land concession near the village. All were aged between 46 and 70, except for the *achar* and the elder who were aged respectively 81 and 72. 11 were men and three were women: women comprised the village gender focal person, who was also the local midwife and nurse and a Cambodian Red Cross volunteer; a commune councillor who was also a wealthy money-lender and businesswoman in the commune; and the commune chief. All were CPP members, except for the commune chief who represented the Sam Rainsy Party (SRP).

The election of an SRP commune chief in 2007 puts Commune A in a minority of 30 out of 1,621 communes in Cambodia with a non-CPP chief.[16] Different interviewees posited sharply different reasons for this electoral upset. According to the SRP commune chief, her election was the result of the corruption of the former commune chief in relation to the land concession

---

16 The CPP holds 1,591 commune chief positions, the SRP 28 and the royalist *Front Uni pour un Cambodge Independent, Neutral, Pacifique et Cooperatif* (FUNCINPEC) holds 2. Results taken from United Nations Development Program, *Report on the 2007 Commune Council Elections in Cambodia* (Phnom Penh: UNDP, 2007), 23.

which was destroying villagers' livelihoods. Those local leaders representing the CPP regarded their defeat as due to internal party disunity in the area.

Both stories are tenable given the circumstances; and it appears clear that the electoral upset was in part caused by conflict of interest within the CPP. In 1979, Lek[17], a local farmer was appointed commune chief by the Vietnamese and was subsequently confirmed in that position by the 1981 local elections. He served in this position for the next twenty years. In the 2002 election, he was placed in second position on the CPP party list. First place on the list was given to Sok, a local landowner and the brother of a wealthy and powerful businessman, *Oknha* Krouch, who lives in the commune and who does business in logging, rubber plantation and petrol import.[18] *Oknha* Krouch sponsored his brother to gain the first place on the list,[19] and he was duly elected to commune chief, while Lek took the first deputy's position.

According to both Sok and Lek they worked well together during the first mandate from 2002 to 2007; Lek was able to use his longstanding knowledge of the local context to resolve villagers' problems and claims that today villagers still come to him for advice and assistance, even though he is out of power. Sok says that he used his party and business connections to bring considerable development to the village: he sponsored festivals and infrastructure development, including a new road, a pagoda development and a new school. Sok argues that these activities made him well-loved in the village.

However, during this period, Sok's brother, *Oknha* Krouch, was in conflict with the district governor of the area over ownership of a road development; *Oknha* Krouch had built the road and we were told that the district governor wanted to renovate the road and take the credit for it. This dispute, we were told, led to the district governor dropping *Oknha* Krouch's brother from the party list for the 2007 elections and a new candidate was put in his place – a former head of the district education department, with connections in the district governor's office. The CPP lost the election and a new SRP commune chief took over; subsequently, the district governor was fired from his job, opening the way for Sok to stand for office again next time.

Some informants attributed the CPP's election loss in 2007 to the change in the party list and the presentation of new candidates. Others argued that the commune had suffered from the various land conflicts arising from *Oknha* Krouch's land concession. Either way, it is clear that these two leaders were constrained in

---

[17] Names have been changed to protect identities.

[18] *Oknha* Krouch merits the *Oknha* epithet because he has spent over US$100,000 on pagoda donations and infrastructure development in the commune. Interviewees in the village were unsure whether the title had been officially bestowed by the Prime Minister or not.

[19] It is common practice in Cambodia for aspiring candidates to pay for a place on their party's list.

their ability to maintain support in the commune by the pressures coming from three directions: the relationship with *Oknha* Krouch as brother of the commune chief and as a key development patron; the need to retain the political backing of the district party office which controls the party list; and the need to respond to demands for representation and development from villagers. These different pressures entailed that the two leaders were hamstrung, once the various interests of the villagers, *Oknha* Krouch and the district governor came into conflict with one another. The commune leaders did not have sufficient autonomy from either business or the party to be able to act authoritatively in support of the villagers.

The SRP was able to gain a surprise victory and their top candidate, a former schoolteacher, was elected to the commune chief's position. However, one year into her electoral term, the commune chief told us that she had found it difficult to get much done in her new position, for three reasons.

The first reason related to her exclusion from networks within the village. This individual was a relative newcomer to the commune; and because of her party allegiance, she was excluded from the leadership group that possessed the experience and close networks extending down into the villages. This exclusion was evident not only from the commune chief's own comments, but from the comments of CPP leaders in talking about her. It appeared evident that they cooperated with the commune chief only minimally and they regarded her as lacking knowledge of commune affairs. The difficulties this presented a new commune chief was evident from the responses of survey respondents in all three communes: a common finding was that villagers had a strong preference for going for help to officials that they knew personally. The election of a commune chief who did not know many people was a serious problem for the functioning of the commune. However, in this case, the anti-corruption stance of the SRP commune chief may provide a way around this problem. The CPP leaders in this commune grumbled, in interviews for this study, that they had lost some of their income since her election, since poor villagers preferred to go straight to her for signatures and paperwork, since she, unlike the CPP leaders, tended not to charge a fee. This raises a question of how far the predilection amongst villagers for familiar faces is connected with the concern to avoid paying extra fees.

A second source of impotence for this commune chief was lack of access to funds. The commune's state budget is extremely small – only US$8,000 a year. Commune chiefs throughout Cambodia rely heavily on CPP and business contributions to fund development plans. Former commune chief Sok commented:

> Because of my brother I could borrow money and paid my own money to implement commune projects on time and as needed. Then I mobilize

resources to pay back, often a large sum from business people and politicians.[20]

By contrast, the current SRP commune chief told us:

> I want to help my commune and have ideas for initiatives but I don't know who I can ask for help besides NGOs. In addition, I am being excluded from what other councillors in the other party are doing in the commune even though I am the chief.[21]

The third major constraint was the status of the economic land concession. The land concession was clearly the most important determinant of the state of development in the commune for decades to come. It overwhelmed local development planning and made locally produced strategies largely redundant. Yet there was no formal communication between the local authorities and the operators of the land concession. Local authorities and the villagers had not been given any information by the provincial or national level of government about the award of the economic land concession, or its purpose. A clear map of its boundary was not provided; however, it soon became clear that the concession area encroached upon areas that the villagers had used in the past for collecting forest products and even on the private agricultural land of the villagers. This issue was impossible for the commune chief to resolve and she was left trying to calm angry villagers and to negotiate with security guards when they captured trespassing villagers in the forest. The commune chief had tried to lead villagers to complain to Prime Minister Hun Sen when he visited the province, but without success.

From 2002 to 2007, the election of the contractor's younger brother to the position of commune chief ensured that communication between the land concession and the commune office took place: yet, in this relationship the conflict of interest is immediate and obvious. The sponsorship of the commune chief by the *Oknha* suggests that business was in the driving seat, co-opting local government rather than negotiating with it. Interviewed for this study, the *Oknha* commented that he had contributed to the commune's development by using his own machinery and labour to build roads through the commune. However, he acknowledged that the decision to build roads, like the decision on where to locate them, was made with his own business interests in mind; when asked if he had consulted the commune's development plan before building the road, he looked slightly surprised at the idea.[22]

---

[20] Sok, former chief, Commune A, response to interview, 25 April 2008.
[21] Rina, Commune Chief, Commune A, response to interview, 24 April 2008.
[22] Interview with *Oknha* Krouch, May 2008.

Significantly, this *Oknha* was identified as a leader by numerous villagers in the village survey and falls into a category referred to as *thavkae* (big businessman). These big businessmen operate on a level beyond the boundaries of the local. They have national connections and are awarded contracts on a national scale. The commune is the place in which they live, but it is not the stage upon which they primarily act. All three communes in our study were home to one or more of these businessmen. However, not all *thavkae* are regarded as local leaders. In Commune A, *Oknha* Krouch was regarded as a local leader because he had intervened in commune politics, to sponsor his brother into a position of power and because he had donated money for the pagoda and had built local infrastructure. Despite the fact that his business interests were destroying local livelihoods, his donations were gratefully received by villagers. As one villager in Commune A described *Oknha* Krouch, "This leaders' spit is very salty. His spit is not just made of salt; it is mixed with *prahok* (fermented fish)."[23]

This apparently genuine gratitude for gifts from individuals who have become wealthy through the expropriation of the local community's resources has been noted elsewhere in Cambodia in recent years.[24] Drawing on Cambodian conventions of giving and gratitude, it represents a powerful force in the context of economic transformation, defusing potentially explosive conflicts between rich and poor, by allowing the award of development gifts as a palliative in communities threatened with livelihood destruction. The sentiment involved is expressed in a Khmer proverb, "The rich who take care of the poor are like the *sarong* [traditional Khmer skirt] which surrounds a body." Just as the *sarong* covers the naked body, so the rich are obliged to ameliorate poverty in the village; failure to do so is considered as shameful as nakedness. These attitudes suggest that leaders do not actually need to mobilize in order to be regarded as influential: the act of donating is itself regarded as a type of leadership.

Whether these relations of giving and receiving represent either a merely superficial veneer, imposed by a venal ruling elite as a means of mystifying the population, or the first tentative steps towards a welfarist counter-movement organized via patrimonial structures with the aim of protecting the poor from the ravages of marketization, is unclear. However, the emergence of protection for the poor from charitable donations rather than from the meagre resources of elected local governments is a trend that belies the democratic rhetoric of Cambodia's decentralization policies.

---

23 *Prahok* is a Khmer delicacy, made from fermented fish. It is extremely salty.
24 See comments of squatters receiving plots of land far outside the capital city to compensate them for the destruction of their city-centre homes, in Caroline Hughes, "The Politics of Gifts: Tradition and Regimentation in Contemporary Cambodia," *Journal of Southeast Asian Studies*, 37.3 (2006): 484–485.

Commune B: Land Values, Money Politics and Local Leaders

Commune B, situated adjacent to the Tonle Sap lake in the centre of Cambodia, reflects some similar but also some different sets of problems associated with economic transformation. Two major resource conflicts beset commune politics: a conflict with Vietnamese fisherman over fishery resources in the Tonle Sap and conflicts emerging from the problem of distributions of parcels of land within the commune.

With respect to the fisheries conflict, Commune B showed similarities with Commune A. The Vietnamese fishermen who were exploiting resources upon which villagers had formerly depended were, we were told, well connected, paying regular bribes to high-ranking officials. They were consequently beyond the reach of commune officials and, as foreigners, did not engage in the kind of socially mandated gift-giving documented above. This led to disillusionment among villagers with the capacity and effectiveness of the commune level of goverment. This sense of disillusionment had been exacerbated by a conflict between a large number of villagers and the commune authorities over distributions of land within the commune.

As in Commune A, this commune also showed great continuity within the leadership group, although as in Commune A again, the advent of elections and the use of the party list system had offered opportunities for well-connected local party members to get ahead of the officials who had been in place since 1979. In Commune B, an individual who had been a village chief from 1979 to 2002 managed to use personal connections to get his name put on the top of the party list in the 2002 commune elections, at the expense of the incumbent commune chief. Following the elections, the former commune chief became the deputy of the new chief. Subsequently, the commune leadership group was expanded to incorporate deputy village chiefs and village gender focal points, but as in Commune A, aside from some of the commune councillors, all local leadership positions were awarded to former group leaders, militias or party activists belonging to the CPP.

The potential for abuse of power represented by the entrenchment of a long-standing and well-networked leadership group is illustrated by this commune. In the late 1980s, the district authorities had ordered the commune authorities to distribute what was formerly communal land to the villagers as private property. The responsibility to distribute land within each village was given to the respective village chiefs. In one of the villages studied, the then village chief had told the people to wait while the decision was being made on how to distribute the 25 hectares to 105 families within this village. While they were waiting, villagers used the land in question as common land for grazing cows.

At some point during the course of the next fifteen years, perhaps as land prices started to rise in the early 2000s, the local leadership group made a secret plan to share the land amongst themselves. The village chief mentioned above, his successor in this post, the former commune chief (now deputy commune chief), the current commune chief and a few other members of the village and commune councils were in on the deal. In the end, a total of eight families received around three hectares of land each.

The rest of the village found out about the deal only in the early 2000s, as members of the eight families began to enclose the land. 86 families got together and brought the case to the district and provincial levels.

However, the higher authorities were not helpful. As indicated above, the commune chief elected in 2002 won his position through high level connections. Those same high level party connections supported him against his constituents during the land dispute. The district and provincial authorities told the 86 families that they did not have the political power to act against the village and commune authorities and they told the villagers to drop the case.

Two years passed. As a last resort, the villagers decided to call on two high-ranking CPP politicians in Phnom Penh, connected by blood to some of the villagers. Following the intervention of these powerful individuals, the district CPP office asked the commune authorities to deal with the issue. As a result, in 2007, 6.5 of the 25 disputed hectares were given back to the 86 households, while each of the eight families originally in on the deal retained between 1.5 and two hectares each. What made the deal a particularly poor one for the 86 families was that the 6.5 hectares they were given were scattered in different places and situated furthest from the village and the road. People could not make much use of this land, so they decided to sell it and share the proceeds; so far they have been unable to find a buyer. At the time of our study, the villagers were still disappointed and frustrated with the "resolution" of the case, but had no prospect of taking it further.

As in Commune A, there was clear disillusionment with local leaders in the village. One respondent to our survey commented, "The villagers these days are helpless; it is hopeless to talk abut the commune. They do not take care of the people; how can they act as our parents (*mae ov*)?"[25]

As noted above, the commune council included one figure who had been a leading representative of the poor in a previous land case in the same commune. This individual was a wealthy local farmer, who, prior to his election to the council in 2002, had represented villagers successfully in negotiations

---

[25] B8, response to survey, Commune B, 4 June 2008.

over water sharing and in a different land dispute. This individual's leadership was not available to the 86 families in the current land case however: villagers reported that following his election to the commune council, although this individual was quite active in commune affairs, he found it difficult to do anything concrete with respect to the money politics preoccupying his fellow councillors. The advent of elected commune councils thus appears to have reduced the ability of villagers to find leaders to represent them, in this case, rather than increasing it.

In this commune, networks of alliances within the ruling party at commune, district and provincial level eclipsed the sphere of local politics, undermining the democratizing goals of decentralization. As one villager commented, "We feel we are shut down in the dark. They [the commune chief and his group] closed down every door. We feel hopeless."[26] Villagers have little possibility of challenging existing structures of power and money politics in the area.

Commune C: A Settled Commune with a Powerful Patron

Commune C is a rice-growing village in Cambodia's central plains. It is situated in an area where there have been no sudden economic changes and where land ownership is relatively less disputed since the commune has been settled for a long time and ownership rights are clearly established. The area has a fairly stable population, with little inward migration. This has led to even greater stability within the leadership group than in the other cases. Not only have most of the leaders of Commune C been leaders since the early 1980s, but they are also related to one another by blood or marriage. Of the three communes, this is the commune where elders and spiritual leaders such as *achar* have the most influence on the secular sphere of decision-making and resource mobilization, to evidently positive effect:

> In this commune, you know, we listen to *chas tum* very much. For example when Ta Art and his team raised the idea of paving the local paths, we all participated. They are good role models: even though they are old they joined in the work, they didn't just talk about it. Their family members joined in too. So in this commune, we can get things done quickly and effectively.[27]

A particular factor in this commune was the dominance of a CPP patron with very close links to the commune. This patron is a national minister with a major

[26] B4, response to survey, Commune B, 27 May 2008.
[27] C4, response to survey, Commune C, 8 April 2008.

portfolio. In line with the CPP's strategy of assigning provinces and districts to particular ministers, this individual is in charge of the province and district of which Commune C is a part; but he appears to maintain a particular interest in the commune itself. The patron keeps very close contact with the villagers and often visits the area during his free time and at weekends. The large quantities of assistance he provides to the commune causes villagers to view both him and the local authorities very positively. This commune has the same constrained state budget as other commune councils. However, the extra funding from the national patron means councillors are motivated to spend time on development planning:

> I visit villagers every day and collect their needs that I then refer to His Excellency [the patron] for help. He comes and helps us on many development projects in the commune from road, to dam to providing fingerlings [baby fish]. It has been easy for the councils to access him because we know him. One of my sons works for his ministry in Phnom Penh too.[28]

Villagers refer to the national patron as their own patron and they are proud of their ability to seek his help when necessary. The abundance of support provided by this patron has apparently had a very powerful legitimizing effect on the local authorities. One of the village chiefs in this commune is widely referred to as "*Ov*". His status is such that market sellers decline to take payment from him when he shops in the market and villagers often visit his home with gifts of fruit, as a mark of respect. However, another village chief in this commune was widely derided as a drunk, suggesting this legitimacy is not unconditional with respect to personal good character.

At the same time, the commune council finds its own powers constricted by the presence of the patron. We were told that the local authorities were under strict instructions from the national patron not to displease the people and to ensure sound security in the commune. The patron monitors the performance of the local authorities closely:

> Here, we have to listen to and please the people; we are told [by our party patron] to do so[29].

> When villagers refuse to contribute money to local projects, we cannot say anything to them; otherwise, our patron wouldn't be happy. But he also mentioned that we can always request from him the amount of money we couldn't collect from villagers.[30]

---

[28] Ming Yet, Village Gender Focal Person, response to interview, Commune C, 10 April 2008.
[29] Ta Deng, Village Chief, Commune C, response to interview, 10 April 2008.
[30] Ming Yet, Village Focal Person, Commune C, response to interview, 10 April 2008.

The presence of this patron also outshone the potential contributions from local *thavker*. The commune is home to a gasoline seller who is well connected at higher political levels and contributes some money to local development projects. This individual was not in a sufficiently powerful position to dominate the commune authorities, as *Oknha* Krouch does in Commune A, although he may have influence with them and contributes or not to commune development as he wishes. The influence of this *thavkae* was put into the shade by the influence of the national patron, survey and interview responses indicated. Respondents were also strongly aware of the political source of this support. One elder from this commune commented:

> I approached all *neakthum* [big men],[31] not just those from CPP or SRP or Kem Sokha[32] for resource support for my commune. But the only one who can respond and help has been the CPP.[33]

This commune exemplifies the positive features of mass patronage. Here, the party makes available an abundance of resources, making up for the weaknesses in state funding. Public-spirited local authorities with high levels of legitimacy and strong local networks consult on how to spend the money and the result is a feeling of community pride and ownership. However, such examples cannot be taken in isolation. A key issue to take into account is that the patron of Commune C works for a ministry that makes money from Commune A. The two cases are not separate but inextricably linked.

Conclusion

Comparison of the three communes illustrates different aspects of contemporary Cambodian politics. Commune A illustrates the powerlessness of local leaders and local electorates in an area that is being transformed from subsistence farming and forest harvesting to industrial agriculture. Commune B illustrates a different problem: the lure of money politics for local leaders for whom the electoral mandate represents a tenuous resource and for whom political backing is strong. Commune leaders in this commune were in a position to control natural resources; but they did so in their own interests and were able to do so because of their ability to disregard any serious concerns over party discipline or electoral competition.

---

[31] *Neakthum* refers to wealthy or powerful individuals.
[32] Kem Sokha launched the Human Rights Party in 2007; it is now the fourth most important party in Cambodia.
[33] Elder, C1, Commune C, response to interview, 11 April 2008.

Commune C represents the positive face of contemporary Cambodia. In this commune, villagers had, in one of their chiefs at least, the idealized benevolent patriarch. Yet this idyllic relationship was made possible by two contingent circumstances: first, the relatively settled and uncontested nature of land and resource holdings in the village; and second, the presence of an external patron who was able to give them more or less whatever they needed to fulfil their development plans. Abundance of resources and a clear sense of who owned what prevented the emergence of conflicts and allowed the elders and one of the village chiefs to perform their duties in a serenely traditional manner, while the commune authorities enjoyed high levels of support.

Yet the patronage available to Commune C is in large part the profits of the economic transformation affecting A and B, in a system of national patronage operated by the party. Similar patronage is available in Commune A, if not Commune B; but these villagers are faced with the upheavals and dispossessions associated with economic transformation and this considerably reduces the perception of beneficent rule. The question raised is whether such patronage is sufficient, first, to protect the poor from the ravages transformation presents to their livelihoods; and second, to create new opportunities for the poor to assert political demands. The answer to the first of these questions is more likely to be positive than the latter. While patronage has indeed provided infrastructure and welfare in a manner which benefits the poor across Cambodia, it also renders them dependent and constrained. They are powerless in the face of business–politics alliances and participate in development only when invited. The emergence of independent leaders is prevented by strategies of co-optation and enforced dependence upon the good will of national level patrons.

Thus one of the key problems of decentralization is highlighted: while transformation is organized at a national level – indeed, comprises, in Polanyi's thesis, the forging of national markets for labour, money and land – decentralization pushes political participation down to the local level. At this level the best policy outcome is mitigation of the worst effects, rather than the exertion of any real kind of control. Decentralization in this context represents a strategy of disempowerment rather than empowerment. It appears to be a mechanism for preventing the poor from raising their sights beyond a strictly local horizon, at a time when the rich are doing precisely that, in the interests of transformation.

13

ACCOUNTABILITY AND LOCAL POLITICS IN NATURAL RESOURCE MANAGEMENT

Kim Sedara and Joakim Öjendal

IN ITS POST-CONFLICT PHASE, THE depth of Cambodia's democratization has been seriously questioned.[1] Admittedly, Cambodia has only recently taken anything like substantial steps towards in-depth democratization.[2] The move towards democratic decentralization, however, marked by the first local elections in 2002 and established in the second local elections of 2007, set Cambodia on a novel reform path with the aim of substantially deepening democracy. The core principle of this attempt at deepened democracy is the encouragement of a culture of participation and trust between the local state and civil society, which can build local government accountability and enhance local government capacity, as a prerequisite for realizing its democratic potential.

While it is a crucial dimension to democratic development, there is still a lack of in-depth studies on the re-vitalization of the civil society in Cambodia and in particular the nature of community-based organizations and their relations with local authorities.[3] As most would agree, historically, local civil society has

---

[1] Steve Heder, "Hun Sen's Consolidation: Death or Beginning of Reform?", in Daljit Singh (ed.), *Southeast Asian Affairs 2005* (Singapore: ISEAS, 2005), 113–130; Duncan McCargo, "Cambodia getting away with Authoritarianism," *Journal of Democracy* 16.4 (2005): 98–112.

[2] Joakim Öjendal and Kim Sedara, "Decentralization as a Strategy for State Reconstruction in Cambodia," in Öjendal and Mona Lilja (eds.), *Beyond Democracy in Cambodia: Political Reconstruction in a Post-Conflict Society* (Copenhagen: NIAS Press, 2009), 101–135.

[3] David Ayres, *NGOs, Partnership and Local Governance in Cambodia*, discussion paper, Mimeo, Phnom Penh, 2004; Kim Sedara and Ann Sovatha, "Decentralization: Can Civil Society Enhance Local Government's Accountability in Cambodia?," *Cambodia Development Review*, 9. 3 (2005), 1; Caroline Rusten, Kim Sedara, Eng Netra and Pak Kimchoeun, *The Challenges of Decentralisation Design in Cambodia* (Phnom Penh: Cambodia Development Resource Institute, 2004); Kim Sedara, "Local Government Responsiveness: Can Building Civil Society Enhance Accountability in Cambodia's Political Context?", paper presented to

been thoroughly suppressed under whatever state authority has happened to be in power.[4] A change to this pattern would represent a thorough transformation of rural political life, with far-reaching consequences for local livelihoods. Whether this currently is taking place is to a large extent an empirical question. Hence, *To what extent can civil society through CBOs hold local authorities accountable?* is a worthwhile question for study and the focus of this chapter.

In a democratic decentralized system, decisions are supposed to be made openly, rather than in the (semi-) private domain of personalized patron–client relationships; traditional decision-making processes are – with "modernization" and "liberalization" – expected gradually to vanish and be replaced by more liberal democratic practices. While this may be an idealized conception, distanced from Cambodian realities, it is nevertheless pertinent to seek an understanding of how changing modes of decision-making affect the content of political culture.[5] Hitherto, most of the literature on the topic in Cambodia has emphasized the incompatibilities between these different modes of governance.[6] Our point of departure, however, is that as local institutions are altered, local decision-making processes also change, potentially leading to deep transformation in the structure of local governance.[7] These changes may enhance accountability and hold the promise of increased local empowerment, as has been cautiously indicated in early studies of the reform.[8]

Given the vast historical gap – the distance between people and formal authorities – between ruler and ruled in Cambodia,[9] Community-Based Organizations (CBOs) will have a crucial role to play in being *intermediaries* in the "dialogue" between people and authorities now emerging in rural Cambodia. It

conference on *Civil Society in Southeast Asia: Scope and Concepts*, Phnom Penh: Cambodia, 2004; Kim Sean Somatra and Chea Chou, *The Local Governance of Common Pool Resources: The Case of Irrigation Water in Cambodia*, Working Paper 42, (Phnom Penh: Cambodia Development Resource Institute, 2009).

[4] Serge Thion, *Watching Cambodia* (Bangkok: White Lotus, 1993); Michael Vickery, *Kampuchea: Economics, Politics and Society* (London: Pinter/Rienner, 1986); David Chandler, *The Tragedy of Cambodian History: Politics, War and Revolution since 1945* (New Haven: Yale University Press, 1991); Ian Mabbett and David Chandler, *The Khmers* (Cambridge: Blackwell, 1995).

[5] Caroline Hughes and Joakim Öjendal, "Introduction: Reassessing Tradition in Times of Political Change," *Journal of Southeast Asian Studies*, 37.3 (2006): 415–420; Öjendal and Lilja, 2009, op. cit.

[6] David Roberts, *Political Transition in Cambodia 1991–99: Power, Elitism and Democracy* (Richmond: Curzon, 2000); Pierre Lizee, *Peace, Power and Resistance in Cambodia: Global Governance and the Failure of International Conflict Resolution* (London: Macmillan, 2001).

[7] Ann Sovatha, *Patron-Clientism and Decentralization: An Emerging Local Political Culture in Rural Cambodia*, MA Thesis, Northern Illinois University, 2008.

[8] Joakim Öjendal and Kim Sedara, "Decentralization as a Strategy for State Reconstruction in Cambodia", in Öjendal and Lilja, 2009, 101–135.

[9] Mabbett and Chandler, 1995, op. cit.

has already been reported that since the commune councils were established in 2002 they have taken on issues such as forestry communities and community fisheries, which are also the focus of this study.[10] The journey towards good governance, including the exercise of political accountability, may, however, be difficult for the commune councils to travel and the fate of the process to a large extent depends on the quality of collaboration with a civil society that could facilitate for the commune councils to actually represent local concerns.

Hence, the crucial research problem addressed in this chapter is: *To what extent do CBOs enhance local government accountability?* To answer this question we need to link three critical issues associated with the concept of accountability, namely the degree of popular participation, mobilization and support for CBOs; partnership and interaction between CBOs and commune councils; and the power of commune councils in the political system. Empirical analysis of these consecutive links will enable a discussion of whether accountability is emerging as a feature of local politics in rural Cambodia.

Operationalizing Accountability in Cambodia

Decentralization reform has brought political decision-making to rural areas, where the great majority of Cambodians live. Downward accountability for local authorities (i.e. commune councils) has been explicitly emphasized in Cambodia's reform process and was pursued in order to strengthen – some would say compensate for the lack of – overall democratization.[11] A functional democracy depends on the degree of public consent for such a system. In Krishna's words, "consent derives . . . from locally shared notions of legitimacy and appropriateness. So institutions will need to be designed that are both technically proficient and locally legitimate."[12] This is a crucial process which eventually may determine the success or failure of decentralization. Hence, in pursuing a political system with broad legitimacy, accountability[13] is central and some crucial questions emerge. What does it mean to be accountable? Who is accountable

---

[10] Kim Sedara, 2004, op. cit.
[11] Prum Sokha, "Decentralisation and Poverty Reduction in Cambodia," *Regional Development Dialogue*, 26.2 (2005): 114–120.
[12] Anirudh Krishna, "Partnerships Between Local Governments and Community-Based Organisations: Exploring the Scope for Synergy," *Public Administration and Development*, 23 (2003): 361.
[13] Whereas "accountability" is a difficult term in Khmer, it seems so obvious in the English terminology that – although of central importance in the analysis – it is often not defined, explained or even discussed in many studies, for example, *Cambodia at the Crossroads* (Phnom Penh: World Bank, 2004). In Khmer, the term accountability is translated as *kanak neiyapheap,* for example in Royal Government of Cambodia, *Strategic Framework*

to whom? What does accountability entail? How can it be measured? How is it demanded? How can it be acknowledged?[14]

"Accountability" has particularly come to the fore in the debate on the efficiency of decentralization as the conduit for enhanced democratization.[15] In the literature, accountability is generally taken to mean an obligation to answer for actions according to a particular framework such as a constitution or a contract, or, as Moncrieff simply puts it "answering for the use of authority".[16] Having said that, it should be pointed out that it is not normally the case that local authorities are not accountable – they do often answer to various actors such as superior state levels or local elites – but rather the issue here is to what extent they are accountable to the *demos* in order to deepen democracy. This puts a critical focus on what has been called the "demand side" of local governance: By whom and in what way is accountability demanded? Or for whom is accountability in reality demandable?[17]

For citizens in rural Cambodia to experience accountability from their commune councils, realistically a three-phase process needs to unfold. *First*, there must be a relation between the *demos* and its local organizational forms (i.e. CBOs) acting as intermediaries. Are these CBOs widely supported and do they have popular legitimacy for their cause? Are they well organized and efficient? This is the first critical link that was empirically investigated in the cases in this study. *Second*, there needs to be a relation between the organizations in

for Decentralisation and Deconcentration Reforms (Phnom Penh: RGC, 2005). This term is related to responsibility, transparency and honesty.

[14] See Horng Vuthy, Pak Kimchoeun, Eng Netra, Ann Sovatha, Kim Sedara, Jenny Knowles and David Craig, "Conceptualising Accountability: The Cambodian Case," *Annual Development Review* (Phnom Penh: CDRI, 2006), 171–198.

[15] James Manor, *The Political Economy of Democratic Decentralization* (Washington DC: World Bank,1999); Richard Crook and James Manor, *Democracy and Decentralisation in South Asia and West Africa: Participation, Accountability and Performance* (Cambridge: Cambridge University Press,1998); Richard Crook and A. Sverrison, *Decentralisation and Poverty Alleviation in Developing Countries: A Comparative Analysis in West Bengal Unique?*, Working Paper, No. 129 (Brighton: University of Sussex Institute of Development Studies, 2001); Nick Devas and Ursula Grant, "Local Government Decision-making – Citizen Participation and Local Accountability: Some Evidence from Kenya and Uganda," *Public Administration and Development*, 23 (2003): 307–316.

[16] Joy Moncrieff, "Accountability: Idea, Ideals, Constraints", *Democratisation*, 8.3 (2001): 26–50. Schmitter and Karl define political accountability as: ". . . a relationship between two sets of persons or (more often) organisations in which the former agree to keep the latter informed, to offer them explanations for decisions made and to submit to any predetermined sanctions that they may impose", Philippe C. Schmitter and Terry Lynn Karl (1991), "What democracy is . . . and is not," *Journal of Democracy*, 2.3 (1991): 75–88. See also, Schmitter, "Quality of Democracy – The Ambiguous Virtues of Accountability," *Journal of Democracy*, Vol 15. 4 (2004): 47–60.

[17] Jennifer, M. Coston, "Administrative Avenues to Democratic Governance: the Balance of Supply and Demand", *Public Administration and Development*," 18 (1998): 479–493.

question and the local authorities. Are CBOs interacting effectively with local authorities (i.e. commune councils)? Are they in this way enhancing political accountability? This is the second critical link for demanding accountability that was investigated in the empirical reviews. *Finally*, for local accountability to be meaningful, the authority offering accountability must be in possession of some knowledge and power through its position and role in the state system. If not, seeking accountability turns into a charade and local governance turns into hollow rhetoric.[18]

What kind of accountability, then, are we expecting to find? We take a broad, political view of accountability, whereby councils are required to answer for more than just actions taken in relation to project implementation or their narrow mandate, but rather are expected to explain why things are how they are and how local government will respond. This also corresponds to villagers' broad expectations of local government and to the broad mandate awarded commune councils by the central government, which includes supporting national policies, securing law and order, resolving local conflicts, supporting community well-being and protecting the local resource base.[19] In addition, in Article 42 of Commune/Sangkat law, they are required to defend the interests of their citizens vis-à-vis superior state agencies. So, while many particular issues are not the commune councils' task, they are still their concern. For instance, without a specific mandate, various commune councils immediately came to play an intense, controversial, crucial and sometimes successful role in relation to various fishery conflicts, displaying the pent-up need for accountable local authorities.[20]

Research Design and Research Methods – CBOs as an Empirical Focus

With the spread of liberal political sentiments and, in particular, emerging in the aftermath of the first commune elections, local NGOs or what we prefer to call CBOs have sprung up in great numbers.[21] Often without a very solid

---

[18] James Manor, 1999, op. cit.
[19] Cristina Mansfield and Curt MacLeod, *Commune Council and Civil Society: Promoting Decentralization Through Partnerships* (Phnom Penh: PACT, 2004).
[20] Ibid., 41–44
[21] CBO is not necessarily a well-defined term. The definition of a CBO is here taken as an organization arising from the local community, responding to functional needs and being primarily run by local representatives. It has at least a minimal organizational structure and rudimentary ideas of membership. It may have connections to the state machinery and may be financed externally.

institutional framework, always without major funds, but rooted in the local society and sometimes with a legal standing, they are turning into key features in the localization of politics. Although they tend to materialize from particular functional needs, some have a recognizable political face too. By now, it may be generally accepted that organizational density has increased considerably in rural Cambodia.[22] While the presence of such organizations should not be exaggerated, recent research indicates that they are growing in number and scope, further validating the hypothesis that CBO activities are relevant for local politics.[23] Some are, however, more mature and more significant than others and we have chosen to focus on these.

This study limits its scope to two specific types of CBOs, namely forestry communities and community fisheries. These groups are legitimized through national regulatory frameworks by decrees emanating from the relevant ministry, which establish the connection between civil society and the state in these issue areas. Furthermore, they are typically initiated and run by and in, the local community, although there may be more or less covert state or NGO influence. They also share the quality that they aim to protect local livelihoods. As such, they should be able to rely on popular support and enjoy responsiveness from local authorities. Although these types of CBOs are not representative of the entire spectrum of civil society, they may be among those most able to enhance a commune council's accountability. Through purposive sampling, representing various political, geographical and livelihood situations, four different sites were chosen for this fieldwork.[24]

The study employs a qualitative approach based on focus group discussions and in-depth individual interviews. In each of the communes, the focus group discussions were carried out with representatives from the organizations, its members, heads of associations, village chiefs and villagers of both sexes. In total, four focus group discussions were held in each commune. A large part of the empirical input emanates from these. Separate individual interviews were held with commune councillors, heads of the CBOs, heads of the relevant district offices and district governors. Certain leaders of relevant provincial departments were also interviewed. Previous studies have been conducted in

---

[22] Wat or Pagoda Committees, School Support Committees (SSC), Funeral Committees, Midwife Associations (also known as Health Associations), Help the Aged Associations, Water User Associations, Dry Season Rice Cultivation Associations, Saving Associations, Community Fisheries, Forest Communities are among the CBOs we came across.
[23] Joakim Öjendal and Kim Sedara, "Korob, Kaud, Klach: In Search of Agency in Rural Cambodia", *Journal of Southeast Asian Studies*, 37.3 (2006): 507–526.
[24] They were located in the provinces of Battambang, Kampot, Siem Reap, Kratie. Fieldwork was carried out during two months in the summer of 2004 and updated, completed and cross-checked during 2008/9 and 2010.

several of these communes, which supplied us with a considerable amount of background information complementing the findings from this fieldwork. Our empirical investigation focuses on the three different phases of accountability indicated earlier, namely, linking the *demos* to CBOs, CBOs to commune councils and commune councils to the wider political system, which also defines the structure of the presentation of the findings.

The chapter concludes with an analysis of our question in focus and with a discussion about to what extent this process constitutes a part of a "transformation". First, however, a brief review of the chosen CBOs' mandates and activities is offered.

Forestry and Fishery Communities – Mandates and Activities

Although forest management is explicitly excluded from commune council jurisdiction, the role of the commune council in this issue is still crucial for its popular legitimacy. Formally, the Ministry of Agriculture, Forestry and Fisheries (MAFF) is responsible, although it delegates its powers to its provincial departments.[25] According to the government sub-decree on community forestry management, forests are "state and public property and the forestry administration has the right to give official recognition of each community forest boundary".[26, 27] The main objective of this sub-decree is to support the implementation of the forestry law and other legislation regarding local community management of forest resources; to support the government's policies of poverty alleviation and decentralization; to provide an effective means for a forestry community to participate in reforestation, rehabilitation and conservation of natural resources, forests and wildlife; and to enable citizens to understand and recognize the benefits and importance of forest resources through direct

---

[25] Commune councils, according to Article 44 of the Law on the Administration and Management of Communes-Sangkats, have no explicit authority over forest resources but, according to Article 43 of the same law, they have a general responsibility to promote social and economic development, protect and conserve the environment and natural resources and conduct general affairs to meet the needs of the citizens.

[26] Royal Government of Cambodia, *Sub-decree no. 79 of Royal Government of Cambodia on Community Forestry Management*, (RGC: Phnom Penh, 2003).

[27] A study by McKenney et al. notices that numerous names have been used to refer to forestry communities, including "participatory forestry", "co-management forestry" and "social forestry". The general rationale for the forestry community is "to allow villages located in and around forests to participate in forest management and establish a form of partnership or agreement with the government" (ibid: 48). Bruce McKenney, Chea Yim, Phom Tola and Tom Evans, *Focusing on Cambodia's High Value Forests: Livelihoods and Management*, Special Report (Phnom Penh: Cambodia Development Resource Institute, 2004).

involvement in their management and protection.[28] As described in the administrative proclamation on their role and responsibilities, forestry communities have a formal duty to disseminate information on forest protection to villagers; occasionally mobilize labour for reforestation; report illegal logging to relevant authorities; and liaise between different NGOs, state agencies and villagers.

Fishing communities have been encouraged by the government since 2001, when 52 per cent of the private fishing lots was released to local communities. The sub-decree on community fisheries states that community fisheries should be created with the technical and administrative support of the MAFF, as well as emanating from local initiative.[29] In the new framework, the right to form community fisheries as well as the local authorities' role to support and oversee these communities are clearly outlined in the new "Law on Fishery 2007, Chapter 11, article 59–63 on the Community Fisheries". The primary duties of the community fishery are to:

- Safeguard natural resources and the environment;
- Be a watchdog to curb illegal fishing and provide information to relevant authorities;
- Liaise with the fishery department and commune council;
- Educate and disseminate information in order to prevent degradation of natural resources;
- Cooperate with local authorities to counter illegal fishing.

Formally, however there is a longer list of community fishery responsibilities in the sub-decree.[30] Hence, "forest communities" and "community fisheries" are not only serving a similar functional need, but are also operating in a similar context and with similar mandates.

In addition, the law states that the district forestry administration shall assess and analyse the requirements and problems faced by the local communities in order to ensure that the forestry communities are established as requested with the involvement of local authorities. Thus, although driven by local engagement, the functioning of a forestry community is ultimately the responsibility of the local government, including the district technical offices with decision-making responsibility. For fisheries a similar situation applies. Article 41 of 2003 Sub-Decree no. 3 on Community Fishery stipulates that commune/sangkat, district/khan and provincial/municipal authorities are obliged to:

---

[28] RGC, 2003, op. cit.
[29] Royal Government of Cambodia, *Sub-Decree no. 80 of Royal Government of Cambodia on Community Fisheries Management* (RGC: Phnom Penh, 2005)
[30] Ibid.

- facilitate and support the establishment and management of community fisheries,
- cooperate in combating fishery crimes when there is a request from a community fishery with participation from the fishery authority,
- help disseminate government policy in the fishery sector,
- encourage community fisheries to implement their statutes, internal regulations and management plans.

The leaders of the CBOs are elected at the commune level. Usually, there are five to ten active members working closely in order to coordinate the concerned villages. Each village has four or five representatives to the CBO, but ultimately most households are considered members of the communities. Even though village chiefs and commune councillors do not necessarily serve as leading members, they seem always to be active within the CBOs. Once the committee members are elected, they select deputies, a treasurer and a secretary. Usually, the chief and the deputies are invited for management and technical training, which is typically offered by international agencies.[31]

In spite of the formal state connection, it is a fact that the communities are local initiative groups. However, all communities in this field study were formed or established by/with the assistance of international NGOs, with meagre collaboration from technical line departments, such as the Provincial Forestry Administration, *Sangkat* Fisheries, or Department of Environment. Moreover, they largely obtain their technical and management support from international NGOs. Many community leaders interviewed had been individually trained by NGOs on technical and management issues.

Participation and Mobilization for CBOs: Are People Engaging and Supporting Them?

Because of the massive flow of information from NGOs and broadcast media, villagers tend to be aware of the degradation of the environment and threatening depletion of natural resources and, most importantly, because they themselves are suffering from the mismanagement of these resources. This is at bottom what motivates people to volunteer for the forestry and fishery communities, as they see that their resources are in real danger, jeopardizing rural livelihoods.

It appears it is not initially difficult to mobilize people to participate in local communities because they are very keen to safeguard the common resources. The level of participation however tends to depend on the performance and

---

[31] In this case FAO and Danida.

effectiveness of the organization in question. Poor performance and a lack of real power cause frequent disappointment among its members. One typical perception of the idea of efficiency of the CBOs is that they are viewed as symbolic rather than effective. A group of villagers in Kratie revealed:

> The role and responsibility of the forestry community are not clear. This forestry community was just created as a symbol to represent the villagers because it does not have power to stop criminals. If they see crimes, they just report to the district or provincial forest authority, eventually reporting to the commune council, but nothing happens.[32]

At the slightest setback the process enters into a vicious cycle in which support and efficiency, after an optimistic start-up, soon begin to spiral downwards. People do not normally drop their membership, but their participation fades and they hope someone else will do the job.

The communities face limitations also in part because people view them as dealing with common property that ought to be dealt with by the state. Moreover, their participation does not necessarily give them personal benefits, at least in the short run. It may, on the contrary, be dangerous, so mostly only the chief and the deputy of the CBOs are active. The majority do not see, do not understand, or cannot afford to benefit from the significance of being active and the difference it can make in the long run. Or possibly they weigh the pros and cons of spending their time with the community and conclude that they are individually better off spending time in their own fields.[33] Typically, only the chief and the deputies remain committed and hard working. According to a chief of a community fishery:

> It is not difficult in the beginning to mobilize people to participate in the community fishery or the forestry community because they know the risk of declining natural resources and the harm to their livelihoods. But people's expectations of the community fishery are too high. ... After a time, many members stop being active and do not want to hear anything from us. They might offer only moral support and most of them are very individualistic ... This causes the community fishery and the people not to understand one another very well.[34]

---

[32] A group of villagers in Kratie, 25 October 2004.
[33] Historically, failed attempts at collectivization and large-scale violence may have resulted in a tendency for the individual household in rural Cambodia to opt for individual decisions, Jan Ovesen, Joakim Öjendal and Ing-Britt Trankell, *When Every Household is An Island - Social Organizations and Power Structures in Rural Cambodia* (Uppsala: Socialantropologiska institutionen, 1996). Typically peasants then, lacking an overwhelming sense of solidarity, tend to make individual rational decisions, cf. Samuel Popkin, *The Rational Peasant: The Political Economy of Rural Society in Vietnam* (Berkeley: University of California Press, 1979).
[34] Community fishery chief, Kampot province, 19 October 2004.

The perceptions above are similar across the four communes we researched. People seem to have high expectations at the beginning, motivating them to participate in the CBOs, but after a period they lose motivation and commitment, typically referring to the leaders as "show offs" (*mean tae sambak*), when bowing to more powerful actors.[35]

Although somewhat discouraging, the above remark should not be taken as an across-the-board rejection of the CBOs in question. Others working with community fisheries reveal a conviction that the quality of their work really matters. Once the people understand the long-term goal of community work they will, it is hoped, participate. The chief of a community fishery in Battambang province said:

> As community fishery chief and committee members, we must be role models for the villagers. Transparency and commitment are vital. People in this commune now see with their own eyes that the community fishery is working hard to curb illegal fishing. We make every effort with NGOs and the authorities to make this work. Last year and this year things have improved a lot. The district and commune are very cooperative and people now even come to me voluntarily to offer their boat and other equipment... The reason is that, since last year, after we became serious about stopping illegal fishing, the fish harvest has increased in our commune.[36]

An additional difficulty for the CBOs seems to be that they themselves experience legitimacy problems. Many of the community members feel that they are affiliated with, or even staff members of, an NGO or a technical department, rather than part of the local community. They become too dependent on either the authorities, who determine the limits of their work, or the external partner that is financing their activity and/or education. They sometimes acknowledged to us that they on occasion prioritize upward over downward accountability.

How do CBOs and Local Authorities Interact?

A consequence of the initiation of democratic decentralization is that popular demands on the state for protection of local natural resources have been pushed downwards, mainly to the commune councils. After the commune elections in 2002, the gap between commune councils and their constituencies was bridged to some extent, allowing villagers to approach the commune councils asking for

---

[35] Members of Forestry Community in Kampot 22 October 2004.
[36] Community fishery chief, Battambang province, 2 December 2004.

different activities. The interactions between commune councillors and CBO members are frequent.[37] As the head of a forestry community put it:

> The relationship between the forestry community and the commune council is good. Each side has the motivation to work together. But the fact is, people do not understand the laws and to what extent the commune council has the power to decide ... whenever we go to the commune council they help us quickly to find a way to solve the problem. As you know, we are all living in the same community ... no problem at all. If problems occur in the commune, they are easy to deal with, but if it needs intervention from the top, please wait and see.[38]

It is also in the interests of the commune councils to have well-functioning communities; the CBOs to some extent "shield" the commune councils from popular discontent when local resources are mismanaged. But although enjoying overall "closer" relations, regular meetings between councils and CBOs are rare. The primary reason for this is claimed by councils to be their overall workload, which was, everybody agrees, overwhelming in the first years after the reform was initiated. However, that is not the full story, or as the head of a community fishery and its members in Battambang stated:

> Commune councils are not curious and never come to learn about the community fishery. They should listen seriously ... community fisheries have to go to commune councils in times of trouble. There is a lack of information sharing from the commune council to community fisheries.[39]

From time to time, councillors run into members of the associations and they always ask about their activities, but only then, the same informant claimed. It is quite rare that CBOs demand to be informed by, or demand the right to pass on information to, the commune councils and even more rare that the councils take the initiative. The prevailing social norm dictates that villagers/CBOs seek assistance and information from the authorities only if they have a really serious problem.

From a functional point of view, in theory, the CBOs complement the council because they engage in activities for which the commune council does not have the full formal mandate. There is a common perception that before CBOs were established, abuse of the commons was a free-for-all, but that after the

---

[37] Recent research indicates that there has been a remarkable difference – i.e. reduction – of the "gap" between people and power-holders at commune level since the first local election in 2002. See Öjendal and Kim 2006, op. cit.; Öjendal and Kim, 2009, op. cit.; Kim Sedara, "Decentralization in Cambodia", PhD Dissertation, Gothenburg University, 2011 (forthcoming).
[38] Forestry Community chief and members, Kampot province, 19 October 2004.
[39] Chief of Community Fishery and members in Battambang province, 2 December 2004.

forestry communities came into existence, to a certain extent abusers cannot operate openly. In this area, according to the villagers, the forestry community has been working well by reducing abuses, hence legitimizing the commune council in the eyes of the villagers:

> If there is anyone cutting down trees or destroying forest products, the community has to arrest those perpetrators first and then educate them. We do not need to report to the commune councils or technical departments. If we wait for their intervention, the perpetrators could run away. Sometimes we need collaboration from the police in the commune as well. This has been working well because [now] we stop crime on time.[40]

Obviously frustrated with local authorities' inability to deal with the situation, members of one forestry community took concrete action by themselves. This is however a risky business without the blessing of the formal authorities.

Hence, there are also tensions between communities, councils and villagers. For instance, a group of villagers and members of the forestry community in Kratie said,

> When people see forest crimes, we ask ourselves, what is the role and responsibility of the commune council? After many times informing the commune council and realizing that the commune council cannot do anything, it creates a lot of disappointment and mistrust of commune councils and related authorities.[41]

A key source of frustration is thus the fact that when the communities fulfil their task and report to the proper authorities, perpetrators are still not caught and punished. Moreover, many people in the forestry communities recount that they have arrested perpetrators on several occasions and tried to get support from the district or provincial forestry administration for their action, without success, forcing the forestry communities to let the perpetrators go. As a result, most engaged people lose the motivation to continue to work with the forestry communities.

Even worse, sometimes the forestry communities become a scapegoat and perpetrators seek revenge on forestry community members. The decline in motivation among forestry community members was observed in Kratie, where they said:

> Our forestry community has no power to do anything. If we see crimes, we must report to the technical authorities, mainly the forestry administration.

---

[40] A Forestry Community in Siem Reap province, 3 November 2004.
[41] Villagers and Forestry Community members, Kratie, 25 October 2004.

> They do not come as we suggest. If they come, they only take money from the perpetrators and go back, doing nothing. This corruption issue exists within the relevant authorities.[42]

Or as the chief of a community fishery pointed out:

> It seems that decentralization today is just decentralized work, but not devolving power to the commune to do anything. For example, the most prevalent problem in the commune is fishery crimes that the commune is unable to control or prevent. The fishery community is created just on paper, but they can't control or intervene against fishery crimes.

In spite of this critical statement, he also and typically, appreciates that conditions are better now:

> However, the commune now communicates better, so people now are more informed via participation and interaction with commune councils, for example through local contributions and commune development plans. The commune is elected to be accountable to the people, but if the commune council cannot help people when abuses occur, it makes people lose trust in them.[43]

Normally, informants reported, the only place they can report growing problems is to the commune council.

As time passes, there are increasing indications that local groups will eventually blame the commune councils for their lack of motivation to assist the community. This has so far occurred in only one commune in our study. As one group of forestry community members articulated:

> The commune council does not really commit for community or villagers ... Whenever people go to them in time of trouble, they always say it is not their responsibility, but the technical departments'. If the commune keeps on thinking this way, it will not be able to respond to people, how can they be accountable? At the end of the day it will make people lose trust in them, since they are only splashing water at one another and no one is held responsible for the ongoing destruction of natural resources.[44]

While the commune councils may try to be accountable, they face a difficult situation too, since it is common that the constituency is placing unreasonable demands on them. Many councillors express their difficulties in simultaneously

---

[42] Forestry Community members in Kratie, 25 October 2004.
[43] Chief of Community Fishery in Kampot province, 20 October 2004.
[44] Forestry Community members, Kampot province, 19 October 2004.

dealing with villagers and line departments. The commune councils claim that villagers do not understand the law and regulatory frameworks and departments do not respond properly. These resentments were expressed by the chief and members of a forestry community:

> The primary ongoing problem of forestry communities can be phrased as a question: can commune councils in collaboration with forestry communities do anything for the sake of this community and be accountable to villagers? We work closely with the commune council informally, but we do not have regular meetings with it. When we run into forest crimes, the only authority we can report to is the commune council. ... We think that to make forestry communities more effective, commune councils need to be given some executive power to intervene.[45]

Hence, rather than CBO–Council problems, it seems most tension is generated by the less-than-perfect relations between commune councils and the upper hierarchies of the bureaucracy. These views naturally lead us to the third "link" in our investigation.

Do the Local Authorities have Sufficient Political Power to Deliver Accountability?

Natural resources have been under heavy pressure for more than a decade and although some regulations have come into effect, the sector has proved difficult to regulate. Who is to take ultimate political responsibility? Commune councils are now positioned awkwardly between their constituents and higher authorities, being squeezed between the mandate to promote the well-being of residents, which to a large extent depends on access to forests and fisheries, while having no proper mandate in these sectors. It is difficult to act forcefully and at the same time they are in no position to escape from making some kind of response. Thus the most critical issue regarding the work of the CBOs may be the relation between commune councils and other state agencies.

Correct or not, the commune councils are *de facto* held responsible for local wrongdoing. A group of commune councillors explained the situation thus:

> [The commune councillors] are very serious about working for the people. But what can we do? We just report to relevant authorities at the top, i.e. district and relevant departments. Sometimes after a few days we see the same perpetrators come back to commit more crimes. ... The council is

---

[45] Forestry Community members in Kratie, 25 October 2004.

caught between higher authorities and villagers. Obviously, people challenge the commune, not the district or other agencies.[46]

CBOs typically criticize commune councils, as the closest authority and the one with the highest likelihood of acting with accountability. This pattern was found in all four communes in this study. Without full cooperation from all relevant authorities, including the district office, sangkat fishery,[47] commune police and technical ministries, it is impossible for the commune council and CBOs to intervene effectively. If the community fishery and local authorities wait for fishery department staff to come to the area, perpetrators might escape. A commune chief in Battambang reported:

> The Fishery Authority does not delegate power to the Community Fishery to make the arrest when they get the information from villagers... Now everyone has a cell phone, if you wait just five minutes, the perpetrators would be gone. According to the laws, the Community Fishery does not have the rights to arrest and fine on the spot, they need the approval from the Fishery Authority, Commune Councils and district.[48]

He continued:

> The relationship between the Commune Councils and the Fishery Authority is not that good, to be honest. The Fishery Authority always claims that they are the technical agency responsible for everything and blames the Commune Councils and the Community Forestry. As the Commune Council and the Community Forestry we are the ones who suffer from this problem... it's under our jurisdiction and our people are suffering from this problem.[49]

In the absence of more substantial interventions, cooperation and moral support – especially from commune councils and district authorities – are vital to encourage community fisheries to work effectively. A district governor in Battambang explained how moral support has helped the community fishery in his district:

> From the district, we need to give moral support against fishery crimes. The community fishery can confiscate illegal equipment used by perpetrators,

---

[46] Commune councillors, Kampot province, 18 October 2004.
[47] *Sangkat* Fishery is the fishery administration below the provincial department and stationed at the district level – not the sangkat or commune administrative unit.
[48] Commune council chief, Battambang, January/2009.
[49] Commune council chief, Battambang, January/2009.

but does not have the right to destroy it. However, it can keep the confiscated equipment at the commune council office or sangkat fishery and report to relevant agencies.[50]

He elaborated further on what else could be done:

> There are at least three types of intervention for curbing fishery crimes: big intervention, commune intervention and community fishery intervention. The big and commune interventions require cooperation from various authorities, especially the police and the fishery administration.[51]

Inter-agency cooperation is critical for the successful sustainability of the community's work. Moreover, a group of councillors and villagers said:

> The people now are aware that the depletion of natural resources cannot be blamed on the commune alone, but on the departments. This is the reason why the commune and district have given a green light to the community to arrest the criminals and report to the sangkat fishery later.[52]

People then are at times frustrated also with the higher echelons. In one case however effective intervention took place, which is widely believed to be due to the support from the district, including the right for the community fisheries to arrest first and report later. The role of the commune councils in safeguarding fish stocks is to work very closely with community fisheries by allowing community fisheries to arrest first and report to the fishery office later, if they find crimes on the spot. A commune chief in Battambang said:

> The commune has been very active in advocating that more responsibilities be given to community fisheries to intervene against fishing crimes. In the past, community fisheries were not successful in combating crimes because of a lack of cooperation from fishery officer. ... Now the commune has full support from the district in combating fishing crimes. We allow community fisheries to arrest first and report later to fishery officers. This is more effective than before.[53]

Some argue that if this practice were generally accepted by the higher authorities there would be more fish and people would be more capable of reducing poverty on their own. If not, the community fishery will turn into just a symbol with no clout. And not just villagers are frustrated with this:

[50] District Governor, Battambang Province, 30 november 2004.
[51] District governor, Battambang province, 30 November 2004.
[52] Commune councillors and villagers, Kampot, 21 October 2004.
[53] Commune council chief, Battambang, 30 November 2004.

As you know, you need full cooperation from many relevant authorities. This is a complex matter. If you see a crime, you can intervene without cooperation. Please do it right away, since it is in the interests of the people.[54]

The exact limits of this community fishery makeshift mandate are not clear. Any CBO right to arrest is contradicted by the fishery office saying that arresting the perpetrator is their responsibility, not the community's. Normally, cracking down on fishing crimes needs the full cooperation of fishery officials, police, military police and local authorities. A clear commitment from the district and commune is needed to make sure that the community fishery can act on illegal fishing in its jurisdiction.

It might be expected that the district office would shoulder some responsibility for decision-making and the lack of support to the commune councils and forestry communities.[55] A district governor put it this way:

> We stand and watch without making any decisions. Every month, both forestry and fishery offices report directly to provincial departments. Although the report ... is also copied to the district, still the district is not well informed about the situation on the ground since some technical offices bypass local authorities such as the district office and commune councils.[56]

There is a widespread opinion that departments do not execute the work directly by cooperating with elected councilors, but rather just come to inform people about new regulations without giving any clear account of or grounds for making decisions. Ministries are seen to be either too centralized and acting with too much bureaucratic delay, or they are plainly uninterested in local wrongdoing but keen on generating extra-legal incomes. Some claim there are also chains of patronage in which private interests are defended.

In the view of the provincial forestry administrations, there is an unacceptable and confusing lack of local coordination, presenting them with contradictory, unreasonable or even illegal demands:

> Almost all of the forestry communities are established without formal regulations or formal recognition by the government, formed by NGOs with no coordination whatsoever from the forestry administration. We never receive reports from them or NGOs. This is driven by NGOs, we do not know what the process is. Maybe the forestry communities in the commune that you are looking at are just consultative committees, not forestry communities.[57]

---

54 District governor, Battambang, 30 November 2004.
55 For a fuller view of the work and rationale of the district office, see Öjendal and Kim, 2008.
56 District governor, Siem Reap province, 8 November 2004.
57 District forestry administration in Kratie province, 27 October 2004.

According to this view, there is a serious lack of communication and coordination between technical departments and local communities, as well as a lack of political will to assume overall political responsibility in order to improve the situation. There may even be economic interests in maintaining the status quo.

Conclusion

This research initially proposed three related research questions that guided the empirical review. Below, we will present an analysis, before we move to some overarching conclusions and return to the key topic of this chapter and volume.

Participation and Mobilization in CBOs?

A key aspect for achieving accountability in rural Cambodia is the voluntary and broad participation of people in a process in which they are given a voice, which is, as was argued in the Introduction, most efficiently achieved through engagement in CBOs. That is, generating people's participation with CBOs is easier – as compared to individualized engagement with formal authorities – because of the lesser distance between people and the local associations. There is no doubt that participation and engagement in CBOs is much deeper and more "real" than the interaction between individuals and the commune councils. However, the credibility of and popular support for, the CBOs become strictly related to their efficiency in the short-term. But to rapidly and fundamentally alter the situation may be difficult since it challenges major interests, often far beyond the reach of CBOs (irrespective of how well run they are). Moreover, CBOs are torn between loyalty to external NGOs, popular interests and local authorities. Most leaders tend to be more accountable to the NGOs that have helped to set them up than to their local constituents. Paradoxically, many CBOs also suffer from being perceived as a state agency and dealing with issues that should be the state's concerns. In this maze of loyalties and demands, the CBOs try to navigate and at times succeed fairly well.

How do CBOs and Local Authorities Interact?

The partnership remains limited. It is rare for them to meet more frequently than once a month, if at all. Some, but not all, CBOs send regular reports to commune councils. The overarching impression from the interviews, however, is that the commune councils and the CBOs try to get on well with one another and that commune councils do their best to be accountable. Shortcomings typically come from structural factors. These would include the political culture, or social norms as it has been termed at some places in this chapter, hampering easy, direct and institutionalized communication between CBOs and commune councils. Ironically, in contemporary rural Cambodia this legacy may be most tangible with the *demos* rather than with the local authorities; that is, the reformation of the political institutions may be more thorough than the change of mindset with people at large. Moreover, if authority is vague for the commune council, it is not easy to be accountable. Commune councils' weakest spot, we believe, is their lack of capacity to pursue credible, pro-active politics to protect and to be seen as protecting, their constituents.

The Power of Local Authorities in the Political System?

Commune councils have neither substantial financial resources, nor a full formal natural resource management mandate, nor control over the security apparatus, nor sufficient clout in the political hierarchy. Their economic resources consist basically of allocations from the Commune/Sangkat Fund, which give them only a very limited possibility of responding to people's demands. They have the commune police at their disposal, but with a very unclear chain of command. The decentralization and deconcentration reform is so far limping on only one leg, meaning that commune councils are isolated in their openness to accountability. So, when the commune councils try to be accountable, there is very little they can actually contribute. This structural powerlessness of the commune councils may be both the most critical deficiency in the short to medium term. As seen above, some commune councils (and CBOs) try to overcome this gridlock by overstepping their formal mandates. This has an immediate effect on local perceptions of accountability and legitimacy, but it is hardly sustainable and not a long-term solution to the problem. It does however if nothing else show that the pressure the CBOs are putting on the commune councils can work, that the commune councils are receptive to local pressure and that CBOs are to a certain extent capable of channelling public sentiments into a political agenda. Having responded to our key questions, we are now ready to return to the central question of this chapter and of this volume.

Analysing Accountability and Understanding the State of Transformation.

The central query of the chapter was: *To what extent do CBOs enhance local government accountability?* The meaning of accountability was "answering for the use of authority", which is here broken down to: "answering" and "use of authority".

Commune councils – much more than the district and provincial authorities or, in our opinion, any other political body in Cambodia – are trying to "answer", explain and communicate the decisions they make. There are many indications that the commune councils actually try to be accountable, but sometimes are unable to, due either to unclear mandates and lines of responsibility within the state machinery, or to their inability to express themselves in a way that will be understood by ordinary people. While they do not naturally share all information with all concerned parties, they do not really conceal it either. And they are open to receiving requests, reports and informal information. Compared to previous eras, this is a huge change, amounting to a structural transformation of local governance.

The other part of the accountability concept – "use of authority" – is more confusing. The commune councils' weak mandate and lack of financial resources may make it difficult for them to exercise authority. In this respect, they are far from fitting the ideal version of a local government and far from the vision in the decentralization law itself. The lingering suspicion is, however, that in the "trap" in which commune councils have been placed, they frequently choose not to exercise authority because they either are afraid to lose the little authority they have, or themselves simply play into the prevailing social norm of not overstepping their formal mandates.[58] Having said that, it should be remembered that some commune councils are pro-active and act forcefully to satisfy popular demands (e.g., agreeing to CBO demands to arrest perpetrators without a proper mandate). This suggests that the CBOs actually succeed in demanding not only accountability, but also activity.

Hence, commune councils have come a long way towards acknowledging and exercising accountability and the CBOs have played a major role in achieving that. The major weaknesses are to be found above and below the commune council itself. First, people in rural areas are not yet sufficiently confident, capable and organized to effectively demand accountability. Second, commune councils are not getting the support they need from higher levels. This is hardly surprising. While the commune councils since 2002 have operated on the basis of a progressive democratic decentralization reform, the district and provincial authorities are only now experiencing a revision to their mandate.[59] Ideally this would democratize district and provincial authorities,

---

[58] It should be pointed out that resource management is a rough business, often involving violence, top-politicians, vested interests and large amounts of money. For that reason, it is often far beyond the means of a local community/council to deal with the problems that arise.

[59] As of writing this chapter, the "deconcentration reform" is rolling out, with, first, indirect elections to District and Province level having taken place 17 May 2009, to be followed by the conclusion and implementation of a comprehensive road map. Ideally this will transform these levels, making them more unified, operational, internally accountable and, in the end, more responsive to local demands.

harmonize technical offices with commune councils and open up rural areas for a more dynamic development. Whether that will actually happen, however, remains to be seen.

However, there is no doubt that the idea of downward accountability is emerging in rural Cambodia, driven by the decentralization reforms and the process of allowing community-based schemes to emerge. This amounts to a political transformation – downward accountability has never been a dominant feature in (rural) Cambodia – with far-reaching democratic and development consequences. But as with all macro-transformations, it is dynamic, multi-dimensional and unpredictable. In the short to medium term, the most critical enhancement of this transformation would be a rapid and genuine implementation of the deconcentration reform. In the long term, the sense of local empowerment, education and community solidarity would need to be strengthened. So far the commune councils seem to represent the most progressive change and deserve further attention, both in terms of enhanced financial support and a fuller legal mandate.

Authors' Note

The field research for this chapter was supported by Cambodian Development Resources Institute (CDRI). We would like to acknowledge the invaluable contribution and cooperation of the commune councillors and villagers in concerned communes. We gratefully acknowledge the significant input of Ann Sovatha in conducting fieldwork. Robin Biddulph provided very valuable comments on a draft version of the manuscript.

14

NGOs, People's Movements and Natural Resource Management

Roger Henke

THIS ANALYSIS[1] WILL FOCUS ON the concept of "civil society" as a means to understand the problems and opportunities for the poor in the new Cambodian political economy. Like other social science concepts, civil society is a container for many different types of content. For the purposes of this chapter, civil society means the "domain in which people are free to form independent and autonomous associations to mediate with the state and pursue their political goals".[2] Civil society also connotes, drawing on the work of Gramsci, the domain of contestation of ideological hegemony.

The mainstream perspective on Cambodian governance – the "neo-patrimonial" model – insufficiently acknowledges the importance of "ideology" for the organization and legitimation of state practices. But the ideological contests which play out on the terrain of civil society in contemporary Cambodia have been even less analysed. In this chapter, I reflect upon the ways in which the terrain of civil society emerges as a site of social contestation between three sets of forces: the Cambodian elite, via legitimating ideologies rooted in Buddhist *dhamma* (world view) and communist state theory; international donors promoting a "good governance" agenda; and the poor. This reflection is presented by means of discussing recent efforts by international donors to support the emergence of "civil society" actors to perform certain good governance functions in the field of natural resource management in contemporary Cambodia. The story shows how donor requirements regarding civil society as "partners" have resulted in a proliferation of Non-Governmental

---

[1] This article is based on an unpublished report available from the author: Roger Henke, "People's Movements, NGOs, Donors, and the Cambodian State: Reflections from a practitioner's perspective" (Phnom Penh: ICCO, 2009).
[2] Bruce Missingham, *The Assembly of the Poor in Thailand. From Local Struggles to National Protest Movement* (Chiang Mai: Silkworm, 2003), 7.

Organizations (NGOs). The story also shows how the dominance of this NGO-model currently hinders the emergence of a true social movement challenge to state-sanctioned efforts to dispossess the poor from the natural resources on which their livelihoods are based.

Ideological Frames in Contemporary Cambodian Civil Society

Contemporary analyses of the Cambodian state foreground neo-patrimonialism as the most useful model for understanding strategies of state organization and legitimation. With respect to legitimation, the most important ideological frame is that of the *boran*[3] (magical) Buddhist interpretation of the *dhamma*.[4] *Dhamma* has interrelated meanings ranging from ontological reality, animating energy and power, to moral law which sees existence as moral in essence and as being all about balance. Actions in themselves are seen as amoral, but produce inherent "good" or "bad" in their effects on the balance of existence, which implies an acceptance of or tolerance for the "negative" poles of any continuum. There is no high without low, so inequality is natural.

This framing highlights a particular moral–ontological understanding of power: here, power is regarded as expressing fitness to rule, rather than as being dependent upon it. This understanding of power as an expression of legitimacy fuels fierce status competition. As Guthrie describes, the channelling of large amounts of money and resources into rebuilding temples following the war has been a characteristic of recent Cambodian election campaigns. Guthrie argues that in engaging in these activities, politicians are trying to access a type of power known as *parami (bareamey)*, "a Buddhist technical term for 'highest', 'mastery', 'supremacy' or 'perfection'". Guthrie adds that "in contemporary Cambodia, the word *parami* has additional meanings of 'sacred force', 'magical power', or 'energy' . . . [that] can provide real-time benefits . . . *Parami* can provide protection against enemies and help to accomplish certain goals. Access to *parami*, or at least the appearance of having access to *parami*, is a necessary component of political survival in Southeast Asia". Politicians, Guthrie argues,

---

[3] Alexandra Kent, "Compassion and Conflict: remaking the pagoda in rural Cambodia," *Stockholm University Department of the History of Religion Yearbook*. 14, (2005): 131–153.

[4] Roger Henke, "Mistakes and Their Consequences: Why Impunity in Cambodia is Here to Stay", in Edwin Poppe and Maykel Verkuyten (eds) *Culture and Conflict: Liber Amicorum for Louk Hagendoorn* (Amsterdam: Aksant, 2007), 15–42; another observer describing Cambodian Buddhism as overwhelmingly *boran* (including the personal beliefs of its leadership) is Stephen Asma, *The Gods drink Whiskey. Stumbling towards enlightenment in the land of the tattered Buddha* (New York: HarperCollins, 2005).

have varying amounts of this: Sam Rainsy tried to demonstrate his access to this sacred power by spending time as a monk in a monastery. Prince Norodom Ranariddh, First Prime Minister from 1993 to 1997 but now a marginal figures in Cambodian politics, is believed to have squandered the power he had through "corruption and associating with bad people". Hun Sen, on the other hand, "appears to be a *neak mean bon* (a man who has great merit) with access to large amounts of *parami*. His survival amidst Cambodia's turbulent political waters is proof of his parami as is the success of his religious construction projects such as Wat Wiang Chas".[5]

The pursuit of politics and the practice of patronage with this conception of power produce a distrustful and dangerous world characterized by exploitation, deceit, and disproportionate revenge. Cambodian understandings contain both normative rejection of power as exploitation, and a normative acceptance of power as earned. One expression of this is through the mixed messages of generosity and menace that surround gift-giving during election campaigns.[6]

The deployment of reinvented tradition in this manner maintains the legitimacy of inequality of power in Cambodia, but has less to say about the logic of state organization. With respect to the latter, contemporary analysis of Cambodia neglects the importance of the communist character of the contemporary Cambodian state that was built in the 1980s. Bringing this perspective back in enriches the neo-patrimonial approach in explaining the ideological aims of the current government, which is still organized along democratic centralist lines: the explicit and elaborate program of principles for party and state organization underlying communist regimes in Eastern Europe.[7] Relevant elements of this model are one-party rule, no separation of party and state, and no separation of powers. The importance of this alternative model is that it explicitly justifies an authoritarian state, making for a smoother blend of "neo" and "patrimonial" structures and their legitimization than in the mainstream interpretation of what the neo-patrimonial Cambodian state looks like.

In that mainstream understanding the ideological manipulation of tradition by the ruling party is set against the explicit promotion of "good governance" by international actors and local NGOs. However, this latter, non-authoritarian model focuses on the normative question of how government *ought* to be conducted, rather than providing practical guidance on how to more effectively and

---

[5] Elizabeth Guthrie, "Buddhist Temples and Cambodian Politics," in John Vijghen (ed.) *People and the 1998 National Elections in Cambodia. Their Voices, Roles and Impact on Democracy*, Working Paper no. 44 (Phnom Penh: ECR, 2002), 70–71.

[6] Caroline Hughes, "The Politics of Gifts: Tradition and Regimentation in Contemporary Cambodia," *Journal of Southeast Asian Studies*, 37.3 (2006): 469–489.

[7] The party-building history is told by Kristina Chhim, *Die Revolutionare Volkspartei Kampuchea 1979 bis 1989* (Frankfurt: Peter Lang, 2000).

efficiently structure what *is* already there. Therefore, the actual incorporation of good governance ideals has been left to a ruling elite for whom the model of state organization used in the 1980s remains foundational. The result has been an adoption of good governance practices so selective that it makes more sense to assess the donor push for good governance in terms of the opportunities it offers the Cambodian state to strengthen itself, rather than as a real challenge.

What has been the effect of these different ideological frames on Cambodian civil society? Unlike either neo-patrimonial or communist models of governance, both of which strive to co-opt independent organs of civil society quite overtly, "good governance" ideals require a civil society that is organized independently of the state, to play at least two roles:[8] challenging entrenched interests, by demanding the realization of constitutional rights and responsive government; and addressing the needs of particular vulnerable groups and remote communities which government agencies find it "difficult" to access.

The development of civil society since the early 1990s thus reflects two contending forces: the reluctance of government to countenance an independent civil society and the demand by donors that civil society associations should be created who could assist them in their "good governance" programs. Contention over this issue between government and donors, and the difficulties faced by organizations attempting to form on this contested terrain, has resulted in the emergence of organized civil society actors which bear particular characteristics. However, as with understanding the current character of the Cambodian state, understanding civil society development since the introduction of the good governance model requires a look at what was there previously.

Ovesen et al. in a controversial volume published in 1996 posited a historical lack in Cambodia of strong intermediary institutions between households and the state that could operate as loci of collective social responsibility and social sanctions.[9] Critics of their findings have responded by pointing to some apparently indigenous types of collective action, such as committee activity, often associated with the local pagoda, and collective labour exchange and other episodic mutual support arrangements among *bong pa'on* (kin).[10] Because such mutual assistance is all event-focused, organized around short-term

---

[8] World Bank, *Draft Concept Note for a Study of the Civil Society in Cambodia*, internal memorandum, 29 September 2006.
[9] Jan Ovesen, Ing-Britt Trankell and Joakim Öjendal, *When Every Household is an Island: Social Organization and Power Structures in Rural Cambodia*. Uppsala Research Reports in Cultural Anthropology No. 15 (Uppsala: Uppsala University Department of Cultural Anthropology and Swedish International Development Agency, 1996).
[10] See for example, Judy Ledgerwood and John Vijghen, "Decision-Making in Rural Khmer Villages," in Ledgerwood (ed.) *Cambodia Emerges From the Past: Eight Essays* (De Kalb: Northern Illinois University Press, 2002), 109–110.

specific tasks within the immediate local setting, and not based on an enduring formal structure, let alone transcending the boundary of the face-to-face community, this is insufficient to discredit Ovesen, Trankell and Öjendal"s overall characterization.[11] There are no larger kinship or caste groups, and religious affiliation is decentralized with an emphasis on the local pagoda. Villages are administrative entities, rather than "communities" and lack indigenous governance structures. Traditional community-level leadership is normally described as "informal" and "In contrast to some Asian cultures, the Cambodian family is more loosely organized, with less importance given to the extended family".[12] So culturalist perspectives, such as the neo-patrimonial perspective, produce an image of Cambodia as a "loosely" organized society, lacking traditional models for intermediary organizations with enduring governance structures and allegiances beyond the immediate living environment. As this characterization goes, the three decades of civil war, with its accompanying destruction of social life, massive population displacement, and trauma-related breakdown of social trust, has only intensified this "looseness"[13].

As nothing organized enough to implement their agenda existed, it had to be created: which is what donors, international organizations, and international non-governmental organizations (INGOs), have done since the early 1990s. As a consequence, three categories of civil society organizations have emerged: informal membership community-based organizations (CBOs); formal membership organizations, in particular trade unions; and Non-Governmental Organizations (NGOs).

CBOs[14] comprise a great variety of quite different creatures. Indigenous groups with a long-standing pedigree of authenticity are mainly characterized by their event-based character, informal leadership, and independence from either NGOs or government. Pagoda committees, mutual help groups and *tontin* (credit groups) are commonly-cited examples.[15] Population-specific groups (such as women and youth) for purposes such as peer-solidarity and education were organized under state and party auspices in the 1980s. To some extent they have

---

[11] See e.g. the assessment of the literature in Tim Conway, *Poverty, Participation and Programmes: International Aid and Rural Development in Cambodia*, unpublished PhD Thesis (University of Cambridge, 1999).

[12] Bit Seanglim, *The Warrior Heritage. A Psychological Perspective of Cambodian Trauma* (El Cerrito: Bit Seanglim, 1994), 46.

[13] Because of the legitimacy accorded to inequality (through the *boran* understanding of *dhamma* and power), the absence of rule of law, and the absence of intermediary structures between households and the state, Ovesen et al. describe Cambodian society as *prototypically* patrimonial, with patronage the only vehicle for personal security and advancement.

[14] "A typical village would have 3 or more such groups (hence it is estimated there are over 30,000 CBOs in Cambodia," World Bank, *Draft Concept Note* (no page numbers).

[15] See for example, Arnaldo Pellini, *Decentralisation Policy in Cambodia. Exploring Community Participation in the Education Sector*, unpublished PhD Thesis (University of Tampere, 2007).

been revived by NGOs in the 1990s. A third form of CBO comprises self-help groups, mobilized by either government or (I)NGOs around income-related or infrastructure maintenance and management issues. Savings and loans groups are most common, but there are also groups for irrigation, fish-farming and other collective production, livelihood training, and natural resource management (community fishery, community forestry), and user-groups for government services. When the issue involved access to interesting resources, government has adopted NGO-initiated models and created its own, especially community fishery and more recently community forestry committees. The same is true regarding Village Development Committees, non-sectoral committees with a semi-official status, associated initially with the *Seila* programme for channelling donor funds to local development.[16] These are intended to engage rural people directly in local development, promoting bottom-up planning.

Formal membership organizations are basically limited to trade unions, most of which are found in the garment industry. The growth in unionization is to a great extent tied to the garment industry, because respect for labour rights is part of the package guaranteeing Cambodian garments access to US and other international markets. Nevertheless, estimated union membership varies considerably across studies[17], but overall unionization remains low. Unions are typically established at factory level, most are weak, and none are financially independent. Political space for union activity beyond strikes at individual factories has consistently shrunk since the early 2000s, particularly following the killing of high-profile union leader Chea Vichea in 2004.

This leaves the donor-created NGO sector[18]. Databases of NGOs are all incomplete and not up to date so numbers are questionable[19], but it is a sector

---

[16] The *Seila* (literally: foundation stone) program, which operated from 1996 to 2006, was a participatory local development program which mandated the formation of particular sub-national governance structures, including village development committees, to formulate development plans to be funded through the program.

[17] From 160,000, quoted by the US Department of Labor in their report on *Foreign Labor Trends: Cambodia* (Washington DC: US Dept of Labor, 2003) to 337,000, quoted by Dain Bolwell in his *Cambodia Trade Union Survey,* (Phnom Penh: ILO, 2004), 10.

[18] Government and private interests have also started creating NGOs as a means to extend control over civil society. This is similar to the emergence of government- and factory-controlled labour unions. The government NGO is much less prevalent than the government union, although a career change from NGO director to an important position in the bureaucracy or the CPP is, tellingly, not infrequent. See J. Wilson, *Establishing the Rule of Law in Cambodia: the Role of NGO Regulation and Judicial Reform*, Research Paper for the International Human Rights Internship Program (Phnom Penh: Cambodian League for the Promotion and Defense of Human Rights, LICADHO 2005) 16., and Ray Zepp, "The Aid Industry: A frank discussion of local and international NGOs," in Ray Zepp. *Experiencing Cambodia*, unpublished paper (Phnom Penh, 2004), 65–78.

[19] Estimates of the numbers of active local NGOs start from 700 upwards, see Council for Development of Cambodia (CDC), *Report on Mapping Survey of NGO/Association Presence*

with a sizable turn-over, work-force[20] and influence. Seventy per cent of NGOs focus on service delivery; while only seven per cent work in areas of "advocacy", and "democracy and human rights".[21] Nearly all local NGOs are localized INGOs, started as INGO projects or programs, and have been founded with strong foreign advisory support and/or by Cambodians who returned from overseas or refugee camps or more recently were former INGO staff.

Externally initiated and resourced organizations are usually short-lived and do not survive the period of active involvement of their external patron by a substantial period of time.[22] Good governance promoters are aware of this, and good governance model assessments of *current* Cambodian civil society all suggest that civil society remains comparatively weak. An example from a World Bank report published in 2006 is typical. The authors write: "Compared with other countries, civil society is quite weak and not strongly independent in Cambodia". They attribute this first to historical oppression under the Khmer Rouge and Vietnamese occupation, and to the "mixed feelings" of post-UNTAC governments. Furthermore, the authors argue, "The poverty of the country and the relative prominence of donors and INGOs further distorts civil society ... [as do] relatively weak values, stemming from the hierarchical nature of Cambodian society (including CSOs[23]) and limited real "civic-ness". [24]

The most common criticisms of NGO governance tend to mirror criticisms of the Cambodian government, and focus on the apparent attributes of neo-patrimonial culture: authoritarian leadership style, nepotism, corruption, and secrecy. But the much closer control of donors in the NGO sector, as compared to the state sector, unhampered by the "sovereignty" issue, has created organizations which are perhaps more "neo-" than "patrimonial".[25] It highlights the extent of external influence on NGOs, and concludes that "This cadre of 'donor-created' NGOs ... should not ... be equated with the emergence of a broader,

---

and Activity in Cambodia (Phnom Penh: CDC-Natural Resources and Environment Programme and DANish International Development Assistance, 2006).

[20] 24,000 Cambodian staff (CDC *Report on Mapping Survey*).

[21] CDC, *Report on Mapping Survey*, but it needs repeating that all of these figures are guesstimates at best.

[22] Obviously there are many exceptions: to the extent that ownership transfer has occurred they may acquire a life of their own; but many fold up after the removal of foreign support.

[23] Civil Society Organizations.

[24] World Bank, *Civic Engagement in Cambodia: Supplementary Material on Civil Society for the Concept Note for a Study of the Civil Society in Cambodia*, internal memorandum (Phnom Penh, 2006).

[25] The core of the criticism that NGOs operate as sub-contractors for outside agendas is not specific to Cambodian NGOs. See e.g. Anthony Bebbington et al. "Introduction", in Anthony Bebbington et al. (eds), *Can NGOs make a difference. The challenge of development alternatives* (London: Zed Books, 2008).

indigenous Cambodian 'civil society'... [They] are not membership organizations and have no active constituency or social base". This situation, the authors argue, is perpetuated by NGOs' dependence on international funding, which gives them "strong incentives to cater to donors' programmatic priorities and reporting requirements and weak incentives to respond and account to grassroots constituencies". In the end, the report found, "An estimated 100 national NGOs dominate the NGO sector, of which about 30–40 can be considered strong".[26] This finding concurs with the assessment of the Focus on the Global South that, "Most CSOs are trapped in the capitalist development "narrative" themselves and the development industry is a rewarding employer. Many CSOs are involved in important tasks of services provision and crisis management but are unable to challenge the development model that is the source of these crises".[27]

Despite these problems, donors have no other operational model up their sleeve; consequently the creation and maintenance of NGO- and government-CBOs continues.

The Cambodian Government and Ideological Contestation in Civil Society

While Cambodia observers question the relevance of a "civil movement without citizens"[28] the Cambodian government apparently thinks otherwise. On the one hand the government has chosen an extremely liberal policy regarding NGOs, making Cambodia a paradise for NGO operators. This policy reflects a government assessment of the Cambodian incarnation of the NGO-model of civil society organization not as an *inherent* challenge to the existing hegemony, and thus useful in the pursuit of international legitimacy. So donor efforts at strengthening civil society through creating NGOs is supporting rather than reforming existing neo-patrimonial governance. On the other hand, over the last couple of years NGOs have been an increasing target of government control and repression efforts. This development is seen by prominent NGO movement "leaders"[29] as parallel to the ruling Cambodian People's Party's (CPP) acquisition of unchallenged dominance in the political arena.

Three examples indicate this trend. In 2006 the government picked up its stalled efforts to finalize an NGO law – an idea first mooted in the mid-90s. This

[26] Centre for Advanced Studies/World Bank, *Linking Citizens and the State: an Assessment of Civil Society Contributions to Good Governance in Cambodia*, draft report (Phnom Penh, 2008).
[27] Focus on the Global South, *Work plan 2009–2011*, Mimeo (2009).
[28] Kheang Un, *Democratization without Consolidation: The Case of Cambodia, 1993–2004*, Unpublished PhD Thesis (Northern Illinois University, 2004), 272.
[29] Personal communication. during various conversations over October and November 2008.

was the third serious effort, and it was accompanied by a new draft law and, initially, World Bank support in the form of technical advice and the organization of an NGO consultation process.[30] The most recent and, according to the shared assessment of most stakeholders, non-resistible round of announcements that the law will be passed in the foreseeable future kicked off with a post-2008 electoral victory statement by Hun Sen last September. Although NGOs remain divided over the issue of engaging with the government about this law this time round the various actors remain talking to each other, and have managed a common statement[31] which can be read as an indicator that even the pro-engagement, basic social service provision NGOs are aware of the potential threat this law may imply. The human rights NGO LICADHO issued a report which commented on concerns expressed by the Special Representative of the UN Secretary-General on Human Rights Defenders, Hina Jilani,[32] over an international trend in the use of NGO laws to restrict human rights advocacy. Such laws included provisions which criminalize non-registered groups, impose burdensome registration procedures, limit networking, deny registration inappropriately, limit the independence of registration authorities, impose state scrutiny over and interference in organizations' management, objectives and activities; restrict access to funding, and lead to administrative and judicial harassment.

A second example occurred in late 2005, when various prominent civil society personalities – Mam Sonando, owner and director of the independent Beehive Radio station, Rong Chhun, president of the Cambodian Independent Teachers Association, Kem Sokha, President of the Cambodian Centre for Human Rights, his deputy, Pa Ngoung Teang, and Yeng Virak, Director of the Cambodian Community Legal Education Centre – were arrested along with opposition leaders of the royalist FUNCINPEC and the Sam Rainsy Party and detained on defamation charges[33]. Some of these individuals had strong links with the political opposition, and therefore their arrests can be seen as targeting political rather than civil society; but this was not the case with all. Yeng Virak is a prominent NGO figure with no public political affiliations.

---

[30] According to a letter written by the human rights NGO LICADHO to various embassies: "Strong reactions by numerous NGOs prompted the World Bank in June 2006 to scale back the objectives of the consultation process to discussing ways to 'improve the policy environment for NGOs', which it now explains 'may' include the drafting of an NGO law". See LICADHO, *Letter and Background Note on NGO Law to Various Embassies*, unpublished letter (Phnom Penh, 2006).

[31] As part of the *NGO Statement to the 2008 Cambodia Development Cooperation Forum* (Phnom Penh, 2008). Online at http://www.ngoforum.org.kh/Development/Docs/NGOStatement/2008/2008NGOStatement_Final_English.pdf, accessed 15 February 2009.

[32] Hina Jilani, Report of the Special Representative of the Secretary-General on Human Rights Defenders, 1 October 2004, *UN Document no. A/59/401*, 2.

[33] See LICADHO, *Letter and Background Note on NGO Law*.

A third example emerges from the government"s recent successful use of the Bar Association of the Kingdom of Cambodia (BAKC) to target critical NGOs[34]. In June 2007 the BAKC eliminated the donor-funded Legal Fellows Program (LFP) that placed 12 young legal interns with NGOs by refusing to swear in the young interns unless they resigned from the LFP and their respective NGOs. Since then, BAKC has publicly demanded that all NGOs must have a memorandum of understanding with the Bar Association to allow them to employ lawyers, even though there is no legal basis for this statement. The BAKC at the time also insisted, less publicly, that lawyers should not be allowed to work in NGOs as this would prevent them from being independent. In the same period, NGO lawyers defending villagers in the "Keat Kolney"[35] land-grabbing case in Ratanakiri faced a criminal complaint lodged against them with the Ratanakiri prosecutor as well as a complaint with the BAKC accusing the lawyers of inciting villagers in Ratanakiri to file a lawsuit against Keat Kolney to claim their land back; and training villagers in Ratanakiri to talk negatively about Keat Kolney and to misinform the media.

These examples show the government's intention of not only suppressing freedom of association but also establishing ideological hegemony. The pursuit of ideological hegemony is, in Gramscian terms, the objective of all governments; it is more apparent for (ex-)communists, whose governance philosophy is quite elaborate regarding the need for ideological "work". Furthermore, this perspective explains the politicization of another set of civil society voices – the Buddhist *Sangha* (monkhood).

The re-institution of the *Sangha* in the 1980s was organized by the state and the Supreme Patriarch of the major Mahanikay sect, Tep Vong, is a former party official who remains affiliated with the CPP, as does much of the senior *Sangha*.[36] Befitting a communist state, religion has its own Ministry of Cults and Religions that is in charge of appointing the senior leadership of the Buddhist *Sangha*. The institution is currently closely controlled by the government/party. One account describes the situation as follows:

> Like any other Cambodian institution, Buddhism is much politicized and the two main leaders of Buddhism have openly sided with the ruling party since mid 90s. Furthermore, credible information collected has also pointed to high levels of corruption, violence, discrimination and harassment by the

---

[34] The information is based on various internal documents of legal NGOs involved.
[35] For more information on the case, see Andrew Cock's contribution to this volume.
[36] Academic sources documenting the history of this government–Buddhist hierarchy nexus in considerable detail are Heike Löschmann, *Die Rolle des Buddhismus in der gesellschaftlichen Entwicklung der Volksrepublik Kampuchea nach der Befreung vom Pol-Pot-Regime 1979 bis Mitte der achtziger Jahre*, unpublished PhD thesis (Berlin: Humboldt University, 1988) and Ian Harris, *Buddhism under Pol Pot*, Documentation Series No. 13 (Phnom Penh: DC-Cam, 2007).

leading monk, head monks of specific key pagodas and the abuse and presence of Pagoda Boys (PB) in almost all the pagodas in Cambodia. PB is an officially registered NGO in Cambodia. Its head has publicly stated that the NGO receives money from the prime minister and government officials. The NGO acts as an intelligence group reporting to specific head monks and government officials on the movement and actions of monks and people in each pagoda. Investigations have also highlighted that PB are used to fight violently against other students who are demonstrating peacefully on specific issues.[37]

Allowing a Gramscian perspective on civil society should not be read as discounting the relevance of the associational perspective. The two are very much intertwined: ideas need groups to acquire force. When this happens a popular or social movement is born, wherein a large informal grouping of individuals and/or organizations focuses on specific political or social issues, in other words on carrying out, resisting or undoing substantial socio-political change.[38] Ideological control efforts of the government are aimed at preventing the emergence of such a movement. It is telling that "social movements" are not part of the common typology used above to characterize Cambodian civil society. There doesn"t seem to be anything that would fit that label.[39]

An Emerging Social Movement?[40]

In the light of this bleak assessment, donors are quite excited about the emergence of natural resource management activist networks that seem to have a

---

[37] This quote is taken from a confidential memo from a human rights organization to my employer in response to a request for an assessment of the potential of Buddhism in Cambodia to contribute to civic-driven change (Phnom Penh, 20–4-2007).

[38] For a decent overview of social movement theory and research, see David Snow et al. (eds), *The Blackwell Companion to Social Movements (Blackwell Companions to Sociology)* (Oxford: Blackwell, 2004).

[39] Obviously, the observation that donor supported civil society development has been near exclusively focused on supporting NGOs can be read as indicating an equivalent reluctance on the donor side to support the emergence of socio-political movements. Given the importance of social movements in "consolidated" democracies this indicates the prioritization of political stability and the role of the state versus market development "good governance" model over substantive democratization.

[40] The information contained in this section is based on several sources of data: long interviews with foreign advisors to these networks; repeated discussions with various core Cambodian NGO supporters and facilitators; discussions with other donors involved in supporting some of the activities that are part of this development; participation in meetings organized by and/or for network representatives; analysis of informal memoranda, case descriptions, and advocacy material; and on information drawn from other studies and consultancy papers, especially Peter Degen et al., *Taken for Granted. Conflicts over Cambodia's*

social-movement-like quality. The development of these networks has occurred in the last two years and they have so far remained under the radar of academic and most other Cambodia watchers. Until very recently this was an explicit strategy to avoid government attention, but this seems to be changing. How did these networks emerge and how have they developed to date? What are their relationships with donors, NGOs and the state?

The initial impetus for this network development came from the "discovery"[41] by a foreign consultant and four Cambodian collaborators of self-mobilized fishing communities in Kampong Chhnang who put up a fight, without any NGO involvement, against what they perceived as unjust encroachment upon their commons. Some of those who made this discovery were motivated to start Community Organizing (CO) NGOs, to support these struggles. The foreign consultant supported this move, and also prompted an international NGO to recruit community fisheries activists, rather than (only) local NGO staff in its ongoing programme of Active Non-Violence Training. The training had been going on for a couple of years already with NGO staff participants only, without resulting in much follow-up action. This time round things were different. Two months later the community activist trainees put the practical skills acquired into practice at an event when 400 people took a stand against armed guards of a disputed fishing lot concession.[42] Six months later some of these CO NGOs took a Kampong Chhnang activist along to Battambang fishing villages, to explain to her peers what her community had done; subsequently, similar actions started happening in Battambang. More Active Non-Violence Training was organized in both Kampong Chhnang and Battambang.

Freshwater Fish Resources, Paper for 8th International Association for the Study of Common Property Conference (Bloomington, 2000); Graeme Brown, *CFI Ratanakiri Coordinator 2004–2007, End of Contract Report to Community Forestry International,* unpublished report (Phnom Penh, 2008); Shalmali Guttal, *Supporting Knowledge Generation Among Community Led Networks,* Completion Report of the Pilot Phase of the Project (Phnom Penh: Focus on the Global South, 2008); A. Cruz, and Meas Nee, *Options for Future Support to Empowering Community-Based Organisations In Cambodia* (Phnom Penh: Forum Syd, 2006); Meas Nee, CBO working model and strategy for CBO pilot project (Phnom Penh: Forum Syd, 2008); and CORD Asia, "The Community Peace Building Network in Cambodia. A Strategic Review 2008". 2nd Draft for comments (Phnom Penh: February 2009).

[41] Like the 'discovery' of Angkor Wat, the phenomenon may not have been new at all. The *mé khyol* leadership skills required for mobilizing a community in times of an acute crisis or anything asking for "daring" (what Cambodians call "salty spit") may be different from those required to organize socio-cultural events, or periodically recurring mutual assistance, but they are common enough to have been described in the literature: see e.g. Centre for Advanced Study/World Bank, *Justice for the Poor? An Exploratory Study of Collective Grievances over Land & Local Governance in Two Provinces.* Working paper (Phnom Penh, 2006). NGO people and their advisors were just not aware of it.

[42] See Degen et al. *Taken for Granted* about the situation regarding fishery conflicts at that time.

Parallel to this the Fisheries Network of Cambodia's NGO Forum[43] started organizing provincial meetings on the inland freshwater economic fishery concessions (fishing "lots") system. The combination of these community actions and the Forum-coordinated meetings constituted the "fisheries movement", which achieved astonishing success when the government cancelled more than half of the allotted concessions in the run-up to the first commune council elections in 2002.[44]

In the meantime, one foreigner involved in facilitating the fisheries actions developed an interest in the forestry sector and pursued a similar strategy of working with Cambodian collaborators. The group went to forestry concessions to map resin tree tapping and logging, and helped local activists to start CO NGOs. Again NGO Forum was involved and again Active Non-Violence training for community activists resulted in many protest actions, including complaint letters, road blocks, and confiscation of logging equipment. In 2001, NGO Forum organized the first national meeting, concentrating on the illegal logging of resin trees in Cambodia.

The CO NGOs started organizing provincial forestry networks which, by late 2001, had federated into a national network. The forestry concession system, which was supported by a World Bank loan, had been put on hold in 2000 because of an NGO Forum complaint to the Bank about rampant irregularities in the sector, and the failure of the Bank itself to follow its own guidelines with respect to Cambodian forestry. Equally important in focusing international attention on the issue was a public rally held in December 2002, in which 240 villagers from forestry communities requested a meeting with the Department of Forestry and an audience with the King to present their comments on the (mostly inadequate) forestry management plans that logging concessionaires had to produce. The submission of these plans was part of the government–World Bank-agreed procedure of "milestones" to get the logging industry back under control, and free up the frozen loans.

The villagers" action resulted in a government crackdown. Global Witness, at that time the Independent Forestry Monitor appointed by agreement between the government and the World Bank, was kicked out the country and the villagers and all CO NGOs that were involved were harassed to find out who was behind this "incitement". Nevertheless, this "movement" was a success in that the few companies whose plans were finally accepted by the government have not, in fact, started operations again[45].

---

[43] Later to become an independent NGO: Fisheries Action Coalition Team (FACT).

[44] The powerful head of the Department of Fisheries was fired, so one might also assume some infighting over the control of the spoils of the lot system to have been part of what made this success possible.

[45] Good histories of the forestry sector are Philippe Le Billon and Simon Springer, "Between war and peace: violence and accommodation in the Cambodian logging sector", in: W. de

As in fisheries, other factors played into this. A government-organized Forest Crimes Monitoring Unit had been established as part of the World Bank"s support for the logging concession system. Andrew Cock[46] has argued that a major rationale for this unit was the desire of the political faction led by Hun Sen faction to know who was making money from logging, so they could move in and take it. By 2002 that purpose had undoubtedly been fulfilled. Also, by 2002 the government had hit upon an alternative to forestry concessions: economic land concessions, created on land that was judged to be degraded forest, and within which concessionaires were empowered to clear-cut timber in order to establish cash crop plantations. In July 2002 the Tumring rubber plantation was inaugurated in Kompong Thom as the first operating land concession. This conversion of a forestry into a plantation concession woke those focusing on forestry up to a new reality.

From 2001 onwards land disputes emerged on the agenda of the CO NGOs and they started to bring land activists to Active Non Violence Training. But the sector-specific success stories of fisheries and forestry have not proved replicable with land. A major reason is the very muddled land ownership situation: this has produced rival claims referring to different "traditions" of ownership and usage rights, making issues of right and wrong less clear. Lack of clarity regarding the rights and wrongs of land cases placed a burden of proof on the villagers, both from the perspective of the authorities and from the perspective of supportive NGOs from the legal aid, human rights, and policy advocacy sectors.

For about two years the situation regarding economic concessions remained "quiet" with forestry concessions inactive and land concessions mostly not yet up and running. But in November 2003 the powerful Pheapimex Company began ploughing in a land concession planned for pulp and paper production covering more than 315,000 hectares of land in six districts of Pursat and Kampong Chhnang provinces. The community actively opposed the company, and even though violence in the form of a grenade attack was used against the villagers, they prevailed, and Pheapimex stopped its activities here. Instead, it began working on a large concession in Mondulkiri province in 2004.[47] Involved CO NGOs brought

---

Jong et al. (eds), *Extreme conflict and tropical forests* (New York: Springer: 2007), 17–36, and Andrew Cock, "The interaction between a ruling elite and an externally promoted policy reform agenda: the case of forestry under the second kingdom of Cambodia", unpublished PhD Thesis (La Trobe University, 2007).

[46] Andrew Cock, *The interaction between a ruling elite and an externally promoted policy reform agenda*, 176.

[47] As part of the Wuzhishan LS Group; for more information on both concessions, see Environment Forum Core Team, *Fast-wood plantations, economic concessions, and local livelihoods in Cambodia* (Phnom Penh: NGO Forum, 2006).

people from Pursat to Mondulkiri to discuss their strategies. However, established legal aid, human rights and national advocacy NGOs took a different stance: they were very reluctant to support such "semi-legal" community action (road blocks, equipment sabotage, etc.) and told villagers to refrain from such action in their own best interest (which they did). The established advocacy NGOs" stance was, perhaps, a good illustration of the validity of the government"s assessment of the NGO-model as a politically toothless challenge.

What characterized all of the *networking* between activist communities in the examples above was its entirely NGO-driven nature. The initial acts of resistance at the local level were not NGO-driven – although some of them were NGO-supported – but the linkages between activist communities *were* a product of NGO involvement. Two kinds of NGOs were thus involved: the CO NGOs, comprising small community organizers, who all, in one way or the other, had been established with the support of the same international "vehicle" of a core foreign advisor; and some larger established legal aid, human rights and national advocacy NGOs. The former had formed the coordination committee of an active non-violence network covering activities in about 150 villages nation-wide.

By spring 2006 this co-ordination committee had died a natural death. Corruption issues within some organizations, the inability to look beyond their particular sectoral and territorial interest, and bickering over control of the network resulted in a couple of the established support NGOs pulling out and rethinking their networking strategy. The latter had played key roles in the successes of both the fisheries and forestry "movements" but felt very unsure about how to operate regarding the legal morass surrounding land conflicts for various reasons. This may have been partly because they saw their primary role as "protection" rather than the active mobilization of villagers; partly because they felt threatened by their association with active resistance to authority; or partly because they felt threatened by communities deciding themselves what course of action to follow rather than relying upon their "NGO patrons".

At the same time as the shift into contestation over land brought different dynamics into play, things started changing in fisheries and forestry. With the "fight" over the concession system won, the attention of CO NGOs turned from advocacy to promoting demands for community fisheries and community forestry projects (with land in ethnic minority areas this was later supplemented by communal land titling projects). These banked upon reasonable working relationships with local authorities, tried to make use of (new) legal opportunities, and diverted attention from stalled concession fights.[48] They focused hopes

---

[48] In most struggles, time is on the side of the powerful as solidarity is not easy to maintain without an immediate threat, key organizers can be co-opted by individual deals, etc.

on "legalizing" a community''s rights on usually quite small areas of commons – but had the unfortunate implication that the rest of the commons were now up for grabs.[49] This is another indication of the way that Cambodian NGOs end up legitimating, rather than challenging, the existing neo-patrimonial nexus of political and economic power.

By mid 2006 the CO and support NGOs and their foreign advisors started thinking about a new mechanism, different from a coordination committee of NGOs. National networking obviously requires structure but structure is a ticket to trouble, as the first incarnation had proved. Structure always and everywhere tends to empower the better resourced, professional organizations at the expense of more informal local collectives, but implications of permanent structure in Cambodia go beyond that universal. The complement of the earlier-described preference for temporary/episodic indigenous leadership seems to be a fear that permanent formal organizational leadership is bound to be misused. Whatever the new structure was going to look like, the fundamental change made for the second incarnation was to have community people in charge, rather than NGOs. The participants experimented with a mechanism that comprised a network of community activists with a structure of its own, and a linked "advisory" committee of some support NGOs that acts as a channel of funding, takes care of reporting requirements, and provides facilitation and access to other support apart from money (training, national and international networking, etc.). The network rallies around issues, rather than sectors and brings people from different sectors (fisheries, forestry, land, ethnic minorities, unions, students, monks) together. Party politics are avoided because of the assessment that association with the opposition is too risky and would prevent the participation of good people with ruling party connections; and because in any case there is an expectation that change *within* the ruling party is more likely than a change *of* ruling party. This explicit strategy of defining the network's challenges as "issue-based" and not "political" tends to be interpreted by non-Cambodians as acceding to democratic centralist definitions of politics. However, an alternative reading is that this is rather a sensible pragmatic choice for the time being.

A first structure built upon a representative model, with regional network committees sending representatives to a national network committee, but this created conflicts and was quickly abandoned for a more organic model that networks *individual* activists. Some of the regional networks do have an existence of their own, especially in the two regions where they receive funding support from INGOs. There is a core group of around ten individuals representing a national

---

[49] This is not to discredit all of these projects. Some use these as "fronts" for community organizing, but in many cases these projects become ends in themselves.

leadership, half male, half female, from rural communities all over the country, with another 10 to 15 active people within an "assembly" that is much larger. The groups that people come from include the Community Peace Building Network (CPN, the community activists associated with the CO NGO incarnation of the active non-violence training network), a group brought together through community-organized training; the regional networks; and other linked or overlapping groups including a donor-initiated food sovereignty network, unions, urban groups fighting resettlement, and some individual students and monks.

The relationship between the core group and the advisory group has been built over time through getting people to meet informally so as to slowly break down barriers of distrust. This has resulted in a changed dynamic between individuals. Many network members have extensive and often negative experience with NGOs as they have leadership roles within their communities and, as such, often have positions in NGO-created community based organizations. One of the claims that promoters of the network make is that the effectiveness of a CBO is very much leadership dependent; NGOs lucky enough to identify a good leader who then makes his or her CBO work tend to claim the success as theirs. This patronizing bias does not go unnoticed and creates considerable distrust at the community level. Others have been alienated by NGO staff from legal aid or human rights monitoring organizations telling them what to do, as described above.

From early 2007 onwards, with considerable facilitation from supportive Cambodian and foreign advisors, the core group of the network started developing its own advocacy and action plans. Initially everything remained quite fluid and informal, but national-level networking and assistance in building a support structure came with increased exposure to a small but growing group of sympathetic donors who saw this as a social experiment that challenged their assumptions about Cambodian civil society. This has led to the beginning of a "mutually constitutive dynamic", between donor interests and Cambodian leadership potential, similar to the one that initially resulted in the creation of an NGO-dominated landscape in the 1990s.

The problems that keep resurfacing over the history of this movement are not likely to disappear. Initial successes were around specific natural resources, were entirely NGO driven, involving both small CO NGOs and large national NGOs, and would not have been possible without strategic and financial input from some core foreign advisor-activists and "vehicles". This reality is reflected in a continuing dependence of some of the Cambodian activists and CO NGO directors upon their foreign mentor and resentment of this dominance by others. The resentment also reflects differing opinions about strategy amongst these mentors, as their differences hinder solidarity amongst activists who are "affiliated" with them. First, efforts to localize through NGOs quickly brought all the problems of the NGO model (a hierarchical, condescending expert attitude, a self-serving, project and donor-oriented agenda) to the fore, but the follow-up efforts to work towards a community-owned network cannot do without NGO technical assistance and services (like legal aid). That the required attitudinal changes are going to take a lot of time is clear.[50] On the network side of things, the decision to circumvent structure as much as possible and build a network of individuals was an interesting and bold move. Bringing these activists and interested NGO people together informally does seem to have wrought some real change with particular individuals. But they are not the majority and issues of competition, distrust, and naive dependence on outsiders are still prevalent.

Also, as a network of individuals it is not yet rooted in communities. Most members have some kind of leadership role in their community, but for many this is a role tied to a particular natural resource dispute. Although these conflicts have proved to be powerful, and to a certain extent the only rallying points for real larger-scale collective action, this solidarity proves insufficiently enduring once the conflict is over or even temporarily stalled. In addition to this, although hitherto having been at the receiving end of the "NGO experience" and thus often very critical of NGO staff, the only tested model in town for formalizing structures is the NGO model. The quickest way for the activists to achieve recognition as "peers", is for them to NGO-ize. And other actors put great pressure on informal entities like this that are in need of material support and legitimacy to register (government) and acquire the necessary organizational infrastructure to live up to planning, reporting and other paper-production requirements for support (donors).

This account of the historical relationship between NGOs and activist groups in Cambodia is clearly very different from that in, for example, Thailand or the Philippines. The NGO organizational model comprising a professionalized service provider with social rather than profit-maximization objectives might be similar, and come with similar characteristics, but these characteristics produce very different outcomes, depending upon the initial relationship with the social movement that they support.[51]

The case of the Philippines, where many NGOs emerged as political fronts of an armed highly organized movement[52] is therefore different from the case

---

[50] This is a pervasive problem everywhere; for Cambodia it was insightfully described by Moira O'Leary and Meas Nee in their volume *Learning for Transformation. A Study of the Relationship between Culture, Values, Experience and Development Practice in Cambodia* (Phnom Penh: Krom Akphiwat Phum, 2001), but, like anywhere else, this has led to precious little change.

[51] Obviously, more contextual factors are significant, such as the labour market – in Cambodia, until quite recently, an NGO job was the only opportunity for an educated member of the urban middle class who lacked the connections to gain public sector employment to make a decent living.

[52] See e.g. Thea Hilhorst, *The real world of NGOs: discourse, diversity and development* (London: Zed Books, 2003).

of Thailand, where many NGOs emerged as the urban supporters of people"s movements[53]. Thai people's movements were less well organizationd than the armed rebellions in the Philippines, but they did set their own agendas. This is again different from Cambodia, where the organization of "movements" is the outcome of NGO interventions.

The significance of such differences is illustrated by a case in which Filipino trainers were brought in to facilitate training for community organizers in Cambodia. The trainers initiated a strategy of placing community activist trainees as interns with established Cambodian NGOs. In the Philippines, this makes sense, because the NGOs are, in fact, an organic part of the movement. In Cambodia they are not; and therefore a community activist shifting into the NGO world as an intern is very likely to become – or to be seen by others as having become – "NGO staff", with a different status, orientation and set of interests from those she had before.

A further significant factor is the contradictory nature of donor interests and analyses. On the one hand, donors identify this social experiment as an example of "potential people power" that needs support to develop on its own terms, following its own agenda. On the other hand, donors make their own independent assessment of the broader context of economic transformation, and the speed with which this disenfranchises increasing numbers of the poor. In response, donors support the production of sophisticated activity plans, which involve the networks but are not initiated or designed by them. Furthermore, money and technical support from donors comes with accountability requirements attached. At the moment, these latter tendencies are resulting in the group of active community members being engaged, more or less full time, in externally initiated, facilitated and funded trainings, advocacy activities and consultations, most conducted outside their own community. These tendencies on the part of donors undermine the ability of community activist networks to organize themselves, and prompt a process of gradual but inexorable NGO-ization.

Members of the community activist networks are aware of the dangers of NGO-ization. Many of the interested donors are also aware of the problems that their involvement might create. But on both sides the combination of the influence of some individuals who are stuck in their ways and thus indeed create the problems feared, and the more general difficulty inherent in the need to judge plans and activities, not only on their own merits, but also in terms of what they mean in the context of everything else that is already happening, makes for a frenzy of training and consultation activity. These training and consultation

---

[53] See e.g. Bruce Missingham, *The Assembly of the Poor in Thailand*, and Sonchai Phatharathananuth, *Civil society and democratization. Social movements in Northeast Thailand* (Copenhagen: NIAS Press, 2006).

activities are supposed to equip the network of individuals to become more deeply rooted in their communities. However, it is hard to see this happening because the training itself entails that the activists spend less and less time in their communities.

There are certainly interesting and informed analytic discussions amongst and between activists, their advisors and their closest CO NGO supporters. The need for "deepening the roots", for a move from networking individuals to a networking of communities, is widely shared, but analysis has not yet transformed practice. Community organizing requires a variety of roles: internally – from mobilizers (who draw on community anger about resource theft to confront the threat), to organizers (who strengthen community solidarity on a more permanent basis), to livelihood- and culture-oriented local leadership (who co-ordinate the event-based mutual help and other collective action that is always present and needs to become part of the foundation of community solidarity)[54]; and externally – from networkers (linking up with other communities facing similar problems). These roles are often played best by different individuals because they require different skills and personalities. But the "movement" clearly lacks examples of how to support this deepening in ways other than the creation of CBOs, which is very much an imposition of the NGO model at local level.

Another major component in the above-described push for NGO-ization, besides bureaucratization through planning and reporting requirements, is the commodification of activism by the introduction of salaries and per diems. The payment of individuals by NGOs for activities introduces the dynamics of contractual relationships on top of those of the gift relationship that comes with outsiders paying the material costs of activities that activists themselves propose. It creates jealousies and de-legitimizes them as activists because they are now seen as NGO employees. That the NGOs pay different individuals to work on their project, thereby pulling the network apart, obviously weakens it. And that they often pay them for things that they were doing up to that point in time voluntarily weakens it even more.

The narrative presented above recounts developments from the emergence of a network of individual activists that felt strong enough to present itself as a civil society actor in the public domain, to the emergence of centrifugal forces that began to break down this solidarity. The time period over which this story played out was about a year. It is common knowledge that organization always comes with problems, and it is anyone's guess what will happen next: a key characteristic of change is that it can be understood in hindsight better than it can be predicted. But the very obvious power differential between outside

---

[54] This analysis comes from CPN reflections. CPN foreign advisor, personal communication, Phnom Penh, 25 November 2008.

actors with their own money and agendas, and the internal dynamics of a still-fledgling network of individuals trying to develop a shared understanding of and strategy regarding complex socio-economic transformations, while simultaneously trying to more firmly root that understanding in much wider community solidarity, does not bode well.

Conclusions

The story of community activism around natural resource struggles illustrates the three-way ideological contestation ongoing in Cambodian civil society. A series of natural resource management policies initiated by the government, with backing from donors such as the World Bank, in forestry, fishing and land, were and remain potentially disastrous for the poor. Yet the extreme weakness of the poor in a civil society dominated by neo-patrimonial links of co-optation and sponsorship to a centralizing and authoritarian state offered few resources of resistance. Enter the NGOs, established specifically to contest neo-patrimonialism in the name of good governance: yet here too, we find that the practice of resistance is itself speedily undermined by a heavy-handed and ideological pursuit of particularly associational forms and priorities. To the extent that the emergence of a social movement for the protection of the commons is a real civil-society challenge to the ideological dominance of the Cambodian state, the NGO-ization of civil society can only be interpreted as supporting that dominance. Regarding the supply-side of the good governance agenda, Hughes and Un make a convincing argument in this volume for the donor co-creation of the current neo-patrimonial state. Donor efforts regarding the demand-side of that agenda seem to produce a similar outcome: hegemony of the state's agenda, resulting in a further marginalization of the poor.

In general the fast growth of the NGO sector from the 1980s onwards has been accompanied by a continuing debate about NGOs as alternatives to existing (bilateral and multilateral) development approaches. This debate is intertwined with a debate about the inter-relationship between civil society, the state and the market. The understanding of NGOs as part of civil society is at the interface of these two debates. As a relatively recent organizational form, how exactly do they relate to other "more deep-seated" or "more constitutive" social arrangements or social actors[55] like political or religious movements? The question about NGOs as "alternatives" assumes a shared recognition of the benefits of a

---

[55] This terminology and most of the argument is derived from Bebbington et al., "Introduction," in A. J. Bebbington et al., *Can NGOs make a difference? The challenge of development alternatives* (London: Zed Books, 2008), 3–37.

joint existence of movements and NGOs within the struggle against hegemonic and repressive structures manifested through the state"[56] and their corporate supporters. Worldwide this kind of mutually supportive relation of NGOs and more "grounded" movements came under increasing pressure from the early 1990s onwards, with NGOs increasingly assuming the role of a public service contractor which "compromised their innovativeness, autonomy, legitimacy, accountability and ability to continue elaborating alternatives".[57]

It was this already compromised model which was introduced by donors into Cambodia. And the model was introduced into a setting without "more constitutive social movements". This "vacuum" seems to have made co-optation of NGOs in Cambodia even more pervasive than elsewhere. And the story told above indicates that a large and monopolistic co-opted NGO sector is a barrier rather than a challenge to real alternatives. The described "social movement" developments are nowhere close to overcoming the dominance imposed by donors, NGOs and the state. The most realistic assessment is probably that they indicate an emerging political awareness, but not yet a political challenge.

---

[56] Bebbington et al., "Introduction," 12.
[57] Bebbington et al., "Introduction," 14.

15

IMAGINED PARASITES:
FLOWS OF MONIES AND SPIRITS

Erik W. Davis

The Preta are Coming! Cultural Imaginations and Moral Transgressions

To conclude the volume, this chapter takes as its starting point the contention that causes of rural poverty and inequality are wellunderstood by rural Cambodians. This chapter explores resources from the Cambodian imaginary for discussing this inequality and registering opposition to it. The specific contribution in this case is the annual "hungry ghost" festival of *Phchum Ben*. *Phchum Ben* prescribes the proper way of engaging with the dead – with gifts – and portrays the dead as disgusting, hungry, and pathetic. I argue that this particular imagination of proper exchange provides a useful metaphor within which to imagine relations of exploitation in the contemporary economy. Such representations of resentment are not the same thing as active opposition; instead, I highlight how the criticism depends on a set of cultural and religious contexts. Such criticisms are indigenous: local responses to a situation that increasingly lies outside the scope of the indigenous and local power spheres.

During the Fall festival of *Phchum Ben*, people from the cities crowd buses, cars, and small motorcycles to travel along the muddy dirt roads back to the villages of their birth. Almost no one in Cambodia has lived off the farm for more than a generation, and nearly all can identify an agricultural village somewhere in the countryside as "theirs". In 2005, I was crammed into a minibus with fifteen others, mostly elderly women and men, with a few young people clearly returning home after working in the city. We were travelling from the city to the countryside for the festival. Villagers lined the roads to watch the buses and cars rush by, and when they saw the crowded buses often shouted comments like these: "The *preta* are coming! The *preta* are coming! This bus is full of really old *preta*! Hey youngster, make sure that those old ghosts don't grab you!" Those in the buses were being called *preta* by those in the villages. Just like the hungry ghosts of *Phchum Ben*, we were relatives distanced by time and space, and we had returned to our natal villages for sustenance. And then the villagers laughed at us without smiling.

At first I also laughed, but quickly realized that none of my fellow pilgrims found it funny. Instead, their faces fell. Some were angry, but most seemed hurt and dejected. A friend with whom I was travelling kept saying, "They're so angry at us. They really want us to go back home." If the riders in my minibus didn't laugh, the folks standing on the side of the road –skinny shirtless men, older women in faded sarongs, young naked children with taut bellies and reddish hair – more than made up for our lack of delight.

Phchum Ben gathers relatives far and near to celebrate trust, solidarity, and love, during the slow agricultural period when the rice grows fastest. Family members may see each other only once in a while, often when city relatives arrive in their own cars, or on buses and taxis, which remain out of easy reach of rural relatives. *Phchum Ben* is also a period of excess and generosity: both sides of the family make efforts to be hospitable and generous to the other. Families from the city make efforts to give to the limits of their ability – they do not come empty handed to the countryside. They bring food, treats, bread, and rice. They bring candles and cooking pots, toys for children, and packets of bills for distribution at the temple. Country relatives, meanwhile, do a lot of work preparing for the relatives, accommodating them, and cooking for them.

The family members from the city see their own efforts as a great feat of generosity, for which they should be appreciated. And they are appreciated – their food, gifts, money, toys, all go a long way to help create the sense of solidarity and familial love and trust which might otherwise be strained by the tyranny of distance, the length of absence, and the gulf in respective experiences of daily life.

When country folk greet their city relatives – who spend all but the most important religious festivals of the year far away from their birth country – as *preta*, what are they doing? Why is this joke funny to rural Cambodians; why would they denigrate and humiliate the very people who are bringing the food, money, and gifts that make their village festivals so enjoyable? I believe the answer lies in the economic relationships between these two groups, and the differing ways in which social exchange is imagined. We need first to understand the symbols that are being deployed, and their context.

The key to understanding this joke lies in the religious imagination of moral exchange in the festival of *Phchum Ben*, where gift relationships with the dead are reversed for fifteen days, and instead of imploring the ancestors for the blessings of this world, one instead takes pity on the ancestor ghosts' grievous need and dependency.

Part of the proper practice of exchange in a gift cycle is that one must represent each new gift as the return of a previously received gift. Sahlins noted that proper gift economies seem to possess at least three nodes in them, such that the giver never returns directly to the person from whom she receives.[1] In such a system, aggression and inequality are tamed by the existence of a generalized reciprocity made strong by another set of personally fluctuating ideas of which party is currently in which other party's debt. This is why successful giving is represented as the *return* of a previously received gift, and emphasizes *ongoing* reciprocity. The receiver can be humiliated if she or he has suddenly become incapable of reciprocating. In modern Cambodia the city is often widely seen by rural dwellers to refuse to reciprocate or acknowledge the source of its wealth.

In such a situation, the denigration of gifts or givers can help control the status that emerges from gifts given without reciprocation. I will show that this holds true both in unritualized social interactions, such as the joke, and in the religious imagination of *Phchum Ben* and *preta*, and that the two inform and shape each other.

My argument in what follows is simply this: material reasons for widespread rural resentment exist, and the festival of *Phchum Ben* offers a ready-made constellation of imagery which can be used to play on the ambiguity of giving in order to give that resentment voice. In what follows, then, I first offer some relevant economic context. Second, I introduce the festival of *Phchum Ben* and its embeddedness in the practices and imagination that produce value for Cambodian society, noting the dual practices of gift-giving that take place in the *Phchum Ben* celebrations, and the markedly distinct attitudes toward the recipients upon which these practices draw. I also discuss the figure of the *preta* proper – the hungry ghost and its transformation into a beneficent, fertility-possessing ancestor figure, the transformation from *preta* to ancestor.

The third section then deals with gift-giving theory in anthropology, and its relevance to the Cambodian situation. I move from this general treatment of the gift economy to the specifics of the gift in contemporary Cambodia, as simultaneously a valorized practice of moral and social superiority, and a detested practice of power politics which codes its own practices as gifts while embedding other flows of wealth as dependent on aspects of reality beyond mere human control.

Finally I return to the example from the beginning of this essay, and unpack the resentment a bit further, treating especially one additional question relating

---

[1] Marshall Sahlins, "The Spirit of the Gift," in *Stone Age Economic* (New York: Aldine de Gruyter, 1972), 149–183.

to the impoverished nature of one set of migrants – factory workers – and the growth in urban inequality.

Relevant Economic Background

Cambodia is a very poor country, whose poverty is of general interest because it presents a supposed contradiction: Gross Domestic Product (GDP) rates are growing, and absolute poverty remains high. Additionally, inequality is not only relatively high, but rising. Finally, the primary driver of national inequality rates is rising intra-rural inequality. Cambodia's most dramatic distinction remains the old problem of rural and urban inequality, with a few novel twists.

Despite a rapidly growing urban population, approximately eighty-five per cent of Cambodians remain in rural areas. While there are urban sectors of very high absolute deprivation, especially in uncounted groups, poverty is an overwhelmingly rural problem.[2] So the first clear impression of Cambodia's economic and social situation is of a rural area comprising the vast majority of the population, experiencing grave poverty, expressed commonly and tragically in the metric of calorie consumption, whose situation is worsening overall. At the same time, small urban areas comprising very little of the country's population are composed of groups of people who are often the richest of the rich, or at least of that section of the poor that has managed to both work and eat. The geographic distinction is clear and unambiguous – hungry countryside, fattening cities. This is not a new problem in Cambodia.

But the current situation is somewhat more complex than that already sketched, which more closely resembles that of the late Sangkum or early Lon Nol periods. Complicating the situation of rural poverty and urban wealth is the increased existence now of an urban poor, and the rise of new rural classes that are relatively "wealthy". So two questions may be asked: How does the city acquire wealth and the countryside lose it? And second: How do people living in this context represent their own plight, or morally characterize themselves, each other, or those they resent?

Traditionally in Cambodian cities, as indeed in almost all pre-industrial[ized] cities, almost all of the cities' wealth was extracted from the country, in the form of timber, rice, soybeans, rubber, and young factory workers, who primarily work in the garment industry. The wealth produced by those garment workers can be sketched as a figure in the overall figures. Although agricultural work is the primary occupation for 75% of heads of households, the sector only

---

[2] World Bank. *Cambodia: Halving poverty by 2015? Poverty Assessment 2006* (Phnom Penh: World Bank, 2006), 40. Poverty is not only overwhelmingly rural, but increasingly so: Ibid., 85.

accounts for 31% of national GDP. Compared to the relatively small size and greater value produced in the garment industry, which only employed eight per cent of the labour force in 2004, the influence of the factories is striking.[3]

Cambodia also remains barely industrialized. While there has been an increase among the rural poor of young people working in urban factories, and while the garment industry is still in relatively good shape, relative to the ongoing global economic crisis, it has contributed to almost no secondary industrialization. Furthermore, the vast majority of both commodities and profit value produced by the garment sector leaves the country, since most factories are exporting to, and owned by, non-Cambodian groups. Value added to the national productive economy is confined almost solely to the wages retained by the workers. What of those workers?

There are around one quarter million in the sector, and they are overwhelmingly rural and female – 85% are rural women who work in the city and send money back home to the countryside.[4] These remittances are significant; the money these mostly young women send home improves the incomes of up to thirteen per cent of rural households.[5] Moreover, these young women rarely come from the poorest of families owing to job sharking – when a worker must purchase her job – in the industry. So, these jobs can often be part of an equation that leads precisely to the current situation in rural Cambodia – intra-rural inequality is rising, while inequality in the cities is falling.[6] This is also directly reflected in the views of poor rural Cambodians, who believe that their wealthier neighbours are wealthy as a consequence of their urban relatives.[7]

Rural Cambodians are neither ignorant of nor mystified by the reasons for their poverty and the relative wealth of the city; when a "wealthy" peasant starts receiving remittances, the neighbours understand the reason for the changes in the local economy. Some things remain the same: "The poor earn to feed the rich".[8]

While industrial capitalism is indeed contributing to increased rural inequality in Cambodia, and the figure of the garment workers changes social relationships, we must remember that intra-rural inequality still exists largely in an overall context of widespread absolute deprivation.[9] The most conspicuous

---

[3] Ibid., vii, 85.

[4] Ibid., 66.

[5] World Bank 2006, viii. Compare to improvements to nine per cent of all Cambodian households (World Bank 2006, 67).

[6] World Bank, *Sharing Growth – Equity and Development in Cambodia* (Phnom Penh: World Bank, 2007), iii-iv.

[7] Ibid., 34.

[8] Ibid., xiii.

[9] World Bank, Halving Poverty, v, and World Bank, Sharing Growth, 23–29, 50.

mover of extreme inequality in many parts of the countryside is not the existence of a relative in the factories, but of the patronizing gifts given to mostly wealthy rural clients, a type of corruption and connection that not only amplifies local inequality, but speeds up its advance, a fact which also exacerbates the "remote" and peripheral characteristic of some rural areas over others.[10] These flows of wealth sometimes appear momentary, such as when impoverished rural widows receive "personal gifts" from the Prime Minister and his wife on national television. Other instances are marked more permanently, such as when the Prime Minister's initials are painted on schools throughout Cambodia. In all cases these flows of wealth are marked as "gifts". What remittances and political gifts share in common then is a tendency to reproduce and intensify rural inequality, and a tendency to be marked as aid or gifts from the giver. In contrast, the wealth absorbed by the owners of the factories, or politicians and civil servants, is marked only as market or political exchange – certainly not as a gift, but also without a sense that the wage is fair, or even sufficient. Many garment workers personally endure food privation in order to maximize the amount they can remit.

At no other time of the year, except for New Year, is the reversal of the normal flow of wealth from country to city so strongly marked and reversed as during the fifteen days of *Phchum Ben*. And at no other point is the changed connotation of that returning wealth – as "gifts" rather than market exchange – so strongly noted as during *Phchum Ben*, for *Phchum Ben* is a celebration involving travel of people and wealth, creation of new wealth, and giving of gifts. During the two weeks of *Phchum Ben*, the direction of wealth is reversed, like the Tonle Sap river which reverses its flow twice a year, drawing the waters of the Mekong into the giant inland lake that provides sixty per cent of Cambodia's protein consumption. In the rest of this article I argue that the specific conditions of rural poverty, corruption, and inequality underwrite acts of imagination that attempt to set moral relationships in proper balance. That is, the figure of the hungry ghost – the *preta* of *Phchum Ben* – is invoked as a mirror of the parasitic relatives who come back to the villages during the festival period.[11]

To that end, I introduce and briefly characterize *Phchum Ben*, the various living and dead actors involved, before moving on briefly to a discussion of what anthropological studies of the gift might add to our understanding of the cultural nuances of gift-giving in Cambodia, and conclude with a few thoughts on the relevance of this discussion.

---

[10] World Bank, Sharing Growth, vi-vii, 29ff.
[11] I have talked with numerous others about this practice of calling the living *preta* since people tend to recognize it about half the time in any single group.

Preta and *Phchum Ben*

Seasonally, *Phchum Ben* is tied to the social and natural cycles of rural, rice-growing life. It takes place a few months before first harvests and after decreased food availability, and in these ceremonies, specified gifts of rice food are given to, or for, the spirits of dead family members. Ancestors, as "*chidaun* and *chita*", typically, play two roles within the society of the living. They ensure moral behaviour, and ensure wealth, health, and well-being to their descendents. The practice of *Phchum Ben* greatly resembles that type of relationship, with a twist: during *Phchum Ben*, the ancestors are themselves deeply in need of pity and gifts of charity, and the living, again in contrast with normal practice, give publicly and in some cases directly, to the ancestors.

Phchum Ben has significance as a clear example of a well-known type of agricultural ancestral ritual, with the addition that during the season ancestors are objects of charity and disgust rather than veneration and fear. During *Phchum Ben*, it would seem, the ancestor spirits are restored to their status as sources of fertility through the gifts from their living descendents. *Phchum Ben* also includes gifts from the living to the dead by which the relationship of the living descendents to the ancestors is reversed, with the living for once explicitly acknowledged as the source of ongoing value in the cycle composed of dead ancestors and reverent living descendents.

Let us look first at some different figures which evoke the term of the characteristics of the category '*preta*'.

Preta: *morally ambivalent receivers*

Phchum Ben's legendary origins are often assigned to the Indian king Bimbisara, who reigned during the time of the Buddha. He was harassed by the spirits of dead family members who complained of hunger and thirst. He tried to feed them directly with no success, until the Buddha explained that it was only by giving gifts to the monks that the gifts could reach or touch the dead and improve their lot. Once Bimbisara began to give his gifts to the Buddhist monks, his ancestors were satisfied. *Phchum Ben* takes the logic of this story – that morally efficacious gifts can only be made to the dead via the community of monks – and places it on an agricultural calendar, in which the monopoly of Buddhist monks over exchange with the dead is temporarily challenged.[12]

---

[12] Some Cambodians assert that the nineteenth-century king Ang Duong re-established the festival by reducing the period of the festival from the entire three months of the rainy season to its current length of only fifteen days.

Preta are by definition ancestors. Ancestor spirits supply the blessings of fertility; they contribute the abstract forces that make food possible and deflect the danger of hunger. This understanding also fits with a category of agricultural ritual in which the ancestors receive an annual or seasonal sacrifice of wealth. The great anthropologist of the gift Marcel Mauss identified such relationships to which the ancestors receive gifts from the living as the source of all wealth.[13]

But *preta*, or 'hungry ghosts,' are themselves defined by their lack of access to wealth and food. The living descendents of these hungry ancestors must take responsibility for feeding them, providing a new body, a new being, to their forebears, so that they in turn can offer the blessings of fertility and vitality.

The Buddhist textual imagination of the preta

The Buddhist textual discussions of *preta* take place primarily in two texts, the *petavatthu* and the *vimanavatthu*.[14] The former text narrates stories in which a person is reborn as a *preta* after their death as a result of some sin. The living then typically make merit by offering food to a Buddhist monk, at which point the food is transformed and received by the *preta* immediately. There is, in these stories, no need to wait for a subsequent birth in order to enjoy the fruits of meritorious activity, contrary to most other Buddhist writings. On receiving this merit, the *preta* instantly transforms from its hideous state and receives a splendid new body, similar to that of a *tevata*.[15]

Perhaps the most important scripture on the topic of *preta* is the Tirokuddasutta, which is chanted daily during the fifteen days of *Phchum Ben*. This sutta, found in multiple places in the Buddhist canon, describes *preta*, and proper interactions with them, this way:

> They stand at crossroads and outside the walls
> returning to their old homes, they wait at thresholds;
> because of karma, no one remembers them
> when an abundant feast of food and water is served.

[13] Marcel Mauss, *The Gift: the Form and Reason for Exchange in Archaic Societies* (New York & London: W. W. Norton and Co., 1990) and Blake Leland, "Voodoo Economics: Sticking Pins in Eros," *Diacritics* 18.2 (1988): 38.

[14] N.A. Jayawickrama, *Vimanavatthu and Petavatthu* (London: Pali Text Society, 1999). U Ba Kyauw and Peter Masefield, *Peta stories: elucidation of the intrinsic meaning so named the commentary on the peta-stories by Dhammapala* (London: Pali Text Society,1980).

[15] A concise summary of normative stories in the petavatthu is found in David G. White, "Dakkhina and agnicayana: an Extended Application of Paul Mus' Typology," *History of Religions*, 26 (1986): 188–213. White notes that while the immediacy of the fruits of this meritorious giving seem to contravene Buddhist understandings of the working of karma, "The concept of merit-transfer, although quite rare in the Pali canon, is almost totally bound up in the discussion of petas," Ibid., 206.

Those who feel pity therefore, at the right time
give truly pure food and drink to their relatives, rejoicing
"This is for you; our relatives should be happy"

Spectral relations gather and assemble.
Thoroughly pleased with the food and water, they reply
"May our relatives who provide for us have long lives.
We are honoured; giving is not without benefits".

There is no ploughing in that place, and cow-herding is unknown;
no trading, no buying, no selling with gold;
dead preta survive there on what is given from here.

Just as water poured on a hill
flows down and around it, sustaining the land all around,
so a gift from here benefits ghosts in precisely the same way.

Just as the rain from a full cloud
finally meanders to the sea, swelling the tides,
so a gift from here benefits ghosts in precisely the same way.

"He gave to me, he worked for me,
he was my friend, relative, and companion".
Give properly to the ghosts, remembering past deeds.

The weeping, mourning, and laments of relatives are useless
to those who remain in such a way.
But proper gifts dedicated to the *sangha* become useful to them immediately, and for a long time.

The duties toward relatives have thus been shown:
Veneration for the ghosts,
strength for the monks,
and no small merit for you.[16]

This concise text identifies a number of characteristics of the *preta*, and of those who are obliged to give to them. First, *preta* hover outside the walls and doors of temples and homes. Like beggars crowding temple entrances during the *Phchum Ben* season, they do not enter the temples nor participate in the rituals of giving, since they have nothing to give.[17] Second, as dead relatives, they are capable of returning meaningful blessings to the donors.

---

[16] My translation. The *Tirokuddasutta* is found in both the *khuddakapatha* (VII) and the *petavatthu* (I.5). James Egge believes that it may be quite old, relative to both sources. See James R. Egge, *Religious Giving and the Invention of Karma in Theravada Buddhism* (London: Routledge, 2002), 29.

[17] As ghosts, many Cambodians believe they are magically prevented from entering temple compounds. (Some say this is only true of temples that possess a magical power called *baramey*.)

The scripture also identifies the source of their poverty: *preta* have no access to the sources of human wealth: they cannot farm, they have no cattle to herd, and neither commerce nor monetized exchange exists for them. All that the *preta* consume must be given to them as a free gift. They cannot return the gift directly with goods or money of equivalent value, and in spite of the insistence that "the donors are not without reward", the donors do not see an immediate return. The living world intersects with the world of the spirits; a meeting between a world where barter and commerce create the wealth that can be given generously, and the world of the hungry ghosts, where all that is received must be given. Merely mourning their loss – mere remembrance – will not help the dead; they have physical needs as well.

Buddhist monks routinely argue that the only effective way to benefit the dead is through merit-making rituals, that is, by giving gifts to the monks. Giving gifts directly to the dead, according to these same arguments, cannot assist the dead. Instead, the dead must be given their gifts by offering them to Buddhist monks "at the right time". These gifts have the result – the fruit – of benefiting every member of the three-way transaction which creates this gift economy: the monks receive strength from the food they receive and eat, the ghosts receive new bodies and an alleviation of their suffering, and the donors receive blessings from their pleased ancestors and merit from their gifts to the monks.[18] We will see, however, that *Phchum Ben* includes two different gift-giving rituals, and only one includes monks directly.

During the *Phchum Ben* season, Yamaraja, the ruler of hell, releases the *preta* to return to their old homes and villages in search of gifts left at temples for them by their living descendents. *Preta* will search at seven temples, and if they have not found offerings after that point, she or he (or it) will curse the descendents' upcoming year, harvest, and prosperity.

The social imagination of Indic religion, whence the figure of the *preta* arrives, classifies many different types of *preta*, but a standard representation exists: a human-like being with a swollen stomach, impossibly skinny neck, and enormous eyes, and a mouth too small and magically puckered to allow the entry of any food or water. Not only are their bodies foul, they also experience magically restricted perception, and can only perceive foul things. Thus, if they receive food or water, they must find it in dirty and disgusting places, like mud or piles of faecal matter. In their hell, should they manage to get a bit of food to their mouth, it would explode into flame or transform into a mass of maggots. The life of a *preta* is a Sisyphean nightmare of hunger and unsatisfied need.

---

[18] Egge claims the *Tirokuddasutta* does not specifically characterize the ghosts as tormented, but instead "offers the happy prospect of living in a continuing relationship of mutual aid with one's deceased relatives." Egge, *Religious Giving and the Invention of Karma*, 31.

Two more sets of preta

If *preta* are beggar relatives, there are two more types of people whose beggar status may help to clarify the role the *preta* plays in the Cambodian imagination. Both are beggars, but like the dead ancestors themselves, they possess nearly opposed levels of social respect. These two groups are the "real" beggars, politely referred to as *neak som tien*, those who ask for gifts, and Buddhist monks, whose very title, *bhikkhu*, means "one who desires a share".[19]

While beggars are ubiquitous on Phnom Penh's streets throughout the year, some of the poorest of the rural poor go to the city during festival season, when ritual attendees remaining in the city may feel expansive and more willing to give small amounts of food or money to the poor. Here a small irony appears, in that while most urbanites leave the city for the countryside during the holiday, some of the rural poor move to the cities. Like the *preta* in the *tirokuddasutta*, beggars cluster around the thresholds and outer gates of Buddhist temples, and their poverty comes from their lack of access to the activities of farming, herding, trading, or power in the monetized economy. As a result, they too must rely on those who have such access, and who, by entering the ritual space created during *Phchum Ben*, are obliged to give to their "relatives", both those close to them, and those of the seventh generation.

Beggars may receive gifts, but little merit is thought to accrue to the giver as a result. The gift confirms the distance in social status, but does so without reference to any religious or cosmological justification such as the concept of *karma* or merit. From elderly women to street children, they crowd around the walls of temples, and beg for charity from those entering.

Buddhist monks are also beggars. Or at least, so their title, *bhikkhu*, would lead us to believe. However, unlike the beggars described above, giving to Buddhist monks generates a great deal of merit. Most Cambodians I asked explained this understanding by pointing out that Buddhist monks are "better people", and as such supporting them with gifts generates more merit than supporting beggars.[20]

If one gives to a beggar, there is no presumed capacity for return, unless we assume that the merit generated by the gift is a type of return gift, which

---

[19] Steven Collins provided me with the following etymology of *bhikkhu*, which is illuminating: *bhikkhu* is a nominalization of the desiderative form of the verbal root *bhaj*. The root meaning of *bhaj* is "to share in, to participate". Personal communication.

[20] Alternately, monks are described as "higher people", or "studying dharma". Beggars are often, as elsewhere, simultaneously pitied and judged for their poverty. The notion that merit made depends in part on the worthiness of the recipient is at odds with much doctrinal thought in Buddhism, which ascribes merit to the intention (*cetana*) accompanying the act of giving, rather than the worthiness of the recipient. Egge, *Religious Giving and the Invention of Karma*.

seems unlikely; if that were the case, who would fill the role of giver? Moreover, the beggar is presumed to consume the gift himself, rather than give it, or its successive prestation, on to another recipient. The situation of the beggar, who consumes what she or he is incapable of returning, contrasts dramatically with the situation of the *bhikkhu*.

Note first, however, that the *bhikkhu* similarly cannot return the gift directly, nor reciprocate. Having supposedly limited his worldly possessions to a bare minimum, there is very little the monk could give. Similarly, the monk does not himself give merit to the person who donates requisites to him; merit is made in the act, but not given by the monk. Finally, the monk is forbidden from even saying "thank you" to the donor.[21] That monks often occupy the role of merit factory, or "field of merit", in the merit economy is well known, but their behaviour discussed thus far does not identify them as unambiguous members of a gift economy, since they do not actually 'give.'

Monks serve as a conduit to the ancestors whose blessings are the prerequisite for wealth, health, and happiness for their descendents. As is made abundantly clear in Buddhist texts and by Buddhist monks, gifts made directly to the dead do nothing for the dead – the dead cannot "reach" them without the intervention of a monk. It is in this sense alone that the monk serves as the first recipient of the gift network, receiving food which, as the *Tirokuddasutta* explains, strengthens the monk, and passing along the merit, which acts as food for the dead, transforming them from *preta* to *devata*, or from *preta* to ancestor. The ancestor spirit then blesses its descendents, completing the three-point gift exchange, so that all points have both given and received, but not from the entity to whom they gave. Value is created, as Mauss noted, by being reciprocated in an indirect fashion, generalized to the society as a whole, to the "seventh generation".

Phchum Ben

Preta embark on an epic journey during the festival period, from hell to the villages of their relatives. But they are not alone in making pilgrimage. It is expected that all good Cambodians will return to the villages of their birth during *Phchum Ben*, or at least for the final day known as *Phchum*, or the day of gathering. Since *Phchum* should be celebrated in one's home village, the holiday involves massive evacuations of cities to birth villages. Those city-dwellers who are genuinely wealthy will often arrange in advance to donate sums of money or expensive ritual implements for the temple ceremonies, and a catered meal for themselves and a few of their local relatives after the ceremony. In return, some

---

[21] It has been repeatedly explained to me that if a monk says "thank you", no merit will be made.

occupy major roles in communally performed rituals, sit in the best places, and receive more attention from the family and community.

These economic and social distinctions between the city and the village are also points of contention. The generous gifts to the countryside's dead from the city are highly symbolic. They return the countryside's wealth without acknowledging that it had ever previously come from the country.

Phchum Ben means "the gathering of the rice balls", and occurs during the waning moon. The first fourteen days are technically referred to as the days of *dak ben* or *kan ben*, placing or carrying of the rice balls. Traditionally many villagers would share only a few temples, and the village chiefs consult with the temple committees to arrange for "turns", or *ven*, during which each village makes an appearance at the temple during different days of the festival. The last day, *Phchum*, is the day when everyone attends their primary temple – chosen by individual families, usually on the basis of a history of ordination or cremation – at the same time.

These practices of segmentary and shifting solidarity place us within the realm of the gift economy. In Marcel Mauss's classic exposition, societies organized by the gift impose three positive obligations: to give, to receive, and to return.[22] Mauss's primary examples were of societies in which gift economies were most explicit in rituals articulating the relationship between two social groups, such as clans. During *Phchum Ben*, the first fourteen days can be seen to represent a segmentary solidarity of a type larger than the household but smaller than the largest solidarity group. Within each of these groups, smaller, less formalized forms of giving may also be found. In Cambodia, this is found in the household, and its extension via familial networks: the radical idiom of reciprocity is imagined as kinship, "kin of the same flesh" (*sach nhiet*). Ly Daravuth also recognizes *Phchum Ben* as an act of communal identity transcending, among other things, the separation of death.[23]

While this bond of reciprocity through relationship is both practically and symbolically strong, there are a number of ambiguities in the formulation, which result in a particular vision of general reciprocity. Cambodians normally express a certain agnosticism regarding their relatives' status after death – they often have no reason to suppose that deceased relatives have been reborn as *preta*, but give in case they have been. Here we see the image of a generalized reciprocity. Food and merit must be given to relatives. *Phchum Ben* obligates giving to relatives, even if they are dead, and even if we cannot know if they are really in need.

---

[22] Mauss, *The gift*.
[23] Ly Daravuth, "Notes on Phchum Ben," A Working Paper of *Recasting Reconciliation through Culture and the Arts*, Brandeis University, 2005.

This generalized reciprocity is expressed in other ways. In addition to feeding and making merit on behalf of specific, often named, deceased relatives, participants are expected to offer something for all of their deceased relatives, "up to the seventh generation". Since relatives of the seventh generation are almost by definition complete strangers, this formula may in fact operate to express kinship with potentially anyone and everyone.[24]

Two ways of giving to the ancestors

During *Phchum Ben* there are two different forms of giving which entail different imaginary configurations of exchange and different attitudes for different members of that exchange. The most authorized offering is the daytime ceremony of chanting *bangsokaul*, a mortuary chant for the dead. In this offering, gifts of food are given to Buddhist monks. Names of specific dead relatives are usually attached to these offerings, and the monk will chant *bangsokaul* for the dead, transforming the gift into merit that will help the deceased achieve a better rebirth in the future. The ceremony is solemn, and the monks' participation is required – without monks, the *preta* will not be able to receive the gifts. This ceremony is usually performed in family groups.

The *bah bay ben* ceremony, in contrast, is significantly less authorized, and much more iconic. This night-time ceremony usually begins around three-thirty or four in the morning. In stark contrast to the *bangsokaul*, the *bah bay ben* ceremony seems festive, even gleeful. Participants gather usually at the eastern door of the main sanctuary, or *vihear*, and parade around it three times, throwing balls of rice and splashing water into the surrounding ground and mud. Monks have no formal role in this ceremony, and the names of the dead are not necessarily specified.

We can summarize the major differences between the two practices in the following ways. The *bangsokaul* performances emphasize the need for a monk, and gifts given to the monks are transformed into merit given to the spirits. *Bangsokaul* respects the *preta* by treating them in their ancestral aspect. *Bangsokaul* constitutes and imagines a particular type of reciprocity via the metaphors of kinship. Gifts given in such relationships compel and enable their future return, and are celebrated in confidence of the mutual respect involved in the relations.

Bah Bay Ben, on the other hand, emphasizes interaction with the spirits unmediated by monks. It alleviates the hunger which defines the *preta* and treats

---

[24] This sort of generalized reciprocity however has a lot of affective impact for the reason that giving to the seventh generation doesn't create the specific hierarchical relationships instituted by Cambodian society.

them less respectfully, insofar as *bah bay ben* emphasizes their disgusting position by throwing offerings into mud and filth, whence the beggarly ghosts will retrieve their sustenance. *Bah bay ben* then enacts but does not unambiguously celebrate a positive, generalized reciprocity. Instead it challenges the ancestors with gifts given to them unaccompanied by their normal veneration. ***Bah bay ben*** expresses the living world's resentment of the greedy and currently unimpressive dead; most recipients who look like this in the imaginary would clearly be beggars, who cannot be counted on to return the gift later to those who feed them now.

I have given a basic description of the idea of *Phchum Ben*, its relationship to agricultural cycles and imaginaries, and the two primary rituals of giving. I must now present *Phchum Ben* as an example of "the gift" and of giving according to mainstream anthropological thought on the idea. I will indicate the way in which gift exchange is distinct from market exchange in regards to rural relations, and why certain practices so commonly seem to express resentment or aggression on the part of the participants.

Theories of the Gift

The history of thought on the gift and what have come to be termed gift economies within anthropology is foundational, radical, and more than a bit romantic. It is foundational in a number of respects, not least owing to its preeminence in the work of Marcel Mauss, whose essay *The Gift* remains one of the most important texts in the discipline, and which inaugurated the topic as one of core importance. Within that book, Mauss identified gift economies as systems for managing human aggression via the exchange of gifts, rather than via the political and economics mechanisms of state and market exchange.[25]

Mauss's essay challenged the image of the human being as essentially "economic" and figured within the realm of the triumphal State. Mauss argued from a premise similar to that of Hobbes: humanity is composed of individuals, each one potentially at war with every other. But while the State was the answer to this dilemma found in *Leviathan*, according to Mauss gift economies functioned by allowing for antagonistic expressions to be publicly coded as generosity, both when they truly were, and when they were used to shame the recipient. It was this basic expression of solidarity – the gift – that allowed for normal conflict management, and were also, in extreme cases, clear examples of resentment of one's partners in exchange.

This antagonism between givers and receivers is a result of the obligations that the gift exchange imposes on the receiver. In the case of the *potlatch*, the

---

[25] Mauss, Marcel, *The Gift*.

obligation to return *at least* as valuable a *potlatch* may result in extravagant offerings, bankruptcy, or a loss of social face and standing. Leland writes of the anthropological gift, "Masked as generosity, this extravagant giving is really a display of power, since the recipients of the gifts are obliged to gift a *potlatch* in return".[26] In this case one would rather receive fewer presents. But one of the obligations of the gift is to receive; to refuse is unbearably impolite.[27]

The idea that gift economies and exchange economies were necessarily opposed (in the same way that communism and capitalism are opposed) has led to much insightful and productive work, which must also occasionally be criticized as romantic. The romanticism has done little to obviate the importance of the contributions to anthropology however, and some of this has recently begun to be interrogated in ways that do not eliminate the primary opposition, found already in Mauss, of the gift to market exchange and the State.[28]

There have been many influential readings of Mauss's *Gift*, including those which nuanced the original theory. Originating with Mauss, the theory included the notion that the exchange of items of value, which as "total prestations", also embody a portion of the giver themselves and create networks that transmit value, and in so doing, reproduce a society. Second, there is the notion, apparently first made explicit by Marshall Sahlins, that the proper exchange of gifts in a gift economy must take place in a network comprising at least three points: that is, one cannot simply exchange gifts back and forth with a single partner.[29]

While many anthropologists have followed the line that gift economies are opposed to market exchange, perhaps even more have unconsciously accepted the evolutionary notions in Mauss's concept – that the gift economy pre-dated market exchange. In his work on the Kabre, Charles Piot has argued instead that while gift and commodity are separate and antagonistic forms of exchange, they both exist simultaneously for most subjects, who choose to use one or the other depending on the desired relationship with the partner.

Piot's work demonstrates a gift economy in Kabre society in distinction to the market exchange, and one of his most lucid examples focuses on the historical sale of some Kabre people by their relatives, to slave traders. According to Piot, the sale of relatives was indicative of a refusal to engage in "gift relations" with

---

[26] Leland, "Voodoo Economics," 39.
[27] I have already indicated that the double-performance of gift-giving during *Phchum Ben*, found in the *bah bay ben* and the *bangsokaul* ceremonies, reflects this ambiguity toward the dead, and the dependency the living have on them the rest of the year.
[28] See especially Charles Piot, *Remotely Global: Village Modernities in West Africa* (Chicago: University of Chicago Press, 1999). Piot argues that gift economies may in many cases be a relatively recent phenomenon, and at least in the African villages of his own ethnographic work a post-contact response to capitalist exchange, marking an insider-outsider division.
[29] Sahlins, "The Spirit of the Gift."

the slave merchants by replacing these with market exchange in the vernacular of money for human beings.[30]

Whereas market exchange is anonymous and requires no ongoing relationship between the actors, gift relationships function in part precisely because they require the recipient to later give a gift or else be considered cheap, poor, and beggarly, or indifferent. Piot therefore concludes that gift economies are rituals ideally limited to insiders, and market exchanges are preferred when one wishes to escape the obligations and results of a gift exchange.

The consequences of gift exchange that some may prefer to escape include the following: upon receiving gifts from another, you are in a state of "debt" until such time as you return the gift or pass the gift along. Piot is insightful and specific on this point: in order for the gift economy to remain harmonious, the constant alternation of hierarchies, between giver and recipient, must be practised.[31] The gift exchange exists to "produce varying relationships, all of which are in part determined by the relative 'debt' of one partner to the other".[32]

Piot's work demonstrates that in situations where people have access to both gift and commodity as mediums of exchange, the two economies may complement rather than contradict each other. Societies may prefer market exchange in order to mark boundaries with those it considers outsiders, and with whom one does not want to exchange personal stuff, which is, according to Mauss, a requirement of the gift. The gift versus commodity distinction then, exists largely on a moral plane, marking those with whom one is willing to exchange personal stuff in the form of gifts, and those with whom one has no moral relationship. In the gift economy, moral insiders are also mutually policing and evaluating partners.

These are the reasons why some rural Cambodians may resent city dwellers when they first meet up after months of separation. Those coming from the city are not identical, but range from wealthy families, to poor women living and working in factories remitting enormous portions of their salaries to their rural families, to students.[33] Those who return are nevertheless associated in differing

---

[30] Charles Piot, "Of Slaves and the Gift: Kabre Sale of Kin during the Era of the Slave trade," *The Journal of African History* 37.1 (1996): 31–49.

[31] That there should be a hierarchy produced by the exchange is the result of the prestational nature of such gifts.

[32] Piot, *Remotely Global*, 62, 65. Where gift exchange produces difference and mutuality, market exchange produces distance and alienation (47). Sale and market exchange can then on occasion be used to escape hierarchies or other types of unwelcome relationship (48).

[33] Note that the global economic crisis has already hit the situation of the garment workers and other rural poor. Garment workers have taken to foraging for food along the banks of ponds and streams near the factories, in order to get enough to eat. Sam Rith, "As prices rise, workers go foraging," *Phnom Penh Post*, 22 October 2008.

degrees with the city and its wealth, and simultaneously to the countryside's poverty. As I have discussed, the rural poor understand the city's wealth to be based on rural poverty. Moreover, the city comes to the countryside most conspicuously in the guise of someone bearing gifts, via remittances, sponsorship of rituals, or other forms of giving, and each conspicuous gift indebts someone in the countryside. This brings us to the question of political gift giving.

Political gifts appear only in part to be a cynical cultural gesture; but they can also never be adequately returned by a single vote, and one may very well resent the continuing subservience in which one then finds oneself.[34]

This brings us to our final point that, while fora for critiquing elite interpretations of relationships, or their institution, may indeed be rare, Cambodian culture itself contains the resources to criticize both, and to contest the meanings in public, even through semi-anonymous shouts along rural roads.

The Punchline

So we return to the discussion of resentment in the gift. What kind of action is ventured in response to this? In a now-famous article on resentment of gifts, Richard Lee wrote about a personal experience in which he bought a cow to share with his friends in the village where he was staying. He was disturbed and confused when his friends routinely and rudely disparaged and badmouthed his generous offering. When he finally received an explanation, he was told that that this was done to prevent hierarchies from becoming fixed, and to prevent the giver from becoming "arrogant".[35]

> Yes, when a young man kills much meat he comes to think of himself as a chief or a big man, and he thinks of the rest of us as his servants or inferiors. We can't accept this. We refuse one who boasts, for someday his pride will make him kill somebody. So we always speak of his meat as worthless. This way we cool his heart and make him gentle.[36]

The obligations of *Phchum Ben* are fairly clear: gifts of food and merit are to be given to all seven generations of relatives, and such gifts must be accepted. In return, the recipients must bless the givers. The wealth given by the city in the gifting rituals of *Phchum Ben* are rooted in the unmarked flows of wealth and

---

[34] On the question of political gift giving in contemporary Cambodia, see Caroline Hughes, "The Politics of Gifts: Tradition and Regimentation in Contemporary Cambodia," *Journal of Southeast Asian Studies* 37.3 (2006): 469–489.
[35] Richard B. Lee, "Eating Christmas in the Kalahari" *Natural History* (1969): 3.
[36] Ibid., 4.

labour from the countryside to the cities, where commerce, wage labour, and monetized exchange create the wealth that is only partially returned in gifts. In *Phchum Ben* a gift economy with the dead suddenly appears alongside the free-market economy with the living which drives the inequities of modern-day Cambodia, in order to compare one type of exchange with another.

This gift economy is imagined to encompass all one's relatives, even though one may not recognize them – the seven generations. Part of *Phchum Ben*'s communal labour then, is the imagination of all participants as relatives, kin to whom mutual obligations are owed, not out of formal obligations, but because they are kin. A large part of the activity of creating this ritual solidarity is the creation and maintenance of kinship relations through giving. This practice has often been called "fictive kinship".

Fictive kinship is a form of imaginary solidarity. It may or may not lead to real solidarity, but it is a means of expressing a moral and social relationship among people that is understood not to be explicitly or formerly acknowledged. There are at least two forms of imagined kinship during *Phchum Ben*. First, people imagine their dead relatives coming to beg food from them. Second, some rural Cambodians imagine their city-dwelling relatives as these same hungry ghosts coming to the countryside.

This joke relies on the fact that *Phchum Ben* and the image of the *preta* already act as resources for imagining and representing criticisms of contemporary poverty and inequality. The joke relies on an explicit reversal of the ritual imagination: those who receive in ritual context are the ones who should be, and normally are, metaphorized as *preta*. But when city families return to their birth villages in order to celebrate *Phchum*, rather than celebrate in their urban homes, they often return with gifts and offerings, and sometimes see themselves as givers, and the country relatives as the *preta*. Indeed, for the most part the resemblances are more than metaphorical. The Food and Agricultural Organization of the UN routinely notes the disparity in food consumption between the cities and the countryside, where malnutrition results in the swollen bellies, thin stringy hair, and tattered clothing that describe the *preta* of myth. At least a part of our joke relies on a bitter reversal of categories.

Imagining one's city relatives as *preta* implies that it is the city and the people in it that are returning to the countryside, once a year, to ask for what they need. It is the one time of year when Khmer are above their ancestors, and in one of the two giving rituals the living make this clear. This joke, in other words, appears as a product of the religious imagination about *Phchum Ben*, and the practices of giving that are embedded within it, to discuss a problem that ritual cannot solve. The ritual may redistribute some wealth, and destroy more, but families from the city remain significantly wealthier than their relatives in the country. Still, gifts and givers from the city can at the very least be denigrated. Indeed, it is the violent hunger and endless greed of corrupt officials and businesspeople that earns them, in other situations, the metaphorization of the *preta*.[37]

Recipients in such a situation may choose not to celebrate the gift: instead accepting with one hand what they deride with the other. In an essay titled "What makes Indians laugh", Pierre Clastres noted that jokes deriding socially powerful people are funny precisely because of their derision, and the resolution of social contradictions that such transgressions attempt to accomplish:

> The contradiction between the imaginary world of the myth and the real world of everyday life is resolved when one recognizes in the myths a derisive intent: the [Indians] do in mythical life what is forbidden them in real life. . . .. For the Indians, it is a matter of challenging, of demystifying in their own eyes the fear and the respect [that they are supposed to display].[38]

If Clastres's subjects do in mythical life what is forbidden them in real life, rural Khmer appear to be saying in real life one part of what is offered in ritual life: the denigration of the charity of the city. They are insisting instead on a number of things: they are the real givers; they have already returned the gift; the status that is conferred on the ritual givers during *Phchum* should be reversed. This amounts to an attempt to contain the effects of the ritual's imagining of the social world by inverting the roles.

And judging by the reaction of my fellow passengers on the bus, the message was received.

---

[37] A final note about the further ambiguity of the role of the returning garment worker. While clearly a member of the rural poor, she (or rarely, he) may also be the subject of some rural resentment, especially among non-kin members who see her as the cause of local inequality. This fits with the fact that I never witnessed kin in hometowns acting in this manner, but only strangers on the roadside, and when asked if kin would act in such a way, most of those who replied answered that they would not.

[38] Pierre Clastres, *Society against the State* (New York: Zone Books, 1987), 145.

Bibliography

3S Rivers Protection Network. *Abandoned Villages along the Sesan River in Ratanakiri Province, Northeastern Cambodia*. Banlung: 3S Rivers Protection Network, 2007.

Adler, Daniel, Douglas J. Porter, and Michael Woolcock. "Legal Pluralism and Equity: Some Reflections on Land Reform in Cambodia." *Justice for the Poor* 2.2 (2008): available online at SSRN: http://ssrn.com/abstract=1133690, accessed 14 August 2009.

Agence France Presse. "Land Grabs Leave Thousands Destitute in Cambodia's Heartland." News report. Phnom Penh, 14 May 2007.

Agence France Presse. "Cambodia Garments Exports Halve." News report. Phnom Penh, 21 March 2009.

Agence Khmer de Presse. "Cambodian Signs Land Concession Agreement for Sugar Cane Production." News report in English. Phnom Penh, 8 August 2006.

Agence Khmer de Presse. "Guinea to Import Rice from Cambodia." News report in English. Phnom Penh, July 3 2008.

Allen, Bryant J., and Chris Ballard. "Beyond Intensification? Reconsidering Agricultural Transformations." *Asia Pacific Viewpoint* 42.2&3 (2001): 157–162.

Amsden, Alice. "The State and Taiwan's Economic Development." In Peter Evans, Dietrich Rueschemeyer, and Theda Skocpol eds, *Bringing the State Back In*. Cambridge: Cambridge University Press, 1985. 78–106.

Ann, Sovatha. *Patron-Clientism and Decentralization: An Emerging Local Political Culture in Rural Cambodia*. M.A Thesis. Northern Illinois University, 2008.

Apornrath Phoonphongphiphat, and Wilanwan Pongpitak. "Thai Khon Kaen Plans Rising Sugar Exports." *Reuters News*, 22 March 2007.

Aranee Jaiimsin. "Commodities/Sugar Industry Expansion; KSL Joins Partners in Cambodia Venture." *Bangkok Post*, 7 August 2006.

Arulpagasam, Jehan, Francesco Goletti, Tamar Manuelyan Atinc, and Vera Songwe. "Trade in Sectors Important to the Poor: Rice in Cambodia and Vietnam and Cashmere in Mongolia." In Kathie Krumm, and Homi Kharas, ed., *East Asia Integrates: A Trade Policy Agenda for Shared Growth*. Washington, DC: World Bank, 2004. 199–221. Available online at http://siteresources.worldbank.org/

INTEAPREGTOPINTECOTRA/Resources/chapter+9.pdf, accessed 12 August 2009.
Asia Pulse. "Asia Agribusiness." News report. 1 November 2006. Available online at http://www.asiapulse.com/, accessed 12 August 2009.
Asian Development Bank *Technical Assistance to the Royal Kingdom of Cambodia for Rural Credit and Savings Project* (Manila: Asian Development Bank, 1997) online at www.adb.org
Asian Development Bank *Cambodia: Financial sector Blueprint 2001-2010* (Phnom Penh: Asian Development Bank, 2001) online at www.adb.org
Asian Development Bank. *Program Performance Audit Report on the Agriculture Sector Program (loan 1445-CAM[SF]) in Cambodia.* Manila: ADB, July 2003. Available online at www.adb.org/ Documents/PPARs/ CAM/PPARCAM_27154.pdf, accessed 10 June 2009.
Asian Development Bank *Cambodia: Rural Credit and Savings Project* (Manila: Asian Development Bank, 2007) online at www.adb.org.
Asian Legal Resource Centre. "UN Human Rights Council/Cambodia: Landgrabbing, Corruption and the Rule of Law in Cambodia." *Human Rights Solidarity* 17.2 (2007): available online at http://www.hrsolidarity.net/mainfile.php/2006vol16no02/, accessed 3 Feb 2009.
Asma, Stephen. *The Gods Drink Whiskey. Stumbling towards Enlightment in the Land of the Tattered Buddha.* New York: HarperCollins, 2005.
Associated Press. "Cambodia Gives Garment Cos. Tax Holiday." News report. 16 June 2006.
Ayres, David. *NGOs, Partnership, and Local Governance in Cambodia.* Discussion paper. Mimeo. Phnom Penh, 2004.
Backstrom, Maria, Jeremy Ironside, Gordon Paterson, Jonathan Padwe, and Ian Baird. *Indigenous Traditional Legal Systems and Conflict Resolution in Ratanakiri and Mondulkiri Provinces, Cambodia.* Phnom Penh: United Nations Development Programme/Cambodian Ministry of Justice Legal and Judicial Reform Programme, 2006.
Barron, Porter. "Teen Suspected of Stealing Resin Shot Dead." *The Cambodia Daily*, 2 December 2003.
Barton, Cat, and Cheang Sokha. "Keeping Farm in Family Hands." *Phnom Penh Post*, 22 February 2008, online at www.phnompenhpost.com, accessed 8 June 2009.
Batliwala, Srilatha. "The Meaning of Women's Empowerment: New Concepts from Action." In Gita Sen, Adrienne Germain, and Lincoln C. Chen, eds., *Population Policies Reconsidered: Health, Empowerment and Rights.* Boston: Harvard University Press, 1994. 127-138.
——— "Taking the Power out of Empowerment: an Experiential Account." *Development in Practice* 17.4 (2007): 557-565.
Baxter, Will. "Govt to Launch Policy Protecting Migrant Labourers." *Phnom Penh Post*, 14 June 2010.
Bebbington, Anthony, Sam Hickey and Diana Mitlin. "Introduction." In Anthony Bebbington, Sam Hickey and Diana Mitlin, eds., *Can NGOs Make a Difference? The Challenge of Development Alternatives.* London: Zed Books, 2008. 1-15.

Better Factories Cambodia. *Twentieth Synthesis Report on Working Conditions in Cambodia's Garment Sector.* Phnom Penh: International Labour Organization /Better Factories Cambodia, 30 April 2008. Available online at http://www.betterfactories.org/content/documents/1/20th%20Synthesis%20Report%20Final%20(EN).pdf, accessed 12 August 2009.

Bigombe, Betty, Paul Collier and Nicholas Sambanis. "Policies for Building Post-Conflict Peace." *Journal of African Economies* 9.3 (2000): 323–348.

Bit Seanglim. *The Warrior Heritage. A Psychological Perspective of Cambodian Trauma.* El Cerrito: Bit Seanglim, 1994.

Blaikie, Piers, and Harold Brookfield. *Land Degradation and Society.* London: Methuen, 1987.

Bolwell, Dain. *Cambodia Trade Union Survey.* Phnom Penh: International Labour Organisation, 2004.

Boserup, Ester . *The Conditions of Agricultural Growth: The Economics of Agrarian Change Under Population Pressure.* Chicago: Aldine, 1965.

Boston, Jonathan. *Public Management: the New Zealand Model.* Oxford: Oxford University Press, 1996.

Bottomley, Ruth. "Contested Forests: An Analysis of the Highlander Response to Logging, Ratanakiri Province, Northeast Cambodia." *Critical Asian Studies*, 34.4 (2002): 587–606.

Brigg, Morgan. "Disciplining the Developmental Subject: Neoliberal Power and Governance through Microcredit." In Jude Fernando, ed., *Microfinance: Perils and Prospects.* London: Routledge, 2006. 55–76.

Broegaard, Rikke J. "Land Tenure Insecurity and Inequality in Nicaragua," *Development and Change* 36, 5 (2005): 845–864.

Bromley, Daniel W. "Formalizing Property Relations in the Developing World: The Wrong Prescription for the Wrong Malady." *Land Use Policy* 26.1 (2009): 20–27.

Brookfield, Harold. "Intensification and Disintensification in Pacific Agriculture: A Theoretical Approach." *Pacific Viewpoint* 13. 1 (1972): 78–96.

——— *Exploring Agrodiversity.* New York: Columbia University Press, 2001.

Brown, Graham. *CFI Ratanakiri Coordinator 2004–2007, End of Contract Report to Community Forestry International.* Unpublished report. Phnom Penh, 2008

Bryden, Alison, Timothy Donais and Hyder Hänggi. *Shaping a Security Governance Agenda in Post-Conflict Peacebuilding.* Geneva Centre for the Democratic Control of Armed Forces Policy Paper no. 11. Geneva: Centre for the Democratic Control of Armed Forces, 2005. Available online at http://www.dcaf.ch/_docs/pp11_bryden.pdf, accessed 20 April 2009.

Bulletin de Chambre Mixte de Commerce et d'Agriculture de Cambodge. 17 February 1970. Available in the State Archives of Cambodia (ANC), Box 165.

Calavan, Michael, Sergio Briquets, and Jerald O'Brien. *Cambodia Corruption Assessment.* Phnom Penh: USAID Cambodia / Casals & Associates, 2004.

"Cambodia Beckons Thai Firms to Pump in More Investment." *The Nation*, 23 November 2006.

Cambodia Development Resource Institute. *Pro-poor Tourism in the Greater Mekong Sub-Region.* Phnom Penh: CDRI, 2007.

Cambodian Human Rights and Development Association (ADHOC). *Human Rights Situation 2007.* Phnom Penh: ADHOC, 2008.

Cambodian League for the Promotion and Defence of Human Rights (LICADHO). *Letter and Background Note on NGO Law to Various Embassies.* Unpublished letter. Phnom Penh, 2006.

——— *Attacks and Threats Against Human Rights Defenders in Cambodia, 2007.* Phnom Penh: LICADHO, 2008.

Cambodia Microfinance Association. *Information Exchange.* Webpage. 2008. Available online at www.CMA-Network.org/information.htm, accessed 10 April 2009.

Cammack, Paul. "Neoliberalism, the World Bank, and the New Politics of Development." In Uma Kothari, and Martin Minogue, eds., *Development Theory and Practice: Critical Perspectives.* London: Palgrave, 2002. 157–178.

Campion, Anita, and Victoria White. *Non-Governmental Organisation Transformation into Regulated Finance Entities: From Do Good to Be Good.* Bethesda: USAID Microenterprise Best Practices, 2001. Available online at http://www.microfinancegateway.org/p/site/m//template.rc/1.9.28745, accessed 20 August 2009.

Castles, Stephen, and Mark J. Miller. *The Age of Migration. International Population Movements in the Modern World.* New York: Palgrave Macmillan, 2003.

Centre for Advanced Studies. *Child Work and Child Labour at the Chub Rubber Plantation in Cambodia.* Phnom Penh, September 2001. Available online at www.cascambodia.org/child_plantation.htm, accessed 10 June 2009.

Centre for Advanced Studies/World Bank. *Justice for the Poor: an Exploratory Study of Collective Grievances over Land and Local Governance in Cambodia.* Phnom Penh: World Bank/CAS, 2006.

——— *Linking Citizens and the State: an Assessment of Civil Society Contributions to Good Governance in Cambodia.* Draft report. Phnom Penh: World Bank/CAS, 2008.

Chalamwong, Yongyuth. "Government Policies on International Migration: Illegal Workers in Thailand." In Aris Ananta and Evi Nurvidya Arifin, eds., *International Migration in Southeast Asia.* Singapore: Institute for South East Asian Studies, 2004. 352–73.

Chan Sophal and Sarthi Acharya. *Land Transactions in Cambodia, An Analysis of Transfers and Transaction Records.* Working Paper 22. Phnom Penh: Cambodia Development Resources Institute, 2002.

Chandler, David. *The Tragedy of Cambodian History: Politics, War, and Revolution since 1945.* New Haven: Yale University Press, 1991.

——— *A History of Cambodia.* 4th edition. Boulder: Westview Press, 2008.

Chean Sokha. "PM Wants Cambodian Workers in Thailand to Come Back Home." *Phnom Penh Post*, 02 October 2008.

Chetan, Tanmay. "Are Financial and Social Objectives Mutually Exclusive? The Experience of AMK, Cambodia." *Small Enterprise Development* 18.1 (2007): 65–78.

Chhim, Kristina. *Die Revolutionare Volkspartei Kampuchea 1979 bis 1989.* Frankfurt: Peter Lang, 2000.

Chhim Sopheak and Lasse Karner. "Young Man Killed While Trying To Steal Rubber." *The Cambodia Daily*, 21 September 2005, 14.

Christian Outreach (CORD) Asia. *The Community Peace Building Network in Cambodia. A Strategic Review 2008*. 2nd draft for comments. Phnom Penh: February 2009.

Chun Sakada. "Migrant Workers to Get Free Passports." News report. *Voice Of America Khmer*, 24 November 2008.

Chun Sophal and Hor Hab. "Mong Retthy Group Aims for One Million Pigs per Year by 2015." *The Phnom Penh Post*, 8 January 2009. Available online at www.phnompenhpost.com, accessed 12 August 2009.

Clastres, Pierre. 1987. *Society against the State*. New York: Zone Books, 1987.

Cochrane, Liam. "Cambodia: Can't See the Forest for the Thieves." *World Politics Review*, 6 June 2007: available online at http://www.worldpoliticsreview.com/article.aspx?id=829, accessed 13 August 2009.

Cock, Andrew Robert. *The Interaction between a Ruling Elite and an Externally Promoted Policy Reform Agenda: The Case of Forestry under the Second Kingdom of Cambodia 1993–2003*. Ph.D. Dissertation. La Trobe University, 2007.

Coghlan, Mathew. *China's Poverty Footprint in Cambodia*. Hongkong: Oxfam, 2008.

Collier, Paul, and David Dollar. "Development Effectiveness: What Have We Learnt?" *The Economic Journal*, 114.496 (2004): F263.

Condominas, Georges, ed. "Aspects of Economics among the Mnong Gar of Vietnam: Multiple Money and the Middleman." *Ethnology* 11. 3 (1972): 202–219.

——— *Formes Extrêmes de Dépendance: Contributions à l'étude de l'esclavage en Asie du Sud-Est*. Paris: Ecole des Hautes Études en Sciences Sociales, 1998.

Conroy, John. "The challenges of Microfinance in Southeast Asia." In Nick J. Freeman ed., *Financing Southeast Asia's Economic Development*. Singapore: Institute of Southeast Asian Studies, 2003. 120–147.

Consultative Group to Assist the Poor (CGAP). *Good Practice Guidelines for Funders of Microfinance: Microfinance Consensus Guidelines*. Washington: CGAP, 2006. Available online at http://www.cgap.org/p/site/c/template.rc?gbl-searchKeywords=Good+practice+guidelines+funders&type=Search+Vignette&Submit.x=22&Submit.y=8, accessed 20 August 2009.

——— *Key Principles of Microfinance*. Washington: CGAP, 2004. Available online at http://www.cgap.org/p/site/c/template.rc/1.9.2747/, accessed 20 August 2009.

Conway. Tim. *Poverty, Participation and Programmes: International Aid and Rural Development in Cambodia*. PhD Thesis. University of Cambridge, 1999.

Copestake, James. "Inequality and the Polarizing Impact of Microcredit: Evidence from Zambia's Copperbelt." *Journal of International Development* 14.6 (2002): 743–756.

Coston, Jennifer, M., "Administrative Avenues to Democratic Governance: the Balance of Supply and Demand", *Public Administration and Development*," 18 (1998): 479–493.

Coxhead, Ian. "Development and the Environment in Asia: A Survey of Recent Literature." *Asian-Pacific Economic Literature* 17, no. 1 (2003): 22–54.

——— "A New Resource Curse? Impacts of China's Boom on Comparative Advantage and Resource Dependence in Southeast Asia." *World Development* 35, no. 7 (2007): 1099–119.

Craig, David, and Doug Porter. *Development beyond Neo-Liberalism: Governance, Poverty Reduction and Political Economy*. London: Routledge, 2006.

——— "Winning the Peace: Re-Institutionalising Conflict in Cambodia's Politics and Governance." Paper presented at *Critical Approaches to Post-Conflict Policy: Post-Conflict Development or Development for Conflict?* University of Oxford, 25–26 June 2008.

Crone, Donald. "State, Social Elites, and Government Capacity in Southeast Asia." *World Politics* 40.2 (1998): 252–268.

Crook, Richard and James Manor. *Democracy and Decentralisation in South Asia and West Africa: Participation, Accountability, and Performance.* Cambridge: Cambridge University Press,1998.

Crook, Richard and A. Sverrison. *Decentralisation and Poverty Alleviation in Developing Countries: A Comparative Analysis in West Bengal Unique?* Working Paper, No. 129. Brighton: University of Sussex Institute of Development Studies, 2001.

Crouch, Harold. "Indonesia's "Strong" State." In Peter Dauvergne, ed., *Weak and Strong States in Asia Pacific Societies.* Canberra: Allen & Unwin, 93–113.

Cruz, Abelardo, and Meas Nee. *Options for Future Support to Empowering Community-Based Organisations In Cambodia.* Phnom Penh: Forum Syd, 2006.

Curtis, Grant. *A Country Profile*: a *report prepared for the Swedish International Development Authority.* Stockholm: SIDA, 1989.

De Genova, Nicholas P. "Migrant 'Illegality' and Deportability in Everyday Life." *Annual Review of Anthropology* 31 (2002): 419–47.

De Haas, Hein. "International Migration, Remittances and Development: Myths and Facts." *Third World Quarterly* 26.8 (2005): 1269–84.

Degen, Peter, Frank Van Acker, Niek Van Zalinge, Nao Thuok, and Ly Vuthy. *Taken for Granted. Conflicts over Cambodia's Freshwater Fish Resources.* Paper for 8th International Association for the Study of Common Property Conference. Bloomington, 2000. Available online at http://dlc.dlib.indiana.edu/archive/00000245/00/degenp041100.pdf, accessed 9 August 2009.

Deshmukh-Ranadive, Joy, and Ranjani K Murthy. "Introduction: Linking the Triad." In Neera Burra, Joy Deshmukh-Ranadive, and Ranjani K Murthy, eds., *Micro-Credit, Poverty and Empowerment: Linking the Triad.* New Delhi: Sage Publications, 2005. 31–60.

Devas, Nick, and Ursula Grant. "Local Government Decision-making—Citizen Participation and Local Acommune counciluountability: Some Evidence from Kenya and Uganda." *Public Administration and Development*, 23 (2003): 307–316.

DiMaggio, Paul, and Walter Powell. "The Iron Cage revisited: institutional isomorphism and collective rationality in organizational fields." *American Sociological Review* 48.2 (1991): 147–60.

"Donors Pledge More Than $900 Million." *Cambodia Daily,* 5 December 2008.

Dournes, Jacques. "Le Milieu Jörai: Éléments d'Ethno-Ecologie d'une Ethnie Indochinoise." Études Rurales 53–54–55–56 (1974). Available online at http://etudesrurales.revues.org/document584.html, accessed 12 August 2009.

Dove, Michael R. "Theories of Swidden Agriculture, and the Political Economy of Ignorance." *Agroforestry Systems* 1.2 (1983): 85–99.

Deutsche Presse Agentur, "Kuwaitis to Return to Cambodia for Rice Talks — Summary." News report. 6 August 2008.

Dunleavy, Patrick, and Christopher Hood. "From Old Public Administration to New Public Management." *Public Money and Management*, 14.3 (1994): 9–16.
Duong Sokha. "Le Prix à Payer pour Entrer dans la Caste des Oknhas." *Ka-Set Info*. 14 April 2008. Available online at http://ka-set.info, accessed 12 August 2009.
Ear, Sophal. *The Political Economy of Pro-Poor Livestock Policy in Cambodia*. Pro-Poor Policy Livestock Initiative Working Paper No. 26. Rome: Food and Agriculture Organization of the United Nations, 2005. Available online at http://www.fao.org/ag/againfo/projects/en/pplpi/docarc/wp26.pdf, accessed 12 August 2009.
——— "Change and Continuity in Cambodian Human Rights and Freedom of Expression: Learning from Experience." Report for Pact Cambodia Final Draft. 26 May 2006. Available online at http://csua.berkeley.edu/~sophal/pact/pact.pdf, accessed 12 August 2009.
Ebihara, May. *Svay, A Khmer Village in Cambodia*. PhD Dissertation. Columbia University, 1968.
Economic Institute of Cambodia. *Export Diversification and Value Addition for Human Development: Addressing the Impact of the Agreement on Textile and Clothing Expiration on Cambodia*. Phnom Penh: Economic Institute of Cambodia, 2007.
Egge, James R. *Religious Giving and the Invention of Karma in Theravada Buddhism*. London: Routledge, 2002.
Ek Madra. "China to Give Cambodia $215 mln to Build Roads." *Reuters News*. 3 December 2008.
Eng Netra, and David Craig. *Accountability and Human Resource Management in Decentralized Cambodia*. Working Paper no. 40. Phnom Penh: Cambodia Development Resource Institute, 2009.
Eng Sot. *Ka Soeksa Chbab Kruab Meatra Knong Kram Rathpakveni* [Study of Law in Civil Code]. Phnom Penh: Ministry of Justice, 1967.
Environment Forum Core Team. *Fast-wood Plantations, Economic Concessions, and Local Livelihoods in Cambodia*. Phnom Penh: NGO Forum, 2006.
Evans, Peter. "Predatory, Developmental, and Other Apparatuses: a Comparative Political Economy Perspective on the Third World State." *Sociological Forum* 4.4 (1989): 561–587.
——— *Embedded Autonomy: States and Industrial Transformation*. Princeton: Princeton University Press, 1995.
Evans, Peter, Dietrich Rueschemeyer and Theda Skocpol. *Bringing the State Back In*. Cambridge: Cambridge University Press, 1985.
Faist, Thomas. "Migrants as Transnational Development Agents: An Inquiry into the Newest Round of the Migration-Development Nexus." *Population, Space and Place* 14 (2008): 21–42.
Feyzioglu, Tarhan, Vinaya Swaroop, and Zhu Min. "A Panel Data Analysis of the Fungibility of Foreign Aid." *World Bank Economic Review* 121 (1998):29–58.
Fine, Ben, Costas Lapavitsas, and Jonathan Pincus. *Development Policy in the Twenty First Century: Beyond the Post-Washington Consensus*. London: Routledge, 2003.
"Firms Eye Cambodian Agriculture." *The Nation*, 13 March 2006.
Flaming, Mark, Eric Duflos, Alexia Latortue, Nina Nayer, and Jimmy Roth. *Country-Level Effectiveness and Accountability Review: Cambodia*. Washington: CGAP, 2005.

Focus on the Global South. *Work plan 2009 – 2011.* Mimeo. Phnom Penh, 2009.
Food and Agriculture Organisation. *Global Forest Resources Assessment 2005: Progress Towards Sustainable Forest Management.* Rome: Food and Agriculture Agency of the United Nations, 2005.
Fox, Jefferson. "Understanding a Dynamic Landscape: Land Use, Land Cover, and Resource Tenure in Northeastern Cambodia." In Stephen Joseph Walsh, and Kelley A. Crews-Meyer, eds., *Linking People, Place, and Policy: A GIScience Approach.* Dordrecht: Springer, 2002. 113–130.
Frieson, Kate. "The Political Nature of Democratic Kampuchea." *Pacific Affairs* 61.3 (1988): 405–427.
Frings, Viviane. *The Failure of Agricultural Collectivization in the People Republic of Kampuchea 1979–1989.* Clayton: Monash University Center for Southeast Asian Studies, 1993.
Fukuyama, Francis. *State Building: Governance and the World Order in the Twenty-First Century.* London: Profile Books, 2005.
Gammage, Sarah. "Exporting People and Recruiting Remittances: A Development Strategy for El Salvador?" *Latin American Perspectives* 33. 6 (2006): 75–100.
Genova, Nicholas P. De. "Migrant 'Illegality' and Deportability in Everyday Life." *Annual Review of Anthropology* 31 (2002): 419–47.
Gillison, Douglas, and Kay Kimsong. "A Decade of Donor Meetings, Donor Discontent May Not Lessen Donor Largesse." *The Cambodia Daily*, 3 March 2007.
Global Witness. *Cambodia's Family Trees.* Phnom Penh: Global Witness, 2007. Online at http://www.globalwitness.org/media_library_detail.php/546/en/cambodias_family_trees, accessed 10 October 2007.
——— "Latest Threats to Cambodia's Forests." Webpage. Available online at http://www.globalwitness.org/pages/en/threats_to_forests.html, accessed 10 October 2008.
Godfrey, Martin. "Youth Employment Policy in Developing and Transition Countries – Prevention as well as Cure." Social Protection Discussion Paper Series No. 0320. Washington: World Bank Social Protection Unit, October 2003. Available online at http://siteresources.worldbank.org/SOCIALPROTECTION/Resources/SP-Discussion-papers/Labor-Market-DP/0320.pdf, accessed 12 August 2009.
Goetz, Anne Marie, and Rina Sen Gupta. "Who Takes the Credit? Gender, Power, and Control over Loan Use in Rural Credit Programs in Bangladesh." *World Development*, 24.1 (1996): 45–63.
Gomez, Edmund. "Introduction: Political Business in East Asia." In Gomez ed., *Political Business in East Asia.* London: Routledge, 2002. 1–33.
Gottesman, Evan. *Cambodia After the Khmer Rouge: Inside the Politics of Nation Building.* London: Yale University Press, 2003.
Government of the Kingdom of Thailand, and Royal Government of Cambodia. "Memorandum of Understanding on Cooperation in the Employment of Workers." 21 May 2003.
Graeber, David. "Debt, Violence and Impersonal Markets: Polanyian Meditations." In Chris Hann and Keith Hart, eds., *Market and Society: The Great Transformation Today.* Cambridge: Cambridge University Press, 2009.

Grandia, Liza. *Unsettling: Land Dispossession and Enduring Inequity for the Q'eqchi" Maya in the Guatemalan and Belizean Frontier Colonization Process*. Ph.D. Dissertation. University of California, Berkeley, 2006.
Griffith, John. "What is Legal Pluralism?" *Journal of Legal Pluralism* 24. 1 (1986): 1–55.
Grindle, Merilee. "Good Enough Governance: Poverty Reduction and Reform in Developing Countries." *Governance: An International Journal of Policy, Administration, and Institutions* 17. 4 (2004): 525–548.
——— "Good Enough Governance Revisited." *Development Policy Review*, 25.5 (2007): 553–574.
Gruening, Gernod. "Origin and Theoretical Basis of New Ppublic Management." *International Public Management Journal* 4.1 (2001): 1–25.
Guérin, Mathieu. "Essartage et Riziculture Humide, Complémentarité des Ecosystèmes Agraires à Stung Treng au Début du XXème Siècle." *Aséanie* 8 (2001): 35–55.
Guthrie, Elizabeth. "Buddhist Temples and Cambodian Politics." In John Vijghen, ed., *People and the 1998 National Elections in Cambodia. Their Voices, Roles and Impact on Democracy*. Working Paper no. 44. Phnom Penh: Experts for Community Research, 2002.
Guttal, Shalmali. *Supporting Knowledge Generation Among Community Led Networks*. Completion Report of the Pilot Phase of the Project. Phnom Penh: Focus on the Global South, 2008.
Haas, Hein de. "International Migration, Remittances and Development: Myths and Facts." *Third World Quarterly* 26.8 (2005): 1269–84.
Hadiz, Vedi. *Empire and Neoliberalism in Asia*. London: Routledge, 2006.
Hadiz, Vedi, and Richard Robison. "Neo-liberal Reforms and Illiberal Consolidations: the Indonesian Paradox." *Journal of Development Studies* 41.2 (2005):220–241.
Hamre, John, and Gordon Sullivan. " Toward Post-Conflict Reconstruction." *The Washington Quarterly* 25.4 (2002): 85–96.
Harris, Ian. *Buddhism under Pol Pot*. Documentation Series No. 13. Phnom Penh: DC-Cam, 2007.
Harvard Business School. "Worker Rights and Global Trade: The U.S.-Cambodia Bilateral Textile Trade Agreement." Case Study 9–703–034. Cambridge, MA: Harvard Business School Press, Revised 4 November 2004.
Hattha Kaksekar Ltd. "Annual Report 2003." Available online at http://www.hkl.com.kh/Publication.html, accessed 20 August 2009.
——— "Annual Report 2004." Available online at http://www.hkl.com.kh/Publication.html, accessed 20 August 2009.
——— "Annual Report 2006." Available online at http://www.hkl.com.kh/Publication.html, accessed 20 August 2009.
Hayman, Allyster, and Sam Rith. "Boeng Kak Lake Latest City Sell off." *Phnom Penh Post*, 09 February 2007. Available online at www.phnompenhpost.com, accessed 12 August 2009.
——— "Lake Dwellers Among Thousands To Be Evicted." *Phnom Penh Post*, 23 February 2007. Available online at www.phnompenhpost.com, accessed 12 August 2009.
Heder, Stephen. "Hun Sen's Consolidation, Death or Beginning of Reform?" In Daljit Singh, ed. *Southeast Asian Affairs 2005*. Singapore: ISEAS, 2005. 113–130.

Helms, Brigit. *Access for All: Building Inclusive Financial Systems.* Washington: World Bank, 2006.

Heng Sopheab, Knut Fylkesnes, Mean Chhivun, and Nigel O'Farrell. "HIV Risk Behaviours in Cambodia and Effects of Mobility." *Journal of Acquired Immune Deficiency Syndrome* 41.1 (2006): 81–86.

Henke, Roger. "Mistakes and Their Consequences: Why Impunity in Cambodia is Here to Stay." In Edwin Poppe and Maykel Verkuyten, eds., *Culture and Conflict: Liber Amicorum for Louk Hagendoorn.* Amsterdam: Aksant, 2007. 15–42.

—— *People's Movement, NGOs, Donors, and the Cambodian State: Reflections from a Practitioner's Perspective.* Unpub. Ms. Phnom Penh: 2009.

Hildebrand, George, and Gareth Porter. *Cambodia: Starvation & Revolution.* New York: Monthly Review Press, 1976.

Hilhorst, Thea. *The Real World of NGOs: Discourse, Diversity and Development.* London: Zed Books, 2003.

Hing Thoraxy. "Cambodia Country Report." In *Foreign Direct Investment: Opportunities and Challenges for Cambodia, Laos and Vietnam, Hanoi.* Phnom Penh: Royal Government of Cambodia Council for the Development of Cambodia, 2002. Available online at http://www.imf.org/external/pubs/ft/seminar/2002/fdi/eng/pdf/thoraxy.pdf, accessed 12 August 2009.

Hishigsuren, Gaamaa. *Transformation of Microfinance operations from NGO to Regulated MFI.* Decatur: Institute for Development, Evaluation, Assistance and Solutions, 2005. Available online at http://www.microcreditsummit.org/papers/Workshops/3_Hishigsuren.pdf, accessed 20 August 2009.

—— "Evaluating Mission Drift in Microfinance: Lessons for Programs with Social Mission." *Evaluation Review* 31.3 (2006): 203–260.

Hood, Christopher. "The 'New Public Management' in the 1980s: Variations on a Theme." *Accounting, Organizations and Society* 20.2/3 (1995): 93–109

Hor Hab. "Passport Fees for Workers to Drop: PM." *Phnom Penh Post*, 25 November 2008.

Horng Vuthy, Pak Kimchoeun, Eng Netra, Ann Sovatha, Kim Sedara, Jenny Knowles, and David Craig. "Conceptualising Accountability: The Cambodian Case." *Annual Development Review.* Phnom Penh: Cambodia Development Resource Institute, 2006. 171–198.

Horng Vuthy, and David Craig. *Accountability and Planning in Decentralized Cambodia.* Working Paper no. 39. Phnom Penh: Cambodia Development Resource Institute, 2007.

Hughes, Caroline. *The Political Economy of Cambodia's Transition, 1991–2001.* London: RoutledgeCurzon, 2003.

—— "The Politics of Gifts: Tradition and Regimentation in Contemporary Cambodia," *Journal of Southeast Asian Studies,* 37.3 (2006): 469–489.

—— "Cambodia in 2007: Development and Dispossession." *Asian Survey* 48.1 (2008): 69–74.

—— *Dependent Communities: Aid and Politics in Cambodia and East Timor.* Ithaca: Cornell SEAP, 2009.

Hughes, Caroline, and Timothy Conway. *Understanding Pro-Poor Political Change: The Policy Process.* London: Overseas Development Institute, 2004.

Hughes, Caroline, and Joakim Öjendal. "Introduction: Reassessing Tradition in Times of Political Change." *Journal of Southeast Asia Studies*, 37.3 (2006): 415–420.

Hughes, Caroline, and Kheang Un. *Aid That Works, The Phnom Penh Water Supply Authority and the National Response to HIV/AIDS*. Discussion paper. Phnom Penh: World Bank, 2006.

Hugo, Graeme. "Migration and Development: A Perspective from Asia." Geneva: International Organisation for Migration, 2003.

Huguet, Jerrold W., and Sureeporn Punpuing. "International Migration in Thailand." Bangkok: International Organisation for Migration, 2005.

Huot, Caroline, and Sam Rith. "Hope of Justice Lies in School for Judges." *Phnom Penh Post*, 21 November-04 December 2003.

Hutchcroft, Paul. *Booty Capitalism: The Politics of Banking in the Philippines*. Ithaca: Cornell University Press, 1998.

Ibata-Arens, Kathryn, Julian Dierkes, and Dirk Zorn. "Theoretical Introduction to the Special Issue on the Embedded Enterprise." *Enterprise and Society* 7. 1 (2006): 1–18.

In Channy. "From NGO/Project to Micro-finance Institution: The Experience of ACLEDA Bank, Cambodia." Paper presented to the FAO-APRACA Regional Workshop, Bangkok, 2002. Available online at www.microfinancegateway.org, accessed 3 October 2008.

International Crisis Group. *Cambodia: The Elusive Peace Dividend*. Phnom Penh and Brussels: International Crisis Group, 2000. Available online at http://www.unhcr.org/refworld/docid/3ae6a6e74.html, accessed 11 March 2009.

International Monetary Fund. *Cambodia: Statistical Appendix*. IMF Country Report 09/48, February 2009. Available online at http://www.imf.org/external/country/KHM/index.htm, accessed 12 August 2009.

International Organization for Migration. "World Migration. Costs and Benefits of International Migration 2005." Geneva: IOM, 2005.

Integrated Regional Information Networks Humanitarian News and Analysis. "Cambodia: Questions over Legality of Evictions in Name of Development." News Report. Phnom Penh: UN Office for the Coordination of Humanitarian Affairs, 18 August 2008.

Ito, Sanae. "Cambodian Microfinance: A Case of Successful Commercialization?" *Forum of International Development Studies* 37 (2008): 19–33.

Jansen, Kees, and Esther Roquas. "Modernizing Insecurity: The Land Titling Project in Honduras." *Development and Change* 29 (1998): 81–106.

Jayasuriya, Kanishka. "Beyond Institutional Fetishism: From the Developmental to the Regulatory State." *New Political Economy* 10.3 (2005): 383–4.

Jayasuriya, Kanishka, and Andrew Rosser. "Economic Orthodoxy and the East Asian Crisis." *Third World Quarterly* 22.3 (2001): 381–396.

Jayawickrama, N.A. *Vimanavatthu and Petavatthu*. London: Pali Text Society, 1999.

Jessop, Bob, "Knowledge as a Fictitious Commodity: Insights and Limits of a Polanyian Perspective." In Ayse Bugra and Kaan Agartan, eds., *Reading Karl Polanyi for the Twenty-First Century: Market Economy as a Political Project*. New York: Palgrave MacMillan, 2007. 115–134.

Kabeer, Naila. "Conflicts over Credit: Re-evaluating the Empowerment Potential of Loans to Women in Rural Bangladesh." *World Development* 29.1 (2001): 63–84.

Kaboolian, Linda. "The New Public Management: Challenging the Boundaries of the Management vs. Administration Debate." *Public Administration Review*, 58. 3 (1998): 189–193.

Kang Chandararot, and Chan Sophal. *Annual Economic Review 2003*. Phnom Penh: Cambodian Development Resource Institute, 2003.

Kapur, Devesh. "Remittances: The New Development Mantra?" Paper presented at the G-24 Technical Group Meeting, Harvard University and Center for Global Development, 2003.

Kao Kim Hourn, and Sisowath Doung Chanto. "ASEAN-China Cooperation for Greater Mekong Sub-Region Development." In Saw Swee-Hock, Lijun Shen, and Chin Kin-Wah, eds. *ASEAN-China: Realities and Prospects*, (Singapore: ISEAS Press, 2005). 316–328.

Kate, Daniel Ten, and Kay Kimsong. "France to Help Certify Rubber." *The Cambodia Daily*, 29 April 2004.

Kato, Elizabeth. *"We Have the Rights, They Have the Power." A Case Study of Land Expropriation in Northwest Cambodia, Case Study #1*. Phnom Penh: Oxfam Great Britain, 1998.

Kay Kimsong. "Governor: Koh Kong Villagers to Be Paid for Cattle." *The Cambodia Daily (Weekly Review)*, 12–16 February 2007, 6.

Kay Kimsong. "Experts at Asean Conference See Bright Future for Rubber Market." *The Cambodia Daily*, 16–17 June 2007.

Kazmin, Amy. "Villagers Fight for the Right to a Few Hectares of Cambodia's Tilling Fields." *Financial Times*, 10 April 2007.

Kent, Alexandra. "Compassion and Conflict: Remaking the Pagoda in Rural Cambodia." In *Stockholm University Department of the History of Religion Yearbook 2005*. Stockholm: Stockholm University Department of the History of Religion, 2005. 131–153.

Keyes, Charles. *Golden Peninsula: Culture and Adaptation in Mainland Southeast Asia*. New York: McMillan, 1977.

Khan, Mushtaq. "The State and Economic Development: What Role, What Risks?" London: Overseas Development Institute, 2006. Available online at http://www.odi.org.uk/events/states_nov06/ODI%20State%20and%20Development.pdf, accessed 12 August 2009.

Kim Sean Somatra and Chea Chou. *The Local Governance of Common Pool Resources: The case of Irrigation Water in Cambodia*. Working Paper 42. Phnom Penh: Cambodia Development Resource Institute, 2009.

Kim Sedara. "Agrarian Situation in Contemporary Cambodia: Overview of Case Studies in Cambodian Villages." *Cambodia Development Review* 6.2 (2002), 5.

——— "Local Government Responsiveness: Can Building Civil Society Enhance Accountability in Cambodia's Political Context?" Paper presented to conference on *Civil Society in Southeast Asia: Scope and Concepts*. Phnom Penh, 2004.

——— *Decentralization in Cambodia*. Ph D. Dissertation. Gothenburg University, 2010.

Kim Sedara, and Ann Sovatha. "Decentralization: Can Civil Society Enhance Local Government's Accountability in Cambodia?" *Cambodia Development Review*, 9. 3 (2005): 1

Kim Sedara, and Joakim Öjendal. *Where Decentralisation meets Democracy: Civil Society, Local Government, and Accountability in Cambodia.* Working Paper no 35. Phnom Penh: Cambodia Development Resource Institute, 2007.

Kinetz, Erika. "Keeping Workers Safe." *Newsweek*, 12 April 2008.

Kinetz, Erika, and Lor Chandara. "Koh Kong Villagers May Triumph in Land Dispute." *The Cambodia Daily (Weekly Review)*, 13–17 November 2006, 7.

Kinetz, Erika, and Prak Chan Thul. "UN Human Rights Envoy Yash Ghai Visits Ratanakkiri Villagers." *The Cambodia Daily (Weekly Review)*, 2–7 December 2007, 3.

Kinetz, Erika, and Thet Sambath. "Police, Soldiers Block Land Forum in R'kiri." *The Cambodia Daily (Weekly Review)*, 10–15 September 2007, 13.

Kinetz, Erika, and Yun Samean. "Bar Questions Aid Lawyers' Legal Standing over Land-Dispute Case." *The Cambodia Daily (Weekly Review)*, 23–29 June 2007, 5.

Kleih, Ulrich, Sem Viryak and Un Kanika, "Guidelines to Improve Access to Microfinance by Poor Fishing, Processing and Trading Communities" *Cambodia Post-Harvest Fisheries Livelihoods project*, Final Draft, 2006, online at www.nri.org/projects/fishtrade/cphflp_microfinance_guidelines.pdf

Koun Leakhana. "Overseas Agencies Aid Migrant Workers." *Phnom Penh Post*, 13 September 2008.

Krishna, Anirudh. "Partnerships Between Local Governments and Community-Based Organisations: Exploring the Scope for Synergy." *Public Administration and Development*, 23 (2003): 361–371.

Kuch Naren. "Ratanakkiri Villagers Accuse Officials of Grabbing Land." *The Cambodia Daily (Weekly Review)*, 19–23 February 2007, 14.

——— "R'kiri Court Denies Request to Halt Rubber Planting." *The Cambodia Daily (Weekly Review)*, 12–16 March 2007.

——— "R'kiri Land Dispute Villagers Approached for Deal." *The Cambodia Daily (Weekly Review)*, 12–16 March 2007, 11.

Kuch Naren, and Emily Lodish. "UN Envoy to Visit Ratanakkiri to Examine Land Disputes." *The Cambodia Daily (Weekly Review)*, 2–7 December 2007, 11.

Kunmakara, May. "Economic Downturn Hitting Migrant Labour, Official Says." *Phnom Penh Post*, 29 December 2008.

Kyauw, U Ba, and Peter Masefield. *Peta Stories: Elucidation of the Intrinsic Meaning so Named the Commentary on the Peta-Stories by Dhammapala.* London: Pali Text Society, 1980.

Kyle, David, and Christina A. Siracusa. "Seeing the State Like a Migrant: Why So Many Non-Criminals Break Immigration Laws." In Willem van Schendel and Itty Abraham, eds., *Illicit Flows and Criminal Things: States, Borders, and the Other Side of Globalization.* Bloomington: Indiana University Press, 2005. 153–76.

Land Coalition. *Landlessness and Land Conflicts in Cambodia.* Phnom Penh: Star Kampuchea, 2007.

Le Billon, Philippe. "The Political Ecology of Transition in Cambodia 1989–1999: War, Peace and Forest Exploitation." *Development and Change* 31 (2000): 785–805.

——— "Logging in Muddy Waters: The Politics of Forest Exploitation in Cambodia." *Critical Asian Studies* 34. 4 (2002): 563–586.

Le Billon, Philippe, and Simon Springer. "Between War and Peace: Violence and Accommodation in the Cambodian Logging Sector." In Wil de Jong, Deanna Donovan, and Ken Ichi Abe, eds., *Extreme Conflict and Tropical Forests*. Dordrecht: Springer, 2007. 17–36

Ledgerwood, Joanna. *Microfinance Handbook: An Institutional and Financial Perspective*. Washington: World Bank, 2002.

Ledgerwood, Judy. "Rural Development in Cambodia: The View from the Village." In Frederick Z. Brown and David G. Timberman, eds,. *Cambodia and The International Community*. New York: Asia Society, 1998. 128–139.

Ledgerwood, Judy, and John Vijghen. "Decision-Making in Rural Khmer Villages." In Judy Ledgerwood, ed., *Cambodia Emerges from the Past: Eight Essays*. DeKalb: Southeast Asia Publications – Northern Illinois University, 2002. 109–150.

Lee, Chen Chen. *A Study into Exploitative Labour Brokerage Practices in Cambodia*. Phnom Penh: Coordinated Mekong Ministerial Initiative against Trafficking/ United Nations Inter-Agency Project Against Trafficking, 2007. Available online at http://www.childtrafficking.com/Docs/labour_exploitation_study_0607.pdf, accessed 14 August 2009.

Lee, Richard B. "Eating Christmas in the Kalahari." *Natural History* 78 (1969): 1–4.

Leland, Blake. "Voodoo Economics: Sticking Pins in Eros." *Diacritics* 18.2(1988): 38–46.

Lenaghan, Nick. "Pimps up for Hefty Sentences, but Reservations about New Law." *Phnom Penh Post*, 8–21 March 1996, 13.

——— "Officials Implicated in Koh Kong Sex Trade." *Cambodia Daily*, 19–21 April 1996, 1.

Leopard Cambodia Fund. "In the News." *Monthly Newsletter* 9, January 2009.

Lizee, Pierre. *Peace, Power and Resistance in Cambodia—Global Governance and the Failure of International Conflict Resolution*. Basingstoke: Macmillan, 2001.

Loco, Fabienne. *Between a Tiger and a Crocodile: Management of Local Conflicts in Cambodia, An Anthropological Approach to Traditional and New Practice*. Phnom Penh: United Nations Educational, Scientific and Cultural Organisation, 2002.

Löschmann, Heike. *Die Rolle des Buddhismus in der Gesellschaftlichen Entwicklung der Volksrepublik Kampuchea nach der Befreung vom Pol-Pot-Regime 1979 bis Mitte der Achtziger Jahre*. PhD thesis. Humboldt University, 1988.

Lowe, David. *Perceptions of the Cambodian 100% Condom Use Program: Documenting the Experiences of Sex Workers*. Phnom Penh: United States Agency for Internationalo Development/POLICY Project, 2003.

Lum, Thomas, Wayne Morrison, and Bruce Vaughan. *China's Soft Power in Southeast Asia*, Congress Research Service Report, 4 January 2008. Available online at http://ftp.fas.org/sgp/crs/row/RL34310.pdf, accessed 14 August 2009.

Ly Daravuth. "Notes on Pchum Ben." Working Paper on *Recasting Reconciliation through Culture and the Arts*. Brandeis University, 2005.

Lynn, Laurence. *Public Management: Old and New*. London: Routledge, 2006.

Mabbett, Ian and David Chandler. *The Khmers*. Cambridge: Blackwell, 1995.

MacIntyre, Andrew. "Business and Government in Industrializing Asia." In Andrew MacIntyre, ed. *Business and Government in Industrializing Asia*. Ithaca: Cornell University Press, 1994. 1–28.

Maltoni, Bruno. *Impact of Remittances on Local Communities in Cambodia: The Case of Prey Veng*. Draft Report. Phnom Penh: World Bank, n.d.

——— *Review of Labor Migration Dynamics in Cambodia.* Phnom Penh: International Organisation for Migration, 2006.
Manor, James. *The Political Economy of Democratic Decentralization.* Washington DC: World Bank,1999.
Mansfield, Cristina, and Curt MacLeod. *Commune Council and Civil Society: Promoting Decentralization Through Partnerships.* Phnom Penh: PACT, 2004.
Marks, Paul. "China's Strategy in Cambodia." *Parameters,* 30.3 (2000): 92–105.
Markussen, Thomas. *Land Titling in Cambodia—Findings From a Field Trip.* Mimeo, February 2006.
Marston, John. *Cambodia 1991–94: Hierarchy, Neutrality and Etiquettes of Discourse.* PhD Thesis. University of Washington, 1994.
Marubeni Corporation. *Summary for Rubber Tree Afforestation in Mondul Kiri Province, Cambodia.* March 2004. Available online at gec.jp/gec/en/Activities/cdm/FS200317SE.pdf, accessed 10 June.
Matras-Troubetzkoy, Jacqueline. "L'Essartage chez les Brou du Cambodge: Organisation Collective et Autonomie Familiale." Études Rurales 53–54–55–56 (1974). Available online at http://etudesrurales.revues.org/document579.html, accessed 19 August 2009.
——— *Un Village en Foret: L'Essartage chez les Brou du Cambodge.* Paris: Selaf, 1983.
Mauss, Marcel. *The Gift: the Form and Reason for Exchange in Archaic Societies.* New York: W. W. Norton and Co., 1990.
May Kunmakara. "Processing Plant Aims to Boost Trade with Vietnam." *Phnom Penh Post,* 12 November 2008. Available online at www.phnompenhpost.com, accessed 8 June 2009.
McCargo, Duncan. "Cambodia: Getting away with Authoritarianism." *Journal of Democracy* 16.4 (2005): 98–112.
McKenney, Bruce, Chea Yim, Phom Tola and Tom Evans. *Focusing on Cambodia's High Value Forests: Livelihoods and Management.* Special Report. Phnom Penh: Cambodia Development Resource Institute, 2004.
Mcleod, George. "Microlenders Weather the Storm." *Phnom Penh Post* 14 January 2009. Online at www.phnompenhpost.com, accessed 13 March 2009.
McNaughton, Andrew. *The Cambodian Cashew Industry: Assessment of Opportunities and Constraints for Rural Employment and Export Revenue Generation.* Phnom Penh: McNaughton and Associates/GTZ Cambodia, 2005.
Meas Nee. *CBO Working Model and Strategy for CBO Pilot Project.* Phnom Penh: Forum Syd, 2008.
Mengin, Françoise. *La Présence Chinoise au Cambodge Contribution à une Economie Politique Violente, Rentière et Inégalitaire.*" Les Études du CERI No 133. Paris: CERI-Sciences-Po, 2007.
Microcredit Ratings International Ltd. "The Impact of Rating . . . on Banking Practice and Resource Flows." Powerpoint Presentation. Gurgaon, 2002. Online at http://www.sa-dhan.net/Adls/Microfinance/Rating/Impactofratingonmicrobanking.pdf accessed 5 November 2008.
Microcredit Summit Campaign. "What is Microcredit?" Webpage. Available online at www.microcreditsummit.org, accessed 14 February 2009.

Middleton, Carl, and Sam Chanty. *Cambodia's Hydropower Development and China's Involvement*. Phnom Penh: International Rivers/The Rivers Coalition in Cambodia/ NGO Forum on Cambodia, 2008.

Miesel, Nicolas, and Jacques Ould Aoudia. *Is "Good Governance" a Good Development Strategy?* Working Paper 58. Paris: Agence Française de Developpement, 2008. Available online at http://www.afd.fr/jahia/webdav/site/myjahiasite/users/admirecherche/public/DT/WP_58_GB_pour_mise_en_ligne.pdf, accessed 12 August 2009.

Minder, Raphael. "Cambodia Holds Land Deal Talks." *The Financial Times*, 20 November 2008. Available online at http://www.ft.com/cms/s/0/2506f3c6-b72e-11dd-8e01-0000779fd18c.html, accessed 12 August 2009.

Mintz, Sidney W. *Sweetness and Power: The Place of Sugar in Modern History*. New York: Elisabeth Sifton Books, Penguin Books, 1985.

Missingham, Bruce. *The Assembly of the Poor in Thailand: From Local Struggles to National Protest Movement*. Chiang Mai: Silkworm, 2003.

Moncrieff, Joy. "Accountability: Idea, Ideals, Constraints." *Democratisation* 8.3 (2001): 26–50.

Moore, Mick. "Declining to Learn from the East? The World Bank on Governance and Development." *IDS Bulletin* 24.1 (1993): available online at http://old.ids.ac.uk/UserFiles/File/publications/classics/moore_24_1.pdf, accessed 13 August 2009.

Mosedale, Sarah. "Policy Arena. Assessing Women's Empowerment: Towards a Conceptual Framework." *Journal of International Development* 17.2 (2005): 243–257.

Mund, Jan Peter, and Seyha Sok. "Mapping Land Cover Changes." Paper presented at Tropentag, Witzenhausen, Germany, 9–11 October, 2007. Available online at http://www.tropentag.de/2007/proceedings/node355.html, accessed 8 June 2009.

National Bank of Cambodia. *Prakas Relating to the Implementation of Law on Banking and Financial Institutions*. Phnom Penh, 2000. Available online at www.nbc.org.kh/upload/english/prakas/Sup-Prakas2000.pdf, accessed 5 November 2008.

——— *Annual Report 2006* (Phnom Penh: National Bank of Cambodia, 2006) online at www.nbc.org.kh, accessed 20 August 2009.

Network of Sex Work Projects. *The 100% Condom Use Policy: a Sex Workers Perspective*. Webpage, 22 January 2003. Available online at http://www.nswp.org/safety/100percent.html, accessed 13 August 2009.

NGO Forum on Cambodia. *NGO Statement to the 2002 Consultative Group Meeting on Cambodia*. Phnom Penh: NGO Forum on Cambodia, 2002. Available online at http://www.ngoforum.org.kh/Development/Docs/ngo_2002/ngo_2002.htm, accessed 12 August 2009.

——— *Fast-wood Plantations, Economic Concessions and Local Livelihoods in Cambodia*. Phnom Penh: NGO Forum on Cambodia, 2006.

——— *Land Alienation in Indigenous Minority Communities: Ratanakiri Province, Cambodia*. Phnom Penh: NGO Forum on Cambodia, 2006.

——— *The PRSP and CSO's Participation in Cambodia*. Report prepared for the Roundtable Discussion on NGO/CSO Experiences in PRSP Monitoring & Advocacy. Phnom Penh: NGO Forum on Cambodia, 2006. Available online at http://www.ngoforum.org.kh/Development/Docs/PRSP%20in%20Cambodia.pdf, accessed 12 August 2008.

―――― *Land Titling and Poverty Reduction: A Study of Two Sangkat in Prey Nup District, Sihanoukville Municipality*. Phnom Penh: Analyzing Development Issues, NGO Forum on Cambodia, 2007.

―――― *NGO Statement to the 2008 Cambodia Development Cooperation Forum*. Phnom Penh: NGO Forum on Cambodia, 2008. Available online at http://www.ngoforum.org.kh/Development/Docs/NGOStatement/2008/2008NGOStatement_Final_English.pdf, accessed 15 February 2009.

North, Douglass. "Institutions." *Journal of Economic Perspectives* 5.1 (1991): 97–112.

Nyberg-Sorensen, Ninna, Nicholas van Hear, and Poul Engberg-Pedersen. *The Migration-Development Nexus: Evidence and Policy Options*. Geneva: International Organisation for Migration, 2002.

O'Connell, Stephen, and Yin Soeum. "All That Glitters Seems To Be . . . Sokimex." *Phnom Penh Post*, 28 April – 11 May 2000. Available online at www.phnompenhpost.com, accessed 3 Feb 2007.

Odugbemi, Sina, and Thomas Jacobson, eds. "Introduction." In Sina Odugbemi and Thomas Jacobson eds., *Governance Reform: Citizens, Stakeholders, and Voice*. Washington, DC: World Bank, 2008. 1–11.

Oldham, Geoffrey P., and Brett Delahunt. *Cambodian Decorations of Honor*. Auckland, N.Z.: Milymen Books, 2004.

Organisation for Economic Cooperation and Development. *DAC Guidelines and Reference Series Applying Strategic Environmental Assessment: Good Practice Guidance for Development Co-operation*. Paris: Organisation for Economic Cooperation and Development, 2006.

―――― *Glossary of Statistical Terms*. Paris: Organisation for Economic Cooperation and Development, nd. Available online at http://stats.oecd.org/glossary/detail.asp?ID=7235, accessed 23 December 2008.

Öjendal, Joakim, and Kim Sedara. "*Korob, Kaud, Klach*: In Search of Agency in Rural Cambodia." *Journal of South East Asian Studies*, 31.3 (2006): 507–526.

―――― "Decentralization as a Strategy for State Reconstruction in Cambodia." In Joakim Öjendal and Mona Lilja, eds., *Beyond Democracy in Cambodia: Political Reconstruction in a Post-Conflict Society*. Copenhagen: Nordic Institute of Asian Studies Press, 2009. 101–135.

Oldham, Geoffrey P., and Brett Delahunt. *Cambodian Decorations of Honor*. Auckland: Milymen Books, 2004.

O'Leary, Janet, and Meas Nee. *Learning for Transformation. A Study of the Relationship between Culture, Values, Experience and Development Practice in Cambodia*. Phnom Penh: Krom Akphiwat Phum, 2001.

Olson, Mancur. "Big Bills Left on the Sidewalk: Why Some Nations are Rich, and Others Poor." *Journal of Economic Perspectives* 10.2 (1996): 3–24.

Ovesen, Jan, Joakim Öjendal, and Ing-Britt Trankell. *When Every Household is An Island – Social Organizations and Power Structures in Rural Cambodia*. Uppsala: Socialantropologiska Institutionen, 1996.

Padoch, Christine, Emily Harwell, and Adi Susanto. "Swidden, Sawah, and In-Between: Agricultural Transformation in Borneo." *Human Ecology* 26. 1 (1998): 3–20.

Page, Sheila, and Adrian Hewitt. "The New European Trade Preferences: Does 'Everything but Arms' (EBA) Help the Poor?" *Development Policy Review* 20.1 (2002): 91–102.

Pak Kimchoeun. "*Oknha* and Advisors in Cambodia." Unpublished brief, 11 June 2008.

Pak Kimchoeun, Horng Vuthy, Eng Netra, Ann Sovatha, Kim Sedara, Jenny Knowles, and David Craig. *Accountability and Neo-Patrimonialism: A Critical Literature Review*. Working Paper No 34. Phnom Penh: CDRI, 2007.

Pak Kimchoeun, and David Craig. *Accountability and Public Expenditure Management in Decentralised Cambodia*. Working Paper no. 38. Phnom Penh: Cambodia Development Resource Institute, 2008.

Pasuk Phongpaichit, and Chris Baker. "Introduction." In Pasuk Phongpaichit and Chris Baker, eds, *Thai Capital After the 1997 Crisis*. Chiang Mai: Silkworm, 2008.

Pearson, Eliane. "Underpaid, Overworked and Overlooked. The Realities of Young Migrant Workers in Thailand." Bangkok: International Labour Organisation, 2006.

Pellini, Arnaldo. *Decentralisation Policy in Cambodia: Exploring Community Participation in the Education Sector*. PhD Thesis. University of Tampere, 2007.

Peou, Sorpong. *Intervention and Change in Cambodia: Towards Democracy?* New York: Palgrave MacMillan, 2000.

Perlez, Jane. "China Competes with West in Aid to Its Neighbours." *The New York Times*, 18 September 2006.

Phann Ana, and Matt McKinney. "Jobless Rubber Workers Evicted From Homes." *The Cambodia Daily*, 22 March 2002. 18.

Pickens, Mark, Meas Thavy and Keo Kang. *Savings-Led and Self-Help Microfinance in Cambodia: Lessons Learned and Best Practices*. Phnom Penh: PACT, 2004.

Piot, Charles. "Of Slaves and the Gift: Kabre Sale of Kin during the Era of the Slave Trade." *Journal of African History* 37.1 (1996): 31–49.

――― *Remotely Global: Village Modernities in West Africa*. Chicago: University of Chicago Press, 1999.

Pirie, Iain. "The New Korean State." *New Political Economy* 10.1 (2005): 25–42.

Pisani, Elizabeth. "Cambodia's Top Investor Scoffs at Rumors About Shady Past," *Asia Times*, 12 March 1996. Available online at http://www.ternyata.org/journalism/features/teng_boonma_profile.html, accessed 21 October 2008.

Polanyi, Karl. *The Great Transformation: The Political and Economic Origins of our Time*. Boston: Beacon, 2001.

Popkin, Samuel. *The Rational Peasant: The Political Economy of Rural Society in Vietnam*. Berkeley: University of California Press, 1979.

Porter, Gina. "NGOs and Poverty Reduction in a Globalizing World: Perspectives from Ghana." *Progress in Development Studies* 3.2 (2003): 131–145.

"Poverty Down, Inequality up in Cambodia: World Bank." *Kyodo News*, 12 June 2007.

Prak Chan Thul. "Sugar Tycoon Is Taking Village Land: Rights Groups. " *The Cambodia Daily (Weekly Review)*, 22–26 January 2007, 3.

――― "Koh Kong Land Protestors Still Waiting in Capital. " *The Cambodia Daily (Weekly Review)*, 12–16 March 2007, 14.

――― "Lawyer Insists R'kiri Land Deal Is Valid." *The Cambodia Daily (Weekly Review)*, 2–6 April 2007, 11.

——— "3 Officials Questioned in R'kiri Land-Dispute Case." *The Cambodia Daily (Weekly Review)*, 23–27 April 2007, 9.
——— "Jarai Villagers Abandon Gov't Doorstep Tactics." *The Cambodia Daily (Weekly Review)*, 16[sic]-22 June 2007, 10.
——— "Villagers Summoned by R'kiri Court in Keat Kolney Land Case. " *The Cambodia Daily (Weekly Review)*, 16[sic]-22 June 2007, 14.
——— "Villagers Say Keat Kolney Did Not Grab Land. " *The Cambodia Daily (Weekly Review)*, 21–27 July 2007, 11.
——— "Ratanakkiri Villagers Paid in Keat Kolney Case: SRP Official. " *The Cambodia Daily (Weekly Review)*, 30 July – 3 August 2007, 16.
——— "Fearing Trickery, Villagers Reject CPP Donations." *The Cambodia Daily (Weekly Review)*, 19–23 November 2007, 10.
——— "R'kiri Police Turn Hoses on Land Protesters. " *The Cambodia Daily (Weekly Review)*, 17–21 December 2007, 1 & 3.
Prak Chan Thul, and Erika Kinetz. "Keat Kolney Files Complaint against 10 Lawyers." *The Cambodia Daily (Weekly Review)*, 23–29 June 2007, 14.
——— "Keat Kolney Files Complaint over Land Dispute." *The Cambodia Daily (Weekly Review)*, 23–29 June 2007, 11.
——— "R'kiri Villagers Take Land Dispute Door-to-Door." *The Cambodia Daily (Weekly Review)*, 11–15 June 2007, 9.
Prak Chan Thul and John Maloy, "Government Wants To Privatize Rubber Plantations, " *The Cambodia Daily*, 23 May 2007.
Prud'homme, Rémy. *L'Économie du Cambodge*. Paris: Presses Universitaires de France, 1969.
Prum Sokha. "Decentralisation and Poverty Reduction in Cambodia." *Regional Development Dialogue*, 26.2 (2005): 114–120.
Ricklefs, Merle C. "Land and the Law in the Epigraphy of Tenth-Century Cambodia." *Journal of Asian Studies* 26.3 (1967): 411–420.
Riggs, Fred Warren. *Thailand: The Modernization of a Bureaucratic Polity*. Honolulu: East-West Center Press, 1966.
Roberts, David. *Political transition in Cambodia 1991–99: Power, Elitism and Democracy*. Richmond: Curzon Press, 2000.
Robison, Richard. "Authoritarian States, Capital-Owning Classes and the Politics of Newly-Industrialising Countries: the Case of Indonesia." *World Politics* 41.1 (1988): 52–74.
Robison, Richard, and Vedi Hadiz. *Reorganising Power in Indonesia: the Politics of Oligarchy in an Age of Markets*. London: Routledge, 2004.
Robison, Richard, and Kevin Hewison. "Introduction: East Asia and the Trials of Neoliberalism." *Journal of Development Studies* 41.2 (2005): 183–196.
Ros Soketh and Paul Vireze. "Green Trade Plans Venture With Indonesian Firm." *The Cambodia Daily*, 15 August 2008, 29.
Royal Government of Cambodia. *Subdecree No. 52 on the Creation of a National Permanent Commission for Coordinating the Privatization and Promotion of Rubber Plantations*. Phnom Penh: 6 September 1994. Available online at www.moc.gov.kh/laws_regulation/part8_sustainable/ank52_94_rubber.htm, accessed 10 June 2009.

——— *Sub-Decree No. 57 on the Export of Khmer Labor to Work Overseas*. Phnom Penh: RGC Council of Ministers, 20 July 1995.
——— *Sub-Decree No. 78 on Community Fisheries Management*. Phnom Penh: RGC, 2003.
——— *Sub-DecreeNo. 79 on Community Forestry Management*, Phnom Penh: RGC, 2003.
——— *National Strategic Framework for Decentralisation and Deconcentration Reforms*. Phnom Penh: RGC, 2005.
——— *Sub-Decree No. 70 on the Creation of the Manpower Training and Overseas Sending Board*. Phnom Penh: RGC Council of Ministers, 25 July 2006.
Royal Government of Cambodia Council for Development of Cambodia. *Report on Mapping Survey of NGO/Association Presence and Activity in Cambodia*. Phnom Penh: RGC Council for Development of Cambodia Natural Resources and Environment Programme and DANish International Development Assistance, 2006.
——— *The Cambodia Aid Effectiveness Report 2007*. Phnom Penh: RGC Council for the Development of Cambodia, 2007. Available online at http://www.cdc-crdb.gov.kh/cdc/aid_management/AER-Report-2007-FINAL.pdf, accessed 19 September 2007.
Royal Government of Cambodia Council of Ministers. *The Rectangular Strategy for Growth, Employment, Equity and Efficiency in Cambodia*. Presented by Samdech Hun Sen to the First Cabinet Meeting of the Third Legislature of the National Assembly. Phnom Penh, July 2004. Available online at http://www.cdc-crdb.gov.kh/cdc/aid_management/RGC_Rectangular_Strategy_2004.pdf, accessed 12 August 2008.
——— *Governance Action Plan*. Phnom Penh: RGC Council of Ministers, 2006.
——— *National Strategic Development Plan 2006–2010*. Phnom Penh: RGC Council of Ministers, 2006.
Royal Government of Cambodia Forestry Administration and Working Group on Natural Resource Management. *Forest Sector in Cambodia Part I: Policy Choices, Issues and Options*. Independent Forest Sector Review. Phnom Penh: RGC Forestry Administration and Working Group on Natural Resource Management, April 2004.
Royal Government of Cambodia Ministry of Commerce. *Estimated Cambodian Export Data Under GSP/MFN Scheme to the Main Markets*. Phnom Penh: RGC Ministry of Commerce, 2008.
Royal Government of Cambodia Ministry of Commerce and Mekong Private Sector Development Facility. *Cambodia and the WTO: A Guide for Business*. Phnom Penh: RGC Ministry of Commerce and Mekong Private Sector Development Facility, March 2005. Available online at http://www.mpdf.org/images/en/content/E3/Wed-Apr-20-03-16-11-CST-2005.pdf, accessed 12 August 2009.
Royal Government of Cambodia Ministry of Economics and Finance. *The Medium-Term Expenditure Framework for Cambodia 2005–2007*. Phnom Penh: RGC Ministry of Economics and Finance, 2004. Available online at http://www.mef.gov.kh/hnaron/mtef-2004/mtef7.htm, accessed 4 January 2007.
Royal Government of Cambodia Ministry of Health, National Centre for HIV/AIDS, Dermatology and STD, National AIDS Authority and UNAIDS. *The Review of*

the *100% Condom Use Programme in Cambodia*. Phnom Penh: NCHADS/NAA/ UNAIDS, 2003.

Royal Government of Cambodia Ministry of Labour and Vocational Training and International Labour Organisation. *Experiences and Lessons Learned on Child Labour Monitoring: Rubber, Salt and Fishing Sectors in Cambodia*. Phnom Penh: RGC Ministry of Labour and Vocational Training/ILO, 2005. Available online at www.ilo.int/public/english/region/asro/bangkok/library/download/pub05-13.pdf, accessed 10 June 2009.

——— Prakas No. 108 on Education of HIV/AIDS, Safe Migration, and Labor Rights for Cambodian Workers Abroad. Phnom Penh: RGC Ministry of Labor and Vocational Training, 31 May 2006.

Royal Government of Cambodia Ministry of Land Management, Urban Planning and Construction. *Strategy of Land Policy Framework: Interim Paper*. Phnom Penh: RGC Ministry of Land Management, Urban Planning and Construction, 6 September 2003.

——— *Land Valuation Study Report*. Phnom Penh: Ministry of Land Management Urban Planning and Construction Land Management and Administration Project, 31 May 2005.

Royal Government of Cambodia Ministry of Planning. *Cambodia Human Development Report 2007*. Phnom Penh: RGC Ministry of Planning, 2007.

Royal Government of Cambodia Ministry of Tourism. *Tourism Highlights: Visitor Arrivals, Average Length of Stay, Hotel Occupancy and Tourism Receipts 1993–2003*. Web page. Phnom Penh: Ministry of Tourism. Available online at http://www.mot.gov.kh/statistics/tourism_highlight.pdf, accessed 12 August 2009.

Royal Government of Cambodia Supreme National Economic Council. *The Report of Land and Human Development in Cambodia*. Phnom Penh: RGC Supreme National Economic Council, 2007.

Royal Government of Cambodia/Development Partners Technical Working Group Forestry and Environment. *Forest Cover Change in Cambodia 2002–2006*. Paper prepared for Cambodia Development Cooperation Forum. Phnom Penh, 19–20 June 2007.

Royal Government of Cambodia/Development Partners" Technical Working Group on Forestry and Environment. *Forestry Outlook Cambodia 2008*. Phnom Penh: RGC TWG on Forestry and Environment, 2008. Available online http://www.phnompenh.um.dk/NR/rdonlyres/3602743D-2288-4248-8FEB-2E1C57043785/0/ForestryOutlookCambodia2008.doc, accessed on March 30, 2009.

Russell, Ray. "Land Law in the Kingdom of Cambodia." *Property Management* 15. 2 (1997): 101–110.

Rusten, Caroline, Kim Sedara, Eng Netra and Pak Kimchoeun. *The Challenges of Decentralisation Design in Cambodia*. Phnom Penh: Cambodia Development Resource Institute, 2004.

Sahlins, Marshall D. *Stone Age Economics*. New York: Aldine Transaction, 1972.

Samakum Thieng Tnaot. "Quarterly Summary of Land Conflicts in Cambodia." *Cambodia Eviction Monitor* 2 (July, 2007): 3–4.

Saing Soenthrith. "UN Envoy and Villagers Discuss Land Complaints." *The Cambodia Daily (Weekly Review)*, 11–15 December 2006, 12.

Sam Rith. "As Prices Rise, Workers Go Foraging." *Phnom Penh Post*, 22 October 2008.

Sardenberg, Cecilia. "Liberal vs. Liberating Empowerment: A Latin American Feminist Perspective on Conceptualising Women's Empowerment." *IDS Bulletin* 39.6 (2008): 18–27.

Sarker, Abu Elias. "New Public Management, Service Provision and Non-governmental Organisations in Bangladesh." *Public Organisation Review* 5.3 (2005): 249–271.

Schmitter, Philippe C. "Quality of Democracy—The Ambiguous Virtues of Accountability." *Journal of Democracy* 15. 4 (2004): 47–60.

Schmitter, Philippe C., and Terry Lynn Karl. "What Democracy Is . . . and Is Not." *Journal of Democracy* 2.3 (1991): 75–88.

Schneider, Ben and Sylvia Maxfield. "Business, the State, and Economic Performance." In Maxfield and Schneider eds. *Business and the State in Developing Countries*. Ithaca: Cornell University Press, 1997. 3–35.

Sciaroni, Bretton. "The State of the Private Sector." Remarks made at the Consultative Group Meeting, December 5–7, 2004. Available online at http://www.cdc-crdb.gov.kh/cdc/7cg_meeting/7cg_document/the_state_private_sector.htm, accessed 12 August 2009.

Selznick, Philip. *TVA and the Grass Roots*. Berkeley: University of California Press, 1949.

Shay, Christopher. "Illegal Migration Surges Despite Persistent Dangers." *Phnom Penh Post*, 6 February 2009.

Shelton, Tracey. "Cashew Market Crumbling." *Phnom Penh Post*, 29 September 2008. Available online at www.phnompenhpost.com, accessed 3 May 2009.

Sinha, Sanjay. "Cambodia Microfinance Miracle." *Economics Today*, 1–15 January 2008. Available online at http://www.etmcambodia.com/Categories/Economics_Business.asp?Nav=3&odrField=tblarticles_eng.title&odrBy=asc&search=, accessed 20 August 2009.

Skeldon, Ronald. "Migration and Poverty." *Asia-Pacific Population Journal* 17. 4 (2002): 67–82.

Slocomb, Margaret. "Commune Elections in Cambodia: 1981 Foundations and 2002 Reformulations." *Modern Asian Studies* 38 (2004): 447–467.

——— *Colons and Coolies: the Development of Cambodia's Rubber Plantations*. Bangkok: White Lotus, 2007.

Sok Hach. "The Political Economy of Development in Cambodia: How to Untie the Gordian Knot of Poverty?" *Political Economy of Development* (Phnom Penh: Economic Institute of Cambodia, October-December 2005), 3. Available online at http://www.eicambodia.org/downloads/files/ER10_politicaldevelopment.pdf, accessed 12 August 2009.

——— "Cambodia's Economy: from Donor Dependence to Self-Sustaining Growth?" Powerpoint presentation delivered at the workshop on Capital Market Development in Cambodia. Phnom Penh, 30–31 May 2007.

Sokha Pel, Pierre-Yves Le Meur, Vitou Sam, Lan Liang, Setha Pel, Leakhena Hay, and Sothy Im. *Land Transaction in Rural Cambodia: A Synthesis of Findings from*

Research on Appropriation and Derived Rights to Land. Phnom Penh: Centre d" Etude et Development Agricole Cambogien (CEDAC), August 2007.

Sonchai Phatharathananuth. *Civil Society and Democratization: Social Movements in Northeast Thailand.* Copenhagen: Nordic Institute for Asian Studies Press, 2006.

Sopheng Cheang. "Cambodian Senate to Be Joined by Prominent Tycoons." *Associated Press Newswires,* 13 February 2006.

Sovannarith So, Sophal Chan, and Sarthi Acharya. "An Assessment of Land Tenure in Rural Cambodia." *Cambodia Development Review* 5 (October-December 2001): 1.

Special Representative of the Secretary-General for Human Rights in Cambodia. *Land Concessions for Economic Purposes in Cambodia: a Human Rights Perspective.* Phnom Penh: COHCHR, November 2004.

Special Representative of the Secretary-General for Human Rights in Cambodia. *Economic land concessions in Cambodia: A Human Rights Perspective.* Phnom Penh: Cambodia Office of the High Commission for Human Rights, 2007.

Special Representative of the Secretary-General for Human Rights Defenders, *Report,* UN Doc. A/59/401, (Geneva: High Commission for Human Rights, 2004).

Stanfield, David, Edgar Nesman, Mitchell Seligson, and Alexander Coles. *The Honduras Land Titling and Registration Experience.* Madison: University of Wisconsin Land Tenure Center, 1990.

Stewart, Devin T. "Damning Public Opinion: The Risks of China's Diplomacy in Cambodia." *Carnegie Ethics Online,* 4 April 2008. Available online at http://www.cceia.org/resources/ethics_online/0020.html, accessed 12 August 2009.

Stiglitz, Joseph. *More Instruments and Broader Goals: Moving Toward the Post-Washington Consensus.* Helsinki: United Nations University/World Institute for Development Economics Research, 1998.

Strangio, Sebastian, and Chhay Channyda. "Who Owns the Lake? Debate Rages." *The Phnom Penh Post,* 03 October 2008. Available online at www.phnompenhpost.com., accessed 12 August 2009.

Suy Se. "Chinese-funded hydro-dams bring hope and fear to Cambodia." Agence France-Presse, Phnom Penh, 29 June 2008.

Swedish International Development Agency. *Employment and Growth in Cambodia: an Integrated Economic Analysis.* Stockholm: Swedish International Development Agency, 2006.

Thai News Service. "Thailand: Thais and Foreigners Interested in Investing in Sugar Industry." News report. 1 September 2006.

——— "Thailand: Khon Kaen Sugar Industry to Go Ahead with Investments in Sugar Mills in Laos and Cambodia." News report. 20 August 2007.

——— "China/Cambodia: Chinese Arrive with Millions in Aid." News report. 5 December 2008.

"The South Korean Embassy Denies That The Shukaku Inc. Company Comes from Korea." *The Mirror,* Phnom Penh, 28 October 2008.

Thelen, Kathleen. "How Institutions Evolve: Insights from Comparative – Historical Analysis." In James Mahoney, and Dietrich Rueschemeyer, eds., *Comparative – Historical Analysis in the Social Sciences.* Cambridge: Cambridge University Press, 2003. 208–240.

Thet Sambath. "Police Block Human Rights Forum in R'kiri." *The Cambodia Daily (Weekly Review)*, 26–30 November 2007, 7.

Thion, Serge. *Watching Cambodia: Ten Paths to Enter the Cambodian Tangle*. Bangkok: White Lotus, 1993.

Thong Lim. "Country Report." Paper presented at the Asia-Pacific High-level Meeting on International Migration and Development. United Nations Conference Center, Bangkok, 2008.

Twining, Charles H. "The Economy." In Karl D. Jackson, ed., *Cambodia 1975–1978: Rendezvous with Death*. Princeton: Princeton University Press, 1989. 109–150.

Un, Kheang. *Democratization without Consolidation: The Case of Cambodia, 1993–2004*. PhD Thesis. Northern Illinois University, 2004.

UNAIDS. *Country Profile: An Overview of the HIV/AIDS/STI Situation and the National Response in Cambodia*. 5th Edition. Phnom Penh: UNAIDS, December 2004.

United Nations Capital Development Fund (UNCDF). *Microfinance and the Millennium Development Goals: A Reader's Guide to the Millennium Project Reports and other UN Documents*. Geneva: UNCDF, 2005. Available online at www.yearofmicrocredit.org/docs/mdgdoc_MN.pdf, accessed 14 February 2009.

United Nations Childrens Fund. *Cambodia: Statistics*. Webpage. Available online at http://www.unicef.org/infobycountry/cambodia_statistics.html, accessed 12 August 2009.

United Nations Development Program. *Report on the 2007 Commune Council Elections in Cambodia*. Phnom Penh: UNDP, 2007.

United Nations High Commission for Human Rights. "Joint Public Statement: The United Nations Special Representatives of the Secretary General for Human Rights in Cambodia and the Special Rapporteur on the Independence of Judges and Lawyers Express Concern Over Judicial Independence in Cambodia in the Light of Recent Judicial Appointment." Geneva, 23 August 2007. Available online at Cambodia.ohchr.org/download.aspx?ep_id=334, accessed February 8, 2008.

US Department of State, Bureau of East Asian and Pacific Affairs. "Background Note: Cambodia." June 2008. Available online at http://www.state.gov/r/pa/ei/bgn/2732.htm#econ, accessed 11 October 2008.

Van Acker, Frank. *Hitting a Stone with an Egg? Cambodia's Rural Economy and Land Tenure in Transition*. Discussion Paper No. 23. Phnom Penh, Centre for Advanced Studies, 1999.

van de Walle, Nicholas. *The Path from Neo-Patrimonialism: Democracy and Clientelism in Africa Today*. Working Paper no. 3. Ithaca: Cornell University Center for International Studies, 2007.

Van Sou Ieng. *Biography of Mr Van Sou Ieng*. E-mail from an informant, 9 November 2008.

Vannak Chou, Simone di Castri, Sophea Hoy, Sovannsoksitha Pen, and Engchhay Soung. *IDLO Microfinance Policy and Regulation Survey N1* (Rome: IDLO, 2008) online at http://www.idlo.int/Microfinance/Documents/Publications/1E.pdf

Vickery, Michael. *Kampuchea: Economics, Politics and Society*. London: Pinter/Rienner, 1986.

VietnamNet. "Rubber group to expand plantation in Cambodia." *Business in Brief.* 10 January 2008. Available online at http://english.vietnamnet.vn/biz/2008/01/763511/, accessed 10 June 2009.

Voan Lim. *Land Regime In Cambodia.* Unpublished ms, 1997.

Vonthanak Saphonn. *HIV Incidence Among Sentinel Surveillance Groups in Cambodia, 1999–2002.* Power point presentation. Phnom Penh, 11 May 2004. Available online at http://www.nchads.org/Publication/dissemination/presentation%20in%20dissemination%20workshop%20english.pdf, accessed 12 August 2009.

Walsh, Nick Paton. "Cambodia Farm Land Sold to Wealthy Nations." *Channel 4 News.* 29 January 2009. Available online at http://www.channel4.com/news/articles/politics/international_politics/cambodia+farm+land+sold+to+wealthy+nations/2914582, accessed 12 August 2009.

Wasson, Erik, and Kay Kimsong. "Tax Holiday Extended, Bond Market Approved." *The Cambodia Daily (Weekly Review),* 17–18 June 2006. 6.

Wasson, Erik, and Yun Samean. "R'kiri Villagers File Complaints over Land Sale." *The Cambodia Daily (Weekly Review),* 22–26 January 2007. 1, 6.

Weber, Heloise. "The Global Political Economy of Microfinance and Poverty Reduction: Locating Local 'Livelihoods' in Political Analysis." In Jude Fernando, ed., *Microfinance: Perils and Prospects.* London: Routledge, 2006. 37–54.

Weber, Max. *The Protestant Ethic and the Spirit of Capitalism.* Translated by Talcott Parsons. London: Routledge, 1992.

Wells, William. *A Case Study of the Continuum of Care for People Living with HIV/AIDS in Cambodia: Linkages and Strengthening in the Public Health System.* Phnom Penh: NCHADS/World Health Organisation, 2006.

Wells-Dang, Andrew. "Agent Orange in Cambodia: the 1969 Defoliation in Kampong Cham." Available online at www.ffrd.org/AgentOrange/cam1969.htm, accessed 10 June 2009.

White, David G. "*Dakkhina* and *Agnicayana*: an Extended Application of Paul Mus' Typology." *History of Religions,* 26 (1986): 188–213.

Williams, Shaun. *Where Has All the Land Gone? Land Rights and Access in Cambodia.* Phnom Penh: OxfamGB, Cambodia Land Study Project, 1999.

Williamson, John. "Democracy and the Washington Consensus " *World Development* 21.8 (1993): 1329–1336.

Wilson, J. *Establishing the Rule of Law in Cambodia: the Role of NGO Regulation and Judicial Reform.* Research Paper for the International Human Rights Internship Program. Phnom Penh: Cambodian League for the Promotion and Defense of Human Rights (LICADHO), 2005.

Woolcock, Michael, and Lant Pritchett. *Solutions when the Solution is the Problem: Arraying the Disarray in Development.* Paper no. 10. Washington DC: Center for Global Development, 2002.

World Bank. *Cambodia: Enhancing Service Delivery Through Improved Resource Allocation and Institutional Reform.* Phnom Penh: World Bank, 2003.

——— *Cambodia: Legal and Judicial Sector Assessment.* Phnom Penh: World Bank, 2003.

——— *Cambodia at the Crossroads.* Phnom Penh: World Bank, 2004.

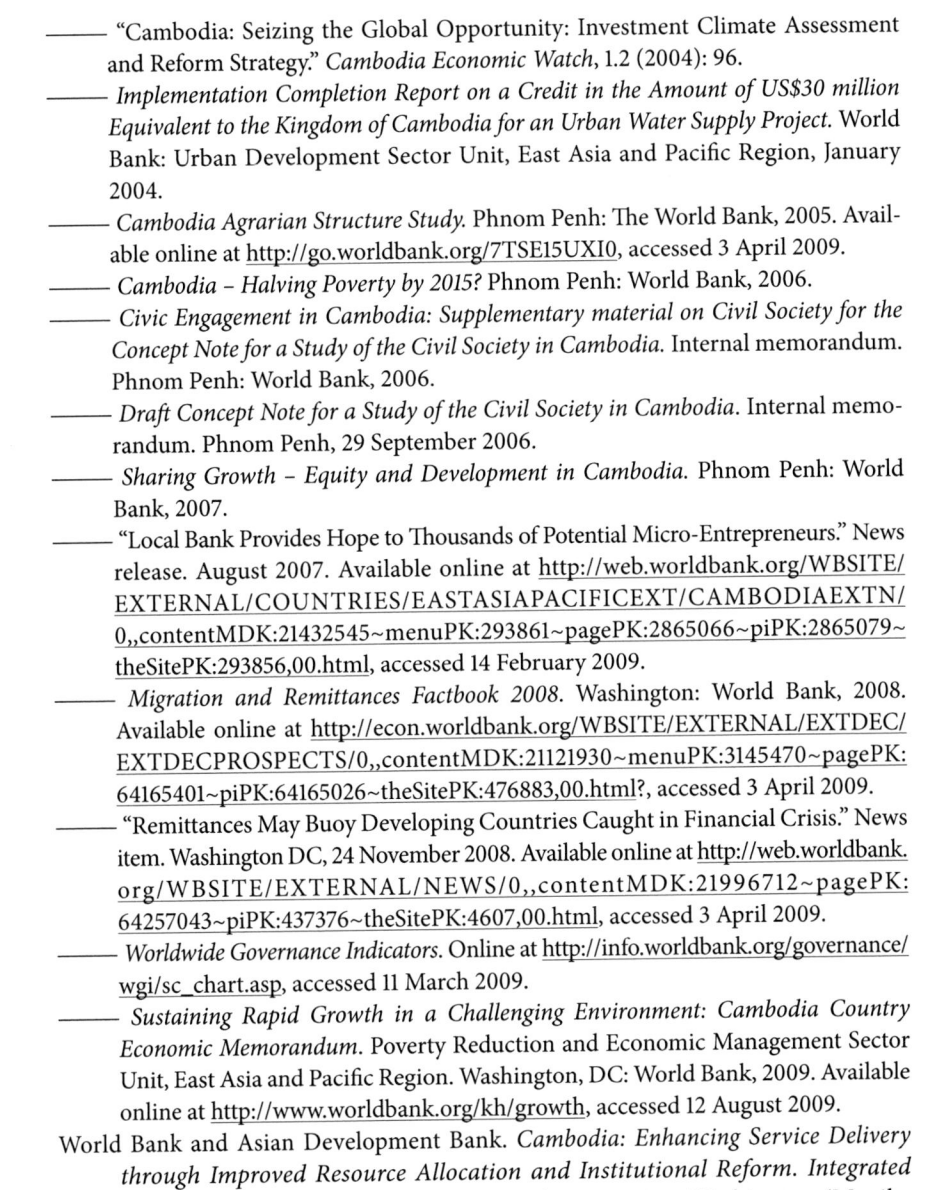

―――. "Cambodia: Seizing the Global Opportunity: Investment Climate Assessment and Reform Strategy." *Cambodia Economic Watch*, 1.2 (2004): 96.

―――. *Implementation Completion Report on a Credit in the Amount of US$30 million Equivalent to the Kingdom of Cambodia for an Urban Water Supply Project*. World Bank: Urban Development Sector Unit, East Asia and Pacific Region, January 2004.

―――. *Cambodia Agrarian Structure Study*. Phnom Penh: The World Bank, 2005. Available online at http://go.worldbank.org/7TSE15UXI0, accessed 3 April 2009.

―――. *Cambodia – Halving Poverty by 2015?* Phnom Penh: World Bank, 2006.

―――. *Civic Engagement in Cambodia: Supplementary material on Civil Society for the Concept Note for a Study of the Civil Society in Cambodia*. Internal memorandum. Phnom Penh: World Bank, 2006.

―――. *Draft Concept Note for a Study of the Civil Society in Cambodia*. Internal memorandum. Phnom Penh, 29 September 2006.

―――. *Sharing Growth – Equity and Development in Cambodia*. Phnom Penh: World Bank, 2007.

―――. "Local Bank Provides Hope to Thousands of Potential Micro-Entrepreneurs." News release. August 2007. Available online at http://web.worldbank.org/WBSITE/EXTERNAL/COUNTRIES/EASTASIAPACIFICEXT/CAMBODIAEXTN/0,,contentMDK:21432545~menuPK:293861~pagePK:2865066~piPK:2865079~theSitePK:293856,00.html, accessed 14 February 2009.

―――. *Migration and Remittances Factbook 2008*. Washington: World Bank, 2008. Available online at http://econ.worldbank.org/WBSITE/EXTERNAL/EXTDEC/EXTDECPROSPECTS/0,,contentMDK:21121930~menuPK:3145470~pagePK:64165401~piPK:64165026~theSitePK:476883,00.html?, accessed 3 April 2009.

―――. "Remittances May Buoy Developing Countries Caught in Financial Crisis." News item. Washington DC, 24 November 2008. Available online at http://web.worldbank.org/WBSITE/EXTERNAL/NEWS/0,,contentMDK:21996712~pagePK:64257043~piPK:437376~theSitePK:4607,00.html, accessed 3 April 2009.

―――. *Worldwide Governance Indicators*. Online at http://info.worldbank.org/governance/wgi/sc_chart.asp, accessed 11 March 2009.

―――. *Sustaining Rapid Growth in a Challenging Environment: Cambodia Country Economic Memorandum*. Poverty Reduction and Economic Management Sector Unit, East Asia and Pacific Region. Washington, DC: World Bank, 2009. Available online at http://www.worldbank.org/kh/growth, accessed 12 August 2009.

World Bank and Asian Development Bank. *Cambodia: Enhancing Service Delivery through Improved Resource Allocation and Institutional Reform. Integrated Fiduciary Assessment and Public Expenditure Review*. Washington /Manila: World Bank / Asian Development Bank, 2003. Available online at http://www-wds.worldbank.org/servlet/WDS_IBank_Servlet?pcont=details&eid=000090341_20030924104425, accessed 12 August 2009.

World Bank and International Finance Corporation. *A Better Investment Climate to Sustain Growth in Cambodia:Second Investment Climate Assessment*. Poverty Reduction and Economic Management Sector Unit, East Asia and Pacific Region. Washington, DC: World Bank, January 2009 .

Xinhua News Agency. "Cambodia Grants Sale of 6,000 Tons Broken Rice to Senegal." www.chinaview.cn, April 23, 2008. Available online at http://news.xinhuanet.com/english/2008-04/23/content_8036128.htm, accessed 12 August 2009.

Xinua News Agency, "Cambodian Garment Exports up 7% in 2008," 18 February 2009, online at http://news.xinhuanet.com/english/2009-02/18/content_10838964.htm, accessed 14 September 2011.

Yun Samean. "R'kiri Land Dispute Petition Blocked, Claim Villagers." *The Cambodia Daily (Weekly Review)*, 5–9 February 2007, 13.

Yun Samean, and Douglas Gillison. "R'kiri's Indigenous People Losing Land, Culture." *The Cambodia Daily (Weekly Review)*, 5–9 February 2007, 9.

Yunus, Muhammad, "Grameen Bank, Microcredit and Millennium goals" *Economic and Political Weekly* 39.36 (2006).

Zepp, Ray. "The Aid Industry: A Frank Discussion of Local and International NGOs." In Ray Zepp, *Experiencing Cambodia*. Unpublished ms. Phnom Penh, 2004. 65–78.

INDEX

bold=extended discussion or term highlighted in text;
f = figure; n = footnote; t = table;
[–] = intermediate page leapfrogged.

A

accountability 15, 50, 56–7, 61, 63–4, 67–9, 76, 89, 170, 206, 210, 220–1, 225, **237–8**, 306, 309
 definition 285
 key question **285**
 operationalization **268–70**
 party financing **238–41**
 party financing of local investment projects (implications) **241–4**
 political power **280–4**
 terminology 268–9
accountability and local politics in natural resource management **266–87**
 CBOs as empirical focus **270–2**
 empiricism 267, 268, 269–70
 purposive sampling 271
 research design **270–2**
achar (lay preacher) 249, 255, 262
ACLEDA (Association of Cambodian Local Economic Development Agencies) 175t, **176–7**, 178n, 252
ACLEDA bank 25
Active Non-Violence Training 299, 300, 301, 304
'Advisors' 30n, 42, 62n, **71–6**
Agence Française de Développement 168n
Agence Khmère de Presse (AKP) 43, 43n, 84n
agri-business **60–3**
agricultural intensification 124n, 128n, 131

agriculture 11, 40–1, 82t, 89, 155n, 159, 200, 230, 324
 see also subsistence agriculture
Agriculture Sector Programme 100, 106n
aid donors 6, 24, 27, 29, 33, 48, 89, 90, 99, 100, 103, 113, 137, 158, 166, 168–74, 178–9, 181, 209, 215, 220, 234, 288, 292, 298, 305, 309
 compromise **58**
 interests and analyses (contradictory nature) 306
 'mutually constitutive dynamic' 304
 Western 26, 39, 49
 Western (playing into hands of PRC) **54–8**, 58–9, 67, 69
 see also good governance agenda
AMRET 175t, 178n
An Samnang (judge) 34, 39n
An Yang Yin Chang 62
ancestors **323–4**, 328
 chidaun and *chita* 316
Andong (plantation) 101
Andong Meas district 120
Ang Duong, King 316
Angkor Kasekam Roongroeung (AKR) 87
anthropology 312, 315, 317, 324, 325
Arbitration Council (garments) 88, 90
armed forces 6, 7, 8, 38, 205, 206, 214–15, 216
Asian Development Bank (ADB) 8, 41, 64, 65, 75n, 100, 100n, 105, 168, 171–2, 177–9, 210

357

Index

Asian Financial Crisis (1997) 4, 19, 20, 21, 55
Asian Legal Resource Centre 137
Association of South East Asian Nations 8, 40, 86, 104

B

bah bay ben ceremony 323–4, 325n
bangsokaul (mortuary chant for dead) 323, 325n
bankers/banking 92–3, 167–8, 176
Banlung (provincial capital) 36, 38
Bar Association of the Kingdom of Cambodia (BAKC) 297
Battambang Province 96t, 156n, 222, 271n, 276, 281, 282–3, 299
best practice 161, 164, 169, 170, 173–4n, 209, 242
Better Factories Cambodia programme (ILO) 78, 79, 88, 90
bhikkhu ('one who desires a share') 320–1
big business 26
 three communes 25, **245–65**
Bimbisara, King 316
Bin Sam Ol 44, 45
Boeung Ket (rubber plantation) 100, 101, 104
'booty capitalism' 16, 27–8, 28n
boran (magical) interpretation of *dhamma* 289, 289n, 292n
Brao ethnic group 130n, 132n
bribery/'bribe tax' 32, 76, 77, 80, 150, 157, 260
Buddhism 224, 227–8, **297–8**, 316, 320
Build-Operate-Transfer (BOT) 65
Bunrong company 6
bureaucracy 15–16, 24, 26, 48, 170, 184, 199–201, 238–9, 280, 283
 land disputes **31–9**
 see also patrimonial administrative state
bureaucratic capitalism 29
bureaucrats 17–19, 205
 'government officials' 72, 78–9, 160, 225, 234
 see also local government officials
bureaucratization 21, 23, 307
business–politics alliances 265
bwa kuli (manual labour) 133

C

cadastral authority 141, 141n, 149, 153–4t, 154–5
Cadastral Registry Unit 155n
cadastral sustainability 138, **139–48**, 156–8
Caisse Française de Développement 101
Cambodia
 economic background **313–15**
 economic transformation (historical and theoretical frameworks) **1–26**
 growth of microfinance **166–9**
 integration into world economy 42
 PRC aid **50–69**
 PRC aid (benefits and costs) 65
 PRC investment and development **63–9**
 see also CLMV
Cambodia: Halving Poverty by 2015? (World Bank, 2006) 14–15
Cambodia Agricultural Development Study Centre (CEDAC) 148, 148n, 149
Cambodia Development Resource Institute (CDRI) viii-x, 11n, 57n, 152n, 156, 238n, 245n, 249n, 287
Cambodia Entrepreneur Building Ltd 178n
Cambodian Bar Association 34, 35n
Cambodian Centre for Human Rights (CCHR) 37–8, 44n, 45, 296
Cambodian Centre for Independent Media 37n
Cambodian Chamber of Commerce 97, 97n
Cambodian Chinese General Assembly 56
Cambodian Constitution (1993) 204
Cambodian Development Cooperation Forum (CDCF) 53
Cambodian diaspora 81n, 188
Cambodian Economic Association 81
Cambodian Free Trade Union 66
Cambodian Human Rights Action Committee 32
Cambodian Human Rights and Development Association (ADHOC) 33, 38, 137
Cambodian Independent Teachers' Association 296
Cambodian Investment Board (CIB) 51
Cambodian League for Promotion and Defence of Human Rights (LICADHO) 44n, 45, 45n, 137–8, 296, 296n
Cambodian Micro-Finance Association 167n, 173, 173n, 175t
Cambodian People's Party *see* CPP
Cambodian Red Cross 231, 232n, 255
Cambodian Rubber Research Institute (CRRI) 101, 104
Cambodian Socioeconomic Survey (2004) 146
Cambodian state 9–10, 12, 47, 49, 52, 68–70, 275, 284, 290, 292n, 308, 309
 alliance with business 159–60
 business relations with CPP **71–4**
 fragmentation 201
 modus operandi 208

neo-patrimonial model **57–8**
Canadian International Development Agency (CIDA) 65
capital 104, 104n, 131
   external/foreign 24, 40, 42
   regional or national 24
capital accumulation 16, 28, 47
capitalism 12, 39, **110–35**, 314, 325n
cashews 24–5, **110–35**
Central Highlands (Vietnam) 116–20
Center for Advanced Study, Phnom Penh (CAS) 102, 106, 107, 299n
Cham Prasidh 81n, 89, 89n, 182n
Chamcar Andong (rubber plantation) 98, 100–1, 104, 106–7
Chan Sarun 43, 81n, 87, 206
Chan Sophal 118, 147n
Chea Sim 8, 73
Chea Vichea (d 2004) 24n, 293
cheap labour 106, 109, 194
Chhan Saphan 31, 34, 37
Chi Khor (village) 44
Chi Khor Loeu commune 42
chiew (supervisor) 195
children 102, 133–4, 219, 311
China (PRC) 4, 25, 41, 79, 89, 94
   aid to Cambodia **50–69**
   foreign policy objectives 50, 54–5, 56, 59
   investment and decision-making **58–60**
   projection of soft power in Cambodia **54–8**, 68
   surge of investment in Cambodia **51–3**
China Exim (bank) 59
China Hong Kong Macau Expatriate and Business Association of Cambodia 66
Chinese Chamber of Commerce 56, 64, 65n, 66
Chinese Wuzhishan concession 63
Chouk village 46
choun tam samnaumpo ('granted according to your request') 219
Chrap estate (rubber) 101, 102
'chronic indebtedness' 179, 181
Chun Sakada 186n
Chup estate (rubber) 99–104, 106–7
cities 310–13, 321–2, 326–7
   'urban areas' 26, 155n, 158
Civil Code (1920) 141, 142, 142n
civil society 32–3, 63, 163, 180n, 252, 266–7, 268
   definition 288
   Gramscian versus associational perspectives 298

   ideological contestation **295–8**
   ideological frames **289–95**
   'two roles' 291
   weakness **294–5**
civil society organizations (CSOs) 294–5
Clinton Administration 78
CLMV 40, 41
coffee 41, 116–17
Cold War 1–2, 3, 18, 20, 51–2
collective action 25, 26, 81, 85, 88, 91, 160, 291, 305, 307
collectivization 1, 135, 142–3, 275n
colonial era 126n, **140–2**, 147, 246
commodification 131, 184, 245
common property rights 127–9
commune budgets 257–8, 263, 285
commune chiefs 157, 223, 229, 232–4, 236, 246–9, 251, 255–6, 260–2, 281
   constraints on power **257–8**
commune councillors 249–50, 252–5, 258, 260, 271, 274, 287
commune councils (2002–) 268, 271–3
   accountability (three-phase process) **269–70**
   interaction with CBOs **276–80, 284–5**
   mandates 254, 256, 264, 270, 277, 280, 285–7
   political power to deliver accountability **280–4**
commune elections (2002) 5, 7, 229, 233, 248, 260–2, 276–7, 286
   (2007) 229, 233, 255
Commune/*Sangkat* Fund (CSF) 220–1, 227, 228t, 231, 233, 237, 285
Commune/*Sangkat* law (March 2001) 270
communes 26, 32, 225–6, 236
   functions (2001–) 248
   local leaders and big business 25, **245–65**
communism 288, 290, 306
community fisheries *see* fishing communities
Community Legal Education Centre (CLEC) 32–5, 39, 44n, 45, 296
Community Organizing (CO) NGOs 299–304, 307
Community Peace-Building Network (CPN) 304, 307
Community-Based Organizations (CBOs) 180n, 267–70, 286, **292–3**, 304, 307
   definition 270n
   empirical focus **270–2**
   examples 271n

interaction with local authorities **276–80**, **284–5**
key question **268, 285**
legitimacy problems 276
participation and mobilization **274–6, 284**
political power **285**
popular engagement and support **274–6**
Compagnie des Caoutchoucs du Cambodge 101, 102
Compagnie du Cambodge 101n
Condom Use Policy (CUP) **214–15**, 217
Consultative Group (CG) 53–4
Consultative Group to Assist the Poor (CGAP, 1997–) 163–4, 171, 172
Continuum of Care for People Living with HIV/AIDS 214
Contract Decree (No 38, 1988) 149
corruption 6, 8–9, 13–15, 18–19, 50–1, 53, 58, 68, 71n, 74–5, 77, 84, 100, 108, 158, 199–201, 206, 210, 221, 255–6, 257, 290, 294, 297–8, 302, 315, 329
 'informal fees' 155–7
Corruption Perception Index (TI) 72
Council for Administrative Reform webpage 51n
Council for Development of Cambodia (CDC) 293–4n
Council of Ministers 72, 75, 79, 85
 Decorations Department 73
counter-movement (Polanyi) 23, 25, 252, 259
County-Level Effectiveness and Accountability Review (CGAP) 171
coups d'état (1970) 95, 251
 (1997) 206
court system 31, **33–5**, 39
CPP (Cambodian People's Party) 1–3, 5–8, 23–6, 37, 46n, 52–3, 57, 62, 68, 70, 72–4, 93, 102–4, 209, 216, 248, 250, 253–4, 260–1, 295, 297
 commune elections (2007) 255–6
 district headquarters 221
 elite and mass patronage 25, **219–44**
 financing **238–41**
 fund-raising **222–3**
 national, central, subnational arrangements **222–3**
 officials 221
 patronage **262–4**
 political economy of 'good governance' reform **199–218**
 provincial development reports 230
 support to commune (2003–7) 228t

working group structure 224f
CPP: Central Committee 204, 223
CPP: District Working Groups 222, 226t
CPP: Provincial Working Groups 225, 226
CPP working groups **223–36**, 242
 hierarchy **225–6**
Creation of Commission for Privatization of Rubber Plantations (sub-decree, 1994) 99
Credit Committee for Rural Development (CCRD, 1995 p 168, 171
crime 280–1, 286n
 see also fishery crime
crony capitalism 16, **17–20**, 22, 119n, 199

D

dak ben or *kan ben* (placing or carrying of rice balls) 322
dams 231t, 232t, 234, 263
 'hydroelectric dams' 41, 51, 59, 65, 66, 69, 85, 126
decentralization 220–1, 243, 246, 248–50, 254, 266–9, 272, 276, 285, 286–7
 key problem 265
deconcentration 220–1, 248, 285, 286–7
decision-making 28, 30, **58–60**, 61, **267**, 273, 275n
deforestation 113, 114, 115, 252
democracy 2. 50, 64, 180n, 294
Democratic Kampuchea (DK, 1975–9) 98n, 142, 142n, 143, 246, 250n
democratization 266, 268–9
Department of Environment 274
Department of Fisheries 300n
Department of Forestry 300
Department of Forestry Administration (DFA) 206, 207
devata (ancestor) 321
development 8, **63–9**, 228, 265, 272n
 approaches 58–9
developmental institutionalist perspective 26
developmental states **15–21**, 23–4
dhamma (Buddhist world view) 288, 289, 292n
dharma xi, 320n
dignity (concept) 165
'disembedding' (Polanyi) 111, 111n, 134–5
District Cadastral Office 155, 157
district elections (2009) 286–7n
district governors 223, 230, 234, 256–7, 271, 283
District Land Governance office 141
district offices 227, 230, 281, 283, **283n**
Dith Monty 203

E

East Timor 23
economic development 162, 208
economic growth 2, 10–11, 14, 15, 27, 60, 68, 74
    constraints **75–7**
    'despite poor governance' 70, 90
economic influence
    conversion into political power 47
Economic Institute of Cambodia (EIC) 78, 118
economic liberalization **39–47**
economic reform (1989) 146, 147
economic transformation **10–12**, 254–5, 264–5, 306
    good governance perspective **12–15**
education 6, 56, 81n, 92, 191, 217, 227, 231–2, 235t, 237, 241, 292
educational attainment 6, 192, 250
Ek Sonn Chan **210–13**
elders 249, 252, 255, 262, 264–5
Électricité du Cambodge (EdC) 213
electricity 71n, 80, 84, 196
elite clientelism patronage **239**, 239n
elite pact 8
elite patronage **239–40**, 241, 242
    tuy yo (pipe) or *ksae* (line) 240
elites **16–20**, 48, 87, 103, 135, 203, **219–44**, 247, 269, 288
    bureaucratic 27–8, 29–30, 47, 72
    business 29–30, 61, 63
    national 42
    political 30, 34, 47, 112
    politico-economic 50, 57, 67–8
    regionally-networked oligarchic 30
    see also ruling elite
'embedded autonomy' (Evans) 16–17, 19, 23
employment 66, 69, 82t, 91, 94, 100, 151, 207, 314
    see also 'labour export'
empowerment 161–2, 164–5, 181, 265, 267, 287
'enslaved migrants' 192
environment 61–2, 272n, 274, 301n
ethnic minorities 207, 254, 302, 303
    see also Jarai highlanders
European Union 44, 46, 83, 88, 89n, 90
Everything But Arms (EBA) initiative (2001–) 44, 44n, 88, 90
exports 10, 71n, 74, 77, 89n, 97, 99, 100, 208
    garments **79–83**
    rice **83–9**
external pressure 91

F

'face' 224–5
fallowing 111, 114–15, 122, 124, 128, 140
family 47, 121–2, 124–5, 127, 129, **133–4**, 138n, 143, 164, 183, 194, 198, 222, 224, 239, 254, 261–2, 292, 311, 318
    dead members 316
    see also preta
Farmer's Hand (NGO) 174n
FDI 10, 50, 51, 60
    'foreign investment' 105
'fictive kinship' 328
Financial Sector Development Plan (2001–10) 166
fisheries 9, 245–6, 252, 260, 268, 270, 301, 303, 308
    see also Sangkat Fisheries
Fisheries Action Coalition Team (FACT) 300n
Fisheries Law (2007) 273
fishermen 189, 190, 192, **194–6**, 233
fishery crime/illegal fishing 273, 274, 276, 279, **281–3**
    see also forestry crime
fishing communities **299–300**
    'community fisheries' 271, 274–7, 279, **281–3**, 293, 302
    mandates and activities **272–4**
    primary duties 273
    sub-decree 273
'fixed asset registration' (1925–) 141, 142
Focus on Global South 295
food 131, 179, 190, 315, 317
foreign exchange 94, 98, 108, 183
forest crime 275, **278–9**, 280
    illegal logging 38, 61, 119, 207, 273, 300
Forest Crimes Monitoring Unit (FCMU, 2001–) 207, 301
forest management **205–8**
Forest Management Plans (2002–) 206
forest products 126, 258, 278
forestry 9, 10, 32, 93, 268, 300–1n, 301, 303, 308
forestry administration 206–7, 273–4, 278, 283
forestry communities 271, 277–80, 283–4, 300
    'community forestry' 277n, 279n, 281, 293, 299n, 302
    general rationale 272n
    mandates and activities **272–4**
forestry law 44
    (2001) 9, 207
    (2003 sub-decree) 272, 272n
forests 112, 130n, 133, 145f, 151, 245, 255

France 81, 86, 98n, 104, 188
fraud 32, 32n, 33
Free Trade Union Workers of the Kingdom of Cambodia 80
freedom of expression 78–9
FUNCINPEC 3, 3n, 6, 7, 52, 233, 235–6, 255n, 296
funeral associations 252

G

G8 (2004) 163–4
garment industry 3, 7, 9, 11, 24, 60, 65–6, 70–1, 74, 76, **77–83**, 88–91, 93, 100, 107, 293, 313–15
   constraints 75, 80, 86
Garment-Manufacturers' Association of Cambodia (GMAC) 66, **81–2**, 88, 90, 91
garment workers 326n, 329n
GDP 75, 77–9, 82t, 83–4, 188, 313, 314
general elections 68, 72, 108, 200, 289, 290
   (1993) 2, 3, 52, 53, 203, 233, 247
   (1998) 2, 3, 52, 57, 223, 233, 247
   (2003) 7, 233
   (2008) 2, 78, 219, 220, 221, 229, 235–6, 241, 296
Ghai, Y. (UN Special Representative for Human Rights) 38–9
gift-giving 312, 315, 317, 322, **324–8**
global commodities markets 120, **126–30**
global economic crisis (2008–) 3–4, 10, 51, 66, 80, 187, 326n
Global Witness 7n, 61n, 119n, 206–7, 300
globalization 20–1, 40
'good enough governance' 70–1, 82, 85, 90–1
good governance agenda 2–4, 8, **12–15**, 21, 24–5, 27, 33, 39, 42, 48–9, 64, 268, 288, **290–1**, 294, 295n, 298n, 308
   absence of vested political interests 209, 210, 215
   political economy **199–218**
   separation of public and private 74
Governance Action Plans 200–1
governance failures 5, 13–14, 75, 80, 86–7
'Governance Focal Monopoly' 87
governance and growth
   outlook and implications **89–90**
governance reform 18, 53, 67, 69, 83, 244
   sustainability 201
   weakness of aid donors **54–8**
government
   and ideological contestation in civil society **295–8**

government-donor relations 34, 35, 50, 54, 200
Government-Private Sector Forum 19
Grameen Bank (1983–) 162, 165
Gramsci, Antonio. 288, 297–8
Grand Land Agricultural Development 62n
'Great Transformation' (Polanyi) **22**, 131, 131n
Greater Mekong Subregion (GMS) 8, 41, 64
Green Trade Corporation (GTC) 84–7

H

Hanoi Declaration on Narrowing Developmental Gap (2001) 40
Hattha Kaksekar Ltd (HKL) **174–6**, 178n
health 25, 75, 80, 185n, 190–1, 195, 208, 236, 316
hegemony 288, 297
Heng Brothers 105n, 119, 119n, 125, 133
Heng Bun Phann 36, 36n
Heng San 44
hierarchy 224, 225–6, 239, 242, 251, 297, 297n, 304, 326, 326n, 327
Hing Thoraxy 75
HIV/AIDS 185n, 199, 201, **213–18**
Hong Kong 56, 66, 67, 186
Hor Namhong 85
houses/housing 107, 125–6, 134, 151, 189, 191, 196, 227t, 252, 255
human development indicators 8, 10, 13, 14
human resource management 209, 241
human rights 44–5, 61, 67, 69, 78–9, 138n, 247, 294, 296, 301, 302, 304
Human Rights Party (2007–) 264n
Hun Sen, *Samdech* 8, 24n, 27, 32, 36, 38, 40n, 42, 49, 58–61, 62n, 68, 76n, 83n, 106n, 112, 160, 166, 192, 197, 206, 230, 238–9, 243, 258, 290, 296, 301
   'Advisors' 73
   consolidation of power 52–3, 57
   visit to Kuwait (2009) 85
Hun Sen schools 6, 7, 220, 224, 234, 315
Huon Chundy 35
Huot Chea 92

I

ideological contestation 308
   government and civil society **295–8**
ideology 288
   civil society **289–95**
In Channy 176
Independent Forestry Monitor 300
Independent Trade Union of Cambodian Labourers (1998–) 107

India 17, 88, 89, 116
indigenous communities 31–9, 44, 45
individuals 164–5, 307–8
Indonesia 16, 20, 30n, 41, 75, 84–5, 182
  'Dutch East Indies' 95
'industrial agriculture' 11
industrialization 22, 64, 314
inequality 26, 40n, 135, 138, 139, 152, 158, 163, 190, 312–15, 328, 329n
  'legitimacy' 289, 292n
  rising in countryside, falling in cities 314
infrastructural projects 41, 57, 59, 60, 64–7, 69, 128, 219, 240, 242, 244
infrastructure 8, 71n, 75, 87, 210, 256, 265
inheritance 111, 128, 133–4, 146–7
institutional layering 242, 242n
institutionalist approaches 5
institutions 243
  see also good governance
'intensive' transactions 244
International Committee for Reconstruction of Cambodia (ICORC) 53
International Crisis Group 112n
International Finance Corporation (IFC) 71n, 77
international financial institutions (IFIs) 11, 14, 40
International Labour Organization 78, 83, 91, 107, 162–3, 168n, 176
  International Programme on Elimination of Child Labour (ILO/IPEC) 102, 106
International Monetary Fund 12, 51, 75n, 83n, 168, 170
international NGOs (INGOs) 168, 274, 292–4, 303
International Rubber Association 101
Intertek Testing Services 90
investment 14, 42, 57, 63–9, 90, 241–4
  by PRC 25, 51–3, 58–60
  see also FDI
investors 24, 25, 46, 73, 91
irrigation 85, 87, 227, 230, 232–3, 235t, 293
isomorphism 242
Ith Mathoura 32–3n, 39

J

Japan 41, 64, 186
Japan: Ministry of International Trade and Industry (MITI) 18, 23
Japanese International Cooperation Agency (JICA) 65

Jarai highlanders xi, 24, 31–9, 131–2, 135
  agricultural calendar 123t
  marriage and inheritance 133–4
  swidden system 120–6, 128
Joint Monitoring Indicators (JMI, 2004–) 54, 200
Joint Technical Working Groups (TWG, 2004–) 54
judiciary/judicial system 8–9, 150–1, 160, 199, 201–5, 240, 244

K

Kabre society 325–6
Kamchay hydropower project 51, 59, 65
Kampong Chhnang Province 62, 114, 299, 301
Kampong Speu Province
  land transactions (mode) 153t
  landholding survey by Sokbunthoeun So (2007) 144t, 145f, 145, 153–4
  transfer of land holdings (1979–2007) 144t
Kampong Thom Province 43n
Kampot Province 65, 96t, 271n, 275–6, 280–1
Kampuchean People's Revolutionary Party (KPRP) 1, 2
kanak neiyapheap (accountability) 268–9n
Kandal 155n, 156n
Kang Chandararot 118
karma xi, 317, 317n, 320
Keat Chhon 31, 88
Keat Kolney case 31–9, 42, 44, 45, 47, 48–9
Kek Galabru 45n
Kem Sokha 45, 264, 264n, 296
Keo Kang 173n
Kep province 65
Kheng Sameth Company 150
Khieu Kanarith 36
Khmer Republic (1970–5) 95[-]97
Khmer Rouge 1–2, 46, 111, 114–15, 119, 135, 206, 229, 246–7, 250n, 294
  dissolution (1999) 52
khnang ('boss', 'back') 211, 213, 240
khnorng (likewise, 'boss', 'back') 72
Khon Kaen Sugar Industry Plc ('KSL') 42n, 43, 44
khsae (connections to powerful figures) 8, 72, 73, 203, 206, 211–13
Khtum Krang commune 144t, 146
khuddakapatha 318n
khum (commune office, 1908–) 141, 142
kin/kinship 250, 322–3, 329n
Kinh (Vietnam's national ethnic majority) 117

Kirivong 8
Kith Meng, *Neak Oknha* 74
klach (fear) 237
'klepto-patrimonialism' (Evans) 15
'kleptocratic elites' (Global Witness) 207
Koh Kong 8
Koh Kong Plantation Company **39–47**, 63
Koh Kong Sugar Industry Company 43, 45, 46, 63
Kompong Cham 24, 94, 96t, 97, 97n, 100, 101, 156n
Kompong Speu 156n
Kompong Svay district 85
Kompong Thom 94, 96t, 101, 103, 148, 301
Kong Yu village **31–9**
koruap (respect) 237
kram (decree) 95
Kratie Province 43, 94, 96t, 101, 271n, 275, 278–9
Kreditanstalt für Wiederaufbau 176
Krek (plantation) 101
krom (sub-village unit) 223
Krom Samaki (agricultural collectives) **143**
kromhun 129–30n
Krouch, *Oknha* (pseudonym) **256–9**, 264
ksae bandanh (extensive networks) 229
Kuwait 85, 86, 186

L

Labansiek (Ratanakiri Province) 98n
labour 12, 21, 22, 93, 99, 105, 120n, 123–4, 131–5, 265, 305n
  bonded 111
  indentured 102, 106, 108
labour export 24, **182–98**
  background/theory **183–7**
  causes 188–9
  'development agent' versus 'vulnerable victim' 182, **187–92**, 196
  illegal migrants **186–7**
  sub-decree (1995) **184–5**
labour law 78, 107
labour productivity 95, 98, 106–8
land 21–2, 24–7, 82t, 86, 91, 112, 120, 127, 129, 131–2, 229, 245, 303, 308
  agricultural 155n, 159
  markets **126–30**
  national market 265
Land Coalition 10
land concessions **60–3**, 64, 85, 105, 114–15, 119, 123–5, 128, 151, **255–9**, 301

land disputes 30, **31–9**, **39–47**, 48, 63, **136–9**, 251, 253, **260–2**, 301, 302
land eviction 159–60
land holding practices **149**
land law 44, 62, 127, 149, 207
  (1884) 140–1
  (1992) 136, 147, 147n
  (2001) 9, 31–3, 61, 114, 136, 152, 154–5
land ownership 40n, 110, 138, 301
land registration **136–60**
land sales 125n, 134
  forced 150–1
  legality 31, **32–3**
land scarcity **128**
land tenure 115, 138–9, 140
  boundary conflicts 149
  forced transactions **149–50**
land tenure insecurity **148–53**
  judicial system (shortcomings) **150–1**
  threat of expropriation 151
land tenure institutions **158–60**
land titles 153
  expropriation risk 159
  registration 'too costly/complicated' 154t, **154–8**
land transfer system ('quasi-formal') **139–48**
  limits **148–53**
Land Valuation Study Report (RGC, 2005) 156n
land-grabbing 35n, 45, 113, **136–7**, 138n, 160, 247–8, 253, 297
landesque capital (Blaikie and Brookfield) **126**
landlessness 10–11, 94, 138n, 249
Laos 41, 44, 46, 55, 114, 126, 192
Lapavitsas, C. 163n
Lau Meng Khin, Senator 62, 62n
Law on Administration of Commune (2001) 248, 272n
leadership 253n, 292, 304, 305
  see also local leadership
legal aid 31, 33, 301–2, 304–5
Legal Aid of Cambodia (LAC) 32, 34, 45n
Legal Fellows Program (LFP) 297
'legal pluralism' **151–2**
'legal vacuum' (Jansen and Roquas, 1998) 139n, 146
legitimacy 2, 25, 201, 241, 244, 264, 268, 269, 272, 285, 290, 292n, 309
  international 68, 295
legitimation 6, 208, 241, 263, 271, 288, 289
Leland, Blake 325

Licensed Financial Institutions (LFIs) 172–3, 175t, 178
livestock 88n, 89, 92, 93, 126, 129
local elections 239n
  (1981) 246–7, 256
  (2002) 226, 256, 266
  (2007) 228, 256, 266
local government 26, 242, 245, **246–9**
  accountability **266–87**
  accountability (power to deliver) **280–4**
  'demand side' 269
local government officials 31, **35–9**, 44, 45, 148, 150–1, 154–5
  see also local leadership
local investment projects
  implications for democracy **241–4**
local leadership
  and big business in three communes 25, **245–65**
  land values and money politics **260–2**
  on margins of land concession **255–9**
local politics
  natural resource management **266–87**
Lon Nol 114–15, 313
longhouses 110–11, 118, 133–5
ludn (slaves and debt-bondsmen) 135
Ly Chhuong Construction Company 119n
Ly Daravuth 322
Ly Yong Phat, Senator 42, 42n, 44, 45, 46n, 62

M

Ma Vichit, 38, 38n
mae-ov (idealized leader *in loco parentis*) 251, 261
Mahanikay sect 297
Malaya 95
Malaysia 17, 51, 186
Mam Sonando 296
mandates 15, 79, 127, 204, 206–7, 235t, 248, 254, 256, 260, 264, 270, 272–3, 277, 280, 283, 285–7, 293n
manufacturing 11, 12, 41, 66, 78, 82
market forces 14, 70, 167n, 308, 326, 326n, 328
marketization 21, 23, 25, 170, 259
markets **21–3**, 46, 177, 179, 265
marriage **133–4**
Marubeni Corporation 104–5n
'mass clientelism' (van de Walle) 220, 239, 239n
'mass patronage' (Craig and Pak) **219–44**, 247, 249, **262–4**, 265
mé khyol leadership skills 299n

Mean Chivun 215
mean tae sambak ('show-offs') 276
media 37n, 93, 100, 100n, 103, 136, 182, 191–2, 274, 297
mekhum (commune chief) 141, 142, 142n, 143, 144
mekhyal
  'broker' 192, 194, 198
  'masters of wind' 253
  contested usage 253n
Mekong Basin 40–1
Mekong Migration Network 186n
Mekong Project Development Facility (MPDF) 77
Mekong River Commission (1995–) 41
Memot (plantation) 100, 101, 104
Men Sarun, Senator *Neak Oknha* 86
merit (Buddhist) 320–3
Mey Sokhan 38
micro-credit 24, 162n, 169
Micro-Credit Ratings International (M-CRIL, 1998–) 174, 174n, 178
micro-finance **161–81**
  borrowers 175t
  commercialization **171–7**
  conceptual origins **161–2**
  global mainstreaming **162–6**
  government role (theory) 172–3
  key principles 163–4
  versus 'micro-credit' 162n
  social and commercial tensions **177–80**
  terminology 162n
'Micro-Finance in Cambodia' (summit, 2006) 166
micro-finance institutions (MFI) 147, 148, 168, 175t
migrant workers 185
  'biggest provider of foreign aid' 183
  death 191
  exploitation **191–2**, 197–8
  illegal **189–98**
migration 115, 251, 252, 262
  see also 'labour export'
migration costs 188–90, 194–5
'migration industry' (Castles and Miller) 198
militias 247, 250, 260
Millennium Development Goals (MDGs) 13, 164, 166
Ministry of Agriculture, Forestry and Fisheries 87, 89, 100, 147, 206, 272–3

MAFF: General Department of Rubber Plantations 102
Ministry of Commerce (MoC) 66, 72, 77, 82n, 87, 91
Ministry of Commerce: CamControl 80, 89
Ministry of Cults and Religions 297
Ministry of Economy and Finance (MEF) 72, 100, 103, 156
Ministry of Health 6, 199, 201, **213–18**, 234
Ministry of Industry Mines and Energy (MIME) 59, 65, 89
Ministry of Interior 37, 72, 80, 214, 222, 248
Ministry of Irrigation 230
Ministry of Justice 203–4
Ministry of Labour 197
    Department of Employment and Manpower 185
Ministry of Labour and Vocational Training **184–5**
Ministry of Land Management, Urban Planning and Construction (MLMUPC) 31, 34, 155, 156n
Ministry of National Defence 72, 214
Ministry of Planning 138
Ministry of Rural Development 234
Ministry of Social Welfare, Labour, and Veteran Affairs 184
Ministry of Water Resources 230
mobile telephones 189, 196, 281
Mobutu, Sese Seko 28
Mok Kim Hong, *Oknha* 103
monarchy 139–40, 204
Mondulkiri Province 43n, 62, 63, 105, 115, 301–2
money 22, 24, 110–11
    'hot' versus 'cold' 237
    national market 265
money politics **260–2**, 264
Mong Retthy Group 7, 79n, 104
moral transgressions **310–13**
Muong Poy 33, 37, 38
Muhammad Yunus 162, 162n, 165
Multi Fibre Agreement (MFA, 1974–2004) 11, 13, 65–6, 88, 91
    or 'Agreement on Textiles and Clothing' (ATC) 88n
Myanmar/Burma 55, 193

N

Nab Bun Heng 38
National AIDS Authority (NAA) 214n
National Assembly 63, 66, 78, 103
National Assembly Construction Committee 119n
National Authority for Resolution of Land Disputes (NARLD 2006) 137
National Bank of Cambodia 166–8, 172–4, 175n
National Cambodian Rice-Millers' Association 87
National Council for Democratic Development (NCDD) 221n
National Council for HIV, AIDS, Dermatology and Sexually Transmitted Infections (NCHADS, 1998–) 213–14, **215–16**, 217–18
National Poverty-Reduction Strategy 166, 207
National Programme to Rehabilitate and Develop Cambodia (1994) 53
National Strategic Development Plan (NSDP, 2006–10) 53, 61, 166
natural resource management 199, 201–2, **205–8, 288–309**
    accountability and local politics **266–87**
    'rough business' 286n
natural resources 25, 26, 40–2, 54, 64, 112, 245, 251, 264
neak mean bon (a man who has great merit) 290
neak som tien ('those who ask for gifts') 320
neakthum (wealthy/powerful individuals) 264, 264n
neo-classical economics 170
neo-liberalism 4, 5, 15, 19–20, 24–5
    poverty-reduction strategies **161–81**
neo-patrimonial state **57–8**, 239
    donor co-creation 308
neo-patrimonialism 8, 10, 18, 21, 28, 67, 152, 202, 205, 241, 288–92, 294–5
neo-Weberianism 15, 16–17
Network of Sex Work Projects 217n
networking 223, 296, **302**, 303–5
networks 8, 39, 47, 52–3, 58, 67, 80, 160, 196, 198, 202–3, 205, 208, 215, 216, 222, 229, 234, 257, 260, 262, 264, 300, 306–7, 325
New Public Management (NPM) 161, **169–71**, 177, 180, 201–2, 206, 209, **242–3**
NGO Forum 33, 33n, 83n, 154n
NGO Forum: Fisheries Network 300
NGO-ization 305–8
NGOs 23, 31, 36, 38, 44–5, 50, 63, 76n, 93, **161–81**, 175t, 182, 191–2, 258, 283–4
    draft law 295–6, 296n
    individual activists **303–4**
    'localized INGOs' 294, 294n

people's movements and natural resource management (chapter fourteen) 26, **288–309**
pragmatism 303
transformation into microfinance institutions 161, **171–80**
Ngy San 32
Nhang commune 118, 128n
'no-strings attached' approach 56, 67, 69
noam chenh (export) 184
'non-interference' principle 55, 58, 59, 67, 68
non-state leaders 251–3
Nooy **190–1**
Norodom Ranariddh, Prince 52, 290
Norodom Sihanouk
  King 8, 300
  Prince 52, 115, 251, 254
  Samdech Ov (Lord Father) 251
  Sangkum era 98n, 313
Northeast Cambodia 8, 45, **110–35**, 246, **255–9**
  economic transformation **112–14**
Ny Chandy 34

O

OECD 9–10, 10n
oil 65, 213
Oknha (businessman) **62**, **71–4**, 75–6, 81, 85–6, 91, 103, 213, 255–9, 264
'oligarchs' 27, **39–47**
oligarchy 28, 29, 29n
'oligarchy-building' (Hutchcroft) **47n**, **47–9**
Ou Sopheary 92
Ou Virak 38
Oum Mean 197
Oum Sothea and Sok Hach (economists) 103
ov (father) 250–1, 263
Overseas Development Assistance (ODA) 60, 187–8
Oxfam 67, 136–7, 174n

P

Pa Ngoung Teang 296
Pagoda Boys (PB) 298
pagodas/temples 227–8, 231, 234–5, 256n, 289, 291–2, 318–22
Paknam ('Kambuja City') **193–4**
parami (*bareamey*) **289–90**
Paris Accords (1991) 53, 113, 247
party financing 25, **219–44**
Pate commune 31, 35

'patrimonial administrative state' 27, 29–30, 35, 158
patrimonial administrative tendencies 31, 42
'patrimonial oligarchic state' 28, 28n, 29–30, 47, 49
'patrimonialism' (Weberian concept) 28
patron-client networks 8–9, 18, 80, 199, 201–2, 216, 234, 267
patronage 6–7, 25, 26, 30n, 39, 72, 81, 202–5, 208, 251, 254, 283, 290, 292n
  personalized 149, 222, 237, 239, 242, 267
  powerful **262–4**, 265
Peam Cheang estate 101, 102
peasantry/peasants 239, 251, 275n, 314
Pen Bonnar 33
Peng Seng 92
People's Republic of Kampuchea (PRK, 1979–89) 1, 98, 142–3, 147, 246
petavatthu (text) 317, 317n, 318n
Peung Yok Hiep 32
Phchum Ben ('hungry ghost' festival) 26, **310–13**, 315, **316–24**, 328–9
  meaning (gathering of rice balls) 322
  obligations 327
  two ways of giving to ancestors **323–4**
Pheapimex 62, 114, **301–2**
Philippines 16, 27, 28n, **29**, 75, 85, 89, 182, 183, 305–6
Phnom Penh 11, 37, 51, 65, 104–5, 135–6, 155n, 156, 185, 225–6, 229, 261, 320
  Sino-Khmer community 55–6
  water supply 199, 201
Phnom Penh Chamber of Commerce 62n, 81n
Phnom Penh Post 159
Phnom Penh Water Supply Authority (PPWSA) **208–13**, 215
  autonomy principle 210–11
  collection of water fees 212–13
  staffing structure 210
  western management models 211–12
Phou Mady Investment Group 62n
Phoy Svagn 36
Phu Rieng Rubber Company 43, 105
phung (wife's matrilineal clan) 133–4
plantations 27, 62, 113, 115, 117, 301
  see also rubber plantations
Pneay commune 144t, 146, 153t, 157n
Poipet 8
Pol Pot 1–2, 3
policing 38, 45n, 195, 214–16, 244, 247–8, 278, 281–3, 285

political economy 70, 113n, 124n, 134, 288
  'good governance' reform 25, **199–218**
political power 72–4, 95, 112–13, 149, 152, 208, 261, **285**, 290, 292n, 325
  commune councils and accountability **280–4**
  definition 289
  structures **158–60**
political stability 15, 52–3, 57
politics of gifts 259, 259n, 260
politics of markets **21–3**
post-conflict reconstruction 4–5, **5–10**, 57, 67, 93, 136
Post-Washington consensus 163, 163n, 164
potlatch **324–5**
poverty 4, 5, 10, 13, 21–6, 40n, 45, 84n, 151, 158–60, 189, 244, 252, 254, 265, 288, 294, 306, 308, 310, 314–15, 320, 326n, 328, 329n
  'economically active poor' versus 'poorest of poor' 179–80
  'overwhelmingly and increasingly rural' 313n
poverty-reduction 11, 61, 65, 69, 70, 184, 259, 272
  'commercial culture' versus 'social dimensions' 179
  global agenda 163
  'mission-drift' 177, 177n, 179, 180
  national strategy 166, 207
  neo-liberal strategies **161–81**
Poverty-Reduction Strategy Papers 163
Powell, W. 242n
prahok (fermented fish) 259, 259n
Prak Chan Thul 34–6n, 45n
Prak Soeun 34, 35
Prakas 172, 172n
Preah Vihear Province 96t
Preah Vihear temple crisis 192
prebendalism 239–40, 241
preta (hungry ghosts) 310–13, 315, **316–24**, 328–9
  Buddhist textual imagination **317–19**
  morally-ambivalent receivers **316–17**
  two sets **320–1**
Prey Tumpung village 189, 190–1
Prey Veng province 8, 107, 189, 190
PricewaterhouseCooper 176
Prime Minister's Office 63
primitive accumulation (Marx) 128n
private property 22, 23, 25, 130, 139, 260
Private Property Regime Management **202–8**
private sector 9, 12, 23, 75–7, 151, 160, 167n, 172–3, 241

privatization 24, **99–104**, 111, 143–4, 163n, 170, 177
Procedure for Privatization of Public Enterprises (sub-decree, 1995) 103
profit motive 64, 86, 192, 198
Progressive Farmers' Association 37
provincial elections (2009) 286–7n
Provincial Forestry Administration 274
Prud'homme, R. 98, 106
PSDD (Project Support to Democratic Development through Decentralisation and Deconcentration) 228t, 231n
public goods and service delivery **208–18**
public-choice theory 170
Pursat Province 62, 114, 301–2

Q

Qatar 85, 186
quasi-formal system **139–48**, 155, 158
  limits **148–53**
quotas 78, 80, 83, 88n, 91, 247

R

Racharvali (conglomerate) 84–5
Ratanakiri Province **31–9**, 96t, 105, **110–35**, 137, 148, 297
  see also 'Kadon Village'
Ratanakiri Province: Agriculture Department 117
Ratanakiri Provincial Court 32, 33–5
rational choice theory 170
Rayong (Thailand) **193–6**, 198
reciprocity (generalized) **322–3**, 323n
recruitment agencies **184–6**, 197
Rectangular Strategy for Growth (2004) 13, 53, 53n, 83n, 200
reform agenda (1994–) **99–104**
regional [international] integration **39–47**, 47, 48–9
Relative Comparative Advantage 41
remittances 183, 183n, **187–92**, 196
  urban--rural 314, 315, 327
rent-seeking 18, 27–9, 48, 50, 68, 87, 160, 207
resentment 310, 312–13, 324, 326–7, **327**, 329n
rice 70, 71, 77, 81n, **83–9**, 119, 123t, 127, 132, 189, 190, 231t, 233, 237, 246–7, 313, 316
  'highland' versus 'lowland' 126
rice sector 24, 74, 90
  constraints 86–7
  'Mafia-like element' 86, 91
rice-milling 84–8, 90–1, 93

roads 41, 64–6, 69, 115–16, 125, 145f, 146, 227, 231–2t, 235t, 236–7, 247, 258, 263
Rong Chhun 296
Royal Government of Cambodia (RGC) 58–60, 81–2, 84, 91, 95, 99, 108
rubber 24–5, 31–3, 36n, 41, 133, 256, 313
   advantages (Cambodia) 99
   history 94, **95–9**
   state role (post-privatization) 104–8
   privatization **94–109**
rubber plantations 99–100, 119–20, 126
   French 94, 95
   'state-owned' versus 'family-owned' (1968) 96t, 97–8
   working conditions 102, **106–8**, 108–9
rule of law 6, 15, 33, 39n, 108, 199
   'law enforcement' 61
   'law and order' 270
ruling class **30n**
ruling elite 31, 48, 259, 291
rural areas 26, 39, 61, 63, 155n, 156, 158–60, 166–7, 169, 179–80, 183, 185, 187, 220, 245, 267–9, 271, 284–7, 304, 310–15, 326–9
   development schemes 48
   see also Phchum Ben
Rural Development Bank (RDB) 177–8
rural population 12, 82t, 83, 94
rural votes 6, 7

S

saboraschun (charitable person) 220
sach nhiet ('kin of the same flesh') 322
Sam Rainsy 35, 105, 290
Sam Rainsy Party (SRP) 238, 250n, 255–8, 264, 296
sambot (border pass) 194–5
sang sang ('doing construction') 219–20, 222, 236, 242
Sangha 297, 318
   'monks' 290, 303, 304, 316, 317, 320, 320n, 323
Sangkat Fisheries 173, 274, 281, **281n**, 282
Sangkum Reastr Niyum 251
Sanitary and Phytosanitary (SPS) measures 74, 89, 90
Sar Kheng 8, 222
Sector-Wide Approach Programme (SWAP) 89
Seila program (1996–2006) 230, 293, 293n
Seilanithih Ltd 175t 178n
self-help 164–5, 252, 293
Senate/Senators 72–4

services sector 9, 11, 12, 76
sesame 123t, 126
Sesan River 118–19
Sev Kem (villager) 32
Sev Nhang 35
Sev Rith 37
seventh generation 320, 321, 323, 323n, 327–8
sex workers **214–17**
Seyha Sok 115
Shay, C. 186n
Shukaku Inc. 62n, 159
Siem Reap (city) x, 11, 14n, 155n
Siem Reap (province) 148, 150, 271n
Sihanoukville (port) 11, 71n, 80, 87, 93, 155n
   Prey Nup District 154n
Sihanoukville (province) 65, 96t, 148, 156n
Sin Kheam 44
Singapore 4, 17, 20, 98, 186
Sinohydro Corporation 59, 65
Sino-Khmer community 55–6, 62, 81, 81n, 95, 254
Sirik Matak 95
slavery 111, 126n, 325–6
Smallholder Rubber Plantation Project (1999–2012) 100–1
smallholders 95, 116, 120, 122, 127, 249, 254
Snoul (plantation) 101
sobaraschon donations 228
social capital 81, 181
social class 29, 305n
social movements
   'emergence' **298–308**
   'more constitutive' 309
Société Nationale d'Exportation et d'Importation (Sonexim) 95
Socio-Economic Development Plan 166, 207
SOFRECO (French company) 104
'soft infrastructure' 40
soft loans 59, 60
soft power 54–5
Sok An 203, 222, 239
Sok Hach 76n
Sok Kong, *Oknha* 6, 213
Sok Na 38
Sokimex company 6, 71n, 213
Somrongtong district (Kampong Speu Province) 145
Sour Sitha 44
South Korea 4, 17, 20, 21, 23, 62n, 85, 186, 189, 234

Sre Ambel district (Koh Kong province) **39–47**, 63
srok komnaoet (family homeland) 224, 230
state, the 16, **23–6**, 324–5
    rational-legal 51, 57–8
    see also Cambodian state
State Archives of Cambodia (ANC) 96–7n
'state land' 159
'state private land' 159–60
'state public land' 159
state of transformation **285–7**
state-owned rubber enterprises (SOREs) 103, 104, 108–9
Structural Adjustment Programmes 163, 163n, 170
'structure of incentive' (Olson) 158
Stung Atay project 59
Sub-Decree on Economic Land Concessions (2005) 61
Sub-Decree on Manpower Training Board (2006) 185n
subsistence agriculture 9, 11–12, 126, 140, 146
    shift to market production 110–11, 131, 264
    see also swidden agriculture
sugar 41, 62, 120n
    see also Koh Kong Plantation Company
Suharto, President 23, 28
Suos Yara 85
Supervision Office for Specialised Banks (1997–) 168
'support' NGOs 303
Supreme Council of Magistracy (SCM) 204–5
Sustaining Rapid Growth in Challenging Environment (World Bank, 2009) 71n, 90n
Swedish International Development Agency 245n
swidden agriculture 114, 115, **120–6**
Syndicat de Mimot 101n
Systematic Land Registration programme (SLR) 137, 138, 159
    limits **153–8**
    cadastral sustainability **139–48**
    provinces and cities initially included 145n

T

Ta Art 262
Ta Mok 3
Taiwan 17, 42n, 52, 55
Tak Khmau 11
Takeo province 65 , 222
Tan Binh Rubber Company 105
'Tang Kadon' (pseudonym) 110n, **110–12**
economic transformation (cashews, cash, capitalism) **114–16**
great transformation **130–5**
Jarai agricultural calendar 123t
Jarai farming system 121f
land sales (2003–8) 129t, 130t, 130, 132–3f
location 118
'remote village' **118–20**
Tanmay Chetan 177n
Tapao (Kompong Cham Province) 98n
taxation 75, 79, 207–8, 239, 240
    versus aid flows 76
    see also cadastral sustainability
Technical Secretariat on Economic Land Concessions (2006–) 61
Teng Bunma 6
Teng Lao 105
Tep Vong 297
teuk moat prai (ability to get things done) 212, 253, 253n, 259, 299n
tevata 317
Thailand 4, 16, 20, 21, 25, 28, 41, 42n, 51, 75, 84, 87, 88, 91, 186–93, 239, 305–6
    'Siam' 114
    trade agreement with Cambodia (2006) 42–3
    work and life (for Cambodian migrant labour) **192–6**
Than Kang 37
Thaneakea Phum Ltd 175t 178n
thavkae (big businessman) 259, 264
Thelen, K. 242n
Thet Sambath 37–8n
Thmar Pitt [Pich] estate 101, 102–3
timber 9, 112, 126, 313
    logging 7, 100, 113, 206, 115n, 246, 255–6, 301
    logging (illegal) 38, 61, 119, 207, 273, 300
time **223, 302n**, 307
tiproeksa (advisor) **73–4**, 227
Tirokuddasutta **317–18**, 318–19n, 320, 321
Tonle Sap Lake 246, **260–2**
Tonle Sap river 315
tontin (credit groups) 292
'total prestations' 325
tourism 11, 77–8, 83
Trade Agreement on Textiles and Apparel (TATA, US-Cambodia, 1999–2004) 66, 78, 78n
trade unions 23, 24n, 292, **293**, 293n, 303, 304
transparency 25, 50, 56–7, 59, 60–1, 63–4, 67–8, 69, 100, 103, 109, 158, 204, 210, 217, 269n, 276
tukchet (trust) 237
Tumring plantation 103–4, 301

U

unemployment 183, 187, 193n
United Kingdom: Department for International Development x, 92, 245n
United Nations 52, 58, 69, 162–3, 296
  UN FAO 10, 113, 274n, 328
  UN High Commission for Human Rights (UNHCHR) 61–2n, 63, 136, 204, 248n
  UN World Summit 164
  UNAIDS 214n
  UNDP 118n, 166, 168, 168n, 176, 255n
  UNICEF 168
UNTAC 1, 4, 136, 203, 216, 223, 294
United States 11, 13, 18, 20, 54–5, 79–80, 91, 97, 188
  soft power (post-Cold War) 55
  trade preferences 78, 83
  US Department of Agriculture 84
  US Department of Labor 293n
  USAID 77, 77n, 168n, 176
'unofficial payments' (terminology) 77
'use of authority' **286**

V

Van Sou Ieng 81
Varenne's Labour Code (1927) 107–8
Ve Wong Corporation 42n
ven ('turns') 322
Vietnam 43, 51, 78n, 79, 84–5, 87–8, 91, 101–2, 114, 116, 126–7, 255–6, 294
  see also CLMV
Vietnam Rubber Corporation 43n
Vietnam Rubber Group 105
vihear (main sanctuary) 323
village chiefs 129t, 246–51, 254, 260–1, 263, 265, 271, 274, 322
Village Development Committees, 293, 293n
village gender focal person/point 248, 250, 255, 260
villages 26, 292
  natal 237, 310, 321, 328
vimanavatthu (text) 317
violence 63, 138, 149, 150, 240, 247–8, 297–8, 301
Voar Sar commune 144t, 146, 153t
voice (indicator) 15
Voice of Democracy (VOD) radio 37

W

Washington Consensus 163n
Wat Wiang Chas 290
water 25, 89, 230–3, 253, 262, 323
  wells 231t, 231, 232t, 235t
welfare dependency 165, 179
Wen Jiabao 51
women 66, 79, 80n, 102, 111, **133–4**, 164, 189n, 190, 192, 194, 248n, 250, 253, 271, 292, 304, 310, 314, 315, 320, 326, 329n
Woolcock, M. **151–2**
Working Group Helping Local Level (*krom kangea choh moulthan*) 223
World Bank **12–15**, 71, 75n, 76, 78n, 82–3n, 90n, 99, 100n, 117n, 162–3, 166, 170, 188, 209, 210, 252–3, 294, 296, 296n, 299n, 300, 301, 308
  governance indicators 15
  report (2004) 108
  report (2007) 40n
World Bank–Netherlands Partnership Program 92
World Food Programme (WFP) 232
World Microcredit Summit Campaign (1997–) **164–5**
World Health Organization (WHO) 217
World Trade Organization (WTO) 80, 88, 88n, 89
World Vision 168n
Worldwide Governance Indicators (World Bank online) 15n
Wuzhishan LS Group 301n

Y

Yamaraja (ruler of hell) 319
yang (spirits) 128, 130n
Yeng Virak 296
yok yual knea tov vinh tov mok (reciprocity and empathy) 212
youth 292, 310

NIAS Press is the autonomous publishing arm of
NIAS – Nordic Institute of Asian Studies, a research institute
located at the University of Copenhagen. NIAS is partially funded by the
governments of Denmark, Finland, Iceland, Norway and Sweden
via the Nordic Council of Ministers, and works to encourage and
support Asian studies in the Nordic countries. In so doing, NIAS
has been publishing books since 1969, with more than two
hundred titles produced in the past few years.

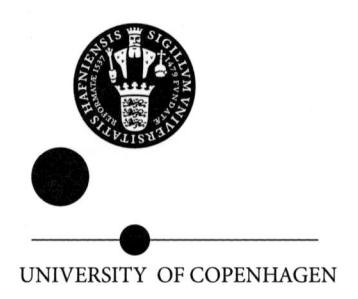

UNIVERSITY OF COPENHAGEN

norden

Nordic Council of Ministers